TH

EROS REVIVED

EROS REVIVED

Erotica of the Enlightenment in
England and America

PETER WAGNER

SECKER & WARBURG
LONDON

For Odile, Anne-Claude and Marie-Laure

First published in England 1988 by
Martin Secker & Warburg Limited
54 Poland Street, London W1V 3DF

British Library Cataloguing in Publication Data

Wagner, Peter, 1949–
    Eros revived: erotica of the enlightenment
in England and America.
    1. Sex in the arts — History — 18th
century
    I. Title
    700   NX650.E7

ISBN 0–436–56051–8

Set in 11/12½ pt Linotron 202 Sabon by
Fakenham Photosetting Limited
Printed and bound in Great Britain by
Butler & Tanner Ltd, Frome & London

Contents

List of Illustrations

Acknowledgements

My first debt of gratitude is for a generous grant I received from the *Deutsche Forschungsgemeinschaft*. It enabled me to do the research for this book in Europe and America. Special thanks are due to Professor Butler and my former colleagues at the University of Bath, and to Christopher Upward of the University of Aston, for help and advice. I received assistance from the staff in the British Library, Bath Public Library, Bodleian Library, Bibliothèque Nationale, and from the employees in the university libraries of Bath and Aston. To Mr D.W.C. Stewart, librarian at the Royal Society of Medicine, London, I am grateful for allowing me access to the library; and I acknowledge the friendly help of the librarians of the American Antiquarian Society (Worcester, Massachusetts), the Institute for Sex Research Library (the former Kinsey Institute at Bloomington, Indiana), the Library of Congress, and the staff of the Historical Society of Pennsylvania and the Maryland Historical Society. I am especially thankful for the detailed information I received from the librarians at Colonial Williamsburg and at the College of William & Mary in Williamsburg, Virginia.

I should also like to express my gratitude to those who have contributed to this book with their advice and criticism. My colleagues in France, particularly Jean Dagen, Gershon Legman, and my good friend, Georges Lamoine, made many useful suggestions. Paul-Gabriel Boucé accompanied the final stages of a more scholarly version of the manuscript with expert information and advice, based on his vast and detailed knowledge of eighteenth-century literature. He arranged for me to submit this version as a doctoral dissertation at the Sorbonne in September 1986. Professor Boucé's own prodigious work taught me that there is nothing odious about Enlightenment erotica and that our understanding of the eighteenth century can only profit from the kind of research that was undertaken for this book.

Among the scholars in Britain who provided me with information, I am glad to mention Giles Barber, Günter Berghaus, Dennis Fletcher, David Foxon, Christopher Frayling, Ludmilla Jordanova, Roy Porter, David Profumo, Pat Rogers, W.A. Speck, John Styles, Keith Thomas, Roger Thompson, Peter Wagstaff, and P. Winnack. Mr Charles Skilton kindly offered me a number of bibliographies, now out of print, which I found extremely useful. In Germany, Uwe Böker, Ursula Brumm, Roland Hagenbüchle, Winfried Herget, Mary Lindemann, Viktor Link, Herbert Mainusch, Edgar Mertner, Heinz-Joachim Müllenbrock, Hansgeorg Nitschke, Hermann-Josef Real, and H.J. Vienken gave me some help. In Canada and the United States, I acknowledge the assistance of Vern L. Bullough, the late Richard Beale Davis, Robert Darnton, Arthur N. Gilbert, Leo Lemay, Robert P. Maccubbin, Michael McGiffert, Stephen Parks, Ronald Paulson, E.W. Pitcher, George S. Rousseau, Peter Sabor, Thad Tate, Randolph Trumbach, Ron Walters, Richard J. Wolfe, and P.M. Zall. My special thanks go to my friends Carl and Joan Dolmetsch, and to Roy and Elsa Diduk, whose help and encouragement I have appreciated over the years.

I also want to thank Karl-Heinz Birzele and Karlheinz Donaubauer for their assistance with the pictorial material, and particularly Richard Bonnin for his unfailing and friendly help with the locating and ordering of source material and critical literature. The friendliness and help of the staff at the libraries of the University of Eichstätt remain unsurpassed. I must also thank Michael Hulse for his critical comments on several chapters of this book; and to Allen Gilbert I am deeply indebted for his generous assistance with my research in the United States and for his critical reading of the manuscript.

Peter Grose, now at Heinemann, has shown great patience while waiting for the final version of this book, so special thanks are due to him too; and I also acknowledge with great pleasure the very constructive editorial help I received, at various stages, from Sue Moore, Linda Martin, Helen Wythers and Maggie McKernan.

Sections from chapter 1 originally appeared as 'The Discourse on Sex – Or Sex as Discourse', in Roy Porter and G.S. Rousseau, eds., *Sexual Underworld of the Enlightenment* (Manchester: Manchester University Press, 1988); and as 'The Veil of Science and Morality:

Some Pornographic Aspects of the *Onania*', *British Journal for Eighteenth-Century Studies* 6 (1983): 179–84.

Sections from chapter 4 originally appeared as 'The Pornographer in the Courtroom', in P.-G. Boucé, ed., *Sexuality in Eighteenth-Century Britain* (Manchester: Manchester University Press, 1982): 120–41; and as 'Trial Reports as a Genre of Eighteenth-Century Erotica', *British Journal for Eighteenth-Century Studies* 5 (1982): 117–21.

Sections from chapter 7 originally appeared in my edition of John Cleland, *Fanny Hill or Memoirs of a Woman of Pleasure* (Harmondsworth: Penguin, 1985); and as 'The Assertion of Body and Instinct: John Cleland's *Memoirs of a Woman of Pleasure*', in P.-G. Boucé and Suzy Halimi, eds., *Le corps et l'âme en Grande-Bretagne au xviiie siècle* (Paris: Publications de la Sorbonne, 1986): 139–57.

Sections from chapter 8 originally appeared in my *Lust und Liebe im Rokoko/Lust and Love in the Rococo Period* (Nördlingen: Greno, 1986).

Chapter 9 originally appeared in a slightly different form as 'Eros Goes West: European and "Homespun" Erotica in Eighteenth-Century America', in W. Herget and K. Ortseifen, eds., *The Transit of Civilization from Europe to America* (Tübingen: Narr, 1986): 145–65. Another section of this chapter was published in an enlarged version as ' "The Female Creed": A New Reading of William Byrd's Parody', *Early American Literature* 19 (1984): 122–37.

Peter Wagner
January 1987

PICTURE CREDITS

American Antiquarian Society, 92; British Library, 1, 2, 3, 5, 6, 8, 9, 10, 12, 14, 17, 21, 31, 32, 40, 44, 49, 51; Institute for Sex Research (Indiana University), 18, 27, 41, 50; Georges Bataille, *L'Érotisme* (Paris, 1957), 92; *Bilderlexikon der Erotick*, 8 vols. (Hamburg, 1961), 38, 88; Antoine Borel, *Cent vignettes érotiques gravées par Elluin pour illustrer sept romans libertins du dix-huitième siècle* (Nyoms, 1978), 52; Joseph Burke and Colin Caldwell, *Hogarth: The Complete Engravings* (1968), 34, 71; *Dix-huitième Siècle* (1980), 55, 65; Eduard Fuchs, *Geschichte der erotischen Kunst*, 2 vols. (1908–26), 7, 19, 22, 23, 28, 39, 53, 87, 89; Eduard Fuchs, *Illustrierte Sittengeschichte*, vols. II–III (Munich, 1910–12), 20, 24, 29, 42, 43, 45, 47,

66, 78; Eduard Fuchs, *Die Frau in der Karikatur* (Munich, 1906), 25, 56; Eduard Fuchs and Alfred Kind, *Die Weiberherrschaft in der Geschichte der Menschheit*, 2 vols. (Munich, 1913), 4, 26, 37; Cornelius Gurlitt, *Das Französische Sittenbild des 18. Jahrhunderts im Kupferstich* (Berlin, 1912), 66, 68; Jean H. Hagstrum, *Sex and Sensibility* (1980), 60, 61, 78; P.F.H. Hancarville, *Monumens de la vie privée des douze Césars* (1780; repr. Dortmund, 1979), 62; Jean Hervez, *Les sociétés d'amour au XVIIIe siècle* (Paris, 1906), 68, 70, 71; Draper Hill, *The Satirical Etchings of James Gillray* (New York, 1976), 36; Derek Jarrett, *England in the Age of Hogarth* (1976), 13, 15, 16; George Paston, *Social Caricature in the Eighteenth Century* (1905), 35; Ronald Paulson, *Hogarth: His Life, Art and Times*, 2 vols. (1971), 11, 31, 73, 74, 75, 76, 77; Ronald Paulson, *Representations of Revolution* (1983), 63; Thomas Rowlandson, *Allerlei Liebe* (Dortmund, second edition, 1980), 30, 33, 48, 55, 57, 58, 81, 82, 83, 84, 85, 86; Gert Schiff, ed., *Johann Heinrich Füssli* (Munich/Zurich, 1973), 90, 91; Peter Webb, *The Erotic Arts* (1975), 46.

Introduction

In a cartoon of 1786 entitled *A Sale of English-Beauties, in the East Indies*, James Gillray offers his own account of the sexual scene in late eighteenth-century England (plate 1). Though the location is India, the details refer to London. A shipload of English courtesans has just arrived in Calcutta and is being auctioned. Given that actual women, as well as aphrodisiacs, contraceptives, and erotic literature, are among the objects for sale, Gillray's satire is not realistic so much as downright brutal. In the foreground, two ladies are being taxed on their physical assets, the one above the waist and the other below, while the bare bosom of a third lady provides the gentleman beside her with an obvious source of excitement.

What is interesting in this picture, apart from the commodities to be auctioned off, is what Gillray has to tell us about the current market in the literature of eroticism and pornography. The auctioneer stands on a case inscribed 'British-Manufacture', and adorned, by way of a hint at sexual flagellation, with crossed birch rods. At his feet a smaller case bears the words 'For the Amusement of Military Gentlemen' – and a list of titles that provides an idea of the scope of eighteenth-century erotica. Better-known works include John Cleland's *Fanny Hill*, Crébillon's *Le sopha*, and Voltaire's *La pucelle d'Orléans*; *Moral Tales* is probably a translation of a collection of licentious stories entitled *Contes moraux*; and *Crazy Tales* refers to several obscene books of verses, songs and stories by Thomas Hamilton, sixth Earl of Haddington. Among other titles are *Female Flagellants*, a work of sexual perversion; *Berchini's Dance*, a collection of anecdotes on flagellation

1 Gillray, *A Sale of English-Beauties, in the East Indies*, 1786

figuring an English noblewoman of the time; and *Elements of Nature*, possibly one of the ambiguous sex guides of the period, read both for information and for their power to stimulate.[1]

Gillray's allusion to these titles, incidental as it may seem, is an illumination of what English and colonial purchasers of the time understood by the literature of eroticism – not only fiction and poetry but sex guides and books on perversion. It also indicates that French books, whether in the original or in translation, were of importance.

It is this vast and varied field of erotica, as read both in England and America during the eighteenth century, that this book attempts to sketch. I use the words 'attempt' and 'sketch' with deliberation, for after five years of almost uninterrupted work I have come to realise that nothing could be more ludicrous than a claim to exhaustiveness. In view of the source material from various subjects and disciplines, my approach has to be interdisciplinary, for eighteenth-century erotica comprise not merely fiction, poetry, and drama, but also scientific treatises, para-medical works, 'faction' (a strange combination of fact and fiction embodied in frequently satirical 'chroniques scandaleuses', for instance), satire, and − last but not least − erotic art. No single person can possibly read the thousands of erotic books, pamphlets, and broadsides the British and American reading public were offered in the Age of the Enlightenment, and I can only hope that this book, if it achieves anything, may stimulate further research into the areas I have mapped out.

I assume that in the 1980s a book on the representation of sex in the cultures and literatures of eighteenth-century England and America is not in need of a moral justification; for the works of Paul-Gabriel Boucé, Michel Foucault, David Foxon, Jean H. Hagstrum, and Lawrence Stone, to name just a few outstanding scholars in a fertile field of research, have made the subject of sexuality, if not over-exploited, then at least respectable. Hagstrum, in his recent study of ideal and erotic love from Milton to Mozart, does deplore the absence of scholarly and critical works on love in the literary culture of the Restoration and of England in the eighteenth century. However, had he inquired further, he would have found such valuable studies as those by Roger Thompson, Peter Naumann, and Peter Webb, as well as a number of French books which I have discussed in the chapter on prose fiction. Applying some of the results of Lawrence Stone's earlier study to literature, music, and art, Hagstrum himself has done an admirable job in tracing the radical change in '*mentalité*' over more than a century.[2]

A few words need to be said about the method as well as the definitions I have used in this book. In his pioneering study of libertine literature from 1660 to 1745, David Foxon remarked that 'every time a major pornographic book appeared on the continent, it was known in England within a year, and in many cases appeared in translation right away' and that 'the intelligentsia who were familiar with foreign languages provided a substantial enough market for erotica'; and I indeed have frequently had to ask myself what was genuinely English in, for example, erotic fiction and art. The answer this book gives is that France dominated in almost every area of erotica, with the result that England and America became the recipients, producing little homegrown pornography, although in the field of bawdy verse they were more prolific.[3] Analysing lists of erotic books in the catalogues of the private libraries of eighteenth-century writers, one is again struck by the influence France exerted on American and English authors and readers. Swift owned major classical erotica, works by Lucian, Terence, Virgil, Ovid, and Suetonius, some in French editions, and had

120 volumes of French books (a fifth of his whole library), among them the more erotic works of Rabelais, La Fontaine, Voltaire, and Bussy-Rabutin. Fielding, too, owned French erotica, while Sterne, as can be expected of a novelist who adored France, was a connoisseur who had in his possession the licentious novels of Crébillon, Le Sage, the Marquis d'Argens, and Voltaire as well as numerous 'chroniques scandaleuses' about the sex lives of 'Anne d'Autriche', Madame de Pompadour, and Louis XIV. Sterne also owned para-medical works on sexology, midwifery and VD, of French authorship, and many classical erotic books in French translation. The catalogue of the library of Francis Douce, who died in 1834 and bequeathed his holdings to the Bodleian Library, is another treasure trove for erotic titles, giving an idea of the vast number of French fictional and factual erotic and pornographic books an English gentleman could buy in the late eighteenth century.[4] The books discussed in the following chapters are important, not because Fielding, Sterne, and other luminaries exploited them, but because people read them in the eighteenth century and because they helped form widely held opinions and prejudices. What we have filtered out in the twentieth century as 'major eighteenth-century fiction' does not provide a realistic picture of the literature of the period.

Several words I use continually in this book need to be defined. To begin with the title, Eros is as elusive as a mythical figure as he is as a driving force of human behaviour. In Plato's *Symposium*, Aristophanes explains to his listeners the services men require from Eros. In the beginning, thus the tale of Aristophanes, man was a perfect and happy androgynic being. Equipped with the attributes of man and woman, it was sexually self-sufficient. This being had four legs and four arms, and of course two faces, and was in shape as round as a ball. But it soon became vainglorious and hence caused the ire of the gods. They punished the androgynic being by cutting it in halves, calling them man and woman. Ever since, male and female human beings have been looking for their 'missing half' with bleeding souls. In their search, the 'half-men' have often enlisted the help of Eros – for it is only he who can unite what belongs together. Eros, however, is an ambiguous figure, neither god nor man: another participator in the *Symposium*, Diotima, calls him a 'daimon' living between wisdom and foolishness. Thus the myth.[5] Erotic literature is one of the recognisable attempts of man to find his/her missing 'half' after the cutting, so to speak. The eighteenth century harked back to the classical ages, thus creating Neoclassicism, and tried to revive Eros and the culture of love connected with the figure. However, Eros, the Greek man-god, and his Roman successor, Amor, had stood at the head of hedonistic cultures in which neither sexuality nor its representation by artists was associated with sin or shame. The writers and artists who attempted to revive the culture of Eros in the eighteenth century had against themselves a Christian tradition confining sex to marriage while condemning the visual or literary representation of human sexuality. The audience, too, had changed. One of the most interesting phenomena of the reception of erotic books in the eighteenth century is the gradual appearance on the scene of a middle-class readership. The rise of pornographic fiction is a concomitant development which has a few direct links with the bourgeois mentality.

Erotica, in this book, is a comprehensive term for bawdy, obscene, erotic, and pornographic works, including scatological humour and satire, which often employ sexual elements. The terms bawdy (a), used synonymously with ribald, obscene (b), and erotic (c) should cause no difficulties, denoting (a) the humorous treatment of sex; (b) a description whose effect is shocking or disgusting; and (c) the writing about sex within the context of love and affection. The stumbling stone is pornography. Entire books have been written on the question, what is pornography?[6] A few points have been clarified. Thus Susan Sontag has shown that to separate literature and pornography is misleading and that sexual stimulation can be a legitimate aim of literature as well, while Morse Peckham has gone as far as to claim that art can be expressed in pornography.[7] While almost every critic seems to be familiar with the etymology of the word (i.e., meaning the writing of, on, about, or even for, whores), nobody seems to have considered the first appearance of the term in the English language. The *Oxford English Dictionary* lists no references to the words 'pornographic' or 'pornography' before 1857, when the noun is proved to have appeared in a medical dictionary. 'Pornographer' is first recorded in 1850 in a translation from the German. This would seem to relate the origin of the modern notion of pornography to the Victorian period – and I think this is significant. The *OED* rather vaguely defines the term as 'the expression or suggestion of obscene or unchaste subjects in literature or art'. Anthony Burgess has rightly ridiculed such a definition by carrying it to its logical extreme. 'If anything that encourages sexual fantasy,' he wrote, 'is a pornograph, then pornographs lie all about us – underwear advertisements, the provocative photographs in the non-class Sunday papers.'[8] Pornography is difficult to define because both its function and reception are variables changing from one historical

period to another. Significantly, pornography has been defined in the
past on the basis of its function, with the implication that the principal
aim of pornography can only be sexual stimulation. This is definitely
not so. There are a few features of pornography that are not subject to
change. As a branch of literature, for instance, pornography generally
aims at disorientation and dislocation, and it is certainly no coincidence that the production of pornography reached an apogee in
France, and in Europe, during the period of the French Revolution.
Historically speaking, there has been pornography at least since the
time of Pietro Aretino in the sixteenth century. There is an almost
uninterrupted line from his *Ragionamenti* to John Cleland's *Memoirs
of a Woman of Pleasure*, as Peter Naumann has shown; but the
function of pornography in the various societies from 1500 to 1800
was not the same. Initially, pornography served entertaining and
didactic purposes and gradually became a vehicle of protest against
the authority of Church and State, and finally against middle-class
morality. By the eighteenth century, pornography was like a chame-
leon, appearing in various guises – literary mimicry is one of its aspects
– and assuming different functions.[9]

The growing discourse on sex in the medical field, by moralists, and
by Enlightenment writers, was exploited by pornographers like
Edmund Curll, who published material that excited the prurience of
the reading public. Literary hyping, then as now, made 'pornographic'
books out of works that were mildly erotic at best. Eighteenth-century
pornography of this kind was pseudo-didactic, with the *Onania*,
discussed in chapter 1, being a prime example. Socio-political protest
became the principal vehicle for the literary pornography of the
Enlightenment. However, some time after mid-century, a point was
reached when the pornographic aims began to displace and over-
shadow the political ones. Numerous French libertine novels were set
in monasteries, describing the sexual acrobatics and the immoral life
of monks and nuns. What had started as an attack on Catholicism,
moral confinement, and Church authority, soon gained additional
aspects with the increasing pornographic dimensions of these books.
Eventually, pornography becomes an aim in itself, trying to bring
down the established moral and sexual order. Apart from these didactic and socio-political functions, pornography and licentious literature
have a literary dimension, reaching back to Sappho's songs and
poems. Some of the literary functions of pornography were revived in
the eighteenth century, but – and this needs to be repeated – for an
English readership that, for the most part, associated sex with sin.

Hence the desperate attempts in England – not so much in France – on the part of writers and publishers to look for non-offensive styles and forms.

If the functions of pornography change in a given society, so does its reception. Roger Thompson's definition of 'pornographic' as 'writing or representation intended to arouse lust, create sexual fantasies, or feed auto-erotic desires' is unacceptable because of the use of 'intention', a rather ambiguous term which tends to obscure the fact that there may be, and often is, a great discrepancy between authorial intention and actual reception of a text or picture. From a twentieth-century viewpoint, how are we to determine what produced a genital response in an eighteenth-century reader? James Boswell found *Fanny Hill* 'most inflaming' in the eighteenth century, while George Steiner, one of our contemporary staunch opponents of pornography, considers Cleland's novel a 'mock-epic of orgasm' in which 'any sane man will take delight'. What was Cleland's 'intention', then: 'erection (at least) in the pornophile', as Thompson defines the aim of pornography, or laughter, as Steiner sees it?[10] This dilemma is, of course, directly related to the changing conditions of the reception of a pornographic work over the centuries, which means, in this case, that one age may find a novel highly pornographic while a later one perceives more its humorous aspects, or vice versa. Bearing in mind that both the function and reception of pornography are dependent on the value system and the socio-political conditions of a given society, I would define eighteenth-century pornography as the written or visual presentation in a realistic form of any genital or sexual behaviour with a deliberate violation of existing and widely accepted moral and social taboos.[11]

In examining what the eighteenth century understood by each of these terms, I hope this book will show how the literature and art of Eros in the Age of the Enlightenment were by no means set apart from the rest of contemporary culture and history. For better or worse, not only did such works reflect the society that produced them, but they had in turn a telling effect upon the economic and political thought and deeds of their time.

❧ I ❧

Medical and Para-Medical Literature

Spurred on by Enlightenment enthusiasm in some cases, in others by the wish to make fast money, a whole army of eighteenth-century writers applied themselves to hitherto unexplored aspects of human sexuality. The area of knowledge on which they sought to inform their readers had, they claimed, been made accessible for one overall reason, namely a growth in recent knowledge of medicine.

All kinds of people suddenly decided to voice their opinions on sex. There were learned doctors and professors, steeped in the medical knowledge of their day, and there were tinkers and quacks who became self-styled experts on such issues overnight. A voluminous literature recorded the growing discourse on sexual problems – creating new disciplines in satire as well as in medicine. Most authors were well aware of writing within the larger area of erotica, and some made good financial use of the fact that their wares were titillating. The publications themselves propagated sexual prejudices along with Enlightenment ideas, and often provide fascinating combinations of folklore with modern eighteenth-century notions of medical knowledge.

I THE SEX GUIDES

In 1784, when young Francis Place, later to become a prominent parliamentary reformer, had reached the age of thirteen, he faced a major problem. Although, by now, he was 'pretty well acquainted with what relates to the union of the sexes', he continued to be puzzled by the 'accounts of the Miraculous Conception in Matthew and Luke'. He decided to solve the enigma by consulting 'a book at that time openly sold, on every stall, called *Aristotle's Master-Piece* ... a thick 18 mo, with a number of badly drawn cuts in it explanatory of the mystery of generation'.[1]

Aristotle's Master-Piece, published with slightly differing titles in two, three, or four parts, was an eighteenth-century best-seller.[2] Designed to appeal to the innocent and the prurient alike, it was a combination sex guide and obstetrical instruction manual which went through more than thirty registered editions before the end of the century. Probably Place read an edition containing *Aristotle's Complete and Experienced Midwife* and *The Family Physician*, which was quite frank even in its early versions around 1700. It treated 'of the Benefit of Marriage ..., Signs of Insufficiency in Men and Women ..., of Virginity, of the Organs of Generation in Women ... The Use and Action of the Genitals ... With a Word of Advice to both Sexes in the Act of Copulation.'[3] The frontispieces of most eighteenth-century editions show a naked woman standing beside a scholar at a desk (see plate 2), while earlier editions contain an additional woodcut of a black child and a 'hairy maid' clutching one of her breasts. The text has frequent poetic insertions and occasionally lapses into bawdy jargon. As evidence that it was meant to have a strong erotic appeal, one must take into account a lavish emphasis on the female sex and on virginity.

The evidence of this is external too. A print entitled *The Compleat Auctioner* (*c.* 1700), by Sutton Nichols, shows *Aristotle's Master-Piece* alongside works of pornography.[4] In addition, the *Master-Piece* was at the centre of a minor 'sex scandal' in the parish of Jonathan Edwards in Northampton, Massachusetts, where in 1744 certain young men were reprimanded for having talked to some women in a very lascivious manner.[5]

Combining folklore, speculation, and the medical facts known about sexual relations and gynaecology, the book in its various versions is a typical example of an eighteenth-century popular medical work concocted mainly by English hacks. It was probably first published in 1684. There is no denying the fact that the popularity of the manual was due in part to its erotic appeal.[6]

It is hardly surprising that a century which adored both science and sex should have produced a plethora of literature on the medical aspects of sexuality and sexual behaviour. Enlightenment ideas affected medicine; and, filtered down through such channels as essays,

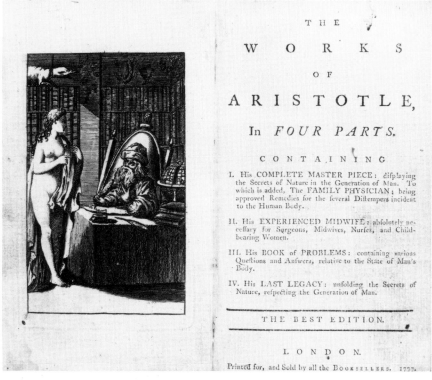

2 *The Works of Aristotle,* 1777

fiction, and conversation, these ideas eventually had an impact on sexual practices and the ideas behind them. Besides the popularisation of medical knowledge, several other factors spawned an amazing variety of works, which both satisfied and exploited needs and expectations. Despite some radical changes, notably in the field of surgery, eighteenth-century medicine preserved a strong element of credulity and quackery, remaining in this respect unenlightened. Even in the serious, trained quarter of the medical profession a blending occurred between rational and empirical elements. In that science as such stepped out of the shadow of the Middle Ages, doctors and quacks were able to improve their status. Although doctors throughout the century did not have the best of reputations and remained a staple diet for satirists, former apothecaries became practising doctors, and surgeons managed to dissociate themselves from the trade of barber. Given the place of sex in eighteenth-century life, it was merely a logical step to make it an object of both science and philosophy. La Mettrie, to name just one writer, tried to rehabilitate the erotic in his *L'art de jouir* (*c.* 1748) and *La volupté*.[7] A phalanx of authors wrote medical treatises, although they could do little against the ill effects of myths, speculation, and error. This situation led to the production of works containing sexually ambiguous material. The diction in these books was at times more poetic than scientific, increasing their erotic appeal rather than clarifying medical matters. Writers of such books were joined by hacks, quacks, and charlatans, for whom the combination of sex and speculation was extremely inviting and often lucrative. Unlike serious medical authors, they had no moral scruples in fighting over the profitable market of mostly urban readers with pornographers of Edmund Curll's ilk, who also dabbled in this field. More often than not, science served as a veil and morality as a pretext for the discussion of topics that were otherwise taboo or even obscene.[8] Literature on sexual matters was circulated to the public from medical, para-medical, and religious quarters. This included marriage and sex guides, a spate of works on masturbation, VD, sexual malfunctions, and perversions, as well as treatises on eunuchs, hermaphrodites, and experiments in medicine. It was either inherently erotic or written with the knowledge that prurient readers would be interested.[9]

Apart from *Aristotle's Master-Piece*, two major works deserve to be mentioned. The first is Joannes Benedictus Sinibaldus's *Geneanthropeiae sive de hominis generatione decateuchon* (Rome, 1642), a giant folio from which selections were translated into English as *Rare Verities, or the Cabinet of Venus Unlocked* (1658). Potted versions of Sinibaldus were sold in Britain after 1670 and in the early eighteenth century, some under the name of Dr Salonici of Venice.[10] In the original translation, the author, Erotodidasculus, presents his 'amorous readers' with discussions of the lustfulness of maids, women, and men, as compared to beasts. He also inquires into the possibilities of changing one's sex and shows how to 'inlarge [sic] the pudenda to a fit proportion, in case it be neither long, nor thick enough', and 'how to shorten the Yard being too long'.[11] Nicolas Venette (1632–98) popularised Sinibaldus. His *De la génération de l'homme, ou tableau de l'amour conjugal* (Amsterdam, 1687) first appeared in English as *Mysteries of Conjugal Love Reveal'd* in 1703 and was often republished in the eighteenth century. Leonard de Vries and Peter Fryer, in their delightful anthology of eighteenth-century erotica, provide an idea of the erotic attraction of a version published around 1740, entitled *The Pleasures of Conjugal Love Explain'd*, which had chapters on 'What hour of the day or night one ought to kiss one's wife', 'How many times one may amorously caress one's wife in a night', and on 'Whether the man feels more pleasure in enjoyment than the woman'.[12]

One of the few writers who wanted to avoid salacity while describing human sexual relations was the French naturalist, Buffon (1707–88). Extremely dissatisfied with the choice between either physiological or licentious jargon, he tried to teach others a lesson by developing a 'langage humaniste', which he tested rather successfully in his description of the female sexual organs and the stage of puberty. Buffon did not place a rhetorical veil over the topics he discussed, thus bereaving his readers of the pleasure of taking it off; but without using too much technical vocabulary or launching into bawdry he remained nonetheless precise.[13]

The majority of the popular medical sex guides were still very much indebted to the Middle Ages and antiquity, their common denominator being the rejection of the intellectualisation of medicine. Given the residue of folklore, superstition, and myths, as well as the poetic rather than scientific diction of these works, it is obvious that erotic and obscene elements seeped in – and were even meant to be included, in order to gain more attention. Myths were an integral part of highly respected and respectable works. A writer by the name of Menken, who was the rector of the University of Leipzig, accused medical authors in particular in his *De la charlatanerie des savans* (The Hague, 1721), arguing that 'la Charlatanerie est la cinquième & même la principale Partie de la Médecine'.[14] A particularly good example of erotic and obscene elements in serious, learned medical works on sexual problems are the publications of Martin Schurig, in particular his *Spermatologia historico-medica* (Frankfurt, 1720), *Muliebra historico-medica* (Dresden/Leipzig, 1729), and *Gynaecologia historico-medica* (Dresden/Leipzig, 1730). With their mixture of quasi-scientific and erotic material, these works assemble 'facts and anecdotes', repeated from volume to volume, and can be considered as prototypes of what came to be known as 'Sittengeschichten'. Written in Latin, with lengthy quotations in German, Italian, and Dutch, they were reserved for medical circles. *Spermatologia* is chiefly concerned with the act of generation, but shows, in its abundance of curious anecdotes, the influence of Sinibaldus and Venette. Thus Schurig provides examples of women changed into men; he also has a remarkable chapter on copulation; compares the size of the nose with that of the penis; and quotes writers affirming that Adam was an hermaphrodite.

His *Muliebra* contains detailed discussions of the genitals of women and has additional material on 'tribades', sodomy 'committed in three ways', the 'usus vaginae', and an extraordinary example of female lubricity. The *Gynaecologia* is the most interesting of Schurig's books. While the main focus of the work is on woman's part in coition, there is also a spate of anecdotes about Messalina and Cleopatra, as well as on cuckolds, and the difficulties of deflowering virgins. We are also informed about men who 'performed' twenty times in a row; the various ways in which sodomy is practised by different peoples; how bestiality may be committed with various animals; and about sex with maids, or demons, and even with statues.[15]

In addition to Schurig's exclusive *Muliebra*, there were more popular sex guides, treating of women's sexual difficulties and containing potentially pornographic material. Closely related to these handbooks for ladies were the popular directories for midwives, which, by their very nature, offered pabulum for the prurient. Laurence Sterne, the great master of the *double entendre* and of the sexual allusion in the eighteenth-century novel, was the proud owner of Maubray's *Female Physician* and Nihell's *Treatise on the Art of Midwifery* (1760), in addition to several books on VD. Such works combined a hotchpotch of correct information, half-truths, folklore, and salacious stories. One favourite topic among the writers or compilers of these treatises was the clitoris, whose function, manipulation, and possible malformations received ample attention. Midwifery gained additional attention through the fact that in the eighteenth century women were gradually excluded from the medical profession and even lost ground in midwifery. This was a consequence of the introduction of the forceps in the 1720s and the concomitant claim of surgeons to deliver children, as well as the changing habit of middle-class women, who were beginning to emulate the upper class; there, it was rather fashionable to have a male doctor or 'accoucheur' supervise the birth of a child. Man-midwives became the butt of satires, which usually exploited the possibilities for amorous dalliance between the man-midwife and his patient, such as *The Man-Midwife Unmasqu'd* of 1739. Even some of the more serious publications, while condemning male practice, used the promise of salacious stories as a come-on to ensure commercial success.[16]

A delightful if peculiar genre of sex guide are those written in verse. Poetry served many purposes in the eighteenth century, from social criticism and lampoons to love letters and epitaphs. Nobody objected to its employment in the description of sexual relations. Successful doctors like John Armstrong used verse to express their medical opinions. His *The Art of Preserving Health: A Poem* (1744), although not particularly erotic, was often read, seeing a second edition in 1745, which was followed by numerous reprints. Armstrong also wrote a poetical treatment of sex, which found as much interest as his health guide. *The Oeconomy of Love. A Poetical Essay* (1736) first described the time and signs of puberty in both sexes, and pronounced warnings against early love affairs. Making love, after choosing and marrying a 'soft nymph', is the focal point of the following passage:

> Now with your happy Arms her Waist surround,
> Fond-grasping; on her swelling Bosom now
> Recline your Cheek, with eager Kisses press
> Her balmy Lips, and drinking from her Eyes
> . . .
> Stretch'd on the flow'ry turf, while joyful glows
> Thy manly Pride, and throbbing with Desire
> Pants earnest, felt thro' all the obstacles
> . . .
> Then when her lovely Limbs,
> Oft lovely deem'd, far lovelier now beheld,
> Thro' all your trembling Joints increase the Flame;
> Forthwith discover to her dazzled sight
> The stately Novelty, and to her Hand
> Usher the new Acquaintance. She perhaps
> Averse will coldly chide, and half afraid,
> Blushing, half pleas'd, the tumid Wonder view
> With Neck retorted and oblique Regard;
> . . .
> Perhaps when you attempt
> The sweet Admission, toyful she resists
> With shy reluctance; natheless you pursue
> The soft Attack, and push the gentle War,
> Fervent, till quite o'erpower'd the melting Maid
> Faintly opposes. On the Brink at last
> Arriv'd of giddy Rapture, plunge not in
> Precipitant, but spare a Virgin's Pain . . .

A true follower of Enlightenment ideas, Armstrong then warns against dedicating too much time and attention to love, advises 'those that pursue Amours . . . to be discreet and secret', and is in accordance with other writers in his rejection of homosexuality and perversion:

> For Man with Man,
> And Man with Woman (monstr'ous to relate!)
> Leaving the natural Road, themselves debase

> With Deeds unseemly, and Dishonour found.
> *Britons*, for shame! Be Male and Female still.
> Banish this foreign Vice; it grows not here,
> It dies, neglected; and in Clime so chaste
> Cannot but by forc'd Cultivation thrive.

The view that buggery, sodomy, and kinky sexual behaviour were of foreign origin, especially Italian or eastern European, was quite common among English writers until well into the nineteenth century. Armstrong's poem is designed to facilitate the finding of special, titillating passages, in that line references and contents are given on a page entitled 'The Argument', which precedes the actual text.[17]

The Love-Encounter, an eighteenth-century satire, published 'At Cnidus' without any date, mocks the practice of medical jargon in combining the poetic and the scientific. Formally, this satire is a parody of a medical treatise on sexual intercourse, in 'The First Section' describing the male genitals:

> The erect Vehicle by which it is hurried thither, varies its Figure according to Diversity of Circumstances; and appears now haughty, now mild, now elate, now humble; a true Representative of the Vicissitudes of Life.
>
> There are some who partially ascribe to the Activity of the MALES, the entire Glory of Propagation, and look on the FEMALES but as meer passive Recipients.
>
> I think quite otherwise, and that the Mothers can lay Claim to a great Share in this wonderful Operation; for if we find in them an instrumental Apparatus almost similar to that which we see in the Sires, by the Rules of *Analogy* the Effects ought to be at least similar.

In 'The Second Section', interspersing verse with prose, intercourse is described:

> But see the Conqueror approaches, high crested and big with the Idea of his pleasing Triumph; lazure Streaks chequer the Smoothness of his Form; adorn'd with Locks like those that curl over the Front of JOVE, he is, like him, by SATELLITES attended.
>
> As the DEITY advances, the NYMPHS retire, CLITORIS rages, HYMEN disappears.
>
> By mutual Embraces the true Lover's Knot is made; interchanging Passions blaze in their Eyes; each Nerve Exerts its utmost Vigour, and clung Lips transfuse their mingling Souls – It is all a Storm of tender Violence, until the rosy visag'd Hero dissolves into ambrosial Tears.

The end of the 'treatise' resumes the attack on quacks and medical jargon, praising this 'Physico-medico-facto-chymico Medley Piece' and promising help to those in whom the 'love-arrow' is defunct.[18]

Almost as popular as the sex manuals were the publications on venereal diseases. Always a subject for ridicule in the seventeenth century, VD also began to interest scientists and quacks. The wide prevalence of VD around 1750 only boosted the sale of treatises. In any case, it was a rewarding ground for peddlers of erotica, who cashed in on the tradition of bawdy references to syphilis and gonorrhea while exploiting the ambiguities of such subject matter for their own purposes.[19] The preoccupation of the eighteenth century with discourse on sex and the danger of VD is to some extent mirrored by the introduction into general usage of the term 'condom', a protection that was common in the better brothels.[20]

2 THE LITERATURE ON MASTURBATION

Enthusiasm for the ideas of the Enlightenment led to analysis of many aspects of human sexuality. While a number of people may have profited from such treatises as G. Archibald Douglas' *The Nature and Causes of Impotence in Men, and Barrenness in Women, Explained* (1758), which did some good despite its errors and myths, the combined efforts of medical and moral writers did not necessarily produce positive results.[21] In fact, the massive literature on masturbation that originated in the eighteenth century is dominated by a tone of total and repressive sexual intolerance. Various arguments have been put forward to explain the sudden mania about 'self-abuse', and its alleged dreadful consequences, as manifestations of misconceptions on the part of almost all writers on the subject. R.P. Neumann believes that the noticeable anxiety of doctors, moralists, and parents must be seen as 'a confused response to the earlier onset of puberty in Western Europe, and also the product of certain middle-class sexual concepts which mirrored and reinforced other economic values and social attitudes'.[22] The powerful and long-lasting misconception that masturbation is a specific cause of mental and physical diseases was the brainchild of moral writers in the religious field, who, at the turn of the seventeenth century, demanded more strictness in an age which they saw as dominated by apostasy and uncleanness. However, it was the medical teaching on masturbation which proved to be most repressive, as T. Tarczylo has shown.[23] The enormously successful publication entitled *Onania, or, The Heinous Sin of Self-Pollution, and All its Frightful Consequences in Both Sexes, Considered* must be seen as one of the major forces spreading the false news of the evil effects of masturbation; although the concern with 'the secret sin' did not start with the appearance of this work in 1708, but had developed slowly, over two decades.[24]

Published by a clergyman-cum-quack probably called Balthazar Beckers (or Bekkers), *Onania* grew from a short booklet of about 60 pages to 194 pages, receiving a supplement of 142 pages in the sixteenth edition.[25] Apart from making a false connection between masturbation and venereal disease, the work in its eager attempt to point out the noxious and immoral effects of the 'sin of self-pollution', also provides an erroneous interpretation of the account of Onan in Genesis 38, 4–11, where the reference is to coitus interruptus and not to masturbation. While the errors and myths in the *Onania* have been studied in great detail, no author has yet provided a sufficiently convincing explanation of how a religiously oriented work, despite its elements of anxiety and fear, and a strong awareness of sin, went through at least nineteen editions, probably selling close to 38,000 copies.

The letters to the author, reprinted by him on pp. 73–193 and in the *Supplement of the Onania*, constitute some of the most titillating material of the whole work. One very sensible reader charged the author with lack of explicitness and a failure to point out alternatives for unmarried people, who, if they wanted to have a sex life at all, only had the choice, according to *Onania*, between the sin of fornication and the sin of masturbation.[26] The majority of the letters describe particular problems and the way *Onania* provided help. A confessional situation is thus created, which allows the reader of these letters to listen in, so to speak, on men and women describing allegedly sinful sexual behaviour. By replacing the author, to whom the letters are addressed, the reader becomes a voyeur. It should be recalled that masturbation, and in particular masturbation by women, is one of the necessary themes, if not staple diets, of eighteenth-century pornography. It plays an important part in such successful novels as *Thérèse philosophe*, *Histoire de Dom B.*, and *Fanny Hill*.[27] One example will suffice to demonstrate this aspect in *Onania*. The author claims that a young lady sent the following letter to him:

To the commendable Author of ONANIA.

Sir,   Oct. 16, 1735

This Letter comes from a young Female Creature, but an old Transgresser in the Practice of that filthy Pleasure which you have so justly exploded and condemned in your ingenious Book of *Onania*, which I happily met with about ten Days ago: But in all the Cases therein enumerated, there is not one that is parallel to mine, which, as my Welfare requires it, I must be obliged to relate, and is what I question, Sir, whether you have ever once met with: Nor could I tell it, though, at the same Time, I bless the Opportunity, but that I am sure you no more know the Writer of it, nor ever will, than I know the author of *Onania*, or desire it. I began, Sir, the Folly at eleven Years of Age; was taught it by my Mother's Chamber-Maid, who lay with me from that Time all along till now, which is full seven Years, and so intimate were we in the Sin, that we took all Opportunities of committing it, and invented all the Ways we were capable of to heighten the Titillation, and gratify our sinful Lusts the more, as being prompted to it by *Aristotle's* saying, That Women might procure to themselves, *cum Digitis, vel aliis Instrumentis*, a Sensation, *non multo minor Coitu Voluptas*. We, in short, shamefully pleasured one another, as well as each ourselves; but whether by the hard Usage of my Parts by her, or myself, or both, or whether from any Thing in Nature more in my Make than is customary to the Sex I do not know; but, for above half a Year past I have had a Swelling that thrust out from my Body, as big, and almost as hard, and as long or longer, than my Thumb, which inclines me to excessive lustful Desires, and from it there issues a Moisture or Slipperiness, to that Degree, that I am almost continually wet, and sometimes have such a forcing, as if something of a large Substance was coming from me, which greatly frightens both me and my Maid.[28]

She then bemoans her fate and asks the author for speedy advice. Most of the letters are answered dutifully with a metaphorical wagging of the finger at the masturbator. In this instance, the reader is informed that the young lady's case,

> through the Height of her Lust, and Force and Frequency of abusing herself, and probably the unnatural Propendance of the Part, is no more . . . than a Relaxation of the Clitoris, a Thing common to many of the Sex, both single and married, who are vigorous and lascivious, and have given themselves to the Practice of Self-Pollution . . .[29]

This story is followed by remarks on hermaphrodites, who are in this case equated with women suffering from an enlarged clitoris. Beckers quotes from the *Book of Anatomy* of Dr Drake:

> Dr. Drake. . . . tells us, that the extraordinary Size and Laxness of the *Clitoris*, hanging out of the Body of some Infants, has made the Women mistake Children for those Sort of Monsters they call *Hermaphrodites*. Of this Sort, says he, I had one brought to me upon another Occasion, whose *Clitoris* hung out of the Body so far, at about three Years old, that it resembled very much a *Penis*, but it wanted the Perforation . . . so that the Parents mistook it for a Boy . . . It is certain, that in some Women, especially those who are very salacious, and have much abused themselves by

SELF-Pollution, the *Clitoris* is so vastly extended, that, upon its thrusting out of the passage, it is mistaken for a *Penis*; such have been called *Fricattrices*; by *Gaelius Aurelianus*, *Tribades*; by *Plautus*, *Subigatrices*, and accounted *Hermaphrodites*, because, as is said before, they have been able to perform the Actions of Men with other Women.[30]

Hermaphrodites being generally considered as monsters, their equation with masturbating women is obviously meant to frighten the latter.[31]

Clearly, the success of *Onania* was due to several factors. Not only did it introduce an important topic of sexuality, hitherto considered taboo, into general public discussion, but it also loaded it with sin and anxiety, to deter the young. The inclusion of salacious material and its presentation in a voyeuristic situation of epistolary confessions must have increased the popularity of the book and should not be underestimated. Ironically, even the religious quarter used the topic as a come-on for the sale of its moralistic tracts; and these more religiously oriented publications, which contained a quantity of erroneous medical information, ruled the field until about the middle of the eighteenth century, when the medical writers joined forces with the moralists. Considering the 'genital liquor' as something precious, an idea which was cherished in classical times and throughout the Middle Ages, the physicians argued unanimously that it must not be wasted. Lengthy lists of dreadful physical consequences were drawn up in order to deter masturbators.[32] A Swiss doctor by the name of Samuel Auguste André David Tissot (1728–97) became the outstanding authority on the subject. He was a fellow of the Royal Society of London, a member of the Medico-Physical Society of Basel and of the Oeconomical Society of Berne, and his word carried weight, especially in Catholic countries, which honoured his place as one of the personal counsellors of the Pope on medical matters. Tissot's *L'onanisme, ou dissertation physique sur les maladies produites par la masturbation* (Lausanne, 1760) became one of the most influential and widely read medical works in the eighteenth and nineteenth centuries. It was first translated into English by Dr Hume in 1766, as *Onanism: or, A Treatise Upon the Disorders Produced by Masturbation: or, The Dangerous Effects of Secret and Excessive Venery*, reaching a fifth edition in 1781.[33]

Tissot's major *opus* consists of four parts, which treat of the symptoms, the causes, and the cure of masturbation, as well as 'accessory or relative diseases'. The first part includes a chapter on the terrible consequences female masturbators have to face; but he is generally more concerned with men.

Tissot's neglect of discussing female masturbation in greater detail was amended by the French physician M.D.T. de Bienville, whose most successful book was translated by Dr Edward Sloane Wilmot (an obscure Englishman resident in Italy and not to be confused with the eminent physician-in-waiting of King George III) and appeared as *Nymphomania, or, a Dissertation Concerning the Furor Uterinus* (1775). Paying frequent homage to Tissot, de Bienville claims that his book is a strict application of the latter's methods. Like Tissot, he offers no analysis of pleasure and reproduces the same results and failings. De Bienville does not recognise an autonomous female erotic ego. In his opinion, clitoral masturbation is bound to bring about hysteria and nymphomania. It is obvious that he could not avoid discussions leading him upon tricky, sexually equivocal ground. In Part II he provides 'a general description of the Nymphomania':

> To this disorder, young widows are frequently liable, especially if death hath deprived them of a strong, and vigorous man, during a commerce with whom, by acts briskly repeated, they had acquired an habitude in pleasures, the delicious remembrance of which too often affects them with that bitter regret ... when once they yield themselves to this disorder, are uninterruptedly busied with equal perseverance and eagerness in the search of such objects as may kindle their passions and the infernal firebrand of lubricity.[34]

His erotic passages include a detailed description of the erogenous zones and 'observations on the imagination, as connected with the Nymphomania'. These observations contain the history of Julia, a girl who is initiated into the art of love by a waiting-woman. Julia's sexual development occupies the author for about twenty pages. He also gives a detailed account of her gradual mastering of masturbatory practices, against which he pronounces severe warnings.[35] The underlying belief in the destructive violence of female sexual desire that this work betrays is best exemplified by the methods of cure de Bienville prescribes. These methods are dependent, in his opinion, upon the stage the 'furor uterinus' has reached in the female patient. In the first stage he suggests that three indications be followed.

> The first indication is the necessity of tempering, and cooling the blood ... The second indication is the necessity of moistening, and relaxing all the internal face of the matrix, and of the vagina. The third indication is the necessity of withdrawing the patient from her obscene thoughts.[36]

The possibilities of using bleeding and purgatives are also considered, while in desperate cases he is all in favour of the strait-jacket.

Thus the rejection of masturbation was almost total in the eighteenth century, since the writers of the Enlightenment, equally, condemned it, although their reasons may have differed from those of doctors and moralists. Voltaire and Rousseau, for instance, also believed in noxious physical consequences of masturbation; but they were more concerned with the fact that in the thought of their time it was 'unnatural' and that it enhanced the danger of a decreasing population. Boucé has shown that opposition on the part of writers to masturbation reached down into sub-literary strata. The only noteworthy exception is a work entitled *La masturbomanie, ou la jouissance solitaire*, which seems to be of early nineteenth-century origin and sings the praise of the 'solitary pleasure'.[37] If this lonely voice from France ever reached the shores of England, it must have found a bad reception.

3 FREAKS AND KINKY SEX

The writings of the *philosophes* tend to make us forget that the eighteenth century could be cruel and unenlightened. Homosexuals, if caught in the act, were put to death – unless they were aristocrats, in which case they went abroad if prosecution threatened. Sexual freaks were ridiculed, while unusual sexual behaviour – which the twentieth century would label as being still within acceptable limits – was equated with perversion. But there was no shortage of writings on the more freakish aspects of sex, discovered by the eighteenth century, following remarkable development in the refinement and sophistication of manners. Eunuchs and hermaphrodites had received mostly scabrous attention in literature from Roman times throughout the Middle Ages; but flagellation and strangulation, in a sexual context, do not seem to have interested many readers and authors before the eighteenth century. While the literature on flagellation as a means of sexual stimulation only reached its heyday after 1800, in the eighteenth century the public appetite was already being whetted.

Jacques Boileau (1635–1716), one of the numerous French *abbés* who acquired more fame in the field of erotica than in religion, seems to have been one of the first writers on flagellation with his *Historia flagellantium, de recto et perverso flagrorum usu* (Paris, 1700). This was made accessible to a wider public with a French translation, *Histoire des flagellants* (Amsterdam, 1701). The book claims to be an historical survey of flagellation as a punishment in nunneries and monasteries. Along the way, however, the reader is also served titbits of indecent details in the description of punishments with the rod or whip which naked 'Christians', not always of the same sex, inflicted on each other.[38] Boileau's treatise was apparently well known in England, for two ancillary publications took it for granted that readers were acquainted with the *abbé*'s book. The first appeared in 1783 and bore the alluring title, *The History of the Flagellants: otherwise, Of Religious Flagellations among different Nations, and especially among Christians. Being a Paraphrase and Commentary on the* Historia Flagellantium *of the Abbé Boileau, Doctor of the Sorbonne, Canon of the Holy Chapel, &c.* Written by 'one who is not a Doctor of the Sorbonne' (i.e., J.L. Delolme), the book is an implicit attack on religious practices, ridiculing Quakers and, above all, Catholics. Apart from mocking bishops, cardinals, and popes who condoned flagellation, Delolme takes an obvious satirical delight in the description of the 'discretionary powers of flagellation ... established in the Convents of Nuns, and lodged in the hands of the Abbesses, or Prioresses', (Chapter XII) and in the 'story of a female Saint appeased by a flagellation' (Chapter XXII).[39]

According to Ned Ward's monthly *London Spy*, a periodical flourishing around the turn of the seventeenth century, the rod was very much in demand among the elderly customers of brothels. The main character of the satirical *Spy*, an innocent countryman guided by a friend through the pits and snares of the immoral metropolis, one night visits the 'Widow's Coffee-House', a modest name for a bordello. When a 'sober Citizen ... about the Age of Sixty' enters the establishment, the bawd immediately asks one of the ladies in attendance whether there are any rods in the house.

> The Wench answer'd, *Yes, yes, You know I fetch'd six penny worth but Yesterday.* Upon the Entrance of this grave Fornicator, our Ladies withdrew themselves from our Company, and retir'd like *Modest Virgins* to their Secret *Work-Room* of Iniquity; and left the *Old Sinner*, in the *Winter* of his *Leachery*, to warm his *Grey-Hairs* with a Dram of *Invigorating Cordial*, whilst we pay'd our Reckoning.

When the countryman asks his London acquaintance about the meaning of the question concerning the rods, he is told that the

> Sober seeming Saint ... is one of that Classis in the Black School of *Sodomy*, who are call'd by Learned Students in the Science of Debauchery, *Flogging Cullies*. This Unnatural Beast gives Money to those Strumpets

3 Curll, *A Treatise of the Use of Flogging*, 1718

which you see, and they down with his Breeches and Scourge his Privities till they have laid his Leachery. He all the time begs their Mercy, like an Offender at a *Whipping-Post*, and beseeches their forbearance; but the more importunate he seems for their favourable usage, the severer Vapulation they are to exercise upon him, till they find by his Beastly Extasie, when to withhold their Weapons.[40]

Ward abstained from downright pornography but sailed close to the wind. By 1718, however, Edmund Curll, one of the tsars of early eighteenth-century English pornography, thought the time had come to exploit the obscene aspects of erotic flagellation. Adding an explicit frontispiece (plate 3) and a *Treatise of Hermaphrodites* to an English translation of John Henry Meibomius' *De usu flagrorum* (Leyden, 1639; 2nd edn, Frankfurt, 1670), he published *A Treatise of the Use of Flogging In Venereal Affairs*, for which he was later prosecuted.[41] This treatise was republished in 1761, with a cover before the title, reading, 'The use of Flogging, as provocative to the pleasures of love. With some Remarks on the Office of the Loins and Reins'. In the preface, Curll defended himself against accusations of pornography, arguing that 'the Fault is not in the Subject Matter, but the Inclination of the Reader, that makes these Pieces offensive'.

Flagellation, though not always in a sexual context, continued to interest publishers and readers. Discussions and letters dealing with the art of flogging can be found in the periodicals throughout the century, from the respectable *Gentleman's Magazine* in the 1730s to the erotic *Bon Ton Magazine* in the 1790s.[42] A print dated 1752 depicts the erotic joys of flagellation as well as voyeurism. In 1782 the subject gained a legal dimension when a judge by the name of John Buller declared that a man could legally chastise his wife, provided he used a stick no thicker than his thumb. Several cartoons immediately satirised the words of this learned man. Toward the end of the century, flagellation mania, or at least the discourse about it, seems to have increased, foreshadowing what came to be known as the Victorian vice. The two volumes of *Exhibition of Female Flagellants in the Modest and Incontinent World* were published in 1775 and 1785, and in 1792 followed *The Cherub: or, Guardian of Female Innocence*. All these works contain scenes of sexual flagellation, often in boarding schools, and show traces of paedophilia, which was to be developed by Victorian pornography. Gillray's satire on the auction already included a hint at the new vice; but it was Gillray himself who made it obvious, with his sketch in 1786 on *Lady Termagant Flaybum Going to Give her Step Son a Taste of Her Desert after Dinner* (plate 4).[43]

Like flagellation, 'amorous strangulation' found much interest with those seeking extraordinary or vicarious ways of sexual stimulation. In the early eighteenth century the case of Peter Motteux, a literary hack who edited a magazine and translated Rabelais, caused some stir in London's satirical circles. His accidental death in 1718 was apparently the result of sexual strangulation in a bawdy house. Several ribald satires alluded to his case in the years to follow. The theme of strangulation for erotic purposes united both pornographers and medical quacks of late eighteenth-century London. Their relationship is highlighted by the accidental death of Franz Kotzwara, a composer whose music was popular in England and America until well into the twentieth century. Kotzwara's penchant for wine and women, together with a sexual abnormality, were the causes behind his 'accident' in 1791, which in turn started a trial at the Old Bailey. According to a rare manuscript trial report, the musician arrived at the house of one Susannah Hill, a prostitute, and first provided her with some money to procure liquor and food. Subsequently, he made perverse sexual suggestions to her, requesting some form of sexual mutilation.

LADY TERMAGANT FLAYBUM *going to give her* STEP SON *a taste of her* DESERT *after Dinner* / *Scene performed every day near Grosvenor Square to the annoyance of the neighbourhood*

4 Gillray, *Lady Termagant Flaybum Going to Give her Step Son a Taste of Her Desert after Dinner*, 1786

When she refused these requests, he proposed that she hang him up for some time so that he might gain some sexual gratification from this. Susannah bought a rope with the money she received from Kotzwara and he made a noose which she attached to the knob of the door. He then suspended himself for about five minutes. When Susannah cut him down, he was apparently dead. A few days later, she was put on trial, charged with the murder of Franz Kotzwara by hanging him with a rope. After the examination of two witnesses, Judge Gould directed the jury to acquit the prisoner. The Court regarded the case as extremely indecent and wanted to prohibit the publication of the circumstances. Hence it was ordered that the shorthand reporter tear up the notes he had taken, before the whole court. While the official record was thus destroyed, the existence of a manuscript copy indicates that someone may have considered a publication of this case. This never happened, although several newspapers covered the trial and published the gist of the proceedings.

During the time that Kotzwara became a victim of his strange inclinations, an eccentric quack named Martin Vanbutchell was engaging in the promotion of suffocation and strangulation for sexual pleasure. He published cryptic advertisements in London newspapers and may very well be the author of a bizarre pamphlet, probably published about a year after Kotzwara's death, whose title reads, *Modern Propensities; or, An Essay on the Art of Strangling, &c. Illustrated with Several Anecdotes. With Memoirs of Susannah Hill, and a Summary of Her Trial at the Old-Bailey, on Friday, September 16, 1791, on the Charge of Hanging Francis Kotzwara, at Her Lodgings in Vine Street, on September 2.* This work, of forty-six pages, consists of three parts. The first, the essay, contains references to James Graham's 'Celestial Bed', which was supposed to bring relief from sterility. The dangers of Graham's device for the elderly are then pointed out. Instead of 'internal excitements', the pamphlet proposes 'external expedients' and launches into a discussion of flagellation, trying to show that pain promotes, and is a concomitant of, pleasure. At last, the main part of the essay is reached with the introduction of suffocation and the 'vital emotions' it produces. The author states:

> That every thing which produced irritation in the lungs and thorax, produced also titulation in the generative organs: that the blood by such means being impeded in its regular velocity, rushed to the center, and there formed, by sudden and compulsive operations, a redundancy of those vivifying secretions which animate and invigorate the machinery of procreation.

Allegedly, criminals went to their deaths more happily, once they had been informed of this physiological reaction. A prison chaplain, 'Reverend Parson Manacle', is said to have expired while indulging in the practice of hanging himself. However, this sad conclusion could be avoided according to the pamphlet:

> It were therefore to be wished that *gentlemen* who are obliged to acquire the powers of procreation through the physical medium of strangling, would devise some certain means of watching its progress, and checking an inordinate indulgence of its paregoric influence; and for this purpose there is no medical or surgical artist better calculated than the celebrated Patent Inventor of Spring Banks, in Mount-street, who ... could very probably invent not only a safe but an agreeable mode of suspension...

Unfortunately, this wonderful apparatus was still to be built, and the author therefore recommends that practitioners of strangulation have recourse to Dr Vanbutchell's astonishing nostrum, approved by Dr John Hunter, and sold under the name of *Vanbutchell's Balsam of Life.* The final paragraph continues to praise the products of Martin Vanbutchell. Vanbutchell may also have had a hand in the writing of some articles on strangulation, in several issues of *The Bon Ton Magazine* in 1793. One of them discussed the 'Origin of Amorous Strangulation' and another one, the 'Effects of Temporary Strangulation on the Human Body'. The latter appeared in the September issue of the magazine and is written in much the same tone as *Modern Propensities*:

> The strangulation of Kotzwara, however, whimsically fatal, has not entirely discouraged the practice of animal suspension. It unfortunately appeared, from the *private* examination of the fair object who assisted that eccentric paramour in the operation, that for some moments before his final exit, he actually did evince, *certain signs* of ability, which clearly demonstrated the good effects of his expedient – she was, indeed, rather gross and direct in *her* description, but, speaking with technical delicacy, *we* will say, that during those concluding *paroxisms*, *spasms*, and *corporeal fidgettings* which attend total dissolution, she observed a kind of *central tumour* and *pulsation*, which promised fairly an actual reciprocity of *contact*.

Adding a fictional aspect to Kotzwara's sad case, which *The Bon Ton Magazine* exploits without any moral scruples, the article claims that 'a wealthy citizen of Bristol' who was himself 'in want of auxiliary assistance in the private affairs of Venus', decided to 'adopt the antidote, but with more caution'. His efforts with 'a fair Cyprian of Charlotte-street' are shown in a plate (plate 5). All was in vain, however. When the citizen began to choke and quiver,

> the fair one ... examined the parts particularly in question; but, alas! instead of those warm vivifying effects which were expected ... all was cold as a stone! Alarmed at this unexpected and deleterious symptom, our heroine, with more dexterity and coolness than her Vine Street prototype, cut the instrument of suspension, and gently holding her fair bosom against the prominent abdomen of our meretricious adventurer, let him down easy, and just in time enough to save his life...[44]

Those lovers of the joys of Venus who found strangulation and flagellation too dangerous or perverse but wanted additional stimulation, could always have recourse to less spectacular sexual aids. One of them is described by Georges-Louis Lesage (1676–1759), who visited England in 1713–14. According to this French traveller, who is not identical with the author of *Gil Blas*, there were always some women in St James's Park, London, carrying baskets full of dolls which seemed to be in great demand with the younger ladies. Instead of legs, the dolls sported a cylinder, covered with cloth, which was about six inches long and one inch wide. Lesage reports in an anecdote that a

EFFECTS of STRANGULATION.

5 *Effects of Strangulation* – illustration from *The Bon Ton Magazine*, 1793

young woman found her purchase too big and ordered a smaller one. But the saleswoman insisted on being paid in advance, arguing that she would not be able to sell it, if ever the young lady changed her mind, since only big ones were being asked for.[45]

'Signor Dildo', as Rochester called this 'cylinder' in his poem of 1678, was apparently not only known but also in demand and, consequently, a subject of literary comment. It may be of some interest to have a closer look at *Monsieur Thing's Origin: or Seignor D———o's Adventures in Britain* (1722),[46] a rather badly rhymed poem which, despite its mediocre quality, provides some eighteenth-century opinions about the dildo, its alleged origin and uses:

> The Engine does come up so near to Nature,
> Can spout so pleasing, betwixt Wind and Water,
> Warm mild, or any other Liquid softer,
> Slow as they please, or, if they please, much faster.

'Monsieur Thing' afterwards meets a merchant's wife who is immediately very fond of him:

> She boldly work'd him up unto an Oil,
> So did she make the Creature slave and toil;
> She wrought him till he was just out of breath,
> And harrast Seignor almost unto Death.

Its tribulations are not finished with this episode, however. It must satisfy an old maid, and encounters two lesbians. One of the girls ties it to her middle:

> She acted Man, being in a merry Mood,
> Striving to please her Partner as she cou'd;
> And thus they took it in their turns to please
> Their Lustful Inclinations to appease.

The dildo also goes to court, before ending up with some old maids, who enjoy its company in secrecy. The tone of the poem is playful, occasionally lapsing into satire; but the author succumbed to one of the main obsessions of his age, the fear of depopulation. For this reason, the alien instrument was not to be accepted in Britain, as the last four lines make clear:

> Now [sic] doubt but this Uncouth contriv'd New Fashion
> Was to destroy the End of the Creation;
> Like that foul Sin which is as bad in Men,
> For which God did the Eastern World condemn.

Sold at sixpence a piece, *Monsieur Thing's Origin* did not meet everyone's taste. *The Daily Journal* of 9 June 1722 reports that a female bookseller sent constables to stop some hawkers selling the poem.[47]

If the evidence contained in a poem published in 1748 is correct, we can assume that eighteenth-century males with sufficient financial means could order life-size dolls for their private amusement. The preface of *Adollizing: or, A Lively Picture of Adoll-Worship. A Poem in Five Cantos* (1748) justifies the introduction into the English language of a new word and assures the reader 'that the ground-work, from whence the term of adollizing was taken, is a real fact ... A person of high distinction failing in his attempt on the virtue of a young lady ..., resolves to enjoy her at any rate, and thereupon has recourse to the extraordinary method here attempted to be described.' The poem relates the story of Clodius, a young gentleman used to easy conquests, who falls in love with the icy-cold and indifferent Clarabella. His fruitless efforts render him furious:

> Woman, cries he, when man's neglect denies,
> With mimic art the real thing supplies:
> When of dear copulation she despairs,
> At once a dildo softens all her cares.

Clodius decides to do alike and has a doll made for himself, 'as big as life'. Again, it is indicative of eighteenth-century English opinion on the origins of sexual perversity that 'a Latian artist' does the job, and not a morally upright English workman:

> On the arch'd mount, just o'er the cloven part,
> A tufft of hair he fixes with nice art,
> ...
> A seven-inch bore, proportion'd to his mind,
> With oval entrance, all with spunge he lin'd,
> Which warmly mollify'd, is fit for use,
> And will the sought-for consequence produce.

Clodius is very eager to try the invention forthwith:

> Stretch'd on a couch he *Claradolla* lay'd,
> (For so he call'd the figure newly made.)
> Her cloaths uplifted, bare her legs and thighs,
> And all expos'd he feasts his ravish'd eyes,
> Prostrate before the secret seat of bliss,
> The room resounds with ev'ry ardent kiss
> ...
> With this, fierce back the supple joints he flings,
> And his proud matters to a level brings

...
Then breathing quick, lust rushes thro' each vein,
And for that time concludes the filthy scene.

The last line indicates that the poem, despite its bawdy irony, is opposed to the 'unnatural practice' of 'adollizing'. In fact, the hero of the poem, after some further experimenting with his doll, which includes the changing of heads, eventually grows tired of his peculiar hobbyhorse. Clarabella's ice melts away with his ardent declarations of love, and they decide to get married. The author thus showed the 'person of high distinction' how to get rid of his strange passion, also informing him in the preface that he would be exposed, if he did not 'return to Venus'.[48]

The eighteenth century produced a considerable body of literature on freaks or sexually abnormal people. Eunuchs, hermaphrodites, homosexuals, lesbians, and transvestites were the objects of treatises, satirical attacks, moral diatribes, and erotic fiction, which all had one common denominator, despite their different literary origins. This was the calculated effort on the part of publishers to meet and exploit the prurient interest of readers in a notoriously equivocal subject matter, whose mysterious and occasionally frightening aspects literally invited comment, reaching from enlightened speculation to deliberate fabrication.

The castrated male or eunuch received ample literary attention, continuing a tradition which had already flourished in Roman and Greek times.[49] The idea that sexually promiscuous women relied on eunuchs to enjoy fornication without any danger became attached to castrated men for the rest of the century. It is perhaps most evident in fiction. In *New Attalantis for the Year 1762; Being a Select Portion of Secret History Containing Many Facts Strange! But True* (1762), a collection of five 'histories', the first episode describes the 'Amours of Lady Lucian', who is neglected by her husband. A good friend advises her ladyship to take a 'castrato' for a lover since 'these creatures are very tractable; it gratifies their pride to be taken notice of by a woman; and ... they toil like horses'. Lady Lucian decides to try Signor Squalini, a singer, who turns out to her entire satisfaction and is employed as her music master. One day, however, the happy musicians are interrupted by the lady's husband. Passing her room, he

heard his lady cry out in an extatic tone of voice, 'Give what thou can'st, and let me dream the rest.' His lordship was too well read in Pope, not to know where that line was, and the occasion of speaking it; he laid his hand immediately upon the lock of the door, and giving it a push open, for the

lady had omitted to bolt it, he beheld my lady and her master – not playing
the harpsichord, but playing upon it; her ladyship couchant on the instrument, which served her for a sopha, and the master recumbant on the lady,
while every now and then he touched the keys of the harpsichord with his
feet.[50]

Italian musicians continued to provide favourite targets for the satirists throughout the century. An untitled print of 1780, for instance,
shows the Italian composer Cotta in the process of fitting his wife with
false buttocks.

Cases of physical and psychical hybrids fascinated the eighteenth-
century reading public. Many of the hermaphrodites, as the bisexuals,
transsexuals, and transvestites were indiscriminately referred to, were
simply 'cross-dressers', while others were male homosexuals. For
centuries, the problem of hermaphrodites had provoked strong reactions. Real hermaphrodites – extremely rare cases – were put to death
in antiquity, while the Middle Ages knew a tradition of transvestite
female saints. The eighteenth century, which showed a deep interest in
monsters of any kind, continued to be attracted by the ambiguity of
the topic, not least because a number of men and women declared
themselves 'hermaphrodites'.[51] Popular sex guides usually had a section on sexual hybrids. Such cases were duly reported in newspapers
and received the full attention of doctors, theologians – and
pornographers.[52] Edmund Curll's *Tractatus de hermaphroditis: or, A
Treatise of Hermaphrodites* (1718), appropriately published with a
book on erotic flagellation, was obviously supposed to cater to those
looking for salacious entertainment. Part I of this treatise follows
closely in the tracks of Venette's distinctions of the several sorts of
hermaphrodites as laid down in *Le tableau de l'amour conjugal* and
repeats the myth of the enlarged clitoris of these creatures, which was a
favourite topic in the literature on masturbation. As such monsters
could hardly be of English origin, Part II contains 'intrigues' of hermaphrodites in Italy and Spain and also treats of 'the outward Marks
to distinguish them'. This is the actual pornographic part of the short
book of eighty-eight pages, offering explicit and voyeuristic scenes of
lesbian love involving dildos and other forms of sexual stimulation.
One episode introduces Philetus, disguised as a maid, who attempts to
woo Theodora away from the lesbian love of Amaryllis. When
Philetus has finally reached his aim and is making love to Theodora,
she thinks he is employing a dildo,

'till the moment of ejaculation, which was not usual with the same Instrument in her Embraces with Amaryllis: when this happen'd, she was pro-

digiously surpriz'd, and endeavouring to disengage her self from *Philetus*, he folded her more closely in his Arms, and in the greatest Transport told her, he was her constant Admirer *Philetus*.

Theodora is convinced and expresses her vow of reformation in a short verse.

> The Shadow I'll no longer try,
> Or use the pleasing Toy;
> A sprightly Youth I can't defy,
> The Substance I'll enjoy.

A few transsexuals and transvestites became internationally known, and their sexual predilections caused literary, and in one case even political, reverberations. In addition, the eighteenth century continued the literary tradition of bawdy and prurient works on sexual freaks. Antonio Beccadelli's *Ermafrodito* (Bologna, 1425), a collection of erotic epigrams based on the *Priapeia*, Martial, and Catullus; Artus Thomas' *Les hermaphrodites* (1605 and 1610); and the anonymous *L'hermaphrodite de ce temps* (1611?) are some of the more prominent examples known to the cognoscenti.[53]

There are some well-documented cases of transsexualism, i.e., men who felt as women and behaved accordingly, and vice versa. François-Timoléon de Choisy, also known as the Abbé de Choisy (1644–1724), lived the life of a girl from age fifteen to eighteen, then dressed as a man and later adopted the way of life of a 'countess' in the country, teaching young ladies and girls how to behave properly. The rakish *abbé* is alleged to have seduced some of his innocent pupils.[54] The mysterious life and personality of the Chevalier d'Eon, one of the numerous French expatriates in eighteenth-century England, continues to puzzle historians and writers to this very day. Charles Geneviève Louise Auguste Andrée Timothée d'Eon de Beaumont (1728–1810), whose mixed Christian names may serve as an indication of his sexual dilemma, was a French political adventurer equally famed for his transsexual tendencies, his excellent swordsmanship, and his clandestine role as a spy and ambassador for the court of France. Like the Abbé de Choisy, he was dressed in girl's clothes at an early age. In 1755 he wore women's clothes as a secret agent of the French king in St Petersburg. His later life in England was as bizarre. As minister plenipotentiary at the court in London, from 1762 to 1763, he quarrelled with his successor. Once this affair was settled, d'Eon was ordered by his sovereign to dress as a woman – it is not clear why this decision was taken. Bets were laid on d'Eon's real sex. One better, a surgeon by the name of Hayes, claimed he could prove that the chevalier was a woman and sued him. The case was tried in 1777 before Lord Mansfield, and a jury decided on evidence that Hayes was right. D'Eon dressed as a woman until his death. Because of financial trouble, he was compelled in the latter part of his life to take part in exhibition fencing matches, proving very successful until he received a severe wound at the age of sixty-eight. A post-mortem examination established that he was a man.[55]

Among the women who felt an urge to behave like the opposite sex, we have the recorded cases of the negress 'William Brown'; Christian Davies (1667–1739), an Irishwoman masquerading as a man in the army; and Hannah Snell (1723–92), who was also a female soldier. Davies was celebrated in *Life and Adventures of Mrs Christian Davies* (1740; reprinted 1741), an 'autobiography' attributed to Defoe, which – according to the *Dictionary of National Biography* – contains portions 'uniformly disfigured by the revolting details of many unseemly and brutal acts, related in a tone of self-glorification which is suggestive of nothing so much as of an unsexed woman'. Hannah Snell is the protagonist of *The Female Soldier* (1750), which relates her picaresque life as 'James Gray' on board several ships and in the army. She later returned to England to wear petticoats again, became insane in 1789, and was removed to Bethlehem Hospital, where she died, aged sixty-nine. Parts of her biography, such as the five hundred lashes she is supposed to have received after enlisting as a 'man' in Coventry, are written by a hand well skilled in the production of fiction.[56] Contemporary prints on the punishment of transvestites show the public interest in and fear of such people. After the mid-century, there were many other cases of women dressing as men; nine of them are recorded in the *Annual Register*, between 1761 and 1793.[57]

Some of the transvestites were homosexuals, who met with a strong reaction among eighteenth-century writers. Whether they were novelists, scholars, or quacks, all authors agreed that homosexuality, or sodomy as it was called, was one of the most detestable forms of sexual perversion. There is a remarkable unanimity of opinion on this topic in all extant documents that broach the 'unnatural crime', which was punishable by death in England from 1533 onwards. Characteristically, the pornographers, although feasting their own and the public's eyes on the 'mollies', generally abstained from publishing obscene details of trials for sodomy, while transcripts of trials for adultery and rape, for instance, were minutely reported and frequently reprinted. Obviously, sodomy was taboo. The eighteenth century stressed its non-procreative aspects and the fact that it was condemned in the Bible and by the Church Fathers. Since it was unnatural, according to contemporary thinking, homosexuals were perverts. These factors merged with the idea of the homosexual as a passive, effeminate man, which threatened a culture founded on male aggression and aggressiveness. As a logical consequence, homosexual behaviour in women was not as objectionable as it was in men. It would be going beyond the scope of the present work to provide a study of homosexuals in the various social strata and their sub-culture in eighteenth-century England. Several scholars have tried to analyse these issues, notably Randolph Trumbach, A.L. Rowse, and H. Montgomery Hyde. My focus is rather on the literary and sub-literary exploitation of the subject as a vehicle for erotic entertainment.[58]

No medical or para-medical treatises on sodomy seem to have survived. On the Continent, a few isolated voices argued for a moderation of the laws against buggery and sodomy. Montesquieu and Voltaire tried to point out to their unenlightened contemporaries the similarity between the laws against sodomy and against witchcraft, in an age when most intellectuals had rejected sorcery, while the German Friedrich August Braun pleaded for more leniency in the case of sodomites in his *Dissertatio juridica de mitigatione poenae in crimine sodomiae, von Milderung der Strafe beym Laster der Sodomiterey* (Frankfurt, 1750), which he presented in an inaugural address to the faculty of law of his university in 1739. But England, listening to the powerful voice of Blackstone, remained adamant. Indeed, it bespeaks the eighteenth-century English state of mind that Thomas Cannon, author of *Ancient and Modern Pederasty Investigated and Exemplified*, which was published in 1749, was prosecuted – together with his printer John Purser – and had to flee abroad. It was no less a person than John Cleland, author of the best-seller *Fanny Hill*, who instigated the prosecution of the treatise, which defended sodomy as a form of sexual behaviour known and tolerated as far back as Roman and Greek times.[59]

Cannon was the exception to the rule which demanded of an author writing on aspects of the mollies' life that he state the foreign origin of the 'unnatural vice' ('bugger' seems to be derived from 'Bulgarian') and exhibit the homosexuals as effeminate and misogynist. Ridiculing homosexuals as fops and transvestites was a stereotype dramatic pattern that is already noticeable in Rochester's obscene playlet, *Sodom* (Amsterdam, 1684), reputed to have been performed at court, and in John Vanbrugh's *The Relapse* of 1696. It continued throughout

the eighteenth century. Satire pursued the same line. John Dunton's
The He-Strumpets. A Satyr on the Sodomite-Club successfully slandered homosexuals in 1707 and was reprinted four times until 1710.
Edward Ward, in his *History of the London Clubs* (1709–11), attests
to the existence of a 'Mollies Club' in London early in the century. Its
members are described in conventional clichés:

> They adopt all the small vanities natural to the feminine sex to such an
> extent that they try to speak, walk, chatter, shriek and scold as women do,
> aping them as well in other respects. In a certain tavern in the City . . . they
> hold parties and regular gatherings. As soon as they arrive there they begin
> to behave exactly as women do, carrying on light gossip as is the custom of
> a merry company of real women. Later on, one of their brothers – or rather
> 'sisters' – (in their feminine jargon) would be dressed in a woman's
> nightgown with a silken night-cap, and thus representing a woman, bears
> a 'child' (a dummy being to hand for this purpose), which is afterwards
> baptised, while another man in a large hat plays the part of a country
> midwife, a third that of a nurse, the rest of them acting as unseemly guests
> at a christening. Each had to discourse at length and with great improprie-
> ty of the pleasures of a 'husband' and children, and praise the virtues of the
> former and the wonderful talents of the latter. Some others, in the role of
> 'widows', lamented the deplorable loss of their 'husbands'. Thus each
> imitated the petty feminine faults of women gossiping over coffee, in order
> to disguise their natural feelings (as men) towards the fair sex, and to
> encourage unnatural lusts.[60]

Although Ward occasionally embellished his history with fictional
accounts, he can be trusted in this case, for we have additional evidence confirming the existence of several places in London where
sodomites could meet. Like Paris and other great European cities,
London had a homosexual sub-culture in the very first decades of the
eighteenth century, which, in the absence of a police force, remained
relatively undisturbed. When the street robber James Dalton was
arrested in 1728, he gave evidence of his 'biting the Women of the
Town, his detecting and exposing the *Mollies*, and a Song which is
sung at the Molly-Clubs'. Dalton's confession confirmed that
homosexuals openly solicited in the streets, and enacted mock marriages and childbirths, and that there was a danger of being blackmailed if one responded to their advances.[61]

Most publications, whether they were satires or moral diatribes,
ascribed the increase of sodomy, which they seemed to perceive, to the
'Modish way of bringing up young Gentlemen', and to the 'Effeminacy of Dress and Manners', such as kissing each other, a habit 'brought
over from Italy (the Mother and Nurse of Sodomy)'. Eighteenth-

century fashion for men, not to mention the extravagant style of ladies, reached extremes, such as the Macaronis and their way of dressing, which invited satirical treatment by writers, painters, and engravers. Since descriptions of the homosexual sub-culture, which were written to entertain the general public, invariably emphasised its effeminacy, it is hardly surprising that the public eventually believed that all sodomites were effeminate, misogynist, and hence perverse. These erroneous ideas would explain the violent treatment, by the crowd, of homosexuals punished by the pillory for attempts to commit buggery. By requiring that they stand at least once in the pillory of the area where they were best known, the courts made sure that convicted sodomites lost their reputation and were fiercely attacked with bricks, clubs, and stones. In 1761 a young homosexual of Cornhill, London, who had been sentenced for an attempt of buggery, was almost lynched by the furious mob. Two years later, two men, similarly sentenced, were killed by the crowd.[62] When another unfortunate sodomite faced the rage of the public in 1763, a broadside folio was produced to celebrate the merry occasion (plate 6).

Since sodomites were regarded as such despicable creatures, a mere accusation of buggery, however ill-founded, was liable to damage a person's reputation and lead to his ruin. Naturally, blackmail and extortion thrived in such conditions, and the case of Samuel Foote, the well-known actor and dramatist, illustrates the dangers of being falsely accused.[63] Foote fathered several illegitimate children, but was nevertheless reputed to be homosexual, mainly because of the roles he played in his theatre and because he was not married. In 1776 he was dragged into a scandal whose roots reached back to other events. As a playwright, Foote had used the character and the well-publicised bigamy of the Duchess of Kingston in his play, *A Trip to Calais*, which she succeeded in suppressing. Foote also satirised an Irish clergyman called Jackson, who was ridiculed as Dr Viper in *The Capuchin*. Deeply offended, the Duchess and the priest were waiting for a chance to hit back. It is not quite clear whether the Reverend Mr Jackson was solely responsible for the instigation of Foote's trial for sodomy. At any rate, Jack Sangster, a coachman dismissed by Foote, accused his former master of indecent assault. It transpired at the trial that Sangster had unknown helpers, who had provided him with money to prefer a bill of indictment against Foote. The jury acquitted the actor without even leaving the jury box. Soon after the trial, a satirical attack appeared, obviously written by Jackson and perhaps commissioned by the Duchess of Kingston, which bore the title, *Sodom and Onan, a*

a man at Shalford in the pillory Ap. 1763. was killed by the populace.

This is not the T H I N G:

O R,

M O L L Y   E X A L T E D.

Tune, *Ye Commons and Peers.*

YE Reversers of Nature, each *dear* little Creature,
  Of soft and effeminate fight,
See above what your fate is, and 'ere it too late is,
  Oh, learn to be—all in the *Right*.
        Tol de rol.

II.
On the FAIR of our Isle see the Graces all smile,
  All our Cares in this Life to requite ;
But such Wretches as You, Nature's Laws wou'd
  undo,
For you're *backward*—and not in the *Right*.
        Tol de rol.

III.
Can't Beauty's soft Eye, which with Phœbus may vie,
  Can't her rosy Lips yield ye Delight?
No :—they all afford sweets, which each Man of
  Sense meets,
But not *You*,—for you're not in the *Right*.
        Tol de rol.

IV.
Where's the tender Connection, the Love and
  Protection,
Which proceed from the conjugal Rite?
Did you once but know *this*, sure you'd ne'er do
  amiss,
But wou'd always be—all in the *Right*.
        Tol de rol

V.
The *Sov'reign* of ALL, who created this *Ball*,
  Ordain'd that each Sex should unite ;
Ordain'd the soft *Kiss*, and more permanent Bliss,
  That ALL might be—all in the *Right*.
        Tol de rol,

VI.
But a Race so detested, of Honour divested,
  The Daughters of *Britain* invite,
Whom they leave in the Lurch, to well flog 'em
  with Birch ;
Shou'd they flay 'em they're—all in the *Right*.
        Fol de rol.

VII.
Press ye *Sailors*, persist, come ye *Soldiers*, inlist,
  By *Land* or by *Sea* make 'em fight,
And then let *France* and *Spain*, call their Men
  home again,
And send out their WIVES—to be *Right*.
        Tol de rol.

VIII.
Now tho'many good Men, have so frolicksome been,
  Our Pity and Mirth to excite,
Yet may these worthy Souls have the uppermost
  Holes
In the PILLORY ;—all is but *Right*.
        Tol de rol. &c.
        Ap. 1763.

To be had at the *Bee-Hive, Strand* ; and at all the Print and Pamphlet Shops in *Great Britain* and *Ireland.*

Satire, Inscribed to ————— Esq., Alias the Devil upon Two Sticks. In this short work of twenty-nine pages, Foote and homosexuals in general are held up to ridicule. There are veiled hints at the actor's alleged assault on his servant in a stable:

> In splendid Mansion finding no resource,
> Fain he'd defile the Chamber of the Horse.

The judge, the jury, and Foote's witnesses are accused of bending the law:

> ... the Laws leave Avenues,
> Which powerful Sod'mites frequently abuse;
> Tamper with Gold, and terrify with Threats,
> 'Till the astonish'd Ignorant forgets.

Continuing the attack on sodomites, readers lodging in hotels are advised:

> Observe this rule: – ne'er pull your Breeches off. –
> From Health restoring Slumbers strive to keep,
> Or ten to one you are B———'d in your Sleep.

Foote was completely unnerved by the circumstances of the trial and the concomitant damage to his reputation. His acting deteriorated and he died the following year. Popular prejudices made life difficult even for the high and mighty, who normally indulged their passions without objection by the public. Homosexual aristocrats had to tread carefully in order not to be slandered by their political opponents. The example of John, Lord Hervey (1696–1743) is typical. While he did not lose his position because of his sexual predilection, his enemies knew that his homosexuality was an excellent weapon to be used against him in the political arena. The situation was similar for noblemen in France during the Revolution.[64]

Lesbians found much more leniency with the writers of the day. *Satan's Harvest Home* (1749), for instance, merely contains a mild rebuke for sapphic ladies. The weaker sex, argues the author of the pamphlet, 'not content with our Sex, begins *Amours* with her own, and teaches the Female World a new Sort of Sin, call'd the *Flats* ... practis'd ... at Twickenham at this Day'. While homosexual men were exposed, ridiculed, and ostracised, lesbians received occasional poetic praise. Possibly influenced by such French works as *Poésies de Sapho* ('Londres', 1781), English authors celebrated lesbians in satires like *A Sapphic Epistle from Jack Cavendish to the Honourable and Most*

6 *This is Not the Thing: or Molly Exalted*, 1763

7 Illustration by Fragonard, undated, for an edition
of Voltaire's *Candide*

Beautiful Mrs D (c. 1782), a bawdy attack on a Mrs D. and her lesbian
adventures in Italy; and *The Sapphoan, An Heroic Poem, of Three
Cantos. In the Ovidian Stile, Describing the Pleasures which the Fair
Sex Enjoy with Each Other* (17—?). Lesbianism in literature and
society was much discussed in eighteenth-century France as well. A
lesbian club was founded, around 1770, by Madame de Fleury. Its
members are alleged to have indulged in erotic rituals. Two decades
later, Mademoiselle Raucourt became the notorious butt of several
publications, among them *Anandrina, ou confessions de Mademoiselle Sapho* (1789); and *La liberté, ou Mademoiselle Raucourt à toute
la secte anandrine assemblée au foyer de la Comédie Française* (1791).

Actresses like Miss Raucourt were thus not afraid to show their inclinations: Fragonard gave expression to the talk about lesbians in an engraving (plate 7); and England imitated, as usual. Having heard of Madame de Fleury, Mrs Yates, of the Drury Lane Theatre, thought that English thespians could not stand back, and founded a lesbian club. Johann Wilhelm von Archenholtz, a German traveller, recorded the existence of 'Anandrinic Societies' and the prevalence of lesbianism among actresses in late eighteenth-century London.[65]

To the writers at least, the behaviour of homosexual women seems to have been less objectionable, since they remained female in their manners and did not adopt features of the opposite sex, like the dreaded mollies. Clearly, the strongest sexual taboo of eighteenth-century England concerned male homosexuals, whose behaviour seemed to threaten the independence and aggression traditionally associated with the male.[66]

4 THE SCIENCE OF SEXOLOGY

The Enlightenment, it has been stated, progressed from an interest in the philosophy of sex to a kind of sexual religion. In this process, one can discern a remarkable growth in the discourse on human sexuality. Sexual quackery constituted an integral part in the spreading of the new gospel. The cases of Marten, Spinke, and the later Vanbutchell indicate that eighteenth-century quacks were a curious and motley lot. With a medical profession still in its formative years, almost anyone could declare himself or herself a doctor and begin practising. Thus a jobbing tailor like William Read, who was to receive a knighthood and an appointment as Oculist-in-Ordinary by Queen Anne, and a dry-salter like Joshua Ward, who later treated George II, turned into MDs overnight. Many chose the field of medicine since it paid well and enabled quite a few practitioners to experience the rags-to-riches story in an unbelievably short time.[67] Naturally, many suffered, and an unknown number of patients died at the hands of inexperienced charlatans, while the trained medical world waged war with, and raised its voice against, the impostors and 'empiricks' in the field. But it was not only the quacks who brought medicine into disrepute. The constant squabbles and feuds between the recognised medical authorities further lowered the doctors in the esteem of the public. These conditions created a fertile ground for satire. When the doctors and surgeons Richard Mead and John Woodward had a minor disagreement in 1719, they were immediately mocked in *Tauronomachia or A*

*Description of a Bloody and Terrible Fight between Two Champions,
Taurus and Onos, at Gresham College.* The predominantly negative
picture of the physician in eighteenth-century literature is a direct
consequence of the low esteem in which the medical profession was
held. Tom Brown says of the 'Country of Physick' that 'the language
that is spoken here, is very Learned; but the People that speak it are
very Ignorant ... When a Sick Man leaves all for *Nature* to do, he
hazards much. When he leaves all for the Doctor to do, he hazards
more: And since there is a Hazard both ways, I would sooner chuse to
rely upon *Nature*; for this, at least, we may be sure of, That she acts as
Honestly as she can, and that she does not find her Account in
prolonging the Disease.' The physicians in Christopher Anstey's *The
New Bath Guide*, first published in 1766, instead of attending to the
patient who called them, discuss political and economic questions
before prescribing a 'peppermint draught' on their way to another bad
case.[68] Doctors, like priests, were also satirised because they had
access to women in strict privacy, a privilege denied to ordinary
mortals. Thus the dallying doctor became a favourite topic with those
who produced erotic and pornographic prints (plate 8).

This negative impression of the medical world was certainly not
improved by the dabbling of both quacks and doctors in such equivocal fields as abortion, aphrodisiacs, contraceptives, and venereal diseases, where the sharks of the pornography business were roaming as
well. Some quacks did not hesitate to use downright lies in order to
further their business. The greatest absurdities went down well with a
credulous audience. The Age of Reason was still gullible enough to
believe in such impostors as Richard Hathaway, the apprentice who in
1700 vomited nails and pins, claiming he had been bewitched by an
old woman. Occasionally, doctors announced to the public that they
had witnessed the birth to women of monsters or animals – and they
were believed. I have already mentioned John Maubray's report in his
Female Physician (1724) of the alleged birth of a 'sucker'. Two years
later, he was outdone by Mr Nathaniel St André, a native of Switzer-
land and an ex-dancing master, who had set up as a doctor in London.
He was eventually appointed 'Anatomist to the Royal Household' by
George I. St André became known with a pamphlet of forty pages,
entitled *A Short Narrative of an Extraordinary Delivery of Rabbits,
Perform'd by Mr John Howard* (1726). The news of the reported case
spread all over London, and the pamphlet sold extremely well. St
André described in this 'treatise' how he himself had delivered Mary
Tofts of Godalming in the county of Surrey of two rabbits and how she

The Wilful Mistake; or the
Medical Metamorphosis.

8 *The Wilful Mistake; or the Medical Metamorphosis –*
   frontispiece of *The Bon Ton Magazine*, 1793

9a–b *The Doctors in Labour, 1726/7*

Help help good people—fetch another—Neighbour—
Her pains are strong—she'll quickly fall in labour.
Here Doctor—here goodwomen help to hold her
—nay thing she faints—take care you hurt her shoulder
Bless me... Whats this you've brought to town—O Mary
three late legs, and a may Skin all hairy.

Take notice Gentlemen how from her—breaſt
the Milk ſquirts out as ſron as čr— he Preſt
From whence with Reaſon it may be believ'd
I ſtrongly wonder'd Fœtus 'tis certain'd.
What can i'th aye think—Why man of Reading
Will ſoon conclude that She's a Rabbet breeding.

Nay—tis as I ſuppoſe'd—for let me tell ye
I feel the Rabbets leaping in her—belly
Nay feel your ſelves—obſerve the motion truly
ſuch Evidence muſt make convince ye fully
The Devil is't if this can be a bite
Or you can longer—doubt my notion's right.

Now Mary ſtruggles with a ſecond Pain
The Doctor now attends her throw's again.
But ah too late—Impatient of delay,
Bum thro' his Burrough work himſelf a way
The next ſo ſlily but the Doctor ſpies him
And fallows with deſign t'Anatomize him.

Is this a Rabbit or a Cat—in troth
Tis hard to ſay it looks ſo like 'em both.
But hold—this thing will join decide ye Matter,
By this I judge it cannot be the latter
And by its weight—I can as ſafely ſwear
Tho it has ſhit—It never breath'd in Air.

The Doctors here and Midwives all conſult
If 'tis a fœtus Rabbit or adult
When up the learned Merry Andrew ſtarts
This Animal quoth he in all its parts
Does with a Natural Rabbit well agree
And therefore it muſt Preternatural be.

Now to the Bagnio flock the Town & Court,
T'improve their Judgment ſome and ſome for ſport,
They're welcome all to Mary—all that will
May in her Warren for a Rabbit feel.
But we'll take care they don't of Trick diſcover,
For then the Merry days will all be over.

Tis an unhappingly to be Lamented,
That people near know when to be contented,
Had breeding ſeventeen Rabbits ſatisfied
Poor Mary ſo't the Plot had ſtill been hid!
But fond to make the Number up a Score,
The prying World the Secret did explore.

ſtrange turn of Human life—unhappy Moley
I mas to Bridewell carry'd to Mill Dolly,
The loney Warren's ruind and no more,
Muſt Ferrits hunt there as they did before,
Poor Andrew ſits upon Reporting ſtool,
Curſing his fate in being made a fool.

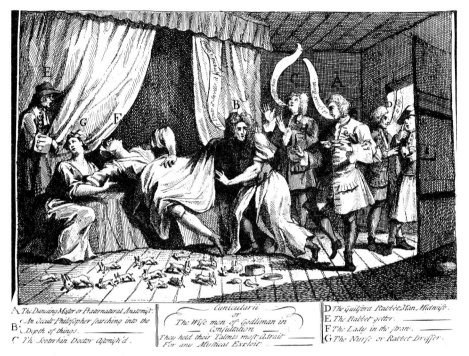

10 Hogarth, *Cunicularii or The Wise Men of Godliman in Consultation,*
    1727

gave birth to a litter of seventeen 'coneys'. Added to the text were the
oaths of several persons confirming the strange birth. The 'Anatomist
to the Royal Household' was to regret his lies. It later transpired that
he had merely received a report by his apothecary friend John
Howard, the local 'accoucheur' in Godalming. St André went there,
but never actually extracted a rabbit from Mary Tofts' uterus, as he
claimed in his *Narrative*. The whole story could be studied in a series
of bawdy cartoons under the title *The Doctors in Labour; or A New
Whim Wham from Guildford* (plates 9a–b). Hogarth used the story as
well in 1727 and again in 1762 (plates 10 and 16).[69]

Time and again, quacks were able to exploit the ignorance of a
superstitious and gullible public. Readers were especially keen on
treatises discussing the mysterious aspects of sexuality, such as artificial insemination and conception without intercourse, which had been
discussed before the eighteenth century. Sex developed into a new
science and was discussed freely by such people as James Graham, a
self-styled expert in Sexology.[70]

Anti-Religious Erotica

Several factors merged in the eighteenth century to create a climate favourable to anti-religious erotica in which it achieved an unprecedented popularity. Both the systematic atheism of the Enlightenment, and libertines of the time, revolted against Christianity itself. Even within the Catholic Church there existed a history and tradition of licentious criticism, expressed in occasionally erotic parodies of such religious forms as sermons, the Catechism, the Commandments, and prayers. Mock-sermons like *A Dissertation Wherein the Meaning, Duty, and Happiness of Kissing are Explained* continued to be popular throughout the eighteenth century. In this 'sermon', a comic-erotic parody of Genesis 29, 11, the readers are enjoined 'to imitate the shining Example of ... Jacob, and embrace every Opportunity of doing as he did when "he kissed Rachel"'.

Clerics of all denominations have always attracted the projection of sexual ideas; and clergymen were most successfully ridiculed by association with such unholy topics as lewdness and scatology. Satire and burlesque have their own tradition of erotic humour and obscenity, and the age of satire was in great need of these integral parts of literary attack. Michel Foucault has shown that from 1700 onwards sexual desire found expression in discourse as a result of political, economic, and technical incitement. He sees what he terms the 'confessional technique' as typical of our society as opposed to the 'ars erotica' of other or earlier cultures. In addition, there are undeniably strong relations between sexual and religious expression, and especially between erotica and devotional literature. Much of eighteenth-century pornographic fiction, for instance, was expressed in the form of 'confessions' and can, in fact, be traced to the Augustinian confession. The sublimation of the sex instinct in literature found an early expression in religious writings voicing a burning love in terms elsewhere reserved to sensuous lovers. Devotional writing developed an erotic terminology which, in the eighteenth century, can be detected, for example, in Charles Wesley's hymns, 'Wrestling Jacob' and 'Jesu, Lover of my Soul'. Ribald and obscene satire often availed itself of this religious erotic terminology. There is an equally interesting connection between obscenity and pornography on the one hand and religious topics and localities on the other. The tendency of obscene writings to shock, and to violate existing taboos, provoked a preoccupation with monastic life and clerics. Anti-religious erotica either employ obscenity as a vehicle to achieve other aims, such as an attack on the Pope, or – more often – they use the genre as a cover for pornography.[1] Like the seventeenth century, of course, the Age of Reason did not confine itself to the Catholic Church in its attack on religion. Although by 1720 Puritanism, at least in bawdy and obscene satire, had almost been flogged to death, it was the Church of England, and Dissenters, above all the Quakers and Methodists, who continued to provide targets and who, more often than not, were the main pretexts for the publication of pornography.

I LIBERTINISM IN BRITAIN

In his historical survey of the exclusion of sex from the realm of normal behaviour and everyday life, Wayland Young distinguishes two periods of libertinism. The first came to an end in the seventeenth century, while the second ran from about 1700 to the French Revolution. It was, according to Young, 'a revolt against Christianity itself, and had affinities with the ... atheism of the Illumination'. Unfortunately, Young confines his discussion to Restoration rakes in England, and then deals with eighteenth-century French libertines, whose ideas were directed against chastity and religion.

In England and Scotland the tradition of the rake, which survived openly until well into the fourth decade of the eighteenth century, virtually guaranteed a continuation of atheism, blasphemy, and anti-religious satire. In the first two decades many impious clubs were in existence, in which atheism was a principle. This was continued afterwards, although rakes and libertines had to meet in secrecy. On 28 April, 1721 George I, probably urged by the purity movements, released an order against 'certain scandalous Clubs or Societies of young Persons who meet together . . . insult the most sacred Principles of our holy Religion . . . and corrupt the Minds and Morals of one another'. The order was reprinted, and published with *The Hell-Fire-Club: Kept by a Society of Blasphemers. A Satyr* (1721). The verses of this pamphlet of twenty-three pages, sold at three shillings, are dull, and hardly deserve the epithet 'satirical', since the moral and didactic purpose is much too obvious. 'The very worst of Men' are exposed in a description of their blasphemous swearing, revelry, and immorality. The pamphlet attests to the existence of clubs whose affluent members excelled in drinking, gambling, wenching, and blasphemy. These 'societies' consisted of full-time members, and young sparks. It was William Hogarth who, with a keen eye for the foibles of his contemporaries, caught the life-style of some of these parasites of society in a series of eight prints, published under the title *A Rake's Progress* (1732). The message may be heavily moral, but Hogarth provided a good impression of the dissolute life of the rake (see plates 11a–h). Since public opposition gradually forced the rakish clubs into making their activities clandestine it is difficult to obtain reliable evidence of their proceedings, although some clubs did keep records of their meetings. In England, for example, there is a great gap of information between Hogarth's prints, in 1732, and the scandal of the Medmenham Monks, revealed during the Wilkes affair, in 1763.

The 'Order of St Francis at Medmenham Abbey' was indeed a most peculiar club of rakehells and blasphemers, some of whom held important positions in political and public life. Sir Francis Dashwood, Lord Le Despenser (1708–81), was the founder of this 'Hell Fire Club', whose members, in allusion to the Catholic order and to Dashwood's Christian name, took the name of Franciscans. His anti-Catholicism, and his atheism, date from his traditional aristocrat's Grand Tour of France and Italy. He was to become the master rake of his age, combining life as a rakehell with a wide variety of other activities – he was later appointed Postmaster General by Pitt. Dashwood founded the blasphemous order of Medmenham 'monks', whose meetings took place in the cells of a ruined Cistercian abbey near Marlow, around the year 1755. In time, he initiated into his 'order' such prominent men as Frederick, Prince of Wales; the third Earl of March; the fourth Earl of Queensberry; the fourth Earl of Sandwich; William Hogarth; Thomas Potter, the son of the Archbishop of Canterbury; John Wilkes; and George Bubb Dodington. Writers like Charles Churchill and Paul Whitehead were awarded honorary ranks

in the order by the 'prior' Dashwood. As the actual records of the club are lacking, we have to rely on second-hand information. The libertines met in the garb of monks and followed the motto, 'Fay ce que voudras', borrowed from Rabelais' *Gargantua*. Allegedly, they had in attendance their mistresses and a number of prostitutes, who were addressed as 'nuns' and 'abbesses'. It would seem that the Medmenhamites produced the equivalent of, or approximated to, the Black Mass, and also mocked other religious forms and rites (plate 12). John Wilkes (1727–97) is said to have had a collection of erotica in the abbey, some of them bound as Books of Common Prayer or other religious works. The blasphemous and sacrilegious songs which the 'monks' chanted in their mock-masses included productions from the pens of John Wilkes and his chum, Thomas Potter.[2] When Wilkes was excluded from the House of Commons, in 1763, because of the notorious No. 45 of his *North Briton*, some of his former friends, notably Lord Sandwich, turned against him, and he was expelled from the 'order' as well. The hypocritical Sandwich, himself a Medmenhamite, read portions of Wilkes' obscene *Essay on Woman* to the House of Lords, the while feigning disgust. This infamous *Essay* (1763) was seized by government agents in a raid on Wilkes' premises, where they also found some appended poems which may have been sung by the Medmenhamites. An obscene and blasphemous parody of Pope's *Essay on Man*, the *Essay on Woman* was probably written by Thomas Potter, although Wilkes was charged with having produced it. The work consists of ninety-four lines, divided into an invocation and three main parts. The poem starts with a *double entendre*: an allusion to Fanny Murray, the courtesan, and 'fanny', a slang term for vagina:

> Awake my Fanny! leave all meaner things;
> This morn shall prove what rapture swiving brings!
> Let us (since life can little more supply
> Than just a few good fucks, and then we die)
> Expatiate free o'er that loved scene of man,
> A mighty maze, for mighty pricks to scan;
> A wild, where PAPHIAN THORNS promiscuous shoot,
> Where flows the monthly Rose, but yields no Fruit.
>   . . .
> 1. He who the hoop's immensity can pierce,
>   Dart thro' the whalebone fold's vast universe,
>   Observe how circle into circle runs,
>   What courts the eye, and what all vision shuns,
>   All the wild modes of dress our females wear,
>   May guess what makes them thus transform'd appear.

But of their cunts the bearings and ties,
The nice connexions, strong dependencies,
The latitude and longitude of each
Hast thou gone through, or can thy Pego reach?
Was that great Ocean, that unbounded Sea,
Where pricks like whales may spout, fathom'd by Thee?

II. Presumptuous Prick! The reason would'st thou find
Why form'd so weak, so little, and so blind?

. . .

Then, in the scale of Pricks, 'tis plain,
God-like erect, BUTE stands the foremost man
And all the question (wrangle e'er so long)
Is only this, if Heaven placed him wrong.

. . .

Then say not Man's imperfect, Heaven in fault,
Say rather, Man's as perfect as he ought;
His Pego measured to the female Case,
Betwixt a woman's thighs his proper place;
And if to fuck in a proportion'd sphere,
What matters how it is, or when, or where?
Fly fuck'd by fly may be completely so,
As Hussey's Duchess, or your well-bull'd cow.

III. . . .

Pleased to the last, she likes the luscious food,
And grasps the prick just raised to shed her blood.
Oh! Blindness to the Future, kindly given,
That each may enjoy what fucks are mark'd by Heaven.
Who sees with equal Eye, as God of all,
The Man just mounting, and the Virgin's fall;
Prick, cunt, and bollocks in convulsions hurl'd
And now a Hymen burst, and now a World.
Hope humbly, then, clean girls; nor vainly soar;
But fuck the cunt at hand, and God adore.
What future fucks he gives not thee to know,
But gives that Cunt to be thy Blessing now.

This is all there is to what has been termed the most scandalous poem
of the second part of the eighteenth century. It was not the poem itself
that created such a reputation, but the talk about it, and the concomitant affair of Wilkes' overall reputation. Appended to the obscene
'essay' by Potter, with notes by Wilkes (which he ascribed to Warbur-
ton), were several obscene parodies of prayers and hymns. They had
circulated among the Medmenhamites and may have been used in
their Black Masses. 'The Universal Prayer' consists of thirteen stanzas,
with four lines each, including notes. The first and last stanzas run as
follows:

Once on a Time, as Fame reported,
When Friar Paul St Frances Courted,
Thus Frances answer'd, your no Novice,
You well deserve the Jewel-Office.
A Place of Trust your Faith will suit,
You shall demand it of Laird Boot.
Your *MANNERS*, Morals, Virtue, Grace
Call loudly for a goodly Place.
Success attend you, I'll be blunt
My dearest Brother here is ———

1765

12 *The Secrets of the Convent*, 1765

> Mother of all! in every Age,
>   in ev'ry Clime ador'd,
> By Saint, by Savage, and by Sage,
>   if modest, or if whor'd
> …
> To thee whose Fucks thro'out all space,
>   This dying World supplies,
> One Chorus let all Beings raise!
>   All Pricks in rev'rence rise.

This is obviously a feeble parody of Pope's poem of the same title. 'The Dying Lover to his Prick' is a ribald parody of Pope's 'Dying Christian to his Soul', and explodes religious terminology and enthusiasm by means of sexual associations:

> Happy spark of heavenly flame!
> Pride and wonder of Man's frame!
> Why is pleasure so soon flying?
> Why so short this bliss of dying?
> Cease, fond Pego, cease the strife,
> And yet indulge a moment's life.
>
> Hark! Cunt whispers, don't she say,
> Brother Pego come away?
> What is this absorbs me quite,
> Seals my senses, shuts my sight,
> Draws my spirits, draws my breath?
> Tell me, my prick, can this be death?
>
> Now you recede, now disappear!
> My eye looks round in vain, my ear,
> Fanny, your murmur rings:
> Lend, lend your hand! I mount! I die!
> O Prick, how great thy Victory!
> O Pleasure, sweet thy stings.

Similarly, 'Veni Creator; or, the Maid's Prayer', parodies Dryden's translation of Maurus' hymn:

> Creator Pego, by whose aid
> Thy humble suppliant was made
> O Source of Bliss, and God of Love,
> Shed thy influence from above;
> Come, and thy sacred Unction bring
> To sanctify me while I sing.
>
> On thee all day and night I call,
> Great promised Comforter to all;

Martyrs and Prophets have of old
Thy wondrous energy foretold;
Come, and awhile vouchsafe to dwell
In my dark unfrequented Cell.
Thy secret influence impart
To charm my senses, fire my heart;
Come, pour thy joys on womankind,
Be all my frame to Thee resign'd,
And, oh! Thou rulest a willing mind!
From loathed Hymen set me free,
Enter a Temple worthy Thee,
Where thou a heavenly Guest shalt prove,
Happy in me to live and *move*,
And have a Being worthy love.

Immortal Honour, endless Fame,
Almighty Pego! to Thy name;
And equal adoration be
Paid to the neighbouring pair with Thee,
Thrice blessed Glorious Trinity.

The Medmenham Monks were not an exception, even if they reached extremes in the sacrilegious and blasphemous mock-rites that they directed against religious forms and religion as such. Other private clubs, such as the Beef-Steaks and the Humbugs, cherished the libertine tradition of obscene verse and songs. In Scotland, in the early eighteenth century, the Beggar's Benison of Anstruther had readings of pornography; and, if the records are to be believed, members masturbated in groups. John Hall Stevenson, author of the satirical and bawdy *Fables for Grown Gentlemen* (1761) and *Crazy Tales* (1762), headed a society of libertines called 'Demoniacs', who counted Laurence Sterne among their members. Thomas Hamilton, sixth Earl of Haddington, seems to have founded a similar club, at 'Crazy Castle', and published ribald tales, such as 'Pious Ejaculations', in his *New Crazy Tales* (1783). Some clubs, such as the Beef-Steaks, although founded by men with rakish interests, later developed into honoured societies.[3]

To be sure, the members of these clubs were a minority, recruited from the aristocracy and upper social strata. Nevertheless, they gave expression to a new ideology, combining sexual libertinism and anti-Christian attacks. This attitude surpassed the licentiousness of the Restoration rakes, and was influenced by writers of the Enlightenment. Wilkes, for instance, was a frequent guest of Paul Heinrich Dietrich d'Holbach (1723–89), who belonged to the coterie of the *encyclopédistes* and attacked the Christian faith and the priesthood in his *Christianisme dévoilé* (1767); *De l'imposture sacerdotale* (1767); *Prêtres démasqués* (1768); and *Système de la nature* (1770), his major opus, which had a bearing on the works of de Sade. Similar works were written, and discussed in the salons of the time, by Helvétius and Voltaire. This simultaneous phenomenon in French aristocratic circles should not be overlooked. R.F. Brissenden has noted that 'sexual freedom among the French aristocracy was not merely tolerated but encouraged to a degree unknown across the channel'. The rakish males of England's upper class, mobile and multi-lingual as they were, must have welcomed, with interested motives, the ideas and the practical example of France's debauched aristocracy. The affluent in both countries enjoyed a lively cultural exchange, despite the several wars of the period between France and England; and it is hardly accidental that both nationalities should have reached sexual debauchery combined with atheism at the same time. They put into practice the ideas of the avant-garde of the *illuminés* who advocated pleasure and passion as the guide-lines of one's life, while some French Jesuit theologians went as far as suggesting the cultivation rather than the denial of human nature.[4]

2 EROTICA AGAINST THE CHURCH OF ENGLAND AND DISSENTERS

Given the tradition and preponderance of anti-Catholic erotic and obscene satire, as well as attacks on Dissenters, it is understandable that very little of a similar nature was produced against the Church of England, although the clergy and their behaviour were occasionally vituperated in ribald prose and poetry. Adrian Beverland (1651–1716) seems to have been one of the few exceptions; but then he was not born an Englishman, a fact which might explain his 'unpatriotic' flinging of obscenities against his enemies, or rather those whom he perceived to be enemies, within the Church. Beverland grew up in Holland and studied theology at Leyden, where his undergraduate pranks of publishing classical Italian and other pornography annoyed the theologians to such an extent that he was banned and had to go to England. After a short sojourn in Oxford and in London, he joined the Church of England, in the early 1690s. In 1697 he made an attempt to appease his critics in Holland, with the publication of *Hadriani Beverlandi de fornicatione cavenda admonitio*, in which he deplored his youthful sins and gave advice to his readers on how to avoid

fornication in order to lead a chaste life. However, the expected
pardon did not arrive from Holland, and the dissatisfied Beverland
decided that an attack might produce better results. He again put pen
to paper, and wrote *Seignor Perin del Vago's Letter to Mr. Hadrian
Beverland* (1702), which contains some rather foul language and
which was reprinted several times, under different titles, up to 1710.
Beverland developed a growing persecution mania and continued to
lash with obscene words in print those in the Church of England and in
Holland whom he suspected of working against him. *A Hue and Cry
After the Bulls of Bashan* (1702 and later) was an enlarged version of
his first attack and was followed by several editions of a pamphlet
entitled *Although my Innocence is Shelter'd* (London, 1709–12). By
1710 Beverland was mentally unstable and physically ill, and six years
later he died.

By all one can tell, the Church of England remained a sanctum, if not
taboo, for otherwise iconoclastic satirists, who aimed at the clerics but
spared the institution. Like their 'Romish' brethren, the Anglican
clergy provided such satirists with material for erotic lampoons
throughout the century. Some ordained men, like Daniel Maclauchlan
and Laurence Sterne, even joined the ranks of those who wrote against
their own profession. While much has been written on the great
Yorkshireman's erotic and scatological references in *A Sentimental
Journey* and *Tristram Shandy*, less is known about the young clergyman from Scotland who is the author of *An Essay Upon Improving
and Adding to the Strength of Great Britain and Ireland, by Fornication, Justifying the Same from Scripture and Reason* (Dublin, 1735),
published under the pseudonym, 'Philosarchos'. Maclauchlan had
earlier been accused in Scotland of intemperate drinking, swearing,
and singing obscene songs and, in 1735, was imprisoned in London on
suspicion of being the author of the *Essay*, a work of forty-three pages,
reprinted in an enlarged edition of fifty-five pages in 1755. The
Church was far from being amused at this ribald and sacrilegious
satire, and the unfortunate Maclauchlan was deposed and excom-
municated in 1737. He ended up in Jamaica, where he died in 1745.

The theme of the lecherous parson dominates much of what remains
extant in ribald satire from this period. It is beautifully and most subtly
exemplified in Hogarth's *The Sleeping Congregation* of 1728 (plate
13): while the preacher in this print has managed to make his flock fall
asleep with his sermon, the lustful clerk is secretly eyeing the shapely
bosom of a young sleeping beauty beside him.[5] Richard Newton,
towards the end of the century, resumed the theme, and in his *The*

13 Hogarth, *The Sleeping Congregation*, 1728

Progress of a Divine. A Satire, Richard Savage, another Scotsman, uses poetry as a vehicle for his attack and describes clergymen as gluttons and fornicators:

> Lux'ry he loves; but, like a priest of sense,
> Ev'n lux'ry loves not at his own expense.
> Tho' harlot passions wanton with his will,
> Yet av'rice is his wedded passion still.
>
> See him with napkin o'er his band tuck'd in,
> While the rich grease hangs glist'ning on his chin;
> Or as the oil from Aaron's beard declines,
> Ev'n to his garment-hem soft-trickling shines!

He feeds and feeds, swills soup, and sucks up marrow;
Swills, sucks, and feeds, till leach'rous as a sparrow.
Thy pleasure, Onan! now no more delights,
The lone amusement of his chaster nights.
He boasts – (let ladies put him to the test)
Strong back, broad shoulders, and a well-built chest.
With stiff'ning nerves now steals he fly away,
Alert, warm, chuckling, ripe for am'rous play;
Ripe to caress the lass he once thought meet
At church to chide when penanc'd in a sheet:
He pants the titillating joy to prove,
The fierce short sallies of luxurious love.

Not fair Cadiere and Confessor than they
In straining transport more lascivious lay.

    Conceives her womb while each so melts and thrills?
He plies her now with love, and now with pills:
No more falls penance cloth'd in shame upon her,
These kill her embryo and preserve her honour.

To recount all the instances in fact and fiction in which amorous parsons constituted the objects of erotic satire would be a most tedious and repetitive enterprise. I shall spare the reader. It will suffice to give one example taken from the leading erotic magazine towards the end of the century. One would indeed be rather astonished if *The Bon Ton Magazine* had not in some way exploited the theme. No. 31, of September 1793, has a tale which is a sort of crystallisation of the theme, cherished by the satirists for almost two centuries, of the lecherous divine in the Church of England. *The Jolly Buck Parson and the Hibernian Matron*, published with an erotic frontispiece (plate 14), relates how an Irish baronet employs a 'buck parson' as a tutor for his son. The young clergyman, however, prefers to dedicate his attention to the ladies of the household, who are taken in by his appearance. The lady's maid, Abigail, recommends the parson to her mistress, who soon falls in love with him. At the occasion of a masquerade,

our hero flipping off a black domino, assumed the character of a hooded friar, and taking our heroine into a remote corner, insisted upon hearing her confession. Some wit and vivacity ensued; the frail matron, under her supposed concealment, confessed that she was married, and yet in love with another, whose person, profession, and manners she delineated with a degree of accuracy, which could not be possibly mistaken. Clear in the knowledge of his conquest, our hero now not only assumed the power of

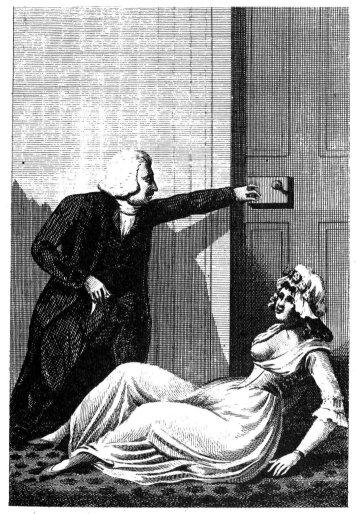

The Jolly Buck Parfon *and the* Hibernian Matron.

14 *The Jolly Buck Parson and the Hibernian Matron* – illustration from
The Bon Ton Magazine, 1793

absolution, but that of divination also – whispered that he knew her
favourite, and upon being laughed at for his presumption ... disclosed his
own more fascinating visage....

After this adventure, our readers will naturally suppose that no great

time was lost in scrupulous punctilios; the truth is, that the evening of the
ensuing day, while the Knight basked in the delights of Bacchus, the
amorous and impatient parson stole un-heeded to his wife's chamber ...
and finding her in a state of unresisting lassitude, threw himself, as Zanga
says, *all upon her*, and enjoyed a possession which, from interest as well as
inclination, he had long panted for.

The watchful Abigail, however, surprised him on a subsequent occasion.

> Our Jolly Buck Parson, finding his connexion discovered, and dreading the
> rage and jealousy of Mrs. Abigail, took an early opportunity of obtaining a
> tête-à-tête; when, after swearing that his visit was nothing more than
> merely Platonic ... he confirmed his innocence by a vigorous proof of
> unexhausted manhood.

But Abigail remains suspicious and jealous and finally discovers that
the parson and her mistress are meeting somewhere in a country
cottage. When she reports this to the unsuspecting knight, he decides
to investigate the matter forthwith.

> Near to the cottage was an umbrageous grove, where nature had erected
> flowery beds of dalliance; where the gentle zephyrs fann'd ambrosial gales,
> and where the power of love himself might have resided: here it was that
> our amorous lovers occasionally met, and this, from a thorough know-
> ledge of its convenience, was the place to which the Baronet resorted: the
> rustling leaves, the heaving sighs, which he saw and heard as he
> approached, gave evidence of guilt – he rushed upon the confounded and
> astonished pair, and saw them in the fullest moment of meretricious
> excess!

The tale concludes with the news that the enraged and cuckolded
knight is seeking a speedy sentence of divorce.[6]

If the seventeenth-century satirists had attacked the Puritans as
furtive lechers and sanctimonious fornicators, their successors of the
next century still had the Quakers as potential targets, and were soon
revelling in erotic and obscene attacks against the Methodists. Roger
Thompson has noted that the Quakers suffered sexual slander in the
later Interregnum and throughout the reign of Charles II. This continued into the eighteenth century. *A Comical New Dialogue Between
Mr. G...ff, a Pious Dissenting Parson, and a Female-Quaker, (a
Goldsmith's Wife) near Cheapside; Whom the Reverend Preacher
Pick'd up. With the Discourse that Pass'd Between Them, and the
Treatment He Gave Her* (1706), which was based on a true incident,
figures the familiar type of the seducing preacher. The amorous parson

accosted the goldsmith's wife in the street and made plain to her what he wanted. He carried on, despite a strong rebuke from the woman:

> Diss. Parson: Don't make Noise – it's a good Convenient Place – I must satisfie my self a little further. (Goes to put his Hand under her Petticoats)
>
> Gold. Wife: Out Villain. I cou'd spit a Leprosie on you – help, help.

Some people then entered and arrested him, whereupon he insulted the woman, claiming that she was lying.

> Diss. Parson: Thou art an Imp of Satan . . . a faithless Delilah, and wou'dst betray me into the Hands of the Philistines.

The dialogue ends with a warning against preachers who bemoan the lewdness of the town while they are secretly indulging the flesh.

The satirists loved to poke fun at the pious jargon of the Friends, which is often juxtaposed with the Quakers' very human and ungodly desires. Curll's *Post-Office Intelligence* (1736), a fictitious 'Collection of Love-letters, Written by Persons, in all Stations, from most Parts of the Kingdom', features two letters whose humour is based on this principle. The first is from a Quaker lover to his sweetheart and uses biblical language for a declaration of love (Letter No. II). Letter No. XXVI is from 'James Wyborne (a Quaker) to his Friend William Bastick . . . Describing the Acts, and Consequences of promiscuous Copulation, metaphorically explained and illustrated by Similes'. The topics of lust and fornication are dealt with in a pious jargon which occasionally lapses into bawdiness. Thus the fornicating friend is warned about the dangers of venereal disease, with the example of another young man who 'thrusts his rustling Pole into an overheated Oven, where it takes such Fire, that half a Year's Penance with Ten Pounds worth Doctor's Assistance will scarce quench'. By the fourth decade of the eighteenth century, the bawdy and obscene attacks against the Quakers were petering out, not least because a new sect was on the rise whose members soon eclipsed the Quakers as the butts of erotic satire. One of the last ribald works directed against the Quakers with a sexual flavour overshadowing the satirical purpose is *A Merry Conversation which Lately Pas'ed Between a Very Noted Quaker and His Maid, Upon a Very Merry Occasion. The Third Edition* (1739). This is written in the tradition of the whores' dialogue, in which an older person usually initiates an inexperienced youngster into the arcane mysteries of love. In this case John, the master, and Mary, his maid, are discussing a sermon of the last meeting. Mary wants John to explain to her the passages from the Bible which were quoted and which she did not understand, specifically, 'and he went in unto her, and Adam knew his Wife Eve; and why the Laud slew Onan for spilling his Seed'. John proposes to show her in practice and with brotherly love the meaning of all this and, after dissipating her religious and moral scruples with much biblical talk, they begin to 'enjoy the Comforts of Carnal Copulation':

J.: Let me feel thy Breasts; for they are like two Roses, which are Twins, feeding among the Lillies.

M.: My Brother! My Spouse! How Fair is thy Love.

J.: . . . . Doest thou feel nothing *Mary*?

M.: Yea, I feel something stiff against my Belly, as it were the Horn of a Unicorn.

J.: My Undefiled, speak not of Unicorns, for there is nothing of the Beast between these Sheets: This is that Part of Carnal Man which riseth and falleth according to the Spirit within. This is that which entereth into the Secrets of Woman, and filleth them with the Blessings of Posterity, so that their Memories shall not perish.

M.: May I not feel too? Oh *John*! Where are the Chariots of *Israel*, and the Horsemen thereof? for here are two of the great Wheels!

J.: Now, in the Fear of Heaven, will I take up thy lower Linnen, for Time calleth me to feel thy Belly and the Secrets.

M.: Thou seest I am free, yea, very free: do unto thy Hand-maid as seemeth good in thine Eyes.

J.: How beautiful is my Beloved!

M.: What hast thou found there *John*?

J.: Thy Belly, and thy secret Parts of Generation; thy Belly is like a Field of Wheat, set about with Lillies, and thy Navel is as a round cup which wanteth Liquor; Embrace me, *Mary*; Embrace me in thy Arms.

M.: I will, I do *John*, I will embrace thee; thou shalt lie between my Breasts.

J.: Yea, I will lie betwixt thy Thighs: Give Way to thy Beloved; spread one Thigh towards the *North*, and the other towards the *South*, I will exalt my Horn, I will enter with Courage and Resolution, *and beat down Satan before me.*

M.: Oh! *John*, I have seen many go out of this World, but never knew how they came into this World before; Oh! *John*, thou hast filled me with the Spirit of Life, and with the Dew of Knowledge.

Both continue to describe their satisfaction in pious language until Mary asks:

M.: When will the Spirit move thee again, Friend John?

J.: I will seek the Laud, and he will give us many Opportunities: but, Mary, take great Care of thyself . . . be sure thou publish it not in the Streets of Ascalon, lest the Uncircumcis'd triumph over us.

M.: I will be as tender of that as of the Apple of mine Eye.

Although seduction and fornication are at the centre of this erotic dialogue – it is, in fact, a parody of the whore dialogue – it is obvious that any sexual stimulation is suffocated by the humour resulting from the juxtaposition of holy language and some very unholy subjects.[7]

Early in 1739 John and Charles Wesley established the first Methodist society, in Bristol. It did not take long for scurrilous anti-Methodist broadsides to appear on the market of literary satire. The novelists, too, chimed in, concentrating on the now almost tedious type of the lustful preacher. Thus Henry Fielding's prurient *The Female Husband* (1746) portrays the Methodists, and in particular their ministers, as hypocritical perverts keen on lesbian and homosexual activities, which the eighteenth century considered the most detestable form of sexual perversion. Laurence Sterne included obscene and scatological references to George Whitefield, one of the principal voices of the movement in its early years, in Volume III, Chapter 38, of *Tristram Shandy*. In addition, the theatre, with its branch of comedy and farce, was usually not very far behind other developments on the literary scene. Samuel Foote wrote *The Minor*, in 1760, another satire against Whitefield and his followers, and Christopher Anstey ridiculed a fornicating Methodist preacher in his verse satire, *The New Bath Guide* (1766). From Bath, Miss Prudence informs Lady Betty in a letter about the way she was 'elected to Methodism by a Vision':

> Blessed I, tho' once rejected,
>   Like a little wand'ring sheep;
> Who this morning was elected
>   By a vision in my sleep:
>
> For I dream'd an apparition
>   Came, like *Roger*, from above:
> Saying, by divine commission,
>   I must fill you full of love.
>
> Just with *Roger's* head of hair on,
>   *Roger's* mouth, and pious smile;
> Sweet, methinks, as beard of *Aaron*,
>   Dropping down with holy oil.
>
> I began to fall a kicking,
>   Panted, struggled, strove in vain;
> When the spirit whipt so quick in,
>   I was cur'd of all my pain.
>
> First I thought it was a night-mare
>   Lay so heavy on my breast;

> But I found new joy and light there,
>   When with heav'nly love possest.
>
> Come again, then, apparition,
>   Finish what thou has begun;
> *Roger*, stay, thou soul's physician,
>   I with thee my race will run.
>
> Faith her chariot has appointed,
>   Now we're stretching for the goal;
> All the wheels with grace anointed,
>   Up to heav'n to drive my soul.

There is a tongue-in-cheek footnote in which the editor

> begs to be excused giving the public the sequel of this young lady's letter;
> but if the reader will please to look into the bishop of Exeter's book,
> entitled, *The Enthusiasm of Methodists and Papists Compared*, he will
> find many instances (particularly of young people) who have been elected
> in the manner above.

'Roger', the Methodist preacher's name in the poem, is of course also a *double entendre* if one considers its slang meaning, i.e., sexual intercourse.

It was again the ingenious William Hogarth who captured the spirit of erotic anti-Methodist satire. In 1760 he produced a painting, based on his earlier *The Sleeping Congregation*, which showed the inside of a meeting house very much like the one in which George Whitefield preached in Tottenham Court Road (plate 15). As is usual with Hogarth, there are several levels to the satire. The preacher in a harlequin's robe is exposed as a Catholic monk threatening his congregation with both God and the Devil, while the dog whose collar reads 'Whitefield' barks at a raving flock munching and devouring the body of Christ. In the right-hand corner, Hogarth makes an allusion to contemporary bawdy satire: a pious cleric is about to reach into the bosom of a transported maid while a statue of Christ is tumbling to the ground. In the foreground, the pious bawd, Mother Douglas (who was converted to Methodism), hugs the figure of Christ in a manner suggesting that her convulsive fits are due to physical as well as spiritual stimulation. As the Christ images might have given offence, Hogarth never published this picture in its original form. After two years of waiting he made some alterations, to put into visual terms his hatred of Methodists, who are represented as reviving the worst superstitions of Catholicism and ancient magic. The altered version

15 Hogarth, *Enthusiasm Delineated*, 1760

was entitled *Credulity, Superstition and Fanaticism* (1762) and incorporated the notorious cases of Richard Hathaway, the boy who
vomited pins and nails, claiming to have been bewitched, and Mary
Tofts (Mother Douglas in the original version; plate 16). Despite such
venomous criticism, Methodism was becoming respectable by the
1760s, when the Countess of Huntingdon had begun to spread the
new faith in the upper social stratum. But the literary myth of the
hypocritical and fornicating Methodist preacher died hard. It was still
alive when *The Bon Ton Magazine* went into production in the 1790s.
Number 31 of this periodical (1793) featured a story on 'The Priest-

16 Hogarth, *Credulity, Superstition and Fanaticism*, 1762

Ridden Washerwoman; or, the Birth of Mahershalalhashbaz', accompanied by a suggestive frontispiece (plate 17). The hero of the short tale is conveniently dubbed Crab, a pun on 'grab' and on (anal) crab lice. After exploiting several of his converts, Crab decided to lodge in the house of 'Sister Tabitha Puckneedle, a pious washerwoman', who, when he entered,

> was busily employed in washing out a pair of Nankeen breeches. Never did pious washerwoman labour more assiduously to present her work fair and unpolluted; she rubbed, she wrung, she wrenched, she washed and wrenched again, but all to no purpose: the best intentions in the world are

17 *The Priest-Ridden Washerwoman* – illustration from *The Bon Ton Magazine*, 1793

not always practicable; still there appeared one spot, and that none of the smallest, which defied all her care and solicitude. The said spot ran down in an oblique direction, traversing that part, where the twin divisions of these *inexpressibles* of the male attire first meet and unite in one. Every one knows, that Nankeen breeches, provided the stuff be really genuine, (and can saints be supposed to wear any other?) have always something of a yellow cast: the contrast, therefore, exhibited by the said spot, in hue somewhat resembled that appearance in the firmament which philosophers distinguish by the name of Galaxy, or milky way. 'What aileth thee, sister Tabitha?' cried Crab, perceiving her embarrassment, 'what aileth thee? and wherefore is thy countenance fallen?' ... The eyes of sister Tabitha immediately reverted, or fell upon that part of Crab's dress, whose counterpart at that very moment gave her so much trouble and uneasiness. Crab's breeches, however, being of black plush, defied in the present instance the test of examination ... 'See, brother, (replied sister Tabitha) the garment spotted by the flesh,' as Jude says, ' 'Tis even so (quoth Crab); this proceedeth from the man of sin. Touch not, sister Tabitha, taste not, handle not! O most abominable pollution of the sons of Belial!'

Tears stood in the eyes of Crab, as well as in those of sister Tabitha. Both fell down on their knees in prayer; sister Tabitha's heart beating all the time so high, that Crab was fain to thrust his hand into her bosom, for fear the throbbing tenant should fairly bounce out. What further followed, we are not authorized to relate; so much, however, is certain, that our prophetess, at the expiration of nine months, brought forth a second Mahershalalhashbaz.[8]

Satire is unfortunately limited in that it has to rely on exaggeration, myth, and stereotype, which do not allow much variation of a given theme. The pious style of the Methodist preachers, their enthusiasm in an age which believed in reason, and the ecstasies of the followers in their crowded meetings, were the aspects of Methodism most obvious to the outsider, as evidenced in parodies and lampoons. It is noticeable that all dissenting religious groups, from the seventeenth century onwards, were subjected to sexual slander and obscene attacks, both very efficient means of ridiculing and ostracising political or religious adversaries. When Thomas Rowlandson produced his pornographic illustrations, in the early nineteenth century, he could draw on a tradition of anti-clerical satire of more than a hundred years old. His *The Sanctified Sinner* is the very apogee of the sexual slander of clergymen: the preacher receiving sexual services from a girl is a hypocrite who privately reads the Earl of Haddington's *Crazy Tales*. His pretence has become a part of his false nature, and not even sexual passion can change it.

3 EROTICA AGAINST THE ROMAN CATHOLIC CHURCH

Venus in the Cloister or The Nun in Her Smock was one of the more successful pornographic books of the early eighteenth century. Written by Jean Barrin, precentor of Nantes Cathedral and vicar-general of the diocese, it was first published in 1683. By 1692, it had reached a sixth edition and appeared in London in an English translation published by Henry Rhodes, a young bookseller who, like Edmund Curll, also specialised in pornography. Curll usually had an ear to the ground in this field and, in the absence of copyright, hardly ever missed a good seller. In 1724 Curll published the book, too, and was very pleased to be able to announce a second edition in the following year. With most of his salacious ware, Curll knew exactly how far he could go or how to veil the true nature of his books by inventing pretexts for their publication. In this case he reckoned he was on safe ground. If Rhodes had published the book without any legal trouble, why should not he earn good money with it as well? In addition, *Venus in the Cloister* provided excellent cover in its professed attack on the Roman Catholic Church. But with the rise of the purity movements and the societies for the reformation of manners, the times and public tolerance were changing. To his great surprise, Edmund Curll found himself charged with obscene libel for publishing *A Treatise of the Use of Flogging*

(1718) and especially *Venus in the Cloister*. Lord Fortescue was one of the three judges who heard the case. While his colleagues, Raymond and Reynold, were convinced of the obscenity of *Venus in the Cloister*, Fortescue disagreed with them and later confessed, 'I thought it rather to be published on Purpose to expose the ROMISH Priests, the Father Confessors, and Popish Religion.' Thus Curll hoodwinked at least one victim into his trap, although it did not help him much since he was later found guilty.[9]

Lord Fortescue's view explains the production as well as the official toleration if not encouragement of a huge wave of eighteenth-century erotica with a strong anti-Catholic flavour. Ever since Henry VIII fell out with the Pope, Roman Catholics had been the traditional whipping-boy of English satire, much of it written in the form of ribald or obscene attacks. Almost anything, including pornography, could be levelled against the Catholics, an opportunity thoroughly exploited by Curll and those who shared the field of erotica with him.[10]

For most English writers of the eighteenth century the Roman Catholic Church remained in the pillory, where it had been for more than a century; and the peccadilloes of the Catholic clergy, whether invented or true, were the staple diet of bawdy satire. Almost any treatise or pamphlet sold if the anti-popery flag was properly hoisted in the title. These critical and satirical attacks must be seen as a reaction to the imminent danger of a powerful Catholic France and the worldly, mercantile enterprises of the Jesuits in the Western hemisphere. Examples from the early eighteenth century are Cipriano de Valera's *A Full View of Popery, in a Satirical Account of the Lives of the Popes ... Written by a Learned Spanish Convert* (1704) and the anonymous *Popery Display'd: or, The Church of Rome Described in Her True Colours* (1713).[11]

Bawdy and obscene treatises or pornographic works with an anti-Catholic stance had an important part in the general mud-flinging against the Pope and his Church. Anti-Catholic writings had been flourishing for some time in England, and for a much longer period in Catholic countries and within the Church itself. France exerted a powerful cultural influence on England, and this included the anti-Catholic attitudes of enlightened writers and the unabashed ribald or obscene works of Catholic clerics. To be sure, France had her own tradition of bawdy attacks on the Roman Catholic Church. Like the Italian novella, the occasionally virulently anti-clerical *fabliaux* expressed their criticism in sexual and scatological humour. They influenced the frivolous collections of love stories in the style of Boccaccio's

Decameron, such as *Les cent nouvelles nouvelles* of 1486, and Marguerite d'Angoulême's (also called Marguerite de Navarre) *L'heptaméron*, which was written in 1542–9 and published in 1559.
Eighteenth-century authors and readers in England knew these works,
and they knew even better Jean de la Fontaine's *Contes*, published
between 1655 and 1685 and often reprinted in the following century.
The *Contes* are very much indebted to the fables, the *contes-en-vers*,
and such writers as Aretino, Boccaccio, and Rabelais. La Fontaine's
lecherous monks guaranteed the popularity of his tales, which were
also published with explicit prints (plate 18).[12]

18 *Le religieux*, 1740

In this field Voltaire remained unrivalled, with his ribald epic poem
La pucelle d'Orléans (1762). Through this work he generally aimed to
ridicule the Catholic doctrine of virginity and the belief in saints and
miracles, and he also expressed much venom against the priests and
the orders. The first canto was translated into English in 1780, and the
complete poem in 1796.

There was also a prodigious erotic and anti-Catholic literature produced by libertine *abbés*. In particular the '*abbés de cour*' did not hold their clerical titles and offices in great esteem. Many of them treated their vocation more as a joke than as an obligation, having been destined from their births for the clerical career. It is well known that some of the '*abbés de cour*' were amongst the most notorious rakes at the court of Louis XV. Ironically, the title '*abbé*' thus became a naughty incentive for readers if used in the title-pages of erotic works. Voltaire, for instance, called himself 'Abbé Bazin' in some of his licentious works. The better-known *abbés* who wrote erotica with an anti-Catholic bias included Jacques Boileau, Timoléon de Choisy, Claude-Henri Fusée de Voisenon and Guillaume Hyacinthe Bougeant.

In addition, a vast body of anti-monastic erotica was eagerly received, translated, and imitated in Protestant England. By the 1790s, the sexual exploits of the clergy in France had attained the status of a literary cliché, flogged to death in such pieces as P.J.B. Nougaret's *Aventures galantes de Jérôme, frère capucin* (1797), which had first appeared in 1765 as *La capucinade*.[13] For their own bawdy and obscene anti-Catholic works English writers thus had a formidable source that could be constantly tapped. English novelists gave expression to the themes of popular literature as well as to the anti-Catholic ideas of the eighteenth-century English *Zeitgeist*. Sterne, whose library contained books on the Cadière–Girard scandal in France and on the moral corruption of the Jesuits, found many occasions to criticise and ridicule the 'Romish Church' in his *A Sentimental Journey* and *Tristram Shandy*, while Smollett, who disliked both Frenchmen and Catholics, created an *abbé* for his *Ferdinand Count Fathom* (1753), who leads a boisterous, drunken party to a Paris brothel. One of the favourite areas of muck-raking was the celibacy of the clergy and of the Pope. As the head and representative of his Church, the Pope was a natural target for those who intended to ridicule Catholicism with ribald satire and obscene attacks. An early example is *A Full and True Account of a Dreaded Fire that Lately Broke Out in the Pope's Breeches* (London, 1713), an anonymous bawdy satire consisting of six pages of verse. It relates the story of a London courtesan and her friend, Signor Nicolini (one of the castrato singers in London), who takes her to Rome. There, her beautiful voice and buxom looks eventually attract the attention of 'St Peter's Chair'. In a private audience, the following conversation ensues:

> Pope. —————————— Ah! my Dear,
> Come sit thee down in *Peter's* Chair;

Here's *Peter's Key*, and as you Sit,
Let's try how *Peter's Key* will fit
Thy *Key-hole*; for even those who Sin most
Their Secrets must unlock, tho' inmost,
Unto their Ghostly Father, who
From all their Sins does them undo;
For those who practice Holy Living,
Must to their Priests go off a Shriving.
This said, St. *Peter's* Key he stole,
As he suppos'd, to the Key-hole,
And then began to push it in,
In order to unlock her Sin.

She.   With that, O Holy Sir, cry'd She,
I doubt you've pitch'd too low your Key:
I'll pitch it for ye, if you please,
And then you may unlock at Ease.
Then strait she did it with a Touch,
His Holiness too thank'd her much,
And withal this excuse did make,
In the behalf of his Mistake.

Pope. Saying, he seldom had of late
Us'd his Key to ope fore-gate;
Therefore, dear Madam, 'tis no wonder,
That now my Key had made a Blunder.
Now as he thrust the Key in Hole,
Amaz'd, he cry'd, upon my Soul,
The Key goes in most wondrous easy,
What is the Key-hole broke, or Greasy?
Hah! it turns round not very hard,
I fear your Lock has ne'er a Ward;
Pray what's the Reason of it, Madam?
You must tell Truth by good St. Adam.

She.   Ah! Sir, if it must be then spoken,
My Key-hole is a little broken;
As to the Wards, I do declare,
They were knock'd out in *Angleterre*.

Pope. In *Angleterre*, Damn'd Hereticks!
Damn 'em to the bottom of *Styx*!
I'm out of Patience, marry am I,
I'll turn my Key no more, G——d d——n me.
By C——— and by St. *Peter's* Rock,
I'll put my Key out of thy Lock,
This said, he let down T———s's Smock.

Some Three Days after, this Apostle
In's holy Codpiece had strange Bustle,

Which when he found he sent forthwith
For Learned able Pintle Smith,
To Cure his Fleshly Key's disaster,
Which he soon did by Pill and Plaister.
As soon as e're the Pope grew well,
He curst poor T———s by Book and Bell,
And vow'd to keep, in fright of Whores,
His Key for to unlock back Doors.

Thus, Sirs, you see how *T———s* has pepper'd,
The Codpiece of the *Romish* Shepherd.
We could not burn the Pope at Home,
But *T———s* has burnt the Pope at *Rome*.
What may not Hereticks then hope,
Since even at *Rome* they've burnt the Pope.

As in this satire, cast in the form of the popular ballad, the Pope as a lecher was a common theme in anti-Catholic erotica, drawing on seventeenth-century English works, and on contemporary publications by disgruntled insiders and apostates, such as Christian Gottlieb Koch's *De obscoenis pontificorum decimis* (Flensburg, 1707) – just one example of the numerous erotica which continued to appear in Latin – and Antonio D. Gavin's *A Master-Key to Popery* (Dublin, 1724), which soon appeared in a second edition in three volumes (London, 1725–6). A native of Saragossa, Gavin left Spain and the Catholic Church after a falling-out with the latter and, as a protégé of the Earl of Stanhope, joined the Church of England. According to the *DNB*, his *Master-Key* is 'a farrago of lies and libels, interspersed with indecent tales'. The clever mixture of little fact and much fiction made the work a best-seller. Apostates like Gavin poured their hatred of Catholicism into vitriolic, fictitious publications which found a credulous public in Protestant England. As late as 1779 Anthony Egane, 'Late Confessor General of the kingdom of Ireland, and afterwards, through the mercy of God, Minister of the Gospel, according to the Reformed Religion', as he states on the title-page of his *The Book of Rates Now Used in the Sin Custom House of the Church of Rome*, inscribed his curious pamphlet to the Edinburgh societies for promoting the Protestant interest. Egane had a section on 'Certain Decreed Impositions of the Chancery Court of the Church of Rome' in which it is maintained that the Catholic Church granted dispensations for mortal and carnal sins, provided that specified amounts of money were paid. According to the pamphlet, 'dispensations for bastards' were thus regulated:

	£	sh.	d.
For admitting a bastard after the manner to holy orders; and to capacitate him to hold a living, wherein is a cura animum [sic], he pays	5	1	1
...			
For a Mendicant's bastard turning Monk; his dispensation is	6	2	3
For a Mendicant to be made provincial of an order, or first guardian ... if Monks that have revenues ... they may have a dispensation for as high as an abbot, for	1	1	9

Allegedly, the provisions made for carnal sins and buggery were the following:

	£	sh.	d.
A Priest or friar, having lain or carnally sinned with a woman of whatsoever sort or degree, whether a *Nun* or kinswoman, or a relation, or with any other, whether married or single, whether within the bounds or cloisters of his monastery or elsewhere ... it gives him power to exercise his function, and to hold his livings: and that together ... is only	36	9	6
And if besides this, there be an absolution for Buggery, or for unnatural sin committed with brute beasts, a dispensation ... will come to	90	12	1
A simple absolution for the sin of Buggery, or the sin Contrary to nature, that is to say, with brute beasts, together with a dispensation and the inhibitory clause, is	36	9	0
A *Nun* having played the whore very often *aut intra, aut extra, sepia Monasterii*, is to be absolved, and rehabilitated to hold the dignity of her order, for	36	0	0
An absolution for one that keeps a whore at bed and board, with a dispensation to hold a benefice, is	4	5	6
For all act of whoring, or such dishonesty committed by a layman, he is to be dispensed with, for	6	2	6
A layman, having committed incest, is to pay	4	6	0
A layman having committed adultery, is to be absolved for	4	0	0
But if it be adultery and incest together, he is to pay	6	2	6
For the adulterer and adulteress together, is	6	6	0

Gavin's largely fictitious *The Frauds of Romish Monks and Priests* has many amorous episodes originating in the confessional, generally seen as the main cause, along with celibacy, of the lustfulness of the priesthood. This first appeared in 1691 and had reached a fifth edition in two volumes by 1725; its second part was entitled *Observations on a Journey to Naples. Wherein the Frauds of Romish Monks and Priests are Further Discover'd* (London, 1725). Other virulent works against the Catholic clergy were *Reasons Humbly Offer'd For a Law to Enact the Castration of Popish Ecclesiastics, As the Best Way to Prevent th[e] Growth of Popery in England* (London, 1700) and *The Priest Gelded: or Popery at the Last Gasp. Shewing … the Necessity of Passing a Law for the Castration of Popish Ecclesiastics in Great Britain, as the Only Means to Extirpate Popery etc. To Which is Added a List of the … Religious Houses Abroad Maintained by the English Papists* (London, 1747). The latter was translated into French in the same year as *Le prêtre châtré* and is a vitriolic tract of thirty-six pages against the Catholic clergy and the monks. Aiming at the vow of celibacy, the anonymous author argues that when monks, 'inspired with amorous Sentiments, go abroad from their Monasteries, they are like so many fed Horses, neighing after every Woman they see: And if they have not Opportunity of giving vent to their Lusts that Way, they many Times do it by other Methods, which Nature as well as Religion forbids to name'. He accuses the Church of Rome of deliberately tolerating the fornication of priests in order to gain power and make converts. 'The Priest's Testicles,' he maintains, 'are the greatest Promoters of the Pope's Empire,' and he therefore suggests gelding as the most efficient means of solving the problem of immoral Catholic priests, who would thus be driven out of the kingdom. He cites the example of Italy, where boys were allegedly gelded to be singers at the opera 'or to be Catamites to Cardinals, and other Dignitaries of the Romish Church … the Roman clergy are much addicted to that damnable and unnatural Crime; and such of them as are not, keep lewd Women almost constantly'. The pamphlet concludes with a list of fifty-one 'Monasteries, Nunneries, Colleges, and Religious Houses abroad, maintained at the Charge of the English Papists', thus supposedly demonstrating the influence and power of the Catholic Church in Protestant England.

It is obvious that in this example, and many others, imagination and hatred guided the hands of writers who begrudged the priests their right of privacy with women. There may have been an element of truth in the rumours about the confessional, confirmed by Father Girard's seduction of his penitent (see Chapter 4); the result was the cliché, in pictures, folklore, and literature, of the confessional as the 'lechery office' and of the Catholic priest as the artful, experienced seducer who, in his capacity as confessor, has acquired an extensive knowledge of all sorts of sexual perversions. An anonymous engraving of

19 *Father Paul and the Blue-Eyed Nun of St Catherine*, 1770

c. 1700 shows a double scene in the confessional. In the scene on the left, the monk says, 'By St Patrick I never hear this Woman's Confession, but my Virtue is very much staggered. I will enjoyn her Flogging for Pennance, & administer it myself for my own Consolation –.' In the scene on the right, while administering the punishment, he pronounces, 'She is a delicious Morsel, her Beauty dazzles like the Sonn [sic] in the Meridian ...' Monks are also the focus of *Father Paul and the Blue-Eyed Nun of St Catherine* (1770; plate 19). Other examples are Rowlandson's *Symptoms of Sanctity* (1801) and the anonymous *Friar Bald-Pate's Absolution to his Fair Penitent.*[14]

This stereotype was equally applied in the attacks against the Catholic orders. It is indicative of the reputation which the orders enjoyed in eighteenth-century England that bawdy houses were jocularly referred to as 'nunneries'. Thus Volume I (February 1769) of *The Town and Country Magazine* figured a description, on pp. 64ff., of a brothel run by Charlotte Hayes, entitled, 'The Monastery of Santa Charlotta'. In an advertisement at the end of the erotic poem *Mimosa*, probably published in 1779, the following work was announced, in two volumes and at the price of seven shillings if bound: *Nocturnal Revels; or, the History of Modern Nunneries . . . Comprising also The Ancient and Present State of Promiscuous Gallantry, with the Portraits of the Most Celebrated Demireps and Courtezans of this Period . . . By a Monk of the Order of St. Francis.* Contemporaries immediately understood the hints at the Wilkes scandal and the Medmenham-ites, as well as at the allegedly wanton Franciscans. One can discern several historical and political reasons, in addition to traditional Protestant hatred of Catholicism and opposition by the Enlightenment, which would seem to explain the spate of works against Catholic monks, and the members of the Society of Jesus in particular. To begin with, the vows of chastity and celibacy required of the members of the orders ran counter to eighteenth-century ideas of the natural propagation of the human species and of natural sexual behaviour. In the eyes of English Protestants, monastical celibacy came close to abnormality if not perversion. The orders, and especially the busy Jesuits, posed further problems to the Protestant world, through their efforts and success in the Counter-Reformation and their mercantile enterprises in America and in other colonies. Since the Jesuits were the most fervent supporters of papal claims, opposition to their influence and power was growing in the eighteenth century. Even within the Catholic Church the orthodox disagreed with the methods of the Society of Jesus, which had a reputation for cherishing casuistry and moral relativism. Many Catholics objected to the practice of the Jesuits in China, where they had won the confidence of potential converts by pretending sympathy with the teaching of Confucius. In South America and the French West Indies, the Jesuits were commercial competitors and rivals of England and the Catholic European countries. When England destroyed the French colonial trade, the head of the Society of Jesus in the West Indies, Père Lavalette, went bankrupt, and thus there started an investigation which led to the abolition of the order in France in 1762. For the Jesuits, this came as a hard blow, since in 1757 they had already been expelled from Portugal and Brazil. But worse tribulations were to come. In 1767 they lost their stronghold, Spain, and in July 1773 Pope Clement XIV, by the Bull *Dominus ac Redemptor*, dissolved the Society. It can be assumed that such private sexual scandals as that of Père Jean-Baptiste Girard played a part in this final decision by the Holy Father. Both in France and England, the Girard–Cadière affair (1730s: see Chapter 4) kept the clandestine anti-Catholic presses in business for several decades. Voltaire, short and precise as was his wont, summed the scandal up in four lines:

> Le père Girard, remply de flamme,
> D'une fille a fait une femme;
> Mais le Parlement plus habile,
> D'une femme a fait une fille.

A large part of the welter of eighteenth-century licentious popular writings directed against Catholic monks and nuns has today disappeared. It was France that provided a sizable part of the literature against the Church, some of it of seventeenth-century origin, that was translated or imitated in England. One of the many attacks on the Jesuits allegedly based on fact was *Love in All its Shapes: or the Way of a Man with a Woman. Illustrated in the Various Practices of the Jesuits of the Maison Professe at Paris, with Divers Ladies of Quality and Fashion at the Court of France* (London, 1734). First published in France as *Les Jésuites de la Maison Professe* (1696), it was rather successful and in the course of the eighteenth century was reprinted several times. Sold at one shilling, the fifty-eight pages of this work give an allegedly genuine account by former members of 'la maison professe' of the sexual escapades of several Jesuits and their 'Father-Guardian'. Almost all the themes and myths of anti-Jesuit erotica are put to use in this book. The first part traces the amorous tracks of the Reverend Father de la Rue, possibly a hint at the scandal of the Abbé des Rues in 1723, an account of which Curll had published in 1725. The priest falls in love with his penitent, Ninon, and demands her maidenhead as a penance while promising to keep it secret with 'the doctrine of St. Dennis'. At a clandestine meeting he reveals this doctrine, 'a thing of divers colours' which the innocent Ninon begins 'to take pleasure in handling'. The Jesuit, 'finding by her languishing and tender air that she would not be displeased at knowing it to the bottom, threw her upon a little Bed, where he taught her all its Wonders'. The thankful Ninon promises to allow him 'refreshments' after her marriage. The focus of attention then moves on to Father Bourdalou, who satisfies a young lady of quality whose husband is apparently not doing enough for her. This tale shows the Jesuits as casuists who can even prove with quotations from the Bible that adultery is not a sin. Father Bourdalou is so taken in by his young lady that he begins to hallucinate during his sermons when, to the amusement of his congregation, he exclaims: 'What raptures! Quick, my pretty dear, take my Nag, and put him into your Stable before he is quite spent.' While the Father-Guardian reprimands him for this public *faux-pas*, he is quite prepared to accept Bourdalou's sexual desires, especially so since he, too, is allowed access to the generous young lady. Upon the Father-Guardian's visit, however, she discovers 'that Father Bourdalou's *Doctrine* was worth infinitely more than *his*, and that it penetrated farther'. There follow some outright attacks on the Jesuits, who are shown as bending religious doctrines to make them suit their sexual immorality. The quality of the humour is rather poor. Meanwhile, the two Jesuits take turns with the young lady, a marchioness; and the imprudent Father-Guardian is discovered by the marquis *in flagrante delicto*. He manages to escape, and the marchioness is sent to a convent. The next part deals with Father Le Comte, who first 'converts' a Turkish maiden and then directs his attention to the wife of a doctor. When she confesses his advances to her husband, they plan to set up the Jesuit. He is lured into her bed and then seized by the porters, who lash him severely. This upright doctor also exposes the King's confessor, Father La Chaise. This is, however, to no avail. The Catholic Church as a whole is shown as powerful and immoral, in that when the bishop and archbishop are informed of Father La Chaise's fornication with a girl disguised as a page in his service, they make haste to look him up – not to punish him but to partake in his sensual pleasures. The story culminates in the last episode, when De la Rue, Bourdalou, and Le Comte ask a bawd to provide them with whores, who enter the monastery disguised as novices. One of these 'nuns' 'peppers them off with the Pox', from which they recover with much pain. In the tradition of popular erotica, the lecherous monks are thus punished for their wickedness while the reader gets a good laugh.

Memoirs of the Voluptuous Conduct of the Capuchins in Regard of the Fair Sex: Represented In a Variety of Curious Scenes, Exhibited to Public View by a Brother of the Order (London, 1755) is another English translation of a French popular best-seller, dating back to the seventeenth century. The French versions usually had erotic or satirical frontispieces and pornographic plates, while the English translation was unillustrated. The English title gives the publication an air of authenticity and truthfulness, which is soon put into question by the anonymous author's attacks on the Capuchins, depicted by their former brother as unabashed liars. He claims to have once held the position of alms gatherer in a French convent near Paris. Maintaining that he was taught to lie in order to procure money, he soon launches into the sexual immoralities of monastical life. Starting with a display of the expert knowledge of sexual practices the monks acquired through the confession, he demonstrates the various methods they purportedly employed to seduce their penitents, who are divided in such categories as young maids, dissatisfied women, female bigots, and virgins. After several anecdotes illustrating the lewdness of the monks and their complicity with the police, the author moves on to a description of his sexual adventures as a monk in the country, where he was gathering money with his superiors. In one of their many feats of debauchery, they visit the house of a rich family where the Provincial makes love to the lady of the house, while the Father Secretary and the author satisfy other female members of the household:

> The Door was close shut, but seeing a Window half open, I was desirous to look in, which I did, and I saw our Provincial, who held in his Arms the Lady of the House, whose petticoat was tucked up so as to afford me the delightful Prospect of a Scarlet Stocking, neatly drawn on, a Garter accurately tied, and a Bit of plump Flesh as white as Alabaster. I retreated with Precipitation ... and sought to keep myself concealed in some Part of the Grove ... But another Adventure happened to me; for passing into a great Thicket, I observed the Father Secretary rise briskly, and advancing towards me all in a Sweat, he said in embracing me: Hah! Brother *Leonorus*, how transported am I to see you here, come partake of our Joys, and share in our Delights. At the same Time he took me by the Hand, and led me to the Place where the Gentleman's Sister was sitting, to whom he said, Miss, I am vexed to the Heart, that the too great Ardour of my Passion opposed your and my Desires; you assuredly have Reason to be dissatisfied with me, but if I have failed to compleat your Wishes, I believe you will meet in Brother *Leonorus* wherewithal to content them. Retire, said she, as in a Passion, I should not have a Desire stirred up in me without seeing its Accomplishment; in the Brother I hope to find Matter for a proper Satisfaction; and your Presence serves only to retard the Pleasures I expect to taste with him.
>
> He retired, and these Words having given broad Hints of the Combat I was to engage in, my Arms were soon ready for the Charge, I mounted to the Assault, and behaved so gallantly that the young Lady confessed, she was exceeding glad of the Adventure ... During these Transactions the Provincial came upon us: He was surprized to see me in a lascivious Posture, and he might well have fallen into a fainting Fit, very different from that which seized him undoubtedly in the Summer-house; he knew not how he should construe the Thing; but Miss having related the History how it happened, he laughed heartily, and said to me with a paternal Heart, Cheer up, dear Brother, proceed as you begun, this is a lovely young Lady, you must employ all your Strength to content her, and you must rejoice in the happy Occasion that has so unexpectedly presented itself.

The gallant monks then make their way to a convent of nuns 'to perform a Nine-days Devotion' and the author becomes an eye-witness of, and a participant in, various acts of fornication including group sex between three monks and two nuns. Although the nuns are separated from their confessors by grates, they find ways and means to overcome this difficulty, as the author tells us in a voyeuristic scene:

> I went up Stairs to the Parlour of the Prioress, where he usually conversed with one or other of the Nuns. I opened the Door without knocking, tho' the contrary is punctually observed by Monks and Nuns: But I had so raised the Latch, that I did not well know what I was about. I beheld, on opening the Door, shall I say! our Reverend Father Provincial making Preparatives for conveying very luscious Ideas to the Imagination; he lay extended on his Back, upon the Shelf that was placed before the Grate; his Eyes full fraught with the Glances of amorous Passion, were eagerly fixed on one of the beautiful Nuns on the other Side, who displayed Charms not to be told, and whose Hand, to avoid Idleness, went through the ceremonious Part of a certain Office. This Spectacle surprized me so much, that I drew the Door after me with more Precipitation than I opened it, and ran in quest of the Secretary, without knowing why, or wherefore; my Head was so distempered with Wine, and what I had seen, that I rushed suddenly into the Parlour where he was, and broke the Bolts which he had the Prudence to keep the Door secured by, for Fear of a Surprize. But if my Astonishment had been great on Sight of the Condition of the Father Provincial, that in which I found the Secretary was much worse. He was stretched on two Chairs, his Visage pale, his Cord loose about him, his Sandals at a Distance, his Gown carelessly raised, and a young Lady held him by the Hand across the Grate. I ran to succour him, but the Posture in which I saw the Lady as I approached, convinced me that he was only dead to partake of the Effects of a more pleasing Resurrection. She assured me that his Debility would be attended with no fatal Consequences.

Back in Paris, the author follows the example of his Provincial and sends to the nuns 'certain Waters, to make subside the hydropical Humours which Love might have engendred'. The rest of the *Memoirs* is concerned with the scandals in convents involving Capuchin monks, which the author claims to have heard from his brethren.[15]

Popular as they were, anti-monastic erotica had a pervasive influence on other literary genres. The works of the great eighteenth-century English novelists, in particular those of Smollett and Sterne, thrived on the rich humus of anti-Catholic satire. The sentimental and Gothic novels published in the second half of the eighteenth century also drew extensively on previously published anti-Catholic erotica and, to a certain extent, are a continuation of anti-monastical writings.[16]

It is worth noting that the sexual slander of Catholic clerics had developed literary stereotypes well before the seventeenth century. Disagreement on political and religious issues between secular and ecclesiastical powers is to be seen as one of the main causes behind this slander, quite apart from the acceptance in literature of the cliché-ridden 'types' developed by folklore and oral satire. There is no doubt that, with the growth of libertine literature in the seventeenth century, and even more in the Age of Reason, attacks on Church representatives also increased. However, it would be wrong to see the wave of anti-clerical erotica after 1700 exclusively as an expression of revolutionary feeling and of the Enlightenment. Such a view underestimates the pervasive power of literary stereotypes. Admittedly, the libertines and the *philosophes* united in their mud-flinging against the Church of Rome; but their ammunition had been provided by others before them. I would argue that the stereotypes of Catholic clerics as lechers and fornicators had an essential, if not central, place in anti-Catholic erotica during the Age of Enlightenment. This era did not, however, invent them, but merely made them more popular. It was as early as 1542 that Marguerite de Navarre began to write her collection of tales, modelled on Boccaccio, that first appeared, in 1558, as *Histoire des amans fortunez*, the original version of what came to be known as the *Heptaméron*. A considerable number of the tales of the third, fourth, and fifth days in this book are concerned with the sexual adventures of monks. The devout Marguerite had had a few tiffs and arguments with the Franciscans; and in the *Heptaméron* she revenged herself on the monks who had caused her this trouble. In one of the tales a sex-crazy Franciscan kills all the members of a household to abduct the lady to a monastery. Another Franciscan takes advantage of the confidence of a virgin, while other monks fool husbands to get at their wives. Thus a number of themes and allegations as well as types in eighteenth-century anti-monastic erotica can be found in the literature of the Renaissance. The *Heptaméron* was often reprinted during the eighteenth century, some editions including erotic illustrations; and the genre was also practised by writers, including La Fontaine. Eighteenth-century writers of anti-monastic erotica thus found ready-made motifs, types, and stereotypes, to which they added aggressively, through obscenity and pornography.[17]

❦ 3 ❧
Anti-Aristocratic Erotica

Several factors contributed to the extraordinary increase in the eighteenth century of the obscene libels, bawdy lampoons, ribald personal satire, and downright political pornography directed against the nobility and aristocracy. There was the European – mainly French – literary tradition of the 'chronique scandaleuse', reaching back to the times of Aretino and even Suetonius. English writers thrived on this. In order to survive, the pamphleteers and writers of 'libelles', more often than not of Grub Street origin, resorted to sexual slander and obscene attacks, forms of aggressive satire that had proved rewarding for scandalmongerers for almost two thousand years. The high life of the members of the nobility, both in England and France, provided more than sufficient material for such writers, and their clandestine publishers, in low life. The development of the press and the concomitant advancement of literacy guaranteed a corner for those who earned their living by slandering the high and mighty. Some attacks on clerics and aristocrats, triggered by the spirit of the Enlightenment and hunger for money, were carried on in the literary underground, where publishers and their badly paid hacks could remain anonymous and thus escape prosecution. The libel laws of eighteenth-century England had large loopholes that opened opportunity for innuendo while hampering prosecution. Both Viktor Link and R.C. Kropf have shown convincingly the connections between the laws concerning defamation, and Augustan satire. In fact, such laws encouraged personal satire in the form of innuendo. Literary history has perceived the rise of satire in the eighteenth century in relation to the revival and reception of classical authors like Horace and Juvenal. The libel laws, however, had an equally important influence, as far as form and expression of satire were concerned. Oblique attack and *double entendre*, both essential parts of eighteenth-century satire, are in essence a consequence of writers' fear of the law.

It is impossible to exclude France from a survey of English anti-aristocratic erotica and political pornography, although one might well be tempted to do so in view of the daunting number of publications produced in the literary underground of the Old Régime. Not only were French revolutionary ideas, dressed up as obscene 'libelles', exported to England; but London also became a haven for a motley group of French expatriate and disgruntled 'libellistes', who exploited the British freedom of the press by producing slanderous pamphlets. These were either then offered for sale to the French court before publication, or printed in London, Amsterdam or Neuchâtel to be smuggled into France in secret. Obscenities published in France against the nobility during the revolutionary period also had an effect abroad in England.

I FRENCH ANTI-ARISTOCRATIC EROTICA

The extravagant lifestyle and general excesses of French court nobility in the eighteenth century were an invitation to literary and sub-literary attack. Due to severe censorship in France, satire and slander were eventually written mainly underground or abroad. The Revolution finally allowed the gutter press writers to abandon their anonymity, bringing great change; but it also brought death, not only for the nobility but for several pamphleteers, too. The sub-literary genre of the journalistic 'chronique scandaleuse', as developed in the second part of the eighteenth century, was indebted to literary history. One predecessor of eighteenth-century 'colportage' was Pierre de Bourdeille, Sieur de Brantôme (1540–1614). At the end of the sixteenth century he started to record his memoirs, in the form of anecdotes containing bawdy gossip and erotic adventures. Providing the names of male protagonists, while protecting the ladies' reputations through anonymity, Brantôme arranged his material according to topics, such as 'on ladies engaging in amorous adventures and cuckolding their husbands', 'on the charm of beautiful legs', 'on the question who is the most arduous: women, widows or young girls', etc. Structurally, the influence on him of Montaigne's essays is undeniable, in that Brantôme establishes a thesis and then proves its validity with

exemplary stories. His anecdotes circulated for some time in manuscript form, which was also common for eighteenth-century writings,
and were first published as *Mémoires de Messire Pierre de Bourdeille,
Sieur de Brantôme, contenant les vies des dames galantes de son temps*
(Leyden, 1666). Numerous editions followed. The year before, the
Histoire amoureuse des Gaules, by Roger Comte de Bussy-Rabutin
(1618–93), had been published. This is a 'chronique scandaleuse' of
the court of Louis XIV and, with the English court recently residing in
France, had a significant influence on English writers. Laurence Sterne
owned a book by Rabutin, who took his plot from the *Satyricon* of
Petronius, fleshing it out with love affairs, intrigues, and slander.
Rabutin's mentioning of names produced a scandal; and one of the
persons concerned, his cousin Madame de Sévigné, paid him back in a
similar publication. Edmund Curll's *Court Secrets: or, the Lady's
Chronicle Historical and Gallant From the Year 1671 to 1690. Extracted From the Letters of Madam de Sevigne* [sic], published in
1727, attests to the international influence of such works and to their
reception in the course of the eighteenth century. Since Rabutin had
ridiculed Louis XIV, in remarks on the king's affair with Louise La
Vallière, he was sentenced to sixteen months in the Bastille, one of the
first pamphleteers to suffer at the hands of the court. However, his
history, later enlarged, sold well, particularly abroad, and was often
republished, under such titles as *La France galante*, or *Amours des
dames illustres de nostre siècle*. Brantôme and Rabutin found worthy
successors in Gédéon Tallemant des Réaux (1619–92) and Catherine
Lamothe, Comtesse d'Aulnoy. Tallemant's *Les Historiettes.
Mémoires pour servir à l'histoire du XVIIe siècle* was not published
until 1834/5, but its manuscript version was well known and read.
D'Aulnoy's spate of 'chroniques scandaleuses', written around 1700,
were concerned with European courts and aristocrats. Her numerous
works were a mixture of gossip, actual events, and fabrication and
flooded various European countries, English translations reaching
several editions.[1]

The genre continued to prosper in the eighteenth century, when
reprints of earlier titles were competing with new 'chroniques scandaleuses'. The genre of the 'chronique scandaleuse' is a hybrid form,
with literary, semi-literary, and sub-literary branches offering many
degrees of fact and fiction. It is not always easy to make clear-cut
distinctions. One source of the novel, for instance, must be seen in the
'chronique scandaleuse'. The titles one encounters most often in this
varied field are 'Confessions de', some of them genuine personal

confessions of celebrities; and 'Mémoires secrets'. The title of John
Cleland's best-selling novel, *Memoirs of a Woman of Pleasure*, indicates both its proximity and its indebtedness to the 'chronique
scandaleuse'.[2] The general interest of the reading public in the open or
secret sex life of European royalty, and especially in the affairs of the
members of the French court, was satisfied by an avalanche of books,
such as the monumental *Mémoires secrets tirés des archives des souverains de l'Europe, depuis le règne de Henri IV*, published in thirty-six
volumes (Amsterdam and Paris, 1775–84). This was a collection
dating from the seventeenth century. It was compiled by Vittorio Siri,
an Italian, and translated into French by Baptiste Requier. A similar
work was *Mémoires secrets sur les règnes de Louis XIV et de Louis
XV, par feu M. Duclos* (Paris, 1790), published in two volumes.[3] The
common denominator of all these works is their indebtedness to
literary history. They owe more to earlier models, both in form and
content, than to any sort of social protest caused by the ideas of the
Enlightenment. The readers of these generally mild erotica were mainly members of the gentry and aristocracy living in style and splendour
– this is confirmed by the fact that such relatively benevolent 'chroniques scandaleuses' mostly appeared as expensive books the
'bourgeois' and lower middle classes could not often afford. Up to the
revolutionary period, there was a sort of officially tolerated 'chronique scandaleuse' (as opposed to the underground publications) that
was not deemed noxious by the censor. The audience for such works
was international. Baron von Pöllnitz's record, embellished with fictional conversations, of the sex life of Frederick-Augustus II was read
in France and Germany, and in England, where it appeared in a
translation in 1734. Many 'chroniques scandaleuses' first became
known in manuscript form in the salons, and were then printed at the
behest of the authors' friends; or sometimes even against their wish or
anonymously, as Mirabeau's *The Secret History of the Court of Berlin*
(1789).

But there was also a substantially different and much more aggressive branch of this genre. Produced underground or abroad, and
banned by the censor, anti-aristocratic erotica of this kind at first
comprised entertaining bawdy satires, and gradually absorbed political and social protest. In the late 1770s one can discern in these
writings a change not merely in style and content but also in the
intended readership. While the traditional and officially tolerated
'chronique scandaleuse' was in many cases written by noblemen for
noblemen and for the 'nouveau riches', the new wave of underground

pamphlets, produced after the mid-century, came from the pens of poor gentlemen, or ordinary hacks pretending to be gentlemen, and were addressed to 'le peuple' and not to the nobility.

Why this sudden appearance of a virulent, obscene, and porno-graphic underground literature?

It was a result of political events and personal intrigues at the court; but also and above all of severe literary censorship, suppressing all sort of criticism of the aristocracy and the court. And there was a lot to criticise. Living extravagantly, and frequently in debt, the French nobility were becoming unpopular, not least because of the privileges they enjoyed. The commoners began to interpret hitherto accepted legal and social injustice as exploitation, especially towards the 1780s, when the bourgeois became virtually excluded from higher posts in the administration and in government. When in 1737 the Chancelier Daguesseau took the office of 'garde des sceaux', or official censor, he was instructed that his main job was to reduce the growing amount of licentious literature. His strict censorship seems to have been success-ful in France; however, he unwittingly created a new and busy world of publishing, abroad and underground. Because of this watchful censor, manuscripts were sent to Holland or England to be printed, or were given false foreign locations of publication on the title-page. Within a few decades, underground publishing in France and abroad became a world of its own, attracting crooks, blackmailers, impostors, political adventurers, and pornographers. Receiving their information from disgruntled aristocrats, they exploited for their own purposes half-truths and other reports of the sexual liberties of court circles. If the pamphleteers survived, and, for some time, even did well, it was because their victims were afraid of having their true or invented sins made public, offering money to the 'libellistes' when other means failed of silencing them. Few had the courage and perspicacity of Voltaire. When Théveneau de Morande, a minor king among black-mailers, threatened in a letter that if Voltaire did not pay a certain amount of money he would write a pamphlet against him, Voltaire simply published Morande's letter and was left in peace, having thus shamed him into silence.

2 FRENCH ÉMIGRÉ WRITERS IN LONDON

The most vicious of these attacks came from a group of French expatriates in London. Here Théveneau de Morande ruled unchal-lenged when it came to making money from salacious details about the sex life of those who had chased him out of France. Morande spent his early life among pimps and prostitutes, and tried his hand at several illegal professions before being imprisoned. His literary career as a pamphleteer began with his flight to England in 1769. Attacking the corrupt morals of the French court, in *Le philosophe cynique* (London, 1771), he achieved his first major success with *Le gazetier cuirassé, ou anecdotes scandaleuses de la cour de France* (1771). This pamphlet sold well in London because of its combination of spicy sexual detail with witty comment. Ostensibly written to defend public morals and to exhibit the moral turpitude of Louis XV and his mistress, Madame Dubarry, *Le gazetier* offers a titillating mixture of salacious anecdotes, based on café gossip, and a punchy, aggressive prose that set the tone for the yellow press of the future. Dubarry's story of sexual success is told in a way which was to influence a whole wave of pamphlets, into the late 1780s. Starting with her alleged illegitimate birth as the daughter of a servant girl seduced by a monk, *Le gazetier* comments on her career as a whore and courtesan, her exploitation of the king's power, and her lesbian relations with maids. One of the many scabrous details about Madame Dubarry that the astonished London reader could find in this defamatory pamphlet was the information that she was accustomed to perfume the interior of her genitals in order to keep her lover, Louis XV; and that his great attachment to her was the result of her efforts to douche her genitals daily with amber. Noticing his success with a concoction of slander, wit, and sexual perversity in high places, Morande continued to exploit this new line in aggressive pamphleteering. In his *Mélanges confus sur des matières fort claires* (1771), he attacked the custom of the French court of awarding military ranks to undeserving noblemen; he slandered the members of the Académie Française; and he furnished further details from the bed of Louis XV and the Dubarry: this time she was charged with having venereal disease. Naturally, Louis XV and his government began to worry about Morande. Unfortunately, they took his defamations too seriously, and Morande, through his contacts with the émigrés and his sources in Paris, got wind of the French court's concern. He decided that this was the right moment to make a fortune, through blackmail; and he announced the immediate publication of *Mémoires secrets d'une femme publique*, yet another secret report about the turbulent events in the much-frequented bed of the Dubarry. At the same time he approached the French court, asking for a payment of 5,000 *louis*, and a pension of 4,000 *louis* in return for not publishing the pamphlet. Louis XV first tried diplomatic channels and demanded Morande's extradition. When this was denied him, he dispatched a group of secret policemen to London, in 1773. But Morande was informed of their arrival. After borrowing money from each member of the French party, he informed the London papers that French spies and policemen were secretly operating in London, trying to kidnap upright émigrés who were enjoying English liberty after their escape from French tyranny. The papers roused the patriotic ire of the population and the exposed policemen had to leave in a hurry, while Morande kept the money he had borrowed from them. Louis XV now decided to negotiate with Morande, and engaged Beaumarchais as a go-between. The author of *Le barbier de Séville* and *Le mariage de Figaro* went to London and bought the whole edition of the pamphlet, offering Morande a great deal of money in addition to a pension.

After the death of Louis XV, in 1774, there was no mistress to attack and hence no money to be made; so without any scruples Morande changed sides, and became a secret agent for the new French king among the émigrés in London. Morande was not the first among them to take this job. Consisting of criminals, banned noblemen, and ex-courtiers, as well as defrocked priests and monks, such agents spied on each other; slandered the French court or worked for it, depending on what paid most; and were never sure of their security in London.[4] The duty of the French government's agents in London at that time consisted in dealing with and spying on the 'libellistes', and getting book dealers to destroy or retain pamphlets by offering them money or threatening legal action. One of these agents was Goezman, who assumed the name of Baron de Thurn. Through his friend Boissière he bought up entire editions of pamphlets against the French court. Boissière was a bookseller at whose house the French expatriates used to meet. With his first-hand information and good contacts abroad – he collaborated with Gosse *fils* in The Hague – Boissière soon directed a profitable racket in political slandering and extortion, dealing with several European sovereigns, and in particular with the French court. Both Boissière and Goezman earned a lot of money by playing French émigrés and their 'libelles' against the king in Versailles, receiving bribes from both sides. They also spied on the English court. After a while, the French court seems to have discovered that Goezman was unreliable, and had kept some of the money he had been given with which to silence the 'libellistes'. When Théveneau de Morande was asked to work as a secret agent for Louis XVI, it was because the court no longer trusted its current informers.[5]

Political events were to play into the hands of the London pamphleteers. When Louis XV died, they were left with the by now often repeated and reprinted sex life of Madame Dubarry. Morande and others may have had a hand in late versions, and in such desperate last attempts to exploit a waning interest as *Anecdotes sur Madame la Comtesse du Barri* (1775); *Anecdotes secrètes sur la Comtesse du Barry* (1776); and *Vie d'une courtisane du dix-huitième siècle* (1776). But there was now a new royal pair in Paris, whose private life was to furnish welcome material for clandestine attacks and political pornography. Marie-Antoinette and the future Louis XVI were married in 1770. For seven years the marriage was not consummated, owing to difficulties of the Dauphin, who had an impediment under his foreskin. Never before had the literary mud-slingers had a more excellent source for slander. As the genuine reason for the absence of children was not known in the country, the king was suspected of impotence and the queen of barrenness. Marie-Antoinette, who was never very popular in Versailles or in France, engaged in a hectic social life to compensate her frustration at being married to a king mainly if not exclusively interested in hunting. She visited theatres, and spent fortunes on clothes and jewellery, and in gambling. Her preference for a selected clique of people at the court was eventually slandered as adultery and lesbianism. Politically, she was unwise in siding with the Austrian faction at the court, which made her many enemies; and her youthful short temper increased the number of courtiers who were all too willing to furnish the pamphleteers with 'information' about her sex life. By 1777 much damage had already been done; and although the king was operated on in that year and finally consummated the marriage, the birth of a girl in 1778 was accompanied by much literary sniggering. When in 1781 Marie-Antoinette gave birth to a boy, the question of his paternity was debated by several pamphlets. Some of these, like the *Naissance du Dauphin*, were of London origin. The last blow came with the diamond necklace affair of 1785, which hastened both her fall and that of the French monarchy.[6]

The scandal centred upon a famous diamond necklace originally made to be bought by Louis XV for Madame Dubarry. In 1784 a jeweller had offered it to Marie-Antoinette at the price of one and a half million francs; but in view of the desolate state of the royal coffers the queen had to refrain from a purchase. At this point, enter Jeanne de St Rémy de Valois, also known as Madame de la Motte, the wife of a cheat and adventurer, and the mistress of the Cardinal Prince de Rohan. Rohan had not been in favour with the court for some time.

His mistress easily convinced him that to offer the necklace to Marie-Antoinette was a good chance to win back the sympathy of the royal pair, which could have meant more influence for Rohan. The money, Madame de la Motte suggested, could later be paid back in instalments. In order to persuade the Cardinal to go ahead with the plan, she arranged a nocturnal meeting in the park of Versailles between Rohan and a prostitute by the name of Le Guay d'Oliva, who was instructed to play the part of Marie-Antoinette. She seems to have done her job well enough to assure Rohan of the queen's change of mind regarding his person. One Rêtaux de Villette was then employed to forge Marie-Antoinette's handwriting in a few letters which Rohan used to buy the necklace, the jeweller being convinced that it was for the queen. The ever-serviceable Madame de la Motte offered to take the necklace personally to the queen. But Marie-Antoinette never received her present. La Motte's husband was probably in on the deal and took the necklace to England; there it was broken up to be sold. When in 1785 the fraud came to light, Louis XVI asked for an open trial to prove Marie-Antoinette's innocence. For ten months, the whole of Europe read, and heard, about rumours, lies, credulity, and stupidity in a sensational affair in which even poor Cagliostro, who just happened to be in Paris, was suspected of participation. Rohan was acquitted, but deprived of his offices. Madame de la Motte received a sentence of life imprisonment; but in 1787 she escaped from the terrible Salpêtrière to join her husband and to share the spoil of their coup with him in London.[7]

While the French monarchy took a giant step towards its own downfall with the diamond necklace scandal, the pamphleteers in London and France set about dealing their final, fierce blows against the royal pair and the court at Versailles. The clandestine presses produced an incredible stream of malicious pamphlets ranging from the obscene and pornographic to the bawdy and burlesque. While Louis XVI was mostly portrayed in minor roles, as an impotent, cuckolded fool, Marie-Antoinette had to bear the full brunt of the slander. The participants in the scandal of 1785, joined by d'Artois, Lafayette, and a few courtiers, appear as the major characters in the slanderous obscenities hurled against Versailles. In the pornographic *L'autrichienne en goguettes, ou l'orgie royale* (1789) Louis XVI is asleep on a sofa while, beside him, d'Artois satisfies the Duchesse de Polignac and Marie-Antoinette. Later on, the *gardes du corps* join the orgy. The *Bordel royal*, also published in 1789, is staged in Marie-Antoinette's bedroom in Versailles and stars Rohan as a leading figure who, like other aristocrats in the piece, engages in sexual intercourse with the queen and with several men. A similar 'libelle' is *Bordel national sous les auspices de la reine, à l'usage des Confédérés Provinciaux, dédié et présenté à Mlle Théroigne, présidente du District des Cordeliers, & du Club des Jacobins* ('A Cythère, Et dans tous les Bordels de Paris'; 1790). It provides a description of what life is going to be like under the auspices of Mlle Théroigne, who is all in favour of 'fouterie jour et nuit'. To enter this brothel royalty must pay most while the common people are charged very little. The main part of the pamphlet is a play in eight scenes with Mlle Théroigne, Marie-Antoinette, Lafayette, Bazin (the *valet de chambre* of Marie-Antoinette), Mirabeau l'aîné, Danton, and Marat. The action takes place in the circus of the Palais Royal. In Scene II, Lafayette has intercourse with Marie-Antoinette while being buggered by Bailly. Everyone expresses their sexual joy and satisfaction, Marie-Antoinette avowing that she prefers being mounted by a man to being handled by lesbian women in Versailles. In the next scene the whole action assumes a Sadeian dimension, the stage directions specifying 'Barnave fout la Théroigne en con; et Bailly encule Barnave; la Fayette remonte sur La Reine qu'il refout avec vigueur'. Marie-Antoinette then affirms that her only pleasure is to be 'foutue en con' and wants to engage a whole regiment as well as several monastical orders to assuage her ardour. Other characters appear, including Mirabeau and Marat, trying various positions and partners. Between 1789 and 1791 there was a series of such obscene or pornographic pamphlets against Marie-Antoinette and those around her. Many 'libelles' had pornographic engravings illustrating their highlights and central scenes (plate 20).[8]

What is interesting with these publications, apart from their aggressive obscenity and moral-political message, is their literary form and their indebtedness to a literary tradition which historians tend to ignore, perceiving mainly the revolutionary aspect of the pamphlets. It is remarkable that a considerable number of writings are presented in the form of dialogues and scenes, thus indicating a theatrical influence. *L'autrichienne*, for instance, is entitled an 'opéra-proverbe', and *Le branle des capucins ou le mille et unième tour de Marie-Antoinette* (1791) a 'petit opéra aristocratico-comico-risible en deux actes'. The *Bordel royal* is basically a play like the *Bordel national*, which has eight scenes. The very form of these erotica is, of course, a hint at Marie-Antoinette's private theatre in the Trianon, where many a salacious play is said to have been performed. Aristocrats too had

20 *Invocations à Priape*, undated

private stages. France also knew a tradition of a boisterous and burlesque erotic theatre, whose scatological and obscene branches came to the fore during the Revolution. The successful plays of Grandval *père* and *fils* had set the tone during the earlier decades, and it is quite probable that a play by Grandval *fils*, entitled *La nouvelle Messaline. Tragédie en un acte par Pyron, dit Prépucius. Se vend à Chaud-Conin & à Babine ... A Ancone, Chez Clitoris Librairie rue du sperme, vis-à-vis la fontaine de la semence à la Verge d'Or* (1773), was the first tongue-in-cheek theatrical slander of Marie-Antoinette.

The writers of the 'chronique scandaleuse' were not interested in producing 'good literature' for posterity but had a message to convey. And they knew that the best way to do this was to write in popular literary forms which entertained while driving home subconsciously a moral message. Their message was conveyed through verses and songs that could be easily remembered, to be afterwards recited and sung in the streets, and through powerful clichés that were repeated until the readers took them for reality.[9]

The Revolution of 1789 brought an end to the production of political pornography by French exiles in London. Overnight, almost, they rose from the miserable existence of malicious Grub Street hacks to the admired position of political heroes, a status most of them wanted to exploit back in France. The Revolution devoured its own begetters. The tsar of the London pamphleteers, Théveneau de Morande, returned in 1791 to Paris, where he engaged in Revolutionary journalism and helped to bring down the hated monarchy. Accused of nymphomania, VD, impotence, and homosexuality, the aristocracy became a symbol of depravity. Physical diseases were eventually seen as social diseases; charges of lust and filth ostracised the upper classes. If the *philosophes* had an influence on the events that brought about the Revolution, so had the writers of the bawdy and obscene 'chronique scandaleuse'.[10] It is remarkable that, when the forces of the Revolution finally struck, sexual atrocities committed especially against the nobility seem to have been inspired by sinister and malicious allegations from political pornography, which had harped in particular on the sexual perversion of the mighty. The pamphleteers probably never realised what bloody consequences their writings would lead to. The Princess Lamballe, Marie-Antoinette's 'confidante', was torn from her prison, undressed, and raped by several soldiers, who then forced her to kiss bloody corpses. Before decapitating her, they cut off her breasts and pubic hair, which together with her head, were then carried around the town. The Countess Pérignon and her two daughters were also undressed and then covered with oil to be slowly roasted. One wonders whether the pamphleteers were present at such occasions.[11]

When the French exiles in London set sail for Paris with the beginning of the Revolution, they left behind literary seeds which were to flower immediately. Their aggressive sexual slander had opened new literary terrain so far shunned by writers of the traditional 'chronique scandaleuse'. Apart from the spate of French anti-aristocratic erotica openly available in London, the English reader in the early 1790s had the choice between accounts of the necklace scandal, in English and

French, and such pieces as the *Memoirs of Antonina* (London, 1791). This, which concludes our survey of the overwhelming influence of France in the field of political pornography, is an English contribution to the slander of Marie-Antoinette. The *Memoirs of Antonina* consists of two volumes, the first providing the story of Antoinette's upbringing, with the names of courtiers in anagrams, and the second allegedly from her own pen. We are informed that Antonina 'brought with her to the court of Abo [i.e., Versailles], the germ of every vice, even that of an unbridled love of her own sex'. The whole court is shown as corrupt and foolish, the king being 'an absolute nullity ... both in mind and body'. Antonina then develops her lesbian and nymphomaniac tendencies while looking for lovers to replace her impotent husband. Her mother advises her to get a tall and strong prince to make her a child. Several anecdotes then describe Antonina's attempts to seduce courtiers. Impregnated by a duke in a theatre box, she carries on with lesbians, fooling the king, who believes that their first girl is his own. After the birth, Antonina has more extramarital sex, with an officer of the body-guard:

> He led her to a bower: on the way his language was such as the fiercest desire could dictate; and, finding it well received, the moment they arrived at the destined spot, he prepared for that conflict which he justly thought his fair adversary was willing to sustain; one hand had already pressed her bare bosom; and the other, more enterprising, was rapidly advancing towards the seat of love.

But as she is afraid of discovery, the officer this time has to cool his ardour. Antonina carries on both with men and women, organising mock marriages in the park of Versailles followed by orgies in arbours and gardens. Even the clergy join in. A bishop is thus introduced:

> Having been long fascinated by the white globes which embellished the tempting bosom of Mrs. Sarud, he was at length induced to convince himself whether their firmness and size were real or artificial. Finding that the lady was solely indebted to Nature for those delightful ornaments, the curious prelate was tempted to pursue his investigation, and to enquire whether Nature had been equally bountiful in the decoration of her favourite seat ... Gratitude required he should sacrifice at her shrine, and her priestess was so much charmed with his zeal, fervour, and ability, that she resolved to give him a lasting proof of her friendship ... a bouncing boy.

Volume Two is presented in the form of a secret confession of Antoinette, divided into chapters on her scheming, intrigues, and affairs. She reports on the orgies in the bowers and accuses her husband of impotence and homosexuality, recalling the example of Henri IV. Her adventures with d'Artois and one of her lady friends are thus described:

I flew, with the velocity of a star, to Nonairt, where I was soon joined by my dear count, to whose caresses I submitted myself, and with whom I enjoyed the sports of Venus, heightened by a variation of postures, and by every amorous incitement which our heated imaginations could suggest. But wherever he be, let him not imagine that he *monopolized* my person, at this period. With him, indeed, I enjoyed the *solidity* of pleasure, but I seasoned it with the enjoyment of others. Miss Tavrod ... had fixed my attention by her beauty. The brilliancy of her eyes, and the delicate whiteness of her bosom, excited my desires; the impulse soon became irresistible, and I determined to gratify it. The mode I adopted is too curious to be omitted. ... I observed a mole on her right cheek, and immediately remarked that she must consequently have another mole beneath her right breast ... I therefore desired she would pull off her stays, which she did with a blush, and discovered to my enraptured sight the most lovely pair of snowy orbs that woman was ever blessed with ... I moulded them with my hands – sucked their rosy nipples – and, in short, acted the part of an impassioned lover ... Never was woman better formed for amorous disport; and never did any one sacrifice to Venus with greater zeal and ardour than this sweet girl.

The rest of the 'autobiography' is concerned with Antoinette's love letters to men and women and further sexual conquests. Her tale of erotic adventures includes an episode of sexual intercourse with a priest on a sofa. The Revolution abruptly puts a stop to her report. This is obviously the kind of stale erotic fiction that was offered in the more licentious magazines of the day. On occasion it comes close to pornography, availing itself of the anti-royal stance as a pretext and veil. Antonina's tale has more historical than literary value.[12]

3 ENGLISH ANTI-ARISTOCRATIC EROTICA

Socially accepted extramarital affairs and the high life of the nobility were the staple themes of the 'chronique scandaleuse' of English provenance. Unlike its French counterpart, licentious literature concerned with English libertines and their mistresses did not become a vehicle of political protest; although social satire certainly entered the picture after the mid-century. Literary censorship in the last forty years of the eighteenth century was not as severe as in France; but it was nevertheless determined by the government's fear of political revolution and of increasing literacy. Most such publications celebrate the erotic exploits of nobles and their changing courtesans. Satirical and essentially moral criticism of fornicating noble ladies, supported by popular satirical writings on the war of the sexes, soon increased; but it was often mitigated by ribald laughter. The viciousness of the French underground pamphlets never seems to have been adopted in England, not even in the 'wickedest age', under George III; the relative moderation of English aristocrats, as compared to the excesses of their French equals, and early democratic reforms, took the wind out of the sails of licentious anti-aristocratic satire.[13]

Inspired by the French 'chronique scandaleuse' and the erotic novels of Mrs Haywood and Mrs Manley, early eighteenth-century English erotica concerned with aristocrats were still thriving on the scandals of the Restoration, with accounts 'of the most considerable amours in the court of King Charles II', while only gradually focusing on the 'amours of the present nobility'. *The Amours of Edward the IV* (1700) is one of the numerous novels containing mildly erotic anecdotes. If contemporary personages were referred to, they appeared under the veil of classical names. Special keys were published, either appended to the books or separately, informing the readers of the true identities of the participants in erotic tête-à-têtes. In John Oldmixon's *Court Tales*, for instance, Lord Harcourt figures as Hortensius and the Earl of Oxford as Faustus. This inoffensive branch of the 'chronique scandaleuse' found readers up to the end of the century.[14]

While the 'gallantry' of other countries' noblemen was always an interesting topic for English readers – Baron von Pöllnitz's *Les amusements de Spa: or, The Gallantries of the Spaw* [sic] *in Germany* was an international success – England also had an abundance of noblemen who were to go down in history as womanisers, rakes, and Don Juans. Their affairs and scandals were busily recorded in chapbooks and pamphlets, and countless volumes of secret memoirs in the Continental tradition. From the lecherous Colonel Charteris and the rakish Duke of Wharton in the first half of the eighteenth century to the aristocratic members of the Hell Fire Club, and later libertines, such as William Douglas and the Regency rakes, all found biographers and authors describing them as worthy followers of Giacomo Casanova. A voluminous literature traced every minor step in the private lives of the 'persons of distinction'. Pamphlets and chapbooks of trial reports highlighted erotic episodes in the cases of divorce and adultery; portraits of persons concerned in scandals appeared in engravings; and the 'chronique scandaleuse' itself spawned such fictional offshoots as the *History and Matrimonial Adventures of a Banker's Clerk, With the Pretended Lady Ann Frances Caroline Boothby, Otherwise Sister to the Duke of Beaufort* (1762). Graphic personal satire on the aristocracy sometimes took a ribald or bawdy bent, especially when their dissolute conduct was the butt of the attack. A print of 1763/4 shows John Montague, the fourth Earl of Sandwich, in company with Wilkes, Dashwood, and other members of the Hell Fire Club; Kidgell is receiving a copy of the *Essay on Woman*. On the right, Sandwich is depicted as 'Jemmy Twitcher [his nickname] in High Life', surrounded by prostitutes demanding money and presents from the swearing lord for their sexual services (plate 21). Gillray's *Fashionable Contrasts: or, the Duchess' little Shoe yielding to the Magnitude of the Duke's Foot* was published in 1792 and mocks the contemporary discussion in the newspapers of each and every move of the Duchess of York. The allusion to sexual intercourse reduces the Duchess to common human standards, but is not as obscene as comparable French satires from this period. As late as 1812 Rowlandson's *Plucking a Spoony* satirises aristocratic debauchery in whoring, drinking, and gaming – but again this is done by allusion in the tradition of Hogarth: the pictures on the wall express more than the central scene of rakes and a whore.[15]

The Toast, by the Reverend William King, is an outstanding personal satire of the bawdy kind that ranks among the best written in the eighteenth century, although in literary histories it has unjustly been eclipsed by Pope's satires. *The Toast* is a literary retribution for the hardship King suffered at the hands of Frances Brudenell, Countess of Newburgh. He had lent her and her husband, his uncle Sir Thomas Smyth, some £3,000, which they refused to pay back. According to King, the countess hired killers to get rid of him. When the plot failed, she started a law suit that dragged on beyond her death in 1736 and which King finally won after heavy costs. King poured his anger and frustration into a ribald satire owing much to the popular poems on Myra by George Granville (1667–1735). In 1730 King composed the first part of *The Toast* (in eighteenth-century slang this meant a beautiful woman whose health is drunk by gentlemen), which is inspired by ballad metre and entitled 'Ode to Myra', mocking the old age and ugly appearance of the Countess:

> Wou'd the modest Fair excuse
> Some few Freedoms in the Muse,
> I'd unveil a nobler Part,
> Touch it with Dan Ovid's Art:
> Not compare it, like a Sloven,
> To a Furnace, or an Oven;
> To a Gobbet, or a Bowl,
> Large as thy capricious Soul!

21 *Jemmy Twitcher in High Life*, 1793/4

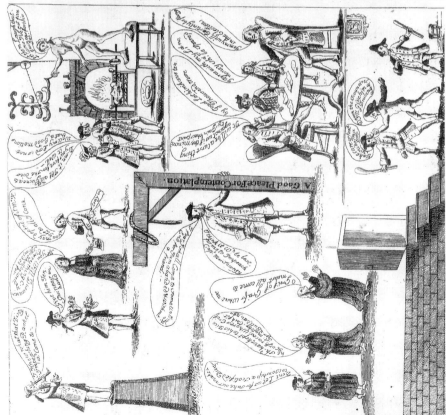

. . .
For I'd swear, that thou art chaste;
True to every Husband's Bed,
To their Mem'ry, when they're dead:
That thou never had'st Affair
With a Prelate, or a Player;
With the Bully Chevalier
Or with Centry Grenadier

. . .
What if Sappho was so naught?
I'll deny that thou art taught
How to pair the Female Doves,
How to practice Lesbian Loves:
But when little A——n's spread
In her Grove or on thy Bed,
I will swear, 'tis Nature's Call,
'Tis exalted Friendship all.[16]

Salacious details of the sex scandals of English aristocrats were discussed *ad nauseam*, in collections of facetious, erotic poems on court personalities in the style of *Court Whispers: or, A Magazine of Wit* (1743), and in reports contained in the periodicals catering to the 'beau monde'. After 1750 there was a considerable number of such periodicals of amusement. *The Court Magazine, or Royal Chronicle*, later continued as *The Court, City and Country Magazine*, had regular sections on 'secret histories of the court'. The journals of pleasure-seeking high society, such as *The Bon Ton Magazine* and *The Rambler's Magazine*, towards the end of the century revived erotic stories and memoirs of earlier decades or centuries. Thus *The Rambler's Magazine* featured a series in five parts on the 'amours of the Earl of Essex and the Countess of Rutland, supposed to be written by Herself', while *The Bon Ton* had an equally long sequence of 'secret anecdotes of many illustrious personages of this and the neighbouring kingdoms'. In the political debates and controversies of the second half of the century, sexual calumny of opponents was attempted a few times, but the journalists and publishers responsible were all prosecuted, and served prison sentences or suffered in the pillory, and paid heavy fines. The literary 'chronique scandaleuse', for all its prurience, remained harmless when compared to the malignant attacks of French pamphlets.[17]

The acceptance of the sexual double standard allowed aristocratic males to have mistresses. If courtesans had a vital role at the court of Versailles, their equals in London's high society were no less known and influential. On 16 April 1768 the Duke of Grafton, Prime Minister of England, took Nancy Parsons, his mistress, openly to the theatre, in the presence of the queen, other aristocrats – and his own wife. Miss Parsons was just one of an illustrious line of high-class whores. They made both political and literary history, in newspapers, pamphlets, and books tracing their rags-to-riches stories via the bedrooms of the nobility.

Unlike their street-walking sisters, whose sad fate was recorded by Swift in *A Beautiful Young Nymph Going To Bed*, they shared the lives of the mighty, and were sometimes even married by them; although quite a few such courtesans ended in poverty once their physical attractions had waned. Several times during the century both English and French surveys were published of the 'filles célèbres' and their affairs with 'persons of high distinction'. A number of mistresses had their portraits painted or engraved; and each decade produced its outstanding courtesan dominating the sexual 'bon ton' in high society, much like the Hollywood sex stars of the twentieth century.

Mistresses of aristocrats were generally not despised. The spate of benevolent erotica, in prose and verse, dedicated to them is proof of this; one such case is that of Martha Ray, mistress of John Montague, Earl of Sandwich. When she was killed, in 1779, by one James Hackman, a preacher madly in love with her, the whole of London took notice, while Sir Herbert Croft published a fictitious correspondence between the killer and his victim, entitled *Love and Madness*. Lord Nelson's mistress, Lady Hamilton, also appeared in graphic satire. *Lady H. ... Attitudes* alludes to her career as Dr Graham's rosy sex-goddess, while *The Night Mare* (plate 22), a print which parodies Fuseli's famous picture and was also sold as *The Nightmare or the Source of the Nile*, is an oblique political satire on her affair with Nelson.[18]

It was the wives of aristocrats who came under literary and graphic satirical attack, often in the form of ribald and obscene pamphlets. A broadside of 1746 pretended to be a petition of *The Union of the Breeches and Petticoats. With a Letter from the Bawds, Whores, and Jilts* addressed to the king. In this 'letter' the ladies of the night complained that 'many Ladies of Quality privately practice OUR OCCUPATION, and (like Poachers) seize our Game'. The socially accepted rule of the double standard demanded that women be chaste before and after the wedding, while men were allowed greater sexual freedom. But aristocratic ladies were not quite willing to submit to this rule. Those who emulated their libertine husbands, however, found

22 *The Night Mare, c.* 1798, a parody of Fuseli's painting

their names in bawdy poems and obscene skits with a moral message
suggesting that these women were to be regarded as whores. The
satirical *Satan's Harvest Home* claimed in the late 1740s that upper-
class women had 'turn'd the Tables upon the Men, and very fairly
begun openly *to keep their Fellows*' and that they 'visit them publickly
in their Equipages'. In *Drive on Coachman. An Humorous Tale.
Occasioned by an Affair Lately Discover'd in a Family of Quality*
(1739) the story pits lusty lower-class males like Robin the coachman
against an elderly and impotent Sir John, thus producing an anti-
aristocratic slant. Sir John's new wife, much too young for him, sadly
realises after the wedding that any action in the conjugal bed will
consist merely of Sir John's snoring. The frustrated wife first deceives
him with a handsome footman, who is soon tired with her lust. So
Robin, the coachman, takes over. One afternoon, the surprised husband wakes up in bed to see his coachman and his wife in the act beside
him. However, since his lordship is very keen on getting an heir, Robin
has nothing to fear:

23 Isaac Cruikshank, *The Duties of the Footman*, 1791

> Since my Lady wants a Son;
> I know she'll have her Bus'ness done;
> So! – welcome, *Robin*, Pray drive on.

Isaac Cruikshank gave pictorial expression to the theme of the cuck-olded aristocrat. In a satire dating from 1791 (plate 23), a lady is being served sexually by her footman. The tags read (valet): 'Who would not work themselves to Death for such a Mistress'; and (maid): 'Oh the Ungrateful Dog, don't he say he lov'd only me … Now I'll be re-venged, I'll go to the Coachman'.

In England, bawdy satires on the debaucheries of the aristocracy took a moral rather than a political turn. The English government in the last forty years of the eighteenth century feared revolution, and attempts were made to tighten the screws of literary censorship. 'Junius' had attacked monarchs, ministers, and public figures in an abrasive style in the *Public Advertiser*, from 1769; Grafton, Lord North, and the Duke of Bedford often provoked his ire. Personal political satires generally were on the increase, especially after the

Wilkes affair; and it is hardly surprising that the wily Charles James
Fox, in 1791, introduced a bill in the Commons to give juries the right
to decide on what was libellous. This bill was at first thrown out by the
Lords; but Fox tried again in 1792, and got the Libel Act which was to
bear his name. As a consequence of moderation both by satirists and
censors, very few anti-aristocratic attacks of English origin breathe the
French revolutionary spirit. *The Female Jockey Club* by Charles Pigott
is an exception, in that it describes the sexual adventures of several
aristocratic ladies. One of them, Lady Wallace, seems to have had an
affair with the Abbé de St F——re in Paris, where he was 'the first
person present at her levée, the last at her couchée [sic]'. One night her
apartment was searched, for political reasons:

> The doors were forced in an instant, leaving *my Lady* scarce time to make
> the smallest necessary arrangements. The aide-decamp [sic] entered, and
> discovered his trembling victim, we cannot say in *virgin* sheets, but in a
> superb Parisian bed, decorated with costly looking glasses, *dished neatly
> up*, so as to offer a voluptuous temptation to the most squeamish appetite.
> The son of Mars no ways agitated by the *delicious* spectacle before him,
> was only mindful of his order ... It were impossible to describe what
> passed in her Ladyship's bosom during this *critical* and *tremulous* interval
> ... Nothing that could justify the slightest suspicion of criminality could be
> found, but at length a petit cabinet contiguous to *my Lady's garde robe*
> was opened, when lo! appeared the poor *palpitating* Abbé, perishing with
> cold ... who presented a *nudity* to the *astonished* soldiers. Here, however,
> the national gallantry of a Frenchman shone forth conspicuous. The
> Aidecamp immediately ordered off his party and retired; leaving the lovers
> to recover their spirits, and pursue their ———— *lucubrations* without
> further interruption.

There was no better place where sexual slander could thrive than in
the relatively new art of political graphic satire, which seems to have
developed at the same speed as political events in Europe in the late
eighteenth century. Caricatures with a political bent were often based
on contemporary debates in the columns of newspapers. Print-shops
were mushrooming all over London, and people of fashion paid daily
visits to them to see their caricatures. The better-known caricaturists
of the later eighteenth century, Rowlandson, Gillray, Newton, and
Woodward, sold their works in these shops through their patrons,
such as Holland and – for Gillray – Miss Humphrey. One shilling was
charged for entrance to these exhibitions; but there were also prints in
the windows for the poorer sort, while the well-heeled could use the
lounges inside. The more fashionable shops in the Strand or in Bond
Street sold 'folios of caricatures', or lent them out for the evening at the

rate of two shillings and sixpence a day, sometimes even by the year. Political caricatures were definitely in. Any sort of satire was allowed against foreign potentates who endangered England's security, even the obscene and scatological. Thus Maria Theresa of Austria was ridiculed in rough ribald verses attached to a print alluding to the Seven Years' War (1756–63). The debunking elements of this satire are the Queen's urinating and her bad English. Similarly, Gillray had Pitt poking Catherine the Great of Russia in a sensitive part in *The Balance of Power*, published in 1791. The empress's alleged nympho-maniac tendencies were a favourite subject for caricaturists, and not only in England; in *L'enjambée impériale* (1792), a French satire, military, aristocratic, and ecclesiastical personalities from various European countries are looking up, commenting on what they see above their heads. The Pope on the right pronounces, 'here is an abyss ready to engulf you', and the Russian soldier on the left proudly affirms, 'I, too, have helped to make it bigger'. Rowlandson was even more direct, in his obscene satire on Catherine II, entitled *The Empress of Russia Receiving her Brave Guards*. Unabashed obscenity was still the best means to ridicule political enemies, and had the advantage of both official and public approval. Gillray knew this when he showed the Turkish plenipotentiary presenting his incredible member to the astonished George III, in his *Presentation of the Mahometan Credentials or the Final Resource of French Atheists*, in 1793.

Where domestic English politics were concerned, caricaturists had to be more careful if they wanted to avoid pillory and prison. In the 1780s Charles Fox and his powerful lady friends were among the targets of satirical prints with bawdy allusions. Even abroad, books were published on *Les amours et les aventures du Lord Fox* (Geneva, 1785), and in England he was mocked in the election campaign of 1784, when the Duchesses of Portland and Devonshire supported him.

However, often the decency of the prints in England showed that members of the royal family were generally not insulted by the carica-turists – although on occasion scatology did go beyond the limits of what was deemed permissible. A suggestive print from the 1780s merely hints at the impotence and old age of the King (plate 24); and even caricatures of the time on the Prince of Wales never went too far.[19]

The son of George III was nonetheless a welcome butt for pictorial satire. Married to a woman he did not like, he engaged in a hectic social life with rakes like the Barrymore brothers and his uncle, the Duke of Cumberland. As early as 1787 he became the object of bawdy

A NEW COCK WANTED.

Or WORK FOR THE PLUMBER.

24 *A New Cock Wanted, c.* 1780

allusion, in a serialised novel in the *Rambler's Magazine* which was published as *The Adventures of Moses M. Fun*. In this novel one Mrs Handcock has sighted a 'cock' in her neighbour's garden and wants to have it. The narrator promises her that her wish will be fulfilled:

> By heavens! if it were the Prince of Wales's you should have it. The Prince of Wales's, Sir! (echoed Mrs Handcock). Oh, if it was his I wanted, I should not long be in need: for, God bless the Prince! he is too good, too generous a soul *in that way*, to refuse me such a *small favour*.

Such stories of the Prince's sexual prowess were a common reaction to his dissolute life. After a brief affair with Mrs Robinson, a twenty-year-old actress playing Perdita in *A Winter's Tale*, he fell madly in love with Mrs Fitzherbert, a plump yet pretty widow who had twice been married and was of the Roman Catholic faith. When she refused to be his mistress – she could not be his legal wife under the Royal Marriages Act – he staged a dramatic near-suicide. But Mrs Fitzherbert still did not change her mind, and escaped to France. The Prince pursued her with passionate letters until she returned to marry him in secrecy in her own drawing-room in 1785. Although Fox denied it openly, rumours of the secret wedding were soon circulating, and members of the House of Commons were asking nasty questions; however, the Prince did enjoy Mrs Fitzherbert for quite a while. In 1792 Pitt convinced him to break with her, an event a satirist depicted with a classical allusion in *The Rape of Helen*. The marriage of the Prince of Wales to Princess Caroline of Brunswick had been an arranged one and was never happy, despite periods of temporary truce. When the Prince ascended to the throne in 1820, he staged a trial for divorce against his wife – one of the last of a long series of criminal conversation cases that made sub-literary history – to get rid of her. All the details of the trial could be found in the daily papers and were often rehashed. The queen was acquitted in the same year, but died in 1821. Several pictorial satires commented on the case. *Eunuchs Attending a Circassian Beauty in the Bath*, published in 1819, compares Caroline to the biblical Susannah, who appears in a picture on the wall; but the gestures of the men and her own expression are as equivocal as the voyeur behind the curtain (plate 25).[20]

One notices again an overwhelming influence of France in the field of anti-aristocratic erotica. The main difference between the 'chronique scandaleuse' in France and that produced in England was that in France a severe censorship ironically helped to create an aggressive underground version with political aims, while in England the satirists

25 *Eunuchs Attending a Circassian Beauty in the Bath*, 1819

had more freedom, and pursued moral aims in their exposure of vice.
Works on the sex life of male aristocrats were often benevolent, if not
laudatory; and the worst that could happen was ribald laughter.
Aristocratic ladies did not fare as well; and the attacks they suffered
from writers of the 'chronique scandaleuse' are due to the double
standard and to the fact that some did behave like their husbands.

Sexual slander of aristocracy, whether based on fact or fabrication,
is a timeless weapon of satire. Before the present Prince of Wales
married, satirical magazines like *Private Eye* ran series on his alleged
womanising and fornication; by all one can tell, the 'chronique scandaleuse' is far from dead.

✤ 4 ✤
Trial Reports and 'Criminal Conversation' Literature

In late 1687 Marie Aubrey, a midwife of French extraction, killed her English husband, Denis, in London. It was a most brutal murder, committed with a meat cleaver, and the right material for sensational crime reporting. Several trial reports were published soon after Marie Aubrey had been sentenced to death at the Old Bailey, in January 1688, and illustrations depicted gory details of the assassination (plate 26). The case proves that the reporting of crime was well developed before 1700 and that it was as irresistibly fascinating for readers in late seventeenth-century England as it is for many of us today. Although as early as Elizabethan times crime chapbooks were published to gratify the desire of a public yearning for sensational news, it was only in the last decades of the seventeenth century that a diverse crime literature emerged. By that time, such writings were catering to the special tastes of a growing readership.[1] This chapter provides a brief survey of the emergence of criminal conversation or 'crim. con.' literature – i.e., the journalistic exploiting of cases of adultery, rape, seduction, and sodomy – from the background of trial reporting.

I CRIME AND SEX

In the early eighteenth century, several branches or genres of crime literature can be discerned. Apart from the still very popular chap-books (for which crime was, of course, merely one topic among many others) and similar broadsheets and pamphlets, at least three other distinct branches were vying for public attention. The first, and

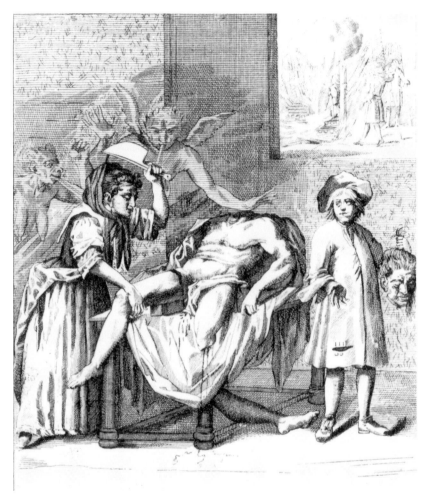

26 Mary Aubrey (or Hobry) killing her husband, *c.* 1688

initially probably the most important, of these were the *Old Bailey
Sessions Papers* (*OBSP*), reports about the single monthly 'sessions' of
the Old Bailey, which were published eight times a year. The *OBSP*
survive from 1674 and in their early format are very much like the
chapbooks, offering sensational sucker-trap titles and a lot of moral
instruction. These features gradually disappeared from the Sessions
Papers as they underwent major changes in size, content, and function,
from chapbooks to 'sessions newspapers' to true law reports. This last
stage was reached in the early 1740s, when the reports contained
about forty pages and were considered as a quasi-official publication.[2]

The *OBSP* were competing with a parallel series of pamphlet reports, written by the prison chaplains who held the post of Ordinary of Newgate Prison. The accounts which these clergymen published after – occasionally even shortly before – each hanging all bear the same title, *The Ordinary of Newgate, His Account of the Behaviour, Confession, and Dying Words of the Malefactors Who Were Executed at Tyburn*. Although, like the *OBSP*, the format and layout of the *Account* changed considerably in the eighteenth century, its internal structure did not. Already, at the beginning of the eighteenth century, the *Account* had gained a semi-official status; but it remained a moralising tract on the backgrounds, the criminal careers, the behaviour in prison as well as the execution of the convicts who had been condemned to death at the Old Bailey. Parts of the Ordinary's *Account*, such as the third section, containing narratives allegedly based on individual confessions, display rhetorical devices which can be found in most other types of eighteenth-century criminal biographies.[3]

The *OBSP* and the Ordinary's *Account* were thus two very important types of a burgeoning crime literature catering for what has been termed a 'trans-Atlantic plebeian culture'.[4] They were competing in this market not only with each other and, later on, the newspapers, but also with specialists turning out pamphlets and books of criminal 'lives', and with the printers and hack-writers of Grub Street. Collections like *The Tyburn Chronicle: or Villainy Display'd in All its Branches. Containing an Authentic Account of the Lives, Adventures, Tryals, Executions, and Last Dying Speeches of the Most Notorious Malefactors*, published in four volumes (*c.* 1768), and *The Newgate Calendar or Malefactor's Bloody Register*, which appeared in five volumes (*c.* 1773), were popular, especially if they contained illustrations; *The Newgate Calendar* had fifty of these, with crucial scenes engraved by Samuel Wale.[5] To make competition even tougher, a third form of trial reporting developed in the early eighteenth century which, with the exception of the newspapers, eclipsed all other forms. This was represented by separately published trial reports or collections drawing on, and 'embellishing', the reports in the *OBSP* and the Ordinary's *Account*.[6] From the many criminal offences covered by trial reports, a special type emerged, which, initially, concentrated on cases involving crime in combination with sex, such as rape, incest, and adultery followed by murder. An early example, indicating subsequent developments, is *News from Tybourn* [sic] *Being an Account of the Confession & Execution of the Woman Condemned for Committing*

Buggery With a Dog, Which Was Also Hanged on a Tree by Her. This pamphlet of eight pages merely expresses disgust at the unnamed woman's 'carnall copulation with a little Dog, about ten inches high', abstaining from further details and describing her way to the gallows.[7]

Trials of a similar nature, also made lasting by print, were those in which clergymen were charged with rape or seduction. Around the year 1700 a catchpenny life of the Reverend Peter Vine, vicar of Heartland, appeared – probably in London – promising the reader 'an impartial Account' of the Reverend's life, character, behaviour, and of his execution for rape and murder, 'the first committed on the body of a Child Eleven Years of Age . . . and the second on the Body of Roger Ashton'.[8]

For Protestant Englishmen, there was nothing more exciting in this field than sex scandals involving Catholic priests. Edmund Curll, the jack-of-all-trades in early eighteenth-century erotica, knew this when he published his case of 'seduction' in 1725 (the date of publication on the actual title-page, given as 1726, is wrong), which dealt with the trial of the Abbé des Rues in Paris.[9] Expecting one hundred and thirty-three rapes upon virgins, as promised in the title, the reader is sorely disappointed. The ninety pages of the proceedings merely present the case of the defence against the charge of having seduced Jeanneton Le Fort and of having bought the 'favour' of Mrs Le Roy's daughter, at a price of two hundred pounds. The other cases, not mentioned, apparently concern prostitutes produced as witnesses by the prosecution.[10] The reader or buyer of this book could not know, of course, that in his civil trial the Abbé was accused of only two instances of 'seduction'.[11] The two cases of the book have absolutely no erotic or obscene details and are supplemented by a discussion, according to canon and civil law, of the 'rape of violence' as well as the 'rape of seduction'. Curll relied entirely on his readers' prurience.

The case of Father des Rues was eclipsed in 1731 by a scandal in Toulon, France, which caused unprecedented activity in the seamy world of Grub Street publishing. It involved a Jesuit priest by the name of Jean-Baptiste Girard, and his young penitent, Cathérine Cadière, who charged her confessor with 'Quietism, Sorcery, Incest, Rape, Abortion', and several other crimes. Girard was a renowned preacher, who had acquired a good reputation at Aix and was then appointed 'Recteur du séminaire royal de la marine de Toulon', where Mlle Cadière insisted that he become her confessor. She was a girl given to religious fits and pretended to hear heavenly voices. Girard was at first quite taken in by the girl's piety and often spoke to her. Towards

Easter of the year 1730 she claimed to have received stigmata from an archangel in a vision. Girard decided to inquire into this claim and shut himself up with her in her bedroom. Finding that she had been telling lies, he tried to break with the false saint, while Miss Cadière started a law suit against her former confessor. It is difficult to get all the details of this case from reliable sources, because there are not many such sources available. Miss Cadière was urged by her new confessor to take Girard to court; and it is obvious that he was trying to blacken the Jesuit order as much as Girard's person. The populace was quite upset about the trial, for Girard was acquitted by thirteen votes to twelve, and it was rumoured that the Jesuit order had had a hand in this decision. Cadière, who had the reputation of a saint in Toulon, was also acquitted and received in triumph by the people of the town, while Girard left in secrecy and died two years later in his native town of Dôle.

Publishers of erotica set to work immediately, fleshing out the case to their liking. Trial reports were turned out for many years in France, England, and Germany, which harped on the Protestant claim that Catholic priests were lechers taking advantage of the secrets they heard in the confessional. A wave of trial reports exposed every detail of the case for the prurient. The Marquis d'Argens based his novel, *Thérèse philosophe* (1748), on the scandal – it was soon translated, as *The Philosophical Theresa* – and England saw the publication of such obscene burlesque poems as *Spiritual Fornication* (1732). Published by the pseudonymous 'Jeremy Jingle', this is a satire of three cantos with an explicit, though badly done, engraving. A verse on the title-page voices the familiar warning of Protestants against the lewd Catholic clergy:

> Priests, whether Jesuits or Fryars,
> Are Pious Cheats, Religious Lyars;
> Who use their Function as a Gin,
> To catch unwary Maidens in.

Canto I exposes 'ecclesiastical lechery' and Girard's immorality:

> Of Wantons he had half a dozen
> Whom he religiously did couzen;
> To him, Adult'ry, Fornication,
> Were nothing more than Recreation.

Canto III contains the obscene parts of the affair, including the whippings and the rape of Cadière:

Now with impetuous Lust grown bolder,
He flings her Cloaths up to her Shoulder;
Three tender lashes then he gave,
Which she did willingly receive.
This done, he rules her Back, her Bum
He kis'd, and eke her Modicum
   . . .
But had Miss Polly been so kind
To send her Thunder from behind,
While he was playing at Bo beep,
Or else perhaps at Creep Mouse, creep,
Tho' it might make him start and stare,
Each sense would then have had a share.
   . . .
Stark naked stripp'd he lays her down,
And now his eager Hopes to crown
He mounts the Saddle, rides Tantivee,
Tickling those Parts that are most privy.
   . . .
Thus every Day, for three Months space,
This pious, holy *Babe of Grace*,
Renew'd his Sport, play'd with the *Same*
And yet he could not quench his Flame.

The poem then relates the details of the abortion, Polly's (i.e., Cadière's) removal to a nunnery, and the subsequent investigation of the bishop, which brought the scandal to light. The concluding lines deal another blow against the Jesuits:

But tho' each Crime was fully proved,
Yet still it seemed that it behoved
The whole Society to join,
And save a brother by their Coin;
A Brother-Villain, in degree
Of Crimes not one so great as he.
Ten hundred thousand *Livres* spent,
Sav'd him from condign Punishment.
And now this Matter to decide,
Not guilty Twelve brib'd Judges cry'd,
Guilty the righteous Twelve reply'd.[12]

Ordinary folks made headlines if charged with adultery and cruelty, or with such 'unnatural' crimes as buggery and sodomy. In the early 1780s, for instance, a trial report was advertised that dealt with 'the most brutal and unheard of Cruelties inflicted on Jane Prescott' by her

27 Gillray, *The Monster Going to Take His Afternoons Luncheon*, 1790

28 Gillray, *Swearing to the Cutting Monster*, 1790

husband, Captain Isaac Prescott.[13] It was James Gillray who exposed the prurience of the public and the courts, in two prints commenting on the 'Cutting Monster of 1790' (plates 27 and 28).

   The seventeenth century had witnessed two trials for sodomy that caused much stir at the time. The first was the case of the Earl of Castlehaven, tried in 1631; and the second concerned John Atherton, Bishop of Waterford and Lysmore in Ireland, who was hanged in 1640 for the crime of 'unnatural lewdness'. The most spectacular account of these was the first to be republished, in 1699, as *The Tryal and Condemnation of Mervin, Lord Audley Earl of Castle-haven, at Westminster ... for Abetting a Rape Upon His Countess, Committing Sodomy With His Servants, and Commanding and Countenancing the Debauching of His Daughter.* Mervyn Touchet, second Earl of Castlehaven (1592?–1631), was apparently psychologically disturbed, and had a most bizarre sex life. When his son, James, was only thirteen years old, he forced him to marry Elizabeth Brydges, the daughter of his second wife, Anne. Elizabeth was then forced by her stepfather into 'criminal intercourse' with one Skipwith, who was the Earl's servant and catamite. Lady Castlehaven, a woman of great sexual appetite, endured life with the Earl for more than five years, but took action against him in the autumn of 1630. Together with James, who was disgusted at the many scenes of sexual perversion he had to watch at home, she was instrumental in bringing Castlehaven to justice. The republication of this trial, as a journalistic report in 1708 and again, by Curll, in 1710, indicates its popularity, and the extent to which publishers could earn money with it. The report presents the main pleas in the trial, and the depositions of the witnesses. Religion played an important part in Castlehaven's trial; for he became a Catholic after Skipwith, an Irishman, had entered his service. The prosecution, having quite obviously Puritan sympathies (Heath, the Attorney General, later dismissed the court for this reason), tried to prove that the Earl's crimes were a consequence of his not having been 'constant to ... religion'. His sexual offences as described by the witnesses are outrageous. The Countess deposed that her husband wanted her to have sexual intercourse with two servants and that she was raped – upon Castlehaven's command – by the servant Brodway while the Earl was holding her hands and one leg. The servants FitzPatrick and Skipwith confirmed that they had had sexual relations with the Earl and that they had been ordered to have intercourse with Castlehaven's stepdaughter and wife. Skipwith confessed

That the Earl often sollicited him to lie with the young Lady ... and that she was but Twelve Years of Age when he first lay with her; and that he could not enter her Body without Art, and that the Lord *Audley* fetch'd Oyl to open her Body, but she cry'd out and he could not enter, and then the Earl appointed Oyl the Second time, and then *Skipwith* enter'd her Body and knew her Carnally; and that my Lord made him lie with his own Lady ... That the Lord *Audley* made him lie with him at *Founthill*, and at *Salisbury*, and once in the Bed, and emitted between his Thighs, but did not penetrate his Body; and that he heard he did so with others.

The evidence was confirmed by the footmen and other witnesses. Castlehaven was found guilty by the House of Lords, forming the court, of abetting a rape on his wife and, by fifteen votes to twelve, of committing sodomy in two cases. Initially sentenced to death by strangulation, the most ignominious punishment for a nobleman, the sentence was later modified to decapitation, and carried out on 14 May 1631. The trial report concentrates on the juicy depositions, with many tedious parts, of no interest to a prurient reader, summarised. In the typical style of the later Edmund Curll it offers obscene details while claiming moral aims – sin and perversion are punished by death.[14]

In February 1710, Curll published *The Cases of Unnatural Lewdness*, a reissue of the Castlehaven and Atherton trial reports. This was followed by one of Curll's come-on titles, *The Case of John Atherton, Bishop of Waterford in Ireland; Who Was Convicted of the Sin of Uncleanness With a Cow, and Other Creatures; For Which He Was Hang'd at Dublin*. If a reader had one shilling to spare for this publication, he was offered Nicholas Bernard's 'A Relation of the Penitential Death of Bishop Atherton', as well as two letters of Atherton to his wife and children. An additional funeral sermon complemented a work which – despite its title – contained nothing erotic or obscene.[15] While those who were disappointed with their purchase kept quiet about it, others had moral objections against Curll's publishing methods, and said so.

Trials for sodomy found much attention between 1720 and 1730. Commenting on homosexuals of this period, a satirical attack on the morals of the time claimed, 'our Sessions-Papers are frequently stain'd with the Crimes of these beastly Wretches; and tho' many have been made Examples of, yet we have but too much Reason to fear, that there are Numbers yet undiscover'd, and that this abominable practice gets Ground ev'ry Day.'[16] It is, however, indicative that such trials were not as much exploited for commercial purposes as the cases of adultery, around which a vast body of literature developed. It is therefore not surprising to find that few trial reports on cases of sodomy have survived. One example will suffice. The title provides the gist of the report: *A Faithful Narrative of the Proceedings in a Late Affair between the Reverend Mr John Swinton and Mr George Baker, both of Wadham College, Oxford . . . To which is Prefixed a Particular Account of the Proceedings against R. Thistlethwayte . . . Warden of Wadham College, for a Sodomitical Attempt upon Mr W. French, Commoner of the Same College* (1739). The narrative was allegedly written by friends of George Baker. The first part deals with Robert Thistlethwayte, accused of an homosexual affair with W. French, while the second part charges John Swinton with having had similar affairs with the Warden and others. According to French's statement, the Warden one day committed an act of sodomy with him 'of which the Particulars are judged too gross and obscene to be repeated'. Before he could be formally charged in court, the Warden disappeared, not without making a last unsuccessful attempt to silence French with the promise of money. It was later found that Thistlethwayte had made other attempts in the college. Since the Reverend Mr Swinton had acted for, and defended, the Warden before his disappearance, he too was suspected of having had sexual intercourse with Thistlethwayte. Baker was able to produce a boy who declared

> that he used to lie in the Bed with Mr. Swinton; that Mr. Swinton used to tickle and play with him in the Morning; that he used to play with Mr. Swinton's Cock, which used to stand; that Mr. Swinton used to kiss him. Mr. Baker asked him, Whether Mr. Swinton used to put his Tongue in his Mouth? to which the Boy answered, No. And then being asked, whether Mr. Swinton did not use to get upon his Back, he answered, No; but said, that he used to get upon his Belly, between his Thighs, and that he used to put his Cock into his A-h-, and that he felt something warm come from him, and that he sometimes made him wet between his Thighs.

But the college prosecutors later doubted the statement of the witness, on account of his alleged idiocy. Since Baker could not really prove his charge, he reluctantly signed a form of recantation.[17] Homosexuals were never popular in the eighteenth century; but it was cases of adultery involving the high and mighty that most interested a great many people; and thus it was that crim. con. literature was born.

2 'CRIMINAL CONVERSATION' LITERATURE

The reporting of crime and sex was, as has been indicated above, a common feature of several types of crime literature. But it was the eighteenth century that for the first time successfully exploited trial reports as potential pornographic material. This was particularly true for the numerous so-called 'crim. con.' cases, which, though not an invention of the eighteenth century, are almost a hallmark of the age. The genesis of this type of trial report was the result of changing relations between Church and state in the seventeenth century and of the concomitant emergence of a surprisingly varied crime literature. Originally and until the late 1640s, the Church tried cases of adultery, incest, ribaldry etc., in its own hierarchy of more than 250 courts, the 'bawdy courts'. However, Charles II abolished the Courts of High Commission and the *ex officio* oath, thus removing criminal jurisdiction from the ecclesiastical courts. Matrimonial and divorce cases were transferred to the quarter sessions and assizes. This was a re-markable judicial and social revolution; not only was sin now disting-uished from crime, a fact which entailed considerable intellectual and moral upheaval, but the trials were also made public. Among the people who attended the sessions of the Old Bailey, for instance, which was the court trying cases of serious crime in London and the con-tiguous county of Middlesex, there were some who took notes of the proceedings. These were then published, more or less fully, and some-times even before sentence had been passed.[18]

It was from individually published trial reports that a peculiar genre developed, which soon turned into pornography. The advantage this new branch had over its main competitors was its relative independ-ence, which the others – given their quasi-official status – did not have. In the case of the Chaplain of Newgate, it was obvious that his *Account*, albeit not devoid of luridness, was unable to compete in a market demanding erotic or obscene details. The same was true to a lesser extent for the *OBSP*, although they put up a long fight and continued to include cases of bigamy, incest, rape, and even sodomy.[19] But these reports did not differ in length or format from others, such as cases of murder. The separately published trial reports, however, were usually much longer than the *Sessions Papers*, relying more and more on their salacity as the century grew older.

Until the Matrimonial Causes Act was passed in 1857, a husband could bring an action for damages against his wife's paramour, an action for 'criminal conversation' (hence 'crim. con.'). This was a common law suit, and the damages were at times extraordinary. The new act abolished this procedure, thus also pulling out the carpet from under the feet of the publishers of crim. con. literature.

Eros Revived

29   Crim. Con. scene, undated

From the time of Henry VIII, divorces attracted much attention, especially if those involved were the high and mighty and if the case had to do with criminal conversation, impotence, or sexual perversion. In order to get a private divorce bill through Parliament, it became usual, after the Norfolk case in 1700, to require a crim. con. judgment in the courts beforehand.[20] Around the turn of the century, public taste had already been whetted by some publishers, notably John Dunton and Edmund Curll, who had quickly noticed the existence of a section of the reading public interested in the sort of obscene details that can be found in the trial reports of some unusual cases in the seventeenth century.[21] Without realising it, Curll found another goldmine in 1714, which he and others began exploiting soon afterwards. He published two volumes on the trial between the Marquis de Gesvres and his wife, Mademoiselle Mascranny, a case which in 1712 was 'more taken Notice of all over Europe, than any case of the same Nature hitherto known'.[22] Mademoiselle Mascranny charged the Marquis with impotence, after three years of cohabitation, and pleaded for nullity of the marriage. The first volume contains the plea of her ladyship, the interrogation of the spouses, and the reports of the physicians examining the Marquis, as well as a few remarks on 'The Difference between a Maid and a Widow'. Medical reports in the divorce trials played an important part in the sale. Playing on the reader's prurient interest, the 'physicians' account' was often mentioned in the title-page and – as in this case – made obvious in the text, by special print. The doctors examining the Marquis – he was allowed to nominate them himself – were careful in their judgment. 'We have view'd,' they wrote,

> and carefully examin'd the Marquis de Gesvres, and find that his exterior Parts serving for Generation, have the requisite Figure, Size and Dimensions; but as these Conditions are not sufficient for judging of the Consummation of Marriage, because there is occasion for Erection and Ejaculation, which did not appear to us, we cannot absolutely decide, whether he be able to discharge the conjugal Duties or not.[23]

The next volume has similar documents from the trial, complemented by a discussion of virginity, 'artificial maidenheads', and 'Examples of some remarkable Cases of natural Impotence'. The pseudo-scientific and essentially erotic contents of the two volumes, and the person of the Marquis, who was descended from one of France's best families, were confidently supposed to attract readers. The case must have appealed to the prurient for several reasons. It highlighted the sometimes bizarre sex life of the aristocracy while at the same time exposing them to ridicule. In addition, a lady charging her husband with impotence was a rare event indeed in a macho century. To make it even more attractive, this work contains quite a few blows against France's aristocracy, with two of their members (the Marquis and his father) shown as impotent and the king sharing a mistress, Madame de Maintenon, with a duke.[24] What Curll had tapped here was the rich source of the 'chronique scandaleuse', in this case its factual division. In France, as in England, an erotic and basically prurient trial literature developed around 'les causes célèbres', a genre that was started in 1734 with the first collection of famous cases, in a volume published by François Gayot de Pitaval as *Causes célèbres et intéressantes avec les jugements qui les ont décidées*; by 1788 twenty-three volumes had appeared under this title.[25]

Edmund Curll prepared the ground very well for others to follow. The reading public at the beginning of the fourth decade of the eighteenth century was more ready than ever to treat trial reports as entertainment. Publishers in turn were beginning to make changes in the presentation of their material in order to cater for and accommodate such tastes in their customers. By 1730 a great many cases of criminal conversation had provided publishers with excellent sources. One case in particular, which occurred in 1729–30, caused much stir in London's polite world, and was reported in all the newspapers. This was the trial of Colonel Francis Charteris. Exhibiting the prevailing attitude towards rape among the male members of the upper class, this unusual trial also yields a good picture of contemporary social mores. At the same time it provides us with an example of the leniency which noblemen could expect, even if convicted of rape. Charteris was charged in 1729 with the rape of Ann Bond, a spinster, who had been in his service only a few days when he began to make improper advances. Ann Bond told the court

> That on the 10th of November, the Colonel rung a Bell and bid the Clerk of the Kitchen call the Lancashire Bitch into the Dining Room, That she going in, he bid her stir the Fire, while she was doing it, He lock'd the Door, and took her and threw her down on the Couch, which was nigh the Fire, in the farther Corner of the Room, and forced her down with Violence, and lay with her; that she shove what she could, and cry'd out as loud as she could, and he took off his Night Cap and thrust it into her Mouth, and then had carnal Knowledge of her.

The court then insisted on further details of what had happened:

> Being asked whether the Prisoner had his Cloathes on? She reply'd, he was in his Night Gown. – Being asked whether she had not her Petticoats on? She reply'd, yes; but he took them up, and held her down upon the Couch – Being asked, whether she was sure, and how she knew he had carnal Knowledge of her? She reply'd, she was sure he had, and that he laid himself down upon her, and entered her Body. – She was also asked how it was afterwards? She reply'd, that there was a great deal of wet ... That he endeavour'd to pacify her with Promises of a great many fine Cloaths, &c. if she would hold her Tongue, and say nothing of it.[26]

Since other servants confirmed Ann Bond's deposition, Charteris was found guilty and sentenced to death. This was quite a shock, as it was unusual for a gentleman to be punished in such a harsh way for what many contemporaries considered an act of gallantry. Bond's lawyer remarked in his opening speech that servant girls being raped by their masters 'were now-a-days made little Account of by too many Persons of Levity'.[27] Like many other upper-class males, Charteris had seduced and raped a sizable number of country girls in his service. Generally, he preferred lower-class women and girls for his sexual adventures, for it was easier that way to escape prosecution, and pregnancies could be dealt with with money. One result of this habit of upper-class males, which they considered a part of their amusement and entertainment, was a high rate of infanticide. The price for what the upper class termed gallantry was thus paid by servant girls who would rather kill their own babies than face the common fate of pregnant servants, which was prostitution. If some servants rejoiced after the sentence which Charteris received, they were soon silenced, for he had friends among the aristocracy who persuaded the king to pardon him, in April 1730; another proof of the dominant opinion among the nobility that raping a servant was gallant adventure at best and at worst a misdemeanour; but certainly not a crime.[28]

By the fourth decade of the eighteenth century, newspapers had become strong competition for the publishers of crim. con. cases and similar trial reports. For obvious reasons, the papers were hard to beat in the race for readers. More often than not, publishers of books had to be content with commenting on or satirising affairs which had previously been exploited by the papers. As a consequence, between 1737 and 1770, very few trial reports appeared in book form.[29] The case to end this long dry spell for publishers was reprinted because success was guaranteed by the fact that the whole of England was talking about it. It was *The Trial of His R.H. the D. of C. July 5th, 1770 For Criminal Conversation With Lady Harriett G...r*, and appeared in 1770. This trial report about the Duke of Cumberland and Lady Grosvenor went into more than five editions. The Earl of Grosvenor recovered £10,000 damages when the Duke was found guilty of criminal conversation with the Countess Grosvenor.[30] The publisher of the trial report endeavoured to make his work more entertaining with the help of editorial comments. As a matter of fact, this publication is another big step forward towards the presentation in the last two decades of the century of trial reports as pornographic and erotic literature. 'Adultery is become so fashionable', writes the editor in his introduction, 'and Divorces so frequent, that it may admit of some debate in the polite world whether the first is criminal or the latter dishonourable.' In the years to follow, only cases involving well-known personalities appeared as reprints. Cases of adultery, and divorce of commoners, had to have an element of perversity to attract the publishers. Trial reports with spectacular sentences were also popular. In one instance Mr Foley, the plaintiff, received £2,500 damages from the Earl of Peterborough. Like Lady Grosvenor, Lady Foley became one of the 'noble whores' of the century, celebrated in lampoons and erotic poems. Her many love affairs are the subject of *The Life and Amours of Lady Ann F-l-y*, which also contained the juicier depositions of a crim. con. trial in which John Davis, a mason, declared that he knows Lord Peterborough and Lady Ann, and that he saw them on the 30th of September last, in the shrubbery, near the grotto, a few minutes after six o'clock in the evening. That he first heard Lady Ann cry out ... 'Oh dear! you hurt me!' which induced him to look that way; and going towards the pales, he look over them, and saw Lord Peterborough and Lady Ann together. That his Lordship had Lady Ann round the middle, and that her Ladyship's coats were up; and, at the same time, he saw her Ladyship's naked legs and thighs round Lord Peterborough's hams; and her arms round his Lordship's neck.[31]

John Motherhill, charged with 'committing a rape on the body of Miss Catherine Wade', was acquitted in 1786, although the prosecution was able to prove that he did rape the victim; and in 1789 Mr Cooke, accused of adultery with Mrs Walford, had to pay £3,500 damages to the lady's husband.[32] In the same year Francis Plowden published his monumental *Crim. Con. Biography*, in twelve volumes, which included numerous erotic prints.[33] Foreign visitors touring London before the turn of the century frequently expressed their disbelief at the popularity of crim. con. literature and related trial reports, which were now sold and read as pornography. A German visitor with apparently strong moral principles remarked that

> the most scandalous literature in London consists of the reports of Crim. Con. and Divorce Cases which are printed without expurgation. No book is asked for so frequently in the lending library, and the editions, reprints and extracts from them prove their popularity.[34]

Clearly, the publishers of trial reports were profiting from the increase of literacy, and from the concomitant interest of the middle stratum of eighteenth-century urban readers in the sexual peccadillos of the nobility.[35]

The apogee of the development of this genre towards pornography was reached with the publication, in 1793, of *The Cuckold's Chronicle*. The select trials for adultery, incest, ravishment, etc., presented in two volumes, are not merely reprinted or reported. In order to ensure that his readers received the best possible entertainment, the editor cut out 'longueurs' in speeches and in parts dealing with moral issues. Instead, he added generous comments of his own, which are mostly ironic in kind. In the trial of Mrs Errington, for instance, several statements of witnesses are ridiculed by editorial remarks. Fun is also poked at a scene in which Mrs Errington and a parson were together in a bedroom. Some of the editor's comments add to the bawdiness of the publication. Describing Mrs Errington's gallant adventures with Captain Southby, he gives his own interpretation of the deposition of

Molly Mitchell, a witness who confirmed that her mistress and the captain had had 'carnal knowledge of each other' at the occasion of a dinner at Mrs Errington's house. 'Mrs Errington', writes the editor,

> paid but little attention to her dinners, when matters of more consequence were transacting. We cannot absolutely say how she was engaged while the repast was cooling, but we can give a shrewd conjecture; and Molly Mitchell appears to favour our opinion. The Captain and she, it is supposed, were taking a wet and relish together; or he might probably be instructing her in some new evolutions, with the modern methods of attack and defence. She is a woman who thirsted after knowledge, and if the Captain had any thing new to communicate, she was sure to pump it out of him. Molly Mitchell supposes the Captain discharged his musket, for, though she did not hear the report, she smelt the powder; and Mrs Errington appeared to have been very much heated in the engagement.[36]

Trials for criminal conversation during that period also appeared in abbreviated form in erotic magazines and books, which seemed to thrive on the sexual content of the cases and the accompanying obscene prints.[37] The caricaturists, too, wanted to have their share of the profits and chimed in on the theme of 'adultery à la mode'. It was, above all, Rowlandson who satirised the genre of crim. con. literature (plate 30).

Around the turn of the century, then, crim. con. cases and similar trial reports had fully developed as a genre of erotica. The genre took a last turn in 1830, before being finally stopped by the activities of the Vice Society and the Matrimonial Causes Act of 1857.[38] On 20 November 1830 appeared the first number of *The Crim. Con. Gazette; or, Diurnal Register of the Freaks and Follies of the Present Day*. Mainly – although not exclusively – concerned with the reports of trials for adultery and divorce, this publication changed into *The Bon Ton Gazette* in its eighth issue, and died an early death, in 1831.[39]

It bespeaks the preoccupation of the eighteenth century with sex that trial reports containing equivocal material were published and read for erotic reasons. Starting as a slow trickle in the seventeenth century, the genre was gradually shaped after 1700 and eventually flowed as a full stream in a century which made sex a major topic. Several factors produced a climate of deep sexual interest in the eighteenth century, calling for the production of sex literature. To begin with, many people in the upper class led a life marked by permissiveness if not licence, which stood in sharp contrast to the behavioural patterns prevalent in the middle stratum of eighteenth-century society. A phase of licentious sexual behaviour among the aristocracy had begun at the court of Charles II in the previous

30 Rowlandson, *The Observers*, early nineteenth century

century, where sexual promiscuity was almost a hallmark of fashion. Whether this astonishing release of the libido is to be seen as a direct reaction against a 'Puritan ascetic morality' is not altogether clear.[40] Of equal importance for the increasing interest in sexual matters was the habit among the aristocracy of arranging marriages with a view to money and influence. The personal feelings of the parties concerned were rarely considered. A French engraving of the time, entitled *The Manners of the Age*, has a motto, reading 'one marries a woman, lives with another one and loves but oneself'. Freudenberger's picture and motto are equally valid for the English nobility; among them very many men had extramarital affairs, and an ever increasing number of women did the same.

Lawrence Stone has argued that lower down in the social hierarchy, marriages were in the majority of cases 'based on prior personal affection, sexual attraction or love', and that when this 'attraction eventually dried up ... many husbands sought variety elsewhere'.[41] While this may have been the case, one should, however, not underestimate the exemplary position of the aristocracy and the attempts of the lower echelons of the gentry to imitate fashionable attitudinal or behavioural patterns. In the eighteenth century it became a common practice, and eventually a status symbol, for the London aristocracy to keep one or even several mistresses. This in turn had an impact on social as well as moral values. Given the frequency of extramarital relations, a word like adultery almost lost its former connotation with sin. The new usage of words of love was partly influenced by French romances of seventeenth- and early eighteenth-century origin: formerly negative words were upgraded. Thus adultery became gallantry; a love affair was an amour; and an attempt at seducing someone was labelled intrigue. The titles of the published divorce trials bear witness to this gradual change of usage and, in particular, to the euphemistic application of the term gallantry to what in essence was nothing else but adultery.[42] Other features contributing to the treatment of sex in the various genres of literature were the excesses of beaux, rakes, and libertines, and a growing wish to recognise the needs of the body – including its sexual needs. In addition, one ought to consider the amount of leisure time available to many members of the upper social stratum who had very little if any sexual interest in each other. To be sure, there is plenty of evidence suggesting substantial differences of moral and intellectual attitudes between the aristocracy and the nobility on the one hand, and the gentry and commoners of the middle stratum on the other hand. One also has to take into account London's exceptional position, which meant that attitudinal and behavioural patterns were rather different in the country.

While the gentry and the middle stratum, for various reasons, may have been unwilling or unable to emulate the sexual behaviour of their social betters, we are still confronted with the phenomenon of an enormous amount of homespun English pornography in the eighteenth century (France continued to be a major supplier until the 1750s and even beyond), which was one consequence of the existing interest in sex and the needs arising from it, especially among the literate. It is quite possible that this literature served as a kind of 'ersatz' for the less fortunate people who were trying to imagine what it would have been like to live a life of free-wheeling sexual promiscuity. The evidence of the trial reports, in particular the prefaces and the moral justification for their publication, would suggest that this sort of literature was read above all by male literates lower down in the social hierarchy. They were admiring, and possibly also hankering after, the extramarital liaisons of the rich and mighty which they could not afford to have.

It is obvious that most members of the upper class had not as urgent a need as the lower echelons of society to be acquainted with the sexual adventures of people of their own status. For the former did every day what others were reading about. It is a moot point whether such pornographic materials as the trial reports contained could satisfy the needs of a large number of people from various walks of life. There are some indications that trial reports did fulfil such alleviating functions. This is rather tricky ground, however, for even today we do not know exactly what pornography does, although some people seem to be quite sure about its noxious consequences. As to the eighteenth century, erotica of the time were not merely the result of a preoccupation with sex but also the prolongation of what came close to an obsession, created by changing attitudes and behavioural patterns.

❧ 5 ❧

Matrimony and the War
of the Sexes

Adultery, cuckoldom, fornication, matrimony, prostitution, and virginity were the major heads under which eighteenth-century writers
discussed the social implications of sexual relations between men and
women. Given the literary predilection of the age, a sizable part of
what was written is bawdy satire rather than serious, learned investigation, although the latter usually served as a starting-point for the
former. Restoration drama usurped the satirical treatment of love and
sex to such an extent that the themes of the cuckold and of extramarital relations were almost flogged to death in theatrical writing.
Outside the field of fiction, writers like Defoe claimed moral reasons
for their contribution, knowing very well that ambiguous subject
matter was a virtual guarantee for a large readership interested in
writings on the war of the sexes, and on sex in and out of wedlock.

I PROSTITUTION

What more exciting topic for writers of bawdry and pornography than
prostitution? The vast body of eighteenth-century literature, both
factual and fictional, on the whore and her trade attests to the perennial personal interest of readers in – and the literary exploitation of –
an area of human life that has always been surrounded by fear,
prejudice, rumour, and taboo. If the prostitute became a cherished
topic in literature and a cause for concern of the public, it was because
England's capital and fashionable resorts like Bath, right from the

beginning of the century, were swarming with ladies of pleasure. Their public behaviour was a thorn in the side of allegedly moral citizens like Daniel Defoe, John Dunton, and the members of various reforming societies. Defoe, himself an incipient pornographer, made a benevolent whore the heroine of his novel *Moll Flanders*, and joined contemporary discussion of prostitution with *Some Considerations Upon Street-walkers* (1726), which, although not devoid of sympathy for the London 'strumpets', had nothing better to suggest in 188 pages than an encouragement of matrimony, and the whipping-post, the work-house, or transportation to the colonies for obstreperous whores. Around 1700, John Dunton published a monthly periodical called *The Night Walker, or, Evening Rambles in Search After Lewd Women*. According to Dunton, it was 'well received' and ran successfully for eight months. Pretending to aim at a reformation of the prostitutes he 'interviewed' at night, it was obvious that Dunton also counted on the prurient interest of his readers. The sternest adversaries of prostitution, however, were the self-proclaimed apostles of morality, who seemed to gain in public influence as the century advanced. While the early Societies for the Reformation of Manners fought a losing battle against man's carnal lust, the repression of prostitutes became one of the special concerns of the Society for the Suppression of Vice and of people like Wilberforce and Hannah More. They joyfully published their black lists of successfully prosecuted whores and brothel owners and took delight in such pious pamphlets as Martin Madan's *An Account of the Triumphant Death of F.S.: A Converted Prostitute who Died April 1763; Aged 23*. It was not before the third decade of the nineteenth century, however, that their efforts were rewarded, with the consequences that both prostitution and sexuality lost their former place in everyday life and were replaced by a sham Victorian prudery.[1]

    In the Age of Reason, there were of course also a number of advocates of prostitution. Two years before Defoe suggested a harsh treatment for the cure of what he considered a public nuisance, Bernard Mandeville had published his *A Modest Defence of Publick Stews: or, An Essay Upon Whoring, as it is Now Practis'd in These Kingdoms*. Mandeville expands upon arguments set forth ten years earlier in a piece entitled *The Fable of the Bees*, adding a tongue-in-cheek dedication to the Societies for the Reformation of Manners to his *Modest Defence*. His rumbustious prose ridicules their plan to suppress bawdy houses, and outlines a proposal for state brothels intended to cover the needs of London's males. Mandeville estimates that two hundred houses with about two thousand girls would be sufficient, and recommends that physicians be employed in these establishments to stamp out 'the French pox'. This was a spirited treatise; but its content proved too equivocal for pornographers to resist the temptation of exploiting it. At first republished anonymously as *A Conference on Whoring*, it was then pirated in 1740 by the ubiquitous Edmund Curll, who sold it as the product of 'Luke Ogle' under the title, *The Natural Secret History of Both Sexes*, thus giving Mandeville's treatise a completely different bent. Later in the century, Restif de la Bretonne was to rely on Mandeville's work, which had then been translated into French, when he sketched a plan for the regulation of prostitution in Paris in his *Le pornographe*.[2]

The contributions of satire to the literary discussion of prostitution were partly written in response to the over-serious attempt on the part of the Reforming Societies to stamp out whoring altogether. Writers like Edward Ward dealt with the subject more superficially when satirising 'The Miseries of Prostitution & Debauchery'. More often than not, the satires left their moral message in the dark and propelled themselves into the realm of bawdry and erotic entertainment. Hogarth's pictorial series, *A Harlot's Progress*, of 1732 (plates 31 a–f), and Swift's poem, *A Beautiful Young Nymph Going To Bed*, of 1734, are, for all their seeming bawdiness, warning examples or shock treatments, so to speak, meant for the prostitute as well as for her customer. But many literary adaptations of Hogarth's prints stressed the ribald rather than the moral element of Moll Hackabout's short whore biography. In *The Harlot's Progress: or, the Humours of Drury Lane*, for instance, the poor and still innocent Moll is delivered into the hands of the 'Stallion *Don Francisco*', i.e., the notorious rake, Colonel Charteris:

> With muckle Een, like Saucers twa,
> He gaz'd, as tho' he'd leek'd her thra;
> With his left Hand he tip'd a Broad-piece,
> And put his other Hand in's Codpiece:

> Said he, *Here's Gold, and precious Stones,*
> *Girl, take all my Riches all at once.*

> This said, the *Tarquin* flew at *Hackabout*,
> Who scream'd, and from him turn'd her Back-about;
> But he, as void of Grace as Fear,
> Began to charge her in the Rear.

> And *Bent-y* held her, *Plene dolens*,
> Whilst he o'ercame her *Nolens Volens*.[3]

Many writings provided a modicum of information on the world of the whore, mostly with a sham moral pretext for the publication hidden in the preface, Edmund Curll-style, while speculating on the lure of an equivocal subject. Tongue-in-cheek satires like *Pretty Doings in a Protestant Nation: Being a View of the Present State of Fornication, Whorecraft, and Adultery, in Great Britain, and Territories and Dependencies Thereunto Belonging. Inscrib'd to the Bona-Roba's in the Several Hundreds, Chaces, Parks, and Warrens, North, East, West, and South of Covent-Garden: and to the Band of Petticoat Pensioners, etc.* (1734) and *Satan's Harvest Home* of 1749 were definitely inspired by seventeenth-century prototypes. Despite their ribald tone, they contain valuable remarks on the miserable life of prostitutes in eighteenth-century London. One moral gentleman proposed in 1758 the opening of workhouses – public laundries, for instance – where prostitutes would 'obtain an honest Livelihood by *severe* Industry', but an anonymous pamphlet laughed the idea out of court. If there is to be repression of whores, argued the author, one ought to consider the various 'Gradations of Whores in this Metropolis, which I believe will stand thus,

> Women of Fashion, who intrigue
> Demi-Reps
> Good natured Girls
> Kept Mistresses
> Ladies of Pleasure
> Whores
> Park-Walkers
> Street-Walkers
> Bunters
> Bulk-mongers

As the first Four of the List, are entirely excluded from the present Argument ... we must consider whether *Ladies of Pleasure* and *Whores* (to speak *technically*) or *Park-walkers, Street-walkers, Bunters*, and *Bulk-mongers*, are the greatest Pest to Society. The first comprehend those in continual Waiting (in the House or at the Door) of *genteel Brothels*; the other compose the Furniture of (what you call) *low-infamous Bawdy-houses*.

If all whores were justly prosecuted, the argument goes on, their number would amount to several thousands in London alone. And how were girls to be kept from plying this trade as long as there were such promising financial prospects, as high-class whores and courtesans daily proved:

Fanny M-y [i.e., Murray] and *Lucy C-r* [i.e., Cooper], have made more *Whores* than all the Rakes in *England*. A *Kept-Mistress*, that rides in her Chariot, debauches every vain Girl she meets – such is the Presumption of the Spectator, she imagines the same Means will procure her the same Grandeur. – A miserable *Street-walker*, who perhaps has not Rag enough to cover her Nakedness, more enforces *Chastity* – I had almost said *Virtue* – than all the moral Discourses, and even Sermons that ever were wrote or preached.[4]

Apart from such cheerful defences of prostitution, there were also professedly didactic pamphlets and books on the ruses of bawds and whores, and guides or 'pocket pilots' to London with sections of advice on ladies of pleasure. They were written and published with the knowledge that male readers too shy to venture into the realm of the whore would find it a most titillating experience to imagine a night in the 'Hundreds' of Drury Lane, or in a bagnio, while reading about it from the safe distance of an armchair. Some titles speak for themselves. An amazingly detailed poetical analysis of the work of procuresses and bawds was published as

The Bawd. A Poem. Containing all the Various Practices these Diabolical Characters make use of to decoy Innocent Beauty into their Snares, with their Behaviour to them, and the means they are made to employ to entertain their numerous gallants, many of whom are here described in the most *glowing* colours, And is, in the whole, a high-seasoned dish cooked up for the Bucks, Bloods, Choice Spirits and Demy Reps, of the Present Age. By a Distinguished Worshipper in the Temple of Venus. For the Author. London [*c.* 1782].

This sketches the career of a bawd until the point when she acquires a hotel,

> Where Bucks and Bloods a wish'd reception find;
> A sisterhood of Nuns, well drest and gay,
> Attend, to pass the joyous hours away;
> Skill'd in each wanton art which can allure
> The am'rous mind, and make destruction sure;
> The *leering* eye, the soft lascivious air,
> Their cov'ring light, the *bosom wholly bare*;
> Each *limb display'd*, the fancy to invite
> All those who seek *venereal delight*;
> . . .
> [The men] daily to the mother Abbess run
> And pay to have a *fine, fresh, blooming Nun*;
> . . . and still to crown the jest,

> Some *maidenheads* are sold *ten times* at least;
> To take you *in*, they have a happy art,
> To tighten soon the oft' extended part.

Subsequent pages describe how bawds discover young girls and turn them into money-making whores. A favourite place for this recruiting seems to have been the 'office', where girls applied for work, either in England or in the colonies. By bribing the clerks, the bawds even had girls sent to their establishments. Another catching place was the country; there the bawd travelled accompanied by a 'neat dress'd Nun' to help her to get innocent girls to town under pretence of protecting them from the snares of the evil city. Impregnated by one of her first customers in London, the debauched girl is then offered to

> Lord Spindleshanks, who long'd for something new,
> (And none but *virgins*, e'er with him will do)
> . . .
> Revels in Pleasures never felt before,
> Chuckles to think he's made a Maid a Whore!

The old lecher pays one hundred pounds, only to be blackmailed by the bawd a little later, who maintains that he is responsible for the girl's pregnancy. Bawds, the poem continues, will not hesitate to buy children from poor parents to train them for their business:

> Yes, *infants* have been purchas'd for the *trade*,
> And e'er they know what Virtue was, betray'd;
> Pamper'd in school, if schools they might be nam'd,
> Where that was taught which always must be blam'd;
> *Babies not in their teens* come tutor'd there,
> For old rich fools to comb their glossy hair;
> Others (believe me it is no romance)
> Come to behold the *naked Graces* dance;
> Some just to kiss the *part* where *pleasure* lies
> Like *spaniels lick the centre* of all joys.

Not only do bawds practise child prostitution, they also force girls into their service:

> The *Bawd* has private rooms and private doors,
> Against their wills to make the *Virgins* Whores;
> Some *Irish bullies*, who obey command,
> And all the wretch'd business understand,
> Whom no fond cries or virgin tears can move,
> *Who, 'gainst their wills, will give them what they love*;
> For such the language which they're taught to say,
> To them, when victims do for mercy pray.

The pamphlet concludes with a description of the miserable death of bawds, commonly alleged to die of VD. Pictorial satire took up such themes, mocking the 'plucking' of dotards in 'bagnios', or the reconstruction of the maidenhead, one of the perennial topics of ribald laughter.[5]

Satirical 'reports' about London's night life appeared regularly in most of the London guide books. *The Midnight Spy* of 1766, for instance, had chapters on 'Adventures at certain Taverns in the purlieus of Covent Garden; View of certain Night Houses with a Description of the Company; Transactions at certain Bagnios; Views of several Famous and Infamous Houses, between the Hours of Two and Three in the Morning; and General and particular Descriptions of the Women of the Town'. In addition to these semi-erotic guides and descriptions, the connoisseur and man of pleasure could consult pornographic catalogues of lists of whores in London. Such lists were already popular in antiquity and reappeared in the Renaissance, spreading from Italy to France and from there to Holland and England. In 1758 a commentator remarked on such a catalogue of the London ladies of pleasure:

> He pulled out a LIST, containing the Names of near FOUR HUNDRED, alphabetically ranged, with an exact Account of their Persons, Age, Qualifications, and Places of Abode. To me ... this List was more entertaining than the real Objects of its Description, and I perused it with great Attention.

Obviously, the catalogues were also sold as erotica. The most popular in London was probably *Harris's List of Covent Garden Ladies*, published between 1760 and the early 1790s. *Kitty's Attalantis for the Year 1766* is a little different, including bawdy poems and riddles but also brief descriptions of the London whores and their particular specialities. Here are two examples:

> The cautious Miss *Sally C-ts*. This lady has fought through life, for many Years, without exposing herself to bagnio or tavern; little, and freshcolour'd, without cosmetics. – In keeping at a useful shop in *Royal-street, Leicester-fields*.

> The lustful Miss *Yo-ng*, or rather Mrs. for she was really married; but she, poor girl, having an uncommon itching after the male kind, was caught twice by her husband in the fact ... she ... is at this juncture so amorous, that if she misses her *quantum* one day, she goes whining about the house like a dog-drawn bitch ... Margaret-street, Cavendish-square.

Other cities apparently aped the London fashion of publishing such lists. In Edinburgh, it became a custom to sell broadsides, with ribald descriptions of whores, at horse races. The *Genuine List of Sporting Ladies* thought it rather funny to compare some of the assembled prostitutes to the horses.

> Mary Fiddler, a fine blooming lass of 18, her – is like silk itself, and bubbles as white as snow; she is just in her prime, and fit for business, she is broke in this spring, by a well-known gentleman of the turf. Her movements are regular, her pace elegant, and her action is good; and when you mount her, she begins to f-k away to the tune of the 'Dandy, O'. Her price, 5s. 'She riggles her a-e su' cantily.'
>
> Peg Simpson, an old stage-player, her dam had the honour of parading through the streets of this town ... Her movements are according to price; kindly palm her hand with gold, and if you have the vigour of a stallion, the letchery of a goat, the continuance of a boar, or the repetition of a sparrow, she will always meet you with the same energetic ecstacy; standing or falling ... Ten shillings.
>
> Eliza Booth, a fine country girl of 20, tall and slender, fine blue eyes ... and good legs; when mounted, she starts at full speed, and while in the act, she causes her rider the most pleasing delirium, and entertains you with the admired song of 'Come cuddle me, Cuddie, now or never'. A sovereign.

The eighteenth-century English male considered this ribald entertainment: women as the butt of bawdy laughter.[6]

2 THE CUCKOLD AS A LITERARY FIGURE

Although by the eighteenth century the horned husband was an over-used literary figure of fun, having been exploited almost *ad nauseam* in Restoration comedy, cuckoldry remained a popular object of satire, not least because of the growing literature on extramarital affairs. The songs and poems on cheated husbands sung and recited in taverns, and mock-treatises like *The Benefits and Privileges of Cuckolds* (1728), ridiculed a subject which in real life was far from hilarious. In many ways, the abundance of erotic and bawdy satire on cuckoldry seems to bespeak the unconscious and pressing sexual fears of eighteenth-century males, an anxiety that was projected on stock figures of comedy. The themes of most of these ephemeral pieces on the cuckold – male impotence, female lust or nymphomania, and the risible folly of old men marrying young girls – were, of course, not of eighteenth-century origin; they were already known to the theatregoers of classical Rome. Hence it would be erroneous to attribute the wave of bawdy

satire on the cuckold solely to social circumstances and sexual relations in the eighteenth century. As in other literary genres of erotica,
heritage played an important role. When John Dryden lent his pen to a
translation of the notorious Sixth Satire of Juvenal shortly before
1700, he wrote of 'Marriage-Beds' that 'creak'd with Foreign Weight'
and rendered the Roman's rhymes into aggressive English verse in the
description of unfaithful wives in contemporary England:

> She acts the Jealous, and at Will she cries:
> For Womens Tears are but the Sweat of Eyes.
> Poor Cuckold-Fool, thou think'st that Love sincere,
> And suck'st between her Lips the falling Tear:
> But search her Cabinet, and thou shalt find
> Each Tiller there with Love-Epistles lin'd.
> Suppose her taken in a close Embrace,
> This you wou'd think so manifest a Case,
> No Rhetoric cou'd defend, no Impudence out-face:
> And yet ev'n then she cries, the Marriage-Vow
> A mental Reservation must allow;
> And there's a silent Bargain still imply'd,
> The Parties shou'd be pleased on either side:
> And both may for their private Needs provide.
> Tho' Men your selves, and Women us you call,
> Yet *Homo* is a common Name for all.
> There's nothing bolder than a Woman caught;
> Guilt gives 'em Courage to maintain their Fault.

Dryden's version of Juvenal's invective against lustful and adulterous
wives was a major literary source for eighteenth-century satire. By
1735 his translation was selling in its sixth edition and had made its
impact on writers like Jonathan Swift.

Like a number of other satires, *The Praise and Profit of Cuckoldom*
(1743) pretended to defend cuckolds, in order to heighten its satirical
effect. As a 'consolotary oration delivered by an eminent teacher, to
the two congregations of London and Westminster', it parodies the
sermon. Arguing that the cuckold's fate is alleviated by the fact that he
has numerous 'fellow-sufferers', the kind preacher points out the
advantages of cuckoldom. Pictorial satire recorded and varied the
literary theme of the cornuto cheated by his wanton wife. *Folly of an
Old Man Marrying a Young Wife* (plate 32) depicts the familiar
satirical topic of the rich old man whose money is not enough for his
lustful spouse; while the satisfied and amused lover takes his silent
leave, the young lady leads her husband by the nose. Thomas Rowlandson's *The Old Husband* (plate 33) applies the theme of cuckoldry

32 *Folly of an Old Man Marrying a Young Wife, c. 1800*

to erotic art, with touches of the grotesque. Plagued by gout, which is quite obviously due to excessive eating and drinking, the husband cherishes the heat of the fireplace to find soothing solace; the young wife, in the background, being in heat – so to speak – has no need of a fire while she is being serviced by a young gallant.

The gloating if not malicious joy expressed by both literary and pictorial satire whenever cuckoldry was treated betrays the underlying male attitude towards women in the eighteenth century. A large majority of men considered married women as chattels. As one watched one's property, so wives had to be watched. The rich man victimised by a thief or an adulterer was sure to encounter public ridicule; in the case of cuckoldry, laughter on the part of the observers was a traditional response.[7]

33 Rowlandson, *The Old Husband*, early nineteenth century

3 MATRIMONY

Hogarth's series of engravings on the modern marriage, published in 1746, contains most of the themes occurring in the bawdy satires on matrimony (plates 34 a–f). A marriage, made for purely financial

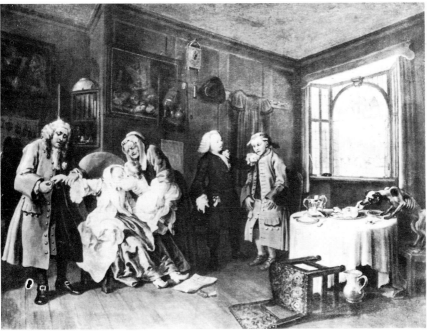

reasons, soon leads to loss of interest of the spouses in each other, both engaging in their own diversions. While the wenching husband contracts VD and berates a quack doctor for his useless nostrums, his wife enjoys the 'bon ton' of social life and falls prey to the amorous pursuits and schemes of her counsellor, Silvertongue. In a dramatic scene obviously inspired by the theatre, Hogarth has the Earl die in a bagnio. The last picture shows the death of the Countess Squander-field, who has taken an overdose of laudanum after reading about the hanging at Tyburn of her treacherous lover.

The popularity of this series in England was due, on the one hand, to the deep interest the subject was able to arouse, and, on the other, to a literary preoccupation with marriage, which included sober moral treatises as well as ribald satire. With a slightly prurient eye, Daniel Defoe, Peter Annet, and a number of anonymous writers thus investi-gated 'conjugal lewdness' and 'cohabiting unmarried'. It is indicative that the passing of the two major eighteenth-century laws regulating matrimony – Lord Hardwicke's Marriage Act of 1753 and the Divorce Act of 1771 – were preceded, accompanied, and followed by a spate of publications from humorists, moralists, and satirists.[8]

Writers of bawdry and satire, by all one can tell, seem to have been divided on the issue of whether marriage was to be commended. However, the advantages of married life were extolled in John Arbuth-not's *The Pleasures and Felicity of Marriage* (1745). Writing under the pseudonym of Lemuel Gulliver, he displays his intimate knowledge of Ovid's *Ars Amatoria* when he describes the wedding night in the first of the ten books which make up his work:

Fortunate Lover! You have now vanquished, and are triumphing over all your potent Rivals, who can imagine your Joy! Whatever you are em-ploy'd about, your Thoughts continually glance upon the near Approach of your Happiness. – Your beautiful Mistress is now willing; Denials are laid aside; nothing remains but a small Degree of Shame and Fear, which a little Time will eradicate. What Mortal can desire a greater Happiness than you now participate! Your Will and Desires are hers, and her Desires augment your Pleasure. Now may you tumble and regale yourself in a Bed of Lillies and Roses; for her disdainful Looks are exchanged for inviting Smiles. Those panting, snow-white Breasts, which before you hardly could presume to look upon, much less to touch with one Finger, you may now survey all o'er with eager Eyes, and imprint with burning Kisses. What shall I add! The delightful Place, the Haven of all your Joys, which heretofore you hardly durst approach in Thought, much less express in Words, you have now an uncontrollable Liberty to visit, embrace and enjoy, while you have any Capacity for that most ravishing Exercise. But, O victorious Lover, let not however your exulting Mind ruminate too much upon these dazling Enjoyments; be a little temperate in your Plea-sures; because there may possibly happen in the Course of Things some cross-gain'd Obstructions: For I have frequently experienced, that those imaginary Joys, which you are now indulging, introduce a numerous Train of Anxieties. Perhaps the very Mouth upon which you are bestowing so many rapturous Kisses, and amorous Epithets, and which now flows with the sweetest Language, may hereafter oftener open to overwhelm you with Reproach. Those heaving Breasts, which now you fondly call the *Hills of Nectar*, and *Banquet of the Gods*, may perhaps hereafter sink in the Comparison. Moderate therefore your extatic Descriptions, and amorous Praises, till you have been longer accustom'd to the delicious Banquet *Hymen* has prepared for you.

If Arbuthnot saw nothing but bliss in marriage, writers of bawdry were eager to prove that it was not to be commended.[9] *Reasons Against Coition* (1732), a mock-sermon breathing the spirit of Swift's prose satires, explained the 'benefit arising in not touching women' and 'the perpetual Wretchedness of Posterity' caused by matrimony or fornica-tion. 'What is the cause of *Vertigoes*', asked the pamphlet,

> sudden pains in the *Head*, *Paralytick* disorders, frequent *Hystericks*, *Rheumatism* and *Gout*? – Coition! for whoever saw an Eunuch afflicted with these Diseases? Thrice happy Species! not only exempt from these Maladies, but from Children also . . . Let therefore the Name of *Eunuch* be no more a term of Reproach, but an appellative of Happiness. Let 'em be respected as those favour'd by Heaven; and though we have not the *mighty blessing* to be of the Number, let us imitate their Example, let us always have 'em in View and follow their Steps, so shall Peace and Tranquility be in our Days.

After a rundown of the medical and theological teachings on the evil effects of fornication, the reader is urged to ignore women:

> Be free from *Women, and you're free from Care*, is an Axiom, that has no need of a Comment; and shall *Man*, the Lord of the *Universe*, be subdued by that trifling *Sex*? A Sex, notorious for their *Pride* and *Affectation*! recorded for their *Vanity* and *Self-Opinion*; and distinguished for the Fomenters of *Mischief*! A Sex, as difficult to be discover'd as the *North-East-Passage*! The Generality of *Women* are formed of such a Medley of Principles, either in their *Minds*, or in their Dress, that they quite efface their natural Structure.[10]

The dichotomy between marriage, which was often arranged with a view to money and social status, and affectionate love could not be resolved in the eighteenth century. Love matches were still the excep-tion rather than the rule. No wonder then that several authors prop-osed the alternative of polygamy, which they deemed a better solution than an unhappy monogamous marriage. Eighteenth-century writers thus drew on the discussions of earlier Catholic casuists and writers of other denominations, whose works were read and reprinted up to the seventeenth century. Quite naturally, literature took up contemporary issues of debate. It is significant for eighteenth-century literary tastes that Henry Neville's *The Isle of Pines* of 1688 was taken out of the drawer and republished one hundred years later. In this prototype of the exploration novel, later elaborated by Defoe, one George Pine finds himself alone with four women on an island after a shipwreck in the Indian Ocean:

> Idleness and fullness of every thing begot in me a desire of enjoying the women. Beginning now to grow more familiar, I had persuaded the two maids to let me lie with them, which I did at first in private; but after, custom taking away shame, there being none but us, we did it more openly, as our lust gave us liberty. My master's daughter was also content to do as we did. The truth is, they were all handsome women, when they had clothes, and well shaped, feeding well. For we wanted no food, and living idly, and seeing us at liberty to do our wills, without hope of ever returning home, made us thus bold. One of my consorts, with whom I first accompanied, the tallest and handsomest, proved presently with child. The second was my Master's daughter. And the other also not long after fell into the same condition. None now remaining but my Negro, who seeing what we did, longed also for her share. One night, I being asleep, my Negro, with the consent of the others, got close to me, thinking it being dark to beguile me, but I awaking and feeling her, perceiving who it was, yet willing to try the difference, satisfied myself with her, as well as with one of the rest.

After forty years Pine's offspring allegedly counted five hundred and sixty-five children.[11]

Another satirical line of writing, with its usual departments of ribaldry and obscenity, which the eighteenth century inherited from earlier periods, was the war of the sexes, and misogyny. In the seventeenth century satire on women figured prominently in chapbooks on courtship and sex. The eighteenth century continued this line with the revival of classical slanderers of women. As early as 1707 James Read and Angell Carter were indicted at the Guildhall quarter sessions for printing and publishing *The Fifteen Plagues of a Maidenhead*. This was a satire in fifteen stanzas in which a maid describes the disadvantages of virginity, and her several efforts to be made a woman.

The Second Plague

...

But ah! 'tis my Misfortune not to meet
With any Man that would my passion greet,
Till he with balmy Kisses stop'd my Breath,
Than which one cannot die a better Death.
O! stroke my Breasts, those Mountains of Delight,
Your very Touch would fire an Anchorite;
Next let your wanton Palm a little stray,
And dip thy Fingers in the milky way;
Then having rais'd me, let me gently fall,
Love's Trumpets Sound, so Mortal have at all.
But why wish I this Bliss? I wish in vain,
And of my plaguy Burthen do complain;
For sooner may I see whole Nations dead,
E'er I find one to get my Maiden-head.

The Sixth Plague

Pox take the thing Folks call a Maiden-head,
For soon as e'er I'm sleeping in my Bed,
I dream I'm mingling with some Man my Thighs,
Till something more than ord'nary does rise;
But when I wake and find my Dream's in vain,
Return to Sleep only to Dream again,
For Dreams as yet are only kind to me,
And at the present quench my Lechery.

The Ninth Plague

By all the pleasant Postures of Delight,
By all the Twines and Circles of the Night,
By the first Minute of those Nuptial Joys,
When Men put fairly for a Brace of Boys,
Dying a Virgin, once I more do dread,
Than ten times losing of my Maiden-head;
For though it can't be seen nor understood,
Yet it is troublesome to Flesh and Blood.

The Fourteenth Plague

If any man does with my Bubbies play,
Squeeze my small Hand, as soft as Wax or Clay,
Or lays his Hands upon my tender Knees,
What strange tumultuous Joys upon me seize!
My Breasts do heave, and languish do my Eyes,
Panting's my Heart, and trembling are my Thighs;
I sigh, I wish, I pray, and seem to die,

35 Hogarth, *Morning (Four Times of the Day)*, 1738

In one continu'd Fit of Exstacy;
Thus by my Looks may Man know what I mean,
And how he easily may get between
Those Quarters, where he may surprize a Fort,
In which an Emperor may find such Sport,
That with a mighty Gust of Love's Alarms,
He'd lie dissolving in my circling Arms;

> But 'tis my Fate to have to do with Fools,
> Who're very loth and shy to use their Tools,
> To ease a poor, and fond distressed Maid,
> Of that same Load, of which I'm not afraid
> To lose with any Man, tho' I should die,
> For any Tooth (good Barber) is my cry.

Largely indebted to a religious and French tradition – the satire is in fact a parody of an old French prayer – *The Fifteen Plagues* provoked a long-lasting series of similar ribald works on the fifteen 'comforts' or 'plagues' of cuckoldom, matrimony, whoring, and virginity.[12]

Eighteenth-century satire certainly had it in for women. Those who rejected sexual advances were termed prudes in their youth and later classified as old maids. Like the cuckold and the bachelor, the old maid became a figure of amusement; and even such a compassionate artist as William Hogarth, in Plate 1 of *Four Times of the Day* (plate 35), could not resist the temptation to make fun of her. The pious old lady is on her way back home from church and is obviously shocked at the loose behaviour of the rakes fondling the women in the market. What Hogarth contrasts in this picture is the dissolute yet joyful conduct of young men, representing youth, and the old woman's piety, serving as an 'ersatz'. Hogarth's sympathy is recognisably on the side of youth.[13] An anonymous 'True Penitent' wrote a diatribe against *The Folly, Sin, and Danger of Marrying Widows, and Old Women in General*, in which he argued that it was 'unnatural' for a young man to marry an old woman, for once married

> he loaths the Embraces, the Conversation, the Presence of his Wife, and goes in search of those Gratifications abroad, which it is impossible he should find at Home. He now gives a Loose to every inordinate Desire, revels in the pestilential Arms of the Harlot, in the poisonous Delights of the Bottle, and in the ruinous Diversions of the Gaming-table; till at length, his Health, his Wealth, his Reputation being destroy'd, and nothing left him but Poverty and Contempt, he applies himself to infamous Practices for a wretched Subsistence.

The true penitent provides some examples to support his argument that widows are given to cuckolding their husbands with servants and male friends. Relating the story of his own misfortune in marrying a widow, he revives the cliché of the oversexed old woman:

> My Wife, tho' sixty-five years old, still preserved a lusty, warm, and vigorous Constitution, and had not the least Aversion to the Pleasures of Youth. But as for me, my Habit of Body was weakly and cold, and the Fretting and Vexation which I daily endured, from the termagant Be-

haviour of my Wife, had worn me to a Skeleton. Hence it naturally followed, that I did not give unto such Conjugal Exercises, as some married Folks, who are better matched, possibly may; and, as it seems, my amiable Consort wished I should. This prompted her to charge me with wronging her in that Article which no Woman can suffer with Patience, declaring 'that my Affections were placed upon some former Mistress whom I still kept, or some new one: Adding, that her dear first Husband never gave her the least Cause of Complaint on this Head, and that if I did not do her Justice, she would expose me to all her Acquaintance, Relations, &c.' Tho' conscious of my Innocence with respect to this Charge, yet, as I knew she was capable of inventing and asserting any Falsehood, I confess her Threats had such an Effect upon me, that, rather than provoke her to do any thing prejudicial to my Reputation, I constrained myself to endure her too frequent Embraces, and did her Justice, as she called it, till a Surfeit ensued; after which, all Advances on my Part ceased, being glad to lie by, waiting her Motions. At the End of two Months more, finding my Aversion to the Drudgery increase to such a Degree, that to consent to her was little better than Suicide, I fell into *statu quo*, and turned my Complaisance towards her into Compassion for myself. This again roused her Resentment, and a terrible Quarrel ensued; when I had the Courage to assure her, 'That since she was not content with my best Endeavours, I would have nothing further to do with so ungrateful a Creature, but for the Future should chuse to lie alone.' This desperate Resolution mortified her not a little, as it could not fail of exposing the Affair to the Servants, and indeed I did not like that myself; however I persisted in it, and we never after lay together.

The frame of the satire may have tempered such attacks; but even their humour cannot cover the seriousness of the theme, in an age when men were often more interested in the dowry of a woman than in her person.

Around 1700 John Dunton and Edward Ward were the principal writers of innocuous bawdy works on the war of the sexes and marriage, stressing laughter and entertainment rather than social criticism. As the century grew older and women gained more sexual liberty, above all in the upper reaches of English society, the tone and content of these popular works underwent a slight change, the stress shifting from laughter to harsh criticism of what most male authors saw as an 'unnatural' sexual freedom for women. The ribald fun of seventeenth-century comedy and erotic folklore is still apparent, meanwhile, in such satires from the beginning of the century as *Love Given Over* (1709), and 'An Essay on Matrimony', which is contained in a scatological pamphlet and has this joke to tell:

In a Manuscript, taken out of the *Vatican* Library, and sent me from *Rome*, I have read the following short Tale, which I have endeavoured to put into an *English* Dress, hoping it may be as entertaining to the Reader, as it has been diverting to me.

As a numberless Multitude were crowding one Day about the Gate of Heaven, a pale, meagre, little Man stept forward and knocked at the Wicket. *Peter* asked him immediately what he wanted? To which the diminitive [sic] Gentleman answered, He desired Entrance into Heaven. Have you passed through *Purgatory*, says *Peter*? Yes, replyed the Gentleman, – I have been *married*: Alas! Alas! come in, said *Peter*. Amidst the crowd stood One, who hearing upon what Terms the other had gained Admittance, *waddled* up to the Gate with a Paunch and a Face as *large* and as *red* as a Cardinal's. He thundered at the Wicket with as much Authority, as if he had been a *Pope*; and *Peter*, with a Countenance somewhat discomposed, demanded in a rough Tone, what he would have? I want to come in, sayd the Fellow. *Peter*, having interrogated him, whether he passed through *Purgatory*? Yes, yes, answers the corpulent Man, I have passed through Purgatory with a Witness; I have been *twice* married. Have you so, says *Peter*? Stand back, stand back, *Fellow*, Heaven is not a place for *Fools*; upon which he shut the Door in his Face, which, I humbly conceive to be no great Sign of polite Manners.[14]

The popular writings published on the subject of marriage held the view that entering into wedlock meant – at least for the majority of the satirists who dealt with the topic – the loss of a man's sexual freedom. Hymen, the god of matrimony, may offer beautiful young wives with nice dowries; but those who take them will also have to accept the manacles of conjugal life with its disagreeable aspects.[15]

Many of the bawdy attacks on women found their butt in the eighteenth-century extravagances of fashion. Although the beau or fop was certainly not exempted from such satire – he was one of the stock figures of early eighteenth-century comedy, the craze of male fashion reaching its apogee with the Macaroni of the early 1770s – it was mainly female follies that were castigated in the traditional ribald tones of popular satire. John Dunton's *Bumography: or, A Touch at the Ladies' Tails* (1707), reprinted as *The Rump* (1708), is just one of numerous bawdy writings on female fashion, ridiculed around 1700 by John Brown, Edward Ward, and other Grub Street writers. In the early decades of the century the 'hooped-petticoat' was under attack. In 1719 an anonymous writer let loose against ladies of fashion in *A Rod in Piss for Hooped-Petticoats*, and was immediately answered by a colleague, who pretended to side with the victims, in *A Modest Defence of the Ladies*, where he asserts the advantages of the new fashion, such as the hiding of an uncomely physical shape or an embarrassing pregnancy. 'Did I not say before,' he asks, tongue-in-cheek, 'Hoops were designed as a *Fortification*? And have not your *Moats Circumvallations* one within another, not to say any thing of the *Hornwork*? That when one *Trench* is forced in such Extremity Men may retire to another.' The rest of the pamphlet continues in the same way, with frequent *doubles entendres* and erotic allusions. *Whipping-Tom: or, a Rod for a Proud Lady* (1722) was intended to 'touch the Fair Sex to the Quick', and also used much ribaldry while inveighing against 'the Foppish Mode of Taking Snuff; the Expensive Use of Drinking Tea; their immodest Wearing of Hoop-Petticoats'. Apart from condemning the 'extravagance of a lady's toilet', this humorous piece also makes fun of the alleged lust of women, in interspersed poems like 'A New Satyr, For the Use of the Female Voluntiers in Hyde-Park' and 'The Virgin's Dream'.

Around the mid-century an increasing resentment on the part of male authors can be felt against the attempts of women to show their newly acquired sexual liberty in daring manners of dressing. 'The Conduct of the Ladies in appearing in Publick quite Naked', wrote the sarcastic 'Adam Eden, Esq.', in 1755,

> from the Top of the Head, almost to the Waist, discovering their Neck, Shoulders, Breast, and part of their Waist quite bare, and shortening their Petticoats almost to the Knees, sufficiently shew their Intention of returning to the original Custom of going naked; and if any should doubt the Truth of a Design to shake off all Prejudices that favour Chastity too, let him but consider how industrious they have been in contriving all Means of shewing the World their Contempt of it; their appearing at Masquerades more frequently than before they were understood to be calculated for Intrigue; let him consider the Behaviour of the Ladies at that Diversion; let him remember that those *called* modest Ladies, who used by every Means to shew their Contempt for Women of Pleasure, have of late set them up as Patterns of Imitation in Dress and Behaviour; let him consider the great Increase of late of Routs and Card-Assemblies, those Seminaries of Intrigue, contrived to give Ladies an Opportunity of indulging their amorous Inclinations, without the Fear of Interruptions from Father and Husbands.

Sarcastically, he suggested a plan to speed up the process of shortening dresses:

> I have spent much Time, and have applied myself with great Industry to assist the Ladies in their glorious Undertaking; I have invented, that the Decrease of the lower Part of their Garment, may keep pace with the upper, a Fashion to take off as much in proportion, from the Petticoats, as has lately been taken from the Stays. I have not observed any Lady discover more of her Legs, than to the Calf, therefore to induce them to expose more of their pretty Limbs, I have invented some new-fashion Garters, to tempt

36 Gillray, *Lady Godina's Rout*, 1796

them to diminish the Length of their Petticoats to discover these Garters, which will be a sort of Bracelets, to adorn and set off a well-shaped Leg ... and that the Decrease of the Dress below, may not be in greater Degrees than that above, I have invented a beautiful Girdle, in Imitation of the famous one worn by *Venus*, which had that valuable Quality of creating Love and Desire in every Beholder, for that Female that wore it. If therefore the Stays which now reach a little above the Waist, shall be cut so as to reach a little below it, every Female that wears this Girdle, which shall be contriv'd to supply the vacant Part, this last lessening of the Stays has left, will soon become sensible of a Warmer Affection and more ardent Desire in the Men, than they perceived before ... and they may be satisfied that when this Reformation has proceeded as far as the wearing the Girdle I mentioned, a Breach of the Laws concerning Matrimony, will be as little regarded, as the Breach of those prohibiting Gaming, and other genteel Amusements on a *Sunday*; and the World will be as much reconciled, that the Women live publickly with the Men without the Sanction of the nuptial Union, as they have been for Ages, to this Practice among the Men.

In the final section of his vindication of the 'reformation among the ladies to abolish modesty and chastity' he demonstrates how easy it had become by 1755 to seduce respectable women. Selecting one to prove his argument, he first took her to bawdy plays, like *The Old Batchelor* and *The Chances*, and then further fired her imagination with the *Memoirs of a Woman of Pleasure*. When the lady was still very concerned about her reputation, he accompanied her to some

WEARING THE BREECHES

37 Newton, *Wearing the Breeches*, 1794

'routs', i.e., parties with games of chance (plate 36), where she got so much into his debt that she yielded to him, at the occasion of a masquerade. The final pages of this satire explain the particular advantages of the new scheme proposed by the author. He explains that, in addition to the reduction of the money spent on fashion, his proposal for women to go naked would also mean the abolition of private whoring.

In her instructive historical survey of misogyny in literature, Katherine M. Rogers has not included such popular satires. Concentrating on writers, like Swift, who treated women harshly or condescendingly, she argues that towards the end of the eighteenth century a gentler criticism, and an 'insidious' belittlement, of women ensued. This may be the case for novelists from Swift to Sterne; but a different picture emerges from the popular literature and bawdy satire introduced in this chapter. Rogers has ignored the literary sub-soil, and the tradition in which Swift and his successors wrote. The change in women's sexual role is well exemplified in the pictorial caricatures of the last decade of the eighteenth century. Newton and Woodward, for instance, caught the fear and impotent rage of the English male at the progress of female sexual freedom. Richard Newton's *Wearing the Breeches* prominently figures a superior wife, who is merely amused at her husband's futile rage (plate 37). Significantly, the conjugal bed in the background remains empty. The caricature suggests that the Englishwoman had gained a new sexual status, and a freedom she was willing to defend. Women in the upper and middle classes were becoming aware of their new advantageous position and were beginning by 1800 to reject the traditional sexual roles. In the first part of the eighteenth century women had been nothing better than chattels for men, sexual objects of pleasure one could buy like horses. Warning all bachelors against marrying widows, a satirist reminded men that

> If I am to purchase a Horse, I can mount the Saddle, and walk, trot, pace, or gallop the Creature, in order to form a Judgment of its Motions and Properties before-hand. If a Mare hath been ill broke when a Colt, or any Ways spoiled by the Ignorance or Boisterousness of the first Rider; if she hath been over-hackney'd, jaded, founder'd; or had any latent Distemper, occasioned by the Carelessness or foul Play of the Seller, or any other former Proprietor; yet, in such Cases, if I have any Skill in Horses, I shall discover the Imperfections before I pay my Money, and am still at Liberty to seek further, till I can suit myself to my Liking: But it is not so with Widows.

For all its ribald laughter, the comparison is telling. But this was to change as the century grew older. It had been a common theme of erotic pictorials to show women wearing chastity belts. While they might try to cheat their inhuman husbands by inviting the local locksmith to open the dreaded belts – a common theme of erotic folklore – the fact remained that wives were regarded as valuable objects that could be locked up by their proprietors. However there is a pictorial satire by Woodward where a man-wife has put a giant chastity-lock on her demure husband, telling him that the 'shop' is now closed and that he will not be able to run after housemaids any more (*The Padlock c.* 1800).

Admittedly, caricatures exaggerate; and henpecked husbands had been a familiar topic of bawdy satire for several centuries. But caricatures comment on social themes, too; and the evidence of both pictorial and popular satire towards 1800 suggests that the English male had been made to feel somewhat insecure in his traditional role as the absolute 'owner' and protector of a woman. If eighteenth-century matrimonial and related satire has a message for us – a message often lost in bawdy humour and plain fun as the sole aims of a great number of works – it is that of increasing liberty in the sexual relations of upper- and middle-class women with men. The unconscious or deliberate resentment of male writers against this growth of freedom lay at the bottom of much of the bawdry written against women.[16]

✀ 6 ✀

Poetry and Facetiae

Much of the history of erotic poetry in eighteenth-century England remains to be written. The standard literary surveys have concentrated on the 'genus grande', i.e., Petrarchism, while ignoring popular forms of the 'genus medium' and the 'genus humile', which found expression in mostly witty libertine and coarsely humorous or facetious verse. One gets the distinct impression that literary historians are prejudiced against what they consider to be 'lower' forms devoid of seriousness and value. The notion that erotic poetry must be grave, solemn, and spiritual to deserve attention is a fairly modern one, and developed in the eighteenth century. From classical times until well after 1750 the tradition of facetious and jocose erotic verse had been almost uninterrupted; but it was to be challenged by the moral ideas of the rising eighteenth-century middle class, whose members eventually determined literary taste. Bawdy and facetious verse came to be equated with the moral depravity of the aristocracy and court circles. When the new middle class applied its concepts of morality to the classical eroticism of much extant poetry the result of this juxtaposition was a reduction of such poetry to lewdness and superficiality – the work ethos of a new literary audience henceforth allowed negligible value to be perceived in bawdy and ribald verse. Writing in the early nineteenth century, Francis Place is a typical representative of the new middle class who were now to assess literature. In the early decades of the nineteenth century he looked back at his youth and at what he now considered bad taste in poetry. The bawdy and scatological travesties of the classics – always very popular in the eighteenth century – and many notorious writers of ribaldry 'would be a disgrace to any respectable bookseller', wrote Place, applying to his quoted examples such words as 'gross' and 'filthy'. Such opinions explain the gradual disappearance of facetious poetry towards the end of the eighteenth century. The public dispersion and reception of bawdy verse came to a halt or went underground, surviving in the private clubs of *bon vivants* and belated libertines. As far as literary histories are concerned, moral judgments by members of the late eighteenth-century bourgeoisie of a traditionally amoral bawdy poetry have been upheld to this day.[1]

I THE TRADITION: ANTIQUITY, THE CONTINENT, AND THE RESTORATION

The notable absence of any particular poetic forms specific to the genre makes it difficult to impose an order upon erotic verse, an area whose humorous aspect called for a mixture of forms, both high and low. The various elegies, epigrams, madrigals, verse tales, odes, songs, and epistles are for the most part in lyrical form, although the epic was also present, especially in the popular combination of verse and prose known as the *genre mêlé*. This found expression in the 'love letter', with a history dating back to Greek authors like Alciphron and Aristainetos. One of the few common denominators in this field of varied forms is the brevity of these pieces, which distinguishes them from the prose tale, the novella, and the novel.

If the English writers of jocose erotic verse turned towards the ancients for inspiration in the early eighteenth century, it was because they knew that eroticism had had an unchallenged place in the literature of the Greeks and Romans. It is significant that Greek mythology tells of the nine daughters of Zeus and Mnemosyne, the Muses, who were led by Apollo and lived on Parnassus; one of whom was Erato, the muse of erotic poetry and love lyrics. Classical writers had developed about three-quarters of the poetic forms later to be revived in the Age of Reason. The Eros of the Greeks and the Amor of the Latins each had a hand in the creation of Cupid, the patron of modern eroticism. Jean Hagstrum has shown that pagan verse was dignified in its early-eighteenth-century forms. In the tradition of the ancients, love was described as an entertaining Arcadian game, thus keeping out Christian morality. Although there was much imitation of classical erotica, the eighteenth century did not accept completely the authority of the ancients, for that would have meant, among other things, the acceptance of aristocratic Greek homosexuality and pederasty, as codified in literature. The eighteenth century could neither condone nor praise such sexual relations, for 'Nature' and 'Reason' – the major authorities for writers in the Augustan Age – seemed to suggest that they were unnatural. This was not too serious a problem, however. One way to get around it was suggested by translations of the homoerotic verse of Anacreon, the Greek bard of love and wine, which performed a miraculous sex operation on Anacreon's catamite, Bathyllus: in quite a few eighteenth-century versions the boy Bathyllus has turned into a girl, Bathylle, thus making acceptable the love lyrics Anacreon wrote for him/her. In this way, more recent eroticism dissociated itself from the Greek ideas of homosexuality and lesbianism while retaining a classical joy and playfulness in descriptions of physical love between men and women.[2]

Who were these ancients, translated, imitated, plagiarised, and satirised by their eighteenth-century acolytes? Among the Greek authors, Anacreon and Sappho rank highest among those who found attention. Anacreon had almost sunk into oblivion when his work was reintroduced into literature by the *Carmina Anacreonta* of the Romans, serving as a basis for the seventeenth-century translations by Cowley, Oldmixon, Stanley, and others. Addison lent his prestigious support to an edition of *The Works of Anacreon ... To Which is Added the Odes, Fragments, and Epigrams of Sappho* (1735). The notorious bisexuality of both authors certainly contributed to the vogue they enjoyed, with numerous editions and translations up to the end of the century. Like Germany and France, England had her 'Anacreontic' circles; so had Scotland, with The Beggar's Benison of Anstruther. The genuine and would-be libertine members of such clubs as the Beef-Steaks and the Humbugs had a natural penchant for the Greek poet of wine, women, and song. Captain Charles Morris, publisher of several song collections, dedicated his *Festival of Anacreon* [sic] (1788) to the 'Anacreontic Society', and achieved nine registered editions with this anthology of songs and short bawdy poems. Lampoons of the time played on the reader's acquaintance with Sappho's sexual predilections. *A Sapphic Epistle from Jack Cavendish to the Honourable and Most Beautiful Mrs D...* (*c.* 1782) makes fun of the alleged lesbian adventures of a certain Mrs D. while in Italy. The unnamed author praises Sappho's kind of gentle love which he mockingly juxtaposes with the 'inhumanity' of a maid being deflowered by a man:

Small's then the touch-hole, not being old,
The colour lead, or carrot gold,
  Or brown, or white or black:
But think what a fair maid must bear
When some rough marksman to a hair,
  Shoots at the little crack.
. . .
'Tis martyrdom small wits declare,
To torture such a beauteous fair,
  On such a monstrous spit.

With the revival of the erotic works of the Greek poets the love stories of mythology also came into fashion. Intensifying the sexuality of the original, Dryden, in 1697, translated the story of Queen Dido and Aeneas from Virgil's *Aeneid*. Scatological travesties, such as Charles Cotton's *Scaronnides* (a mock poem on the first and fourth books of the *Aeneid*, featuring a storm of farts), which had reached its tenth edition by 1715 and was still selling in the 1770s, were as popular as the actual myths and legends, exploited in erotica like Curll's *Consummation: or, The Rape of Adonis* (1741) and E.M. Diemar's *The History and Amours of Rhodope* (1780). Diemar's modern adaptation is concerned with the love of Aesopus for the nymph Rhodope and includes 'An Hymn to Venus'.[3]

When Latin poetry was taught to future gentlemen, they were bound to discover, at one time or another, the twelve books of epigrams by Martial on sodomy, pederasty, fellatio, irrumination, cunnilingus, and tribadism; the love songs of Catullus to his 'Lesbia' and of Propertius to 'Cynthia'; and the poems and songs of Laberius and Tibullus. Most cherished, however, was the master of playful, elegant erotic verse, Publius Ovidius Naso; his love elegies (*Amores*), poetical sex manual (*Ars amatoria*), and antidote to love (*Remedia amoris*) were all-time favourites. The translations of Ovid's works by Dryden, Congreve, and others asserted his sexuality, and revived his myths and heroic stories of wild passions and hetero- and homosexual love. In the department of ribaldry, neoclassical poets had recourse to Juvenal. According to Dryden, Juvenal's *Sixth Satire* against women was the source 'whence all the Moderns have notoriously stolen their sharpest Railleries'.

In addition to the Latin, French, and English editions of these individual Roman authors, several anthologies had come down to the eighteenth century – the *Priapeia* from the tenth century AD, for instance, and the *Anthologia Latina*, with its obscene 'Pervigilium

Veneris', from the sixth century – and were again popularised by the translations of Jean Bonnefons (1554–1614), which continued to be reprinted throughout the century, in Paris, Amsterdam, Leyden, and London. Edmund Curll published several versions of Bonnefons's poems, one of them appropriately entitled *The Pleasures of Coition* (1721). This collection of 'lovepieces', as Curll termed them, celebrates the unrestrained joys of copulation. After a brief prefatory homage to the translator, from Clermont, in Auvergne, thirty-one translated stanzas of the 'Pervigilium Veneris' make up Part One. Here are stanzas XII and XIII:

> Whilst now in Bed compos'd she lies
> My Fires with Force redoubled creep
> To that dear Flame that gave 'em Rise,
> Like Rivers to their Parent Deep.
> Prostrate I traverse o'er her Form Divine,
> Embracing ev'ry Park where nameless Graces shine.

> Our Legs in *Cupid's* Fetters lock'd,
> Our Lips, like Birdlime, sticking fast,
> Our Limbs by graceful Venus yoak'd,
> Round her white Neck my Arms I cast;
> Fix'd on her panting Breasts, like Glew, I dwell,
> And closely, gently press, the *Part* I like so well.[4]

Italy was not far behind France in her international influence on erotic poetry. Pietro Aretino's 'sonetti lussuriosi', originally only a sort of poetic appendix to Giulio Romano's pornographic plates depicting the various positions of sexual intercourse, set the tone for later writers like Giorgio Baffo (1694–1768). Baffo's poetic erotica at first circulated in manuscript form, and got him into trouble in Italy. It was Lord Pembroke who had *Le Poësie di Giorgio Baffo* published, in four volumes in a London edition entitled *Raccolta Universale delle Opere di Giorgio Baffo* (1771 and 1789).

The indebtedness to the classical and Continental tradition of describing in verse the pleasures of copulation is apparent in numerous English collections, some of which went into several editions. *The Cabinet of Love, or, Cupid's Pastime* (1718) and *Cythera, or New Poems Upon Love and Intrigue* (1723) are comparatively mild material even eighteenth-century ladies could read without blushing. But *The Festival of Love*, sold in its sixth London edition around 1770, and *Hilaria. The Festive Board* (1798) have quite a few obscene passages.

Bawdy songs were openly sung and seem to have found little objection; and ribald verse was recited in the clubs of rakes and libertines. Like the bawdy parodies and travesties of cherished eighteenth-century masterpieces – Pope's *Rape of the Lock*, for instance, was mocked by Joseph Gay's *The Petticoat* (1716) and Giles Jacob's *The Rape of the Smock* (1727) – the ribald erotic poetry of the genus medium was meant to produce laughter. Sexual allusions and obscenities are the spices in this basically humorous literature, which, unlike pornography, is not interested in building up sexual stimulation in the reader. If this ever happens, the final punch line explodes any sexual tension, and the reader's laughter is thus also at the expense of his or her own prurience. Ribald laughter is what much of humorous erotic folklore is concerned with. It should be pointed out that many authors of such bawdry have today fallen into oblivion, although they were quite popular in their day. Hildebrand Jacobs, for instance, is a name modern literary histories will hardly ever record; but his *The Curious Maid* (1720/21) was a ribald poem frequently imitated and parodied following its publication.[5]

2 SONGS, JESTS, AND RIDDLES

In 1705 an anthology of obscene and facetious writings was published in London which indicates the range of current erotic folklore, including the 'genus humile' of erotic poetry. It was *The Compleat Academy of Complements: Containing First, Choice Sentences, with Variety of Similitudes, and Comparisons; Also the Best Complemental Letters. Second, The Art of Courtship and Genteel Breeding, with Discourses Proper for this Ingenious Age ... Together with a Collection of the Newest Songs that are Sung at Court House and Play-House.* This is a typical example of the many printed collections of hotch-potch mixtures of short humorous erotica in which the bawdy song figured prominently. One should bear in mind that there was a strong oral tradition in this field and that the obscene songs and riddles, in particular, were favoured by drinking clubs, which thus continued a popular line of erotica that has often been overlooked. Francis Place noted that ribald songs were openly sung by men and women in the streets and taverns of eighteenth-century London; and the examples he quotes surprise even a twentieth-century reader by their sexual frankness and occasional obscenity. 'The Jolly Waggoner' is an example of the songs that were contained in *The Fond Mother's Garland* (Newcastle, *c*. 1770):

As I was driving my Waggon one Day,
I met a young Damsel, tight, buxom and gay;
I kindly accosted her with a low Bow,
And I felt my whole Body, I cannot tell how.
    Hey gee Dobin, gee ho Dobin, gee gee Dobin
    gee ho, gee ho.

I longed to be at her, and gave her a Kiss,
She thought me but civil, nor took it amiss;
I knew no recalling the Minutes were past,
So began to make Hay while the Sun shine did last.
    Hey gee Dobin etc.

I've six Score of Sheep, and each Ram has his Ewe,
And my Cows when they lack to the Parson's Bull go;
We are made for each other, so prithee comply,
She blush'd, her Eyes twinkl'd, she could not tell why.
    O poor Jenny etc.

I kissed her again, she reply'd with Disdain,
No Kisses I want, prithee take them again;
Then whisper'd me softly, the Weather was hot,
And her mind run on something, she could not tell what.
    O poor Jenny, etc.

Then down in my Waggon this Damsel I laid,
But still I kept driving, for Driving's my Trade,
I ruffl'd her Feathers, and tickl'd her Scut,
And I play'd her round Rubbers at two-handed Put.
    O brave Roger, Drive on Roger, etc.

Her Breasts they were soft and white as new Cream,
And her Motion kept Time with the Bells of my Team,
As her Bubbies went up her plump Buttocks went down
So the wheels seem'd to stand, and the waggon go round.
    O brave Roger, etc.

Thus to and again to our Pastime we went,
And my Cards I play'd fairly to *Jenny's* Content,
I worked at her Pump till the Sucker was dry,
And then I left pumping, a good Reason why.
    O poor Roger, broken back'd Roger, etc.

I thought e'er we parted to have t'other Blow,
When slap went the Waggon Wheel into a Slough,
Which shatter'd her much out of repair,
Then *Roger's* pump Handle run the Devil knows where,
    O poor Roger, broken back'd Roger, etc.[6]

The history of obscene and ribald jests, anecdotes, and riddles is as long as that of the bawdy song, the English tradition drawing on Restoration comedy, Shakespeare, Chaucer, and The Exeter Book; and the Continental line being influenced by, among others, Gian Francesco ('Poggio') Bracciolini's *Liber facetiarum* of 1470. The prime example of the sexual or scatological joke in rhyme, the limerick, is by now well researched and documented. So-called 'dirty jokes' were popular; *The Merry Andrew* of 1772, written by 'Ferdinando Funny', contained such jokes as these two:

> Some Men and their Wives, who all lived in the same Street, and on the same Side of the Way, being a merry-making at a Neighbour's House, said one of the Husbands, it is reported that all the Men in our Row are Cuckolds but one: His Wife, soon after being a little Thoughtful, What makes you so sad my Dear, said her Husband, I hope you are not offended at what I said? No replied she, *I am only considering who that one can be in our Row that is not a Cuckold.*

> One wished a young married Man Joy, for she heard his Wife was *quick* already. *Ay*, said he, *quick, indeed, for I have been married but six Months and she was brought to Bed Yesterday.*

The Puzzle: Being A Choice Collection of Conundrums (1745) is an example of the joke books which were made up of two parts. The first twenty-eight pages contain the questions, and Part Two ('The Nutt Crack'd') provides the answers, in thirty pages. Most are as simple as Number Three:

> Why is a bad Fire like an old Maid?
> Because it wants poking at the Bottom.

Many of the longer bawdy jokes and riddles were published in separate broadsides and chapbooks, such as *A Riddle of a Paradoxical Character of an Hairy Monster Often Found Under Holland* (*c.* 1725), a poetical *double entendre* based on allusions to the vagina. These short ribald writings were the salt of erotica like *Kitty's Attalantis for the Year 1766*, containing the following riddle, which appeared again in *The Trial of Wit* (1782):

> What's that in which good housewives take delight,
> Which, though it has no legs, will stand upright,
> 'Tis often us'd, both sexes must agree,
> Beneath the navel, yet above the knee;
> At the end it has a hole; 'tis stiff and strong,
> Thick as a maiden's wrist and pretty long:
> To a soft place 'tis very oft apply'd,

And makes the thing 'tis us'd to, still more wide;
The women love to wriggle it to and fro,
That what lies under may the wider grow:
By giddy sluts sometimes it is abus'd,
But by good housewives rubb'd before it's us'd,
That it may fitter for their purpose be,
When they to occupy the same are free.
Now tell me merry lasses if you can,
What this must be, that is no part of man?

The answer: 'A Rolling Pin'. Ribald verse satires occasionally also contained riddles. Thus *A Merry Conversation which Lately Pass'd Between A Quaker and A Maid* (1739) included 'The Button Hole. A Riddle':

I'm a Hole tho' too narrow when first I am try'd,
The Thing I was made for will stretch me out wide;
Tho' at first Entrance, perhaps, I may teaze ye,
Soon after I commonly prove but too easy.
Tho' I'm nothing but Mouth, no Teeth you can find,
And tho always before, I am likewise behind;
When whimsical Folks would have used me quite bare,
The Kings, Lords, and Commons took me into their Care,
Crying out, with one Voice, they wou'd have me with Hair.
The Members stood to 't, and like Creatures betwitcht
Said the Nation was lost, if I was not well stitcht.

Three other examples from *The Trial of Wit* are the following:

Pleasantly growing in a bed,
Of complexion white and red,
The fairest lady in the land,
Desires to have me in her hand,
And put me in her hole before,
And wish she had two handfuls more.
                                 A Strawberry

There is a thing long and stiff
And at the end there is a cliff;
Soft moisture from it doth flow,
And makes fair ladies pleasant grow.
                                 A Pen

My lady has thing most rare,
Round about it grows much hair,
She takes delight with it in bed,
And often strokes its hairy head.
                                 A Lap-Dog

Jonathan Swift's scatological and obscene riddles in verse are not, as has been suggested, a sign of his pathological penchant for ordure, but indicate his closeness to contemporary folklore.[7] Here is one of his riddles:

Written in the Year 1725

Depriv'd of Root, and Branch, and Rind,
Yet Flow'rs I bear of ev'ry Kind;
And such is my prolific Pow'r,
They bloom in less than half an Hour:
Yet Standers-by may plainly see
They get no Nourishment from me.
My Head, with Giddiness, goes round;
And yet I firmly stand my Ground:
All over naked I am seen,
And painted like an *Indian* Queen.
No Couple-Beggar in the Land
E'er join'd such Numbers Hand in Hand;
I join them fairly with a *Ring*;
Nor can our Parson blame the Thing:
And tho' no Marriage Words are spoke,
They part not till the *Ring* is broke.
Yet hypocrite Fanaticks cry,
I'm but an Idol rais'd on high;
And once a Weaver in our Town,
A damn'd *Cromwellian*, knock'd me down.
I lay a Prisoner twenty Years;
And then the Jovial Cavaliers
To their old Posts restor'd all Three,
I mean the Church, the King, and Me.
                    A Maypole.

One of the most important publications of the time was *The Dictionary of Love*, which held first place, until it was surpassed, in 1783, by Francis Grose's *Classical Dictionary of the Vulgar Tongue*.[8]

3 THE VERSE TALE

Coarse humour and ribaldry are the main characteristics of short verse tales and satires circulating in the seventeenth and eighteenth centuries. La Fontaine's erotic-hedonistic *contes-en-vers* and Chaucer's bawdy tales (*The Court of Love*, for instance) reappeared on the eighteenth-century literary scene, thus keeping alive a most interesting genre of erotic poetry, which left its traces in anonymous verse satires like *The Adulteress* (1773), and such successful works as Charles

Hodge was a Miller, & Joan was his Wife,
And Years they'd liv'd threescore;
Joan lov'd — tho' she was Old,
But Hodge could do it no more.
A beautiful Daughter they had, in her Eyes
You kiss me, Sir, might read:
Her pouting Bubbies softly told
Her of a Buxome Breed.
Hodge & his Wife left the Damsel, to go
To Town one Market-Morn;
Anon comes Will, the Farmer's Man
To grind a Sack of Corn.
Father's gone out, Says the Lass w.th a Smile,
But we'll do't without Delay:
On then cries Will we'll have a —
To pass the Time away

O'erjoy'd at the Sound, to the Oven she ran,
And seem'd to be much afraid:
But Will soon into the Oven got,
And Pegs into the Maid:
Will was for ganging, when finish'd y' Job;
But she demanded Toll:
So once again he kiss'd the Maid,
And paid her in the Hole.
What a sad Accident hapd you shall hear
In came Roger and Joan.
And, wounds cries Roger, in a Rage,
Where is our Daughter flown?
Above and below the Damsel they sought,
But all their Search was vain:
O ho! thought Joan, when I was young,
And in the — Vein

Snug in the Oven she lay conceal'd,
And spent an Hour or two:
My Girl, perhaps, takes after me,
'Tis what we all will do.
Snug to the Oven she snigg'd the old Maw,
With forceful Peal in Hand;
And had not Time his Matters tam'd,
The Sight had made him stand.
Ecstacy melted the amorous Pair,
Their Legs hung dangling out:
Take 'em to Task when the Work is done,
'Twere Sin to baulk the Bout
Thus let each Mother her Daughter befriend,
Who knows she's done the same;
For sure the Damsel Acts but right
To play her Mother's Game.

38 *The Surprised Lovers*, undated

Churchill's *The Rosciad* (1761), of which more than nine editions are recorded. Popular in France and England, the verse tales varied in length, from the simple broadside to the chapbook versions. In the closed circles of London's *beau monde* minor incidents were apt to provoke epic verse satires. When in 1773 one Sally Harris eloped with a Mr Lyttleton, John Courtney put pen to paper and produced *The Rape of Pomona* (1773). Among the short verse tales published as a single sheet there was a rather curious combination of suggestive illustration and bawdy verse, placing this kind of broadside halfway between facetious joke and ribald tale. Many of these writings were concerned with some humorous aspect of sexual intercourse, an engraving showing a crucial scene of the appended tale in verse.[9] *The Surprised Lovers*, for instance, recounts the story of illicit country love in an oven (plate 38):

> Hodge was a Miller & Joan was his Wife,
>   And Years they'd liv'd threescore;
> Joan lov'd – tho' she was Old,
>   But Hodge could doe it no more.
> A beautiful Daughter they had, in her Eyes
>   You kiss me, Sir, might read;
> Her pouting Bubbies softly told
>   Her of a Buxome Breed.
> Hodge & his Wife left the Damsel to go
>   To Town one Market-Morn:
> Anon comes Will, the Farmer's Man
>   To grind a Sack of Corn.
> Father's gone out, says the Lass with a Smile,
>   But we'll do it without Delay:
> On then, cries Will, we'll have a ——
>   To push the Time away.
> O'erjoy'd at the Sound to the Oven she ran,
>   And seem'd to be much afraid:
> But Will soon into the Oven got,
>   And Pego into the Maid.
> Will was for ganging, when finish'd ye Job,
>   But she demanded Toll:
> So once again he kiss'd the Maid
>   And paid her in the Hole.
> What a sad Accident hap'd you shall hear:
>   In came Roger and Joan.
> And, wounds cries Roger in a Rage,
>   Where's our Daughter flown?
> Above and below the Damsel they sought,
>   But all their Search was in vain:

Jack and his Master a wager laid,
  Of Threescore Shillings and ten:
Which of them had the longest —
  The Wager he should win, Tot. &c.
They measur'd the Length, and measur'd y Breadth,
  And they measur'd them round about:
But Jack he beat his Master far,
  By Four Inches and the Snout.
The Maid she went behind the Barn Door
  For which she was muckle to blame,
And when she saw the Wager won,
  She ran and told her dame.
The Old Woman went behind the Barn Door,
  To do as she was wont,
And stooping down occasionally
  A Mouse jumpt into her —.

The Old Woman cry'd out to the Old Man,
  As loud as she could cry,
There's a Mouse crept into my Belly,
  And without your Help I die.
The Old Man laid her on a Jack,
  As oft he had done before:
But he could not touch the Mouse's Tail
  By Four Inches & more.
The Old Man cry'd out to his Man Jack,
  As loud as he could cry,
Here's a Mouse crept into thy Dame's Belly
  And without thy help she'll die.
Without you'll double my Wages, quoth Jack,
  It shall you'll double my Price.
When you'll double my Wages quoth Jack,
  My — shall hunt in Wee.

I'll double thy Wages, quoth the Old Man,
  And give thee a Hat and Coat;
And for to buy thee a Button and Loop,
  Thy Dame shall give thee a Groat.
Then work it a-m-ig my bonny Boy Jack,
  For thou needest not to fail:
A little further Jack she said,
  And you'll touch the Mouse's Tail.
The Old Man stood upon the Barn's Floor,
  With the Beesom in his Hand,
To knock the Mouse all on the Head,
  As soon as it should land.
Come all ye merry Maids of Yorkshire,
  If you will me believe,
When thou old Harry had got ... enough!
  So let the Mouse out of her Sleeve.

---

39 *The Mouse's Tail*, 1753

O ho! thought Joan, when I was young,
   And in the —— Vein,
Snug in the Oven I lay conceal'd,
   And spent an Hour or two:
My Girl, perhaps, takes after me:
   'Tis what we all will do.
Strait to the Oven she dragg'd the old Man,
   With forceful Peat in Hand;
And had not Time his Matters tam'd,
   The Sight had made him stand.
Extacy melted the amorous Pair,
   Their Legs hung dangling out:
Take 'em to Task when the Work is done,
   'T were a Sin to baulk the Bout.
Thus let each Mother her Daughter befriend,
   Who knows she's done the same;
For sure the Damsel Acts but right
   To play her Mother's Game.

The Mouse's Tail, a bawdy ballad from Yorkshire, published in 1753, is also situated in a rural milieu, and focuses on the competition between Jack, a farmhand, and his master (plate 39):

Jack and his Master a Wager laid,
   Of Threescore Shillings and ten:
Which of them had the longest –
   The Wager he should win.
   Tol. etc.
They measur'd the Length and measur'd ye Breadth
   And they measur'd them round about:
But Jack he beat his Master far,
   By Four Inches and the Snout.
The Maid she went behind the Barn Door,
   For which she was muckle to blame,
And when she saw the Wager won,
   She ran and told her Dame.
The old Woman went behind the Barn Door,
   To do as she was wont.
And stooping down occasionally
   A Mouse jump'd into her –

The woman then cried for help; but her husband, equipped with an insufficient 'tool', could not help her. So poor Jack was called to the job. He exploited his employer's predicament, and first asked for a pay increase before setting to work with the old woman:

> A little farther, Jack, she said,
>   And you'll touch the Mouse's Tail.
> The Old Man stood upon the Barn Floor
>   With the Beesom in his Hand.
> To knock the Mouse all on the Head
>   As soon as it should land.
> Come all ye merry Maids of Yorkshire,
>   If you will me believe,
> When this Old Whore had got – enough
>   She let the Mouse out of her Meeve.

Longer verse tales were for the most part sold in chapbooks, at a price of sixpence. An example of this very popular genre is *Kick Him, Jenny. A Tale*; it was published in 1733, and within four years had reached eleven editions. The tale relates the story of Jenny, a naive country maid, who wants her sweetheart, Roger, to make love to her as a sign of his sincere wish to marry her. Jenny's idea of what making love means is rather vague; she has heard it means 'kissing her breech' and asks her mistress for advice. This lady cannot dissuade her from her plan to make love, so Jenny arranges a rendezvous with Roger in her bedroom. Meanwhile, the lady has informed her husband of her maid's curious yearnings and naivety. So both decide to watch the scene through peepholes. Randy Roger appears and sets to work:

> So, on her Face, upon the Bed,
> He lightly down my Damsel laid;
> Her Petticoats he o'er her Head throws,
> And pins 'em tight unto the Bed-cloaths.
> . . .
> Now down his Leathern Trowzers dropt
> And out a monstrous live Thing popt.

Innocent Jenny wonders what Roger is about, since she expected a 'kiss'.

> So round her Thighs his Hands he cast
> Lifted her up and held her fast.

At this point, her ladyship, still watching the action through the peep-hole, decides to intervene on Jenny's behalf, telling her in a loud voice

> Kick him – why kick him, Jenny, kick him.

But the peeping squire has put his money on Roger and will not have his sport spoiled by his wife:

> Mad at his wife, he cou'd have struck her.
> Aloud cry'd, – her, Roger, – her.
> Kick him as loud the Dame went on;
> – her, still louder cry'd Sir John.

The tale then continues with an obscene description of the eventual penetration of the unsuspecting Jenny:

> Inch after Inch he thrust it then
> Nor stopt 'till he had given her Ten.

Even Jenny's moanings are rendered in rhyme. Before concluding with a happy ending – Roger marries his Jenny – the anonymous author takes a few snipes at the ladies of the upper class. Allegedly, they never get into Jenny's position on the bed, for fear of pregnancy:

> Thus in a Chair the cautious Dame,
> Who loves a little of That Same,
> Will take it on her Lover's Lap,
> Sure to prevent, this Way, Mishap:
> Subtle Lechers! Knowing that,
> They cannot so be got with Brat.
> I grant, indeed, they may, with Ease,
> When resting on their Hands and Knees.

The author, however, prefers it in a different manner:

> No – let me lean upon the Breast,
> And bite their Lips, as at a Feast;
> Behold 'em roll their dying Eyes,
> And see the kindling Blushes rise;
> Feel their Arms wreath around my Waist,
> Their Hands on Honour's Mansion plac'd;
> At ev'ry Thrust their Bodies heave,
> Pant, riggle, quiver, warmly cleave
> …
> 'Till all entranc'd in bliss we lie,
> And in dissolving Raptures die.

The bawdy verse tale had its origins in common with the erotic prose tale and the novella, both greatly in vogue between 1660 and 1800, when the collections of Boccaccio, Cervantes, Chaucer, La Fontaine, and the bawdier parts of the *Heptaméron* and the *Cent nouvelles nouvelles* were reprinted, 'reinvented', and plagiarised. In 1721 Edmund Curll printed a title, *Three New Poems*, which assembled such older writings; these were 'Family duty: or, the monk and the merchant's wife. Being the shipman's tale from Chaucer. Moderniz'd';

'The curious Wife . . . Moderniz'd'; and 'Buckingham-House, a poem'. This edition was republished in 1727 as *The Altar of Love*. Some verse tales were so popular that they were reprinted over the centuries. Gershon Legman has shown that Alexis Piron's 'Le Placet', a *conte-en-vers* contained in his *Oeuvres badines*, which was published in several editions in the latter part of the eighteenth century, is still being told in modern versions in England and America today. In the original version, a nobleman receives a pretty young girl, who wants to submit a petition. The nobleman does not take his time to read the petition, but seduces the girl forthwith. On reading her 'placet' he finds that it is a complaint against the doctor who had not been able to cure the girl of venereal disease. François de Neufchâtel adapted this tale at the time of the French Revolution, as 'La consultation épineuse', replacing the nobleman with a lawyer. English translations substituted a priest for the lawyer.[10]

Other tales were sold in verse and prose. *The Secret History of an Old Shoe* (1734) has a versified story of a girl impregnated by a knight, with digressive interludes in prose in which the author talks to the reader in *doubles entendres*. An example of a tale sold in prose and verse is *The Surprize: or, The Gentleman Turn'd Apothecary* (1739). This tale, 'versified in Hudibrastics', according to the title-page (plate 40), had been written by Jacob de Villiers in 1670, as *L'apoticaire de qualité*. First translated as *The Gentleman Apothecary*, by Roger L'Estrange, in the same year, the tale proved successful for more than a century. The 'Hudibrastics' of John Ellis in *The Surprize* of 1739 are not particularly suited for this tale, whose plot and characters indicate the aristocratic origin of the *conte galant* in French literary circles. But the fact that the well-known tale was given a new, albeit ill-fitting, coat of verse suggests that the publisher reckoned he could make some money with it in the popular line of the verse tale. *The Surprize* starts out with a report about 'Parisian Dames' and their use of the 'clyster' in the interest of beauty and health. Amarinta (later in the text spelled Araminta) is one of the dedicated followers of this custom. One day, she asked her maid to administer the enema in the usual procedure:

> The Lady, as before we said,
> In such a prone Position laid,
> As serv'd effectually to blind her,
> Unless she'd also Eyes behind her.

On this particular day, however, the ordinarily reliable maid had forgotten something and went out to fetch it, leaving her mistress in the position which is shown in the frontispiece of the tale. As the door had been left open, a visiting gentleman, Timante, surprised Amarinta in this state of affairs:

> But finding no Apothecary,
> Resolv'd the Task himself would dare he;
> And so he did, and play'd the Part
> Like a top Master of the Art
> …
> This done, without a Mortal's View,
> He secret as he came withdrew.

THE

SURPRIZE:

OR, THE

GENTLEMAN

TURN'D

APOTHECARY.

A TALE Written Originally in *French* Profe; afterwards Tranflated into *Latin*; and from thence now Verfified in *Hudibraftics*.

——*Virgo Pretiumque & Caufa Laboris,*
By Mr. John Elis   OVID.

LONDON:

Printed and Sold by the Bookfellers of *London* and *Weftminfter*. MDCCXXXIX.

[*Price,* Two Shilings Stich'd, Two Shillings and Sixpence Bound]

N.ᵗ Parr Sculp

40 Frontispiece and title-page of *The Surprize*, 1739

When the maid returned, she was of course as perplexed as her mistress, who claimed that she had been served satisfactorily. Timante later met Amarinta, in a circle of friends to whom he told the story without mentioning the name of the lady. What follows is much in the tradition of the French sentimental tale, with some friends intervening to get the lovers together – Timante has fallen in love with Amarinta, who refuses to speak to him for a while. The love letters of Timante are cited in the text, and the action takes a new turn with the return from the country of Lycander, Amarinta's lover, who challenges Timante to a duel but is humiliated by him. Timante then addresses another letter to his beloved lady, explaining why he fell in love:

> Ne'er, Madam, found I any Thing,
> In all my Life so ravishing,
> As *That*, by me so lately seen, –
> Your Ladyship knows what I mean.
> Its Form and Graces, when conjoin'd
> By Recollection in my Mind,
> Convince me, that the World around,
> Its Equal is not to be found;
> So sweet, so plump, so gently rising,
> Its Symmetry thro'out surprising.

There is, of course, a happy ending, with the marriage of Timante and his beloved lady:

> The Clyster thus, as it fell out,
> Was what the Marriage brought about.
> . . .
> Timante well had played his Part,
> And was rewarded for his Art.

Finally, two genres ought to be mentioned with an influence on the verse tale. They are the fable and the oriental tale. An example of the fable in verse is Edward Moore's *Fables For the Female Sex* (fourth edition, 1755), containing sixteen fables, none of which is exceptionally erotic – not even No. XV, 'The Female Seducers'. The contemporary literary fashion of the oriental tale is parodied in *A Chinese Tale. Written Originally by that Prior of China the Facetious Sou Ma Quang. A Celebrated Mandarine of Letters, Under the Title of Chamyam-tchochang, or, Chamyam with Her Leg upon a Table* (1740). Alluding to successful erotic tales in this genre by Crébillon *fils*, d'Argens, and others, this tale introduces a Chinese beauty at a court – although the surroundings described are more reminiscent of ancient Greece and Rome. A mandarin attempts to seduce her; but his efforts are in vain, and he has to resort to the help of a maid, who hides him in Chamyam's bedroom. He watches her masturbate – a scene recorded in the frontispiece (plate 41) – and finally rapes the girl. This

41 Frontispiece of *A Chinese Tale*, 1740

cruel ending is in sharp contrast to the usually romantic oriental tale, and introduces into the satire an element of shocking realism.

Towards the end of the century, the salacious verse of Thomas Hamilton, sixth Earl of Haddington, embodies most of the character-istic traits of the 'genus medium' of erotic poetry. Originally written for his friends and companions in a private club, most of his bawdry circulated in manuscripts and was not published until half a century after his death (Hamilton died in 1735). Like John Hall Stevenson's *Crazy Tales* of the 1760s, Hamilton's *New Crazy Tales, or Ludicrous*

Stories, Facetiously Told for the Entertainment of Young Gentlemen and Ladies ... Printed at Crazy Castle (1783) cover the *topoi* of erotic verse. The tales are all in ballad metre and, in their anti-Catholic stance, remind one of similar works by Boccaccio; the *Heptaméron*; and La Fontaine's 'contes'. Thus tale No. 3 is entitled, 'The Ax laid to the Root of Popery'. No. 11, 'The Longing Woman', resumes the anti-religious theme, with the story of a neglected wife impregnated by a parson. Other tales in this collection are simply erotic love poems (tales No. 4 and No. 5), or obscene extended metaphors on the vagina (No. 1, 'The Wonderful Grot') and lovemaking. No. 7, 'The Incendiary', presents a girl in front of a fireplace, dreaming that she is having sexual intercourse:

> With panting breasts and dying eyes,
> Fancied she seiz'd the manly prize:
> Her legs she canted in the air,
> Thinking to seize the phantom there;
> Then to her gap her hand applies,
> Clinging close her legs and thighs.

The little damsel gets so excited that her dress catches fire. She wakes up and makes a narrow escape.[11]

4 SCATOLOGY

Scatology was an unquestioned part of erotic folklore, and did not disturb eighteenth-century readers in the least. While a twentieth-century reader will probably have little difficulty in the assessment and appreciation of ribald verse from the Age of the Enlightenment, the same cannot be said of scatological poetry and the entertainment eighteenth-century writers saw in it. In fact, with the exception of Jonathan Swift's so-called dirty poems, which have received some attention over the last years, scatological literature, although rather popular in the eighteenth century, is still an area which most scholars prefer to ignore. One reason must certainly be due to the fact that we find it hard today to see the entertaining aspects of, for instance, stercoraceous jokes. Twentieth-century American English usage has virtually banned 'unclean' ideas and things from everyday conversation. American students seem to live in constant fear of having 'body smell', apparently a terrible disease which can only be avoided by taking at least two showers a day; and the words 'toilet', 'urine', and 'faeces' are absolute taboos, with the consequence that American English has dogs and horses 'going to the bathroom'. Given such hygienic attitudes, which find scatology unacceptable if not inhuman, it is understandable that American critics in particular tend to see Swift's scatological verse as expressing a sort of pathological or even perverse penchant for stercoraceous matters. They have failed not only to understand Swift's aims but also to recognise an essential part of eighteenth-century humour. Admittedly, this humour was rather coarse, and does not seem to fit into established and accepted pictures of the fashionable and genteel Age of Reason; but to ignore it for twentieth-century reasons of propriety is hardly helpful if we want to arrive at a genuine impression of eighteenth-century literary tastes and attitudes.[12]

In this context it is essential to remember what eighteenth-century sanitary conditions were like. Both physically and mentally people then seem to have had a much more natural attitude towards the biological functions of the body. Public toilets were non-existent; people relieved themselves, men and women alike, in the streets. When Giacomo Casanova visited London he was shocked to see people defecating near main roads. In Italy, he remarked, men looked for doorways or courtyards if they wanted to urinate; but in London they turned toward the middle of the road and apparently did not mind being watched by passing coach passengers – an unacceptable behaviour for the polite Italian. Human excrement was perhaps a disturbing part of daily public life; but it was nevertheless accepted. The prevalence of scatological humour, always a sign of a culture's rural links, indicates the proximity of eighteenth-century English society to the simple life of the country. Although of French origin, *L'odorat* (plate 42), by Le Vasseur, expresses the general eighteenth-century attitude towards excrement: the lady in the picture may find the odour disagreeable, but she does not object to the physical necessity of defecating. Woodward's caricature of 1801 shows the beginning of the subsequent Victorians' prudery: *Modesty* (plate 43) figures a lady and her maid passing a gentleman who is relieving himself. The lady tells Mary, the maid, 'my dear, let me know when I am past that I may open my eyes – 'Tis a shameful thing!' And Mary agrees, 'Tis indeed Ma'am a vile shameful thing – I wonder such things are tolerated in a Christian Country!' Victorianism minded the mere bodily functions, and not only people relieving themselves in public.

If the scatological works of Pope, and more particularly those of Swift, have been misunderstood in the past it is mainly because of our ignorance of the tradition of literary scatology. Only a fraction of this literature has come down to us; and the few extant works have often

L'ODORAT

Il est des cas ou les regards d'autrui   Ami lecteur, qui vous en chagrines,
Gênent beaucoup, loin d'être nécessaires;   Vous avez tort mettez vous a votre aise,
On s'en passeroit bien; mais les gens d'aujourd'hui Traitez tous vos secrets comme la traite Blaise,
N'ont point assez de leurs propres affaires.   Vous verrez si quelqu'un ose y mettre le nez.

42 Le Vasseur, *L'odorat*, undated

been dismissed as ephemeral and worthless.[13] The mostly satirical scatological pamphlets written after 1700, and sold and read in the London coffee-houses and taverns, catered to a sense of humour which had been shaped by various literary and popular traditions. On the one hand, there was the influential line of ribald and scatological obscenities contained in the seventeenth-century chapbooks and related erotic folklore; on the other, literary scatology was propagated

43 Woodward, *Modesty*, 1801

by writers like Rabelais, and Poggio Bracciolini, whose *Liber face-tiarum* (*c.* 1470) was one of the first collections of dirty jokes. They continued to be read and imitated in the eighteenth century. Educated English readers who were keen on French literature had a rich choice among the numerous pamphlets that were imported from French presses in Paris and Holland. Underestimating his own country's contributions in this field, H.S. Ashbee wrote towards the end of the nineteenth century that the French 'delight in making the Cloacinan rites the subject of their wit, and even the most respectable French

THE PISSING CONFLICT.

A correspondent has sent us the following dialogue, with the annexed drawing, which he says will give our readers a compleat idea of a late whimsical affair at a tavern near Westminster-bridge; and as we endeavour to seize every opportunity of amusing our readers, we have engaged *an eminent wooden engraver* to *cut* Sir Joseph for the *simples* upon the occasion.

DRAMATIS PERSONÆ.

Sir J. M. Mr. W. Waiter, and Intruders.

Scene a Room at a Tavern.

Mr. W. WELL, sir, you know upon what occasion you met me here.

Sir J. No—not in particular—to drink a bottle, and have a little chat.

Mr. W. A little chat will go a great way upon this occasion.

Sir J. I hope, sir, you an't angry.

Mr. W. No, I'm not angry—but I beg no farther trifling.

Sir J. Trifling, sir! I do not understand you.

Mr. W. Oh, we shall soon come to an explanation.

(Spits in Sir J—'s face—Sir J— endeavours to do the same, but having drank hard over night, his mouth is dry.)

Mr. W. Have at you—(strikes Sir J. and he falls.)

Sir J. For heaven's sake, do not kill me—consider my dignity.

Mr. W. Damn your dignity! If it was not doing you too much honour, I'd piss upon you.

Sir J. No, indeed, it won't be too much honour!

Mr. W. Say you so, then have at you.

(Lugs out and lets fly.)

Sir J. Oh heavens! I shall be drowned—this is *distilling* upon me with a vengeance.

(The waiter and some gentlemen now rush in, when the baronet is raised up, and he pulls out a *moidore* to purchase pistols; but the *moidore* being light, no arms can be had, and he considers this pissing assault as nothing more than the effects of the *diabetes*, with which his antagonist is violently afflicted.)

POETRY.

44 *The Pissing Conflict* – illustration from *The Covent Garden Magazine*, 1773

women of the present day do not hesitate to listen to jokes, and even to make them, upon subjects which among females of the corresponding class in England would be deemed highly improper'. French satires and humorous pieces on the 'cloacinan rites' were certainly as much read as those written in England.[14]

Most of this literature had flourished almost uninterruptedly from the more scurrilous classics like Juvenal to the medieval antifeminist scatology and down to Rabelais, Nashe, Rochester, Oldham, and such early eighteenth-century Grub Street writers as Tom Brown and Ned Ward. One should not forget that Latin was still being read in the eighteenth century; thus, partly comical treatises like *De flatibus humanum corpus molestantibus commentarius*, and collections such as the *Amphitheatrum*, both of sixteenth-century origin, were sources that were constantly tapped by writers after 1700. A few satirists, especially Swift, Pope, and Sterne, made judicious use of scatology in their works; but a great deal of what appeared was written with less ambition and meant merely to entertain. Some of these hilarious pieces of scatological humour are collected in *An Essay on Wind* (1783); *The New Boghouse Miscellany, or a Companion for the Close-Stool* (1761); and *The Merry-Thought: or, the Glass-Window and Bog-House Miscellany* (1731). In 1773 the rather fashionable *Covent Garden Magazine* published a piece which provides an idea of what was considered scatological fun in that decade. The dialogue, accompanied by an engraving and allegedly sent in by a reader, is entitled *The Pissing Conflict* (plate 44).

Given this scatological tradition in writing, and especially in satire, it is not surprising to notice that major authors like Swift and Sterne availed themselves in their satirical works of what had been written. In *A Tale of a Tub*, Swift mocks 'Enthusiastick Preachers' (i.e., Methodists) by associating them with an ingenious device for catching their farts to conduct them to their 'panting Disciples' greedily 'gaping after the sanctified Breath'. Ridiculing one's adversary in a scatological piece of writing was one of the more successful means of satirical attack. Ensuring the laughter and sympathy of the reading audience while creating a prejudice against the intended victim, scatology was used both in literary and in pictorial satire. *Frontis-piss*, from the 1730s (plate 45), which has been attributed to Hogarth, is a scatological comment on the contemporary disputes between Newton and Hutchinson. A theologian and writer, John Hutchinson tried to refute the Newtonian doctrine of gravitation, in *Glory and Gravity* (1733), maintaining that the Bible contained all elements of natural

45 Hogarth (?), *Frontis-Piss*, c. 1733

philosophy. The satirist has the Man in the Moon urinating on what he regards as ephemeral works that will rot and be forgotten in a short time.[15]

Since Jonathan Swift's scatological verse has been reassessed during recent years, it may be of some interest to comment on this discussion and to point out what remains to be done. Gradually, scholars seem to be recognising that a psychological, analytical approach is hardly a rewarding way to achieve a better understanding of Swift's scatology, especially if contemporary literary and popular backgrounds are not taken into account. In the case of Swift's so-called dirty poems it is particularly important to explore erotic folklore and the kind of popular writing Swift drew on, which we ignore or do not know. The Dean continued a two-fold tradition, that of classical writers like Juvenal and that of his own time. Harry Solomon has recently shown that if Swift is seen within his background, much of his scatological verse fits into the line of writing established by Rochester, Etheridge, D'Urfey, James Thurston, and Allan Ramsay. Most of these scurrilous and indecent works were published as pamphlets, and some in chapbooks; what has been recorded in bibliographies is just a small fraction at best, and even less is still extant. That Swift has been credited with a number of humorous scatological pieces from the early eighteenth century indicates, indeed, our ignorance of the background and the extent of popular scatological satire. It has been erroneously assumed that just because the Dean produced some scatological satires and poems he must have been singular in that respect. *Human Ordure, Botanically Considered* (1733); *The Grand Mystery* (1726); and *The Benefit of Farting Explained* (1722), as well as *A Dissertation upon Pissing* (1726), have all been attributed to him but are probably not by his hand. They are all humorous mock-treatises brimming with stercoraceous jokes. *The Grand Mystery, or Art of Meditating over an House of Office* was even translated into French, the translation claiming that the original was from the Dean's pen. This short satire has an ironic dedication to Dr Woodward, a well known physician and surgeon, and suggests that politics could benefit from the inspection of faeces, if the right people were charged with this duty. The author proposes the founding of academies where young people may learn to empty their bowels properly and in style. The final section drafts a project in twelve points for the building of public conveniences in London and Westminster. It is worth quoting the full title of the third piece, whose antifeminist stance has induced critics to ascribe it to Swift:

The Benefit of Farting explained: or, the Fundament-all Cause of the Distempers incident to the Fair Sex inquir'd into: Proving à posteriori most of the Disordures in-tail'd on 'em are owing to Flatulencies not Seasonably vented. Wrote in Spanish, by Don Fart in hando Puff-in-dorst, Professor of Bum bast in the University of Craccow. Translated into English; at the Request and for the Use of the Lady Damp, of Her-fart-shire. By Obadiah Fizle, Groom of the Stool to the Princess of Arse-Mini in Sardinia. The Sixth edition revis'd by a College of Fizz-icians. London 1722.

Swift's major scatological satires against women and the folly of love have found many commentators. Recent research puts Swift into a literary tradition starting with Juvenal and Ovid's *Remedia amoris* and reaching up to Restoration satires against women. But Swift's minor pieces have often been ignored, although they seem to show best his proximity to popular English humour of the beginning of the eighteenth century. There is, for instance, *Clad all in Brown*, a parody on the tenth poem of Cowley's *Mistress*, which shows Swift as a true disciple of Rabelais:

To Dick

Foulest Brute that stinks below,
   Why in this Brown dost thou appear?
For, would'st thou make a fouler Show,
   Thou must go naked all the Year.
Fresh from the Mud a wallowing Sow
Would then be not so brown as thou.

'Tis not the Coat that looks so dun,
   His Hide emits a Foulness out,
Not one Jot better looks the Sun
   Seen from behind a dirty Clout:
So T—rds within a Glass inclose
The Glass will seem as brown as those.

Thou now one Heap of Foulness art,
   All outward and within is foul;
Condensed Filth in e'ry Part,
   Thy Body's cloathed like thy Soul.
Thy Soul, which through thy Hide of Buff,
Scarce glimmers, like a dying Snuff.

Old carted Bawds such Garments wear,
   When pelted all with Dirt they shine;
Such their *exalted* Bodies are,
   As shrivelled and as black as thine.
If thou wer't in a Cart, I fear
Thou would'st be pelted worse than they're.

Yet when we see thee thus array'd,
  The Neighbours think it is but just
That thou shouldst take an Honest Trade,
  And weekly carry out our Dust.
Of cleanly Houses who will doubt,
When *Dick* cries, *Dust to carry out?*[16]

5 THE EXTENDED METAPHOR

Poets have always grappled with sex as a literary topic. Given the taboo character of sex and sexual relations, direct use of explicit sexual vocabulary in poetry and prose was often impossible; when it did occur it was in the form of an attack on social and moral standards. The poet's dilemma of not being allowed to use explicit language in the description of erotic topics gave birth to what Peter Fryer has termed the extended metaphor. This was, and still is, the poetic method of depicting the genital anatomy, and sex, in biological, geographical, mechanical, and historical-political analogies. The technique of describing the sexual organs of the human body in a language that is allusive and inoffensive can be traced back to Roman and Greek authors. In the eighteenth century this way of writing was again popularised, by such works on copulation as Charles Borde's *Parapilla* (1776), a free adaptation of Antonio Vignale's 'La novelle dell' Angelo Gabriello' from *Il libro del perchè* of 1757, and published with obscene and pornographic illustrations; and M.P.J. Bernard's (*alias* Gentil-Bernard) *L'art d'aimer*, a successful poetic manual of love. The border between such erotic-allusive poetry and aggressively obscene writings like *La foutro-manie* (1780), also printed with engravings, was not always well defined; ribaldry often became obscenity. Here is an example from England, entitled *The Members to their Sovereign*, which likens the penis to a king.

What, tho' with Blood thy Conquests oft are stain'd,
To either Party's Joy they still are gained;
Nor doest thou swell, Vainglorious, with Success,
But after Action still retir'd, and less,
The Hero and the Sage at once confess.
. . .
Strong as thou art, thy stubborn Neck must yield,
One day, reluctant, thou must quit the Field,
Then shall the Nymphs thy drooping Head deride,
Tho' now the Maiden's Dream, and Matron's Pride.

...
Rather when old, and loaded with Renown,
A Priapism all your Labours crown,
And may you prove the D–do of the Town.[17]

The majority of English ribald facetiae exploiting the historical-
political metaphor have French or Italian ancestors. Influential works
were Godard de Beauchamps, *Histoire du prince Apprius* (1728); the
sixteenth-century *L'origine des cons sauvages*; and *Il libro del perchè*.
Originally written as a satire against the Regent, Godard's 'history'
proved equally successful in England, when Curll had it translated, in
1728; and its popularity endured until the last decade of the century
and its final publication, in *The Bon Ton Magazine*. *The History of
King Apprius* provides a brief description of the 'upbringing' of the
king (i.e., Priapus or penis), with anagrams, or almost anagrams, being
used throughout the tale, and traces his travels through the land of the
Gnifers (fingers) and the evil Grifeggs (friggers). Saved by Prince
Stoperiors (posteriors), Apprius soon loathes the country of this
potentate, which gives the author ample opportunity to ridicule
homosexuals. Eventually, Apprius makes the acquaintance of Princess
Gontue (tongue), and is led by her to Queen Nicnulia's (cunnilingus)
court. There he meets, among other characters, the Barits (tribades),
Litocris (clitoris), and the Liddoes (dildoes). When the Stoperiors start
a war, Apprius valiantly defends Nicnulia, and then 'encounters' the
queen in triumph.

   Admittedly, from what we consider an advantageous modern viewpoint, many of these humorous erotica employing analogies seem
childish, if not primitive; but the fact remains that they were popular
in the eighteenth century and are part of an erotic folklore which,
ignored by our 'literary' histories, has almost completely disappeared.
These writings were hardly ever pornographic, and mirror the taste
of a readership that was not as sophisticated as one might have
expected.[18]

   A great deal has already been written on geographical or topographical allegory in eighteenth-century erotica, notably by David
Foxon, Peter Fryer, and Roger Thompson.[19] The botanical-biological
allegory in erotic facetiae is much more in need of research. What has
been ignored in the past is the close relation between scientific research
and its satirical reflection in humorous short writings. Such satire
indicates the immediate reaction to the publication or discussion of
research results that many writers and their readers were not prepared
to accept. The shady and seedy world of quackery provided more than

sufficient material for criticism by satirists. Behind the satirical attacks on scientists and would-be-scientists there also lurked a surprisingly unenlightened spirit, condemning progress and, since it was now unfashionable to talk of devilry, trying to ridicule with scatological and ribald satire scientific advancement. To understand ribaldry about botany, as published in the eighteenth century, it is necessary to recall that by 1700, in several European countries and even in America, hundreds of devotees were engaged in botanic research. What irritated the moralists and tickled the fancy of satirists in particular was the terminology and the classification system of the botanists, who claimed that plants had a sex life. In 1672 Nehemiah Grew and Thomas Millington discovered the sexuality of plants; in 1694 their findings were confirmed by a German, Jakob Camerarius. And in 1716 Cotton Mather, New England's busybody in theology and science, provided evidence of plants' sexuality in a letter from America to the Royal Society. By the third decade of the century – especially after Philip Miller had reported on plant fertilisation by bees, in 1721 – it was almost generally accepted by biologists that plants had a sort of sex life. Both Miller, in his *Catalogus Plantarum* of 1730, and Linnaeus, in his monumental new classification system published in the following years, put much emphasis on this. In the *Systema Naturae* (1735), for instance, Linnaeus used as a basis for his system the presence and kind, or the absence, of reproductive organs in plants, dividing them into 'phanerogams' (plants with visible organs) and 'cryptogams' (plants with hidden reproductive structures). Linnaeus was a religious man and a firm believer in God – his *Nemesis Divina* is sufficient proof – and he used a terminology inspired by religious-moral teaching on sexuality. Hence his delight in personifying plants, and the almost sacramental description of their reproduction. Linnaeus speaks of 'weddings', and uses expressions like 'the nuptial bed', and 'husbands and wives enjoy separate beds'. This insistence on the sexuality of plants caused much criticism. Where moralists objected, satirists attacked with laughter and irony. In the wake of Miller's catalogue of 1730 a number of ribald satires made fun of botanists and gardeners. Thomas Stretser's *Arbor vitae: or, The Tree of Life* (1732) was one of the first works to become well known. It was often emulated. By 1741 the *Arbor vitae* sold at sixpence and consisted of twenty-one pages, the first part being in prose while Part II was in verse. This quotation will show how *The Tree of Life* parodies contemporary botanical terminology, in *doubles entendres* and sexual allusions.

The tree is of slow Growth, and requires Time to bring it to Perfection, rarely seeding to any purpose before the Fifteenth Year; when the Fruits coming to good Maturity, yield a viscious Juice or balmy SUCCUS, which being from Time to Time discharged at the *Pistillum*, is mostly bestow'd upon the open *Calyx's* of the FRUTEX VULVARIA, or FLOW'RING SHRUB, usually spreading under the Shade of this Tree, and whose Parts are by a wonderful Mechanism, adapted to receive it. The ingenious Mr *Richard* BRADLEY is of Opinion, the FRUTEX is hereby impregnated, and then first begins to bear; he therefore accounts this SUCCUS the FARINA FAECUNDANS of the Plant; and the learned LEONARD FUCKSIUS, in his HISTORIA STIRPIUM INSIGNORIUM, observes the greatest Sympathy between this Tree and Shrub, THEY ARE, says he OF THE SAME GENUS, AND DO BEST IN THE SAME BED; THE vulvaria ITSELF BEING INDEED NO OTHER THAN A FEMALE arbor vitae.

In *Wisdom Revealed: or The Tree of Life Discover'd . . . By a Studious Enquirer Into the Mysteries of Nature* (1750), which admits its indebtedness to the 'arbor vitae' in the preface, young Philander meets a girl in the country. Forced under a tree because of rain, they begin a conversation, and hit upon the tree of life, a plant the girl only knows from the Bible. Philander, however, informs her that in Jamaica it is called the 'dildoe Tree'. Asked about its height and texture, he explains to her:

> The Height, quoth He, some Folks will tell ye,
> Would (with Submission) reach your B—y;
> . . .
> For tho' a Lady's Hand 'twill kiss,
> Should she with too much Ardour touch:
> Should the Sensation move too much.

As can be expected, Philander ends up by exhibiting his own 'tree' to the girl.

Mimosa or the Sensitive Plant (1779) has been attributed to James Perry, and slanders aristocrats such as the Duke of Queensberry (his mistress, Kitty Fisher, is referred to in the 'dedication'), while also ridiculing botanists and scientists like Banks, Miller, Hale, and Owen. Sir Joseph Banks was Scientific Adviser to the Royal Gardens at Kew. He became associated with sexual promiscuity, through reports of the customs of Tahiti, which he had visited with Cook on the *Endeavour* voyage. In the introduction to *Mimosa*, Banks is mocked as a botanist with great experience of the plant (i.e., penis) who has 'planted the seed of the sensitive Plant in so many different soils'. Familiar metaphors like 'plants' and 'flowerbeds' are then exploited for the umpteenth time, and applied to members of the aristocracy:

> So said the Marchioness of C –
> When she was broght to *feel*, and *see*
> Her L–ds–p's *plant* erected.
> His Grace now says, the Lady's touch,
> For his poor *plant*, was over much;
> It shrunk and grew dejected.

The fate of an impotent nobleman's wife is thus reported:

> Who does not pity Lady B.
> Fated, nor to feel, nor see
> The plant, altho' she's wed.
> What, tho' my Lord is two *yards* high;
> She cannot, for her life descry,
> One y... when he's abed.

After a comparison of the English mimosa with foreign samples, Perry explains how homosexuals make use of the plant, again slandering various aristocrats:

> And tho' most singers are without
> Yet Hali–x did find it out,
>   And praised it in Leoni.
> . . .
> Can Botanists find out the cause,
> That contrary to nature's laws,
>   Some people can abuse it?
> St–t claps it in his valet's b–m;
> H–ll fingers it, and some
> Like Dorm–r never use it.

Those who could not decipher the names, some of them already quite obvious, could find help in the footnotes, which alluded to various affairs of the persons mentioned.

It would be surprising if the female genitals, after so much ribaldry on the 'tree' and the 'mimosa', had not been made an object of bawdy humour in this context. If Stretser, Perry, and their nameless imitators celebrated the 'arbor vitae', the anonymous 'Philogynes Clitorides' wrote thirty-six pages in 1741 on *The Natural History of the Frutex Vulvaria or The Flowering Shrub*. It offers the same sort of entertainment as can be found in the writings cited above.[20] In 1746 was published *Teague-root Display'd: Being Some Useful and Important Discoveries Tending to Illustrate the Doctrine of Electricity, in a Letter from Paddy Strong-Cock to W(illiam) W(atso)N*. This ridicules useless discoveries, and mocks the Fellows of the Royal Society. Apparently, one scientist had published a treatise on how to light spirits with an electrified finger (when one could use a light instead); and the poem proposes to try the same experiment with 'Teague-root'. The female specimen is thus described:

> It would divert you to see a Female Root, where it is highly electrical, how it will wriggle itself about, twist, squeeze, and gape, as if it would swallow the Male in its voracious Jaws.

The author reports that such roots can also be 'electrified':

> It is to be observed, that these Roots are truly Electricals per se, because, lay them near one another, only in the same Room uncover'd, they become Electrical ... Either of them may be made Electrical by Friction only; without the Intervention of each other ... I know a certain Virtuoso-Lady, that constantly imports a Cargoe of Male-Roots from IRELAND to divert her.

Finally, the author proposes to the Fellows of the Royal Society a 'parcel of fresh young female Roots' that 'have never yet been Electrify'd by Contact'.

James Perry's *The Electrical Eel: or, Gymnotus Electricus* (1777), which he published under the telling name of 'Adam Strong', also alludes to contemporary experiments with electricity. Inscribed to the 'honourable members of the Royal Society', the poem drew on a series of satirical ribaldry from other pens, some of these answers allegedly written by ladies addressing themselves to the 'eel'. One 'Lucretia Lovejoy, sister of Mr Adam Strong', published *An Elegy on the Lamented Death of the Electrical Eel* (1778). This satire made fun of the eel as well as of Gray's famous poem of 1750, the *Elegy Written in a Country Churchyard*. Ridiculing, among other notables, the 'Chevalier-Madame D'Eon de Beaumont', the poem speaks in praise of the great achievements of the deceased eel:

> That Eel which stood erect in beauty's pride,
>   And nodded to and fro its coral head,
> Worship'd by untaught Indians far and wide,
>   Like other creatures, is not stiff, tho' dead.
>
> Limber and lank the heaven-born charmer lies,
>   From every virgin's hand with scorn 'tis hurl'd;
> No maid can make the poor Torpedo rise,
>   Limp as a dish-clout – it forsakes the world.
>
> ...
> For him no more the baking-stones shall burn,
>   Or loving housewife make her evening care;
> No more for butter shall he move her churn,
>   Or climb her knees – the eager kiss to share.

Now weep, Ambition, all thy pride is sunk,
  And, Grandeur, feel – if ought can make thee feel!
The equal bliss of peeress and of punk
  Is dead – and gone in the ELECTRIC EEL.

The satire brims with such *doubles entendres* and sexual allusions to contemporary nobility, and ends with an 'inscription' to the Chevalier D'Eon and the Countess of H[alifax?]:

Here
Rests – without further Hope of Resurrection,
The Elastic
Body
of
THE ELECTRICAL EEL, or GYMNOTUS ELECTRICUS
which
Hath been proved by those who dive deep –
into the Secrets of Nature,
to be
That sinful Serpent – that seduced Eve.
Since
which Paradisiacal Period – it hath been held
in universal
Estimation by the Fair-Sex,
In all Hours, in all Climes, in all Seasons, and in all Families,
it hath been kindly taken in:
Nursed, cherished, delighted and enraptured:
The secret Confident of the most secret Characters:
which Confidence
Was never betrayed by Words – but,
by Births.
No Creature in Nature was ever so coveted;
not Man excepted.
Maids, Wives, and Widows,
made it
Their Darling and Delight:
and such
was their Courtesy, Reverence, and Worship
of it –
That whenever it rose in their Presence,
Like adoring Persians,
They fell flat to it – but not upon their Faces.
In Camps, in Courts, in Cabinets, in Cots,
in
Fields, in Lanes,
in
Groves and Meads,

It was the Solace of the secret Hour:
The
Maiden's Wish – and lovely Wife's
Delight.
. . .
It
filled the Hands of a Peasant's Wife, and
slipped through the Fingers
of a Queen.
Yet with all its Faults and Virtues,
Vices and Qualities – it was
the RARA AVIS of the World,
and not
unlike the Neck of a black Swan.
To its
Illustrious Uses, and noble Feats,
in Armour and without,
the
COUNTESS OF H———————, AND MADAME
EON DE BEAUMONT,
have erected these precious Stones;
on
which this Inscription is engraved, to
the Honour
and
Memory of
THE   ELECTRICAL   EEL;
in
the Year of the world 5782,
and of its Age.

Among the numerous ribald replies to the 'eel' it will suffice to quote from *The Torpedo*, which, within a year of its publication in 1777, was selling in a fourth edition, and was still being advertised two years later. It mocked John Hunter, the surgeon, and Lord Cholmondeley. The latter was thus addressed:

> You descend to every thing. You have the goodness to make the Female World your particular care, and to take the Ladies under you, to whom you have an uncommon method of conveying instruction, uniting Pleasure with Improvement ... Have you not been remarked for your laudable enquiries after Innocence?

The poem itself, in ballad metre, is concerned with the history of the 'torpedo' as recorded in mythology:

> Job, too, if Scripture you believe
> Us'd to feel me from morn till eve,
>   And wish'd for nothing more:
> So fond he grew of my warm touch,
> He took by chance a stroke too much,
>   And made himself *all sore*.
>
> …

Several noble ladies are mocked along the way, among them Lady Grosvenor and the Countess of Strathmore:

> Though oft electrified before,
> Still pants the Countess of St—thm—e
>   For one more stout and boney.
> Long has she tasted, some folks say,
> Each different sort from Black to GRAY
>   But fixt on that of St—n—y.

The Torpedo ends with the almost customary attack on the 'mollies':

> Me only Sodom's Sons disclaim,
> Born for foul deeds, which but to name
>   Would shock the modest mind:
> Bent on destroying all our race,
> Assassin-like, they shun the face,
>   And meanly stab behind.

In the early nineteenth century Thomas Rowlandson summed up this ribald tradition of writing about 'eels' and 'torpedos', in a picture entitled *Meditations Among the Tombs* (plate 46): the illustration alludes both to Gray's solemn elegy and to the libertine tradition of celebrating the joys of copulation.[21] French publications of a similar nature also circulated in England.[22]

When assessed today, erotica concerned with sexual allegory are for the most part of little poetic value. A modern reader has trouble appreciating the humour of these works, which cover the obscene as well as the scurrilous and mildly salacious. To many of us, this poetry seems coarse, often childish and primitive. One often tends to forget that such ribald satire was extremely popular and represents an oral tradition in literature. Reading prose and reciting poems to friends and acquaintances came to a halt some time in the nineteenth century. If today we cannot appreciate a large part of what has been discussed in this chapter, it is partly because we find its blatant sexism disturbing, and partly because much of this literature was meant to be heard in convivial gatherings, rather than to be read privately. Edward W. Pitcher has shown that eighteenth-century short fiction has strong oral

46 Rowlandson, *Meditations Among the Tombs, c.* 1815–20

narrative patterns; but, in the twentieth century, reading has become a private experience. When the members of the pseudo-knightly Beggar's Benison club, of Anstruther, Scotland, met in the eighteenth century, they were entertained with ribald poetry, prose dissertations on the act of generation and on the male and female organs, and – on one occasion in 1737 (if the records can be trusted) – with a reading of the manuscript of *Fanny Hill*. Ribald poems and jests were a common form of entertainment in clubs, pubs, and coffee-houses. To read them privately, of course, reduces these erotica to essentially humorous writings; but at the same time they are subjected to a process of aesthetic reception that drains them of the value achieved through public recital. We ought to bear in mind, therefore, that much of this literature was written to be delivered orally, and that we have lost this oral tradition.[23]

❦ 7 ❦

Erotic Prose

To the modern reader, the literature produced between 1700 and 1800 presents a problem, in that there exists no clear-cut distinction that would help to isolate 'short story' from 'novel', 'novella' from 'tale', and fictional narrative from non-fictional narrative. Short tales were often published as 'novels', tales appeared 'versify'd', and novels were printed in the form of rhymed letters. The picture is even more confused when one looks at the erotic fiction which frequently parodied literary genres.

Any order that is imposed on this period of the rise of the novel must therefore be an artificial one, that helps the modern reader by creating categories unknown to eighteenth-century writers. In view of this dilemma a division of erotic fiction into short prose writings and the novel would seem to be an acceptable solution.[1] This chapter provides an idea of the scope of eighteenth-century erotic prose fiction in its various genres, from short tales to the novel, and including journalism and plays. Its central part is the rise and proliferation of the erotic novel and of pornography.

I SHORT PROSE FICTION

It is especially in the various forms of short prose fiction that the long literary tradition of the erotic novella and the tale can be seen, from Apuleius and Lucian, whose story about a man 'metamorphosed' into an ass was often revived, to Boccaccio, Cervantes, Chaucer, and La Fontaine (plate 47). Erotic tales by these authors, and those from the

Il deviendra parfait ce Commode Cuvier :
Je vois autour de lui que plus d'un ouvrier
Apousser le travail d'un grand cœur se présente :
Aucun deux ne paroît de ses membres perclus ;
L'un frape par dedans, l'autre coigne dessus
L'un répare des trous, l'autre bouche une fente

Le Cuvier

47 Gravelot, *Le cuvier*, 1740, for an edition of the tales by La Fontaine

Heptaméron and the *Cent nouvelles nouvelles*, appeared as reprints throughout the eighteenth century, and served as models for modern adaptations. Thus the ten tales assembled in Juan Manuel's *The Spanish Decameron: or, Ten Novels*, translated by Sir Roger L'Estrange and selling in a third edition by 1712, are clearly written in the manner of Boccaccio. Although some titles in this collection of short tales totalling between thirty and fifty pages sound titillating – for example, 'The Libertine', 'The Virgin Captive', and 'The Perfidious Mistress' – they are quite decent by eighteenth-century standards, and more soporific than erotic. An interesting English collection from the early part of the century is John Curll's *Atterburyana* (1727), a hotchpotch of miscellanies including two tales by John Clarke, 'The Virgin-Seducer' and 'The Batchelor-Keeper'. What makes both tales noteworthy is that they try to combine libertine with moral elements.

Like novelists, writers of erotic tales quarried any literary genre in their search for promising material, including the 'chronique scandaleuse'. Numerous fictional publications promised 'secret memoirs', for example, *The Fair Adulteress* of 1743; or 'secret histories', as did *The Fair Concubine* (1782). *The Fair Adulteress* is a tale of forty-eight pages, 'translated from the Greek', and is concerned with the intrigues of 'a certain noble family in the island of Cyprus'. It holds to a veiled and circumstantial style in the description of erotic encounters and is thus typical of the sentimental novel. *The Fair Concubine* displays a similar diction relating the 'secret history of the beautiful Vanella' and her 'amours' at the Greek court. The tale follows her way up, so to speak, through the beds of several princes, until one of them rewards Vanella with a house and a pension. The numerous love scenes are written in a manner which female readers of the time would not find offensive. Other examples obviously catering to a female readership are Cleland's *The Surprizes of Love* (1765) and the anonymous *The Midnight Ramble: or The Adventures of Two Noble Females* (1754).

The bawdy tale, however, continued to prosper as well. Essentially, it had the characteristics of its sibling, the verse tale. Comic situations are described in a realistic and sometimes coarse language, the general aim being ribald laughter. In *A Spy on Mother Midnight* (1748) a young man writes to his friend about his successful seduction of a country girl. Disguised as a woman – 'Miss Polly' – he engages his intended victim in a conversation turning into bawdy talk. This fires the spirits of the young lady to such an extent that she wants 'Miss Polly' as her bedfellow. Once in bed, the girl confesses she would like to try a dildo, and the disguised lover offers to guide it for her. Of

course, she does not realise until the end that what 'Miss Polly' uses is
not a dildo but something quite natural. Such bawdry was obviously
written by men for men, and sold in pamphlets and chapbooks,
sometimes with engravings. Examples are *A Curious Collection of
Novels* (1731); Edmund Curll's *The School of Venus, or The Lady's
Miscellany* (1739), which deliberately hints at Michel Millot's well-
known pornographicum, *L'escole des filles*; and *The Cabinet of
Amorous Curiosities*, published by 'R. Borewell' in 1786.

Related to this coarsely humorous branch of short fiction are those
tales which deal with prostitution and rakes. In 1711 *The London-
Bawd* was selling in its fourth edition; it is typical of this genre and
must be seen in the tradition of Boccaccio. The various chapters of this
book introduce the world of prostitution with sketches and dialogues
of bawds, pimps, panders, and whores; but there are also short stories
taken from earlier collections, such as 'How a Young Woman, by the
help of an Old Bawd, Enjoy'd her Lover, and Deceiv'd her Husband',
'How a Citizen went to a Bawdy-House for a Whore, and the Bawd
helpt him to his own Wife', and 'How a Gentleman that fell in Love
with another Man's Wife, through the Advice of a Bawd, enjoy'd her'.
Other examples of such tales can be found among the numerous
writings of Ned Ward, at the beginning of the eighteenth century, such
as *The Metamorphosed Beau* and *The Rambling Rakes* (1700), *Three
Nights Adventures* (1701), and *The Amorous Bugbears* (1725). Brimming with vulgar imagery and vigorous colloquialisms, Ward's prose
is ideally suited for the genre of the bawdy tale. Later ribaldry shows
the influence of Ward's almost journalistic style; *The Progress of a
Rake* (1732), for instance, is a bawdy report in forty-seven pages on
the sexual exploits of a libertine in the famous haunts of London's
Drury Lane.[2]

Towards the end of the century, short prose fiction developed a
most peculiar branch combining sentimental, pornographic, and prurient elements. An anonymous chapbook with the title *Amorous
Sketches: By Master Cupid* (c. 1796) assembled 'six capital engravings' with corresponding texts. The quality of the pictures is as poor as
that of the prose. The tale for plate 1, which shows a couple on a sofa –
the woman with exposed breasts – is 'The Virgin Wife' and recounts in
a sentimental-pathetic manner the tragic love story of a young man in
Hamburgh [sic]. He falls in love with Emilia, his stepmother and the
new wife of his aged father. When the old man dies, the son is
prevented by law from marrying Emilia. However, a friend persuades
them to prove to the court their true love. This can only be done with a

courageous deed to which Emilia agrees. The execution is described thus:

> She flew into my arms, and glued her lips on mine; her bosom heaved like the raging billows in a storm; in the ardour of our embraces, her handkerchief got loose, and my lips became fixed, as if by accident, on these delightful swelling globes. My blood instantly caught fire, and burned to a point, in which all the fluid virtue of my body was concentrated, by the flames that irresistibly continued spreading. Need I, can I, paint the ensuing scene!... We successively, that day, tasted of the forbidden fruit.

The court is informed of these scenes out of wedlock and sends spies to surprise the lovers:

> One afternoon, giving a loose to the delights of Venus, Emilia suffered me to fondle with her on the sopha; till, one encroachment succeeding another, at length I had nothing to request, nor she to grant. Her bosom was again exposed, by what had previously occurred; the tide of passion began again to beat high; I was about to launch once more into the sea of bliss; when a spy of power, who had been artfully hidden under a dressing table ... gave a signal to two associates ... finding us precisely in the situation, as represented by the opposite Plate. So great was our consternation, that we suffered these hirelings to make us prisoners ... and before the judges, we made a full and free confession... The result, however, was close imprisonment – but in different jails. – At the end of four months, I found means to effect my escape, when ... I learnt that the dear partner of my joys had died of rage and disappointment, cursing our persecutors with her latest breath.

The second story, about a fornicating alderman, is as poor in quality; while the other plates are accompanied by direct commentary, one showing 'his grace of Queensberry, peeping at the Curiosities of four abandoned women of the town', and another 'the far-famed Countess of Strathmore in three most critical Situations'.[3]

If there was one genre of fictional narrative that was popular among readers at all levels of the contemporary reading public it was the fairy tale, and its relation, the oriental tale. The fairy tale was at times mimicked in bawdy writings. *The Gallant Companion* of 1746 has two 'fairy tales', one entitled 'The Hobgoblin, or the Amorous Sylph', and the other 'The Cat's Paw'. But it was the oriental tale that became a great fad – and so did its parodies.

It is not always easy to pin down the exact reasons for the emergence of any literary current; but the great vogue of the oriental tale is certainly to be seen in relation to Jean Antoine Galland's translation of *The Thousand Nights and A Night*, published for the first time as *Les mille et une nuits* in twelve volumes between 1704 and 1717.

Montesquieu then conceived of a foreign philosophical traveller, in his *Lettres persanes* (1721), as being a better cover for his own socio-political criticism. He was eagerly imitated, in England by George Lyttelton's *Letters from a Persian in England* (1735); and by his own countrymen: the Marquis d'Argens, for instance, published his influential *Lettres chinoises* in 1739. A handy device for frequently severe satire in France, the oriental tale was less aggressive in England, and did not take long to develop an erotic-satirical branch. By the late seventeenth century England already had an amusement periodical, entitled *The Turkish Spy* (1687 and 1694); and after 1700 a great number of French erotic tales poured into the country, from Holland and France. By 1714 two volumes of *The Persian and the Turkish Tales*, by François Petis de la Croix *fils*, had been published. They were followed in 1736 by T. S. Gueulette's *Mongul Tales* (two volumes), and, still later, by Hawkesworth's *Almoran and Hamet, an Oriental Tale* (1761). It is obvious that in this area, as in the field of the 'conte galant' generally, British short fiction is greatly indebted to France. Whether it was Crébillon's clever parodies of the *conte de fée* and the *conte oriental*, or Diderot's *Ceci n'est pas un conte* (1773), or even the ribald tales by Caylus, Duclos, and de Ligne, they were almost all known and read in England.[4]

The overpowering French dominance in this field is best understood when one considers Hogarth's hidden and subtle hint at Crébillon's *Le sopha* (1742), in his pictorial series, *Marriage à la Mode* of 1746 (plate 34d): on the sofa, beside Counsellor Silvertongue, lies a book whose title reads *Le Sopha*. Assuming that his audience knows what he means, Hogarth merely shows the book title to suggest the moral turpitude of the Counsellor and indeed of the whole circle of sycophants around the Countess. He could do this, because the book, like many other French oriental tales (or rather affected oriental tales), was extremely popular and as much read and discussed as Diderot's later *Les bijoux indiscrets* of 1748. Because of its closeness to the pornographic novel, both in form and content, it is necessary to take a closer look at this particular kind of erotic tale.

Crébillon *fils* has generally been credited with ushering in this wave of licentious 'oriental' narratives; but it is obvious that he borrowed from Galland's translation of the *Arabian Nights*, as well as from the French *fabliaux*, and earlier eighteenth-century works like *Le canapé couleur de feu* of 1714. This tale – often confused with *Le sopha*, and erroneously attributed to Fougeret de Monbron – was astonishingly successful, equal to that of Crébillon's own work. Translated into

English in 1742 as *The Settee; or, The Chevalier Commodo Meta-morphosed*, *Le canapé* parodies the literary genre of the fairy tale, in the story of a knight transformed into a dog, by Pritanière, a 'fée'. Serving as her lapdog, with a *double entendre* in the word, he witnesses several scenes of sexual perversion. The knight-dog proves unwilling to comply with the bizarre sexual wishes of Queen Crapaudine; whereupon she gets extremely angry and transforms him into a sofa. There is, however, a happy ending, showing the 'chevalier' back in his human shape. Crébillon then took this tale as a basis for his *Le sopha*, adding to it elements from *The Thousand Nights and A Night*, metempsychosis, and much political bite. *Le sopha* appeared in 1742 and was immediately translated into English. Hogarth's series, mentioned above, suggests that by 1746 it was a very well-known book. Its narrator, Amanzéi, is charged with entertaining a weary and bored sultan – the parallels with Scheherazade in the *Arabian Nights* are quite obvious – and tells him stories about his former lives. In one of these lives, Amanzéi reports, he was a sofa in Agra (i.e., Paris). The ten episodes he tells about the sofa are to prove his thesis that very few women, from their sofas' viewpoints, are virtuous and chaste. Crébillon is, however, not merely interested in the exploitation of the erotic possibilities the framework of this narrative allows. In a sort of parade on the sofa he also demonstrates the sexual mores of his contemporaries, while developing his own view of love, expressed in the dualism of 'amour', the ideal form; and 'goût', the sensual aspect of love. Thus *Le sopha*, while admittedly being highly erotic, definitely deserves its subtitle – 'a moral tale' – for the sofa becomes a place where representative types of eighteenth-century French society reveal themselves in the double sense of the word. Although not a novel, this is an excellent book of great literary value, and proved extremely influential.[5]

Diderot's *Indiscreet Toys* of 1749 (the French original, *Les bijoux indiscrets* appeared one year earlier) also belongs to this category of licentious oriental tales; though if one judged by length alone one would have to call it a novel. The story is derived from a medieval *fabliau, Le chevalier qui faisait parler les cons*, which Diderot probably read in an adaptation by Caylus, entitled *Nocrion, conte allobroge* (1747). The plot introduces another bored sultan in need of being entertained by someone at his court. Upon the advice of his favourite concubine he calls a ghost, who is to help him find out about the erotic adventures of the court ladies. The ghost hands the sultan a ring with a jewel. When pointed at the 'jewel' (*double entendre*) of a lady, this ring

obliges her to reveal all her amorous escapades. The following is what
Vartanian has termed an 'eighteenth-century Kinsey report in fiction,
with twenty-nine interviews', recording the scandalous involuntary
confessions of the court ladies during public receptions given by the
sultan. It is also surprisingly modern in its treatment of such topics as
dreaming and the subconscious and contains observations confirmed
much later by Freud and his disciples.

When such French prose narratives were translated into English, an
interesting phenomenon occurred. They were originally intended as
satires on French society and what were then called 'les gens du
monde'. As the century advanced they also absorbed much of the
libertine ideology – Crébillon and Diderot are just two examples of a
number of authors. This ideology reached England couched in the
frame of the oriental tale. It is very likely that many of the veiled
allusions in these tales escaped the English readers; and one can also
assume that there was no great response to the libertine message, for
England's social and political situation was, after all, not as explosive
as that of France. Nevertheless, the tales had sufficient erotic appeal to
make them equally popular with English readers. By all one can tell,
the English did not mind any additional political or philosophical
undercurrent. Another reason which may help to explain the great
success of such tales is their similarity with the pornographic novel,
both formally and thematically. Invariably, the tales figure a narrator
reporting from the viewpoint of a voyeur. Often this narrator is not
human; and the form of the report is that of a 'confession'. If one adds
to this the location, frequently a 'nowhere land', the step from the
erotic oriental tale to the pornographic novel seems to be a short one
indeed. Saisselin has argued that for the readers of oriental tales the
harem – a constant *topos* in this literature – became a private male
aspiration if not an obsession. This is confirmed by Thomas Rowlandson's illustrations alluding to oriental tales, such as *The Harem* (plate
48). From a psychological point of view, it is noteworthy that a male
dominates a group of women whose only purpose is to provide sexual
satisfaction for the sultan or 'Pasha'.

Towards the end of the century the gothic tale assumes a similar
function. Like contemporary novels, such tales thrived on the by then
conventional practice of condemning and attacking monasteries as
locations of vice and corruption. Pitcher has shown that such tales as
'The Nun', published in two parts in *The European Magazine* between
May and June 1794, were written as much under the influence of the
gothic taste as of French fiction.[6]

48 Rowlandson, *The Harem*, early nineteenth century

2. THE NOVEL

2.1 *The Erotic Novel*

The appearance and proliferation of the novel were the great literary surprise of the eighteenth century. For some time, critical observers continued to regard it as a new-fangled invention; but its victorious advance could not be stopped. By 1753, a critic voiced his disapproval of novels in *The World*:

> The thing I chiefly find fault with is their extreme indecency. There are certain vices which the vulgar call fun, and the people of fashion gallantry; but the middle rank, and those of the gentry who continue to go to church, still stigmatize them by the opprobrious names of fornication and adultery.

Before long the critics of immorality in literature were in the majority, and began to impose their middle-class standards of what they termed decency upon the new literary genre. The rule of the libertine, at least as far as the nature and content of openly published fiction was concerned, was coming to an end, although the stream of licentious and coarse novels took some time to peter out, until it disappeared into an underground.

The major English novelists did not shy away from the themes of love and sex. Daniel Defoe, in *Moll Flanders* (1722) and *Roxana* (1724), of which chapbook versions with woodcuts also circulated, dealt with seduction, adultery, polyandry, voyeurism, and incest. Defoe's ostentatious prudery covers an incipient undercurrent of pornography that is recognisable in his novels. Richardson, headmaster of bourgeois fiction, tried to contain the erotic within his smug ethics; while Fielding and Smollett offered much coarser substance and a broader style. Richardson and Fielding were antagonists, with different views of how sex was to be treated and shown in the novel. Boucé has shown the central significance in *Tom Jones* of Henry Fielding's handling of the theme of sex. Contemporary illustrations for editions of this novel stressed the erotic-sexual aspect – and so did licentious parodies and sequels like *The History of Tom Jones the Foundling in His Married State* (1750). Smollett's use of bawdry in *Roderick Random* and *Peregrine Pickle* may be conventional, yet it is still quite obvious. Richardson is an even more interesting case, not least because he was concerned about his novels 'debauching' the minds of his readers. A bigot at heart, he wanted the works of Swift, Pope, and Sterne to be burnt, and he charged Fielding with 'lowness'. Ironically enough, it was Richardson's *Pamela* which the Vatican put on its *Index librorum prohibitorum*, the only major eighteenth-century English novel to suffer this fate, except for Sterne's *A Sentimental Journey*. In 1773 *The Covent Garden Magazine* published another, more aggressive, satire on Sterne – *The Life and Opinions of Timotheus Randy, Stay-Maker*. When *A Sentimental Journey* had appeared, it was equally parodied. One 'Timothy Touchit' published *La Souricière – The Mousetrap, a Facetious and Sentimental Excursion through Part of Austrian Flanders and France* (1794), in which there is an over-emphasis on sexual adventures. 'Touchit' continues where Sterne drew the curtain. Here is an example:[7]

The Barometer

I arose early in the morning, and found the *Barometer of health* risen to its *utmost elevation*; and contrary to the *Torricellian Baroscope* when at the highest, the *bottom of the Tube* was greatly over-charged with *Mercury*. – It was not a preternatural tension, though it so abundantly exceeded that on the road from *Ghent* to *Alost* the day before...

Finding, by its great and continued elevation, that, according to *Anatomical cant*, the *Pyramidalia* had been too assiduous in supplying the *testiculi* with an abundant stock of the *vivifying fluid*, I began to be alarmed for the consequence of such a repletion; for where there is irritation we are to expect inflammation, and where there is inflammation a conflagration generally succeeds.

I was contemplating on my situation, and had filled my mind with various apprehensions, just as the *Fille de chambre* knocked at my door to acquaint me it was time to rise. I did not tell her I had *risen* hours before, but went to the door, and unlocking it, desired her in a whisper, to run for *un Médecin*. She came into the room, and I wanted words, in her language, to tell my complaint; but it was *too visible* to be mistaken. She had been used to the care of *sick guests*, and knew something of the cure of diseases. – 'Ne craignez rien,' said she, looking full at me, 'il ne fera plus de mal.' – On this she *prepared what I wanted*, and by *collision* effected a *deliquation*, which produced a very *happy crisis*; and after *repeating the application* three or four times, *pro re nata*, as physicians say, the *elevation of the Barometer* fell down to *changeable*, and I became relieved and composed. – It was a speedy, agreeable cure, and I never knew the *Mouse-trap* more serviceable than it was on this occasion.

You are a good doctor, and are used to these complaints, said I to the *Fille de chambre*. 'O qu'oui, Monsieur, tous les jours,' said she. 'I must now go to a *French gentleman* in the next apartment, who is troubled with *the same disorder*, but not in so violent a degree. *It is trifling*; only *a slight symptom*.'

(II, 1–6)

While it is true that Sterne and other lovers of the *double entendre* wrote in a literary tradition (eighteenth-century translations of Petronius' *Satyricon* indicate how far back this tradition goes), one cannot ignore an overt preoccupation with sex in the eighteenth-century popular novel. What were the reasons for this phenomenon?

Peter Hughes has advanced the theory that in the seventeenth and eighteenth centuries a new literary erotic heroism displaced the older epic ideal of the warrior and the knight driven by heroic fury. Hughes has demonstrated convincingly how the mode of heroic expression changed from metaphor and symbol through allusion to the enactment of erotic fears and dreams. Sexual encounters eventually replaced heroic conflicts. A stylistic analysis confirms this observation. Erotic fiction shows, on the one hand, a development of a specific kind of erotic diction and, on the other hand, the retaining of a military vocabulary in the description of amatory conquests. La Fontaine is situated halfway between the eighteenth-century libertine novel and earlier, less overt fiction. Like many eighteenth-century authors after him, La Fontaine plays with a sort of stylistic veil, thus creating a text which, as Roseanne Runte has shown, invites the reader to undress it. Military or 'heroic' metaphors abound in the prose fiction of eighteenth-century authors when they describe erotic encounters, whether in the novels of Fielding, Smollett, and Sterne or in pornographic works like *Fanny Hill*.

Although Hughes' argument may be convincing, it does not, of course, fully explain the endless production of amatory novels in the eighteenth century, from the 'chronique scandaleuse' with its branches of faction and fiction to the whore biographies, whore dialogues, and pornography. One of the main causes of this proliferation of erotica must be seen in the philosophy of pleasure and sexual libertinism, which originated in France. Embodied in philosophical treaties, but also in licentious and pornographic novels, this philosophy affected English erotic fiction much more than has been assumed. It can be argued that without France supplying themes, plots, ideas, and ideologies, in a wave of 'romans galants' and libertine novels, England's erotic fiction would never have developed in such a prodigious way. A brief excursion into French erotic fiction will help to explain why English readers were so susceptible to it.[8]

2.2 *The French Erotic Novel*

If some day someone has the courage to attempt a study of the French licentious novel of the eighteenth century, their task will be no easier than Sisyphus'. The great variety and forbidding number of fictional erotica make the wish for a comprehensive survey seem like a Utopian idea.[9]

Trying to contribute a little towards a true history of the French novel in the eighteenth century, Jacques Rustin has included in his study of vice minor authors and what has been called, somewhat contemptuously, 'la littérature du deuxième rayon'. The libertine novel emerges in his view as a reaction against the corruption of manners. In its depiction of moral decay it provides a panorama of the development of vice which, for the upper classes, gradually became a behavioural and literary fashion. The sexual manners of the upper class were indeed of paramount importance for the development of the idea of libertinism, as P. Laroch has shown. We have now lost the concept of society and of social relations that governed the French élite in the eighteenth century. The licentious literature this ruling class created was dominated by urbane, unpretentious wit and, according to Peter Brooks, demands understanding on its own terms. The rise of the English novel was accompanied by the growth and eventual influence of a middle-class readership. Realism, in the English novel, came with middle-class authors writing for a bourgeois audience. In France, however, it was the tradition of vice and worldliness, recorded in fiction from Crébillon *fils* to Laclos, which contributed to the development of realism. In this process the domain of the erotic had a central function, for it was here that the crucial connection was established between libertine ideas and literature. Both Robert Mauzi and Peter Nagy, the latter from a Marxist viewpoint, have tried to explore what happened after the fusion of philosophical libertinism and erotic literature. Even before the new philosophy of pleasure and sexual freedom began to make itself felt, there had been a strong erotic current in literature. But, with the coming of the ideas of 'plaisir' and 'volupté', erotic prose fiction took a decisive turn towards 'libertinage élégant', where aims were both philosophical and artistic.

The rehabilitation and assertion of sex in human life was achieved through the writings of La Mettrie, one of the atheist and materialist 'philosophes'. His *L'homme machine* (1748), which appeared in English within two years of its first publication, established the materialist view of man. The logical extension were the works *L'art de jouir* (1748) and *La volupté* (1748); in these he explained that the end of life is found in the pleasure of the senses and above all in sex. Baron d'Holbach resumed this line of thinking in *Le système de la nature* (1770), to which Diderot may have contributed as well. Denying the existence of a deity, the German-born d'Holbach, and La Mettrie (who found refuge at the court of Frederick the Great in Prussia when his ideas became too revolutionary for the countries where he wrote), saw in the universe nothing but matter in movement. They proposed happiness as man's principal aim; which meant that if vice renders man happy (thus d'Holbach's argument), he should love vice. Among the wits, philosophers, and libertines for whom the baron kept open house were Continentals like Helvétius, d'Alembert, Diderot, Buffon, and, for a while, Rousseau; but also men like Garrick, Hume, Sterne, and Wilkes.

The new libertine philosophy attacked the bastions of sexual repression, i.e., the social contract of the state, and foremost, the moral teaching of religion, especially that of the Catholic Church. Religion, argued the 'philosophes', was to be replaced by an enlightened self-interest; and some writers applied this philosophy to their fiction.[10]

In its literary shape, the libertine propaganda, as Nagy termed it, took several forms. Generally, it substituted reason and sexual pleasure for love, while ridiculing passion. Numerous novels focused on the theme of the libertine education.

The appearance of pornographic novels was one result of this practical application in literature of libertine ideas about sex. In many cases it is difficult to decide whether it was the libertine message that was more important or the pornographic description. Pornography, the vehicle of the ideology, frequently developed sufficient drive to make itself independent.[11] With such works as Barrin's *Vénus dans le cloître*, d'Argens' *Les nones galantes* and *Thérèse philosophe*, Mirabeau's *Errotika Biblion* and *Le rideau levé*, and the anonymous *La morale du sens ou l'homme du siècle* (1792) one gets into the grey zone between libertine literature and self-absorbed pornography, especially when such novels were illustrated. This pictorial element has been much underestimated in the past when the reception and influence of French libertine novels were discussed. In the second half of the eighteenth century the majority of illustrations in libertine erotica were obscene engravings; and the books in which they appeared were thus often reduced to mere pornography in the eyes of the public. Even less aggressive novels, such as Restif's *Le paysan et la paysanne pervertis*, Choderlos de Laclos' *Les liaisons dangereuses* (plate 49), and Louvet's picaresque *Les amours du Chevalier de Faublas* (1787–90), all works that carried far less libertine philosophical weight than others, were published with overtly sexual and suggestive prints. Due to the powerful attraction of visual imagery, particularly the erotic, the literary aspect of such illustrated novels was thus often doomed to a secondary place, the erotic representations forming a major source for sexual fantasising.[12]

But, as the century grew older, libertinism was increasingly equated with licence. Libertine attitudes, even in fiction, solidified into conventions and fashions; and although ideas were still being propagated by Mirabeau and de Sade, one notices in the licentious works of Andréa de Nerciat and in Restif's *Anti-Justine* (1798) that nothing remains to be said on the ideological level. As the end is reached of a long development that had taken more than a century, sexual pleasure is the only aim left, a fact both text and illustrations underline in their pornographic details. To be sure, a modern reader is repelled by the

49 Illustration from a 1796 edition of Laclos, *Les liaisons dangereuses*, vol. I

insistence on sexual perversion in the French libertine novel of the last decades of the eighteenth century. But when seen as a logical development of the libertine philosophy of pleasure, these novels can be better understood, although not necessarily appreciated.[13]

In de Sade's works, reason, eroticism, libertine pleasure, and a disdain of emotional passion culminate to produce the specific genre which ever since has born his name. In his novels pain and the wish to destroy, which are normally found among sexual instincts, are unleashed in an ecstasy of sexual pleasure that is bound to end not only in the 'little' death ('la petite mort' was a French eighteenth-century expression for sexual orgasm) of the sexual climax, but in annihilation and thus in the world of Thanatos, Eros' next-door neighbour. Throughout the eighteenth century, it was under such ideological influence, from French libertine erotica, that England's own erotic fiction was produced.[14]

2.3   *The Amatory Novel and the 'Chronique Scandaleuse'*

In the wake of the 'roman galant', English writers produced an avalanche of novels within the borders of the mildly erotic and the frivolous. Historically and chronologically, the amatory novel has its roots in the rogue biography and the picaresque, on the one hand, and, on the other, in the heroic novel. Le Sage's *Le diable boiteux* (1707) and *Histoire de Gil Blas de Santillane*, published in four parts between 1715 and 1735, were prototypes spawning sequels, imitations, and adaptations well beyond 1800. The amatory novel draws the curtain, so to speak, where explicit sexual scenes have their beginning. Containing erotic episodes galore, the amatory novel may verge on the comic as well as the pastoral. Examples are *The Modern Lovers: or, The Adventures of Cupid, The God of Love* (1756) and John Cleland's *Memoirs of a Coxcomb* (1751). French dominance in this field even shows in the titles of such novels as *Memoirs of a Man of Pleasure* (1751), which is a translation of Lasolle's *Mémoires de Versorand, ou le libertin devenu philosophe* (1750), and in parodies of Richardson's *Pamela*, such as *The Philosophy of Pleasure: or, The History of a Young Lady, of Luxurious Temperament and Prurient Imagination, who Experienced Repeatedly the Dangers of Seduction, and Whose Escapes from the Snares of Love are truly Wonderful, Depicting Many and Various Luscious Scenes with Her Lovers ... Freely Translated from the French* (1774). Like *Pamela* and *Fanny Hill*, this is a sort of secularised confession, in which 'Fanny Ramsay' tells about her life, basically a series of erotic episodes. Although never obscene, the novel constantly plays with the reader's prurient expectations, mixing the erotic with the sentimental.[15]

One of the favourite genres of the amatory novel was prose fiction that had inanimate or animal spies as major characters. Such novels owed much to Apuleius' *Golden Ass* and the talking objects in the French *fabliaux*, and developed a large spectrum of protagonists, from coins to vehicles and clothes. It will suffice to introduce two examples, Charles Johnstone's *Chrysal: or, The Adventures of a Guinea* (1760) and Francis Coventry's *The History of Pompey the Little: or, The Life and Adventures of a Lap-Dog* (1751). Coventry's novel went into more than five editions by 1800, several of them published with engravings; and was translated into French within a year of its appearance in England. Written in the tradition of Le Sage's *Gil Blas* and the rogue biography, *The History of Pompey* is also a minor masterpiece of social satire. The hero of the novel is a dog born in Bologna, Italy, a place 'famous for Lap-Dogs and Sausages', as Coventry remarks in a *double entendre* at the beginning of Chapter 2. Pompey soon arrives in England in the company of a nobleman and makes his way through the upper and lower classes of society in London and Bath. Coventry uses the perambulations of the dog as a handy device to shift his attention as a writer and satirist from the intrigues of the noble lady to the daily concerns of the poorer sort, providing an entertaining panorama of eighteenth-century customs and follies. Erotic and bawdy scenes are toned down and are not very prominent in the novel. When Pompey has come into the possession of Lady Tempest, his mistress one day receives 'a little Scroll' from another lady concerning the hero of the novel:

> Dear Tempest,
> My favourite little VENY is at present troubled with certain amorous Infirmities of Nature, and wou'd not be displeased with the Addresses of a Lover. Be so good therefore to send little POMPEY by my Servant who brings this Note, for I fancy it will make a very pretty Breed, and when the Lovers have transacted their Affairs, he shall be sent home incontinently.

Flattered at the compliments extended to her darling dog, Lady Tempest replies:

> Dear ———
> Infirmities of Nature we all are subject to, and therefore I have sent Master POMPEY to wait upon Miss VENY, begging the favour of you to return him as soon as his gallantries are over. Consider, my Dear, no modern Love

can, in the Nature of Things, last above three days, and therefore I hope to
see my little Friend again very soon.

There are a number of such bawdy and also scatological incidents in
the novel, which ends with the sudden demise of Pompey, at a moment
when the author has obviously become tired of his subject.

In the case of Johnstone's *Chrysal*, the several editions of this novel
attest to its great popularity. It served as a model for Smollett's *The
History and Adventures of an Atom* (1769), and, in contrast to *Pompey the Little*, excels in scenes of sensuality and sexuality. Thus an old
general has young girls procured for him, in Volume I, which also
introduces whores and a courtesan with a strong sexual appetite. The
guinea passes from the hands of a thief to a Jesuit characterised by lust
and greed; he not only pardons an army officer for raping, robbing,
and killing his sister-in-law, but persuades the vicious officer to turn
the stolen loot over to the Church and to take holy orders. In Volume II
historical figures, such as George Whitefield ('Dr Hunchback'),
Mother Douglas, a notorious bawd who joined the Methodists ('Mrs
Brimstone'), and the playwright Foote ('Momus'), enter the novel
amid sexual scandal. Containing much social satire, *Chrysal* is
obviously indebted to Le Sage, Crébillon *fils*, and Diderot. The episodes of love and lust which the guinea witnesses establish a picture of
a society interested in the pleasures of the senses. Not everything was
as salacious in this field as *Chrysal*, however. *The History and Adventures of a Lady's Slippers and Shoes* (1754), for instance, is an utterly
boring odyssey – despite the promise of excitement in the preface – of a
pair of 'slippers' from one lady to another.[16]

The erotic 'chronique scandaleuse' encompasses 'faction', i.e., fact
and fiction presented in a series of 'secret memoirs and histories', and
pure fiction. Both are related to the non-fictional and sensational
'causes célèbres' in France and the crim. con. trial reports in England,
as well as to journalistic slander of court circles. The scandal novel in
the early decades of the eighteenth century was largely limited to
imitating Mary de la Rivière Manley and Eliza Haywood – the novels
of these ladies had set the tone. In addition, French 'mémoires' and
'histoires secrètes', such as those of the Chevalier de Mouhy, poured
daily into England. John J. Richetti has shown how these novels
dramatise sexual and social antagonisms. Innocent and helpless
females are ruined by masculine aristocratic libertines; the reverse, a
male youth seduced by a lascivious courtesan, occurs far less often.
While these fictional works provide an ideal location for risqué scenes

in a sensual atmosphere, things are never carried too far in print; moral indignation, expressed at the right moment, exculpates the author and creates distance.[17]

As can be expected, not much of excellence was created where almost anyone who wrote fiction tried his hand. Making an excursion from botany and quackery into the field of prose fiction, John Hill in 1751 wrote *The History of a Woman of Quality*, a novel for a female audience, as were most others of this genre. Hill quickly passes over erotic encounters and draws the curtain of decency whenever coitus is nigh. His presentation of Lady Frail's love affairs thus never deviates from convention. Sentimentalism was indulged with brio, and a modern reader needs a lot of stamina to get through such a novel.

This also applies to the pathetic-sentimental type of fiction, focusing almost exclusively on innocence and the dangers of seduction. Though erotic, these are not 'chroniques scandaleuses'. They are best exemplified in the novels of Eliza Haywood, such as *Love in Excess, or The Fatal Enquiry* (1719). Often plagiarised, Mrs Haywood's novels had a bearing on anonymous works like *The Fair Adulteress*, published as late as 1774. While novels of this type retain numerous erotic scenes, the reader's sympathy is not with the seducing hero, but with the beleaguered heroine. The reader hopes that the innocent protagonist will escape seduction or rape and that she will finally clasp the true hero in her arms; this hope was the major suspense for a female audience, who expected the wicked to be punished.

Such novels provided a double satisfaction for the reader, both in witnessing erotic scenes, and in being on the side of virtue. From here, it was just a short step to the extreme sentimentality of Richardson's *Pamela* and to the gothic pathos of Lewis' *The Monk* (1796). Richardson couched in moralism what is basically an erotic novel; and Lewis incorporated the macabre and grotesque elements of Romanticism, while introducing a strong note of sadistic sensuality. This touch of sadism proved too much for Lewis' contemporaries. His novel transgressed the bounds of decency, by tapping subconscious, forbidden sources; as a consequence Lewis had to cut all objectionable passages for a new edition in 1798. But in the same year *The New Monk*, a partly pornographic parody of Lewis' novel, showed what gothic fiction could be like when the trappings of horror and the grotesque were discarded. With its scenes of flagellation in a boarding school for girls, *The New Monk* revealed the underlying preoccupations of the gothic novel and anticipated Victorian pornography.

John Cleland's *Fanny Hill* is, in many ways, a corrective of both extremes of the perverse and the pathetic. As an anti-*Pamela* and a libertine novel, *Fanny Hill* attempts to combine the sensual with the sentimental.[18]

2.4 *The Whore Biography*

As a genre of erotic fiction, the whore biography is yet another eighteenth-century example of a literary half-breed. With its roots in the rogue biography and the 'chronique scandaleuse', it also borders on pornography – etymologically, pornography means writing of, or about, whores – yet, by dint of a moral element, it was still respectable enough for Defoe to write *Moll Flanders* and *Roxana* in this genre.[19] The vast body of literature on London's high-class whores, or courtesans, is of course a kind of 'chronique scandaleuse' on the periphery of the whore biography.[20] A fictional variation is *Genuine Memoirs of the Celebrated Miss Maria Brown* (1766). This claims to be from the pen of John Cleland, no doubt to achieve better sales.[21] Its title-page and list of contents provide some idea of such picaresque novels laced with erotic episodes.

GENUINE
MEMOIRS
Of the Celebrated
Miss Maria Brown.
Exhibiting
The Life of a Courtezan
in the most Fashionable Scenes of
Dissipation.

Published by the Author of a W** of P***

In Two Volumes.

VOL.   I.

Under how hard a fate are women born?
Prais'd to their ruin, or expos'd to scorn.
If they want beauty, they of love despair,
And are besieg'd like frontier towns, if fair.

Rowe

LONDON:
Printed for I. Allcock, near St. Paul's.
MDCCLXVI.

CONTENTS.

The moral frame in which the whore biography is usually cast allows the writer to present the gaudy world of crime and prostitution to a prurient middle-class audience. In the more factual works, whores die, either through venereal disease or on the gallows. This tragic element is, however, more than balanced by the inclusion of comic and frivo-lous scenes. In chapbook versions of the whore biographies the title-pages often contain the gist of the books, as with *The Secret History of Betty Ireland*, an extremely popular story that kept the presses going for several decades until it was eclipsed by such competitors as the history of the celebrated Fanny Davies (plate 50). What is obvious in these examples is the attempt to lure the reader with the promise of details on scandalous sexual behaviour: the frontispiece of the book on Davies sports the subject in both male and female attire. Fanny Davies was a whore, pickpocket, and cross-dresser; Betty Ireland, like

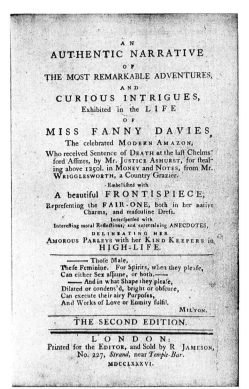

50 Title-page of *An Authentic
Narrative of . . . Miss Fanny
Davies* (the second edition),
1786

Moll Flanders, allegedly engaged in incest. But the promises cannot be
kept by the text itself, for these books steered clear of obscene details,
relying more on the exotic attraction the underworld possessed for
middle-class readers. The title-pages are thus clever come-ons for a
bourgeois readership interested in a titillating combination of crime,
prostitution, and sex.

   With the 'whore letter' we are already into purely fictional territory.
This genre of epic fiction is again difficult to define, being situated
between the mostly pornographic whore dialogue and the whore
biography. However, since the epic aspect in these works is much
stronger than any sort of communication from the protagonist herself,
which is merely indicated formally in a fictive epistolary dialogue, it
would seem justified to include this branch in the survey of the whore
biography. The whore letter found expression in such novels as
*Amusements in High Life; or, Conjugal Infidelities in 1786. In a Series
of Confidential Letters, Between Ladies Who Have Distinguished
Themselves in the Multiplicity and Singularity of Their Amours*

(1786). The two ladies in this book, Caroline and Eliza, write each other letters on their love affairs. Ridiculing their old, impotent husbands, they extol the charms of the youthful lovers consoling them. The letters are never obscene, and display a pathetic style. One of the ladies describes a critical encounter in this way: 'I sunk into his arms on the sopha; nature ruled the helm within me; the tide of love rolled impetuously through my veins, and broke down the barriers of guiding reason.'[22]

The brevity of this epic genre naturally invited satire. Thus *Great News from Hell, or The Devil Foil'd by Bess Weatherby* (1760) not only parodies the more traditional whore letter but also another eighteenth-century literary fad, the letters from the dead to the living. Between 1702 and 1703, and again in 1707, for instance, Grub Street writer Tom Brown and a few of his friends evolved this Lucianic device of dialogues, in a series of scurrilous *Letters from the Dead to the Living*, containing scandalous revelations about contemporary personalities. In *Great News from Hell* the former prostitute Betsy Wemyss writes to her colleague, Lucy Cooper (one of the better-known courtesans of eighteenth-century London), in Covent Garden. Betsy describes life in hell, and the former friends and acquaintances from London she has met. As a sort of punishment, they all have to work twice as much as before – in the same profession. However, upon the arrival of Bess Weatherby, Satan has a feast arranged, and the newcomer is made Queen of Hell. But Lucifer is unable to rule his wife; and when Bess's pimp arrives as well, she joins him instead to rule the nether world. Even for a blasé modern reader, this is a fairly entertaining and ribald satire, extending to fifty-two pages. The whore letter was a well-known literary genre. When Fielding attacked Richardson's unbelievably moral *Pamela*, in his *Shamela* of 1741, he too availed himself of this tradition, replacing the Richardsonian middle-class parents and daughter by an elderly whore (Shamela's mother), and her corrupt daughter, a girl who cherishes such books as *Venus in the Cloister*, and licentious plays in print.[23]

Finally, the erotic pseudo-biographical 'memoirs' and 'histories' bespeak the perennial French influence in this area of the erotic novel. If Crébillon and Diderot were emulated, so were anonymous novels like *Histoire de Mademoiselle Brion* (1754). One example from England is *A New Atalantis for the Year One Thousand Seven Hundred and Fifty-Eight* (1758), with its seven whore biographies. The preface asserts the eighteenth-century aversion to homosexuality: 'We have for a long time been highly displeased at the illicit pursuit of pleasures

a posteriori; which are not only unnatural, but also inconsequential.'
The introduction is concerned with 'the origin of love and gallantry',
which is traced back to Greece. And then the ladies are introduced:
first of all Rocforia, the attraction of Cytherea, who describes
Cytherea's cell (female genitals) and the pleasures it creates:

> The sage politician bows to, and the dauntless warrior lowers his pike to it.
> The grave magistrate chuckles in ermin at the pleasing spectacle . . . In fine,
> it contains the great balm, and sovereign elixier for all the pains and ills in
> life.

The second lady introduced is the lustful Tonzénie. She likes to watch
mating animals, and reads Ovid's *Art of Love*, Rochester's poems, and
the *Memoirs of a Woman of Pleasure*. Tonzénie (a name reminiscent
of Crébillon's oriental tale) also explores the pleasures of masturbation; first with natural means and then with a dildo:

> One of the middle-sized dildo-tribe was procured for her private amuse-
> ment; through it her French maid, well skilled in such practices, would in
> the moment of rapture, dart a warm injection; nay, sometimes artfully gird
> it to her loins, and act the man with her young mistress.

As can be guessed, the dildo only makes her yearn for a man; and
finally a footman is procured. He 'put one of his hands on her glowing
bubbies', and when the French maid in assistance released 'priapus', it
bolted out 'with such violence against the Frenchwoman's face, that it
felled her on the back'. The dutiful footman deflowers Tonzénie and
afterwards pays her several visits, making love in various positions.
Janneton, the French maid, provides a little comic relief via her accent.
Finally, the footman dies of exhaustion, and Tonzénie goes abroad to
look for other victims. The other stories, about Essesia, reading the
Oeconomy of Love, and Petronia, Chimene, Rocketta, and Coquetil-
la, are much the same; they contain explicit descriptions of sexual acts,
and even sacrilegious parodies of prayers. The French philosophy of
pleasure is here put to satirical and ribald use.[24]

The two volumes entitled *Genuine and Authentic Memoirs of a
Well-Known Woman of Intrigue* (1787) allude to John Cleland's
notorious novel; but they avoid overt descriptions of sexual acts.
These 'memoirs' oscillate between sentimentalism and prurience.
Again, it is the confessional form of an 'autobiography' which is
chosen, no doubt to admit an element of voyeurism. Louisa, the
protagonist, begins her story *ab ovo*, so to speak, if not before, for one
of the first scenes is the wedding day of her mother. This lady cheats

her old husband, a clergyman, in the bakery of the house with a lawyer. Due to the numerous love affairs of her mother, the heroine cannot tell the reader who her real father was. Her own erotic life starts at age thirteen, when she is promised to an officer but makes love to someone else in a bower. Tired of her lover, she leaves for London, taking her mother with her. Various love affairs and seductions in London's high society are then described without much detail. One of the *derniers cris* Louisa is acquainted with is a chastity belt, which one of her gallants forces her to wear. A comical scene develops when an amorous gentleman tackles the armoured Louisa:

> He eagerly surveyed the charms displayed to his view. I was set on fire by his burning caresses. He gave way to the raptures of most violent love ... Useless efforts! The temple of voluptuousness was inaccessible to his homage. At length, yielding to despair, and the impetuosity of his desires, he blindly offered his sacrifice against one of the outside pillars of the edifice ... It was necessary to postpone till the next morning, the surrender of a place which could not be carried by storm.

In the morning a charitable blacksmith provides relief for both lovers. Louisa's memoirs end with her twenty-first year, when she finds herself in love with a Russian nobleman. This novel is definitely erotic; yet the stylistic veil allows no obscene details – the reader's imagination must fill the empty spaces.

Such fictional 'biographies' continued to appear, and eventually became the staple diet of erotic magazines; between January and April 1794, for instance, *The Bon Ton Magazine* serialised *The Adventures of a Bar-Maid, a Series of Facts.*[25]

2.5 *The Pornographic Novel*

The pornographic novel is the last stage, or the final product, of a literary development in erotic fiction which had its beginning in the whore dialogue. Initially meant as satire and bawdy entertainment, the whore dialogue gradually changed its function until the sexual stimulation of the reader became its most obvious feature. The causes behind this process are difficult to trace and need not concern us too much, but they are certainly to be seen in relation to changes in literacy; these suggest that a growing audience demanded – and got – changes in both the form and content of the dialogue. As the whore dialogue is essentially important for the appearance of the porno-graphic novel, and since a number of whore dialogues published in the eighteenth century are in fact pornography, the more important and influential titles will be briefly discussed here. David Foxon, and particularly Peter Naumann, have provided detailed studies of the genre.[26]

Pietro Aretino's *Ragionamenti* is the first book that had a major part in the proliferation of European pornography. The whore dialogues in this collection from the early sixteenth century consist of two parts with three dialogues each. In Part I, Nanna, an experienced 'puttana', talks to her friend, Antonia, about her daughter Pippa. Nanna is uncertain about Pippa's future life, hesitating whether to recommend to her life in a convent, or in matrimony, or the career of a 'puttana'. Nanna's problem is that she has some experience in all three areas and cannot decide what to suggest to her daughter. Her friend, however, is more interested in Nanna's past careers, and asks her to relate her adventures. So Nanna's epic reports make up Part I. The beginning of Nanna's first report is concerned with her life as a nun and the sex orgies she witnessed in her convent. This is followed by a description of her life as a married woman, an episode clearly written in the tradition of Boccaccio's tales. The third report is a detailed account of her career as a whore. This last dialogue was afterwards often published separately and appeared in English in 1658 as *The Crafty Whore*, with numerous subsequent reprints. At the end of Part I of the *Ragionamenti* Nanna has reached a decision: Pippa is to become a prostitute, a profession her mother values as a safe and lucrative one. Hence Part II shows Pippa's initiation into the craft of the whore, the 'arte puttanesca'. This is a classic theme of pornography, showing an older, experienced woman teaching a novice about the trade. The *Ragionamenti* popularised the whore dialogue, and with it the bawdy and obscene satire of religion and clerics as well as the description of the voluptuous pleasures of human sexuality.[27]

By 1683 Pallavicino's whore dialogues, *La retorica delle puttane*, had already appeared in an English version, called *The Whores Rhetoric*. What is remarkable about this work is that it was rewritten for an English audience, the sub-title announcing it was 'calculated to the meridian of London'. In actual fact this meant that Pallavicino's salacious anti-clericalism and subversive libertinism were toned down. *The Whores Rhetoric* is made up of two dialogues, in which Mother Creswell, an historical figure who was a well-known English procuress during the reign of Charles II, instructs the younger Dorothea in the art of the courtesan and the mysteries of sexually servicing men. The instructional passages are sometimes rather long, and attain epic qualities. The following is a scene in which Mother Creswell describes how a whore is to deport herself with her customer.

A Whores language is the lascivious dialect, is ever to please the present lover; who always coming to feed on the same dish, ought to enjoy the variety of discourse, in such sort that he be not cloyed with his fare, and by consequence she lose the efficacy and main end of her eloquence. You must seem altogether insatiable in pleasing your lover; and in multiplying his delight; ever pretending to receive therein your self particular satisfaction; if his experience has taught him divers forms in the enjoyment, gratifie him in condescending to his humour therein: provided his particular generosity challenge this particular treatment. During these ravishing minutes be not wanting to afford him a multiplicity of strict imbraces: let your caresses, and ectasies be sometimes inclining to violent, sometimes slow and remiss; but still such as may seem natural, without any artificial constraint, that so he may believe you ravished beyond your self: and be thought, not only to feed him with your body, but to have given likewise your very Soul. Let this be attended with some dying words, soft murmuring sighs, as may be just overheard by your lover. Redoubling the knots of hands and feet, let the Comedy end with some sweet kisses, in which let your tongue gently glide within his lips; that you may seem to have transmitted your Soul that way; whilst he infuses his, in return at another door...

French authors continued the line of the whore dialogue begun by Italian writers, perfecting it as pornographic fiction. It was with *The School of Venus* (c. 1688), which we only know through court records, that a more significant step was taken in the development of the pornographic novel. The book is attributed to Michel Millot and/or Jean l'Ange, and was as popular in 1744 as it was in the century before, when it first appeared in Paris. Instead of whores, two female cousins conduct the dialogues, thus excluding the realm of the whore while including members of the middle class. Again, there is an elderly person with great experience in the art of love, in this case called Susanne, who instructs the innocent Fanchon at the behest of Fanchon's lover, Robinet. At first, anatomical details are explained in didactic episodes, then coitus and sexual pleasure. Susanne spices the dialogues with stories from her own life, before acquainting Fanchon with the techniques of foreplay. In Part II Fanchon relates to Susanne how she successfully applied her newly acquired knowledge with Robinet. Often banned or censored in the seventeenth and eighteenth centuries as what was then termed a lewd and licentious book, *The School of Venus* shares with the pornographic novel a claustrophobic atmosphere, a loss of psychological depth accompanied by an idealisation of sex, and an anarchic message undermining the moral teachings of parents and religion.[28]

The great competitor of this whore dialogue was Nicolas Chorier's *Satyra sotadica*, originally published under the Latin title of *Aloisiae*

Sigaea Toletana Satyra sotadica de arcanis amoris & veneris (c. 1660).
It came to be known in French as *L'Académie des dames* (1680) and
Le Meursius françois; and in English as *The School of Women* (1682)
– a version that is unfortunately lost – and *A Dialogue Between a
Married Lady and a Maid* (1688 and 1740). Other titles of the same
book – *Tullia and Octavia*, for instance, or *Joannis Meursii elegantiae
latini sermonis* – also circulated, in Latin, French, and English. Critics
agree that this is the most advanced piece of pornographic fiction
written in the seventeenth century, and that it was widely read until the
end of the eighteenth century and later. In seven dialogues, Tullia, a
married lady with sexual experience beyond the normal, prepares her
young niece, Octavia, for her wedding night. Tullia reveals herself as a
voyeuse, and goes beyond verbal instruction when sharing a bed with
Octavia at night. Lesbian manipulations, orgasm, and later sadism are
both described and practised. This practical part is a novelty in the
whore dialogue at this stage. There is much male brutality and violence in the description of defloration and flagellation. The same
details are discussed, and only slightly varied, through the introduction of new characters and a number of anecdotes. The stress is
primarily on the sexual and everything related to making love. Comic
elements have disappeared, while the attack on institutions control-
ling sexual morals – matrimony, the Church – has increased to a degree
of striking directness. Peter Naumann has compared the English version of the book of 1740 with its Latin and French predecessors and
found that the depiction of sexual scenes in *A Dialogue between a
Married Lady and a Maid* is longer and more detailed as well as
psychologically more convincing. Patrick Kearney's bibliography lists
eighteen registered and extant editions of this book, most of them in
French and with illustrations, in the eighteenth century. If one bears in
mind that a majority of editions of Chorier's bestseller appeared with
explicit engravings, indicating its relation with the notorious 'postures' of Romano and Aretino (cf. Chapter 8) and underlining the
pornographic element of the whore dialogue, it is obvious that this
book was read if not written for sexual stimulation.[29]

   In the course of the development of the whore dialogue as a literary
genre one notices an increasing exactness in the description of sexual
details. The settings change from brothel to private home, and, eventually, to the monastery. It is in the monastery that the whore dialogue
violates both moral and sexual taboos while exploiting a claustrophobic atmosphere that is most subservient to pornographic aims. Stylisti-
cally, the pathetic is substituted for the comic as the audience and

literary taste change, and pornographic description replaces obscene satire. The epic mode gradually displaces the earlier dialogue forms, leading to autobiographical reports, or confessions about sexual experiences, that include flagellation, homosexuality, orgies, and sadism.

Barrin's *Venus in the Cloister*, of which both French and English versions were marketed in the eighteenth century, can be regarded as the prototype of the anti-monastic novel combining anti-Christian slander with salacity. In many ways it is still a whore dialogue. In fact, the original version consisted of three dialogues between two nuns; but later three epic reports were added that are taken from French collections of tales and novelettes about amorous monks and nuns. The final part introduces two lesbian nuns trying to get out of their convent while denigrating the clerics and the Church, clearly a section of the book that has no relation to the preceding parts. With this novel, pornotopia – as Marcus has called the domain of the pornographic – has finally been reached. Characteristically, *Venus in the Cloister* starts with voyeurism, as the nun Angelica watches through a keyhole how Sister Agnes masturbates. In the ensuing dialogue between the two nuns the inexperienced Agnes gradually accepts the libertine morality Angelica demonstrates in stories on love and lust in the convent. One of these tales is about a nun spying on her lover, a monk of course, who meets another nun in an adjacent room:

> *Angelica.* He then made her come nearer to the Grate, and having made her get upon a Stool of a convenient Height, he conjured her to let him satisfy at least his Sight, since all other Liberties were forbidden. She obeyed him after some Resistance, and gave him Time to handle those Places consecrated to Chastity and Continence. She on her Side would also satisfy her Eyes with the like Curiosity: And the Father who was not insensible, found easily the Means to gratify her, and she obtained of him what she desired, with less Difficulty than what he obtained of her. This was the fatal Moment to them both, and what our Spies desired, who contemplated with a most extraordinary Satisfaction the most beautiful Parts of the naked Body of their Companion, which the Father discovered to their View, and handled with the Transports of a furious Lover. One while they admired one Part, then another, according as the officious Father turned and changed the Situation of his Paramour, so that while he considered her before, he exposed her Posteriors to their View, for her Petticoats on both Sides were taken up as high as her Girdle.

Several levels of voyeurism are involved here. The monk and the nun are eyeing (and handling) each other; Agnes thinks she sees the scene through Angelica's report; and the reader is assigned another func-tion, as a secret observer. In the fourth dialogue Angelica describes her observation of a defloration in a convent:

> He threw her upon the Mattress, and run over her breast and Stomach, and other more secret Parts, with a thousand Kisses, and then proceeded on to Pleasures more particular, which made her, if she was not so before, a perfect Woman.
> *Agnes*. And how came you to know all this?
> *Angel*. I'll tell thee: I thought I saw one of the Workmen enter her Cell and tipping softly along the Dormitory, made up to her Door, which having a large Chink between the Boards, I saw what I tell you. The first Thing I beheld, was *Eugenia* all naked, with *Frederick* sitting by her, holding in his Hand — — which extremely surprized me, imagining to myself that she could never enjoy that Excess of Pleasure I afterwards found she did. Said I to myself, Lord! what Pain must poor *Eugenia* undergo? How is it possible he should not tare [sic] her to Pieces? These were my Thoughts, but I suppose he treated her very gently on Account of her Youth, for she was but bare Fifteen. While I was thus busied in my Thoughts, I heard *Frederic* say, *Eugenia*, my Dear, turn upon your Back, which after she had done, he got up and put his – into her – for my Part I was quite frightened when I heard her cry out as if she were in excessive Pain, this gave me, as thou may'st well imagine, a great deal of Uneasiness, for I did not dare to come in for fear of surprizing of them, which might have had perhaps but very ill Consequences.

Again, this is a scene of voyeurism from which the observer derives sexual stimulation; she tries to convey this to the dialogue partner and to the reader. On one occasion, Agnes gets so excited by Angelica's description of a scene of flagellation that she voices her regret at not having seen it herself:

> ... in order to insult anew, and with greater Violence that opinionated Nature, [she] takes her Discipline in Hand, and pulling up her Coats and Smock to her very navel, and tying them about her with a Girdle, she had no Mercy on her poor Thighs, and that Part which had caused all her Sufferings, which then lay entirely bare and uncovered. This Rage having lasted some Time, her Strength failed her by this cruel Act; she had scarce so much left her as to set her Cloaths at Liberty, which exposed her more than half naked. ... She fell into a very great Weak-ness, but it was a very amorous one, which the Fury of her Passion had caused; and made this young Thing taste such a Pleasure which ravished her to the very Skies. At this Moment Nature inciting all its Forces, broke through all the Obstacles which opposed its Sallies; and that Virginity which till then had been in Prison, delivered it without any Aid or Succour with the utmost Impetuosity, leaving its Keeper extended on the Floor, as a certain Sign of her being discomfited.

Agnes. Ah Lard! I wish I had been present!

Angel. Alas! my Dear, what Pleasure would that have been to thee? Thou
wouldst have seen that Innocent half naked, her Mouth smiling with
those amorous gentle Contractions, of which she knew not the Cause!
Thou wouldst have seen her in an Ecstacy, her Eyes half dying, and
without any Strength or Vigour, fall beneath the Laws of undisguised
Nature, and lose in Defiance to all her Care, that Treasure, the keeping
of which had cost her so much Pain and Trouble.

In *Venus in the Cloister* sex has become a religion. Consequently,
orgasm is described in quasi-religious terms. The new faith, sexual
pleasure, is set down in the books Agnes receives from her *abbé*, all of
them obscene or pornographic, and including such pornographica as
L'escole des filles (i.e., *The School of Venus*) and Chorier's *L'académie
des dames*. Agnes is taught that the illustrations in some of the books
are supposed to heighten her pleasure. *Venus in the Cloister* itself was
published with pornographic illustrations as early as the first decade
of the eighteenth century. The book shows a deep interest in sexual
deviation, particularly sado-masochism. For all their anti-clerical
attacks – sexy nuns meant both anti-Catholic propaganda and prurience – Barrin's whore dialogues were quite obviously intended to
produce sexual excitement for the reader.[30]

It has often been argued that pornography, and in particular the
pornographic novel, did not flourish before the latter part of the
eighteenth century. Donald Thomas believes that just before 1800, an
increasing censorship, ironically, boosted pornography; and Steven
Marcus, correctly relating pornography to the rise of the novel, is of
the opinion that pornographic fiction is a mad parody of the needs
created after the mid-century by more privacy. While it is true that
censorship became tougher, and literacy advanced, though only gently, including more readers from the lower social strata, it should be
pointed out that the pornographic novel and related fiction were in full
bloom before Cleland's *Memoirs of a Woman of Pleasure* appeared in
1748/9. Marcus and Thomas, like most other Anglo-American scholars, have failed to consider two essential points. Firstly, our picture of
pornography in the eighteenth century is far from being realistic. If one
draws conclusions on the basis of extant titles, one should at least bear
in mind that 'most of the erotic books of earlier centuries have almost
entirely disappeared,' as Gershon Legman repeatedly notes in his
Horn Book.[31] Secondly, most critics seem to forget that in the eighteenth century readers of erotica did not make a distinction between
French and English books. The artificial separation of modern critical

studies between French erotica and native English products is hardly a way to do justice to the market in pornographic fiction as the reader found it in the eighteenth century. A great number of French pornographic novels reached England before 1749, most of them also available in English translations. Among the more influential works were those of La Morlière, d'Argens, and Latouche, all of them available in English translations before *Fanny Hill* appeared on the scene. Hence they cannot be ignored in this survey of the pornographic novel.[32]

La Morlière's pornographicum was sold in England as *The Ecclesiastical Laurels*; but since no copies of the translation are extant we depend on the French original. From 1748 on it was published in numerous editions, sometimes with other anti-monastic pornography, until well after 1800. Basically, *Les lauriers ecclésiastiques* is an anti-clerical satire, and straddles the border between 'roman galant' and pornography. An *abbé* confesses his youthful erotic adventures with a marquise in the country home of his uncle, a bishop. The lady's maid, upon seeing the *abbé* in the nude, is inflamed, and visits him in Paris in the disguise of a priest. When their affair is detected, the jealous marquise manages to have the *abbé* sent to a monastery. Until this point a number of pornographic themes, such as voyeurism and transvestism, have been developed. They are then continued and varied in the monastery and in Paris. The hero seduces women and secretly watches his lovers being seduced by others, until he falls in love with a young girl about to be sent to a convent. When their relatives die, the lovers are finally free to leave the monastic world and to get married. It is during the days before the wedding that the *abbé* – in a fit of alleged remorse and repentance – pens his 'confession', a typical convention of popular literature absorbed by the pornographic novel. D'Argens' *Thérèse philosophe* of 1748, soon afterwards Englished as *The Philosophical Theresa*, employed its pornographic content for a demonstration of the new libertine teaching on sexual morals with a strong anti-Catholic current. From the very beginning, this novel was published with explicit engravings, increasing from sixteen in the 1748 edition to twenty-four in 1780 (by Delcroche) and thirty-six in 1782 (by Binet). The varying quality of the illustrations indicates that the book catered to the rich and the poor alike. A 1771 version claiming to be published 'à Londres', for instance, contains poorly executed engravings, reminiscent of seventeenth-century woodcuts (plate 51a–b), for a book that could be slipped into the smallest of pockets and is a cheap edition. Inspired by the Girard–Cadière scandal of 1731, d'Argens created a female narrator who

51a–b Illustrations from a 1771 edition of *Thérèse philosophe*

addresses her teacher in the introduction and admits her indebtedness to the Abbé T. of *The Ecclesiastical Laurels*. Thérèse's confessional autobiography comments on the sexual relations between Girard and Cadière and describes copulation from the viewpoint of the voyeur or voyeuse; but her report is also frequently interrupted by philosophical digressions representing a didactic element of this novel. D'Argens equates sexual orgasm with religious ecstasy, and in the confessional the narrator receives from Abbé T. sexual instructions about various ways of stimulation, including masturbation. Such scenes alternate with others in which Thérèse spies on her friends, the *abbé* and Madame C., until her autobiography arrives at the death of her mother. Accepted by a retired prostitute as a foster daughter, Thérèse records this woman's former adventures. Finally, she makes the acquaintance of her 'comte' and protector – the dialogue partner for whom the novel is written, according to Thérèse – who seduces her with the help of pornographic books and illustrations. In this novel d'Argens avails himself of the long tradition of erotic fiction, combining aspects of the 'chronique scandaleuse', the picaresque novel, the novella, and the whore dialogue with the French philosophy of sexual pleasure and anti-clericism. The anti-Christian element makes it difficult to decide whether the novel is more philosophical libertine propaganda or pornography; but even without the engravings the pornographic potential of the text cannot be denied. However, *Thérèse philosophe* is not just pornography in the sense that its sole aim would be sexual stimulation; the didactic features of libertine ideology, sexual instruction, and the teaching of a new 'natural religion' establish a strong connection between this novel and the French materialism of the Enlightenment.[33]

If one approaches the French and English pornographic novels of the eighteenth century as one body of literature – a view justified by the translations and the reception in England of pornographic French fiction – then it is not John Cleland's *Memoirs of a Woman of Pleasure* which marks the height of the development, but Gervaise de Latouche's *Histoire de Dom B ... portier des Chartreux* (c. 1741/2). English readers could purchase a translation entitled *History of Don B* as early as 1743. It was this book which dominated the field of the pornographic novel until Cleland's *Memoirs* began to compete with it. *Dom Bougre*, to give the novel its full and salacious title, appeared in various guises, such as *Portier des Chartreux; Mémoires de Saturnin*, and *Histoire de Gouberdon*, and was reprinted so often that one can hardly trace every edition. Imitations were equally plentiful. By 1745,

Dom Bougre's sister, 'Soeur Suzon', had become the heroine in a sequel written by Meusnier de Querlon; it was announced as the 'pendant au Portier des Chartreux' and sold under such titles as *Histoire de la tourrière des Carmélites*, *Saint Nitouche*, and others. Still later, Suzon's daughter had the major part in *Histoire de Marguerite* (1784). Clearly, *Dom Bougre* was an important piece of fiction to spawn such a series of books. For the proliferation of the pornographic novel in particular it is of central importance. The plot is the following.

Saturnin, the hero, grows up with a couple – gardeners by profession – without knowing that he is not their child. His first sexual feelings are aroused when one day he watches (through a hole in the wall – the traditional opening for scenes of voyeurism) his stepmother, Toinette, committing adultery with Father Polycarpe. Saturnin's initial attempts at seducing his sister, Suzon, and an acquaintance are both thwarted. A lesbian episode follows, in which Suzon tells Saturnin about her erotic relations with Monique, a nun, whose monastic sexual escapades Suzon reports in detail. These include masturbation, and a rape by a servant in front of an altar. Finding herself pregnant, Monique aborts the child. When her lover is forced to leave the convent, the nun finds solace again in her lesbian activities with Suzon. As Saturnin is very much excited by these stories he suggests sexual intercourse to Suzon. But she declines, being afraid to get pregnant. In order to make her agree to his wishes, Saturnin leads her to the notorious peephole to watch Toinette and Polycarpe repeating their act. Just when Suzon is about to give in to her brother's demands the bed collapses in the heat of passion, and they are discovered and separated. Saturnin is then seduced by his stepmother, and becomes a secret witness to Suzon's defloration by the ever active Polycarpe. After these experiences Saturnin falls prey to the seductive attempts of Madame Dinville, a former acquaintance; and he also tries to satisfy Suzon, who now wants him; but this time he is impeded by a stranger who, disguised as a ghost, interrupts the tryst at a critical moment and attacks Saturnin. There are some further adventures, one of them a sort of 'musical beds' scene, in which the hero, a priest, a monk, two female servants, and a young girl are involved; and at the end of Part I Saturnin retires to a monastery. Part II opens with a description of the hero, his senses dulled by the routine of monastic life and a slave to masturbation. One of the monks introduces Saturnin into nocturnal orgies celebrated by the monks and their girls, with such scenes as this:

Sometimes I was put on a bench, completely naked; one Sister placed
herself astride my throat in such a way that my chin was hidden in her
pubic hair, another one put herself on my belly, a third one, who was on
my thighs, tried to introduce my prick into her cunt; two others again were
placed at my sides so that I could hold a cunt in each hand; and finally
another one, who possessed the nicest breast, was at my head, and bending
forward, she pushed my face between her bubbies; all of them were naked,
all rubbed themselves, all discharged; my hands, my thighs, my belly, my
chest, my prick, everything was wet, I floated while fucking.

Saturnin also discovers a secret cell where the monks keep mistresses;
and one of them turns out to be his real mother. As time advances,
Saturnin's strength wanes; the nocturnal scenes of lust and perversion
take their toll. His superior eventually advises him to hear the confession of young nuns. The first nun who comes along is raped by
Saturnin:

Tired of merely admiring her without feeling sexual pleasure, I put my
mouth and hands with great ardour upon what I had just seen; but hardly
had I touched her, when my dear penitent uttered a deep sigh and began to
show her knowledge while carrying her hand where she felt mine. I kiss
her, my mouth stays glued to hers; my penitent wants to free herself, she
pushes me back; surprised and frightened to find herself on a bed in a
bedroom, she looks alarmed; she tries to find out where she is exactly, she
wants to speak, but her tongue is impeded. My burning ardour produces
the same effect, I do not let go of her; she makes every effort to escape from
my arms, but I hold her back, I throw her down, she gets up again
furiously; she jumps at me and wants to scratch my face; she bites, she
beats me, her whole body is agitated and sweat is running down her
animated cheeks. Nothing can hold me back now, I press my chest upon
hers, my belly upon her belly; I try with my foot to hold her under me and
let her hands do whatever they are told to do by her anger and wish to
defend herself; I use mine to spread her thighs; she holds them together
obstinately, I fail to triumph; anger increases her strength while passion
weakens mine; but I get excited again, gather my strength, spread her
thighs and release my prick, which can hardly await my trousers being
unbuttoned and comes out with the impetuosity of a tree bending back up
when the rope is cut that has held it tied down to the earth; I move it to her
cunt, I push, it gets in: the whole anger of my penitent dissolves, she holds
me in her arms, kisses me, closes her eyes and falls back swooning: I do not
know myself anymore, nothing can hold me back, I push again and again, I
come close to the end, I reach it, I am there. I flood the back part of her cunt
with a torrent of fire: she discharges, we stay unconscious; our minds had
abandoned the rest of our bodies to carry themselves to a place where
pleasure alone ruled with a strong feeling.

The nun turns out to be Monique, whom Saturnin knows from Suzon's report. After the rape, vividly described in the present tense to heighten the reader-voyeur's stimulation and create an impression of immediacy, Monique tells Saturnin her further adventures after leaving Suzon, all of them sexual of course. Saturnin decides to smuggle Monique into his monastery; but he is discovered, and has to escape to Paris. It is in a brothel of the big city that he comes across his step-sister Suzon. This is an occasion for Suzon to provide an epic report of her experiences after their separation. Although Suzon warns Saturnin that she may suffer from VD, he does not heed her words and spends a happy night with her. However, in the morning the police arrive, and they are thrown into prison, where Suzon dies. Saturnin, infected by his step-sister, suffers the loss of his genitals and, in great dejection, returns to a monastery. There he spends his last years as a 'portier' (hence the title, 'Portier des Chartreux'), while penning his memoirs.

What is remarkable in *Dom Bougre* is the ending of the novel: the hero is finally castrated and the plot terminates with the end of Saturnin's sexual activity. This is quite unusual; although other features of the book, such as the final remorse and the retiring to a 'decent' life, are typical of pornography written for a middle-class audience. Fanny Hill, too, must finally come to terms with a bourgeois way of life, to which she has to adapt her libertine sexual drive. Several years before Cleland's famous whore made her entrance into the literary world, *Dom Bougre* represented a typical pornographic novel of the Age of Enlightenment, with its propagation of sexual pleasure as a new religion, its seeming rejection of middle-class ideas on sex, and its double morality – quite obvious at the end of the book – all couched in a parody of the Christian faith. When John Cleland put pen to paper, he thus had a fairly easy job, for he could draw on a long tradition of erotic fiction and a pornographic novel that was already fully developed.[34]

John Cleland's plot in *Memoirs of a Woman of Pleasure* (hereafter *MWP*)[35] betrays his borrowing from the whore biography and especially from Hogarth's *A Harlot's Progress*, although Fanny's fate is a prosperous one and thus a mocking parody of Defoe's and Hogarth's warning moralism. If the better-known whores in English fiction, poetry, and pictorial series before 1748 ended in misery and death through disease or hanging, Fanny Hill rises from poverty to a middle-class existence as wife and mother, via several stages of prostitution. The beginning of the novel is almost identical with Hogarth's *A*

Harlot's Progress. Like Moll Hackabout, Fanny is a naive and innocent girl. The death of her parents forces her to seek her fortune in
London. Left in the lurch by her girl friend, Fanny is picked up at a
registry office by an old bawd, Mrs Brown, who takes her home. Such
scenes had often been described in both pictorial and literary satire,
and Cleland shows his knowledge of this tradition. It is in Mrs
Brown's bawdy-house that Fanny undergoes sexual training, so to
speak, advancing from innocence to curiosity and sexual desire while
schooled by Phoebe, her bedfellow. Phoebe is Fanny's tutor, deputised
by Mrs Brown to initiate Fanny into her new role. At this stage,
Cleland begins to incorporate into his novel the philosophy of sexual
pleasure as it had been propagated by several decades of libertine
French fiction. Through lesbian sex, Fanny discovers erotic pleasure.
But her first male customer, Mr Crofts, an ugly old lecher who has
bought Fanny's maidenhead from Mrs Brown, thoroughly spoils her
appetite. Shocked by his violence, Fanny falls ill. However, Phoebe's
gentle instruction, and, especially, voyeuristic experiences, rekindle
the heroine's sexual interest and desire. The third sexual scene that
occurs in the book, after lesbianism and an attempted rape, gains a
comical-grotesque dimension by dint of Mrs Brown's physical appearance and Fanny's hindsight-report, which creates sufficient distance to
tone down the pornographic aspect of her secret observation of the
encounter between 'the venerable mother Abbess herself' and a 'tall,
brawny, young horse grenadier':

> Her paramour sat down by her. He seemed to be a man of very few words,
> and a great stomach, for proceeding instantly to essentials, he gave her
> some hearty smacks, and thrusting his hands into her breasts, disengaged
> them from her stays, in scorn of whose confinement they broke loose and
> swagged down, navel low at least. A more enormous pair did my eyes
> never behold, nor of a worse colour, flagging-soft, and most lovingly
> contiguous: yet such as they were, this neck-beef-eater seemed to paw
> them with a most unenviable lust, seeking in vain to confine or cover one
> of them with a hand scarce less than a shoulder of mutton. After toying
> with them thus some time, as if they had been worth it, he laid her down
> pretty briskly, and canting up her petticoats, made barely a mask of them
> to her broad red face, that blushed with nothing but brandy ...
>
>   Her sturdy stallion had now unbuttoned, and produced naked, stiff, and
> erect, that wonderful machine, which I had never seen before, and which,
> for the interest my own seat of pleasure began to take furiously in it, I
> stared at with all the eyes I had. However, my senses were too much
> flurried, too much concentered in that now burning spot of mine, to
> observe anything more than in general the make and turn of that instru-
> ment, from which the instinct of nature, yet more than all I had heard of it,

now strongly informed me I was to expect that supreme pleasure which she has placed in the meeting of those parts so admirably fitted for each other.

Long, however, the young spark did not remain, before, giving it two or three shakes, by way of brandishing it, he threw himself upon her, and his back being now towards me, I could only take his being engulfed for granted, by the direction he moved in, and the impossibility of missing so staring a mark: and now the bed shook, the curtains rattled so, that I could scarce hear the sighs and murmurs, the heaves and pantings that accompanied the action, from the beginning to the end: the sound and sight of which thrilled to the very soul of me, and made every vein of my body circulate liquid fires: the emotion grew so violent that it almost intercepted my respiration (*MWP*, pp. 62–3).

After this scene Fanny loses her moral innocence, and masturbates. When she watches Polly's copulation with an Italian customer, Fanny's sexual desire is aroused, a process that is described in minute detail. Neither Phoebe's lesbian manipulations nor Fanny's autoeroticism can now quench the flames of aroused sexuality. Thus Fanny's defloration by Charles, the lover she is to meet again and marry later, may be painful to her, but she had been longing for it. In addition, she loves her ravisher, which makes her bear the pain more easily. This episode introduces the sentimental strain into the novel. Fanny has found her true love in a brothel; but she must leave the world of prostitution for this love to develop in a place more acceptable for a middle-class audience. Hence Charles deflowers Fanny not in a bawdy-house, but in a public house, where both become aware of their love for each other. This discovery of love surpassing mere physical pleasure and attraction is the fourth stage of Fanny's development. It is interrupted by Charles' sudden disappearance, which is instigated by his father, as Fanny learns much later. Perturbed by the end of her bliss, Fanny, now pregnant, suffers a miscarriage. However, these trials have made her much wiser, and she now realises that money is important to survive. It is for this reason that she does not refuse to become Mr H.'s kept mistress, the next stage of her life and learning; though Mr H. is no competitor in view of Fanny's feelings for Charles. She even remains faithful to her new keeper until discovering him one day having sexual intercourse with the serving maid. In a remarkable reversal of the eighteenth-century sexual double standard Fanny turns the tables on him and seduces Mr H.'s footman, Will. She thus not only challenges accepted eighteenth-century sexual roles but becomes a teacher of sex herself while losing what she terms a 'kind of second maidenhead' (*MWP*, p. 112). But her happiness with Will, based on sexual and physical pleasure, is not to last for long. Mr H. surprises her in the act of making love with Will. Rebuked and abandoned by her keeper, but financially better off than before, Fanny advances from kept mistress to woman of pleasure, in Mrs Cole's 'academy' in Covent Garden. This step marks the end of Letter I and Volume I, with Fanny mocking the tradition of the epistolary novel in her final remark, 'for surely it is high time to put a period to this'.

In Mrs Cole's establishment Fanny finds happiness and pleasure again, in the company of pleasant girls and an understanding and reasonable surrogate mother. Mrs Cole runs a 'bagnio' for better customers; and the first part of Volume II is made up of the tales of Fanny's companions, Emily, Harriet, and Louisa, entertaining male customers with stories about the loss of their maidenheads. Here Cleland has quite obviously borrowed from the whore dialogue and erotic tales as far back as Boccaccio and the *Heptaméron*. The tales are followed by a little orgy – Fanny terms it a 'country-dance' – which demands much of the author's skill, for Cleland describes a series of copulations whose only differences are the variations of positions. We are into pornotopia at this point, with several couples in a closed room, the only intention being sexual pleasure and satisfaction by alternately making love and watching others in the act. Borel's illustrations for this scene go beyond the text, alluding to earlier French pornography and anticipating the later de Sade (plate 52a).

With the introduction of Mr Norbert, the novel then turns to the description and parody of defloration mania. Mr Norbert pays dearly for what he takes to be Fanny's virginity but which is only a well-hidden sponge filled with blood. As part of her sexual and libertine education Fanny samples a wide variety of erotic behaviour. Not satisfied with Mr Norbert's nocturnal fumbling, she gives herself to a sailor. The scene takes place in a public house while Fanny is in town; and what is remarkable about it is that Fanny experiences pure voluptuous sensuality without money being involved. Back home at Mrs Cole's house, she has sadomasochistic sex with Mr Barville, a flagellant; fetishist sex; and is witness to the brutish intercourse between Louisa and an idiot. During an outing Fanny also watches a male homosexual encounter at an inn, a scene she describes in detail but immediately afterwards condemns 'in rage and indignation' as criminal (*MWP*, p. 195).

With this scene Cleland went too far. In order to achieve pornographic aims, he broke one of the major eighteenth-century sexual taboos (Fanny actually voices her spite of homosexuals, but only after giving a minute description of the sexual intercourse of two men); and

52a–b Engravings from a French edition of Cleland's *Memoirs of a
Woman of Pleasure*, 1776

when he was prosecuted for writing the novel, a prosecution probably
pressed by Church authorities, the passage about the homosexuals
was at the centre of the debate. The censored version of the novel,
which Cleland produced himself for a 1750 edition entitled *Memoirs
of Fanny Hill*, did not include this passage; and after Drybutter's
reinsertion of the scene in a pirate edition in 1757, for which he was
put in the pillory, it has never again appeared in modern editions,
though such reprints usually proclaim 'unexpurgated' versions without providing sufficient details on the origin of the texts.

Cleland's inclusion of a voyeuristic description of homosexual

52b

copulation between men as seen through Fanny's seemingly shocked eyes reflects an ambiguous attitude towards the male homosexual, as well as the false morality of pornography. Lesbianism is often described and practised in *MWP*, without any warning remarks; but sodomy receives a different treatment. On the one hand, anal intercourse is described for sexual stimulation; but on the other hand this behaviour is then immediately rejected by the heroine, who voices the feelings of a middle-class audience.

Fanny's sampling of sex at Mrs Cole's brothel ends with another orgy, in the bath. When the aged bawd moves to the country, Fanny is ready to enter the next stage of her life. Having saved enough money, she takes leave of Mrs Cole, now retired, and acquires a pleasant house at Marylebone, representing herself as a 'young gentlewoman'. An old bachelor whom she kindly assisted one day takes her into keeping, and she becomes the heiress of a large property upon his death. It is now, after her financial independence, that Fanny remembers Charles, her first and only love. Her distinction between physical and psychic love recalls Prévost's *Manon Lescaut* of 1731 and constitutes Cleland's adaptation of French philosophical ideas of pleasure (of aristocratic-libertine origin) to an English bourgeois heroine and readership. On a trip to her birthplace Fanny is united again with Charles. Fortune has not smiled on her lover, but Fanny has sufficient means for both of them. She can thus retire to a virtuous middle-class existence of domesticity, to the satisfaction of herself and the readers of the novel (plate 52b).[36]

MWP is a novel thoroughly dominated by eighteenth-century bourgeois thought. The heroine rises from the lower class to a middle-class existence – like Pamela, Fanny never wanted more than this status. It is the bourgeois state of mind that controls the smallest details of plot, theme, and language. Financial success is continually stressed; and Fanny reproduces like a good pupil what she has learnt on her social climb, thereby perpetuating clichés and prejudices of bourgeois origin. They are most obvious in Fanny's comments on, and treatment of, her maid while a kept mistress of Mr H.[37] There is no doubt that *MWP* was intended as what was termed in Cleland's day a licentious novel; thirty-nine episodes, roughly one third of the text, are sufficient evidence. Summoned before the Privy Council in 1749, Cleland made clear that his primary motives for writing the book were commercial. He got the idea for the novel around 1730 when a first draft of Volume I was apparently written. This he 'altered, added to, transposed, and in short new-cast,' to use his own words, while in debtors' prison between February 1748 and March 1749. To be sure, the confinement suggests itself as a handy explanation for the elaborate sexual fantasies of the novel. De Sade, too, was in prison when he wrote his pornography-cum-philosophy. But Cleland's assertion that an earlier version existed in the 1730s should not be ignored and is, in fact, confirmed by an entry in the records of the would-be libertine club of the Beggar's Benison of Anstruther, Scotland, asserting that in 1737 *Fanny Hill* was read there.[38]

What Cleland attempted with *MWP* is a fusion of natural sexuality acceptable to a middle-class audience and an aesthetic framework incorporating the current of sentimentalism. It is this point, the fusion of sex and pathetic sentiment, which needs some further explanation, since it concerns the fundamental question of the reception and evaluation of the novel. It has often been stated that *MWP* does not contain a single obscene word, a point frequently made in modern editions to appease the law and defend the publication of the book, the tacit implication being that the absence of obscene language precludes any pornography. Cleland may not violate any verbal taboos – which saved him from prosecution and prison – but he does break those of content. It is quite possible to describe copulation, for instance, with the help of circumlocutions and euphemisms instead of Anglo-Saxon four-letter words. The message or content thus remains sexually stimulating, but the effect of the description, and this is the crucial point, may actually run counter to the pornographic intention. In this context it is important to recall that several critics, notably Morrissey, Slepian, and Shinagel, have perceived a comic element in the description of the sexual scenes in *MWP*; Shinagel even believes that this stylistic comedy was intended by Cleland. This is to be doubted. In Volume II, p. 129, Cleland has Fanny Hill remark on the style of her 'memoirs' while addressing the lady to whom she writes. Her intention in penning her confessions, she says, was to write in 'a mean tempered with taste, between the revoltingness of gross, rash, and vulgar expressions, and the ridicule of mincing metaphors and affected circumlocutions'. In other words, the novel tries to describe sex with the stylistic means employed by contemporary prose fiction. Since Cleland also parodied *Pamela* and the whore biography, the stylistic mimicry of the literary sources was a necessary result. While it is true that the autobiographical form, which implies hindsight and hence a certain distance, allows for a certain comic aspect of *MWP* – as in the first three sex scenes of Volume I – most other sexual scenes are quite obviously not intended as comedy. If we find them comical today we ought to bear in mind that our reception of *MWP* is fundamentally different from that of an eighteenth-century reader used to euphemism and metaphor in the description of sex. It is significant, however, that in fact Cleland has trouble keeping up his 'mean way', often tending to what he termed 'mincing metaphors' ending in pathetic clichés. Especially towards the end of the novel, as Naumann has shown, Fanny finds it extremely difficult to invent still different and more powerful words to convey the feelings of joy and pleasure she experiences in the sexual reunion with Charles.

Since it is the reader who re-creates a novel in the process of reading, a novel's reception and evaluation may vary through the centuries as literary taste changes. This may seem to be an obvious point, especially in the case of the sentimental novel, which we find today to be boring and indigestible, so to speak; but it is easily forgotten in the discussion of the pornographic potential and comical effect of *MWP*. On the basis of the predominant literary taste in England around 1750 one can assume that a mid-eighteenth-century reader would not have found Cleland's style comic or odd. In fact, the reading audience probably shared James Boswell's opinion that it was a 'most licentious and inflaming book'.[39] A quotation of the scene in which Fanny finally joins her beloved Charles again, with body and heart, may demonstrate the ambiguous effect of Cleland's style on the twentieth-century reader.

> I have, I believe, somewhere before remarked that the feel of that favourite piece of manhood has, in the very nature of it, something inimitably pathetic. Nothing can be dearer to the touch, or can affect it with a more delicious sensation. Think then! as a lover thinks, what must be the consummate transport of that quickest of our senses, in their central seat too! when, after so long a deprival, it felt itself re-inflamed under the pressure of that peculiar sceptre-member which commands us all but especially my darling, elect from the face of the whole earth. And now, at its mightiest point of stiffness, it felt to me something so subduing, so active, so solid, and agreeable that I know not what name to give its singular impression ...
>
> I panted now with so exquisitely keen an appetite for the imminent enjoyment, that I was even sick with desire, and unequal to support the combination of two distinct ideas that delightfully distracted me! For all the thought I was capable of was that I was now in touch at once with the instrument of pleasure and the great-seal of love: ideas that, mingling streams, poured such an ocean of intoxicating bliss on a weak vessel, all too narrow to contain it, that I lay overwhelmed, absorbed, lost in an abyss of joy, and dying of nothing but immoderate delight.
>
> Charles then roused me somewhat out of this ecstatic distraction with a complaint softly murmured, amidst a crowd of kisses, at the position, not so favourable to his desires, in which I received his urgent insistence for admission, where that insistence was alone so engrossing a pleasure that it made me inconsistently suffer a much dearer one to be kept out. But how sweet to correct such a mistake! My thighs, now obedient to the intimations of love and nature, gladly disclose, and with a ready submission resign up the lost gateway to the entrance of pleasure: I see! I feel! the delicious velvet tip! – he enters might and main with – oh! – my pen drops from me here in the ecstasy now present to my faithful memory! (*MWP*, pp. 219–20)

The euphemistic style creates a comic effect (whether this is involuntary or not need not concern us here) which obviously jars with the pornographic content. The jaded modern reader, used to hard-core scenes in text and film presented in a realistic and obscene vocabulary, cannot help smiling at Cleland's metaphors ('instrument of pleasure', 'abyss of joy', 'velvet tip') that create a pathetic style bordering, for a modern audience, on the comic if not the grotesque. Comical effects, however, whether in style or theme, are detrimental to any sort of pornography which aims at an immediate sexual stimulation. Thus time has added another dimension to Cleland's *MWP*; and many modern readers may find that, rather than being inflamed as James Boswell, they will be amused at Cleland's mixture of voluntary and involuntary stylistic comedy.[40]

After his survey of the pornographic novel in the second part of the eighteenth century, Naumann concluded that, apart from a few imitations of *MWP*, and sub-pornographic titles such as *The History of the Human Heart* (1749 or 1769) and *La Souricière. The Mousetrap* (1794), no major English pornographic novel appeared before the nineteenth century. This is correct as far as genuine English literature is concerned, which, after Cleland's *MWP*, avoided sexual explicitness. The best example is John Cleland himself with his 'cleaned-up' version of *Memoirs of Fanny Hill* of 1750 and the later *Memoirs of a Coxcomb* (1751), as well as *The Woman of Honour*, published in three volumes in 1768.

If English writers produced nothing new in the way of pornography it was, according to traditional explanations, because of the domination of taste by the middle class, and increased censorship. What has been ignored, though, is that France continued to be a major supplier of erotica. Starting with Fougeret de Monbron's *Margot la ravaudeuse* (1750),[41] the pornographic novel had yet to reach its heyday across the Channel with the works of Andréa de Nerciat, Mirabeau, Restif de la Bretonne, and de Sade. In addition, countless anonymous works, like *Caroline et Belleval, ou les leçons de la volupté* (3rd edition, 1797), and *Confessions de Mademoiselle Sappho* (1789), attributed to Pidansat de Mairobert, continued to be published, and are easily overlooked. With the pornographic fiction of the preceding century and of the early eighteenth century continually being reprinted and pirated, there was no shortage of pornographic novels; nor was there a gap in licentious fiction between 1750 and 1800, as Naumann and others have argued. Cleland was unique anyway and combined the streams of French and English pornography with sentimentalism. After Cleland's *MWP* France regained control of a market that it had never really lost. Many of those who read pornography also read French, and those with no command of this foreign tongue had translations available to them.⁴² French pornography culminated with the Revolutionary period, a remarkable coincidence which Ronald Paulson has further analysed in his recent *Representations of Revolution*. Paulson establishes an interesting connection between the inherent moral revolt of pornography and political violence. England dreaded, but never saw, such events as occurred in France.⁴³ Although libertine French erotica were fundamentally different from prevailing English middle-class ideas, in their propagation of sexual pleasure and criticism of moral authorities, French books were apparently quite capable of catering to the English market. If any subconscious sexual needs of readers remained, they were absorbed by the rising movements of sentimentalism and Romanticism. Both were not without covert sexual currents. Lewis's *The Monk* (1796), for instance, and its pornographic parody of 1798, revealed the latent sexuality in the literature of Romanticism. Isaac Cruikshank underlined it with his engraving of 1801, entitled *Luxury* (plate 53), in which a woman's backside is heated by a symbolic fire while her thoughts are inflamed by her reading of *The Monk* – the result is masturbation.

But the gothic also served as a metaphor by which some English writers tried to understand events in France in the 1790s. The revolutionary drive of libertine literature against the authority of Church and state, noticeable from the 1660s onward, merged with the dark powers of Romanticism and the psychic energy and libido released through pornography. As Paulson has shown, the two most striking phenomena in *The Monk* are Ambrosio's revolt against his imprisonment from earliest childhood in a monastery, and the bloodthirsty crowd that grinds into a pulp the evil abbess who has murdered those nuns in her convent who gave in to sexual temptation. If the prioress represents the Church, what better dramatisation can there be of the fight for freedom through revolution of the individual and of the mob, with all its horrible consequences of the breaking of taboos, and of murder, rape, and arson? It is understandable that de Sade should have considered *The Monk* the finest example of gothic fiction, for its obvious element of the release of sex and violence represents an aspect of pornography the Marquis explored in his own works – the compulsive need to degrade the female body in a useless attempt to satisfy the demands of the libido. Admittedly, the gothic had existed from the 1760s on; but gothic terror and its sexual current in fiction in the 1790s can also be seen as a partial reaction to the fears created in England and Europe by the upheavals in France. It was only the supernatural and the demonic, presented in tales of confusion, blood,

53   Isaac Cruikshank, *Luxury*, 1801

sexual perversion, and horror, that could startle readers after everyday reality had been rendered so horrific by the events in France.[44]

3 EROTIC MAGAZINES

A sizable part of eighteenth-century erotic fiction was published in newspapers and magazines, particularly after 1750, when the more specialised licentious magazines began to serialise novels. In the 1720s papers like *The British Mercury*, basically a political sheet, did not refuse ribald poetry; and later newspapers like *The Craftsman* in the

1740s were preoccupied with the discussion in fact and fiction of venereal disease.[45] Already in the seventeenth century Londoners could buy periodicals of amusement. These were published and edited by Grub Street writers, some of whom developed a coarse and aggressive style. Edward Ward's *London Spy* (1698–1700), for instance, was a monthly sixteen-page folio full of biting sketches of London life, with such 'characters' as the Quack, the Banker, and the Gossip. Tom Brown's *Amusements Serious and Comical* (1700) was less crude than Ward's sheet, but Brown, too, could be as bawdy as any major Grub Street writer. Another example was *The English Lucian*, published between 18 January and 18 April 1698, its sub-title promising 'weekly discoveries of the witty intrigues, comical passages, and remarkable transactions in town and country'. It contained facetious news, often bawdy, from such locations as Old Baly [sic], Drury Lane, Lombard Street, and St James. Such papers were emulated by *The Secret Mercury* (September 1702), for instance, developing an aggressive, cynical journalism that did not mince its words in matters of sex. Examples are *The Wandering Spy* (1705) and Ward's *London Terrae Filius, or Satyrical Reformer* (1707–8).[46]

The more polite magazines, which were to concentrate on cultural life and literature in particular, owe a great deal to the French *Le Mercure Galant* (1673–4; 1678–9; 1710–14), written both for and by members of 'le beau monde'. Peter Motteux, for one, modelled his *Gentleman's Journal* – first published in January 1692 – on this French periodical. It included in the sixty-four octavo pages of its initial numbers news from England and abroad; but also, and this was quite new, history, philosophy, letters, 'novels', translations of foreign fiction, fables, and book notices. In addition, the *Journal* contained woodcuts; poetry by Restoration writers like Prior, Sedley, d'Urfey, and others; and even a 'Lover's Gazette'. Although Motteux's periodical gradually dwindled in size and suffered an early death after a few years – competition was then as tough as it is now – he created the prototype of the later literary periodicals and their special branch, the licentious magazines. The respectable and sober *Gentleman's Magazine* (1731–1914) not only borrowed half its title from Motteux's *Journal* but also its section headings.[47]

From the 1750s on a number of 'polite' magazines catered to England's educated classes. Sex, and sex in fiction, even made inroads into this territory of respectability, albeit in a form that never offended taste or style. Francis Place notes that he once browsed in a volume (probably Volume I of 1750) of *The Ladies Magazine: or, The*

Universal Entertainer (1749–53), where he found trial reports, poems, tales, and a satire on Hill's *Lucina sine concubitu*. In the 1750s *The Entertainer* specialised in gossip and scandal, amusing its readers with occasional barbed advertisements like this one of 17 September 1754:

> Whereas Miss Fitz-Gay had the misfortune to lose her Virtue and Reputation at Vaux-Hall t'other night; this is to give notice, that whoever will bring the same to MRS HELPWELL, at the NAKED WOMAN in RUSSELL-STREET, COVENT GARDEN, shall receive the full reward of half-a-crown, to be paid by MISS FITZ-GAY herself, at her lodgings in CATHERINE STREET.[48]

The Town and Country Magazine, of which twenty-four volumes were published between 1769 and 1797, took a prurient interest in the sexual. In addition to occasional erotic plates, scandals involving adultery and fornication were immediately discussed. The issue of February 1769 sported a description of a brothel run by Charlotte Hayes, entitled 'The Monastery of Santa Charlotta', and Volume V of May 1773 speculates on the obscene novels that Wilkes allegedly kept at Medmenham Abbey. Between October 1772 and October 1774 *The Macaroni and Theatrical Magazine* catered to the fashionable beaux interested in London's entertainment; its early death indicates that periodicals passed away as quickly as fashions. *The Matrimonial Magazine* of 1775, despite its innocent title, also covered divorces and extramarital sex rather than connubial bliss, and featured 'memoirs' of persons of quality drawn from crim. con. trials. In addition, readers could choose between tales of love (in March 1775, for instance, 'The Lover's Auction' was printed, a mildly erotic story), excerpts from novels and non-fiction, and domestic as well as foreign news. Still later, *The Brittanic Magazine* (1793–1809) continued the tradition of including a section of 'Memoirs of Love and Gallantry'.[49]

In his survey of the English novel in the magazines Robert D. Mayo has explained that after the mid-century, when novelists like Fielding, Smollett, and Swift left the scene, serialised English and foreign fiction became affected and egregiously sentimental. There was generally very little interest in what we consider today as important fiction. The magazines printed a large amount of French fiction in translations: above all, stories by such writers as Godard de Beauchamp, Cazotte, Crébillon *fils*, Diderot, Voisenon, and Louvet de Couvray. Mayo ignores erotic fiction as a genre, but notes numerous titles reprinted in the licentious magazines of the second half of the eighteenth century. Since it was in their pages that erotic fiction also flourished, they deserve a closer look, not least because serialisation influenced both form and content in the short fiction and the novels that were published.[50]

Donald Thomas sees mainly commercial reasons behind the increasing publication of erotic fiction in the periodicals after 1750, arguing that the editors and publishers hoped to win subscribers with their cunning manipulation of serialised erotica. There was, however, also a tradition of mildly erotic magazines; and if H. Nitschke, in his meticulous study of a few licentious periodicals published after 1750, finds that in many respects they were a continuation of the bawdy literature of the Restoration, it is because these magazines harkened back to the prototypes at the beginning of the century. In addition, they were published for an urban, worldly audience comparable to court circles and other readers of Restoration bawdry. Although the more licentious magazines took a pronounced stance against sentimentalism, their professed satirical attitude was a sham; for their true aim was not, as they claimed, moral reformation but comic and erotic entertainment. The periodicals were quite aware of a change in sexual morals, making frequent references to the 'unbounded sensuality in the higher circles of society', but their survival depended on the commentary on immorality and not on morality. Hence the licentious magazines were content with the cynical exploitation of sex and scandal, and preferably the combination of both.[51]

The Covent Garden Magazine (1772–5) was one of the first of these periodicals after the mid-century. 'Elegant plates' (plate 54) provided pictorial highlights for the erotic scenes, described in fiction and in gossip about amatory adventures in high and low society. This magazine was then successfully copied by *The Rambler's Magazine; or, The Annals of Gallantry, Glee, Pleasure, and The Bon Ton* (1783–90); *The Bon Ton Magazine* (1791–6); and *The Ranger's Magazine* (1795). The tradition of such erotic periodicals continued well into the nineteenth century. The magazines had various sections, some not erotic (gaming, drama, news), with a predominant interest in sex. According to Nitschke's survey, the following themes and forms were used: travel reports; essays on love and marriage (sometimes serious in tone and treatment); satirical whore dialogues; and lists of whores, inspired by *Harris' List of Covent Garden Ladies*, which was popular in the 1780s. These lists were accompanied by 'curious correspondence', from readers reporting their sexual experiences with various ladies of the night. No doubt these accounts were as 'genuine' as the 'genuine' readers' letters in modern pornographic magazines. Sex scandals had a special heading in these periodicals, usually entitled

54   *The Rash Lover*, frontispiece of *The Covent Garden
Magazine*, February 1773

'amorous intelligence', or 'annals of gallantry'.

In the way of erotic fiction there were short tales dramatising sexual
topics in exotic or mythical locations, and others allegedly based on
actual cases. The staple diet, however, and the major attraction of
these magazines was the serialised erotic novel.[52] Two examples of

tales from *The Bon Ton Magazine* will demonstrate the style, heavily strung with *doubles entendres*, and the stance, of this sort of fiction. Number XXVI (April 1793) of *The Bon Ton Magazine* carried a tale, with an 'annexed engraving', about 'Abused Confidence; Or, Infidelity Exposed and Punished', which in essence is nothing more than a case of adultery, possibly based on a real event. After the stereotype initial tongue-in-cheek speculations on the principal sources of illicit sexual gratification among the British gentry and nobility – idleness is mentioned as one evil – the 'characters' are thus introduced:

> The hero of our present *tete-à-tete* [sic] is the third son of Lord M––t G––t, of the sister kingdom; a young fellow of much spirit, and what is generally understood in society by the word *blood*. ... The fair criminal, whom we must call our heroine, is the wife of Mr P––n, of the Queen's County, and exquisitely beautiful. The Hon. Mr B––t––r, for such is the name and addition of our hero, is in the meridian of juvenile vigour, as is, indeed, his *cornuted friend*, Mr P––n.

In Mr P.'s absence, Mary the chambermaid witnesses the adultery of his wife.

> It is a rule among men of gallantry always to lock the door before they begin to do business, but though our hero was a complete adept in the science of intrigue, he now neglected this universal caution: whether the delay of a few hours increased appetite to impatience, we cannot positively say, but no sooner did he and our frail matron enter the pavilion than the fond sport began. Mary, true to her engagement with William, happened to arrive at the pavilion before her lover; but just as she was about to enter, her ears and her heart were assailed by the sound of soft and short breathings, repeated kisses, and dying murmurs: Mary herself began to breath short, and would have retired, but a sudden impulse of jealousy arrested her intention – she thought that William having probably arrived at the place before her, had met by accident some other female, and was bestowing upon her what she herself expected, and conceived she had a right to; this idea induced her to push the door softly open, when lo! to her agitated feelings, she beheld the lovely limbs of her fair mistress exposed to broad day, and our enraptured hero in the act of vigorously assaulting that Cyprian citadel, which was supposed to be only open to the assaults of its Hymeneal Commander. The surprised and almost suffocated Mary continued to behold the rencontre, until the suspension of all motion declared that of emotion in every breast but her own; she then slipped away, and meeting with William, who she chided for being rather tardy in his motions, she told, as far as modesty would permit, what had been going forward; they both retired, and after waiting until our hero and heroine quitted the pavilion, performed an after-piece, which not coming immediately within this *tête à tête*, we shall pass over.

Betrayed by the servants, the adulterers are horsewhipped by the cuckolded husband, who is said to have 'commenced a *suit ecclesiastic*, and will no doubt shortly obtain a sentence of divorce'.

The frontispiece for the November issue of *The Bon Ton Magazine* was more daring, showing a dallying apothecary disguised as a midwife, and a lady on a bed, both being watched by a masturbating servant (plate 8). The engraving illustrates a tale with the title, *The Wilful Mistake; or, the Medical Metamorphosis*, which is another adaptation of the old myth that priests and doctors are in the most advantageous position for seducing women. The story is about a newly-wed widow, the 'em bon point heroine' Mrs A———n, who becomes a willing victim of Mr B. N———'s seductive attempts.

In a short time after her second marriage, our heroine either found, or feigned, herself to be as women wish to be when joined in wedlock. Sickness, palpitations, faintings, longings, loathings, and all the train of pleasing propensities which attend the fair who succeed in their laudable endeavours at propagation, now assailed her, and the new appointed son of Coronis was, of course, frequently in the exercise of his professional functions.

Being compelled to a remedy of this kind, it became absolutely necessary that a proper skilful female operator should be provided. Accordingly, the old gentleman apothecary was directed to send such a person with all convenient expedition. Not having a female upon his list of Nurse Tenders but who happened at that time to be employed, he applied to our angry hero, who, as an accommodating and friendly neighbour, undertook to send an experienced matron without loss of time.

Having thus accounted for our hero's intimacy in this house of *kind accommodation*, it remains that we fully explain the meaning of his visit; to be brief then, he informed the good lady, that he was called upon to attend a patient then in labour, by her husband, who was a sensible man, and would not trust her life to the care of an unskilful ignorant woman; but that the wife herself had conceived a squeamish idea of immodesty in permitting a man to attend her; that therefore, the husband and he had contrived to put a trick upon her, and that he had called for the assistance of his good friend, Mrs. Goodwill, to help in the deception.

Mrs. Goodwill, whose penetration anticipated his wishes, immediately consented; and our hero was in a short time completely metamorphosed into a midwife. He was rather under the middle size, though well proportioned, and one of the lustier ladies' undresses fitted him to a nicety.

A coach was now called for, and our adventurous hero, in his newly resumed character, drove off to Bishopsgate-street. He was immediately introduced to our heroine's apartment; and being left alone with her, produced his implement of operation, mixed its contents together, and said much in praise of its efficacy ...

The fact is, that our heroine, in a very short while, told her supposed nurse-tender that she mistook her object, and began to recede from the operation, but the former, who by this time had effected what it was too late to remedy, persevered with spirit, and against every entreaty completed his secret purposes.

Our astonished heroine, thus deceived into an act, not criminal on her part, was a very considerable time before she recovered the use of her faculties, so as to know what to make of the event: but her exulting quandum lover and medical friend, soon disclosed all, advising her, at the same time, not to render herself unhappy by a communication of what could not otherwise possibly transpire ...

But, no; our modern heroine knew better, and not only kept the secret from her husband, who might have been disturbed in his mind had he known it, but, on account of its singularity as well as ingenuity, agreed to give the amorous accoucheur as many opportunities as possible of repeating his operations ... at last, neglecting to bolt the door of the bed-chamber, a footboy passing up stairs, was induced by curiosity to peep in, and by the light of a large fire, for the candle was extinguished, saw every thing that passed: and divulging it to the other servants, it soon came to the ears of the cornuto, who is now preparing a libel for a divorce.[53]

Eighteenth-century English erotic magazines were not pornographic. From *The Covent Garden Magazine* to the more belligerent and occasionally obscene *Rambler*, erotic entertainment was the main purpose, not sexual excitement. With cleverly devised suspense at the end of each issue, their serialised fiction mirrors the taste of the macho man-about-town re-living in fiction what his social betters in the aristocracy did in reality. In these erotica women are almost always willing sexual objects, with a passive role in the battle of the sexes. The overall detached and mocking attitude of the periodicals is due to a satirical journalism interested in sensation rather than reformation, and to the influence of plagiarised French sources, whose implicit libertine ideology of sex as enjoyment – for men, to be sure; women had to bear the responsibilities – found a propitiously inclined readership among males who regularly read the English magazines.[54]

4 PLAYS IN PRINT AND IN THE THEATRE

In 1707 one John Marshall was prosecuted, for publishing *Sodom: or, The Quintessence of Debauchery*. The re-publication in the eighteenth century of this obscene play from the Restoration period – often attributed to the Earl of Rochester, but also to Christopher Fishbourne – indicates that there was a literary market for printed theatrical erotica. This is confirmed by many literary sources, as well as library catalogues listing plays and collections of plays among the pabulum for connoisseurs of erotic literature.[55]

Given the united efforts of moralists and politicians in the early decades of the century to put a stop to sexual licence and political satire on the stage, it may be surprising to notice that erotic drama and theatrical bawdry survived. Around 1700 Jeremy Collier and Arthur Bedford, to name just two of the moralists fighting what they saw as a flood of immoral plays, published their own puritan diatribes. Some dramatists, like Congreve, decided to tread more carefully, and toned down their use of ribald language; but it was not so much the moralists who stopped the erotic tide, after the mid-century, as the Licensing Act of 1737, and a concomitant change in taste. To be sure, Restoration plays like Wycherley's *The Country Wife* (1675) continued to appear in print; and by 1710 Edmund Curll had already published the second edition of Thomas Betterton's *The Amorous Widow, or The Wanton Wife* (1706). In 1755 a satirical pamphlet entitled *A Vindication of the Reformation, on Foot, Among the Ladies ... of Going Naked* still described the theatre in the terms of Collier, as a place where ladies of questionable reputation were looking for companions for the night and where bawdy plays by d'Urfey and other authors of ribaldry were performed. The pseudonymous writer lists the following plays as examples of theatrical 'immorality':

> *The Old Bachelor* [Congreve]
> *Love for Love* [Congreve]
> *Friendship in Fashion* [Otway]
> *The London Cuckolds* [Ravenscroft]
> *Chances* [John Gay]
> *The Fair Penitent* [Nicholas Rowe]
> *Sir John Brute*
> *The Trip to the Jubilee* [Farquhar; also
>   published as *The Constant Couple*]
> *The Way of the World* [Congreve]

In such plays it was sex that was at the centre of attention. Sexual relations were, however, not shown but discussed, preferably in *doubles entendres* and allusions. Half a century later, Thomas Rowlandson made obvious in an explicit picture what it would have meant to enact the scenes that were only talked about. His *A Scene in a Farce called 'The Citizen'* may be based on Arthur Murphy's play of 1761 (plate 55), but it also sums up the 'off scene' (the original meaning of obscene) elements in eighteenth-century erotic drama.

55 Rowlandson, *A Scene in a Farce called 'The Citizen'*, early nineteenth century

Secret assignments between theatregoers, but also between actresses, singers, and dancers and the patronising nobility, continued. Caricaturists alluded to this established tradition, in prints and

56 Newton, *Mademoiselle Parisot*, 1802

drawings showing old lechers eyeing buxom young dancers (plate 56). When in 1790, the actress Elizabeth Farren (1759–1829), later the Countess of Derby, appeared naked on stage, to expose herself and the avarice of her niggardly manager, the event made pictorial history. In particular, clergymen among the moralists saw a great danger in beautiful female bodies cavorting in a state of near-undress before theatrical audiences.[56]

Ironically, the Licensing Act of 1737 boosted the bawdy and erotic elements in printed plays. Each newly written play now had to be sanctioned by a Royal Patent or licensed by the Lord Chamberlain. The Act was a consequence of political references and slander on stage, with Walpole figuring as the great bogyman; and by 1747, when theatrical activity was completely halted, theatres had to resort to clever advertising to survive. Patrons were now invited to attend 'exhibitions', 'Coffee and Pictures', etc. to evade the law. It is important to note that censored portions of plays, while not spoken during the performance, nevertheless appeared in print. The pre-censorship of drama meant that plays revised or excised by the Examiner were published in the original full version, by disgruntled authors who sent their manuscripts to the printer after the first performance. The unexpurgated book versions thus contained in print what could not be shown or said on stage. Hence theatre audiences were theoretically more protected than the reading public from political allusions, bawdy language, and profanity; though actors, too, found subtle ways to communicate messages not recorded in the script. Erotic plays thus continued, at least in print; so that by 1780 Colman's *The Genius*, a play about the notorious Dr Graham and his sex goddess, could still be bought.[57]

Catalogues of eighteenth-century book owners, if they list erotica, often contain the odd title of French drama. One can therefore assume that a great many printed French plays were available in England. Like their novelist brethren, French playwrights produced a vast number of erotica, from the mildly licentious to the obscene and pornographic.[58] Some libertine members of one literary society, *L'académie de ces dames et ces messieurs* (1739–76), with the Comte de Caylus as a temporary president, wrote plays, which were then discussed by the 'confrères', the best plays being recommended for printing. An example, according to Rabenalt, is *Le bordel, ou le Jean-foutre puni ... À Ancome* (1736; reprinted 1747), whose title and 'place of publication' (a pun on the word *con*, i.e., cunt), bespeak its content. Among the writers of theatrical erotica it was the Grandval family, 'père et fils', and Delisle de Sales who distinguished themselves. Grandval *père* is credited with *L'appareilleuse*, published with illustrations; and his son, equally known for scatological and obscene writings, followed in the footsteps of the elder Grandval with *La nouvelle Messaline* (1773), which is one of the earliest ribald satires on Marie-Antoinette, as a nymphomaniac Messalina seducing her bodyguard and a few 'Carmelite' monks. The French aristocracy could afford private theatres and paid playwrights for specially ordered plays. The Comte d'Hénin, for one, had the works of 'his' author, Delisle de Sales, performed in his own playhouse.

In the period of the Revolution the scatological and obscene branches of the theatre produced a welter of plays, some merely written as entertainments, like *Les costumes théâtrales ou scènes secrètes des foyers* (1793), which, like other erotica, was illustrated; and others anti-aristocratic in tone, like the plays of de Sade, and anonymous works such as *La France foutue. Tragédie lubrique et royaliste* (1799).[59]

In addition to the French and English theatrical erotica in print, one ought to consider that the eighteenth century also knew performances

57 Rowlandson, *The Jugglers*, early nineteenth century

58 Rowlandson, *French Dancers at a Morning Rehearsal*, early nineteenth century

that were never recorded and yet have much in common with the stage. The 'mimus eroticus', as Rabenalt has termed it, comprises public and semi-public erotic dances at special occasions (the strip-tease has a long history), and bawdy speeches. A few examples may help to throw a little light on this part of the eighteenth-century 'performers' world', which is almost entirely lost to the historian who depends on written sources. Shortly after 1800, Thomas Rowlandson recalled this tradition in several of his pictorial erotica. In *The Jugglers* (plate 57), a fantasy based on Callot's similar phallic etchings, he catches the occasional obscene aspects of the 'commedia dell'arte' and the carnival. Like the spectacular Dr Graham in the medical field, George Alexander Stevens gave public lectures, at first in the Hay-market, London, and subsequently in the provinces and in America. Starting in the early 1760s, these lectures were a combination of pantomime, ribald satire, and cabaret. Stevens' 'Lecture on Heads' is best known, and included 'scenes' mocking beaux, rakes, and prostitutes.

In Plate III of *A Rake's Progress* (plate 11c in Chapter 2) Hogarth has left us a hint at erotic dancing performances in early eighteenth-century public houses. The scene shows the rake and his companions in Rose Tavern, Drury Lane. In this engraving of moral chaos and degeneration a pregnant woman provides music by singing an obscene street-ballad; she is accompanied by a trumpeter and a harpist. A 'posture-girl', the eighteenth-century term for a female stripper, is preparing for her erotic dance, in which she will be using a platter and candle carried in by a waiter. Contemporary visitors like Lichtenberg reported that such performances bordered on the obscene. Rowlandson's *French Dancers at a Morning Rehearsal* (plate 58) would seem to confirm such statements; though the caricaturist, as so often, goes beyond the erotic or the pornographic, by adding grotesque and comic aspects. It seems that in many ways the eighteenth century was as advanced in the 'mimus eroticus' as our present age.[60]

❧ 8 ❧

Pictorial Erotica

In the art of eroticism as in its literature, French influence predominated. The two forms were closely linked, both in England and in France, by a tradition of book illustration. Another international type of erotic art was that known as 'postures', which enjoyed especial popularity – and notoriety – as an offshoot of contemporary interest in classical archaeology. The patronage of the French court, meanwhile, had produced an art, in the Rococo mode, celebrating eroticism in terms purely of pleasure. Not so in England, however, where the more notable artists of the time responded to a largely bourgeois clientele with work whose erotic content was moralising or satirical.

I LITERATURE AND PICTURES – AND VICE VERSA

From about 1500, erotic texts appeared with illustrations. Sometimes there was a short time-lag between the first edition of an erotic book and its first illustrated version. Depending on the text, and the audience they were intended for, such pictorials could be allusively erotic, explicitly obscene, or obviously pornographic. Their relation with the texts they accompanied is comparable to the modern transformation of literature into film; and, more recently, film into literature. Pictorials can be detrimental to a literary text, by reducing textual ambiguity to mere sexuality, which happened to a few sentimental novels and specimens of the 'roman galant'; they are able to enhance a text, as did the engravings by Eisen for Cleland's *Memoirs of a Woman of Pleasure*; or they can complement it by making more obvious a pornographic potential. But in each case illustrations exert a powerful influence on the reader/observer exclusively by dint of their own visual quality. In the case of pornographic pictorials it is obvious that they create more initial interest than the text. An example of how such illustrative erotica can displace the text as a sexual stimulant can be found in a collection of trial reports from 1796, containing the case of an alleged nymphomaniac, Mrs Errington. During her trial for adultery, a witness by the name of Phebe Lush deposed that Mrs Errington had shown her a book on several occasions 'which she said was the WOMAN OF PLEASURE ... that there were a great many indecent pictures in such book, which she seemed to take pleasure in shewing the deponent ... and ... to Mr Branston's daughter'.

Many of the better-known book illustrators of the eighteenth century – Cruikshank, Eisen, Gravelot, Hayman, Rowlandson, Stothard, Vanderbank, and Wale – employed erotic themes in their works; and so did the caricaturists Darly, Woodward, Newton, and Gillray; and, above all, Thomas Rowlandson.[1] In turn, pictorial series themselves exerted considerable influence on literature, both thematically and structurally: the shadow of Hogarth's 'rake' is too obvious in the novels of Fielding (*Joseph Andrews, Tom Jones, Jonathan Wild*) and Smollett (*Ferdinand Count Fathom; Roderick Random*) to be ignored.[2]

If erotic art in literary texts usually served the purpose of increasing the erotic appeal of a book through the graphic or visual representation of selected scenes, there are also a few instances in which pictures show the effects upon readers of erotic texts. In P.A. Baudouin's *Le Midi*, for instance, a novel that is no doubt of the licentious kind has fallen from the hand of a masturbating woman (plate 59). Caricatures also varied the theme of the stimulating and immoral effects of licentious literature. Rowlandson's satires on *The Man of Feeling* (plates 60 and 61) are parodies of Mackenzie's successful sentimental novel, with the same title, of 1771. In the picture from 1785, 'feeling' is given a secondary, obscene, meaning, while the second illustration shows a fat, red-nosed lecher whose state of mind and moral attitude are characterised by a copy of Wilkes' *Essay on Woman* emerging from his pocket. Wilkes' obscene essay, thus the message of Rowlandson's satire, explains the man's fondling of the bosom of a pretty country girl.

2 PORNOGRAPHY: 'POSTURES'

The history of what was generally known in the eighteenth century as

59 P.A. Baudouin, *Le midi*, engraved by E. de Ghendt, undated

Aretine's Postures proves again the close relation between eroticism in literature and in art. *Aretine's Postures* was a notorious book throughout the seventeenth and eighteenth centuries and was considered by many the peak of pornography. It contained sixteen (later twenty) engravings of copulating couples, by Giulio Romano, engraved by Marcantonio Raimondi. To these Pietro Aretino had added sexually explicit sonnets, the sixteen 'sonetti lussoriosi', which first appeared in 1527. None of the original engravings has come down to us, although they were often copied in the eighteenth century. Looking at a somewhat feeble translation from 1920 of Aretino's sonnet number four, one may understand the storm of controversy which accompanied the poems when they were published in other editions and languages.

60 Rowlandson, *The Man of Feeling*, 1785

61 Rowlandson, *The Man of
Feeling*, 1788

Sonnet Number Four

Place your leg, dearest, on my shoulder here,
And take my truncheon in your tender grasp,
And while I gently move it, let your clasp
Tighten and draw me to your bosom dear.

And should I stray from front to hinder side,
Call me a rogue and villain, will not you?
Because I know the difference 'twixt the two,
As stallions know how lusty mares to ride.

My hand shall keep the turgid dart in place,
Lest it might slip and somehow get away,
And I should see a frown on your fair face.

Backsided joys enchant but one, they say,
But surely this both you and me doth grace,
So let us spend and quickly, too, I pray.

And I'll be loth to leave a sport so gay,
Dear one, for such a valiant lance
Was ne'er possessed by any King of France.

The plates in François-Félix Nogaret's *L'Arétin françois* (1787), a book of obscene verse and pictures, are a re-make, so to speak, of Raimondi's engravings of the positions of sexual intercourse. As late as 1802 James Aitken was imprisoned for six months for publishing *The Amours of Peter Aretin*, which, according to the court records, also contained obscene prints.[3]

A good excuse for publishing such illustrations of positions in sexual intercourse could be found in the burgeoning science of archaeology and, with it, ethnology. The ruins of Pompeii were discovered in 1748 and identified in 1763. With the work of Winckelmann on the imitation and history of classical art, from the 1750s on, many artists and 'scientists' were drawn to Italy, and charlatans followed in their steps. It was the combination of climate, beautiful landscape, classical sites, and art treasures that attracted a great many Northerners. For English gentlemen it was almost a social 'must' to include the land of the Romans in the Grand Tour – even Sterne tried, and failed, for his *Sentimental Journey*.

One of the earliest to publish his erotic discoveries of monuments and stones in Italian cities and sites was Pierre François Hugues Hancarville. He was an antiquary and member of the Royal Societies of Berlin and London and, like Cagliostro and a few others, tried to pass for a nobleman by calling himself d'Hancarville. In the 1750s he

Tibére et Mallonia

62 Illustration from P.F.H. Hancarville, *Monumens de la
    vie privée des douze Césars*, 1780

reached Rome, and soon contacted Sir William Hamilton, the British
ambassador to the court of Naples and husband of Admiral Lord
Nelson's Emma. Using some erotic pieces in the collection of Hamilton's antiques as a basis, Hancarville produced etchings which he then
published, in four volumes, with English and French explanations, as
*Antiquités étrusques, grecques et romaines tirées du cabinet de M.
Hamilton* (Naples, 1766–7). Hancarville was just one of a group of
dedicated European connoisseurs exchanging information and objects
of art during meetings at Rome and Naples (plate 62).[4]

Among other Englishmen in Italy was Richard Payne Knight, who is best known for his *An Account of the Remains of the Worship of Priapus, Lately Existing at Isernia, in the Kingdom of Naples* (1786). This 'travel report' of 195 pages, embellished with plates showing penes, plays upon the prurience of readers. Nevertheless, it is an expression of the deep interest among eighteenth-century intellectuals and artists in foreign rites and cultures.[5] The first twelve pages of the *Account* contain a letter by Sir William Hamilton describing the remnants of a Priapus culture in the vicinity of Naples. In Isernia, Hamilton noted, during the feast of St Cosmo and St Damian, 'votive objects of wax, representing the male parts of generation, of various dimensions, some even of the length of a palm, are publicly offered for sale. The "vows" are chiefly presented by the female sex, and the person who was at this fête in 1780 told me that he heard a woman say, at the time she presented her "vow" in church, "blessed St Cosmo, let it be like this".' This is followed by a letter of a person of Isernia, in Italian, and Knight's own report in the guise of a scholarly account of the history of the worship of Priapus. At heart a romantic and sensualist who was masquerading as a scholar, Knight was a leading member of the Society of Dilettanti, founded in 1734 and consisting of genteel libertines. They sponsored some of Knight's research into archaeology as well as into sexual rites. Thomas Rowlandson produced an excellent satire on the craze of his noble and rich countrymen for 'antique' objects and on the romantic triangle of Lord Nelson, Emma Hamilton, and her complaisant, senile husband, Sir William. In *Modern Antiques* (plate 63) the antiquary, Hamilton, pokes his nose into an Egyptian statuette while his wife and her lover have a tête-à-tête inside a mummy case.[6]

3 FOREIGN PICTORIAL EROTICA

Single erotic drawings, engravings, and prints from abroad were as numerous in England after 1700 as 'homespun' pictorial erotica. In works exposed in print shops and at artists' studios, the satirists, notably Gillray and Rowlandson, mocked old and well-heeled lechers eyeing the charms of nubile women in the nude. Trade in erotic art was good; and even better when the art was 'antique'. If it was not, it could easily be made so. Giovanni Battista Casanova, the brother of the diarist and womaniser, thus cheated Winckelmann with falsifications from his 'collection'. England had no shortage of vendors of foreign

63 Rowlandson, *Modern Antiques*, 1811?

and domestic art. In 1802, for example, Baptista Bertazzi, an Italian
hawker, was in conflict with the law for selling obscene prints.[7]

Works from the Continent reached England almost every day. A
few erotica came from Holland; and more from Italy, with the paintings and drawings of earlier periods like those of the Carracci brothers
of the sixteenth century being revived. But it was France that played
the leading role in art as in erotic fiction.

It is noteworthy that Watteau's *Le pèlerinage à l'île de Cythère*
(1717) stands at the beginning of a period in painting and engraving

that made love and sexuality its paramount subjects. The court was among the foremost patrons of French artists; and after it moved from Versailles to Paris, at the death of Louis XIV, there was much work to be done in its new apartments. It was at this period that the Rococo style came into being. This was light-hearted and frivolous, with a touch of candour reminiscent of Antiquity, especially in the overtly erotic pictures of François Boucher. Peter Webb has discussed in an authoritative manner the major erotica of Boucher, Fragonard, and Watteau, as well as Greuze's works towards the end of the century. While his predecessors were frankly and openly erotic, Greuze combines a sentimental streak of morality with sexual titillation. What Greuze wanted to convey was sex, religiosity, and sensibility; but the naked body of the woman in the picture, *Saint Mary of Egypt*, for example, and the execution, well below excellence, leave an impression of sentimentality and sin in a mixture that comes close to erotic kitsch. Greuze's yearning girls, full of sad innocence and complacent depravity, have become well known. *La cruche cassée*, for instance (plate 64), shows one of these 'Lolitas' embodying sin, sensibility, and remorse. It is one of the better pictures, in which a balance is well kept between erotic attraction and the sentimental current of the age. If the combination of sexual titillation and simpering, if not lachrymose, sentimentality in some of his other pictures produces a nauseating effect on a post-modern observer, it is because Jean-Baptiste Greuze gave in to bourgeois demands in the art of his day, catering to the middle class rather than the aristocracy. The difference becomes obvious if one compares Greuze's erotica with French paintings from earlier decades celebrating the joy of sex. *Jupiter with Leda and the Swan*, for instance, a work of one of the members of the Coypel family working for the French court, is uninhibited in its demonstration of sex and sexual pleasure, using characters from mythology.[8] One of the great admirers and patrons of erotic paintings was the Duke of Orléans, Regent of France, who owned a vast collection of such pictures, later dispersed. The two volumes of *Descriptions des principales pierres gravées du cabinet de S.A.S. Monseigneur le duc d'Orléans* (1780 and 1784), by La Chaud and Michel (alias Le Blond), with their 179 plates and 56 'culs-de-lampe', provide a good impression of the beauty and magnificence of the paintings he owned.

In surveys of erotic art, the engravers – Baudouin, Boilly, Boucher, Cochin, Freudenberger, Eisen, Gravelot, Moreau, and Lavreince (i.e., Nils Lafrensen the younger, a Swedish painter and engraver calling himself Nicolas Lavreince in France) – have tended to be forgotten.

64 Greuze, *La cruche cassée*, undated

Gravelot came to England in 1732/3 and stayed until 1749. He
brought from France the vogue of the elegantly engraved book of the
Rococo, and proved influential in transmitting the spirit of Claude
Gillot and Watteau to English artists like Hogarth and Gainsborough.
Gravelot's work, like that of Eisen, was in great demand in eighteenth-
century England. Engravings could be obtained easily and were not
too expensive, which explains their popularity. There is a joy of life, a
subtle allusive erotic symbolism, and an exactness of detail and finish
in the works of Baudouin (plates 65–67), Desrais, Freudenberger
(plates 68–69), Jeaurat, and Lavreince (plate 70), making them unsurpassed masterpieces of erotic engravings. Their quality and their
attractive eroticism explain to some extent why they were so much
liked in England, too; and why many English connoisseurs preferred
French engravings to the works created by Hogarth, Rowlandson, and

65 P.A. Baudouin, *Le carquois epuisé*, engraved by N. de Launay

66 P.A. Baudouin, *Le curieux*, c. 1760

67 P.A. Baudouin, *Les amants surpris*, 1764, engraved by Choffard in 1767

68 Freudenberger, *La visite inattendue*, undated

69 Freudenberger. *Le coucher*, engraved by Duclos, undated

70 Lavreince (Nils Lafrensen the younger) *L'amour frivole*, undated

71 Boilly, *Défends-Moi*, undated

Gillray. The engravings and paintings of Louis Boilly (plate 71), towards the end of the century, mark the end of the lightness of Rococo and announce the Directoire period.[9]

4 ENGLISH PICTORIAL EROTICA

Since French artists so amply and skilfully satisfied the eighteenth-century taste for erotica, it is understandable that England's painters and engravers had to be content with an inferior place in public esteem. English artists' approach to the pictorial representation of love and sex may likewise have been influenced by this; because, unlike the French, they insisted on the inclusion of moral elements. Excepting pornography, this overt moralism is one of the characteristic aspects of English erotica. Hogarth's erotic art, for instance, presents clear moral arguments, especially in his series on the harlot and the rake. He associates sexuality with disorder or with animal lust. In a detail of

72 Hogarth, detail of *Noon*, 1738

Noon (plate 72) – which shows Huguenots leaving church – the English world is in disarray, indicated by a Negro handling a girl's breasts. Tom Idle, in plate 7 of the *Industry and Idleness* series (plate 73), may be in bed with a harlot; but he is too frightened to think of sex, and his bedfellow – despite her exposed breasts – is hardly an attractive woman, and reminds one of Swift's ugly 'young nymph going to bed'.

The erotic *topos* of 'before and after' was often varied by artists. Hogarth's two series, indoor and outdoor, of paintings on this theme, from 1730 to 1731, do not show any voluptuous fantasies in the style

73 Hogarth, plate 7 of *Industry and Idleness*, 1747

of a Boucher or Fragonard, but reduce the joy of sex to uncomfortable lust. The interior scenes are said to have been painted for the Duke of Montagu; they stress the lustfulness of the man and the anxiety of the woman before the sexual act; while the 'after' emphasises not satisfaction and pleasure but post-coital depression. The message of the outdoor scene is even more didactic and moralistic, by dint of its allusion to the obscenity of sex. In the 'after' picture of the outdoor scene the man's sexual organs are partly visible, Hogarth's implication being the beastly aspect of human sexuality and the ephemeral, vitiated pleasures of sexual intercourse. The indoor scene engravings rely for their message on symbolic objects which also tell the story (plates 74–75). In *Before* a number of symbols refer to sex and seduction. Thus the painting on the wall shows Cupid lighting a rocket; and the dog, as in similar French indoor scenes, is on his hind legs. The lady is characterised by the books in her dresser drawer. Her pretended shock about her paramour's wishes is ironically paralleled, and exposed as sham, in the arrangement of the books: *The Practice of Piety* lies ostentatiously open in the drawer, but beside it are placed a 'billet

74 Hogarth, *Before and After* (indoor scene), *c.* 1731

doux', *Novels*, and a copy of Rochester's *Poems*. This book was often quoted in eighteenth-century lists of 'licentious literature' and ridicules the lady's seemingly chaste resistance. But there are also symbolic references underlining the illegitimacy of the scene. Rochester's *Poems*, at least to bourgeois readers, represented literary obscenity if not filth. There is also an ambiguous mobcap fastened to the curtain resembling the face of an onlooker, which brings into the scene an element of voyeurism. (Another interpretation of the cap would be to see it as the representation of the male sexual organs.) In addition, the table, and the mirror on it, are about to tilt over, indicating impending disorder and disaster; and there is even a Swiftean scatological allusion in the chamberpot visible under the bed.

The *After* picture is totally dominated by an impression of disorder, exhaustion, and depression. A second painting on the wall now de-

75 Hogarth, *Before and After* (indoor scene), *c.* 1731

picts Cupid laughing at the spent rocket. The table has been turned over, and the mirror, representing innocence and virginity, has been broken. The broken chamberpot introduces a trace of humour. The dog is asleep – passion is over. The message of the *After* picture is thus not pleasure or sexual joy but an ambiguous mixture of regret and longing on the part of the woman, and exhaustion combined with depression on the part of the man, in front of whom lies a book of Aristotle open at the telling page 'omne animal post coitum triste'.

Similarly, in the satire on the Act against strolling players (June 1737), entitled *Strolling Actresses Dressing in a Barn* (plate 76), the actresses' thighs and breasts are revealed to a voyeur hidden in the roof. His presence suggests something forbidden. Hogarth does not warn against eroticism, which is beautifully conveyed in this engraving: rather he is more concerned with the exposure by way of satire of

76 Hogarth, *Strolling Actresses Dressing in a Barn*, 1737

inappropriate ideals of art (on the stage and in conventional history painting). He conveys his irony by showing the discrepancy between the pretension of the young women (playing gods and goddesses) and the realistic disorder on the stage: the 'vanitas' emblems (crowns, orbs, mitres, heroes' helmets) are being used for all sorts of earthly purposes, and the young girl in the centre, in the role of Diana, the goddess of chastity, is in an unbecoming state of undress.

When Hogarth attempted to convey eroticism, as in *The Lady's Last Stake* (plate 77), produced in 1758–9, and quite obviously influenced by contemporary French genre painting in the style of Fragonard, he was inferior to his French colleagues. Again a warning is pronounced in explicit terms, here by burning fire indicating the disturbing heat of passion, and by the picture on the wall showing a penitent Magdalen in the desert. Significantly, the Cupid in the picture carries a scythe. English art simply could not rid itself of moral or didactic strains even where erotic themes were treated. Sir Joshua Reynolds' *The Death of Dido* (plate 78) catches ecstasy in another

77 Hogarth, *The Lady's Last Stake*, 1758–9

78 Reynolds, *The Death of Dido*, 1781

79 *The Irreparable Loss*, 1780

combination of sex and sensibility. Despite the obvious presence in this picture of erotic symbols, such as the half-open mouth and the thrust-out breast, the allusions to sexual passion and post-coital rigor are balanced if not subdued by arrested sexuality and an artificial pose. It is the juxtaposition of Eros and Thanatos that Fuseli admired in this painting, which was to inspire him for the *Nightmare*.[10] There is a manifest current of puritan bourgeois moralism in English picto-

80 *The Joyous Moment. L'instant de la gaieté,*
undated

rial erotica upheld from Hogarth to the late eighteenth-century caricaturists, such as Rowlandson, Gillray, and Newton. Anonymous engravings, too, bespeak this admonitory attitude (plate 79), stressing
guilt and shame rather than the pleasures of love. Significantly, it was
only in imitations of French originals that English artists forgot their
puritan heritage. As if to excuse the man's caressing of the girl's bare
bosom, the engraving entitled *The Joyous Moment* also bears a French
title, presumably to excuse the frivolity (plate 80).

The engravings of P. Simon after paintings of J. Weathly of 1786 are
not more than allusive and foreshadow the Victorian period. French
painters and engravers mainly catered to an aristocratic audience
interested in the pleasures of life and sex – moral lessons were not
asked for. But English artists, although occasionally producing work
for the nobility (Rowlandson made several drawings for his temporary
friend, the Prince Regent), had a middle-class audience in mind. Like
their audience, they could not ignore the English tradition of didacticism in art and literature. Puritan preachers, followed by the Methodists, had harped on the sinfulness of *enjoying* sex. By all one can tell,

81 Rowlandson, *The Discovery*, early nineteenth century

they duly left an impression; for whenever the artists treated the subjects of love and sex, moral warnings were seldom excluded.

Characteristically, this applies also to English pornography, mainly represented by Thomas Rowlandson's work created shortly after 1800. To be sure, some of his work is frankly erotic, when inspired by literature – an illustration for La Fontaine's *Les lunettes*, for example (plate 81) – or myth, and on occasion he approaches libertine French art in theme and spirit, though not in finesse (plates 82–83). But when he tries to depict voluptuousness and sexual joy his women become insatiable nymphomaniacs (plate 84), with an overpowering and almost repulsive physical presence (plate 85) apt to frighten the devil himself. One of Rowlandson's perennial themes in his erotic art is the futility and grotesqueness of senile male lust, most obvious in the illustrations showing groups of old men eyeing naked and shapely young girls (see, for instance, plate 86). If his pornography is to be seen within a tradition it is not the English tradition but rather that of an aggressive, obscene satire deriding incompatible couples (old, impotent men and young, unsatisfied girls), insatiable women, and the useless sexual yearning of aged males. Schiff has argued that Rowlandson, like de Sade, 'exposed the inevitable perversions and frustrations

82 Rowlandson, *The Gallop*, early nineteenth century

83 Rowlandson, *The Wanton Frolic*, early nineteenth century

84 Rowlandson, *Lonesome Pleasures*, early
nineteenth century

86 Rowlandson, *The Congregation*, early nineteenth century

of the individual in whose self sex is separated from emotion', and
Ronald Paulson, in his latest study, has pointed to the relations between Rowlandson's pornography and the French Revolution. Even
as a pornographer, Thomas Rowlandson can be seen as a revolutionary, which in essence means being a moralist. It is this moralistic
attitude which dominates his caricatures. They display his tendencies
for both eroticism and the grotesque. Hogarth's moral overtones may
be lessened in Rowlandson's work, but they are certainly not absent.
Exposing the nudity of repulsively gross women in *Exhibition Stare-
Case*, he laughed at the art-crazy society in the Royal Academy, not

85 Rowlandson, *The Willing Fair or any Way to Please*, early nineteenth
century

EXHIBITION
STARE CASE.

88 Newton, *Too Much or One Thing Good for Nothing*, 1795

without the salacious wink of a voyeur enjoying both the erotic pictures and the exposed female flesh as well as the erotic positions occasioned by the fall (plate 87).[11]

The comic and the grotesque are also present in the erotic satires of Newton and Marks just before 1800, serving as a means to attack, and as an antidote against, their own implicit pornography. In another variation of his pictures of the French dancer, Mademoiselle Parisot, Newton ridicules the males competing for her charms; and in *Too Much or One Thing Good for Nothing* he laughingly hints at the limits of male sexual stamina (plate 88). The women in both illustrations are attractively painted; but the erotic tension thus created dissolves in laughter and is not developed towards sexual stimulation. In Marks' *The Proposal* the effect of the women's exposed breasts is not obscenity or pornography but again comedy and ribald laughter, due to the grotesque exaggeration of physical details, in the manner of Gillray (plate 89).

Finally, the fact that the erotica Fuseli produced in London were strictly not for publication underlines the moral confinement of artists working in England. The painter who caused a stir with his *Nightmare* was of German-Swiss origin and, between 1770 and 1779, made his art-pilgrimage to Italy, before settling in England. His erotic drawings

89 Marks (?), *The Proposal*, 1795

90 Fuseli, *Change of Roles*, 1770–78

91 Fuseli, *Symplegma of a Bound and Naked Man with Two
     Women*, 1770–78

are more of interest as intensely private productions and expressions
of the personal fantasies and obsessions of an artist's dream-world
(plates 90–91). Almost every artist has left such records of the stirrings
of the libido; the later Turner is a notable example. As the cases of
Fuseli and Rowlandson show, English artists who produced erotica
censored themselves. If they painted or engraved pornographic pictorials at all, it was for aristocratic customers or for themselves – the
law did not have to intervene. It was only after 1800 that the Vice
Society succeeded in having people convicted for selling and publishing obscene prints. By that time, however, public taste had changed
anyway and the erotic in art as well as in literature had gone
underground.[12]

❧ 9 ❧

Erotica in Early America

Up to the end of the eighteenth century, by European standards America had produced little in the way of erotic literature. Among people who did have the means, an American market for such work existed nonetheless; and a variety of books and other writings, whether or not already in published form, were imported from the Old World. In the case of locally derived literature, perhaps the most prominent authors were William Byrd II and Benjamin Franklin. Another cultural import, which often gave expression to the bawdier side of contemporary culture, was the various men's clubs established during that time.

I EROS IN THE WILDERNESS: 1620–1700

One of the persistent and ineradicable myths about the Puritan settlers in early New England is their popular image of killjoys and religious fanatics who took no delight in the pleasures of this world. Created by prejudice and by slanted historical accounts, this image has now become firmly rooted in English usage, 'puritan' having predominantly negative connotations. Early disgruntled colonists or dissenters like Samuel Peters, and plagiarists or fabulators like Ned Ward or Dunton, helped as much to contribute to this view of the New Englanders as the later H.L. Mencken, who sacrificed historical accuracy for the sake of puns and aphorisms. The liberalisation of twentieth-century American manners and morals was achieved at the cost of the Puritan founding fathers, who have since been equated with prohibitionists, at least in popular views. Dunton, who ran a bookshop in Boston for a while, slandered the New England divines as lechers; and in his *Letters from New England* (1686) described a 'Person of Quality' as a 'loose woman':

> Mrs Ab-l . . . came to enquire for the SCHOOL OF VENUS; she was one of the first that pas'd me, in asking for a Book I cou'd not help her to; I told her however, I had the SCHOOL OF VERTUE, but that was a Book she had no occasion for. Her Love is a Blank, wherein she writes the next Man that tenders his Affection . . . she writes Characters of wantonness as she walks . . . She'll deny Common Favours, because they are too small to be granted: She will part with all or none; and it is easier to obtain from her the last favour in private, than a kiss in Public.

The association of this lady with seventeenth-century pornography is of course meant to characterise her; but if there is some truth to it, it merely confirms recent findings that even in Massachusetts 'Persons of Quality' could get indecent books if they had a mind to.

The Puritans did not drop their human foibles in the Atlantic Ocean when they sailed for New England. The court and church records of the colonial period contain ample evidence of sinning saints who were as good and as bad as their unregenerate next-door neighbours. They slandered each other and committed adultery; they drank too much and ignored the Sabbath laws; and their unruly behaviour caused their preachers to create the jeremiad, which was a reaction to what the anxious ministers saw as a sinning, apostate people.[1]

Records about sexual behaviour and erotica may be scant, but we know by now that the Puritans, while believing in moral values, never neglected human nature, of which they took cognisance in the enforcement of their laws. There was no shortage of secular and religious injunctions; yet everyday reality looked quite different from Puritan theory. Intellectual life flourished in early New England, as is evinced by the diaries and book catalogues that have come down to us. Harvard graduates like Elnathan Chauncy, Seaborn Cotton, and Edmund Quincy indulged in erotic literature and tried their hands at imitating poetry. In his sophomore year Quincy owned about one hundred books, among them some Greek classics. The Earl of Rochester's obscene poems were on sale in Boston before 1700; and other erotica that could be purchased included *The London Jilt*, a whore biography sold to America in the 1680s; coarse satire and jest books; 'histoires scandaleuses'; and even pornography like Barrin's *Venus in the Cloister*. Puritan divines kept well-stocked libraries containing classical erotica and occasional modern titles. D.J. Hibler has shown the strain of sexual rhetoric in the literature from this period. Thus Edward Taylor's religious meditations are peppered with scatological and erotic imagery. Like his colleagues, the Mathers, Taylor was an avid reader and well acquainted with the 'Hermaphrodite' poems of John Cleveland, for instance, which influenced him.[2]

For the South, our picture of erotica read and sold is much better, due to the admirable and stupendous work of the late Richard Beale Davis, whom death stopped, in 1962, from bringing up to the year 1800 his survey of intellectual life. Davis and others have proved that Southern colonial bookshelves held an amazing variety of erotica, from the journalistic facetiae of Tom Brown to the better-known novels and plays. While the stock of colonial bookshops was not, as Lehmann-Haupt maintained, a replica of the London establishments of the period in all essentials, except that of size, colonial Americans, time and money permitting, could obtain whatever they craved.[3]

2 THE IMPORTATION AND PUBLICATION OF EUROPEAN EROTICA IN EIGHTEENTH-CENTURY AMERICA

A great amount of European erotica was offered and bought in the New World, from the very beginning of the century. In the Revolutionary period the influx of French books increased, and culminated with the Revolution in France. Among the books imported, the 'ancients' were represented by Ovid and Boccaccio, and the moderns by the works of Le Sage, John Cleland, Sterne, French libertine fiction, 'Arabian Nights', and collections of plays.[4] French books were imported in large numbers between 1750 and 1800. Interest in French novelists was great, and seems to have increased with political events in both countries. H.M. Jones has found that Voltaire, Le Sage, Diderot, and Crébillon were among the more popular authors. In the 1790s there was an outburst of demands for books from France and a flood of 'memoirs' and libertine works like those of Mirabeau soon reached American shores. American circulating libraries even contained the libellous *Courier de l'Europe*.[5] Public figures like Jefferson, who counted among his erotica bawdy Restoration plays, Johnstone's *Chrysal*, and Boccaccio's *Decameron*, were far from being ashamed of owning such books. When Jefferson was asked for advice about a future library by Robert Skipwith, he wrote to him in 1771 recommending the purchase of 379 volumes, which included plays by Terence, Vanbrugh, 'Garric', and Foote; and novels by Le Sage, Smollett, Sterne, and Swift, as well as poetry by Ogilby, Prior, and Churchill.[6] A great deal of scatological and bawdy humour was sold by hawkers, in chapbook versions of which we know very little; English crim. con. cases and anti-papist literature made it to America in such editions, including Antonio Gavin's *Master Key to Popery*, of which, since it was in great demand in New England, there was a reprint, in 1773.[7]

Re-publication of European erotica started early in the eighteenth century. Medical books on midwifery, procreation, and venereal disease served as a kind of 'ersatz' for hard-core pornography. The tenth edition of the semi-pornographic *Onania* was reprinted in Boston in 1724 and again in 1726 and 1746; but New England guardians of morality must have been responsible for the exclusion of the appendix of readers' letters, basically confessions of masturbators, in these abbreviated editions. Bostonians thus had to content themselves with 'A Letter from a Lady (very curious), Concerning the Use and Misuse of the Marriage Bed, with the Author's answer thereto'. The sexually stimulating potential of the numerous *Aristotle* sex guides[8] (as well as their function as surrogate erotica) became obvious in a minor sex scandal that caused much stir in Jonathan Edwards' parish of Northampton, Massachusetts. The revivalist preacher, who held one of the best inland parishes of New England, was informed in 1744 of certain young people in his flock reading 'immoral books'. Edwards considered an inquiry into this affair within the purview of his duties, and called a meeting at his house, gathering testimony from accusers and participants. One of the witnesses, Mary Downing, confessed that

> John Lancton a fortnight ago last Friday was at the farm where I was and was talking of such things and he boasted that he had Read Aristotle he talked about his reading the Book more than once talked about the things that was in that Book in a most unclean manner a long time Betty Jenks and Moll Waters there he spoke of the Book as a Granny Book when I checked him he Laughed and he talked exceedingly uncleanly and Lasciviously so that I never heard any fellow Go so far after he was Gone we the young women that were there agreed that we never heard any such talk come out of any mans mouth whatsoever it seem'd to me to be almost as bad as tongue could express.

John Hunter's treatise 'on the venereal disease ... abridged by William Currie' appeared in two Philadelphia editions of 1787 and 1791, the latter illustrated with six plates; and William Smellie's work on the 'practice of midwifery' was published in Boston in 1786 with thirty-nine plates, and in Worcester and Philadelphia in 1793 and 1797. In the second half of the eighteenth century American doctors had treatises published, too. Alexander Hamilton's *The Family*

Female Physician, recorded in editions at New York in 1792 and 1795, and at Worcester, Massachusetts, in 1793, is an example. Hamilton's contribution to 'the theory and practice of midwifery' was in great demand in the 1790s, as well, and sold in its third American edition by 1797. Outside New England, similar books were written, sometimes anonymously, as *A Treatise on Gonorrhoea. By a Surgeon of Norfolk, Virginia* (Norfolk, Virginia, 1787), which has only thirty-nine pages.[9]

In the area of major erotic fiction Sterne ruled unchallenged. *Tristram Shandy* was especially popular in Virginia, and politicians like Franklin and Jefferson thought as highly of it as common readers. Even plays were based on the plot of *Tristram Shandy*. Sterne's other novel, *A Sentimental Journey*, had its first American printing in 1768, with seven more editions recorded by 1795. The New York edition of 1795 sported a frontispiece that was daring, by American standards (plate 92); although the 'elegant engravings' promised on the title-page are a let-down if the reader expected equally explicit plates. Cleland's *Memoirs of a Woman of Pleasure* was apparently not published, but was read, in America before the nineteenth century; although Isaiah Thomas of Worcester, Massachusetts, wrote to London in 1786 to get a copy and later attempted a printing of the book, which was halted after a few pages. *The Catalogue of All the Books Printed in the United States* (Boston, 1804) lists the following titles: *Letters of an Italian Nun and an English Gentleman*; *Nocturnal Visit*; and *Secret Memoirs of the Court of Petersburgh Toward the Close of the Reign of Catherine II*, thus indicating three branches of erotic fiction. The *Letters of an Italian Nun* are plagiarised from Roger L'Estrange's translation in 1678 of the anonymous *Lettres portugaises traduites en françois* (1669), an epistolary novel which appeared as *Five Love Letters from a Nun to a Cavalier* and was very successful. With its mingling of eroticism, passion, guilt, and love, it fascinated and influenced Richardson, among other writers. *Nocturnal Visit* is a specimen of the gothic fiction that became so popular with the novels of Mrs Radcliffe and Horace Walpole. In 1798 Lewis' *The Monk* was performed as a drama in New York. Finally, *The Secret Memoirs of the Court of Petersburgh* bespeaks the wave of erotica of mainly French provenance that flooded Europe and America in the latter part of the eighteenth century. Two versions of *Memoirs of Marie-Antoinette, Cidevant Queen of France* were reprinted in the United States in 1794, the first comprising 143 pages and six plates, and the second, sixty-six pages and two plates.[10]

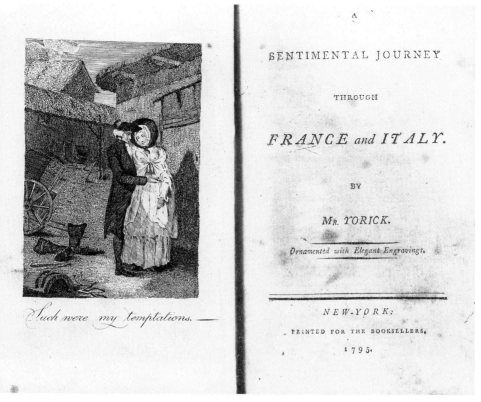

92 Frontispiece and title-page of Sterne, *A Sentimental Journey*, New York, 1795

3 AMERICAN EROTICA

No homegrown pornography was published in eighteenth-century America; although it was perhaps written, as William Byrd's unpublished 'literary exercises' suggest. Various colonial laws would have made impossible the printing of what were termed 'obscene and licentious' books and pictures. By 1712, for example, Massachusetts had a law banning obscene writing and pictorial material. The first cases on record of legal prosecutions of pornography are from the early nineteenth century. Thus censorship seems to have worked as far as books and pictures were concerned.[11]

Nevertheless, Americans did write erotic and scatological poetry and fiction, mostly in the form of satire and published in newspapers and magazines.[12] A good example of popular scatological poetry is

'Upon A Fart', attributed to William Byrd II. If Byrd wrote it, he would no doubt be amused to see that as late as 1980 scholarly battles were waged over the question whether the poem is by Byrd or a contemporary English writer. First published in 1704, 'Upon A Fart' is a parody of 'A Sigh', a poem by Anne Finch, Countess of Winchilsea, and expressed the coarse humour of the age of Swift:

> Gentlest Blast of ill concoction,
> Reverse of high-ascending Belch:
> Th' only Stink abhorr'd by Scotsman,
> Belov'd and practic'd by the Welch.
>
> Softest noat of Inward Gripeing
> Sr Reverences finest part,
> So fine it needs no pains of Wipeing,
> Except it prove a Brewers fart.
>
> Swiftest Ease of Cholique pain,
> Vapor from a Secret Stench,
> Is rattled out by th' unbred Swain,
> But whispered by the Bashfull wench.
>
> Shapeless Fart! we ne'er can show Thee
> But in that merry Female Sport
> In which by burning blew we know Thee
> Th' Amuzement of the Maids at Court.[13]

Scatology and bawdry were major attractions in jest-books, too. Such books, according to P.M. Zall, were 'an amalgam of fables from Sumer, repartees from classical rhetoricians, exempla from medieval preachers, bawdy stories from Italian Humanists, scatology from German burghers, parables from Eastern sages, and current quips from Drury Lane, Fleet Street, and Windsor Castle'.

Here is an example of a bawdy reader's letter from the *Virginia Gazette*, 28 July 1738:

> Last week a Team of five Horses and a Waggon with 2500 Weight of Tea, was seiz'd near Chichester in Sussex, by two Custom-house Officers, assisted by a Guard of Soldiers.
> On Sunday last, Mr. Foster, Surveyor-General of the River, seiz'd a considerable Quantity of Tea at Woolwich, hid under some Hoop-Petticoats. The Owners of those Goods could be no experienced Smugglers, as is plain by their Choice of so improper a Place for Concealment, the Custom-House Officers being generally remarkable for having a natural Itch to rummage under Petticoats. ----- For, some time since, A Custom-House Officer being in the Pit at the Play-house, went to put his Hands up one of the Orange Wenches Petticoats, but the Girl knew him,

and cry'd out, How, now, Mr. Tide-Waiter, there is nothing there *but what has been fairly Enter'd*.[14]

In fiction there was a definite predominance of English and French works; with the result that native American productions were few and far between. However, Americans, when they tried to write ribaldry, could be fairly funny. William Byrd II owned a great number of pornographic books of all sorts and, apart from bawdy poetry, also wrote erotic and ribald fiction. He translated into English erotic episodes from Petronius' *Satyricon* and mocked Catholicism, women, and credulity in a scurrilous prayer-parody which he entitled *The Female Creed*. Like his contemporary, Swift, Byrd let loose in this scatological satire against religious pretensions, termagants, and contemporary social fads. The quote below from the 'prayer' provides some idea of Byrd's satirical humour as well as his scatological satire.

THE FEMALE CREED

1. I believe as all good Catholicks ought to do, in Spirits, Demons and Hobgoblins, that like the Prisoners in New-Gate, they are let out of their Hole anights, and suffer'd to play their Pranks at large in the World. That they appear for the most part to Women and children, their Faith and Imagination being exceeding Strong. I believe that these Spectres with their Horns and cloven feet, and with the Hurly-burly they make in the Dead of night, unluckily scare both the maid and her mistress into a Diabetis. Hence it comes to pass that so many Females in all countrys can scarce hold their precious water, haveing been terrify'd in the Nursery with Bul-beggars and Apparitions. This is the case of the unfortunate Dripabunda, who when She fancy'd She saw the Ghost of her deceast Husband, dy'd away for fear the good man was come to life again. From that fatal moment she lost her Retentive faculty, beyond the Relief of Turpentine Pills and Bristol-water, nor can even Dr. Friend, or Apollo himself intirely stop the Leak, but still whenever she laughs beyond a Simper or a Broad Smile, the liveing Sal-almoniac flows from her. I believe most commonly Spirits delight to haunt old rambleing Houses in the Country, because all sorts of Devils have a passion for Solitude & irregularity, nor do they ever fail to walk in ancient Abbys and Nunnerys, because of the Impurity that was formerly committed therein. In short I believe that all Ghosts hurry back to their dark abode a little before day, because they cant stand the Purity of morning, Besides every body knows they detest the crowing of a Cock worse then the prayers of a Doctor of Divinity, because it brought St. Peter to the bitter tears of Repentance.[15]

Like Byrd, Ben Franklin was a prolific writer; and his works include the odd bawdy piece. Apart from a scatological 'Letter to the Royal Academy at Brussels', he is credited with

The Speech of Miss Polly Baker, said to be delivered by her before a Court of Judicature in the Colony of Connecticut in New-England; where she was prosecuted the fifth time, for having a bastard child, which influenced the Court to dispense with her punishment, and induced one of her Judges to marry her the next day.

Franklin probably had illegitimate children himself; and if this 'speech' is a work of his, then Polly Baker also defends the inventor of the lightning rod. 'Can it be a crime', she asked the judges,

(in the nature of things I mean) to add to the number of the King's subjects in a new country that really wants people?

... I should be stupified to the last degree, not to prefer the honourable state of wedlock, to the condition I have lived in. I always was, and am still willing to enter into it; and doubt not my behaving well in it, having all the industry, frugality, fertility, skill and oeconomy appertaining to a good wife's character. I defy any person to say I ever refus'd an offer of that sort. On the contrary I readily consented to the only proposal of marriage that ever was made me, which was when I was a virgin; but too easily confiding in the person's sincerity that made it, I unhappily lost my own honour by trusting to his; for he got me with child, and then forsook me. That very person you all know; he is now become a magistrate of this country...

You believe I have offended heaven, and must suffer eternal fire: Will not that be sufficient? What need is there then of your additional fines and whipping? ... But how can it be believed that heaven is angry at my having children, when to the little done by me towards it, God has been pleased to add his divine skill and admirable workmanship, in the formation of their bodies; and crown'd it, by furnishing them with rational and immortal souls? ...

But take into your wise consideration the great and growing number of batchelors in this country, many of whom from the mean fear of the expences of a family, have never sincerely and honourably courted a woman in their lives, and by their manner of living, leave unproduced (which is little better than murder) hundreds of their posterity to the thousandth generation. Is not this a greater offence against the public good, than mine? Compel them then by law, either to marriage, or to pay double the fine of fornication every year. What must poor young women do, whom custom has forbid to solicit the men; and who cannot force themselves upon husbands, when the laws take no care to provide them any; and yet severely punish them if they do their duty without them; the duty of the first and great command of nature, and of nature's God, INCREASE AND MULTIPLY; a duty from the special performance of which, nothing has been able to deter me; but for its sake I have hazarded the loss of the public esteem, and have frequently endured public disgrace and punishment; and therefore ought, in my humble opinion, instead of a whipping, have a statue erected to my memory.

This is a remarkable document, breathing the spirit of the Enlightenment. It attacks the sexual double standard as well as Puritan moral thinking, while exposing the sins of those who condemned others for 'crimes' they committed themselves. As a writer of bawdry, however, Franklin is best known for his 'Letter of Advice to A Young Man On Choosing A Mistress', which dates from 1745.[16]

Benjamin Franklin's erotic bagatelles written in France throw some light on his much discussed relations with the ladies of Paris.[17] Several of these works are in the form of familiar letters, most of them in French, to Madame d'Hardancourt Brion and to Madame Helvétius. Credited with at least one illegitimate son, Franklin was far from being sexually inhibited. Although he was over seventy when he laid siege to these ladies, he conducted his love affairs with the ardour of a young man. If his relations with the ladies Brion and Helvétius remained platonic, it was only because they preferred to keep them that way. In his letters to Madame Brion, from the late 1770s, Franklin blended a twofold combination of paternal and erotic love, giving her advice on family affairs while never forgetting his role of an enamoured suitor. He propositioned Madame Brion in 'The Flies', and recorded the memory of a delightful day in 'The Ephemera' (20 September 1778). With Madame Helvétius, who unlike Madame Brion was a widow and thus available for marriage, Franklin was equally unsuccessful, though they seemed to have enjoyed a great degree of intimacy. During the whole of 1779 he pursued her with erotic-romantic proposals. But when in 1780 Franklin indicated that he wanted marriage, Madame Helvétius declared her resolution to remain single for the rest of her life. Obviously disappointed, Franklin compensated his frustration by writing 'The Elysian Fields', in which he is transported to paradise, where he meets Helvétius, now married to Franklin's late wife. Franklin, after returning to the good Earth, challenges Madame Helvétius, 'let us take revenge'. In order to create the impression that his courtship had only been partly serious, Franklin allowed copies of this work, which he had printed on his private press, to circulate; thus the letter found its way into Grimm's *Correspondance littéraire*, where it appeared in April 1780.[18]

No erotic American novel was published in the eighteenth century. *The Coquette or, The History of Eliza Wharton* (Boston, 1797) was published anonymously by Hanna Foster. Its title sounds promising; but it is just another example of the vogue of letter novels brimming with sentimentality. However, as the catalogues and bibliographies of American imprints from the eighteenth century prove, there was no shortage of European erotic fiction for those who wanted it.

Like their European contemporaries, some American gentlemen felt the urge to found clubs where men could be men and did not have to consider the presence of ladies. It was in a number of these clubs that erotica were read and written. When Dr Alexander Hamilton made a tour of the colonies in the summer of 1743, he enjoyed the hospitality of some such organisations; and, on returning home to Maryland, founded what came to be known as the Tuesday Club of Annapolis. This was limited to fifteen members, who were dedicated to raillery and met weekly at the home of a 'long standing member'. The club kept records of its pranks, toasts, and discussions. The toasts were often *doubles entendres* in rhyme and dedicated 'to the ladies'. The club's minutes eventually ran to three volumes, totalling 1,900 pages, which include songs set to music.

While the spirit in such clubs was light and jocular, they never went as far as the European libertine clubs, where blasphemy, fornication, and sexual explicitness were called for. The Beggar's Benison of Anstruther, Scotland, for instance, was a phallic club whose members read obscene poems and pornographic fiction and masturbated openly in groups. Wilkes and the Medmenham 'monks', several decades later, apparently performed black masses and had sex orgies. But Americans chose a middle way, which included bawdry but excluded obscenity.

In toto, then, eighteenth-century Americans could obtain all the erotica their European contemporaries were reading and producing. Some colonial laws, like those of Massachusetts, were strict, if not prohibitive; but they could not prevent clandestine importation, or the acquisition of erotica by American travellers in Europe. The European market offered a choice selection for every sort of taste, which may explain, in addition to their colonial situation, why Americans had to wait until 1849 for the first erotic novel, *Venus in Boston*, to be written and published in America. Thus, although American pornography started around the middle of the nineteenth century, with the exception of *The Memoirs of Dolly Morton* (Paris, 1899), an account of whippings, rapes and social violence preceding the Civil War in America, nothing of any great literary value was produced.[19]

Conclusion

The age of Enlightenment could well be termed the age of Eros. The discourse on sex in expositive writings and in fiction accompanying the attempt to revive the culture of Eros is ideally suited to serve as a test case for the theory of the 'trickling down' of ideas. Sociologists and scholars of literature generally assume that in a given culture, ideas and ideologies are for the most part formulated by the intellectual élite and then percolate down to the masses, as it were, in a complicated process involving oral, literary, and visual channels. But scholars have rarely cared to test this theory by analysing the end of the percolating process they perceive.[1] Peter Nagy's study of what he terms 'propagande libertine' proves for the eighteenth century that in the area of licentious literature a sort of downward osmosis apparently occurred in that a libertine philosophy was absorbed by, and dispersed with, pornography.[2] If, in the present study, I have descended 'down' to the reading matter of the masses, to works produced by Grub Street writers, it is because I wanted to throw some light on a literary and ideological osmotic process that shaped 'mentalités' in England and France and even affected major eighteenth-century novelists and writers to a degree which is often ignored. We are still very much unaware of the links between the canon of so-called 'high literature' and the rich subsoil of erotica.

The findings presented in this book suggest that, despite a remarkable increase in the discourse on sex, Enlightenment ideas made little progress at the level of popular erotica. Clichés and stereotypes abound. This is no reason to ignore this body of literature, but rather a reason to challenge accepted beliefs concerning the influence of Enlightenment thought. In eighteenth-century popular erotica the sexual double standard ruled unchallenged and traditional sexual roles were immutably fixed. Seen from 'below', the age of Rousseau and Voltaire was a machist century adhering to accepted sexual taboos and traditional ways of behaviour.[3]

A brief look at two examples – the cases of Pope's scintillating satire *The Rape of the Lock* and Richardson's deliberately ambiguous *Pamela* – will suffice to demonstrate what Paul-Gabriel Boucé has so aptly termed 'the secret nexus', i.e., the frequently underestimated link between erotica and major eighteenth-century literature.[4] The passages from these works, discussed below, prove beyond doubt that an upward osmosis also occurred in the body of Enlightenment literature, and that research into the fields of erotica and pornography can only help us to establish a better picture of the sexual 'mentalité' that affected the behaviour of such fictional heroes and heroines as Fielding's Joseph Andrews, Tom Jones, Sophia, and Amelia, and Richardson's Mr B., Lovelace, Pamela, and Clarissa.

The very existence of the various genres of erotica that have been assessed in this study explains such recurring themes in the canon of 'high literature' as chastity, virginity, seduction, adultery, and prostitution, to name just a few topics.[5] Seduction and 'rape' as well as the ever popular sexual punning, often in the form of arcane allusions to erotica circulating in the underground, are vital elements in Alexander Pope's *The Rape of the Lock*, first published in Lintot's *Miscellany* in 1712 and subsequently enlarged to five cantos and thus published in 1714. As a matter of fact, a close reading of the poem reveals Pope's constant bawdy playing with the double or triple meaning of words and phrases that have erotic denotations or connotations.[6] This starts with the very title, in which the term 'rape' denotes theft but also connotes seduction or even forcible sexual intercourse imposed on Belinda. In addition, the word 'lock' in the title is not as innocent as it would seem at first glance, especially when related to the sexual meaning of 'rape'. Throughout the poem, Pope develops this erotic and frequently bawdy dimension, so much so that one is tempted to read *The Rape of the Lock* as the metaphorical description of a successful sexual conquest. In Canto II, ll. 19–28, Belinda's locks are first described in highly erotic terms suggesting much more than mere hair. In addition, her paramour's reaction again alludes to the hidden sexual meaning of the locks in a way that is reminiscent of the role of Sophia's muff in Fielding's *Tom Jones*:

> The adventurous baron the bright locks admired;
> He saw, he wished, and to the prize aspired.
> Resolved to win, he meditates the way,
> By force to ravish, or by fraud betray;
> For when success a lover's toil attends,
> Few ask, if fraud or force attained his ends.
>
> (Canto II, ll. 29–34)

The whole passage is a masterwork of *double entendre* in which the lover's erotic wishes are hinted at through the sexual connotations of 'by force to ravish', 'a lover's toil', and 'attained his ends', phrases that were current in early eighteenth-century bawdry.

The actual incident of the cutting off of the lock in Canto·III makes clear that Pope deliberately exploits the ambiguity of the action, 'the rape':

> The peer now spreads the glittering forfex wide,
> To inclose the lock; now joins it, to divide . . .
> The meeting points the sacred hair dissever
> From the fair head, for ever, and for ever!
>
> (Canto III, ll. 147–54)

While it is true that Belinda's outraged reaction may be attributable to her excessive vanity, which is one of the targets of the satire, her indignation appears in a different light if one sees the 'rape' in a sexual context:

> Then flashed the living lightning from her eyes,
> And screams of horror rend the affrighted skies.
> Not louder shrieks to pitying Heaven are cast,
> When husbands, or when lapdogs breathe their last;
> Or when rich China vessels fallen from high,
> In glittering dust and painted fragments lie!
>
> (Canto III, ll. 155–60)

Juxtaposing husbands and lapdogs, at first glance an amusing combination of seemingly incongruous subjects (and as such a common feature of eighteenth-century mock-heroic satires), Pope again provides a sexual dimension. For readers with some background knowledge of bawdy verse and prose knew that the term 'lapdog' was sexually charged and that such dogs were often trained to lick their mistresses' love-grottoes. In fact, in Canto I, Belinda is 'waked', if not aroused, by her own dog, Shock,

> who thought she slept too long,
> Leaped up, and waked his mistress with his tongue.
>
> (Canto I, ll. 115–16)

Earlier in this Canto (ll. 15–16), 'lapdogs give themselves the rousing shake' and are yoked, by the same verse, to 'sleepless lovers'.[7]

At the end of Canto IV, which also brims with erotic innuendo and concludes with yet another daring allusion to sex and the sexual organs, Belinda laments over the loss of her 'lock'. This passage calls to mind similar losses of maidenheads, described in countless humorous erotica:

> 'For ever cursed be this detested day,
> Which snatched my best, my favourite curl away!
> Happy! ah, ten times happy had I been,
> If Hampton Court these eyes had never seen!
> Yet am I not the first mistaken maid,
> By love of courts to numerous ills betrayed.
> Oh, had I rather unadmired remained
> In some lone isle, or distant northern land;
> Where the gilt chariot never marks the way,
> Where none learn ombre, none e'er taste Bohea!
> There kept my charms concealed from mortal eye,
> Like roses, that in deserts bloom and die.
> What moved my mind with youthful lords to roam?
> Oh, had I stayed, and said my prayers at home!
> 'Twas this, the morning omens seemed to tell;
> Thrice from my trembling hand the patch-box fell;
> The tottering China shook without a wind,
> Nay, Poll sat mute, and Shock was most unkind!
> A sylph, too, warned me of the threats of fate,
> In mystic visions, now believed too late!
> See the poor remnants of these slighted hairs!
> My hands shall rend what even thy rapine spares:
> These in two sable ringlets taught to break,
> Once gave new beauties to the snowy neck;
> . . .
> Oh, hadst thou, cruel! been content to seize
> Hairs less in sight, or any hairs but these!'

(Canto IV, ll. 147–76)

Pope's final tongue-in-cheek usage of 'rape' and 'lock' occurs in Canto V, ll. 103–4, where the verb 'restore' (instead of such possible alternatives as return, give back etc.) immediately refers the knowledgable reader to the widely known eighteenth-century habit of restoring lost maidenheads, i.e., broken hymens, a practice that was often described in erotica and is also mentioned by Smollett in his *Roderick Random* (Chapter xxii).[8]

Even if one is reluctant to agree with this reading of Pope's *The Rape of the Lock* as a rape described in protective metaphorical terms to make it publicly and morally acceptable, it is incontestable that the poem is replete with sexual allusions, innuendo, and punning that pay homage to the vast and rich sub-soil of eighteenth-century erotica. From lapdogs giving themselves 'the rousing shake' (Canto I, l. 15) to 'maids turned bottles, call aloud for corks' (Canto IV, l. 54), Pope employs sexual connotations and, in the final Canto, hints at orgasm (or, more suggestively, at the French 'la petite mort'), when one beau 'died in metaphor' and the baron 'thought no more than on his foe to die' (i.e., Belinda; see Canto V, ll. 60 and 78). In Canto II, ll. 117–20, he ridicules both female vanity and chastity by alluding to that ever popular topic of anti-feminist satire, the 'hoop petticoat':

> To fifty chosen sylphs, of special note,
> We trust the important charge, the petticoat:
> Oft have we known that seven-fold fence to fail,
> Though stiff with hoops, and armed with ribs of whale.

More intensely and more jocularly than any major prose fiction – apart from Henry Fielding's *Shamela* – *The Rape of the Lock* shows the vital links between Enlightenment erotica and so-called high literature. As Paul-Gabriel Boucé has pointed out, it does not matter whether Pope had read any specific erotica before composing *The Rape of the Lock*; what is relevant is that in his fine poem he alludes to and – at least for the cognoscenti – plays with erotic and sexual verbal meanings in the same way as the erotica that made use of the extended metaphor, such as Stretser's *Arbor vitae*. A close reading of *The Rape of the Lock* thus proves the importance of contextual 'histoires des mentalités' for a more informed and more comprehensive understanding of eighteenth-century literature.[9]

Similarly, the hidden dimensions of Richardson's essentially prurient pizzicato of sex throughout *Pamela* – but also in *Clarissa* and *Sir Charles Grandison* – his perennial focusing on, and preoccupation with, Pamela's endangered virginity, are fully revealed, even though not necessarily appreciated, when seen in relation with common popular sex lore. For *Pamela*, Richardson had discovered a successful ingredient of best-selling fiction – the heroine in permanent danger of having her virtue assailed. Whereas this theme was often treated humorously and satirically in erotica and underground literature, Richardson decided on a realistic approach. Pamela's personal epistolary confessions allowed him to incorporate both erotic and moral aspects and to describe various attempts at seduction and rape under the cover of 'virtue rewarded', the sub-title of the novel. Eroticism in *Pamela*, whenever it is created, has strong links with contemporary pornographic fiction. In addition to the general structure of epistolary confessional reports that allot the reader the role of a voyeur – as in the classic pornographic novels of the early eighteenth century – *Pamela* contains scenes that seem to be lifted straight from contemporary eighteenth-century erotic fiction. When, in Volume I, Pamela's maidenhead is really in danger for the first time, Richardson has her describe her feelings in terms that suggest an orgasm rather than fright or the danger of rape:

> I found his hand in my bosom, and when my fright let me know it, I was ready to die; I sighed, screamed and fainted away. And still he had his arms about my neck; Mrs. Jervis was about my feet, and upon my coat. And all in a cold dewy sweat was I ... one fit followed another, till about three hours after, I found myself in bed, and Mrs. Jervis sitting up on one side.[10]

The same is true of the ending of the long scene – essentially the titillating description of a strip-tease interspersed with occasional moral reflections and dialogues – in which Mr B., disguised in the maid's clothes and thus adding a touch of the perverse to the event, eventually manages to sneak into bed with Pamela and Mrs Jewkes:

> About two hours after, which was near eleven o'clock, Mrs. Jewkes and I went up to bed; I pleasing myself with what a charming night I should have. We locked both doors, and saw poor Nan, as I thought (but, oh! it was my abominable master, as you shall hear by-and-by), sitting fast asleep in an elbow chair, in a dark corner of the room, with her apron thrown over her head and neck ... All this time we were undressing ourselves. And I fetched a deep sigh ... I looked into the closets, and kneeled down in my own, as I used to do, to say my prayers, and this with my underclothes in my hand, all undressed; and passed by the poor sleeping wench, as I thought, in my return. But O! little did I think it was my wicked, wicked master, in a gown and petticoat of hers, and her apron over his face and shoulders ... Mrs. Jewkes, by this time, was got to bed, on the farther side, as she used to be ... In less than a quarter of an hour, I said, 'There's poor Nan awake; I hear her stir.' – 'Let us go to sleep,' said she, 'and not mind her: she'll come to bed when she's quite awake.'... So I was silent, and the pretended Nan ... seemed to be awaking ... the pretended she came to the bed-side, and sitting down in a chair, where the curtain hid her, began to undress ... I heard her, as I thought, breathe quick and short ... I tremble to relate it! the pretended she came into bed, but trembled like an aspen-leaf; and I, poor fool that I was! pitied her much ... What words shall I find, my dear mother (for my father should not see this shocking part), to describe the rest, and my confusion, when the guilty

wretch took my left arm, and laid it under his neck, and the vile procuress held my right; and then he clasped me round the waist! ... And then I screamed again and again ... and then ... he put his hand in my bosom. With struggling and terror I fainted away, and did not come to myself soon; so that they both, from the cold sweats that I was in, thought me dying.[11]

Pamela's 'fainting away', 'cold sweats', and her 'dying' are proof of her virtue, but they must have caused chuckles with any reader who had some knowledge of erotic fiction and jargon.

Pamela's obsession with virginity, the only treasure she possesses in the bargain for the respectability of marriage and social status, reflects, on the one hand, the cruel economic and ethical dilemma of the majority of eighteenth-century servant girls. More often than not, they gave in to the seductive attempts of their masters in order to keep their places and wages; many left, pregnant and ostracised, and with suicide or prostitution as the only remaining alternatives. On the other hand, Pamela's concern with her maidenhead, which seems overdone and obsessive, also refers to the excessive attention given to virginity – how it could be lost, preserved, and even repaired or restored – in paramedical erotica, such as *Aristotle's Master-Piece* and Venette's *Tableau de l'amour conjugal*, as well as in bawdy satires.

In the case of *Pamela*, the exploration of the 'secret nexus' between eighteenth-century erotica and what we now consider the canon of English literature indicates a sexual 'mentalité' that evaluated women according to the double standard and forced the economically disadvantaged female servants to bargain with virginity as a commodity.[12]

The same link between high and low literature can be detected in Henry Fielding's magnificent *Tom Jones*, as Paul-Gabriel Boucé has proved in his excellent and meticulously researched analysis of the meaning of 'sex, amours and love' in this novel.[13]

As far as sex is concerned, these examples would seem to prove for the age of Enlightenment that ideas, frequently disguised in the powerful forms of myths and stereotypes, did not exclusively trickle from the 'top' (the 'philosophes') to the 'bottom' (the public). Apparently, an upward osmosis also occurred. Eighteenth-century erotica played a vital part in the creation of a sexual 'mentalité' that served as an ever flowing fountain for both the great writers and their forgotten contemporaries from Grub Street.

According to Freud, the advancement of civilisation demands or presupposes the inhibition of the sex instinct. Freud saw in Eros a larger biological instinct and a sort of aggrandisement of sexuality. It was Plato who introduced into Occidental culture the repressive definition of Eros as a culture-building power. In Freud's view, the biological drive eventually becomes a cultural drive.[14] This process seems to have come to a head in the eighteenth century (other crises of this kind occurred in the sixteenth and twentieth centuries) when a revived notion of Eros challenged bourgeois patterns of thought, behaviour, and morality. Significantly, the classical 'ars amoris' was confined to an aristocracy or a propertied oligarchy, and the first readers and revivers of classical erotica in the early modern period were again aristocrats for whom sexual pleasure in fact and print was not immoral but amoral in the classical sense. What stood in the way of a dispersion of this hedonistic notion of Eros was, on the one hand, a Christian heritage restricting sex to matrimony and punishing illicit sex, and, on the other, a rising influence of the middle class in taste and ideology which banned sex from literature. Between 1660 and 1800 a vast amount of classical erotica was translated into English. Although the works of Apuleius, Horace, Juvenal, Ovid, and Petronius were always available in a variety of editions, this tidal wave was not sufficiently strong to overcome the moral fortresses erected and defended by the powerful current of Evangelical religion among the new rising class. While the liberating forces of the Enlightenment, and a revived interest in aspects of classical erotic cultures, resurrected Eros, at least as far as literature was concerned, the new readers from the middle class defined the limits of Eros' realm.[15]

If one excepts the higher aristocracy, who pursued their libertine life styles, it is noticeable that by the eighteenth century even the members of the nobility and the propertied classes began to change their behavioural patterns in sexual relations and attitudes. Both Stone and Flandrin recognised an acceptance among the cultural élite of the eighteenth century of the identity of lust and love and of love and marriage, both relatively new notions for this social stratum. Patterns already firmly established in the lower classes were thus adopted. In the area of erotic literature, these changes meant that lust in print and in pictures was increasingly banned to the domain of the illegitimate, the 'abnormal', and the morally despicable. The newcomers among the readers of erotica, now more and more recruited from the middle class, created the notion of pornography in the eighteenth century and first coined it as a term in the nineteenth century, the age of the bourgeois. The 'ars amoris' thus gained a dimension it had never before possessed – and so did erotic literature: morality entered the process of evaluating erotica and has affected literary judgments down to our present age and day.[16]

It would be erroneous and misleading, however, to see the rise of pornography exclusively as a sociological phenomenon, for there are also literary and psychological causes at its root. It is no coincidence that pornographic biography followed closely upon the heels of spiritual autobiography.[17] The Puritans developed into a fine art the literary spiritual confession, and the pornographic novel, as a parasitical genre, adopted this confessional technique while making itself available as an outlet for sexual fantasies that could not be expressed or acted out otherwise. It is worth noting that the rise of pornography was accompanied by an increasing privacy in social relations, even within the smaller nucleus of the family. More privacy entailed less discourse, and hence also less talking about sex. Although the discourse on sex, according to Michel Foucault, gained in volume after 1600, this is only true for literature, which, by the eighteenth century, clearly began to assume psychological functions. Psychologists are familiar with the German term 'Pseudolismus', denoting the urge to talk about or to record sexual fantasies, one of its variations being erotographomania, which is the habit of writing, or urging others to write, obscene letters. Some psychologists see pornography in this context as a sort of mental masturbation. Even if one disagrees with the psychological viewpoint that there seems to exist something like a need to talk about sex, it is still of interest to notice that as privacy was growing in early modern society so did the need to consume pornography. Psychologically, talking about sex apparently has a liberating function in that individuals attempt to rid themselves of sexual fears and frustrations. Pornography and related areas of erotic literature may well have fulfilled such an alleviating function in literary discourse, although this does not mean that readers underwent a therapy by consuming licentious writings or that authors were able to divest themselves of pathological hang-ups.[18]

Comparing the eighteenth century with our present, seemingly enlightened, age, one is struck by a number of parallels. Crime reporting, and especially its excessively prurient branch covering crime and sex, is as popular now as it was then. Rapists still make headlines, even in such sober and respectable papers as the *Guardian*.[19] As in the eighteenth century, titillation and a secret male yearning for the infraction of sexual taboos can still be discerned behind this sort of sensational reporting. Anti-aristocratic bawdy satire is not as lively and thriving as it was two hundred years ago, but it has not disappeared. After the engagement of Prince Charles and Lady Diana had been announced, the satirical and aggressive *Private Eye* focused on the sexual slander of the royal couple. In a series entitled 'Born to be Queen' Lady Diana was portrayed as an innocent virgin while the Prince of Wales figured as a Pan-like womaniser and Don Juan. Continuing the literary tradition of the licentious 'chronique scandaleuse', the French edition of the magazine *Lui* published a montage, entitled 'un petit prince bien monté', of a masturbating Prince Charles surrounded by naked girls and an equally naked Diana.[20] However, such sexual slander of aristocrats and royalty is neither very popular nor does it carry the political weight of comparable satire from the age of Enlightenment. In an age of democracy when, as Andy Warhol once predicted, everybody will be famous for fifteen minutes, aristocrats have lost their former political and social influence. Hence the 'chronique scandaleuse' has been deprived of one of its traditional targets, although a new moneyed class has emerged that provides enough scandals to keep the yellow press in good business.

Other parallels between the eighteenth and the twentieth centuries suggest that certain forms of sexual humour, frequently on the border of criminal libel, are timeless. Homosexuals were the traditional whipping-boys for eighteenth-century bawdy satire, and this line has been continued by *Private Eye* with its cartoon series on 'The Gays', which is, however, more humorous than aggressive. Occasionally, *Private Eye* also makes fun of Anglican clergymen as potential homosexuals.

In the twentieth century, poetry was initially eclipsed by prose in public esteem and, until the early 1970s, was reserved to a small minority and discussed by a few cognoscenti. With the rise of the younger poets from Northern Ireland, poetry has since seen a remarkable renaissance in Britain. Modern and post-modern poets have not forgotten the tradition of erotic writing. The American e.e. cummings, in the poem cited below, shows his knowledge of the poetic *double entendre* and of the history of the extended metaphor. He catapults that metaphor into the age of the machine, where it provides as much humorous entertainment as the biological or topographical examples in the eighteenth century:

> she being Brand
>
> -new;and you
> know consequently a
> little stiff i was
> careful of her and(having

thoroughly oiled the universal
joint tested my gas felt of
her radiator made sure her springs were O.

K.)i went right to it flooded-the-carburetor cranked her

up,slipped the
clutch(and then somehow got into reverse she
kicked what
the hell)next
minute i was back in neutral tried and

again slo-wly;bare,ly nudg.   ing(my

lev-er Right-
oh and her gears being in
A 1 shape passed
from low through
second-in-to-high like
greasedlightning)just as we turned the corner of Divinity

avenue i touched the accelerator and give

her the juice,good

                (it
was the first ride and believe i we was
happy to see how nice she acted right up to
the last minute coming back down by the Public
Gardens i slammed on
the

internalexpanding
&
externalcontracting
brakes Bothatonce and

brought allof her tremB
-ling
to a:dead.

stand-
;Still)²¹

In the early 1980s, Peter Porter, a cosmopolitan Australian and former
member of the Group (a loosely connected group of poets which
included Ted Hughes), who has lived in England for many years,
wrote a guarded, meditative poetic answer to the post-modern question, 'How Important Is Sex?' His laconic poem provides ironic comments on such twentieth-century developments as the 'scientific'
approach to human sexuality, the reduction of erotic love to

mechanical sex and pornography, and the Freudian view of sex. Porter also alludes to myth:

How Important is Sex?

Not very. Even if it plays a not
Inconsiderable part in misery,
You can be unhappy without reference
To its intervention or its absence.

Our researchers have discovered even
Species whose reproductive processes
Are quite unsexual – and usually these
Are the more efficient and uncomplicated.

But, says the man waiting for a letter
And trying to read an article in a liberated
Magazine, I haven't been able to keep
My mind off sex since I was seven.

Others' minds go further back. Perhaps
Our evolution took the one track
(As the mind has it) into love and found
That those innovatory machines

The genitals, once in place, wouldn't
Be denied their significance. The sight
Of mummy's hair puts us on the spot,
A cave more mysterious than the mouth.

Now flow from it plays and operas
And the horrible spoutings of rancid
Kitchens: a world of novels awaits
The boy taught things by his jokey schoolmates.

But you are talking about love, you'll say.
Yes, and I know the difference,
Taking down a wank magazine,
Then a note more fingered than any photo.

Nevertheless, I am a respecter
Of power, having seen a skinny girl
Screaming in the playground, oblivious
Of boys, wake to her hormonal clock

As Juliana or as Mélisande –
Even the great gods and captains
Might relax with a plaything
As bold and changeable as this.[22]

Pornography has been accepted as a standard component in twentieth-century fiction. There are entire branches and genres catering to all kinds of demands and tastes, from Science Fiction erotica to strip cartoons, and from sado-masochist publications to journals and magazines for male and female homosexuals.[23]

In the novel proper, even in fiction aiming at highbrow audiences, there are no sexual taboos left to be broken, and sexuality has usurped the place of religion and metaphysics. While the eighteenth-century libertine pornographic novel showed what life could be like with a liberated libido controlled only by nature and reason, the modern and post-modern novel focusing on sex portrays human beings completely dominated by their sex drives. More than ever before, sex serves as an 'ersatz' for love, emotional passion, and religious convictions. Thus Eros has been ascribed a multifunctional role he has never had and which he is clearly unable to fulfil. Such novels as John Fowles's *The Collector* (1963) and *Mantissa* (1982), Anthony Burgess's *Earthly Powers* (1980), and, in the United States, the works of John Hawkes, Jerzy Kosinski, and John Updike – to name just three authors who have been fascinated with the role of Eros in post-modern society – are peopled with anti-heroes frantically trying to find a sense to their lives. Their desperate search for truth and happiness in and through sex is more tragic than comic, especially since most of them seem to believe that Eros will help them to ward off Thanatos. Like the characters in an absurd drama, they are unable to realise that they are pursuing an illusion and that their futile attempts, time and again, must culminate not in fulfilment but in what the eighteenth century termed 'la petite mort'. The treatment of sex in the post-modern novel suggests that man is closer to the realm of Thanatos than he seems to know.[24]

Whenever Eros revived in the cultures of the past, poets and artists perceived at the centre of creativity not Eros alone but the association of Eros and Thanatos. Towards the end of the Middle Ages, Niklaus Manuel (alias Nicolas Manuel Deutsch) summed up the idea that sexual love is always accompanied by death, and that death is present in the joys of love, in his picture from the Dance of Death which shows Death as a skeleton seducing a young woman (plate 93). Thanatos accompanying Eros is, admittedly, a late medieval idea and as such a literary and artistic motif – the Baroque and Rococo periods were less preoccupied with Thanatos – but the association of Death and Love was revived by Neoclassicism and has been a powerful, albeit covert and subconscious, current in post-modern fiction. Given new life again in the eighteenth century, Eros went underground in the

93 Deutsch, *La mort en lansquenet embrasse une jeune femme*, 1517 (*Der Tod als Verführer – Death as a Seducer*)

Victorian period but reappeared with Modernism and Postmodernism in the twentieth century. However, he seems to have gained in Thanatos a perennial companion.[25]

The codification of the sacrament of penance by the Lateran Council in the year 1215 proved extremely influential for the optimisation and valorisation of the discourse on sex because it helped develop the confessional technique. With this codification a major step was taken in the transformation of desire into discourse. The eighteenth century saw the rapprochement of two lines of this discourse in the revival of Eros (the 'ars erotica' of the ancients) and the adoption and advancement of the confessional technique in fiction. Sexual desire in medieval literature was cast into subliminal minnesong and then developed into eroticism, a phase that was reached in the eighteenth century. What is left today, in print, pictures, and film, is existential angst and dread drowned in excessive sexual activity that is often dominated by mechanical technique. Eros is waiting to be revived again.[26]

List of Abbreviations

AAA — *Arbeiten aus Anglistik und Amerikanistik*
AC — *American Collector*
AL — *American Literature*
BJECS — *British Journal for Eighteenth-Century Studies*
BL — *The British Library*
BN — *Bibliothèque Nationale*
BSSHM — *Bulletin of the Society for the Social History of Medicine*
C — *Colophon*
CL — *Comparative Literature*
CLQ — *College Library Quarterly*
CQ — *Critical Quarterly*
DHS — *Dix-Huitième Siècle*
DNB — *Dictionary of National Biography*
DOE — *Dictionnaire des Oeuvres Érotiques*
EAL — *Early American Literature*
ECL — *Eighteenth-Century Life*
ECS — *Eighteenth-Century Studies*
EE — *Enlightenment Essays*
EHR — *Economic History Review*
ES — *English Studies*
HJ — *Historical Journal*
HLB — *Harvard Library Bulletin*
HLR — *Harvard Law Review*
ISR — *Institute for Sex Research*
JAF — *Journal of American Folklore*
JEGP — *Journal of English and Germanic Philology*
JHI — *Journal of the History of Ideas*
JHM — *Journal of the History of Medicine*

JIH	– *Journal of Interdisciplinary History*
JMS	– *Journal of Mental Science*
JSH	– *Journal of Social History*
LH	– *Literature and History*
LP	– *Literature and Psychology*
MH	– *Modern History*
MLN	– *Modern Language Notes*
MP	– *Modern Philology*
MSE	– *Massachusetts Studies in English*
NEHGR	– *New England Historical and Genealogical Register*
NEQ	– *New England Quarterly*
NQ	– *Notes & Queries*
PAAS	– *Publications of the American Antiquarian Society*
PCSM	– *Publications of the Colonial Society of Massachusetts*
PMLA	– *Publications of the Modern Language Association*
PQ	– *Philological Quarterly*
RES	– *Review of English Studies*
SECC	– *Studies in Eighteenth-Century Culture*
SEL	– *Studies in English Literature*
SHR	– *Southern Humanities Review*
SL	– *Southeastern Librarian*
SSF	– *Studies in Short Fiction*
SV	– *Studies on Voltaire*
SVEC	– *Studies on Voltaire and the Eighteenth Century*
TLS	– *Times Literary Supplement*
TSLL	– *Texas Studies in Language and Literature*
WMQ	– *The William and Mary Quarterly*

Notes

When not indicated, the place of publication, with English titles, is London, and with French titles, Paris. NY = New York.

INTRODUCTION

1 *The Catalogue of Prints and Drawings in the British Museum. Division I. Political and Personal Satire*, vol. VI (1938), ascribes the first version of this satire (1786) to Gillray: see p. 336 no. 7014. Thomas Rowlandson produced a reduced copy of Gillray's engraving which Grego conjecturally dates 1810: see *ibid.*, 337 no. 7014 A. Hence Lawrence Stone's attribution of the engraving from 1786 to Rowlandson is wrong since Rowlandson's version only contains the first, second and fourth book-titles: see Stone's *The Family, Sex and Marriage in England* 1500–1800 (1977), xxvii, plate 33.

For lampoons on Mrs Phillips see the *Catalogue of Prints and Drawings*, vol. V, no. 5171. In the first place, Gillray's engraving is a satire on the morals of the English in India, but his allusions to erotica provide an excellent picture of the late eighteenth-century English market of licentious books.

In 1872 J.C. Hotten reprinted two volumes in his series 'Library Illustrative of Social Progress' which are entitled *Exhibition of Female Flagellants in the Modest and Incontinent World. Proving from Indubitable Facts, that a Number of Ladies Take a Secret Pleasure in Whipping Their Own, and Children Comitted* [sic] *to Their Care*. According to Hotten, these two books were first published in 1777 and 1785. Although they smack of Victorian kinky sex, their original dates of publication could be correct and accord with Gillray's book title in the engraving. For a discussion of the books see Henry Spencer

Ashbee, *Index librorum prohibitorum* (1877: reprinted NY, 1962), 239 f.

The reference to *Crazy Tales* is probably to Hamilton's *New Crazy Tales* (1783), which were very popular in the 1780s, and not to John Hall Stevenson's *Crazy Tales* (1762; third edition, 1769).

2 See my review of Hagstrum's study in *ECL* VIII 3 (1983). Unfortunately, though, Professor Hagstrum has stayed on well-trodden literary paths; and one wonders how a book that displays 'sex' and 'erotic love' in its title can avoid discussing the rise of pornography, popular erotic literary genres, and *Fanny Hill*. Hagstrum dispenses with pornography in a footnote while ignoring literary erotica for the sake of more promising intellectual speculation. One must conclude that even such a brilliant scholar as Professor Hagstrum is either not aware of the erotic literary sub-soil of the eighteenth century or deems it insignificant. However, five studies must be mentioned which have helped throw some light on the neglected area of erotica between 1600–1800: David Foxon, *Libertine Literature* (NY, 1965), which has much to say on the first half of the eighteenth century; Roger Thompson, *Unfit for Modest Ears* (1979) has given a panoramic impression of the market for erotica in seventeenth-century England; Peter Naumann, *Keyhole und Candle* (Heidelberg, 1976), which is a formidable analysis of John Cleland's *Memoirs of a Woman of Pleasure* and of the rise of the pornographic novel in England; Steven Marcus, although mainly concerned with Victorian pornography, offers some interesting, if not always convincing, ideas on eighteenth-century erotica in his *The Other Victorians: A Study of Sexuality and Pornography in Mid-Nineteenth Century England* (NY, 1967); and also Peter Webb's *The Erotic Arts* (1975), which has a fine chapter on the eighteenth and nineteenth centuries.

The study of eighteenth-century erotica has likewise been facilitated by the appearance in recent years of specialised bibliographies, in particular Pascal Pia, *Les livres de l'enfer du XVIe siècle à nos jours*, 2 vols. (Paris, 1978); Patrick J. Kearney, *The Private Case: An Annotated Bibliography of the Private Case Erotica Collection in the British (Museum) Library* (1981); and Gershon Legman, *The Horn Book. Studies in Erotic Folklore and Bibliography* (1970). For a discussion of the available bibliographies, and of the difficulties of doing research in eighteenth-century erotica, see my review of Kearney's book in *BJECS* VI, no. 2 (1983).

3 See Paul-Gabriel Boucé, ed., *Sexuality in Eighteenth-Century Britain* (Manchester, 1982); Michel Foucault, *Histoire de la sexualité* (1976); David Foxon, *Libertine Literature in England 1660–1745* (NY, 1965); Jean H. Hagstrum, *Sex and Sensibility* (Chicago and London, 1980); and Lawrence Stone, *The Family, Sex and Marriage in England 1500–1800* (1977). I quote Foxon from p. x.

4 See Harold Williams, *Dean Swift's Library* (Cambridge, 1974); *A Catalogue of the Entire and Valuable Library of the Books of the late Henry Fielding, Esq.* (1755), which is to be reprinted soon by AMS Press; *A Facsimile Reproduction of a Unique Catalogue of Laurence Sterne's*

Library, ed. Charles Whibley (London and NY, 1930; reprinted 1973); and the *Catalogue of the Printed Books and Manuscripts Bequeathed by Francis Douce, Esq. To the Bodleian Library* (Oxford, 1840).

5 See Plato, *Symposium*, 189 A–193 B; 202 E–203 D; and Hagstrum, *op. cit.*, 3–4. Greek mythology offers a number of different versions on the origin of Eros. According to Hesiod, Eros originated from Chaos and brought about the union of Uranos (Heaven) and Gaia (Earth). Another report sees Eros as the son of Aphrodite and her lover, Ares, thus possessing the qualities of erotic love and war; and yet another story from classic Greece renders Eros as a winged youth with golden arrows – this view was taken over by the Romans. See *Who's Who in Classical Mythology* (1973), s.v. 'Eros' and 'Aphrodite'.

6 My definitions of bawdy, erotic, and obscene are the same as Roger Thompson's, but I do not agree with his view of pornography; see his *Unfit for Modest Ears* (1979), ix–x. For discussions of pornography see the survey of the critical literature by Peter Naumann, *Keyhole und Candle* (Heidelberg, 1976), 1–8. In addition, see Peter Webb, *The Erotic Arts* (1975), chapter I; C.B. Cox *et al.*, eds., 'Symposium: Pornography and Obscenity', *CL* 3 (1961) 99–123; Douglas A. Hughes, ed., *Perspectives on Pornography* (NY, 1970); Hans Giese, *Das obszöne Buch* (Stuttgart, 1965); Horst Albert Glaser, *Wollüstige Phantasie; Sexualästhetik der Literatur* (Munich, 1974); Eberhard and Phyllis Kronhausen, 'The Psychology of Pornography', in Albert Ellis and Albert Arbanel, eds., *The Encyclopaedia of Sexual Behaviour* (NY, 1961); D.H. Lawrence, *Pornography and Obscenity* (1929); Morse Peckham, *Art and Pornography* (NY, 1971); Norman St John-Stevas, *Obscenity and the Law* (1956); and George Steiner, 'Night Words', in his *Language and Silence* (1979), 91–101.

7 See Sontag's essay, 'The Pornographic Imagination', in Hughes, *op. cit.*, 131–70; and Peckham, *op. cit.*, 4.

8 See Burgess, 'What is Pornography?' in Hughes, *op. cit.*, 5.

9 On the erroneous conceptions and the functional definition of pornography see Herbert Mainusch and Edgar Mertner, *Pornotopia* (Frankfurt, 1971), 121 f. The authors have not, however, taken pornography seriously and see it in opposition to 'works of art'. See also Sontag, *op. cit.*, 144.

10 See Thompson, *op. cit.*, ix; Naumann, *op. cit.*, 3; Steiner, *op. cit.*, 96; and *Boswell for the Defence*, ed. William K. Wimsatt and Frederick A. Pottle (1960), 84.

11 In my definition I have followed the ideas suggested by Naumann, *op. cit.*, 3; and Peckham, *op. cit.*, 40.

I MEDICAL AND PARA-MEDICAL LITERATURE

1 See Mary Thale, ed., *The Autobiography of Francis Place (1771–1854)* (Cambridge, 1972), 45. The Place manuscripts are in the BL.

2 The BL has editions of *Aristotle's Master-Piece* from 1690 until the early twentieth century. Two critical studies with bibliographical

information are Janet Blackman, 'Popular Theories of Generation: the Evolution of *Aristotle's Works*. The Study of an Anachronism', in John Woodward and David Richards, eds., *Health Care and Popular Medicine in Nineteenth-Century England* (1977), 56–88; and Sir d'Arcy Power, 'Aristotle's Masterpiece', in *The Foundation of Medical History* (Baltimore, 1931), 147–78. P.G. Boucé is preparing a modern edition of the Aristotle sex guides which is to be published by Junction Books.

3   See the title-page of the edition published in 1700.

4   Erotic and pornographic aspects of the *Master-Piece* are discussed by Otho T. Beall, Jr, '*Aristotle's Master Piece* in America: a Landmark in the Folklore of Medicine', *WMQ* 20 (1963), 207–22; and Roger Thompson, *Unfit for Modest Ears*, 161–7.

5   See Thomas H. Johnson, 'Jonathan Edwards and the "Young Folks" Bible', *NEQ* 5 (1932), 37–54.

6   For detailed analyses of the Aristotle works see the studies of Beall and Thompson, cited above; Lawrence Stone, *The Family, Sex and Marriage*, 493–4; and Vern L. Bullough, *Sex, Society and History* (NY, 1976), 93–104. Together, these works provide a good idea of the bawdiness and the salacity of the Aristotle manuals.

7   On the development of medicine and the medical profession see Peter Gay, *The Enlightenment: An Interpretation*, 2 vols. (1973), II; Bernice Hamilton, 'The Medical Professions in the Eighteenth Century', *EHR* 4 (1951), 141–69; Lester King, *The Medical World of the Eighteenth Century* (Chicago, 1958); *idem, The Philosophy of Medicine: The Early Eighteenth Century* (Cambridge, Mass., 1978); and *idem*, 'Rationalism in Early Eighteenth-Century Medicine', *JHM* 18 (1963), 257–71; Roy Porter, 'Medicine and the Enlightenment in Eighteenth-Century England', *BSSHM* 25 (1979), 27–40; George S. Rousseau, ' "Sowing the Wind and Reaping the Whirlwind": Aspects of Change in Eighteenth-Century Medicine', in Paul J. Korshin, ed., *Studies in Change and Revolution. Aspects of English Intellectual History 1640–1800* (Menston, England, 1972), 129–59; and Guy Williams, *The Age of Agony: The Art of Healing c. 1700–1800* (1975). On La Mettrie see Aram Vartanian, 'La Mettrie, Diderot and Sexology in the Enlightenment', in Jean Macary, ed., *Essays on the Age of Enlightenment in Honor of Ira O. Wade* (Geneva, 1977), 347–67.

    Also of interest are Jean Donnison, *Midwives and Medical Men: A History of Interprofessional Rivalries and Women's Rights* (1977); and Peter Linebaugh, 'The Tyburn Riot Against the Surgeons', in Douglas Hay, Peter Linebaugh et al., eds., *Albion's Fatal Tree: Crime and Society in Eighteenth-Century England* (1977), 65–118.

8   See P.G. Boucé, 'Aspects of Sexual Tolerance and Intolerance in Eighteenth-Century England', *BJECS* 3 (1980), 173–92; *idem*, 'Quelques aspects de la sexualité au dix-huitième siècle', in Michèle Plaisant, ed., *L'excentricité en Grande Bretagne au dix-huitième siècle* (Lille, 1976), 139–58; Michel Delon, 'Le Prétexte Anatomique', *DHS* 12 (1980), 35–48; and Roy Porter, 'Mixed Feelings: the Enlightenment and

Sexuality in Eighteenth-Century Britain', in P.G. Boucé, ed., *Sexuality in Eighteenth-Century Britain*, 1–28.

On the pornographers thriving in the field of medical writings see Stephen Parks, *John Dunton and the English Book Trade: A Study of his Career with a Checklist of his Publications* (1976); Philip Pinkus, *Grub Street Stripped Bare. The Scandalous Lives and Pornographic Works of The Original Grub Street Writers* (1968); and Ralph Strauss, *The Unspeakable Curll* (1927).

9 See M. Delon, *op. cit.*; and A. Comfort, *The Anxiety Makers* (1967), chapters i–iv.

10 On the pornographic aspects of Sinibaldus see Henry Spencer Ashbee, *Index librorum prohibitorum* (1877), 264–5; A. Comfort, *op. cit.*, 20–7; R. Thompson, *Unfit for Modest Ears*, 162–3, 168–72; and D. Foxon, *Libertine Literature*, 13.

11 Ashbee, *Index*, 265.

12 See A. Comfort, *op. cit.*, 28–9; Thompson, *Unfit for Modest Ears*, 167; and P.G. Boucé, 'Livres de médecine populaire et mythes sexuels en Grande-Bretagne au XVIIIe siècle', *Cahiers de l'université de Pau et des pays de l'Adour 10* (1980); and Leonard De Vries/Peter Fryer, *Venus Unmasked, or an Inquiry into the Nature and Origin of the Passion of Love, Interspersed with Curious and Entertaining Accounts of Several Modern Amours; an Eighteenth-Century Anthology* (1967), 45–68. For editions of Venette see Théodore Tarczylo, *Sexe et liberté au siècle des lumières* (1983).

13 See Denise Brahimi, 'La sexualité dans l'anthropologie humaniste de Buffon', *DHS* 12 (1980), 113–26. See also Marten, *Treatise of All the Degrees and Symptoms of the Venereal Disease* (1708); *Gonosologium* (1708). Also probably by Marten, *An Apology for a Latin Verse in Commendation of Mr Marten's Gonosologium* (1709).

14 See the preface, p. 2. This book first appeared in 1713: see Legman, *The Horn Book*, 339. Other eighteenth-century dissertations include Georg Detharding's *Disputatio inauguralis medica, de erotomania* (1719); Christian Gottfried Stentzel's *Dissertatio medico-iuridica . . . von Liebesträncken* (1726); Hermann Boerhaave's *Institutiones medicae*; John Brown's *The Elements of Medicine*; Robert James' *A Medicinal Dictionary*; John Wesley's *Primitive Physick* (1747); Christian Ulrich Grupen's *Schediasma de amoris illecebris* (1715; repr. 1750 Frankfurt/Leipzig).

15 See Henry Spencer Ashbee, *Centuria librorum absconditorum* (1879), 1–14. On Schurig's sexology see Annemarie und Werner Leibbrand, *Formen des Eros. Kultur- und Geistesgeschichte der Liebe*, 2 vols. (Freiburg/Munich, 1972), II, 253–8. Ashbee, from a nineteenth-century viewpoint, was impressed by, and fond of, Schurig's 'scholarship'. For a critical view of Ashbee's attitude see S. Marcus, *The Other Victorians*, 56–8. Other sex guides include *A Rational Account of the Natural Weaknesses of Woman* (1716); John Maubray, *The Female Physician* (1724): *The Ladies Dispensatory, or, Every Woman Her Own Physician* (1739; repr. 1740).

16 See Jean Donnison, *Midwives and Medical Men*, 21–30; and Claude
   Quillet, *Callipédie ou Art d'avoir de beaux enfants* (1655) translated as
   The Art of Getting Beautiful Children (1712, 1727).
17 J. Armstrong, *The Oeconomy of Love*, 13–8; 42.
18 *The Love-Encounter*, 11–3; 22–3.
19 On VD in eighteenth-century England see Ivan Bloch, *Sexual Life in
   England Past and Present* (1958), 301–19; the works by Marten and
   Spinke cited in the bibliography; Gideon Harvey, *The French Pox* and his
   Great Venus Unmasked; the English and Latin versions of A. Luisinus'
   Aphrodisiacus; John Douglas, *A Dissertation on the Venereal Disease*
   (1737); Thomas Garlick, *A Mechanical Account of the Cause and Cure
   of a Virulent Gonorrhea in both Sexes* (1719); William Buchan, *Observations Concerning the Prevention and Cure of the Venereal Disease*
   (1803); and Jean Astruc, *A Treatise of Venereal Diseases* (1754).
20 See Vern Bullough, *Sin, Sickness and Sanity: A History of Sexual Attitudes* (1977), 99, and chapter 9.
21 A copy of this work is in the US National Library of Medicine.
22 See R.P. Neumann, 'Masturbation, Madness, and the Modern Concepts
   of Childhood and Adolescence', *JSH* 8 (1975), 1. Also P. Wagner, 'The
   Veil of Science and Morality: Some Pornographic Aspects of the *Onania*',
   BJECS 2 (1983), 179–84.
23 See Tarczylo, *Sexe et Liberté*. The title is misleading: the author is
   exclusively concerned with the discussion of masturbation in eighteenth-
   century thinking and writing. In addition, see Boucé, 'Aspects of Sexual
   Tolerance', *loc. cit.*, 175–83; Robert H. MacDonald, 'The Frightful
   Consequences of Onanism: Notes on the History of a Delusion', *JHI* 28
   (1967), 423; Edward J. Bristow, *Vice and Vigilance: Purity Movements
   in Britain Since 1700* (Dublin, 1977), 20–21; and A. Comfort, *The
   Anxiety Makers*, 69–79.
24 MacDonald, *op. cit.*, provides a good analysis of *Onania*. E.H. Hare,
   'Masturbatory Insanity: The History of an Idea', *JMS* 108 (1962), 1–25,
   is not convincing in his determination of the publication date.
25 See MacDonald, *op. cit.*, 424. Quotations from the *Onania* hereafter are
   from the seventeenth edition.
26 *Onania*, 191.
27 See Jean-Marie Goulemot, ' "Prêtons la main à la nature ..." Fureurs
   utérines', *DHS* 12 (1980), 109–10; and Peter Naumann, *Keyhole und
   Candle*, passim.
28 *Onania*, 319–20.
29 *Ibid.*, 321.
30 *Ibid.*, 195.
31 See Marie Delcourt, *Hermaphrodite* (Paris, 1958), for a treatment of the
   dominating opinions on hermaphrodites throughout the ages. Literary
   representations of hermaphrodites, with an emphasis on the eighteenth
   century, are discussed by Jean-Pierre Guicciardi, 'Hermaphrodite et le
   prolétaire', *DHS* 12 (1980), 49–78.
32 See Boucé, 'Aspects of Sexual Tolerance', *loc. cit.*, 177–8; Bullough,

Sin, Sickness and Sanity, 59; and A. Comfort, *The Anxiety Makers*, 74–5.

33 See Boucé, 'Aspects', *loc. cit.*, 177. Another translation is *A Treatise of the Crime of Onan; Illustrated with a Variety of Cases, Together with a Method of Cure* (1766), translated from the third edition of the original.

34 *Nymphomania*, 29–30. See also the comments of Jean-Marie Goulemot, *op. cit.*, passim. The original was published as *La nymphomanie, ou traité de la fureur utérine* (Amsterdam, 1771).

35 *Nymphomania*, 51 f; 156–89.

36 *Ibid.*, 108. For a fuller treatment of Bienville's influence see G.S. Rousseau, 'Nymphomania, Bienville and the Rise of Erotic Sensibility', in P.G. Boucé, ed., *Sexuality in Eighteenth-Century Britain*, 95–120.

37 See Neumann, *op. cit.*, 5–6; Boucé, 'Aspects', *loc. cit.*, 180; and Henry L. Marchand, *The French Pornographers* (NY, 1965), 132.
   A more detailed analysis of masturbation in eighteenth-century medical and moral literature and in fiction is Tarczylo's *Sexe et Liberté*, which is particularly good on non-fictional treatises.

38 See Antoine Laporte, *Bibliographie clérico-galante* (Paris, 1879), sub 'Boileau'.

39 Delolme, *The History of Flagellants*; 4–7; 13, 15.

40 Edward Ward, *The London-Spy Compleat, in Eighteen Parts* (1704); 32–3; cited in Henry Spencer Ashbee, *Centuria*, 449–50; 443. For a discussion of Ward's *Spy* see Walter Graham, *The Beginning of English Literary Periodicals* (NY, 1926), 39.

41 See Thompson, *Unfit*, 164–6. The prosecution was, however, more concerned with Curll's publication of *Venus in the Cloister* than with his translation of Meibomius.

42 See *The Gentleman's Magazine*, January and February 1735, October 1780; *The Bon Ton Magazine*, November 1791, March, April, July 1792, August 1793, February and March 1794, November and December 1795, January and February 1796. This continued into the nineteenth century. See Bloch, *Sexual Life in England*, 385; and Ashbee, *Centuria*, 443 n.

43 See Bloch, *Sexual Life in England*, 320–86; and on *Female Flagellants*, Ashbee, *Index*, 238–49; and *ibid.*, 158–60, for a brief discussion of *The Cherub*. On Gillray's sketch see *The Catalogue of Prints and Drawings*; VI, no. 7011.

44 On Peter Motteux see Charles Reginald Dawes, *A Study of Erotic Literature in England* [typescript] (Cheltenham, 1943), 65; H. Montgomery Hyde, *A History of Pornography* (1964), 158.
   I am grateful to Mr Richard J. Wolfe, curator of rare books and manuscripts in the Boston Medical Library (also Harvard Medical Library), for detailed information on the Kotzwara case. See his article on 'The Hang-Up of Franz Kotzwara and its Relationship to Sexual Quackery in Late Eighteenth-Century London', in my *Sex and Eighteenth-Century English Culture*, SVEC 228 (1984), 47–67.

45 Georges-Louis Lesage, *Remarques sur l'état de l'Angleterre ... dans les*

années 1713 et 1714 (Amsterdam, 1715), 149–50; cited in Boucé, 'Quelques aspects', *loc. cit.*, 151.

46 The BL has a copy of *Monsieur Thing's Origin*. See also the following poems, on the same subject, listed in David Foxon, *English Verse 1701–1750*, vol. I: *Dildoides. A Burlesque Poem* (1706; a copy is held by Trinity College, Dublin), possibly by Samuel Butler; and *The Bauble, a Tale* (1721).

47 See *Monsieur Thing's Origin*, 12, 16, 19, 23; Foxon, *English Verse*, I M 413; *The History of Signor del Dildo* (1732); and *A Voyage to Lethe* (1741).

48 *Adollizing*, preface, iv; and pp. 17, 18–9.

49 See *Eunuchi Conjugium* (Halle, 1697 and later); Charles Ancillon, *Traité des eunuques* (1707) and his *Eunuchism Display'd* (1718).

50 See *The Rambler's Magazine*, I (1783), and *New Attalantis* (1762), quoted by Ashbee, *Catena*, 270–71. No copy of this book seems to be extant.

51 See Marie Delcourt, *Hermaphrodite*; J.P. Guicciardi, 'Hermaphrodite et le prolétaire', *loc. cit.*; Ashton, *Eighteenth-Century Waifs* (1887), 177–203; Ivan Bloch, *Sexual Life in England*, 427–30; Bullough, *Sex, Society and History*, 60–73, 150–60; and Randolph Trumbach, 'London's Sodomites: Homosexual Behaviour and Western Culture in the Eighteenth Century', *JSH* 2 (1977), 18.

52 See Johann Heinrich Wolfart, *Tractatio juridica de sodomia vera et spuria hermaphroditi* (1742); Cregut, *Gründliche wiederlegung eines ungegründet angebrachten facti* (1743); Dr James Parson, *A Mechanical and Critical Enquiry into the Nature of hermaphrodites* (1741).

53 See also Chavigny, *La galante hermaphrodite* (1683); de Foigny, *Aventures de Jacques Sadeur* (1692); de Pauw, *Recherches philosophiques sur les américains* (1771); anonymous, *Description de l'île des hermaphrodites* (1724).

54 On the Abbé de Choisy see *Dictionnaire des oeuvres érotiques*, s.v. 'Mémoires', and Bullough, *Sin, Sickness*, 79, 242. See especially 'Mémoires de l'abbé de Choisy habillé en femme', in Georges Mongredien, ed., *Mémoires pour servir à l'histoire de Louis XIV* (1966). Rose's *Register of Erotic Books*, I. no. 2196, cites a work entitled, *Histoire de Mme La Comtesse des Barres à Mme la Marquise de Lambert* (Anvers, 1735) which could be a version of the *Histoire de l'abbé de Choisy écrite par lui-même*.

55 There is an extensive body of literature on the Chevalier d'Eon. See John Buchan Telfer, *The Strange Career of the Chevalier d'Eon de Beaumont* (1885), and *NQ*, fourth series II, passim. See also Marcel Cadéac, *Le Chevalier d'Eon et son problème psycho-sexuel* (1966); Marjorie Stella Coryn, *The Chevalier d'Eon 1728–1810* (1932); and Valentin Pikoul, *Le Chevalier D'Eon et la guerre de sept ans* (1983). On his trial see *The Gentleman's Magazine* 47 (1777), 346. An interesting and reliable account of his life can be found in the *Dictionary of National Biography*, hereafter cited as *DNB*. *Les loisirs de Chevalier d'Eon de Beaumont sur*

divers sujets importans [sic] *d'administration etc. Pendant son séjour en Angleterre* (Amsterdam, 1774) is by his own hand, while a large number of his manuscripts are awaiting a courageous researcher in the BL: see pressmarks Add. 11339–41; and 29993–4. Newspaper reports, including those of the *London Evening Post*, and some comments in d'Eon's handwriting (London, 1774–1779) are available under the pressmark 1414 b 19 in the BL. In addition to the erotic works cited in the text, see also *The True Story of the Chevalier d'Eon, or The Modern Hermaphrodite by One Who Knew it* (c. 1828), which is cited in Rose, *Register of Erotic Books.*

For prints satirising d'Eon see the *Catalogue of Prints and Drawings. Political and Personal Satires in the British Museum* (1873–1954), vol. V, passim: no. 4872 describes 'The Nuptials of Miss Epicaere d'Eon', published in 1771, which shows d'Eon dressed as a woman being led to the altar by John Wilkes. Two of the many erotic works – pamphlets, prints, lampoons – that were produced on this ambiguous personality in the 1770s are *An Epistle from Mademoiselle d'Eon to the Right Honourable L(or)d M(ansfiel)d ... on his Determination in Regard to her Sex* (sixth edition, 1778), which is a satire in verse, and *An Elegy on the Lamented Death of the Electrical Eel* (1777), which has a bawdy 'inscription' to d'Eon.

56 On Brown, Davies, and Snell see the *DNB*; John Ashton, *Eighteenth-Century Waifs*, chapter ix.; and Charles John Samuel Thompson, *The Mysteries of Sex: Women who Posed as Men and Men who Impersonated Women* (1938; reprinted New York, 1974). Henry Fielding tackled the subject of cross-dressers in his *The Female Husband* (1746), a sadly disappointing piece for the prurient of the middle class. It confirms the eighteenth-century rejection of 'unnatural affections' in sexual relations. On Fielding's erotic book see Sheridan Baker, 'Henry Fielding's *The Female Husband*: Fact and Fiction', *PMLA* 74 (1959), 214–24; and Terry Castle, 'Matters not fit to be mentioned: Fielding's *The Female Husband*', *ELH* 49 (1982), 602–23. See also the reprint of Fielding's *The Female Husband*, ed. Claude E. Jones (Liverpool, 1960).

57 On the cases after 1750 see the *Annual Register*, 1761, 1766, 1769, 1771, 1773, 1777, 1782 and 1793. In addition, see R. Rattrey Taylor, *The Angel Makers* (1958; reprinted and revised 1973), 10; and Derek Jarrett, *England in the Age of Hogarth* (1976), 124.

58 On homosexuals in eighteenth-century England see Bloch, *Sexual Life*, 394–426; Vern L. Bullough et al., *An Annotated Bibliography of Homosexuality*, 2 vols. (NY, 1975); *idem, Homosexuality: A History* (1979), chapter 3; A.D. Harvey, 'Prosecution for Sodomy in England at the Beginning of the Nineteenth Century', *HJ* 21 (1978), 939–48; Bernhardt J. Hurwood, *The Golden Age of Erotica* (1968), 163–9; H. Montgomery Hyde, *The Other Love* (1970): this was published in Boston under the title *The Love That Dared Not Speak Its Name*; A.L. Rowse, *Homosexuals In History* (1977); Lawrence Stone, *The Family, Sex and Marriage*, 541–2; and Randolph Trumbach, 'London's

Sodomites ...', *loc. cit.* See also Trumbach's *The Rise of the Egalitarian Family* (1978), 281–5.

Only a few pornographic trial reports of cases of sodomy were published separately in the eighteenth century, among them the reprinted reports from the seventeenth century of the Earl of Castlehaven and of Bishop Atherton as well as the affair at Wadham College, Oxford. The quasi-official sessions papers of the Old Bailey, for instance, did of course contain the details of almost all the trials, including those for sodomy. See also chapter IV.

59 See Foxon, *Libertine Literature*, 54; and Trumbach, 'London's Sodomites', *loc. cit.*, 13–4. Foxon could locate no extant copy of Cannon's treatise. Braun's dissertation is quoted by Ashbee, *Catena*, 30.

60 On Rochester's *Sodom* and Vanbrugh's comedy see Hyde, *The Other Love*, 60–2. The authorship and the content of *Sodom* are discussed by Thompson, *Unfit*, 125–7. No copy has survived of *The He-Strumpets*: see S. Parks, *John Dunton*, 161. Ward's *History of the London Clubs* is available in an edition from 1711 in the British Library. The quotation is from pp. 28–9. On Ward's work see Howard W. Troyer, *Ned Ward of Grubstreet. A Study of Sub-Literary London in the Eighteenth Century* (Cambridge, Mass., 1946), which has an excellent bibliography including the location of the various works.

61 *A Genuine Narrative ... by James Dalton* (1728), title page and p. 36. See also *Hell upon Earth* (1729), 41–3; and *Satan's Harvest Home* (1749), 45–59.

62 See *Satan's Harvest Home*, 145–8, and Hyde, *The Other Love*, 69; Trumbach, 'London's Sodomites', *loc. cit.*, 21; and the *Annual Register* 6 (1763), 67.

63 For other cases, some of them involving public figures like William Beckford and Charles Fielding, see Harvey, 'Prosecutions for Sodomy', *loc. cit.*, 940; Hyde, *The Other Love*, 69–77; and Trumbach, 'London's Sodomites', *loc. cit.*, 21–2.

64 See *Sodom and Onan* (1776?), 4, 12, 21–9. On Foote, see the *DNB*; *A Biographical Dictionary of Actors*; Hyde, *The Other Love*, 69–70. *Lloyd's Evening Post*, 39 no. 3036, pp. 361–2 of December 1776 has 'particulars of the trial'. On Hervey, see Robert Halsband, *Lord Hervey: Eighteenth-Century Courtier* (1973); and James R. Dubro, 'The Third Sex: Lord Hervey and his Coterie', *ECL* 2 (1976), 89–95. Marie-Antoinette and her coterie were slandered as lesbians while noblemen like the Marquis de Villette were exposed as sodomites in such pamphlets as *Vie privée ... du ... Marquis de Villette* (c. 1792); and *Les enfants de Sodome à l'Assemblée Nationale* (1790).

65 On the 'lesbian' satires directed at Miss Raucourt see Kearney, *Private Case*, s.v. 'Anandrina' and nos. 34–9. Archenholtz's travel report is cited by Bloch, *Sexual Life*, 425: see also *ibid.* for other aspects of lesbianism in eighteenth-century England; and Lillian Faderman, *Surpassing the Love of Men: Love Between Women from the Renaissance to the Present* (NY, 1981). On the prevalence of lesbianism among eighteenth-century French

actresses see Jean de Reuilly, *La Raucourt et ses amies, étude historique des moeurs saphiques au XVIIIe siècle* (1909); *Bilderlexikon der Erotik*, I, 51–4; and chapter v, 'Diderot sexologue', in George May's *Diderot et 'La religieuse'* (Paris, 1954), 98–114.

66 Trumbach, *The Rise of the Egalitarian Family*, 283. On eighteenth-century sexual stereotypes and 'gender logic' see L.J. Jordanova, 'Natural Facts: A Historical Perspective on Science and Sexuality', in Carl MacCormack and Marilyn Strathern, eds., *Nature, Culture, and Gender* (Cambridge, 1980).

67 See Porter, 'Medicine and the Enlightenment', *loc. cit.*, 36–7; *ibid.*, 'Mixed feelings', *loc. cit.*, 8–10. On the role and importance of quacks in the eighteenth century see Jarrett, *England in the Age of Hogarth*, 193–5; and G.S. Rousseau, 'Sowing the wind', *loc. cit.* Studies of the lives and works of quacks are John Ashton, *Eighteenth-Century Waifs*, 287–333; Eric Jameson, *The Natural History of Quackery* (1961); Charles John Samuel Thompson, *The Quacks of Old London* (NY, 1928); G. Williams, *The Age of Agony*, chapter ix. See also Bloch, *Sexual Life*, 301–19; and Donnison, *Midwives and Medical Men*, passim. More recently, the negative image of the incompetent quack has been challenged: see the works of Lester King, G.S. Rousseau, and especially Roy Porter, 'Sex and the singular man', in my 'Sex and Eighteenth-Century English Culture', *SVEC* 228 (1984), 3–25. These studies explain existing schools of thought among the 'empiricks' and see quack doctors as representatives of the moderate Enlightenment. See also Roger A. Hambridge, 'Empir-icomany ...: the socio-economics of eighteenth-century quackery', in *Literature and Science and Medicine* (Los Angeles 1982) 45–102.

68 See B. Hamilton, 'The Medical Professions', *loc. cit.*, 160–61, on the treatises discussing the frauds in medicine. Tom Brown deals with 'phy-sick' in chapter ix of his *Amusements Serious and Comical* (1700), repr. in the facsimile series, *Les introuvables anglais*, ed. Georges Lamoine, pp. 91 and 98.

See also *The New Bath Guide* (fifth edition, 1762), 26–9. Many more literary examples, like the spleeny Dr Slop in *Tristram Shandy*, could of course be added. See G.S. Rousseau, *Doctors and Medicine in the Novels of Tobias Smollett*, unpublished diss. (Princeton, NJ, 1966), chapters i–ii.

The Crafts and Frauds of Physick of 1703, and Dr Pitt's *The Frauds and Villainies of the Common Practice of Physick*, published in 1705, were directed against the quacks.

69 On the dabbling of quacks in the fields of aphrodisiacs and contraceptives see Bloch, *Sexual Life*, chapter xi; and on Richard Hathaway, a black-smith's apprentice, the *DNB*.

The fraud of Mary Tofts and the involvement of the quacks and doctors are described in G. Williams, *The Age of Agony*, 35–8; S.A. Seligman, 'Mary Toft – the rabbit breeder', *MH* 5 (1961), 349–60; and K. Bryn Thomas, *James Douglas of the Pouch and His Pupil, William Hunter* (1964), chapter vi. The fraud was brought to light by Sir Richard

Manningham, the most respected 'accoucheur' of the day. The BL has a collection of tracts relating to Mary Tofts in a volume, shelfmark 1178 h4, which includes the reports of St André and Manningham as well as satirical and critical works. Seligman's article has a good bibliography of bawdy satires and other writings related to the case, too. See also Manningham's *An Exact Diary* (1726), 33–35.

70   On James Graham, sexology, and the literary-commercial exploitation of sex, see Roy Porter, ' "The Secrets of Generation Display'd": *Aristotle's Master-piece* in Eighteenth-Century England', *ECL* 9 (1985, special issue on 'Unauthorized Sexual Behaviour during the Enlightenment', ed. Robert P. Maccubbin), 1–21; 'The Sexual Politics of James Graham', *BJECS* 5 (1982), 199–206; and 'Spreading Carnal Knowledge or Selling Dirt Cheap? Nicolas Venette's Tableau de l'Amour Conjugal in Eighteenth-Century England', *Journal of European Studies* 4 (1984), 233–55; and my own 'The Discourse on Sex – Or Sex as Discourse: Eighteenth-Century Medical and Paramedical Erotica', in Roy Porter and George Rousseau, eds., *Sexual Underworlds of the Enlightenment* (Manchester: Manchester UP, 1988). See also Graham, *Il Convicto Amoroso* (1782); Colman, *The Genius of Nonsense* (1780); *The Rambler's Magazine* (1783).

2   ANTI-RELIGIOUS EROTICA

1   On the revolt of libertinism and the Enlightenment against religion in France see Wayland H. Young, *Eros Denied* (1965; second edition 1968), 223–73. The history of the parody of religious forms and rites is analysed by Peter Burke, *Popular Culture in Early Modern Europe* (1978), 122–4; and Thompson, *Unfit*, 56 n. 56. *A Dissertation ... of Kissing* was published in Norwich, Swaffham, and Lynn and is quoted from p. 18; the copy in the British Library bears no date, but the work is probably of late seventeenth or early eighteenth-century origin. Michel Foucault deals with the discourse on sex in his *The History of Sexuality* (NY, 1978), I, 21–3, and 57–8. On the sublimation of sex in literature and devotional writing see 'Literature and sex', in *The Encyclopedia of Sexual Behavior*, ed. Albert Ellis and Albert Abarbanel, 2 vols. (NY, 1961), II, 637.

2   Young, *Eros Denied*, 212, 219–73. On the influence of *A Rake's Progress* see Jarrett, *England in the Age of Hogarth*, 162–5; and Ronald Paulson, *Hogarth: His Life, Art and Times*, 2 vols. (1971), I, passim. On the verse published with the prints see Naumann, *Keyhole*, 371 n. 67. Background information on the prints can be found in Joseph Burke, Colin Caldwell, *Hogarth. The Complete Engravings* (1974); and Robert E. Moore, *Hogarth's Literary Relationships* (NY, 1969), 44–53.

On the rakish clubs see Edwin B. Chancellor, *The Lives of the Rakes*, 6 vols. (1924–25), vol. iv; Louis C. Jones, *The Clubs of the Georgian Rakes* (NY, 1942), vols. iii–vii; and Iwan Bloch, *Sexual Life in England* (1965), chapter ix. In addition see Ashbee, *Index*, 210–11; Ronald Fuller, *Hell-*

Fire Francis (1939); Daniel P. Mannix, *The Hell-Fire Club* (1970); and Charles Johnstone's *Chrysal, or the Adventures of a Guinea*, first published in 2 vols. in 1760 and then in an enlarged edition of 4 vols. (Dublin, 1766; repr. NY, 1979), which has several chapters on the Medmenhamites in vol. III.

3 On John Wilkes see Horace Bleackley, *Life of John Wilkes* (1917); Raymond W. Postgate, *That Devil Wilkes* (1930); and Adrian Hamilton, *The Infamous Essay on Woman or John Wilkes Seated Between Vice and Virtue* (1972). On the connection between the scandal and politics see D. Thomas, *A Long Time Burning*, 94–5; and Leo Alpert, 'Judicial Censorship of Obscene Literature', *HLR* 52 (1938), 40–76.

Ashbee's *Index*, 207–12 and 231–6, has additional information on the *Essay on Woman* and includes a discussion of the essay and the poems: see pp. 198–236 and 430–2. In addition, see Ashbee's *Centuria*, xiv–xvi; Postgate, *op. cit.*, 76 f.; Eric Watson, 'An Essay on Woman', *NQ* 9, 121 f. Imitations of, and answers to, Wilkes' *Essay* are listed in Ashbee, *Index*, 214. The quotations are from the genuine edition of the *Essay*, identified by Kearney, *Private Case*, no. 1890, and reprinted by Hotten in 1871 (BL shelfmark P.C. 18 b 8). For details on John Kidgell's treatises and on *The Priest in Rhyme* – all of them reactions to Wilkes' *Essay* – see *bibliography*.

On Stevenson's 'Demoniacs' and similar clubs see Jones, *op. cit.*, chapters III–IV; and the *Records of the Most Ancient and Puissant Order of the Beggar's Benison and Merryland, Anstruther* (Edinburgh, 1892; reprinted 1982), with an introduction by Alan Bold.

4 For comments on sexual libertinism and anti-Christian ideologies in England and France during the eighteenth century see Stone, *The Family, Sex and Marriage*, 528 and 535; R.F. Brissenden, 'La philosophie dans le boudoir; or, A Young Lady's Entrance Into the World', *SECC* 2 (1972), 113–41, especially p. 6; René Pintard, *Le libertinage érudit* (Paris, 1943); D. Foxon, *Libertine Literature*, 48–50; and Will and Ariel Durant, *The Age of Voltaire* (NY, 1965), book V. In addition, see Ira O. Wade, *The Clandestine Organization and Diffusion of Philosophic Ideas in France From 1700 to 1750* (Princeton, NJ, 1938; repr. NY 1967), and Olivier Bloch, ed., *Le matérialisme du XVIIIe siècle et la littérature clandestine* (1982). On France's debauched aristocracy see I. Bloch, *Marquis de Sade's Anthropologia Sexualis of 600 Perversions* (NY, 1934); *ibid.*, *Marquis de Sade, The Man and his Age* (Newark, NJ, 1931).

The cultural exchange between England and France in the eighteenth century is treated in Jay Barrett Botsford, *English Society in the Eighteenth Century as Influenced from Overseas* (NY, 1924); Derek Jarrett, *The Begetters of Revolution: England's Involvement with France 1759–1789* (1973); see especially pp. 18–41; C.H. Lockitt, *The Relations between French and English Society, 1763–1793* (1920); George Rudé, *Paris and London in the Eighteenth Century: Studies in Popular Protest* (NY, 1973); and Ronald Paulson, *Representation of Revolution (1789–1820)* (1983).

On the libertine societies and clubs in France see Jean Hervez, *Les sociétés d'amour au XVIIIe siècle* (1906).

5 On Beverland see Eric J. Dingwall, *Very Peculiar People. Portrait Studies in the Queer, the Abnormal and the Uncanny* (1950), 145–77. See also Alard Uchtmann, *Vox clamantis in deserto ad doctissimum juvenem Hadrianum Beverlandum* (c. 1700), published in the Netherlands, of which there is a copy in the *ISR*. For excerpts from Maclauchlan's *Essay* see De Vries/Fryer, comp., *Venus Unmasked*, 10, and 39–46. On Sterne see Michael O. Hounahan, *Sexual Comedy in Tristram Shandy*, doct. diss. (Northwestern University, 1970). See also Curll, *Post Office Intelligence* (1736); *The Polygamist: Or the Lustful Priest ... Written by an Irish Laureate* (1782).

6 See Richard Savage, 'The Progress of a Divine', in *The Poetical Works of Richard Savage*, 2 vols. (Edinburgh, 1780), I, 93–108; lines 99–124 of the poem; and *Post-Office Intelligence*, letters no. vi, 12–13; *The Polygamist*; and *The Bon Ton Magazine* 31 (1793), 239–42.
   For satirical prints of lecherous clergymen see the *Catalogue of Prints and Drawings in the British Museum*, vol. V no. 5447, and passim; and the pornographic pictures of Rowlandson in G. Schiff, ed., *The Amorous Illustrations of Thomas Rowlandson* (NY, 1969), nos. 2, 3, 21, 22.

7 On the bawdy satires against the Quakers see Thompson, *Unfit*, 52. *A Comical New Dialogue*, 3–11; *Post-Office Intelligence*, 42 (letter no. xxvi). On *A Merry Conversation* (1739) see Naumann, *Keyhole*, 56–8, where its relationship with the whore dialogue is discussed.

8 On anti-Methodist satire see Samuel J. Rogal, 'Enlightenment Enthusiasm: Anti-Methodism in the Literature of the Mid and Late Eighteenth Century', *EE* 5 (1974), 3–13. This is a rather sketchy survey, examining the responses of Johnson, Sterne, Smollett, Fielding, and Samuel Foote. See *The Female Husband*, 30–4; and on Sterne's attack on Whitefield see Rogal, *op. cit.*, 8 and 12, where Foote's *The Minor* is quoted. In addition, see *The New Bath Guide* (fifth edition, 1767), 128–30, and the footnote on p. 130. See also my forthcoming edition of this book to be published by Georg Olms Verlag. For a discussion of the details in Hogarth's prints of 1760 and 1762, which refer to Mary Tofts, Richard Hathaway, and the Cock Lane Ghost, see Jarrett, *England in the Age of Hogarth*, 181–2; and Paulson, *Hogarth*, II, 298–301 and 354–7. See 'The Priest-Ridden Washerwoman', in *The Bon Ton Magazine* 31 (1793), 245–6.

9 See John, Lord Fortescue, *Reports of Select Cases* (1748), 100; cited in D. Thomas, *A Long Time Burning*, 82. See *ibid.*, 80–2, on the prosecution of Curll's book in 1725. For discussions of *Venus in the Cloister* see chapter VII and P. Naumann, *Keyhole und Candle*, 43–50.

10 For a survey of erotica directed against the Church of Rome and published from about 1600 to the mid-nineteenth century see Ashbee, *Centuria*, xxii–xlvi and 62–291. Ashbee reveals himself as an anti-Catholic on p. xxxi, dividing the erotica he discusses into works by priests or members of the Church (62–86), works by 'Popish Writers' (87–111), books by apostates (112–44), by those who suffered persecution (145–

56), by Protestants and enemies (157–212), authentic accounts of scandals involving priests (213–59), and slander and fiction (260–91).

Anti-Catholic erotica of seventeenth-century origin are discussed by Thompson, *Unfit*, chapter viii; and Naumann, *Keyhole und Candle*, 91–106. Thompson also has a chapter (iv) on anti-Puritanical writings.

11 See also the Vatican's own *Index librorum prohibitorum* (Rome, 1938), which lists numerous anti-clerical and anti-religious works, most of them French, of eighteenth-century origin. *The Catalogue of All the Discourses Published Against Popery during the Reign of King James II* (1683–1701) in the BL is a collection in twenty volumes of anti-Catholic tracts providing an idea of the kind and scope of the criticism the Catholic Church was subjected to.

12 On Aretino, Boccaccio, Bracciolini, Pallavicino, and Rabelais, see David Frantz, 'Leud Priapians and Renaissance Pornography', *SEL* 12 (1972), 157–72; and Thompson, *Unfit*, chapter I, 134–5, 154. Boccaccio's popularity is confirmed by such republications as *Contes et nouvelles de Boccace*, 2 vols. (The Hague, 1777); *Contes de J. Boccace*, 10 vols. (Paris, 1779); *Le Decaméron de Jean Bocace*, 5 vols. (London, 1757–61). Most of these editions had erotic engravings. Anti-Catholic works by renegades include James Salgado's *The Fryer* (1680) and *Symbiosis* (1681), and G. Leti's, *The Life of Pope Sixtus the Vth* (1704; often reprinted); and also by Leti, *The Court of Rome* (1654); *The History of the Whores and Whoredoms of the Popes, Cardinals and Clergy of Rome* (1678); and his *Il Nipotismo di Roma* (Amsterdam, 1667); and *Il Putanismo Romano* (1669), both often reprinted in various European countries.

On the sexual humour of the French *fabliaux* and *contes-en-vers* see Gershon Legman, 'Toward a motif-index of erotic humor', *JAF* 75 no. 297 (1962), 227 and 236–9, reprinted in his *Horn Book*, 454–94. See *ibid.*, on La Fontaine's *Contes*; and also Henry L. Marchand, *The French Pornographers, Including A History of French Erotic Literature* (NY, 1965), 88 f. See also Rowlandson's illustration for La Fontaine's tale, 'Les Lunettes', in Rowlandson, *Allerlei Liebe*, no. 36.

For a discussion of the following works of prose fiction, with anti-Catholic themes, see chapter VII: La Morlière, *Les lauries ecclésiastiques* (1747); and his *Les délices du cloître* (1760); de Latouche, *Histoire de Dom B* (1743); d'Argens, *Les nones galantes* (1740) and his *Thérèse philosophe* (1748).

On the French anti-Catholic erotica see Paul Englisch, *Geschichte der erotischen Literatur* (Berlin and Stuttgart, 1927; repr. 1932), 318–406; Bernhard Stern, *Geschichte der erotischen Literatur aller Völker und Zeiten*, 2 vols. (Leipzig and Vienna, 1908), II, chapter 5, 'Die Erotiker unter den Geistlichen des 18. Jahrhunderts.' In addition, see *Bilderlexikon der Erotik*, vols. I–IV, which includes the major writers and numerous illustrations; *Dictionnaire des Oeuvres Érotiques*, passim; Marchand, *The French Pornographers*, 114–33. Good bibliographies and discussions can also be found in Jean Leduc, 'Le clergé dans le roman érotique français du XVIIIe siècle,' in *Roman et lumières au 18e siècle* (Paris, 1970), 341–50; Peter Nagy, *Libertinage et révolution* (Paris, 1975); and Jacques Rustin, *Le vice à la mode. Etude sur le roman français du XVIIIe siècle* (Paris, 1979).

Clifton T. Longworth's *The Devil a Monk Would Be: A Survey of Sex and Celibacy in Religion* (1936) has a chapter (14) on clerical celibacy and the confessional but suffers from sweeping judgments, no documentation of sources, and is stridently anti-Catholic as well as racist. Peter Naumann's doctoral dissertation *Keyhole und Candle*, 91–106, discusses eighteenth-century anti-clerical erotica in passing, but for some reason completely ignores the French *abbés*.

Any study of the admittedly vast bulk of eighteenth-century French anti-Catholic and anti-Christian erotica should start with the bibliographies of Daniel Bécourt, *Livres condamnés, Livres interdits, Régime juridique du livre, Outrages aux bonnes moeurs, Arrêts d'interdiction* (Paris, 1961), especially 7–76; Jules Gay, *Bibliographie des ouvrages relatifs à l'amour, aux femmes, au mariage ... par M. le C. d'I*, 4 vols. (Paris, 1893–1900), and Alexandre Cioranescu, *Bibliographie de la littérature française du dix-huitième siècle*, 3 vols. (Paris, 1969). Also of interest are Pascal Pia's *Les livres de l'Enfers*, 2 vols. (Paris, 1978) and Anne Sauvy's *Livres saisis à Paris entre 1678 et 1701* (La Haye, 1972), while Antoine Laporte's *Bibliographie clérico-galante. Ouvrages galants ou singuliers sur l'amour, les femmes, le mariage, le théâtre, etc. Écrits par des abbés, prêtres, chanoines, religieux, religieuses, évêques, archévêques, cardinaux et papes. Par l'Apôtre bibliographe* (Paris, 1879), faulty though it is, remains the principal source for the erotic works of the libertine *abbés*. The influence in the literary salons of these notorious *abbés* is discussed by Nina C. Epton in her *Love and the French* (London, 1959), 191–281.

13 On Voltaire's epithet (Abbé Bazin) see Kearney, *Private Case*, no. 1857. The erotica written by the *abbés* are listed in Laporte's bibliography, which is not reliable as to dates and names and has to be compared with Pia's two volumes on the holdings of the 'Enfer'. On Voisenon's *Les exercices de dévotion* (c. 1780) see Ashbee, *Centuria*, 270 f.

14 On the sex life of Catholic clergymen in the Middle Ages and during the Renaissance see Emmanuel Le Roy Ladurie, *Montaillou. Cathars and Catholics in a French Village 1294–1324* (Harmondsworth, 1980), chapter ix: Ladurie proves beyond doubt that the priests in Montaillou did not suppress their libido, seduced female parishioners, and visited brothels. See also Shulamit Shahar, *Die Frau im Mittelalter* (Königstein, 1981), 181–6 and notes 107 and 108 (p. 274); and Thompson, *Unfit*, 136–7.

As can be expected, the twentieth-century slander of the Catholic Church has focused on this aspect, drawing on half a millennium of ribald satire on the alleged and true sexual incontinency of priests and monks. Longworth's *The Devil a Monk Would Be* and, in Germany, Otto von Corvin's *Der Pfaffenspiegel* (1868; repr. several times); and Karlheinz

Descher's *Das Kreuz mit der Kirche. Eine Sexualgeschichte des Christentums* are examples of such unscholarly and libellous works.

On Koch's *De obscoenis* see Ashbee, *Catena*, 3. Sterne's anti-Catholic books can be found in the catalogue of his library, cited above, pp. 9 and 51. Seventeenth-century bawdy satire against the Pope is discussed by Thompson, *Unfit*, chapter 8. On Gavin's *Master-key* see Ashbee, *Centuria*, 112–22; and Hurwood, *The Golden Age of Erotica*, 80–2. I have quoted Egane's *The Book of Rates* from a copy in the possession of the ISR.

See *L'art de bien baiser*, 22; and *Reasons Humbly Offered*, cited and discussed in Ashbee, *Centuria*, 208–12; and *The Priest Gelded*, 10–12; 16 and 18. Other French anti-clerical erotica are *Les bijoux du petit neveu de l'Arétin* (Paris, 1791), which includes obscene and ribald pieces like 'La consolation des nonnes'; and *Les religieux et religieuses laborieux ou les fruits de la liberté* (Paris, 1790), which is illustrated with obscene engravings and describes the libidinous adventures of *abbés*.

See also the *Bordel apostolique institué par Pie VI* (1790), by the 'abbé Grosier'; *La chasteté du clergé dévoilée ou procès-verbaux des séances du clergé chez les filles de Paris* (1790), which provides the names, status, and residence of those clerics caught with prostitutes before the Revolution; *Le courrier extraordinaire des fouteurs ecclésiastiques, ou correspondance intime, secrète et libertine de quelques prélats de qualité* (1790); and *Liste de tous les prêtres trouvés en flagrant délit chez les filles publiques de Paris* (1790).

15 As early as Shakespeare's time, bawdy houses were nicknamed 'nunneries': cf. the ambiguous use of the term by Hamlet, when he tells Ophelia, 'Get thee to a nunnery'.

On the Jesuits in the eighteenth century see David Ogg, *Europe of the Ancien Régime 1715–1783* (Glasgow 1965), 227–39 and 262–3; Thompson *Unfit*, 138. See Laporte *Bibliographie*, 87 for Voltaire's quatrain; *Love In All Its Shapes* (1734), 11, 17, 22; *Memoirs of ... the Capuchins* (1755), 33–4, 41–9. In addition, see the picaresque novel *The Adventures of a Jesuit* (1771).

For a discussion of the anti-monastic erotica see Ashbee, *Centuria*, 62–291. On 260–4 Ashbee provides excerpts from *The Cloisters Laid Open*. See also Naumann, *Keyhole*, 92.

On the many versions of *Vie voluptueuse* see Naumann, *Keyhole*, 92 n. 89; and Kearney, *Private Case*, nos. 1839–42. Quotations from the *Memoirs of the Voluptuous Conduct* are from pp. 33–4 and 41–9. See also *Adventures of a Jesuit*, 180–84. For additional illustrations of lustful clerics see *Bilderlexikon der Erotik*, vol. IV, 582; and the *Catalogue of Prints and Drawings in the British Museum*. vols. I–V, III (p. 1255 no. 3774), and passim.

16 See Smollett, *Roderick Random*; Sterne, *Tristram Shandy*; and *The Amorous Friars* (1759).

On Smollett's anti-Catholicism and bawdry see Paul-Gabriel Boucé, *The Novels of Tobias Smollett* (1976); on Sterne see Barbara Lounsberry,

'Sermons and satire: anti-Catholicism in Sterne,' *PQ* 55 (1976), 403–17. See also *The Fruit Shop*, I, 102–3, which is discussed by Ashbee, *Catena*, 107–12; and by Bloch, *Sexual Life*, 547–8.

17 A reliable modern edition of the *Heptaméron* is the one published in Berne in 1780/81, which has illustrations by Duncker and Freudenberger. See also the postscript by Peter Amelung in the German translation, published by Winkler Verlag in 1960, 761–84, which stresses the pervasive literary influence and the erotic aspects of this collection of tales.

On the stereotyped stock figures of the randy monk, the cynical cardinal, and the corrupt pope in the satire on clerics written in the popular tradition see Peter Sloterdijk, *Kritk der zynischen Vernunft*, 2 vols. (Frankfurt, 1983), I, 99. Sloterdijk shows that this satire was an important outlet for social, political, and religious protest during several centuries. Ironically, it prevented moral and political reform for a long time while channelling the critical voices into the comparatively harmless fields of satirical writing. It was with the advent of political revolution that this situation began to change.

3 ANTI-ARISTOCRATIC EROTICA

1 On the eighteenth-century English libel laws and their influence on personal satire see C.R. Kropf, 'Libel and Satire in the Eighteenth Century', *ECS* 8 (1974/5), 153–68; and Viktor Link, 'Literatur vor Gericht: zur Wechselbeziehung von Literatur und Landeskunde', *Anglistentag 1979: Vorträge und Protokolle*, ed. Kuno Schuhmann (Berlin, 1979), 121–39.

For a brief survey of classical libels by Suetonius, Lucian, and others see the introduction to Paul Robiquet's *Théveneau de Morande. Étude sur le XVIIIe siècle* (Paris, 1882). On the development of the French 'chronique scandaleuse' see John J. Richetti, *Popular Fiction before Richardson* (Oxford, 1969), chapter IV; Klaus Sasse, *Die Entstehung der 'courtisane vertueuse' in der französischen Literatur des 18. Jahrhunderts. Rétif de la Bretonne und seine Vorgänger*, Ph.D. diss. (Hamburg, 1967), chapters III and IV; Paul Englisch, *Geschichte der erotischen Literatur*, 373 ff.; Vivienne Mylne, *The Eighteenth-Century French Novel. Techniques of Illusion* (Manchester/NY, 1965; reprinted 1970), chapters II and III; and Peter Nagy, *Libertinage et révolution* (Paris, 1975), chapter II, part 1. To date, we have no literary or socio-literary study of French eighteenth-century anti-aristocratic erotica. In her short essày, 'Littérature populaire et littérature de colportage au 18e siècle', published in François Furet's *Livre et société dans la France du 18e siècle*, 2 vols. (Paris, 1965 and 1970), Geneviève Bollème points out that one of the reasons may be the tendency of literary histories to consider popular literature as mediocre and negligible: see vol. I, 61. Robert Muchembled's *Culture populaire et culture des élites dans la France moderne* (Paris, 1978) shows how popular culture, including literature, was suppressed until well into the eighteenth century. Jacques Rustin's recent *Le vice à la mode. Étude sur le roman français du XVIIIe siècle de Manon Lescaut à l'apparition de La Nouvelle Héloïse, 1731–1761* (Paris, 1979) points out the enormous work to be done in this field while providing one of the best studies of the rise of the novel.

The person who seems to have done an enormous amount of research in the most difficult field of clandestine publishing, where anti-aristocratic erotica figured prominently, is Professor Robert Darnton. His several articles appear in *The Literary Underground of the Old Régime* (Cambridge, Mass., 1982). As an historian, Professor Darnton is not so much interested in the literary aspects of the titles he has unearthed. But his studies prove that anti-aristocratic erotica are worth investigating, not only because they may have helped to bring about the Revolution but also as expressions of popular protests, literary traditions, and a field of pornography that served personal and political aims.

One of the many eighteenth-century editions of Rabutin's works is *Mémoires de Messire de Rabutin, Comte de Bussy*, 5 vols. (Amsterdam, 1731). For the 'chroniques scandaleuses' in Sterne's library see the catalogue of his books cited above.

Some of the numerous works of the Comtesse d'Aulnoy are *Memoirs of the Court of England* (1707); Tom Brown's translation of her *Ingenious and Diverting Letters*, published as *Memoirs of the Court of Spain* (1692); *The History of the Earl of Warwick* (1708); *The History of John of Bourbon, Prince of Carency* (second edition, 1723); *History of Hypolitus, Earl of Douglas* (1741): *Memoirs of the Present State of the Court and Councils of Spain* (2 parts, 1701); *Secret Memoirs of the Duke and Duchess of O* (i.e., Orléans) (1708); and *Memoirs of the Court of France* (1692; reprinted 1697).

Several of the influential French high-class whores of the eighteenth century are discussed by J. Christopher Herold, *Love in Five Temperments* (1961). 'Chroniques scandaleuses' titles include *History of the Marchioness de Pompadour* (1765); *Mémoires pour servir à l'histoire d'Anne d'Autriche*; *Life and Reign of Lewis XIV* [sic] (1742); Hamilton, *Mémoires de la vie du Comte de Grammont* (1713); *Chronique arétine* (1789); Imbert, *La chronique scandaleuse* (1783–91), 5 vols.

2   For a discussion of the erotic content of the memoirs of Anthony Hamilton, who dealt with the 'histoire amoureuse' of the court of Charles II in France, see Iwan Bloch, *Englische Sittengeschichte*, 2 vols. (Berlin, 1912), I, 19–65. On the influence of the 'chronique scandaleuse' on the novel see the studies of Mylne, Rustin, and Sasse, cited above, and Naumann, *Keyhole*, chapter III. For works entitled 'Confessions de' and 'Mémoires secrets' see O. Barbier/R. and P. Billard, *Dictionnaire des ouvrages anonymes*, 4 vols. (Paris, 1872–9; repr. Hildesheim/NY, 1983); *DOE*; and Pia, *Les livres de l'enfer*. See also Dunoyer, *Lettres et histoires galantes* (1713); anonymous, *A Discovery of the Island Frivola* (1750); Marchadier, *L'ile de France ou la nouvelle colonie de Vénus* (1752); Fougeret, *La capitale des Gaules ou la nouvelle Babylone* (1759).

3   See the 'Mémoires secrets' by Charles de Fieux, Chevalier de Mouhy;

Mémoires d'Anne-Marie de Moras, Comtesse de Carbon ... 4 vols. (The Hague, 1739); *Les mémoires de Madame la Marquise de Villenemours* ... 2 vols. (The Hague, 1747); *Mémoires de Monsieur le Marquis de Fieux* ... 4 vols. (1735–36). See also Jean-Baptiste d'Argens, *Mémoires historiques et secrets concernant les amours des rois de France* (1739); Charles Pinot Duclos, *Mémoires pour servir à l'histoire des moeurs du XVIIIe siècle* (1751); and Jean Louis Favier, *Mémoires secrets de Mylord Bolingbroke sur les affaires d'Angleterre depuis 1710 jusqu'en 1716 et plusieurs intrigues à la cour de France* ('Londres', 1754). Like Fougeret de Monbron, Crébillon *fils* also used popular literary genres for some of his veiled allusions and criticism of contemporary ideas and affairs. In his *L'écumoire, histoire japonaise* (1734), he employed the oriental tale for a libertine satire.

It is unlikely that a single researcher will ever find the time and the courage needed to explore this vast field of anti-aristocratic erotica, which later in the century included personal memoirs with an erotic touch, such as *Boudoir de Madame de Pooo*; and *Le Vicomte de Barjac ou mémoires pour servir à l'histoire de ce siècle* ... 2 vols. ('Dublin', 1784). A few studies from the beginning of this century exist which provide a little help, as far as they are not erotica in themselves, towards a better understanding of this section of popular literature. See, for instance, F.R. Hervé-Piraux (pseudonyms of François Bournand and Raphaël Viau), *Histoire des petites maisons galantes*, 2 vols. (Paris, 1910–11); Raoul Vèze (writing under the name of Jean Hervez), *Correspondance d'Eulalie ou tableau du libertinage de Paris* (Paris, 1911), a study of high-class whores; and also by Vèze, *La galanterie Parisienne au XVIIIe siècle. La Régence galante, le libertinage sur le trône* ... (1905); *La galanterie Parisienne sous Louis XV et Louis XVI. D'après les mémoires, les rapports de police, les libelles, les pamphlets, les satires, chansons du temps* (Paris, 1910); *Les maîtresses de Louis XV d'après les mémoires* (1910). In addition, see Gaston Capon, *Les maisons closes au XVIIIe siècle* (1903) and his *Les petites maisons galantes de Paris* (1902).

4 On the growing resentment against the nobility see John Lough, *An Introduction to Eighteenth-Century France* (1964). Using evidence from Mercier's *Tableau de Paris*, 12 vols. (Amsterdam, 1783–9), Lough draws a convincing picture in chapter III of the privileged orders, the clergy, and the nobility.

For a definition of the journalistic branch of the 'chronique scandaleuse' see Darnton, *The Literary Underground*, 143. On censorship and prohibited books see *ibid.*, and Albert Bachmann, *Censorship in France from 1715 to 1750: Voltaire's Opposition* (NY, 1934); Jean Paul Belin, *Le commerce des livres prohibés à Paris de 1750–1789* (Paris, 1913; reprinted NY, n.d.). David Pottinger, *The French Book Trade in the Ancien Régime, 1500–1791* (Cambridge, Mass., 1958), is unreliable in its computations but nevertheless helpful; Edgar Mass, *Literatur und Zensur in der frühen Aufklärung. Produktion, Distribution und Rezeption der Lettres Persanes* (Frankfurt, 1981), provides a history of the system of censorship in France demonstrating the limits of toleration. Mass also has an excellent bibliography. See also Sasse, *op. cit.*, pp. 37–40.

Many of the titles published underground were introduced and discussed in the journal of Louis Petit de Bachaumont, which was the basis for his *Mémoires secrets, pour servir à l'histoire de la république des lettres en France depuis 1762 jusqu'à nos jours* ('Londres', 1777–89). Of the thirty-six volumes of this collection Bachaumont edited the first four and half of the fifth. It was continued by Pidansat de Mairobert, Mouffle d'Angerville, and others. Published several times in full and also in abbreviated versions, it contains analyses of plays, remarks on literary circles, notices of prohibited books and pamphlets, anecdotes and political pornography. A good guide is M. Warée, *Auteurs et personnages cités dans les mémoires secrets* (Brussels, Paris, 1866; repr. London, 1970). Mathieu-François Pidansat de Mairobert edited a similar journal, *L'observateur anglais, ou correspondance secrète entre Mylord All'eye et Mylord All'ear* (1777–8), containing spicy memoirs of contemporary affairs. After Mairobert's death in 1779, six more volumes were published anonymously. The entire series of ten volumes was then often reprinted as *L'espion anglais*. For a discussion of this treasure trove of information on eighteenth-century France and England, with an emphasis on erotica, see Ashbee, *Index*, 322–5; and *Bilderlexikon der Erotik*, IV, 726.

Studies of underground erotica written against the French aristocrats and the court are Robiquet, *Théveneau de Morande*; Darnton, *The Literary Underground*; and Malcolm C. Cook, 'Politics in the Fiction of the French Revolution 1789–1794', *SVEC* vol. 201 (Oxford, 1982), ed. Haydn Mason: this is an abridged version of Cook's doctoral dissertation (Warwick University, 1974). In chapter I of *The Literary Underground* Darnton argues that most of the French political pornography is 'dirt' and trash, but Cook provides an analysis of the various literary genres (burlesque, dialogue, letters, drama, novel). Both Cook and Darnton, however, ignore illustrations and fail to explore the relation between the form and message of the pamphlets.

On Lenoir see Maxime de Sans, *Le Noir* … (Paris, 1948); see also Manuel's *Coup d'oeil philosophique sur le regne de St. Louis* (1786), and the letters and pamphlets of Jean-Pierre (or Jacques) Brissot de Warville (1754–93), discussed in Darnton's *The Literary Underground*, chapter II.

5 Literary skirmishes between pamphleteers were carried on in London papers and in coffee-houses, see Bernard, *La gazette de Cythère* (1774). On the pamphleteering of the French émigrés in London see *ibid.*; and Robiquet, *Théveneau de Morande*; Hector Fleischmann, *Les pamphlets libertine contre Marie-Antoinette* (Paris, 1908, repr. 1976); and Iwan Bloch, *Odoratus Sexualis* (NY, 1934; reprinted 1976).

6 See *The Authentic Memoirs of the Countesse de Barré*, discussed in Ashbee's *Catena*, 99–102. The major works of the leading figures among the pamphleteers, in particular Eon de Beaumont, Morande, La Fite de

Pellepore, Brissot, J.F. Bernard, and Imbert, are listed in the catalogues of the BL and BN. Cook's bibliography in his study cited above is not comprehensive. See also Edna Nixon, *Royal Spy: The Strange Case of the Chevalier d'Eon* (NY, 1965). Before the scandal broke, the ground was well prepared by a number of publications such as the diatribe *Avis important à la branche ... XVI* (1774); *Les amours de Charlot et Toinette* (1779); *Le portefeuille d'un talon rouge, contenant des anecdotes galantes et secrètes de la cour de France* (1779).

On the increase of sexual slander of Marie-Antoinette in the early 1770s see Henri d'Alméras, *Marie-Antoinette et les pamphlets royalistes et révolutionnaires* (1907); and *ibid.*, *Les amours de la reine Marie-Antoinette* (1907); Cook, *op. cit.*, and Fleischmann, *Les pamphlets libertins*, chapters III and IV. A good account of Louis XVI and his wife can be found in Will and Ariel Durant, *Rousseau and Revolution* (NY, 1967), 847–55 and 941–3.

7 On the diamond necklace affair see Durant, *Rousseau and Revolution*, 941–43; and *Sittengeschichte der Revolution* (Wien/Leipzig, 1930), 55–122. A more detailed account is Frances Mossiker, *The Queen's Necklace* (New York, 1961).

Some of the works published by, and on, the participants in the diamond necklace scandal are *Authentic Adventures of the Celebrated Countess de la Motte ... Translated from the French. To which is added, a Narrative of her Escape to London, as stated by herself. Also memoirs of her sister, under the character of Marianne* (London, 1787); *The Life of Jane de St. Remy de Valois, heretofore Countess de la Motte ... Written by herself.* 2 vols. (London, 1791); *Mémoires justificatifs de la Comtesse de Valois de la Motte, écrits par elle-même* (London, 1788); *Memoirs of the Countess de Valois de la Motte, containing a compleat justification of her conduct ... Translated from the French, written by herself* (London, 1788); *Mémoire pour le Comte de Cagliostro, accusé; contre M. le Procureur-Général, accusateur; en présence de M. le Cardinal de Rohan, de la Comtesse de la Motte* (Paris, 1786), and the English version, *Memorial, or Brief, for the Comte de Cagliostro, defendant, against the king's Attorney-General, plaintiff: in the cause of the Cardinal de Rohan, Comtesse de la Motte, and others ... With an introductory preface. By Parkyns Macmahon* (London, 1786); *Mémoire pour la Demoiselle L.G. d'O ...* (1786); *Mémoire pour L.R. E. Prince Cardinal de Rohan en présence de la Dame de la Motte*; and by Louis Marc Antoine Rétaux de Villette, *Mémoire historique des intrigues de la Cour, et de ce qui s'est passé entre la Reine ... Madame de La Motte, etc.* (1790). For additional works see the catalogues of the BL and BN.

8 On the malicious obscene and ribald pamphlets against the French court during the revolutionary period see Fleischmann, *Les pamphlets libertins*, chapters v–x. Fleischmann's study is definitely superior to M. Henri d'Alméras, *Les amours de la reine Marie-Antoinette* (1907), and Edmond and Jules de Goncourt, *Histoire de Marie-Antoinette* (1907), works which ignored many obscene pamphlets. But even Fleischmann is too

credulous, assuming in many instances that the allegations of the pamphlets were founded on facts. Nevertheless, his study is indispensable as a survey of the wave of obscene attacks on the queen and her coterie. In addition, see also Paul Englisch, *Geschichte der erotischen Literatur*, 383–87 and 413–23; M.F.A. de Lescure, ed., *Correspondance secrète inédite sur Louis XVI, Marie-Antoinette, la cour et la ville de 1777 à 1792*, 2 vols, (1866); Adolphe Jullien, *La cour et l'opéra sous Louis XVI: Marie-Antoinette et Sachini; Salieri; Favart et Gluck. D'après des documents inédits conservés aux archives de l'État et à l'Opéra* (1878; reprinted 1976); Fernand Drujon, *Catalogue des ouvrages écrits et dessins de toute nature poursuivis, supprimés ou condamnés depuis le 21 octobre 1814 jusqu'au 31 juillet 1877* (1879), and *Essai bibliographique sur la destruction volontaire des livres* (1889); P.L. Jacob, ed., *Catalogue de la bibliothèque dramatique de Monsieur de Soleimne, rédigé par P.L. Jacob, bibliophile*, vol. III (1844), 323–36.

The literature of political pornography written against the court of Versailles after 1785 to the early 1790s is enormous and still waiting to be mined by scholars of literature. Malcolm C. Cook has made a cursory beginning with his chapter on 'politics and pornography' in 'Politics in the fiction of the French Revolution 1789–1794', *loc. cit.* The BL has about 50,000 items from the revolutionary period, many of them obscene or bawdy, while the Bibliothèque Nationale has an even larger collection. On the holdings of the two libraries see Audrey C. Brodhurst, 'The French Revolutionary Collections in the British Library', British Library Journal II (1976), 138–59; a list of titles can be found in G.K. Fortescue, *The French Revolutionary Collection in the British Library*, rev. and augmented by A.C. Brodhurst (London, 1979); and for the BN, *Catalogue de l'histoire de la Révolution Française* (1936–69) which covers the years 1789 to 1799 in 6 volumes.

Special bibliographies containing anti-aristocratic and anti-royal erotica from this period are Pascal Pia, *Les livres de l'Enfer*; Kearney, *The Private Case*; Rose, *Register of Erotic Books*, and the three volumes by Ashbee.

Apart from the titles cited in the text, see the following pamphlets against Marie-Antoinette and her clique: *Fureurs utérines de Marie-Antoinette, femme de Louis XVI* (1791); *Le godmiché royal suivi du Mea culpa* (1789); *Marie-Antoinette dans l'embarras, ou correspondance de La Fayette avec le roi, la reine, la Tour-du-Pin & Saint-Priest* (c. 1790); *Le rendez-vouz de Madame Elisabeth, soeur du roi, avec l'abbé de S. Martin ... dans le jardin des Tuileries* (Paris, 1790); *Soirées amoureuses du général et de la belle Antoinette. Par le petit espagneul de l'Autrichienne.* ('À Persépolis' 1790); *Vie privée, libertine et scandaleuse de Marie-Antoinette d'Autriche ... Ornée de 26 gravures*, 3 vols. (1791–3); *Vie de Marie-Antoinette d'Autriche ... Depuis la perte de son pucelage jusqu'au premier mai 1791, ornée de vingt-six figures* (1793); and *Le cadran des plaisirs de la cour, ou les aventures du petit page Chérubin, pour servir de suite à la vie de Marie-Antoinette, ci-devant reine de France. Suivi de la confession de Mademoiselle Sapho* (c. 1795). In addition, see *La Messa-line Française* ('À Tribaldis', 1789), a novel showing Marie-Antoinette, the Duchesse de Polignac, and Princess d'Henin as lesbians and libertines. For titles after 1792, including novels by Andréa de Nerciat and de Sade, see Cook, *op. cit.*

9 See Darnton, *The Literary Underground*, chapter VI and chapter I. Darnton ignores the literary forms of the pamphlets, which would not have been as influential and important had they been too highbrow or philosophical and less obscene.

10 Malicious and malignant sexual slander with the aim of ostracising political enemies seems to be characteristic of personal satire preceding revolutionary events. See the discussion of this aspect in John H. O'Neill, 'Sexuality, Deviance, and Moral Character in the Personal Satire of the Restoration', *ECL* II (1975), 16–19; Thompson, *Unfit for Modest Ears*, chapter VII; and Stone, *The Family, Sex and Marriage*, 538, where Stone notes that 'on all three occasions in Early Modern times when a King was deposed or executed – England in 1649 and 1688, France in 1793 – the event was preceded by decades of pamphlets and poems, depicting the court as a sink of financial corruption and sexual depravity'. Ronald Paulson's recent *Representations of Revolution (1789–1820)* (1983) examines this thesis in view of the production of pictorial revolutionary satire.

Some obscene, pornographic, and burlesque pamphlets against aristocrats are *Apparution de Thérèse-philosophe à Saint-Cloud* (1790); *Les enfants de Sodome à l'Assemblée Nationale* (1790). The latter ridicules homosexuals; see also *Vie privée et publique du ci-derrière marquis de Villette, citoyen rétroactif* (Paris, c. 1792); *Requète et décret en faveur des Putains, des fouteuses, des macquerelles, et des branleuses; contre les bougres, les bardaches et les bruleurs de paillasses* (c. 1791), and the reaction to this, *Les petits bougres au manège, ou réponse de M. ..., Grand Maître des enculeurs ... à la requête des fouteuses ... A Enculos, Chez Pierre Pousse-Fort* (c. 1791). Titles attacking aristocratic women in particular are *Almanach des honnêtes femmes pour l'année 1790*; and *Les bijoux du petit neveu de l'Arétin, ou étrennes libertines dediées aux femmes ci-devant de qualité ...* (1791).

11 For examples of the atrocities aristocrats, and especially women, had to suffer, see *Sittengeschichte der Revolution*, 74–122; and Paul Frischauer, *Knaurs Sittengeschichte der Welt*, vol. III, chapter 2.

12 See *Memoirs of Antonina, Queen of Abo. Displaying her Private Intrigues, and Uncommon Passions. With Family Sketches, and Curious Anecdotes of Great Persons. Translated from the French* (1791), two volumes in one, I, 14, 20, 41, 65; II, 28–30.

13 On the literary censorship after 1750 see John Brewer, *Party Ideology and Popular Politics at the Accession of George III* (Cambridge, 1976), chapters III and IV; and Thomas, *A Long Time Burning*, 96 f. See Roy Porter, *English Society in the Eighteenth Century*, chapter II, on the English aristocrats and their relations with the commoners. Radicalism in

England during the French revolutionary period is discussed in Albert Goodwin, *The Friends of Liberty. The English Democratic Movement in the Age of the French Revolution* (1979); Alan Lloyd, *The Wickedest Age: The Life and Times of George III* (Newton Abbot, 1971); and Paulson's *Representations of Revolution*, chapters I and II.

14 On the works of Mrs Haywood and Mrs Manley see Richetti, *Popular Fiction*, 119–67; and Peter Naumann, *Keyhole und Candle*, p. 84 f. See in particular Mary de la Rivière Manley, *Memoirs of the Life of Mrs Manley* [Author of the *Atlantis*], *Containing Not Only the History of Her Adventures, but Likewise an Account of the Most Considerable Amours in the Court of King Charles II ... To which is Added, a Compleat Key. Third Edition* (London, 1717; repr. NY 1971); Anthony Hamilton, *Memoirs of the Comte de Grammont* (London, 1963). John Oldmixon's *The Court of Atalantis ... Intermixt with Fables and Epistles in Verse and Prose. By Several Hands* (London, 1714) was reissued as *Court Tales, or a History of the Amours of the Present Nobility. To Which is Added a Compleat Key* (London, 1717 and 1732) and has several harmless episodes, such as 'Calvinio and the Bed' and 'Dolmitius and the Maidenhead': see pp. 12–14 and 45–51 in the edition of 1714, and the appended key for the names of the noblemen. Other works representative of the traditional 'chronique scandaleuse' are *Dirty Dogs for Dirty Puddings. Or, Memoirs of the Luscious Amours of Several Persons of Both Sexes, of Quality and Distinction* (London, 1732); P.L. Saumery, *The Devil Turn'd Hermit: or, the Adventures of Astaroth, Banish'd from Hell ... Exposing ... the Intrigues of Courts; the Ambition, Avarice, and Cruelty of Ministers ... Interspersed with the Portraits and secret Histories of most of the considerable Persons that have lived in Europe within these thirty years past ...* (London, 1741); and *Memoirs of the Love and State-Intrigues of the Court of H[anover]...* (London, 1743). It is remarkable that the genre of the erotic 'chronique scandaleuse' seems to have been popular enough to attract parasitical publishers, who tried to sell sentimental and innocuous ephemera under titles which sounded erotic but were rather misleading: see, for instance, *Memoirs of the Nobility, Gentry, & of Thule: or, the Island of Love* (London, 1742; third edition, 1751).

15 A good survey of the English rakes in the eighteenth century can be found in E.B. Chancellor, *The Lives of the Rakes*, vols. III–VI. Volume III introduces Charteris and Wharton; vol. IV the members of the Hell Fire Club; vol. V is on 'Old Q.', i.e., William Douglas, the fourth Duke of Queensberry, and Richard, seventh Earl of Barrymore; and the last volume is about the Regency rakes, such as George IV, the royal dukes, and the Barrymores. On the Duke of Wharton see also Mark Blackett-Ord, *Hell-Fire Duke. The Life of the Duke of Wharton* (1983).

Chancellor is very much Victorian in his excuses to the reader for having to deal with sexual matters. In vol. II, 127, he refrains from talking 'openly' for fear of hurting the young. In addition to his volumes, see Félix Rémo, *La vie galante en Angleterre* (1888); and Iwan Bloch, *Ethnological and Cultural Studies of the Sex Life in England as Revealed in its Erotic and Obscene Literature and Art*, ed. Richard Deniston (NY, 1972), 275–89. Some examples of erotic memoirs of noblemen are *Confessions of Count de Harcourt, Containing His Amours, with Several Ladies of Quality in the Courts of France, Italy, and England* (1743); and *The Life, Adventures, Intrigues and Amours of the Celebrated Jemmy Twitcher* (*c.* 1770), which is concerned with John Montague, fourth Earl of Sandwich; and *Memoirs of the Amours ... of ... Duke of Grafton* (1769). In the 1770s and early 1780s engravings were published in newspapers and periodicals, mostly oval prints of two heads, of the persons involved in sexual scandals and trials for adultery: see the *Catalogue of Prints and Drawings in the British Museum. Political and Personal Satire*, vols. V–VI, passim. The smallest rumour of an affair had literary consequences. *The Northern Cuckold, or, the Gardenhouse Intrigue* (1731) for instance implicitly relied on the reader's acquaintance with contemporary scandals.

16 *The Toast* was enlarged into 3 volumes by King and the final version appeared in 1736. Quotations from the 'Ode to Myra' are from pp. 57 and 82–6 of the 1732 edition; and her levée in book III is from pp. 96–107 of the 1736 edition.

17 See also *The Court and City Vagaries, or Intrigues, of Both Sexes* (1711), a purely fictional work. *The Court Magazine* was published between 1761–71; for details see Robert D. Mayo, *The English Novel in the Magazines 1740–1815* (1962).

See also *The Rambler's Magazine*, IV (July–November, 1786), for the 'amours of the Earl of Essex'; and *The Bon Ton Magazine*, V (September 1795–February, 1796) for the series entitled 'The Spirit of the Ring. Containing Secret Anecdotes of many illustrious Personages of this and the neighbouring kingdoms'. For comments on the prosecution of sexual slander in London see Louis-Pierre Manuel, *La police de Paris dévoilée*, I, 138–9. Manuel, not an entirely reliable source for England, mentions the name of Griffiths, a publisher of pornography, apparently imprisoned for six months and heavily fined for maintaining that Lady Sarah Bunbury had been impregnated by her nephew, Charles Fox. Other names which Manuel lists are Bates, sentenced to three months for publishing an article on a well-known homosexual; and Finney, a newspaper editor, who went to gaol for six months for slandering Burke: an article in his paper had alleged that Burke had been raised by Jesuits and protected homosexuals.

18 On the Duke of Grafton and Nancy Parsons see Horace W. Bleackley, *Ladies Fair and Frail. Sketches of the Demi-Monde During the Eighteenth Century* (1909), 101–2, and 297–309. Erotic surveys of the London mistresses from the eighteenth century are, apart from *The London Belles* (1707), *Vies et actions des coquettes, maîtresses ... les plus célèbres d'Angleterre* (London, 1721); Jean-Auguste Jullien, *Honi soit qui mal y pense ou Histoire des filles célèbres du XVIIIe siècle*, 2 vols. (London/Paris, 1760; augmented and enlarged in 1766 and 1775); *Memoirs of Love and Gallantry; or the Various Foibles of the Fair, Display'd in a Real History of Several Persons of Distinction* (London, 1732); *The*

Northern Atalantis: or York Spy. Displaying the Secret Intrigues and Adventures of the Yorkshire Gentry: More Particularly the Amours of Melissa, by ... Dr W. King (London, *c.* 1732); *The Genuine Memoirs of Miss Faulkner, otherwise Mrs D...l...n, or Countess of H...x in Expectancy. Containing the Amours and Intrigues of Several Persons of High Distinction, and Remarkable Characters: With Some Curious Political Anecdotes* (1770). See also Archibald Arbuthnot, *Memoirs of the Remarkable Life and Surprising Adventures of Miss Jenny Cameron* (1746); and *Nocturnal Revels or the History of King's Place* (second edition, 1779), which appeared in French as *Les sérails de Londres* (1801).

Not surprisingly, this genre also knew fictional works like Sir Herbert Croft's *Love and Madness – A Story Too True, in a Series of Letters Between Parties Whose Names Would Perhaps be Mentioned, Were They Less Known, or Less Lamented* (1780), based on the assassination of Martha Ray by James Hackman. The prospect of beautiful girls from the lower social strata of attaining the state of noble ladies by becoming the mistress, and eventually the wife, of a nobleman was as good in France as it was in England. On the French aristocrats and their marrying down, as it were, see Manuel, *La Police*, 322–70. Some of the numerous erotica on the London courtesans are the following. On Fanny Murray: *Memoirs of the celebrated Miss Fanny M–* (1758; reprinted Dublin, 1759); *A Humorous Poetical Dialogue Between the Once Celebrated Miss F– M– and the Now Famed Miss K– F–*. (1760); On Kitty Fisher: *Horse and Away to St. James Park, or a Trip for the Noontide Air* (London, 1760); *The Juvenile Adventures of Miss Kitty F–r*, 2 vols. (1759); *Kitty's Stream, or the Noblemen Turned Fisher-Men* (1759); *Kitty's Stream Running Clear* (1759); *An Odd Letter on a Most Interesting Subject to Miss K– F–h–r* (1760); *The Uncommon Adventures of Miss Kitty F...* (1759); on Nancy Parsons: *Memoirs of the Amours, Intrigues and Adventures of Charles Augustus Fitz-Roy, Duke of Grafton, with Miss Parsons. Interspersed with a faithful Account of Miss Parsons' Amours with Other Persons of Distinction* (1769); this was later published as *Intrigues à-la-mode. Biographical Memoirs of the Duke of Grafton, Including Some Remarkable Particulars in the Life of the Celebrated Miss Anna Bella Parsons* (London, *c.* 1812). See also *Memoirs of Mrs Laetitia Pilkington* (1748); and *Apology for the Conduct of Mrs Teresia Constantia Phillips* (1748). Some of these works are further discussed in Bleackley, *Ladies Fair and Frail*, 297–309. For portraits of famous mistresses see *ibid.*, passim; and the *Catalogue of Prints and Drawings*, vol. V, nos. 5177–86. The captions of these portraits are ironic classifications of the various ladies of pleasure; there are 'nuns' of the first, second, and third class, and 'Mother Abbesses' of the same categories.

Nicolas Powell, *Fuseli: The Nightmare* (1973), comments on the success of Fuseli's romantic and pre-surrealist picture and its exploitation for caricatures by Rowlandson, Gillray, and others. See also Gert Schiff, *Johann Heinrich Füssli* 1741–1825 (Munich/Zurich, 1973).

19 On eighteenth-century political satire and the print-shops see Dorothy
    M. George, *English Political Caricature*, 2 vols. (Oxford, 1959), I, 175–
    6; and her equally well-documented *Hogarth to Cruikshank: Social
    Change in Graphic Satire* (1967). Ronald Paulson's *Representations of
    Revolution* has some excellent chapters (V and VI) on Rowlandson and
    Gillray.
        For examples of graphic erotic and scatological satires see the *Cata-
    logue of Prints and Drawings in the British Museum. Political and
    Personal Satires*, vols. II–VII (1690–1800). Often overlooked are *Bowles
    and Carver's Caricatures*, 2 vols. (n.p., 1820); and George Paston, *Social
    Caricature in the Eighteenth Century* (1905). The ISR has a collection of
    British political cartoons of the eighteenth century, all of them by Gillray,
    and some erotic or obscene. There are also a few erotic English engravings
    in John Grand-Carteret, *Le décolleté et le retroussé, trois siècles de
    gauloiseries 1500–1900* (1902).
        German collections are frequently ignored by researchers, although
    they contain much relevant pictorial material. See especially Eduard
    Fuchs/Alfred Kind, *Die Weiberherrschaft in der Geschichte der Mensch-
    heit*, 2 vols. (Munich, 1913); Fuchs, *Die Frau in der Karikatur* (Munich,
    1906 and 1928), reprinted as *Sozialgeschichte der Frau* (Frankfurt,
    1973); idem, *Die Karikatur der Europaischen Völker*, 2 vols. (Berlin,
    1901–3); idem, *Geschichte der Erotischen Kunst*, 2 vols. (Munich,
    1908–26): see especially vol. I, book 2, 'Das erotische Element in der
    Karikatur', reprinted separately (Berlin, 1977); and also by Fuchs, *Illus-
    trierte Sittengeschichte*, vols. II and III, and the supplement volumes for
    each of these. Also see the various volumes of *Sittengeschichte der Kultur-
    welt*, in particular vol. VII: 'Sittengeschichte des Geheimen und Ver-
    botenen' (Vienna, 1930); E. Fuchs, *Die Grossen Meister der Erotik*
    (Munich, 1930); and the volumes of the *Bilderlexikon der Erotik*.
20 On the Prince of Wales and Mrs Fitzherbert see Stella Margetson, *Leisure
    and Pleasure in the Eighteenth Century* (1970), 189–205; Donald A.
    Low, *Thieves' Kitchen. The Regency Underworld* (1982); Lloyd, *The
    Wickedest Age*; and Chancellor, *The Lives of the Rakes*, vol. VI. See *The
    Rambler's Magazine*, V (1787), 231.

4 TRIAL REPORTS AND CRIMINAL CONVERSATION LITERATURE

 1 See *A Hellish Murder Committed by a French Midwife on the Body of
    Her Husband, Jan. 1687/8 for Which She . . . Received Sentence of Death*
    (1688) and three similar pamphlets in the BL.
        On crime in the eighteenth century see James S. Cockburn, ed., *Crime
    in England: 1550–1800* (1977); Peter Linebaugh *et al.*, eds., *Albion's
    Fatal Tree: Crime and Society in Eighteenth-Century England* (1975);
    Christopher Hibbert, *The Road to Tyburn: The Story of Jack Sheppard
    and the Eighteenth-Century Underworld* (1957); Gerald Howson, *Thief-
    Taker General. The Rise and Fall of Jonathan Wild* (NY, 1970).
        The indigenous English tradition of criminal biographies and sensa-

tional pamphlets, which both had a bearing on the rise of the novel, is discussed by F.W. Chandler, *The Literature of Roguery* (NY, 1907); and John J. Richetti, *Popular Fiction before Richardson*, chapter II.

On the reporting of crime see Robert Collison, *The Story of Street Literature* (1973), chapter III; G.A. Cranfield, *The Press and Society. From Caxton to Northcliffe* (1978), chapter III; John H. Langbein, *Prosecuting Crime in the Renaissance: England, Germany, France* (Cambridge, Mass., 1974), especially pp. 45–54 on the crime chapbooks; *idem*, 'The Criminal Trial Before the Lawyers', *The University of Chicago Law Review* 45 (1978), 265–70; Stanley Morison, *The English Newspaper* (Cambridge, 1932); and R.M. Wiles, *Freshest Advices. Early Provincial Newspapers in England* (Ohio State University Press, 1965), chapter VIII.

A good collection of eighteenth-century chapbooks, including titles on crime and criminals, is John Ashton's *Chap-Books of the Eighteenth Century* (1882). Critical studies of such books are Rainer Schöwerling, *Chapbooks. Zur Literaturgeschichte des einfachen Lesers* (Frankfurt, 1980); and Margaret Spufford, *Small Books and Pleasant Histories* (1981).

Also of interest are Leslie Shepard, *The History of Street Literature: The Story of Broadside Ballads, Chapbooks ... and Other Ephemera* (Newton Abbot, 1973); and *idem*, *The Broadside Ballad: a Study in Origins and Meaning* (1962).

2 On the exact titles, the development and the location of the *OBSP* see M.D. George, *London Life in the Eighteenth Century* (1966), 430; Howson, *Thief-Taker*, 325; and Langbein, 'The Criminal Trial', *loc. cit.*

3 See Peter Linebaugh, 'The Ordinary of Newgate and His Account', in Cockburn, ed., *Crime in England*, 246–69.

4 *Ibid.*, 256.

5 See Philip Pinkus, *Grub Street*; and Morison, *The English Newspaper*.

6 For a list of such trial reports see Howson, *Thief-Taker*, 321–5; and Langbein, 'The Criminal Trial', *loc. cit.*, 268 n. 24.

7 *News From Tybourn*, 4.

8 See *Execution of the Reverend Peter Vine* (n.p., n.d.). The ISR, which holds a copy, has dated this after 1700, but it looks more like a late seventeenth-century publication.

9 See *The Case of Seduction* (1725), preface, p. xi; and R. Strauss, *The Unspeakable Curll*, 277, on the wrong dating of this book.

10 See *The Case of Seduction*, 75 f.

11 *Ibid.*, p. x.

12 See *Spiritual Fornication*, 7, 20, 28; and *The Case of Mary Katherine Cadiere* (1731); *The Tryal of Father John-Baptist Girard* (1732). In addition, see also *Recueil général des pièces concernant le procez* [sic] *entre la Demoiselle Cathérine Cadière ... et le P.J.B. Girard, Jésuite ...*, 5 vols. (Aix, 1731); *The Compleat Translation of the Sequel of the Proceedings of Mary Cathérine Cadière, Against the Jesuit Father John Baptist Girard* (1732); *Thirty Two Pieces, Never Before Translated, of

the Proceedings Upon the Tryal of M. Cadière ... (1732); *Memoirs of Miss Mary Cathérine Cadière, and Father Girard* (1731); *The Defence of F. John Baptist Girard. The Fourth Edition* (1732); and in German: *Erstaunenswürdige Historie, des Jesuiten Pater Johann Baptista Girard* (Cologne, 1732); and *Factum der Vertheidigungsschrift Marien Catharinen Cadière* (1732).

    For a reliable account of the affair see Michaud, *Biographie Universelle*, s.v. Girard. Ashbee's survey, in his *Centuria*, 225–53, is well-informed but nevertheless slanted. As a staunch anti-Catholic, Ashbee never doubts the allegations of Cadière's statement.

13 See the advertisement at the end of *The Life and Amours of Lady Ann F–L–Y* (i.e., *Foley*) (n.d.), published after 1782. Such crimes were exploited for bawdy satire: see *A Fair Shoot at a Foul Mark; a Short Account of Some Extraordinary Proceedings Against the Person Who was Shot in Lincoln-Inn-Garden. Written by Himself* (1742).

14 On the Castlehaven case, first published in 1642, see the *DNB*, and Caroline Bingham, 'Seventeenth-Century attitudes toward deviant sex', *JIH* 1 (1971), 447–67. See *The Case of Sodomy* (1708), 6–8, 12, 16–21. See also Iwan Bloch, *Sexual Life in England*, 79.

15 Bernard's *The Penitent Death of a Woeful Sinner. Or, The Penitent Death of John Atherton Executed at Dublin the 5 of December 1640* was first published at Dublin in 1641 and reprinted at London in 1642 and 1651. As the Dean of Ardagh, Bernard had purely religious aims with his work, giving an impression of Atherton before his death. See also *The Life and Death of John Atherton ... Who for Incest, Buggery and Many Other Enormous Crimes ... was Hanged* (1641).

16 See *Satan's Harvest Home: or the Present State of Whorecraft, Adultery, Fornication, Procuring, Pimping, Sodomy, and the Game of Flatts* (1749), cited by Ashbee, *Index*, 338.

    See Ashbee, *Index*, xxxiv, on trials for sodomy between 1720 and 1730.

17 See *A Faithful Narrative*, 7 and 22. For similar cases, see the *Lancaster Gazette* advertising as late as 30 August, 1806 the *Trial of David Robertson, of the Jerusalem Hotel*. See also A.D. Harvey, 'Prosecution for Sodomy in England', *HJ* 21 (1978), 942.

18 See G.R. Taylor, *Sex in History* (1959), 146; and Christopher Hill, *Society and Puritanism in Pre-revolutionary England* (1964), chapter viii.

19 See the cases cited by Langbein, 'The criminal trial', *loc. cit.*, 267, 287, and 301.

20 See Iwan Bloch, *Sexual Life in England*, 15, 70–9; and Roger Thompson, *Women in Stuart England and America* (1974), 170–1.

21 On Dunton and Curll see Pinkus, *Grub Street*; and the list of Curll's publications in R. Strauss, *The Unspeakable Curll*.

22 *The Case of Impotency*, 2 vols. (1714), 2.

23 *Ibid.*, I, 8.

24 See the initial 'Advertisement by the Translator' in this report.

25 On the 'Causes Célèbres' see Jean Sgard, 'La littérature des Causes Célèbres', in *Approches des lumières. Mélanges offerts à Jean Fabre* (1974), 459–70; Hans-Jürgen Lüsebrink, 'Les crimes sexuels dans les Causes Célèbres', DHS 12 (1980), 153–162; *idem, Kriminalität und Literatur im Frankreich des 18. Jahrhunderts* (Munich/Vienna, 1983), 104–72. François Richer edited twenty-two volumes of the 'Causes Célèbres' which were published in Amsterdam 1773–92.

   For English 'Causes Célèbres' see *The Case of Impotency* (1715); *Cases of Divorce for Several Causes* (1715).

   See also Edmund Curll's publications on cases of criminal conversation; *The Cases of Polygamy* (1732); *The Cases of Impotency and Virginity* (1732).

26 See *Select Trials, for Murders . . . Rapes, Sodomy . . .*, 2 vols. (1734–5), II, 200.

27 *Ibid.*, 199.

28 On Charteris see *DNB*; and Chancellor, *The Lives of the Rakes*. Several publications between 1730 and 1739 commented on his acts of 'gallantry', and Hogarth depicted him in plate I of *A Harlot's Progress*: see plate 31a in chapter V. Fielding used the scandal as a background for his satire, *Rape Upon Rape: or, The Justice Caught in His Own Trap*.

29 One reason could be Lord Hardwicke's Marriage Act of 1753. Some cases, however, are still extant; see Naumann, *Keyhole*, 370 n. 62, and the trial reports listed in the catalogue of the holdings of the ISR.

30 The ISR has a sixth edition of this report (London, 1770); see also *DNB* on the Duke of Cumberland.

31 *The Trial of His R.H.* (1770) iii–v, 11; and *The Life and Amours*, 8.

32 Joseph Guerney, *The Trial of John Motherhill*, second edition (1786); and *The Trial of Mr Cooke . . . For the Crime of Adultery with Mrs Walford* (1789).

33 Iwan Bloch quotes this work in his *Sexual Life in England*, p. 75; but the BL only has an edition of 1830 in two volumes without any prints.

34 See the journal *London and Paris* (Weimar, 1800), vol. VIII, 242–3; cited in P. Englisch, *Geschichte der erotischen Literatur*; 624, and translated in Bloch's *English Sexual Morals*, 76.

35 On the increase of literacy in the eighteenth century see A.S. Collins, 'The Growth of the Reading Public During the Eighteenth Century', *RES* II (1926), 428–38; and *idem*, 'The Growth of the Reading Public, 1780–1800', *Nineteenth Century* 101 (1927), 749–58. See also Leslie Stephen *English Literature and Society in the Eighteenth Century* (1904), parts iv and v.

36 See the excerpts from the trial cited in *Venus Unmasked . . . An Eighteenth-Century Anthology* (1967), comp. by Peter Fryer and Leonard De Vries, 84–5, and 94. *The Cuckold's Chronicle* (1793) continued to present adultery trials, peppering them up if they lacked sufficient obscene material.

37 See *The Rambler Magazine* (1783 f.); *The Bon Ton Magazine* (1791 f.); and J. Gill, *A New and Complete Collection of Trials for Adultery*

(1796); and his *New Collection of Trials for Adultery* (1799); Moore, *Annals of Gallantry*. For further details see Ashbee, *Catena*, 329–38.

38 See Hurwood, *The Golden Age of Erotica*, 60. In chapter III he provides an interesting survey of the 'scandalous world of crim. con.', citing many cases and making a few pertinent observations. His study suffers, however, from the absence of any documentation that would allow one to check on his sources. On the Vice Society see Thomas, *A Long Time Burning*, 190–1; F.K. Brown, *Fathers of the Victorians* (Cambridge, 1961); and E.J. Bristow, *Vice and Vigilance*.

39 See Ashbee, *Catena*, 338–9, for details.

40 Cf. Lawrence Stone, *The Family, Sex and Marriage*, 538 and 543; and Edmund S. Morgan, 'The Puritans and Sex', *NEQ* 15 (1942), 591–607. Morgan argues that the Puritans were blamed for the wrong reasons and were not particularly ascetic. See also my own *Puritan Attitudes Towards Recreation in Early Seventeenth-Century New England* (Frankfurt, 1982).

41 Stone, *op. cit.*, 544.

42 *Ibid.*, 530 and 533.

5 MATRIMONY AND THE WAR OF THE SEXES

1 See Thomas D'Urfey's *The Intrigues at Versailles: or, A Jilt in All Humours* (1697); *Love for Money: or, The Boarding School* (1691); and *The Marriage-Hater Match'd* (1692) as late examples of Restoration comedies on love and sex.

On prostitution in eighteenth-century London and England see Bloch, *Sexual Life in England*, 96–194; Vern L. Bullough *et al.*, *A Bibliography of Prostitution* (1977), 106–24, 142–7: there are a few errors in this otherwise good compilation of fictional and historical works. In addition, see Bullough, *Prostitution. An Illustrated Social History* (NY, 1978), chapter IX; Derek Jarrett, *England in the Age of Hogarth*, 103–97; *Sittengeschichte des Lasters* and *Sittengeschichte des Intimsten*, vols. II and X of 'Sittengeschichte der Kulturwelt' (Vienna, 1927–30), and the pertinent supplements. William W. Sanger's *The History of Prostitution* (NY, 1972) is a reprint of an 1859 edition and a superficial survey of several millennia. Eighteenth-century England is treated on a few pages (305–12) in chapter XXIV.

On the repression of prostitutes by the various reforming societies see Bloch, *Sexual Life in England*, 212–27; Bristow, *Vice and Vigilance*, chapter I; Muriel Jaeger, *Before Victoria* (1956), chapters I and II, and W.H. Young, *Eros Denied*. Special studies of the problem of prostitution are T.C. Curtis/W.A. Speck, 'The Societies for the Reformation of Manners: a Case Study in the Theory and Practice of Moral Reform', *LH* 3 (1976), 45–64; and Speck, 'The Harlot's Progress in Eighteenth-Century England', *BJECS* 3 (1980), 127–39.

On Dunton's *The Night Walker* see Pinkus, *Grub Street*, 94–9. Madan's *Account of the Triumphant Death* was republished as *The*

Magdalen: or, Dying Penitent, Exemplified in the Death of F.S. (Dublin, 1789).

2 On Mandeville's work see Bloch, *Ethnological and Cultural Studies*, 281–9; Samuel J. Rogal, 'The Selling of Sex: *Mandeville's Modest Defence of Publick Stews*', *SECC* 5, ed. R.C. Rosbottom (1976), 141–50. The French translation of Mandeville's *Modest Defence* is *Vénus la populaire* (London, 1727): see also Restif's *Le pornographe, ou idées d'un honnête homme sur un projet de règlement pour les prostituées* (London and Paris, 1769). My work on this aspect of prostitution has been facilitated by an unpublished article of Professor Denis Fletcher, University of Durham, on 'The Oldest Profession: Some Eighteenth-Century Views'.

3 See Edward Ward, *The Whole Pleasures of Matrimony* (1714), 141–60; and Troyer's study of *Ned Ward of Grub Street*.

For discussions of the harlot series by Hogarth see Robert E. Moore, *Hogarth's Literary Relationships* (NY, 1969), 24–44; the notes in Burke/Caldwell, *Hogarth*; and the excellent comments by a contemporary, Georg Christoph Lichtenberg, *Der Weg der Buhlerin. The Harlot's Progress* (reprinted Frankfurt, 1969). For Swift's poem on *A Beautiful Young Nymph* see the recent excellent edition of his poems by Pat Rogers, *Jonathan Swift. The Complete Poems* (Harmondsworth, 1983), 453–5. On the moral intentions behind this seemingly bawdy poem see H.J. Real/H.J. Vienken, 'These Odious Common Whores of Which This Town is Full': Swift's *A Beautiful Young Nymph Going to Bed*, *AAA* 6 no. 2 (1981), 241–59. See *The Harlot's Progress: or, The Humours of Drury-Lane* (1732), 14. Other literary adaptations of the prints are cited by Naumann, *Keyhole*, 371–2. Numerous anonymous pamphlets commented in this bawdy tone on the tragic ends of prostitutes. See, for instance, *The Whore* (*c.* 1782), 18–24.

4 Bullough, *A Bibliography of Prostitution*, 319, lists *Pretty Doings*. For an example from the seventeenth century see *The Comforts of Whoreing and the Vanity and Chastity of the Unreasonableness of Love* (1694).

See *Satan's Harvest Home* (1749), 22–7. The chapter on 'whorecraft' in this pamphlet has been reprinted in the anthology compiled by Fryer/DeVries, *Venus Unmasked*, 104–18. The analysis provided in this satire is confirmed by such modern studies as Peter Laslett, *Family Life and Illicit Love in Earlier Generations* (Cambridge, 1978); and Speck, *op. cit.*

Quotations from *A Congratulatory Epistle from a Reformed Rake, to John F...G, Esq. Upon the New Scheme of Reclaiming Prostitutes* (1758) are from pp. 21, 8, 12. 'Demi-reps' were married women who had sexual affairs (hence 'demi-reputation'); they were satirised in such poems as *The Demi-Rep* (1756); and *The Devil Divorced* (1782).

5 London guides had chapters on the tricks of prostitution; see *Roach's London Pocket Pilot; The Frauds of London Detected; The Tricks of the Town Laid Open; The London Jilt* (1683). See *The Bawd*, 6–20.

6 The list of whores of 1758 is from *A Congratulatory Epistle*, 16. On the history of such lists see *Bilderlexikon der Erotik*, I, 282–4. See *Kitty's*

Attalantis, 2, 8, 46; and the broadside, *Genuine List*. For other examples of such ribald descriptions in lists of whores see *List of Sporting Ladies* (c. 1770) and *Harris's List of Covent Garden Ladies ... For the Year 1788*, reprinted in Fryer/DeVries, *Venus Unmasked*, 31–35 and 186–91; *Ranger's Impartial List of the Ladies of Pleasure in Edinburgh* (1775); *List of All the Sporting Ladies who is arrived from the Most Principal Towns in Great Britain and Ireland to take their Pleasure at Leith Races* (Edinburgh, 1777); and *A Complete List of all the Sporting Ladies*.

7 For a survey of the satire on cuckolds throughout history, with particular consideration of the seventeenth century, see Thompson, *Unfit*, chapter 6; and L. Norell, 'The Cuckold in Restoration Comedy', doct. diss. (University of Florida, 1962).

   For Dryden's translation of Juvenal's sixth satire see *The Satyrs of Decimus Junius, Juvenalis: and of Aulus Persius Flaccus. Translated into English Verse by Mr. Dryden. The Sixth Edition* (1735; repr. NY 1979), 66, 77. See also *The Praise and Profit of Cuckoldom*, 14–16.

   Some of the numerous satirical poems were lampoons occasioned by extra-marital affairs of the nobility. See, for instance, the satire on Lady Pendergast, *The Cuckold's Curse Against the State of Matrimony* (Dublin, 1757) and the several poems on the Worseley affair in 1782. In addition, a great many songs and simple poems made fun of the cornuto. Some of these are *The Fifteen Comforts of Cuckoldom* (1706); *The Merry Cuckold and Kind Wife* (1775); *The Cuckold's Cap Garland* (1765?); *A New Song Called the Contented Cuckold* (1790?); *The Four Contented Cuckolds* (1790?); *The Two Cuckolds ... Two Tales in Scottish Dialect* (Edinburgh, 1796). *The Benefits and Privileges of Cuckolds* (1728) is dedicated to the wife of Heidegger, the manager of balls and masquerades in the first three decades of the eighteenth century. It is a satirical dialogue between a cuckold and a jealous man.

8 On Hogarth's *Marriage à la Mode*, of which the paintings were finished in 1743 and the prints in 1745, see Moore, *Hogarth's Literary Relationships*, 53–58; and Burke/Caldwell, *Hogarth*, nos. 193–8.

   See the following moral treatises: Daniel Defoe, *Conjugal Lewdness or Matrimonial Whoredom* (1727); Peter Annet (alias Gideon Archer), *Social Bliss Considered: In Marriage and Divorce; Cohabiting Unmarried, and Public Whoring* (1749); and *The Present State of Matrimony: or, The Real Causes of Conjugal Infidelity* (n.d.), which strongly criticises the habit of matching young people against their will.

   Publications on the Marriage Act of 1753 are *Reflections on the Marriage Act* (1764); and John Shebbeare's novel, in two volumes, *The Marriage Act* (Dublin, second edition 1774), in which adultery is shown to be the consequence of marrying off children without their consent. The Divorce Act of 1771 tried to prevent persons just divorced from marrying the party they had committed adultery with; see Thomas Pollen, *The Fatal Consequences of Adultery* (1772).

9 See *The Joys of Hymen* (1768), Quillet, *Callipaedia* (1710), and Arbuthnot, *The Pleasures of Marriage in Ten Books* (1745), 1–3.

10 *Reasons Against Coition* (1732), 8–9, 33–4; See also Maclauchlan's ribald *Essay Upon Improving and Adding by Fornication* (1735).

11 On the ideas of love and marriage in the eighteenth century see Stone, *The Family, Sex and Marriage*, passim; Jean-Louis Flandrin, 'Amour et Mariage,' *DHS* 12 (1980), 163–76. Seventeenth-century and earlier views of polygamy are discussed by Thompson, *Unfit*, 100–103; Ian Watt, *The Rise of the Novel* (Harmondsworth, 1972), 165–70; A.O. Aldrige, 'Polygamy in early fiction,' *PMLA* 65 (1950), 464–72; and *ibid.*, 'Polygamy and deism,' *JEGP* 47 (1949), 343–60.

On Neville's *The Isle of Pines* – the title may be a pun on penis – see Worthington C. Ford, *The Isle of Pines, 1688. An Essay in Bibliography* (Boston, 1920), which discusses the story and the history of the book and includes information on the author and the translations. The full text is reprinted on pp. 53–91. My quotation is from the London edition of 1768, which was bound with Neville's *The Parliament of Ladies*.

For discussion of polygamy see also Manley, *Court Intrigues*; and his *The True Friend* (1748); Madan, *Thelyphthora* (1780); Lyser, *Polygamia Triumphatrix* (1682).

The True Friend consists of two essays against matrimony, referring to the example of the Old Testament patriarchs and their polygamous marriages. On Lyser and Madan see Bloch, *Ethnological Studies*, 283–4; and *DNB*. A reply to Madan's book was Richard Hill's *The Blessings of Polygamy Displayed* (1781), which is a serious work arguing against polygamy while attacking Madan.

12 On the satirical treatment of the war of the sexes in seventeenth-century popular literature see Margaret Spufford, *Small Books*, chapter VII. An example from that period is *The Academy of Love* (1641). For other examples and early eighteenth-century misogynous pieces, some directly influenced by Juvenal, see Felicity Nussbaum, 'Juvenal, Swift, and *The Folly of Love*', *ECS* 9 (1975/6), 540–52.

See *The Fifteen Plagues of A Maidenhead* (1707), 3–8; and on its prosecution, D. Thomas, *A Long Time Burning*, 77; and Foxon, *Libertine Literature*, ix, 12–13. See also *The Satyrs of D.J. Juvenalis* (1735), 63, 78–80. On similar writings from the seventeenth century see Thompson, *Unfit*, chapter 6. Further examples from the eighteenth century, many written in imitation of the 'maidenhead' satire, are *The Fifteen Comforts of Cuckoldom*; *The Fifteen Comforts of Matrimony*; *The Fifteen Comforts of a Wanton Wife*; and *The Fifteen Comforts of Whoring*, all published in 1706. See also *The Fifteen Pleasures of a Virgin* (1709); and the *Fifteen Plagues of a Lawyer, A Quack Doctor ... A Foot-Man* (1711?). Most of these were indebted to *Les quinze joies de mariage*, a prose satire written around 1400 and published in 1470, which is ascribed to Antoine de la Sale. Such works were originally written in mocking reference to devotional exercises like *Les quinze joyes de nostre dame*: see John Crow, 'The *quinze joyes de mariage* in France and England', *MLN* 59 (1964), 571–7. The *Cent nouvelles nouvelles* introduced these satires to a wider reading public: see Thompson, *Unfit*, 112.

13 An example of satire on spinsters is *A Practical Essay Upon Old Maids* (1768).

On the old maid as a figure of fun in eighteenth-century literature see Paul Denizot, 'La vieille fille, personnage eccentrique du XVIIIe siècle', in Michèle Plaisant, ed., *L'excentricité en Grande-Bretagne au 18e siècle* (Université de Lille III, 1976).

14 See *The Folly, Sin, and Danger of Marrying Widows*, 9–10, 14–15, 28–9 and also *The Pleasures of a Single Wife*. The 'Essay on Matrimony' is from *The Sixpenny Miscellany, or, A Dissertation on Pissing* (1726), 21–2.

15 In addition to the bawdy and prurient works of Dunton and Ward, discussed in the studies by Pinkus, Stephen Parks, and Troyer, cited above, see also the anti-feminist satires by Tom Brown, Richard Ames' *The Folly of Love* (fourth edition, 1700), and anonymous works like *The Art of Knowing Women* (1730). See also *The Pleasures of a Single Life*, 6, 11–23. See also Gravelot's satirical print, *Fore-Warned, Fore-Armed; or, The Bachelor's Monitor – Being a Modest Estimate of the Expenses Attending Married Life*. Such satirical 'estimates' were popular; see also *Cupid and Hymen* (1742), which has an appendix on 'The Batchelor's Estimate of the Expenses attending a Married Life, The Married Man's Answer to it, and a vindication of the estimate, by John Single, of Gray's Inn, Esq'.

16 The Macaroni were young men of fashion calling themselves after the national dish of Italy, which most of them got to know during their traditional Grand Tour of Europe. Between 1772 and 1774 they had their own journal, *The Macaroni, Savoir Vivre, and Theatrical Magazine*, but the fad seems to have died out by 1776. A typical satire on the overdressed male is *The Pretty Gentleman; or, Softness of Manners Vindicated* (1747; repr. 1771), a mock attack on David Garrick who had ridiculed the effeminate beaux in his successful farce, *Miss in Her Teens*, in which 'William Fribble Esq' causes as much laughter as the ridiculous caricature of a beau in Fielding's *Rape Upon Rape*.

I have not been able to locate a copy of *A Rod in Piss for Hooped-Petticoats*. It is referred to in *A Modest Defence of the Ladies*, p. 16. See the chapter heads of *Whipping-Tom, or, a Rod for a Proud Lady* (1722). Edmund Curll, of course, also exploited this popular line of satire with his *The School of Venus; Or The Lady's Miscellany* (1739), which deliberately hints at the English version of a French whore dialogue and has sections on 'The Art of Dress', 'The Hoop Petticoat', *et al.*

See Adam Eden, *A Vindication of the Reformation, On Foot, Among the Ladies, To Abolish Modesty and Chastity, and Restore the Native Simplicity of Going Naked* (1755), 3–4, 25–8. An earlier satirical writing on the same subject, albeit written in sober language, is *Nakedness*

Consider'd: or Reasons for not Wearing of Clothes. By a Gentleman of Great Parts (1729), which attacked the luxury and cost of expensive fashionable clothes.

On misogyny in eighteenth-century literature see Felicity A. Nussbaum, *The Brink of All We Hate. English Satires on Women, 1660–1750* (Lexington, Kent, 1984); Katherine M. Rogers, *The Troublesome Helpmate* (Seattle, Wash., 1966), especially chapter 5; and her article, 'My Female Friends: The Misogyny of Jonathan Swift', *TSLL* 1 (1959), 366–79; Harry M. Solomon, 'Difficult Beauty: Tom D'Urfey and the Context of Swift's *The Lady's Dressing Room*', *SEL* 19 (1979), 431–44; Miller Solomon, ' "To Steel a Hint was Never Known": the Sodom Apple Motif and Swift's *A Beautiful Young Nymph Going to Bed*', *TSLL* 22 (1977) 105–16; and Margarette Smith, 'Smollett and Matrimonial Bawdy', *SVEC* 228 (1984) 39–47. Vera Lee, in *The Reign of Women in Eighteenth-century France* (Cambridge, Mass., 1975), fails to discuss misogyny. For the quotation comparing women to horses, see *The Folly, Sin, and Danger of Marrying Widows*, 13–14.

6 POETRY AND FACETIAE

1 The division of erotic poetry into three genres – the genus grande, genus medium, and genus humile – suggested in Heinz Schlaffer's *Musa Iocosa* (Stuttgart, 1971) is convincing and has been adopted for this study. Although Schlaffer is mainly concerned with Germany, his results are also applicable to eighteenth-century England. Schlaffer points out that contrary to the genus grande, the jocose-erotic and burlesque or facetious pieces of the genus medium and genus humile have hardly found attention among scholars of literature, mainly because they are humorous and do not treat of serious human problems. See *op. cit.*, 1–4. In his study of the evolution of the Stuart love lyric H.M. Richmond, for instance, dismisses popular love poems as flippant or light-hearted and void of imaginative power: see *The School of Love* (Princeton, NJ, 1964), 181. Pat Rogers argues that 'street literature' was marred by stereotypes, was not influential and that serious writers ignored it: see *The Eighteenth Century* (1978), 20: surely a controversial statement from a great scholar.

It is therefore not surprising to notice that most surveys of eighteenth-century poetry fail to discuss popular erotic, facetious, and scatological verse of the genus medium and genus humile. See, for instance, Alan D. McKillop's introduction to *Eighteenth Century Poetry & Prose* (third edition, NY, 1973), xv–xxvii; Bernd Peter Lange, 'Die Theorie lyrischer Dichtung', in his *Die Theorie literarischer Gattungen in der englischen Aufklärung* (Munich, 1979); Victor Lange, *Die Lyrik und ihr Publikum im England des 18. Jahrhunderts* (Weimar, 1935); James Sutherland, *A Preface to Eighteenth-Century Poetry* (Oxford, 1963); all concerned with the genus grande. One of the exceedingly few researchers who has invested much time and energy in the exploration of humorous erotic folklore, of which a large part has found expression in poetry, is Gershon Legman. See his *The Horn Book*, pp. 170–494; the introductions to the New York editions of Ashbee's bibliographies and Kearney's *Private Case*; and his *The Rationale of the Dirty Joke: An Analysis of Sexual Humour*, 2 vols. (NY, 1968 and 1975). The title of Richard Wunderer's *Iocus Pornographicus*, 2 vols. (Schmiden bei Stuttgart, 1969), concerned with the obscene joke, is a contradiction in terms: a joke can hardly be pornographic.

A few examples of eighteenth-century bawdy poetry are contained in De Vries/Fryer, *Venus Unmasked*, 16–21, 30, 35, 120–22, 223–6.

For the comments of Francis Place on what he considered disgraceful eighteenth-century literature, see his papers in the BL, Add MSS. 27825, ff. 20–164 (See f 47). On the long tradition of erotic verse reaching back to Roman and Greek authors, see the *Encyclopedia of Poetry and Poetics*, s.v. 'erotic poetry'; David Loth, *The Erotic in Literature*, chapter III; Jean Hagstrum, *Sex and Sensibility*, 103–12; and Heinz Schlaffer, *op. cit.*, 128 f.

2 For discussions of the variety of ribald verse see Schlaffer, *op. cit.*, chapter I; and Ralph Cohen, 'On the interrelations of eighteenth-century literary forms', in Philip Harth, ed. *New Approaches to Eighteenth-Century Studies* (1974), 33–78. A good although not comprehensive bibliography of the field, with special emphasis on the drolleries, is Arthur E. Case, *Bibliography of English Poetical Miscellanies 1521–1750* (Oxford, 1935), enlarged by Norman Ault in *Cambridge Bibliography of English Literature* (1940), II, 173–256.

On the direct influence of classical erotic verse on popular poetry in England see Schlaffer, *op. cit.*, 6–8, 128–9; Hagstrum, *Sex and Sensibility*, 103–10. The best study is still Paul Englisch's *Geschichte der erotischen Literatur*: see especially pp. 23–56 on influential Greek authors, and pp. 59–86 on Latin poets with a lasting influence. In addition, see François Lasserre, *La figure d'Éros dans la poésie grecque* (Lausanne, 1946); and Peter Green, 'Sex and classical literature', in A. Bold, *The Sexual Dimension in Literature* (1982), 19–49.

3 On the translations and imitations of Anacreon and Sappho after 1700 see Hagstrum, *Sex and Sensibility*, 103; and David Foxon, *English Verse*, s.v. 'Anacreon' and 'Sappho'. Examples are *The Works of Anacreon and Sappho, by Several Hands* (1713), reprinted in enlarged versions in 1760 by F. Fawkes and in another edition in 1768; and Dryden's translation of *The Satyrs of D.J. Juvenalis* (1735; reprinted, NY, 1979). On Juvenal's influence on Swift see F. Nussbaum, 'Juvenal, Swift and *The Folly of Love*', *loc. cit.*

On French works written in the classical erotic tradition see Englisch, *Geschichte der erotischen Literatur*, 406–10; and Henry Cohen, *Guide de l'amateur de livres à gravures du XVIIIe siècle* (Paris, 1887): s.v. 'Anacreon', where many titles published between 1722 to 1794 are listed. Two examples are *Almanach Anacréontique, ou les ruses de l'amour* (c. 1735); and *Almanach des folies de l'amour ou le tribut de l'amitié* (*c.* 1735). The *Beef Steak* and *Humbug* clubs are mentioned in a 1789 edition of *The Festival of Ancareon*.

The quotation from *A Sapphic Epistle* is from pp. 12–13. There are extant editions of Cotton's *Scaronnides* from 1700, 1709, 1728, 1770, 1776 and 1804. A Greek anthology containing erotic poetry is the *Anthologia Graeca*. It was compiled in the thirteenth century by Maximus Planides and served as a treasure trove for later centuries.

4 See also Bancks, *Poems on Several Occasions* (1733); Thompson, *The Court of Cupid* (1770).

5 Many anonymous French collections of erotic verse were published and read in England. On influential French collections of poetic erotica see Englisch, *op. cit.*, 406–10. See especially *L'abbateur de noisettes* (The Hague, 1741); *L'Art de bien aimer* (1781); part II ('Les epices de Vénus') of Nogaret's *L'Arétin françois* (1787); Evariste Parny, *Opuscules poétiques* (Amsterdam, 1779; fourth edition, Paris and London, 1784); and *Momus Redivivus, ou les saturnales françaises* (1796). A modern collection of eighteenth-century French erotic poetry is *Petit enfer poétique du XVIIIe siècle, présenté par Henry Muller* (Paris, 1954), which has works by Vergier, Rousseau, Grécourt, Piron, Collé, Vade, Robbé de Beauveset, Senac de Meilhan, Imbert, Nogaret, Andréa de Nerciat, Parny, *et al.* On influential Continental and English bawdry before 1700 see David Frantz, 'Leud Priapians and Renaissance Pornography', *SEL* 12 (1972), 157–72.

Giorgio Baffo is discussed in *Bilderlexikon der Erotik*, III, 85–90. On Sedley and Sackville see *Restoration and Eighteenth-Century Prose and Poetry*, introduced by Pat Rogers (1983), 81–3, 153–4. Editions of Rochester's poetry appeared in 1710, 1712, 1756, and 1757: see also the standard edition of his poems, *The Complete Poems of John Wilmot, Earl of Rochester*, ed. David M. Vieth (1968). For the erotica of John Bancks, whom Francis Place lists as a writer of smut (see Place papers, Add. MS. 27825 f. 86 in BL), see his *Miscellaneous Works*, 2 vols. (1738), and the *Poems on Several Occasions* (1733). See also *The Poems and Miscellaneous Compositions of Paul Whitehead*, ed. Captain Edward Thompson (1777); and Ed Cray, ed., *The Anthology of Restoration Erotic Poetry* (California, 1965), which has some poems by Rochester, Sedley, Butler and anonymous works. For Hildebrand Jacob's *The Curious Maid* see his *The Works* (1785) of which a reprint is being prepared by G. Olms Verlag. The Bodleian Library has an edition of *The Curious Maid* (Shelfmark Arch Dc 6 [6]) bound with *The Bauble* (1720).

6 On the oral element in erotic folklore, especially in the area of songs and riddles, see Legman, 'The Bawdy Song', *The Horn Book*, 375–9. For comments on such songs see Francis Place, who lists examples in the manuscript of his papers, Add. MS 141–64 (BL).

In addition to the collections cited, see also *The Choice Spirits Museum* (1756); *The Cuckold's Cap Garland* (Newcastle, 1765? and 1780?); *The Frisky Songster. The Ninth Edition* (1788) and Charles Morris' *The Festival of Ancareon. The Ninth Edition* (1788): Rose's *Register of*

Erotic Books lists another edition of this in 1789. A comprehensive collection of songs from the early eighteenth century is Thomas D'Urfey's *Wit and Mirth: Pills to Purge Melancholy*, 6 vols. (1719–20; repr. NY, 1959). See also Ed Cray, ed., *Bawdy Ballads: A History of the Bawdy Songs* (1970).

'The Jolly Waggoner' is quoted from DeVries/Fryer, *Venus Unmasked*, 16–18: see *ibid.* for other songs from *The Fond Mother's Garland*, and *The Compleat Academy of Complements*.

7 See *The Merry Andrew*, 46–7. For the riddles see *Kitty's Attalantis*, 2; and *The Trial of Wit*, repr. in DeVries/Fryer, *Venus Unmasked*, 100–1. See also *ibid.*, 34–7, for 'A Riddle' (1725); and *A Merry Conversation . . .* (1739), 18. For Swift's riddles and poems see Harold Williams, ed., *Swift's Poems*, 3 vols. (second edition, 1966), III, 916 f.; 'The Maypole' is cited from p. 926. See also the notes on the riddles, pp. 757 f., in Pat Rogers' recent edition, *Jonathan Swift. The Complete Poems* (Harmondsworth, 1983). See also the following Edmund Curll publications: *Post-Office Intelligence* (1736); *The Amorous Gallant's Tongue Tipp'd with Golden Expressions.*

8 On the history of bawdy and obscene jests and riddles see Legman, *The Horn Book*, 427–53; R. Schöwerling, *Chapbooks*, 266 f. On Shakespeare see Eric Partridge, *Shakespeare's Bawdy* (revised edition, 1960). A modern edition of Bracciolini's book is Bernhardt J. Hurwood, trans., *The Facetiae of Giovanni Francesco Poggio Bracciolini* (NY, 1968). For discussions and collections of limericks see Legman's two volumes, *The Rationale of The Dirty Joke: An Analysis of Sexual Humor* (NY, 1968 and 1975); *idem, The Limerick* (1974), pp. vii–xxiii; William S. Baring-Gould, *The Lure of the Limerick* (1968), which has a detailed bibliography. Modern collections with examples of eighteenth-century ribald poetry are Alan Bold, ed., *The Bawdy Beautiful*; and *ibid., Making Love.*

An eighteenth-century revival of Greek love letters is *The Love Epistles of Aristaenetus. Translated from the Greek into English Metre* (1773). Aristaenetos, who lived during the fifth century BC, was one of the later epistolographers. His erotic letters contain the major erotic motifs of antiquity. Together with Alciphron, he exerted great influence on later literary periods: see the translation by A.R. Benner and F.H. Fobes, *The Letters of Alciphron, Aelian and Philostratus* (1962). On the French influence in this field and some collections from the sixteenth and seventeenth centuries see DeVries/Fryer *Venus Unmasked*, 12. In addition to Curll's *Post-Office Intelligence*, see part I of his *Atterburyana* (1727); and Charles Freeman's *The Lover's New Guide* (c. 1780).

For a discussion of French erotic dictionaries between 1600–1800 see Englisch, *Geschichte der erotischen Literatur*, xii–xvii. A few examples are Richelot, *Dictionnaire français* (Geneva, 1680; reprinted, 1693 and 1710; and Amsterdam, 1685 and 1706); *Dictionnaire Comique, Critique, burlesque, libre et proverbial* (Amsterdam, 1718; repr. 1752 and 1786); and *Dictionnaire d'amour par le berger Sylvain* (1788).

See *The Dictionary of Love*, repr. in DeVries/Fryer, *op. cit.*, 75–8. Francis Grose's *A Classical Dictionary of the Vulgar Tongue* was reprinted in 1788 and was selling in a third edition in 1796. For quotations and a discussion of its bawdy contents see Hurwood, *The Golden Age of Erotica*, chapter 10.

9 See also *The Bauble* (1721).

10 Standard surveys of English verse satire in the eighteenth century have generally ignored popular verse tales; see, for instance, Raman Seldon, *English Verse Satire 1590–1765* (1978), which only discusses Pope, Swift, and a few minor authors. Thomas Lockwood, *Post-Augustan Satire* (Seattle, Washington, 1979), also ignores salacious verse. On Churchill's bawdy verse see *ibid.*; and Wallace C. Brown, *Charles Churchill, Poet, Rake, and Rebel* (Lawrence, 1953). On the popularity of the verse tale in France and England see Legman, *The Horn Book*, 454–94.

The Surprised Lovers is reprinted from *Bilderlexikon der Erotik*, III, 863; and *The Mouse's Tail* from Fuchs, *Geschichte der erotischen Kunst*, I, book 2, 275. See also *The Bauble* (1721), 3, 5, 6–7; *Kick Him, Jenny*, 17–18, 20–21. The copy in the BL (shelfmark P.C. 26 a 11) has other tales of this kind appended to the poem: see, for instance, *The Contest*, pp. 22–4. Many tales were written by Ned Ward around 1700; see also Thomas James Mathias, *The Pursuits of Literature* (1794).

On the adaptations of Piron's tale see Legman, *Rationale of the Dirty Joke*, I, 36–7.

11 See *The Surprize* (1739), 7, 9, 121, 137–9. See Naumann, *Keyhole und Candle*, 77–8 and note 45 p. 368, on the prose versions of *The Gentleman Apothecary* in the seventeenth and eighteenth centuries. Edmund Curll published an edition in 1726 under the title, *The Gentleman 'Pothecary*. Other versions are *The Artful Lover, or the French Count Turned Doctor* (1751); and *The Female Apothecary Deprived of Her Office* (1753). The BL has a Latin version from 1739, entitled *Nobilis Pharmacopola* (shelfmark 1093 a 16) and a bilingual edition of the same year, listed in the Private Case as P.C. 19 a 14.

See Hamilton's *New Crazy Tales* (1783), tale no. 7. Other such collections by the Earl of Haddington are *Forty Select Poems, On Several Occasions* (1753); *Monstrous Good Things!! Humorous Tales in Verse* (1785). His *New Crazy Tales* was reprinted in 1787 as *Select Poems on Several Occasions, in the Luscious Taste*.

12 Any survey of eighteenth-century scatological literature should start with the following books which contain preliminary surveys and valuable comments: Bloch, *Sexual Life*, chapter XV; John Gregory Bourke, *Scatological Rites of all Nations* (Washington, 1891; repr. up to 1968); Paul Englisch, *Das skatologische Element in der Literatur, Kunst und Volksleben* (Stuttgart, 1928); and Gershon Legman, *Rationale of the Dirty Joke. Second Series* (NY, 1975), chapter 15. Good bibliographies are Paul Jannet *et al.*, *Bibliotheca scatologica* (Paris, 1850), and its supplement by Gustave Brunet, *Anthologie Scatologique* (Paris, 1862). The

Bibliotheca scatologica is itself made up rather humorously, offering alphabetical lists of works in three sections: K (caca); P (pet); and Q (cul). The book covers four centuries.

On the failure of modern hygienists to understand the place and meaning of scatology in eighteenth-century literature see Jae Num Lee, *Swift and Scatological Satire* (Albuquerque, 1971), 121; and Solomon, *op. cit.*

13 On eighteenth-century sanitary regulations see Lawrence Wright, *Clean and Decent: The Fascinating History of the Bathroom and the Water Closet* (1960); and on England and London, Ruth Perry, 'Anality and Ethics in Pope's Late Satires', *BJECS* 4 no. 2 (1981), 139. For Casanova's comments on the coarse manners in England see vol. IX, 302 of *Geschichte meines Lebens* (Frankfurt, 1964).

14 On the functions of scatology in seventeenth-century chapbooks see Spufford, *Small Books*, 184–5 and 192 n. 89–92. Other French works listed under 'K' in the *Bibliotheca scatologia* are the following, *Amusement de la garde-robe* (1712); *Le nouveau merdiana* (1729–1789); *Sauve la peste, ou relation d'un accident terrible ... arrivé aux latrines du Palais-Royal* (1790); and *Le vidangeur sensible, drame en trois actes et en prose* (London and Paris, 1777); the latter is attributed to M. de Nogaret. Further satires on farting are *Le dieu des vents* (1776); and *La facétieuse loterie de pantalon pasquinet, commissaire général des vents méridionaux* (1706). Some of the scatological pieces of Grandval *père* (actually his name was Nicolas Racot) and *fils* (Charles François Racot) have been collected in *Théâtre de campagne ou les Débauches de l'esprit* (1755) and in *Théâtre gaillard* (1803). For eighteenth-century editions of such French collections in the BL see Kearney, *Private Case*, s.v. 'Théâtre Gaillard'. For discussions see Englisch, *Das skatologische Element*, 91–2; and *Bilderlexikon der Erotik*, III, 464–5. See also Gallet's *La péterade ou Polichinel auteur* (n.d.), briefly discussed in Rabenalt, *Voluptas Ludens*, 314. See also Compiègne, *Eloge du pet* (1779); *Histoire et aventure de Milord pet* (1755); *Caquire* (1782); Grandval *fils*, *Les deux biscuits* (1751) and *Sirop-au-cul*; and Grandval *père*, *Le pot de chambre cassé* (1742).

15 On the tradition of scatology in literature and satire see Lee, *Swift and Scatological Satire*, chapters I and II; and Reid B. Sinclair, 'What the World Calls Obscene: Swift's Ugly Verse and the Satiric Tradition', doct. diss. (Vanderbilt University, 1965), chapters III and VII. *An Essay on Wind* contains earlier pieces like *The Benefit of Farting Explained*; *Afterthoughts on Farting*; *The Farto-Turdoniad, a ballad*.

The *New Boghouse Miscellany* was reissued, the title expurgated to *The Wit's Miscellany* (1762). On *The Merry-Thought*, which is not any more in the Private Case of the BL, see Fryer, *Private Case* 79–80.

Plate 44 is a cutting from *The Covent Garden Magazine* contained in the Place MSS in the BL, f. 116. Place included this as an example of what he terms eighteenth-century grossness. See also Swift, *A Tale of a Tub and Other Satires* (1975), 98. On the scatological elements in the works of

Sterne see Robert Alter, 'Tristram Shandy and the Game of Love', *American Scholar* 37 (1968), 316–23; and A.R. Towers, 'Sterne's Cock and Bull Story', *ELH* 24 (1957), 12–29. Plate 45 is from Fuchs, *Illustrierte Sittengeschichte*, III, supplement, 252. The telescope in the picture is an allusion to Newton's works on optics. Hutchinson's works against Newton were *Power Essential and Mechanical, or What Power Belongs to God and What to His Creatures, in Which the Design of Sir I. Newton and Dr Samuel Clark is Laid Open* (1732); *Glory and Gravity* (1733); and *The Religion of Satan, or Antichrist Delineated* (1736).

16 The literature on Swift's scatological poems has assumed dimensions calling for bibliographical surveys. Up to 1973 all contributions on the 'unprintables' are listed in Anthon Murtuza, 'Twentieth-Century Critical Responses to Swift's Scatological Verse: a checklist', *Bulletin of Bibliography* 30 (1973) 18 f. The articles and books, excluding doctoral dissertations from America, written after 1974 up to 1980 are discussed in the excellent survey of Kuno Schuhmann/Joachim Möller, *Jonathan Swift*, vol. 159 of the series *Erträge der Forschung* (Darmstadt, 1981), 167–75.

The best studies of Swift's dirty poems are still Lee, *op. cit.*, Peter Schakel, *The Poetry of Jonathan Swift* (Madison, Wisc., 1978), chapter IV. In addition, see Colin J. Horne, 'Swift's Comic Poetry', in J.C. Hilson *et al.* eds., *Augustan Worlds: New Essays in eighteenth-century literature* (New York, 1978), 51–67; H.J. Real/H.J. Viencken, 'The Syphilitic Lady', *The Scriblerian and the Kit-Kats* 15 (1982) 52–4; and Felicity Nussbaum, 'Juvenal, Swift, and The Folly of Love', *ECS* 9 (1975/76), 540–52. On the questionable psychoanalytic approach, recently applied to Pope by Ruth Perry, *op. cit.*, see Schakel, *op. cit.*, 199; and Real/Viencken, *op. cit.*, passim. On the contemporary influence on Swift see Harry M. Solomon, '"Difficult Beauty,"' *loc. cit.* The question and the issues involving scatology are also discussed in the doctoral dissertation in progress by David Profumo, *The Voices of The Dean: Strategies of Self-reference in the Poems of Jonathan Swift* (King's College, London).

See Lee, *op. cit.*, 153 n. 1, for a discussion of the authorship of *Human Ordure; The Benefit of Farting*; and *The Grand Mystery*. See also *Le grand mystère, ou l'art de méditer sur la garde-robe* (La Haye, 1729); and the slightly different version, *L'art de méditer sur la chaise percée* ('Dublin', 1743). See also *Bibliotheca Scatologica*, 11.

Swift's major antifeminist satires with strong scatological elements are *A Young Beautiful Nymph Going to Bed; The Lady's Dressing Room*; *Strephon and Chloe*; and *Cassinus and Peter*. See the notes on these poems in the editions of Swift's poetry by H. Williams (1966), II; and by Pat Rogers (1983).

See *The Sixpenny Miscellany*, 5; and Swift's scatological poems quoted from the Williams edition, pp. 786 and 917–8 in vol. III. See pp. 919–28 for other such obscene riddles.

17 On the history and eighteenth-century use of the extended metaphor see

364 Eros Revived

Peter Fryer, *Private Case*, 170–3; and Roger Thompson, *Unfit*, 190–4. Borde's *Parapilla* is discussed by Englisch, *Geschichte*, 405; and in *Bilderlexikon*, III, 152–3; and *Dictionnaire des oeuvres érotiques*. The first dated edition of *La foutro-manie* is from 1780: see Pia, *Les livres de l'Enfer*, pp. 542–8. On erotic and sexual love as themes in French literature before 1700, see Roger Gilbert Bougard, *Érotisme et amour physique dans la littérature française du XVIIe siècle*, doct. diss., (Chapel Hill, N.C., 1974). *The Members to Their Sovereign* was published together with *A Merry Conversation which Lately Pass'd Between ... A Quaker and his Maid* (1739), 13–18. Quotations are from pp. 14, 16 and 18.

18 In addition to Godard's *Histoire du prince Apprius*, see also *Anecdotes pour servir à l'histoire secrète des ébugors* (c. 1733), a vicious lampoon on the 'bougres' and 'sodomites'. Curll's translation of *King Apprius* was reprinted in *The Bon Ton Magazine*, October 1794–June 1795. A similar work is *The History of Pego the Great* (1733). See also *The Secret History of Pandora's Box* (1742) and Marini's *The Why and the Wherefore* (1765).

19 See also Cotton, *Erotopolis. The Present State of Betty-land* (1684); Stretser, *A New Description of Merryland* (1740); and lesser-known works like *Little Merlin's Cave* (1773), *A Voyage to Lethe* (1741), *The Potent Ally* (1741), and Stretser, *Merryland Displayed* (1741). See also *A Compleat Sett of Charts of the Coasts of Merryland* (1745), which contained obscene illustrations; its publishers were prosecuted in 1745. On the prosecution see Foxon, *Libertine Literature*, 15–18; and Thomas, *A Long Time Burning*, 84.

For discussions and information on *Erotopolis* and *Little Merlin's Cave*, see Foxon, *Libertine Literature*, 15–8; Fryer, *Private Case*, 73–7; and Thompson, *Unfit*, 190–4.

On *The Potent Ally* see Mertner/Mainusch, *Pornotopia*, 110 and 328; and on *A Voyage to Lethe*, Boucé's article in *BJECS* 3 no. 3 (1980), 173–93. On Curll's false Bath imprint in the *Merryland* book see Neale, *Bath: A Social History* (1981), 23–4; and Foxon, *Libertine Literature*, 15–7: cf. also Kearney, *Private Case*, 319 n. 1750. Stretser's book was translated into French c. 1770 as *Description Topographique, historique, critique et nouvelle du pays et des environs de la forêt-noire*.

20 Stretser's *Arbor vitae* was published as a single folio sheet in 1732, with two pages of prose. Poetic versions also appeared. See Foxon, *Libertine*, 15–17; and Naumann, *Keyhole und Candle*, 367–8. *Arbor vitae* is quoted from the London edition, pp. 2–7 (1/41). *Ridotto All' Fresco*, one of the satires in *The Lady's Delight* of 1732, is cited by Naumann, *Keyhole*, 367–8, quoting from the title-page. See also *Wisdom Revealed*, 6 and 13; *The Crab Tree*, 26; and *Mimosa*, iv, 5–16. See Kearney, *Private Case*, on the attribution of *Mimosa*. Other scurrilous attacks on John Banks are *An Epistle from Obera, Queen of Otaheite, To Joseph Banks* (1774); and *An Epistle from Mr. Banks, Voyager, Monster-Hunter, and Amoroso, to Obera, Queen of Otaheite* (1773). *The Fruit Shop* (1765) is

another satire on the female genitals, but written in prose and as a parody of Sterne's *Tristram Shandy*.

21 See *Teague-Root Display'd* (1746), 16–23. Satirical replies to Perry's poem were *The Old Serpent's Reply to the Electrical Eel* and *The Inamorata. Addressed to the Author of the Electrical Eel. By a Lady*, both published in 1777. *An Elegy on the Lamented Death of the Electrical Eel* is quoted from pp. 2 and 23–8. See also *The Torpedo*, iii, 3, 6, 10, 18, which was advertised in vol. II of *Nocturnal Revels* (1779).

22 See *La confédération de la nature* (1790). On French collections of ribaldry before 1700 see Pierre Brochon, *Le livre de colportage en France depuis le XVIe siècle* (1954), pp. 49 and 69 f.

23 On the poetic tradition of describing garden landscapes and setting poems in such surroundings see Dale Underwood, *Etheridge and the Seventeenth-Century Comedy of Manners* (New Haven, 1957), chapter 2; and H.E.D. Wedeck, *Dictionary of Erotic Literature*, 199. On the *Beggar's Benison* of Anstruther see Alan Bold's introduction to the recently published records (Edinburgh, 1982). See also the review of this edition by Anne Smith in *TLS* March 18, 1983, p. 270; it is the typical modern reaction to ribaldry from earlier centuries. Smith dismisses the recitals and doings of the Scottish rakes as childish and puerile. On the oral tradition in literature see Pitcher, 'On the Conventions of Eighteenth-Century British Short Fiction', *SSF* 12 (1975), 199–212, especially p. 204.

7 EROTIC PROSE

1 Helpful bibliographies for short prose fiction are Andrew Block, *The English Novel 1740–1850*. New rev. ed. (1939); William H. McBurney, *A Check List of English Prose Fiction 1700–1739* (Cambridge, Mass., 1960); and Robert D. Mayo, *The English Novel in the Magazines 1740–1815* (1962). Important studies are Naumann, *Keyhole*, 74–81; Edward W. Pitcher, 'On the Conventions of Eighteenth-Century British Short Fiction: Part I 1700–1760; Part II 1760–1785', *SSF* 12 (1975), 199–212; 327–41; and *idem*, 'Changes in Short Fiction in Britain 1785–1810: Philosophic Tales, Gothic Tales, and Fragments and Visions', *SSF* 13 (1976), 331–54. Pitcher has, however, largely ignored the erotic tales, which is a sad shortcoming of his surveys, especially in the area of the oriental tale. In addition, see Richetti, *Popular Fiction Before Richardson*; and Troyer, *Ned Ward of Grub Street*, which has a good bibliography. Many scholars still believe that much of the short fiction is worthless. Thus Mayo notes on p. 351 that eighteenth-century miscellany fiction between 1740–1800 was 'trashy, affected, and egregiously sentimental'. Pitcher, in his first article cited above (p. 210), maintains that in short prose fiction 'the tendency towards didacticism left little place for the vulgarly comic or for satire'. After one example of a 'somewhat vulgar tale' he heads for more promising grounds, leaving a great number of vulgar satires in the dark. Naumann's survey is too cursory to be

satisfactory; he wrongly attributes *Le canapé* to Fougeret de Monbron (see p. 80).

2 *The Fair Adulteress* (1743) and *The Fair Concubine* (1782) are quoted from the title-pages. See also *The Midnight Ramble*, 26; and *The London-Bawd* (1711), chapters iii–x; the tale about the citizen is reprinted in DeVries/Fryer, *Venus Unmasked*, 21–7.

See Naumann, *Keyhole*, 77–80, for a brief discussion of bawdy tales, including prose versions of *The Gentleman Apothecary*. For a bawdy tale from *A Curious Collection of Novels* see Pitcher, 'On the Conventions of Eighteenth-Century British Short Fiction', *loc. cit.*, 210; and on *The Cabinet of Amorous Curiosities*, Ashbee, *Catena*, 148. For a discussion of Ward's prose see *Restoration and Eighteenth-Century Prose and Poetry*, intr. Pat Rogers (1983), 175–8. In addition to the tales cited above, see also *The Gallant Companion* (1746); and *Venus Unmasked*, 122–31 and 206–23 (excerpts).

The French influence should not be underestimated. See, for instance, such anonymous works as *Les dégouts du plaisir: frivolité* (1755), discussed in Englisch's *Geschichte der erotischen Literatur*, 487; and the collection of better known tales in two volumes, entitled *Les conteurs libertins du XVIIIe siècle* (1904–5).

3 *Amorous Sketches*, 10–11, 13–15.

4 On the oriental tale in France and England see Martha Pike Conant, *The Oriental Tale in the Eighteenth Century* (New York, 1908); M.C. Cook, *Politics in the Fiction of the French Revolution*, chapter 4; M.-L. Dufréoy, *L'orient romanesque en France 1704–1789* (Montreal, 1947), 2 vols., II; François Moureau, 'Le *Mercure galant* de Dufresny (1710–1714) ou le journalisme à la mode,' *SVEC*, ed. H. Mason (Oxford, 1982); and Pitcher, 'On the conventions . . .,' *loc. cit.*, 210–11. Good bibliographies of erotic French tales can be found in Jean Leduc, 'Le clérge dans le roman érotique,' *op. cit.*, and Jacques Rustin, *Le vice à la mode*, 250–91.

Parodies of the 'conte de fée' or 'conte oriental' are Charles Pinot Duclos, *Acajou et Zirphile* (1744); the anonymous *Le canapé couleur de feu*; Meusnier de Querlon, *Psaphion ou la courtisane de Smyrne, fragment érotique* (1748). See also the erotic tales in Caylus' *Oeuvres badines*, 12 vols. (1787); de Ligne's *Contes immoraux* (c. 1785); and the anonymous tales in *L'année galante ou étrenne à l'amour* (1773); *Le cabinet d'amour et de Vénus*, which is a reprint of *La bibliothèque d'Arétin* (1793); *Le calecon des coquettes du jour*; and *La légende joyeuse ou les cent une leçons de Lampsaque*, 2 vols. (1749–50). 'The Hobgoblin' in *The Gallant Companion* (1746) may be influenced by Crébillon's *Le sylphe* of 1730.

On the 'contes' and 'historiettes' in the *Mercure galant* see F. Moureau, *op. cit.*, chapter iv; and on the *Mémoires secrets*, M. Warré's very useful *Table alphabétique des auteurs et personnages cités dans les Mémoires Secrets* (1970).

Voisenon's tale, *Tant mieux pour elle, conte plaisant* (1760) was first translated into English as *Did You Ever See Such Damned Stuff* and later appeared in the *Bon Ton Magazine* (March–June 1795) under the title, *Tant Mieux Pour Elle. Or The Marriage of Tricolore*, this being an abbreviated version: see Ashbee, *Catena*, 103–7, for excerpts and a discussion of the tale. Crébillon's *L'écumoir* (1734) appeared in three French versions; for English translations of his tales see the catalogue of the *BL*, and the modern edition, ed. Ernest Sturm (Paris, 1976). See also Crébillon, *L'écumoire ou Tanzai et Néardarné* (1734). The tales often appeared in magazines such as *Le mercure galant, Mémoires secrets pour servir à la République des lettres.*

5 See also Crébillon's erotic oriental tales *The Amours of Zeokinizul King of the Kofirans* (1749) and *The Night and the Moment* (1770).
   On the attribution of *Le canapé* see Kearney, *Private Case*, 125–6; and Pia, *Les livres de l'Enfer*, s.v. 'Canapé'. For a discussion, see Kearney, *A History of Erotic Literature*, 60. The most reliable study of the works of Crébillon fils is still Hans-Günther Funke, *Crébillon fils als Moralist und Gesellschaftskritiker* (Heidelberg, 1972); see also Peter Nagy, *Libertinage et révolution*, 56–65. Other influential tales were Godard d'Aucour's *Mémoires Turcs* (1743); and *L'odalisque, ouvrage traduit du Turc* (1796), of which Englisch, *Geschichte der erotischen Literatur*, 441–2, lists two earlier editions of 1779 and 1787. The work is probably from the pen of Mayeur de Saint-Paul: see Pia, *op. cit.*, s.v. 'L'odalisque'.
   On Crébillon's *Le sopha*, see Funke, *op. cit.*, passim, and Viktor Link, 'The reception of Crébillon's *Le Sopha* in England: an Unnoticed Edition and Some Imitations', *SVEC* 132 (1975), 199–204. Link shows that between 1742 and 1801 eighteen editions of *The Sopha* are known to have been published. It was exploited in *The Rambler's Magazine*, vol. IV (1786)–vol. VIII (1790), where it appeared in a reprint of a 1781 edition as *Adventures of a Sopha*. It also influenced other serialised novels in this magazine, such as *The History and Adventures of a Bedstead*. See also the modern edition of *Le Sopha*, ed. by Albert-Marie Schmidt (Paris, 1966).

6 On Diderot and his *Les bijoux indiscrets* see Aram Vartanian, 'Érotisme et philosophie chez Diderot', *Cahiers de l'association international des études françaises* XIII (1961), 367–90; and his excellent introduction to the novel-tale in Diderot's *Oeuvres complètes*, ed. Jean Macary *et al.*, III (Paris, 1978), 3–18. See also Vartanian's discussion of La Mettrie's influence on Diderot's *Les bijoux* in 'La Mettrie, Diderot and Sexology', *op. cit.*, 347–67: especially pp. 354–8. In the introduction to the novel, p. 13, Vartanian argues that Diderot got the idea not from Garin's adaptation of the *fabliau, Le chevalier qui faisait parler les cons et les culs* (1747), but from Caylus's *Nocrion* (1747). See also Kearney, *A History of Erotic Literature*, 62–5.
   On the gothic tale see Pitcher, 'Changes in Short Fiction', *loc. cit.*, 331–54; and on the mania for oriental tales, Remy G. Saisselin, 'Room at the Top of the Eighteenth Century: From Sin to Aesthetic Pleasure', *Journal of Aesthetics and Art Criticism* 26 (1967/68), 345–50.

7 See *The World* no. 19, Thursday, 10 May 1753; repr. in Thomas, *A Long*

Time Burning, 88. On the changing taste in literature after 1750 see *ibid.*, 87–91, and Maurice J. Quinlan, *Victorian Prelude. A History of English Manners 1700–1830* (New York, 1941), 61–4. Le Roy W. Smith, in his 'Daniel Defoe: incipient pornographer', *LP* 22 (1972), 166, confirms that about 50 per cent of the titles in McBurney's list appeal to the erotic. John Crow remarks in the preface to Andrew Block's bibliography that there are hundreds of titles defying explanation. See, for instance, *The Adventures of Miss Beverly*, 2 vols. (1768); *The Adventures of Miss Lucy Watson* (1768); *A Butler's Diary*, 2 vols. (1792); *Confessions of a Beauty. From the French*, 2 vols. (1798); *The Confessions of a Coquet* (1785). Such titles and those which Block lists under 'History of', 'Confessions of', and 'Adventures of' can be anything from pathetic-sentimental to bawdy or erotic. See Foxon, *Libertine Literature*, x. Naumann, *op. cit.*, attempted a preliminary survey of the various genres of the erotic novel which, together with Foxon's *Libertine Literature*, remains the best study to date. An excellent anthology is DeVries/Fryer, *Venus Unmasked*, which is far superior to Alan Bold, ed., *Mounts of Venus* (1980), a collection too large in scope to be satisfactory. See also Marianne Thalmann, *Der Trivialroman des 18. Jahrhunderts und der Romantische Roman* (Berlin, 1923); Richetti, *Popular Fiction*; and Donald Furber/ Anne Callahan, *Erotic Love in Literature from Medieval Legend to Romantic Illusion* (NY, 1981). On the English novel in France see Harold W. Streeter, *The Eighteenth-Century English Novel in French Translation: A Bibliographical Study* (NY, 1936).

If we still have no detailed and reliable survey of the erotic novel in eighteenth-century literature it is mainly because of a dauntingly endless list of titles that is liable to frustrate the most courageous researcher. In addition, there are difficulties of definition and classification concerning the nature of pornography and eroticism.

On the veiled pornographic tendencies in Defoe's novels see Le Roy W. Smith, *op. cit.*; and on sex in *Tom Jones*, Boucé, 'Sex, Amours and Love in Tom Jones', in my 'Sex and Eighteenth-Century English Culture', *SVEC* 228 (1984), 25–39. See the 1791 edition of *Tom Jones* for erotic illustrations in the three volumes (by Rowlandson). On Smollett's thematic use of sex and ribaldry see Boucé's introduction to *Roderick Random* (Oxford, 1981), and Margarette Smith, 'Smollett and Matrimonial Bawdy', in *SVEC* 228 (1984), 39–47.

On sex in Richardson's novels see Thomas, *A Long Time Burning*, 86–7; and J. Chalker, '"Virtue Rewarded": the Sexual Theme in Richardson's *Pamela*', *Literary Half-Yearly* II no. 2 (1961), 58–64. Robert M. Lovett, 'Sex and the Novel', in Victor F. Calverton and Samuel D. Schmalhausen, *Sex in Civilization* (1929), 680–3, discusses Richardson, Fielding and Smollett in a very brief way and ignores Defoe, Cleland and Sterne. The *Index librorum prohibitorum* (Rome, 1938) lists only *Pamela* and *The Sentimental Journey* as prohibited novels in the eighteenth century. On Sterne, see Frank Brady, '*Tristram Shandy*: Sexuality, Morality, and Sensibility', *ECS* IV no. 1 (1970), 41–56; and M.O.

Houlahan, *op. cit. The Fruit Shop* is only initially concerned with Sterne and soon launches into a ribald description of the female genitals ('fruit shop'). Quotations are from pp. ii–iv. *La Souricière* is quoted by Naumann, *op. cit.*, 278–9. A more feeble parody of *Tristram Shandy* is *Explanatory Remarks upon the Life and Opinions of Tristram Shandy ... by Jeremiah Kunastrokius* (1760).

8 Eighteenth-century translations of *Satyricon* appeared, for instance, in 1708, 1710, 1713 and 1714. See the *Cambridge Bibliography of English Literature* II, 767. When William Burnaby published his version, *The Satyr of Titus Petronius Arbiter*, in 1694, he wisely left certain sections of the book in Latin because there had been prosecutions before. See Thomas, *A Long Time*, 76–7; and on the influence of Petronius, Englisch, *Geschichte*, 57–87; and Thompson, *Unfit* 3–4. On the reasons for the appearance of the erotic theme in the novel see Peter Hughes, 'Wars Within Doors: Erotic Heroism and the Implosion of Texts', *ES* 60 (1979), 402–21; and on La Fontaine, Roseanne Runte, 'La Fontaine: Precursor of the Eighteenth-Century Libertine', *ECL* III 2 (1976), 47–51.

Critics have so far merely discussed the French influence 'en passant'; thus Ronald Paulson refers to the impact on English literature of Crébillon's *Le sopha*, Diderot's *Les bijoux*, and of the 'chronique scandaleuse', in his *Satire and the Novel in Eighteenth-century England* (London, 1967), 192, but he does not pursue this line. Pat Rogers, in his *The Eighteenth Century* (London, 1978), ix ff., has a table listing major events in literary history and foreign literature. The only French works he lists before 1750 are Prévost's *Manon Lescaut* (1731) and Montesquieu's *L'esprit des lois* (1748). Such titles do not help to explain the appearance in 1749 of Cleland's *Memoirs of a Woman of Pleasure*, which Rogers includes in his list. What Rogers has ignored are the works of Millot, Barrin, Chorier, Crébillon, Diderot, La Morlière *et al.*, which all appeared in English translations but are considered by literary scholars as inferior to the major novelists of the time, such as Swift, Fielding, and Smollett.

9 The French erotic prose fiction of the eighteenth century is so abundant that serious surveys have not been attempted. Jacques Rustin, in his *Le vice à la mode. Étude sur le roman français du XVIIIe siècle de 'Manon Lescaut' à l'apparition de 'La nouvelle Héloïse' (1731–1761)* (Paris, 1979), 21, points out the enormous work to be done: not only major novelists from Crébillon to Andréa de Nerciat remain to be studied, but also the minor authors whose works have been deemed of little value.

Marchand's *The French Pornographers* is unreliable; this is also partly true for Paul Englisch's *Geschichte der Erotischen Literatur*, in which he discusses the major French erotic fiction on pp. 433–88. Nevertheless his contribution is a good beginning, although he does not include minor writers like Cubières, Mercier and Linguet. For a list and partial discussion of the novels and fiction of such minor authors see Émile Henriot, *Les livres du second rayon, irréguliers et libertins* (1948); and Charles-Pierre Monselet, *Les galanteries du XVIIIe siècle* (1862), as well as his

Les oubliés et les dédaignés, figures littéraires de la fin du XVIIIe siècle
(1885). Excellent bibliographies with titles of important erotic and pornographic novels can be found in Robert Mauzi, *L'idée du bonheur dans
la littérature et la pensée françaises au XVIIIe siècle* (1960), 688–95; J.
Rustin, *Le vice*, 250–91. See also Philippe Laroch, *Petits-maîtres et
roués. Évolution de la notion de libertinage dans le roman français du
XVIIIe siècle* (Laval, Can., 1979); Paul Hoffman, *La femme dans la
pensée des lumières* (1977); and Peter Nagy, *Libertinage et révolution*
(1975). Also helpful are Pia's *Les livres de l'Enfer* and the titles published
in the reprint series, *Les maîtres de l'amour*. Nina Epton's *Love and the
French* (1959), chapter iv, is good on the role of sex in eighteenth-century
French literary circles. Although the *Dictionnaire des oeuvres érotiques*
can be of assistance with anonymous works, it is not always to be trusted
with dates and is frequently disappointing even in its résumés. See also
Hoffman, *op. cit.*, chapters iii and iv, who relies too much on Laclos as a
source.

   The best studies to date, however, are those by Rustin, Nagy, Leduc,
and Peter Brooks, *The Novel of Worldliness: Crébillon, Marivaux, Laclos, Stendhal* (Princeton, NJ, 1969), in this order. Also worth reading are
Henri Coulet, *Le roman jusqu'à la Révolution* (1967); Vivienne Mylne,
op. cit., chapters ii and iii; and Klaus Sasse's doctoral dissertation on
Restif de la Bretonne, *Die Entstehung der 'Courtisane Vertueuse' in der
französischen Literatur des 18. Jahrhunderts* (Hamburg, 1967), chapter
iv. See also R. Nelli, *Érotique et civilisations*, 119–22.

   The major novelists have found some attention. See, for instance, the
studies of Crébillon *fils* by Funke, *op. cit.*; Ernst Sturm, *Crébillon fils et le
libertinage au XVIIIe siècle* (1970); and Horst Wagner, *Crébillon fils.
Die Erzählstruktur seines Werkes* (Munich, 1972). See also *Thérèse
philosophe*; Crébillon, *Lettres de la Marquise de M* (England, 1735);
Crébillon, *Les Egarements*; Diderot, *La Religieuse* (1796).

10 See the studies of Rustin, Laroch, Brooks, Nagy, Mauzi (chapter X),
   Leduc, and Nelli cited above. In addition, see Vartanian, 'La Mettrie …',
   loc. cit. On La Mettrie's influence, see Ann Thomson, 'La Mettrie et la
   littérature clandestine', in O. Bloch, ed., *op. cit.*, 235–44.

   On libertine ideas in licentious novels and the developing genres in
prose fiction see Nagy, *op. cit.*, chapter ii. Nagy's categories in libertine
literature, i.e., 'satire, propagande, aventure, education, mirroir des
moeurs', are not quite convincing. Many of the works he discusses would
fit into several of his categories.

11 Typical examples are Crébillon *fils*, *Les égarements du coeur et de l'esprit
   ou mémoires de M. de Meilcour* (1736–8); Godard d'Aucourt, *Thémidore* (1745); Fougeret de Monbron, *Margot la ravaudeuse* (1749–50);
   Dulaurens, *Imirce* (1765); Andréa de Nerciat, *Félicia ou mes fredaines*
   (1775); Perrin, *Les égarements de Julie*; Restif de la Bretonne, *Le paysan
   et la paysanne pervertis* (1787); Mirabeau, *Le libertin de qualité* (1783);
   and de Sade, *Justine* (1791).

12 The *Bilderlexikon der Erotik*, III, 135, 465; and IV, 637, lists erotic

illustrations for Restif's *La Paysanne pervertie* and *Le Paysan perverti*; Choderlos' *Les liaisons dangereuses*; and Louvet de Couvray's *Chevalier de Faublas*. See also Nerciat, *Les aphrodites* (1793) and his *Le diable au corps* (1803).

13 See especially the following works by Andréa de Nerciat, *Félicia ou mes fredaines* (1775); *Le doctorat impromptu* (1788); *Monrose ou le libertin par fatalité* (1792); *Mon noviciat* (1792); *Les aphrodites* (1793); and *Le diable au corps* (1803). On Restif's *Anti-Justine* see the DOE. For a more detailed discussion of the novels of Mirabeau, Andréa de Nerciat, and Restif, see Kearney, *A History of Erotic Literature*, 75–90.

14 On de Sade see Jean Paulhan, 'The Marquis de Sade and His Accomplice', in Richard Seaver/Austryn Wainhouse, comp., *The Marquis de Sade: Three Complete Novels* (NY, 1966), 3–37; and *ibid.*, Maurice Blanchot, 'Sade', 37–73. See also Donald Thomas, *The Marquis de Sade* (1976), and the earlier studies by Iwan Bloch, *Marquis de Sade's Anthropologia Sexualis of 600 Perversions* (NY, 1934); *Der Marquis de Sade und seine Zeit* (Berlin, 1904). In addition, see Kearney, *A History of Erotic Literature*, 90–100.

15 On the amatory novel ('roman galant') see Herbert Singer, *Der galante Roman* (Stuttgart, second edition 1966); and Naumann, *Keyhole*, 81–6. Naumann distinguishes between 'amatory' and 'amorous' novels, both not pornographic, but the difference is not clear.

For a good discussion of the rogue biography see Richetti, *Popular Fiction*, 23–59; and Chandler, *The Literature of Roguery*. Both *Le diable boiteux* and *Gil Blas* were bestsellers. See, for instance, *The Devil upon Two Sticks* (Edinburgh, 1770); and William Combe's sequel, *The Devil upon Two Sticks in England* (1790), 4 vols. In 1791 Combe's book was selling in its third edition in six volumes and was still popular by 1811. Other examples of amatory novels are *The Finished Rake; or Gallantry in Perfection* (1733); and *The Parasite*, 2 vols. (1765). Further titles are discussed by Naumann, *Keyhole*, 83–8.

On the peppering, so to speak, in the twentieth century of *Memoirs of an Oxford Scholar* (1756), a sentimental romance, see Naumann, *Keyhole*, 267 f. The book was reprinted in a reliable edition by Garland Publishing, New York, in 1975. Another come-on title is *The Adventures of Mr. Loveill; Interspersed with Many Real Amours of the Modern Polite World*, 2 vols. (second edition, 1750), which is a sentimental novel.

Also see the anonymous titles, *Memoirs of an Oxford Scholar* (1756); *The History of Will Ramble: A Libertine* (1755); *The History of Charles Jones, the Footman* (1796).

16 See Naumann, *Keyhole*, 307–8, on the spy literature. Examples from non-fiction are Ned Ward's *The London Spy* (1698–1700); and George Alexander Stevens, *The Adventures of a Speculist* (1788), which contains reports about the London prostitutes and night spots. See *The History of Pompey the Little* (1759; reprinted NY, 1974), 55–6.

Amatory spy novels featuring coins are *The Adventures of a Bank Note* (1770–1); *The Adventures of a Rupee* (1782); *Adventures of a Silver*

Penny. Including Many Secret Anecdotes of Little Misses and Masters Both Good and Naughty (1787). Clothes and utensils are protagonists in *Memoirs and Interesting Adventures of an Embroidered Waistcoat* (1751), of which part II appeared as *The Episode of a Petticoat; Adventures of a Black Coat* (1760); *Frailties of Fashion, or the Adventures of an Irish Smock* (1782); *The Adventures of a Gold-Headed Cane*, 2 vols. (1783); *The Adventures of a Cork-Screw* (1775). Vehicles are in the centre of *Travels of Monsieur Le Post-Chaise* (1753); *The Sedan* (1757); and Dorothy Kilner's *Adventures of a Hackney Coach* (1781). See also *A Peep Through the Key Hole* (1761?). Spy novels figuring animals are D. Kilner, *The Life and Perambulations of a Mouse* (1783–4); *The Life and Adventures of a Cat* (1760); *Memoirs and Adventures of a Flea* (1785); *History of a French Louse* (1779); and *The Life and Adventures of a Fly* (1789).

17 On the 'chronique scandaleuse' see Richetti, *op. cit.*, 119–67; and Naumann, *Keyhole*, 83–6. The French trial reports and related literature are discussed by Jean Sgard, 'La littérature des Causes Célèbres', *loc. cit.* On Haywood and Manley see Richetti, *op. cit.*, passim; and Naumann, *Keyhole*, 84. Influential works were Manley's *Court Intrigues* (1711); *The Adventures of Rivella* (1714); *The Secret History of Queen Zarah and the Zarazians* (1705; repr. NY, 1972). See also the following works by Charles de Fieux, Chevalier de Mouhy: *L'amante anonyme ou histoire secrète de la volupté aves des contes nouveaux de fées* (1755); *Mémoires d'une fille de qualité qui ne s'est point retirée du monde*, 4 vols. (Amsterdam, 1747).

18 On Haywood's influence, see Richetti, *Popular Fiction*, 168–210. Bibliographies of the gothic novel are *The Eighteenth-Century Gothic Novel: An Annotated Bibliography of Criticism and Selected Texts* (Folkstone and NY, 1975); and Montague Summers, *A Gothic Bibliography* (London, 1941). Good studies are M. Summers, *The Gothic Quest; A History of the Gothic Novel* (1950); and Devendra P. Varma, *The Gothic Flame: Being the History of the Gothic Novel In England* (1957). The sexual and perverse aspects in *The Monk* and *The New Monk* are discussed by Thomas, *A Long Time*, 181–4; and Naumann, *Keyhole*, 285–6.

19 On the literature on rogues and whores see Frank W. Chandler, *op. cit.*; Richetti, *op. cit.*, 23–59; Karl Heinz Göller, *Romance und Novel. Die Anfänge des englischen Romans* (Regensburg, 1972), 72 f; and Naumann, *op. cit.*, 86–9. The pornographic aspect of Defoe's fictional whore biographies is discussed by LeRoy W. Smith, *op. cit.*

20 On the literature dealing with the courtesans and aristocrats see pp. 104–7 above; and Naumann, *Keyhole*, 87–9.

21 For additional titles of whore biographies see Naumann, *Keyhole*, 87 and n. 72. See also *Nocturnal Revels or the History of King's Place and Other Nunneries* (second edition, 1779).

22 Naumann, *Keyhole*, 63–9, considers the whore letter as a new development of the whore dialogue, but has to admit that the genre is closely

related to biography. On p. 64 he lists many titles of bawdy anti-feminist and anti-aristocratic satire, taking the word 'epistle' in the titles of these works too literally. See also *ibid.*, on the differences between erotic love letters, an old genre, and whore letters as well as whore biographies.

23 See *Amusements in High Life*, 22; and the similar *Conjugal Infidelities, or Authentic Memoirs of Lydia Lovemore*, published in five parts in the *Rambler's Magazine*, VII, supplement (1789)–VIII (April, 1790).

 See Naumann, *Keyhole*, 64, 363 and n. 117, on the revival in the eighteenth century of 'letters from the dead to the living'. On pp. 64–7 Naumann also lists further epistolary whore biographies. Again, the French influence in this section of erotic fiction ought to be taken into consideration. By 1735 Crébillon's *Lettres de la Marquise de M.* were selling in an English translation as *Letters of the Marchioness of M... to the Comte de R.*

24 See also *The Prostitutes of Quality, or Adultery à la Mode* (1757), a collection of fictional 'chroniques scandaleuses'.

25 See *A New Atalantis*, ii, 39, 52, 56; excerpts from this work are re-printed in DeVries/Fryer, *Venus Unmasked*, 196–205. See also the sequel to this book, *A New Atalantis for 1762*, partly reprinted in Ashbee, *Catena*, 268–79; and *The Waiting Woman* (1775), which was trans-lated into French as *Mémoires d'une femme de chambre* (1786): see Ashbee, *Catena*, 174–5. In addition, see *The Prostitutes of Quality* (1757); *Genuine and Authentic Memoirs of a Well-known Woman of Intrigue*, 158.

 See also *La belle allemande ou les galanteries de Thérèse* (1740); *La belle cauchoise, ou mémoires d'une jolie normande* (1788); and *Manuel des boudoirs ou essais érotiques sur les demoiselles d'Athènes* (1787).

 Histoire de Mademoiselle Brion (1754), re-edited in 1774 as *La Nouvelle académie des dames*, thus alluding to a famous whore dialogue: Chorier's bestseller from 1680 on *Tullia and Octavia*. *La belle allemande* is ascribed to Antoine Bret or Claude Villaret and was also published as *La belle alsacienne*, with reprints appearing in 1745 and 1774. See also Paul Barret's (or Baret) *Mademoiselle Javotte* (1757; reprinted in 1788). Some of these titles are briefly discussed in *DOE*.

26 For an excellent discussion of the history of the whore dialogue from Lucian down to the eighteenth century, see Naumann, *Keyhole*, chapter II. In addition, see Thompson, *Unfit*, chapter I; and Foxon, *Libertine Literature*, 25–7. I disagree with Naumann's view of the whore dialogue – although I am greatly indebted to his survey – as a pre- or sub-pornographic form. Some seventeenth-century whore dialogues, such as *Venus in the Cloister* and Chorier's *Satyra sotadica*, were still selling well in the eighteenth century and were definitely pornography. Aretino's *Ragionamenti* was to the sixteenth and seventeenth centuries what Latouche's *Dom Bougre* and Cleland's *Fanny Hill* were to the eighteenth. Literary forms changed, but the conditions of reception are comparable: in the absence of the pornographic novel, which had yet to appear, Samuel Pepys bought a whore-dialogue in 1688, *L'escole des filles*, when

he wanted sexual stimulation. See his *Diary*, ed. H.B. Wheatley, 8 vols. (1962), VII, 261.

27 Aretino's *Ragionamenti* was first published in Rome in two parts in 1534 and 1536, and then reprinted in London in Italian in 1584 and 1597. For bibliographical details, including *The Crafty Whore*, see Naumann, *Keyhole*, 15–19; and Foxon, *Libertine Literature*, 25–7.

28 See *The Whores Rhetoric* (1683); quotations are from the London reprint of 1960, pp. 49–50. On *The School of Venus* see Foxon, *Libertine*, 5, 30–37; Thompson, *Unfit*, 23–8; and Naumann, *Keyhole*, 29–36. A modern edition was edited by Donald Thomas in 1972. For whore dialogues in the wake of *Ragionamenti* see Naumann, *Keyhole*, 20–9, where he discusses *La puttana errante* and *La retorica delle puttane*. See *ibid.*, 21, on *The Wandring Whore* of 1660. French editions of *La puttana errante* from the eighteenth century are listed in Pia, *op. cit.*, and Kearney, *op. cit.*

29 For editions of Chorier's *Satyra sotadica* in Latin, English, and French see Pia, *op. cit.*; and Kearney, *Private Case*, which has five (!) pages of entries for this bestselling whore biography. For discussions see Naumann, *Keyhole*, 36–43; Thompson, *Unfit*, 28–34. See also the imitations and sequels, such as *L'Académie des Pays Bas, ou l'école des voluptueux* (n.p., 1769), which Rose's *Register of Erotic Books* lists among the holdings of Collection Gugitz in Vienna; and *The Cabinet of Love* (1709), a collection of poems drawn from the supposititious works of Rochester and others, and including a long translation of *L'académie des dames* under the title *The Delights of Venus*. A modern translation of Chorier's book in French was published by Euridif in 1976. Both Naumann and Thompson ignore the importance of the illustrations in the book.

30 Naumann, *Keyhole*, 50–2, summarises the characteristics of the whore dialogue. Thompson, *Unfit*, 151, notes that *Venus in the Cloister* owes much to Aretino and Chorier, while Naumann, *Keyhole*, 45, admits that it is not a genuine whore dialogue. Most of the French editions had frontispieces, and from 1737 on, also engravings. A modern French paperback edition was published by Euridif in 1979. Quotations are from the 1725 edition, reprinted in Naumann, *Keyhole*, 358–60. I have followed Naumann's discussion in this case: see *ibid.*, 41 f, 108–10; and 136 f. For comments on *Les délices du cloître*, of which editions are recorded in 1757, 1761 and 1762, see Naumann, *Keyhole*, 92–3; and Kearney, *Private Case*, as well as Pia, *Les livres de l'Enfer*.

31 Francis Place mentions two collections of bawdy salacious tales, *The Spanish Libertines* and *The Reformer*, of which there is no trace.

32 See Thomas, *A Long Time Burning*, 192–3; Marcus, *The Other Victorians*, 284–5; and Legman, *The Horn Book*, 84. See Naumann, *Keyhole*, p. 360 and n. 89–90, for the titles of the pornographic books discussed in *Venus in the Cloister*. For Place's comments on pornographic fiction see his autobiography, MS f 73. *The Spanish Libertines* apparently contained such titles as 'The Life of a Country Jilt', and 'The Town-Bawd', and *The*

Reformer consisted of 'The Debauched Parson', 'The City Lecher', 'The Insatiated Wife', 'The Amorous Maid', *et al.* The BL catalogue attributes *The Reformer; Exposing the vices of the age* (1700) to Edward Ward. This could be the book Place refers to, but I have not been able to ascertain whether it contains the titles mentioned above.

The following brief list of the more important fiction and philosophical treatises provides some idea of the French influence:

Influential French Erotica Before 1749

Year of publication	Title	English Translation
1683, 1702, 1719, and later	Barrin, *Vénus dans le cloître*	1692, 1724/25, 1745
1680 and later	Chorier, *L'académie des dames*	1682, 1688, 1707, 1740, 1745, and later
1655, 1715	Millot/L'Ange, *L'escole des filles*	1688 and 1745
1714	*Le canapé couleur de feu*	1742
1728	G. de Beauchamps, *Histoire du Prince Apprius*	1728
1731	Prévost, *Histoire du Chevalier des Grieux*	
1731–42	Marivaux, *La vie de Marianne*	1736–42, 1743, 1746, 1747, 1765, 1784
1734	Crébillon *fils*, *L'écumoire*	1735, 1742, 1748
1734–5	Marivaux, *Le paysan parvenu*	1765
1735	Crébillon *fils*, *Lettres de la Marquise …*	1735
1736–8	Crébillon *fils*, *Les égarements du coeur*	1751
1740	D'Argens, *Les nones galantes*	(probably translated)
	Duclos, *Confessions du Comte De …*	1775
1742	Crébillon *fils*, *Le sopha*	1742: eighteen editions until 1801
	C. Villaret, *Antipamela*	1742
	Latouche, *Histoire de Dom B.* (often reprinted)	1743
1743	Godard d'Aucour, *Mémoires turcs* (often reprinted)	
1744	Duclos, *Acajou et Zirphile*	
1745	Meusnier de Querlon, *Histoire de la tourrière des Carmélites*	
	Godard d'Aucour, *Thémidore*	
1746	La Morlière, *Angola*	
1748	La Morlière, *Les lauriers ecclésiastiques*	(translated after 1750)
	D'Argens, *Thérèse philosophe*	1748/9
	La Mettrie, *L'art de jouir*	1748
	Diderot, *Les bijoux indiscrets*	1749
	Meusnier de Querlon, *Psaphion ou la courtisane de Smyrne*	
1749	Crébillon *fils*, *Les amours de Zeokinizul*	1749
	Fougeret de Monbron, *Margot la ravaudeuse*	

33 On *Les lauriers* see Naumann, *Keyhole*, 93 and n. 95, where he refers to the English version. See also *DOE*, and for eighteenth-century French

editions, the bibliographies by Kearney and Pia. For a good discussion of *Thérèse philosophe*, see Naumann, *Keyhole*, 95–7. A modern paperback edition in French is available from Euridif (1975).

34 I am indebted in my discussion of *Dom Bougre* to Naumann's excellent analysis in his *Keyhole*, 97–106. See also Marchand, *The French Pornographers*, 119–23; and the *DOE*, which calls it one of the most successful erotica. For bibliographical details see the works of Pia and Kearney, especially no. 806. The only extant English translation was destroyed in Hamburg during World War II. A modern French paperback version was published by Euridif in 1978. Quotations are from pp. 164 and 176 f. of the 1745 edition, reprinted in Naumann, *Keyhole*, 103–4: I have translated the passages into English.

Somewhat surprisingly, Naumann, pp. 100 and 106, sees *Dom Bougre* between the picaresque and the pornographic novel. But the abundance of sexual scenes, the pornographic 'decor', and the illustrations show that this book must be seen as eighteenth-century pornographic fiction. Naumann is too much concerned with showing that *Fanny Hill* was the ultimate form of the pornographic novel to be able to see that it was fully developed before Cleland published his book. For full critical discussion and evaluation of *Fanny Hill*, see my introduction to the edition of the novel published in Penguin English Classics.

35 The original edition, recognised as such by David Foxon, appeared in two volumes in 1748/9. On November 10, 1749, Cleland was questioned about the book before the Secretary of State. Pleading poverty, he was not prosecuted. In March 1750, Cleland had prepared a bowdlerised version of the novel, *Memoirs of Fanny Hill*, which consisted of eleven letters; the first edition is lost. The references are to my own edition of *Fanny Hill* (1985).

36 For a summary of the plot see Ashbee, *Catena*, 87–91; and for a discussion, Naumann, *Keyhole*, 111–56. See *MWP*, 62–63. Editions with illustrations are listed in the bibliographies by Pia and Kearney; Ashbee, *Catena*, 83–6, describes some engravings for the book by George Morland.

37 See Mertner/Mainusch, *Pornotopia*, 293; and Naumann, *Keyhole*, 156–64.

38 On the question of the first draft of *MWP* see Foxon, *Libertine Literature*, 54–63; Naumann, 322–3; and Alan Bold, ed., *Records of the Most Ancient and Puissant Order of the Beggar's Benison* (Edinburgh, 1982). Bold, not a great stickler for bibliographical detail, states in the preface to the new edition of the *Records* that he accepts as genuine the entry about *Fanny Hill* being read in 1737.

39 See Slepian/Morrissey, *op. cit.*; and Shinagel, *op. cit.*, 224; Naumann, *Keyhole*, 250–2. On eighteenth-century commentators see Nitschke, 52. See Boswell, *Boswell for the Defence*, eds. William K. Wimsatt and Frederick A. Pottle, (1960), 84.

40 *MWP*, 219–220. On the hesitance of literary historians to recognise *MWP* as serious fiction see Leo Braudy, '*Fanny Hill* and materialism',

ECS 4 (1970), 21–40, especially p. 21; B. Slepian/L.J. Morrissey, 'What is *Fanny Hill?*', *Essays in Criticism* 14 (1964), 65–75; Roland Mortier, 'Libertinage littéraire et tensions sociales dans la littérature de l'ancien régime: de la "Picara" à la "Fille de Joie"', *Revue de littérature comparée* (January–March, 1972), 35–45; and Frederick R. Karl, *A Reader's Guide to the Development of the English Novel in the Eighteenth Century* (1974), 282–4.

41 For a discussion of *The History of the Human Heart* (reprinted NY, 1974), see Naumann, *Keyhole*, 274 f.; Ashbee, *Catena*, 121–4; Bloch, *A History of English Sexual Morals*, 546–7; and Fryer, *Private Case*, 80–82.

    See Naumann's discussion of *Margot la ravaudeuse* in *Keyhole*, 258–60, who sees more picaresque than pornographic elements in this novel. Cf. R. Mortier, *op. cit.*, who stresses the erotic-pornographic content.

42 See, for instance, the following pornographic novels by Mirabeau, *Le rideau levé, ou l'éducation de Laure*; *Le libertin de qualité*; *Hic et hec, ou l'art de varier les plaisirs de l'amour*, reprinted in *L'oeuvre du comte de Mirabeau* (1921); and by Andréa de Nerciat, *Félicia ou mes fredaines* (1775); *Le doctorat impromptu* (1788); *Monrose ou le libertin par fatalité* (1792); *Les Aphrodites* (1793); *Le diable au corps* (1785); and by de Sade, *Justine* (1791); *Aline et Valcour* (1795); and by Denon, *Point de lendemain*, later reprinted as *La nuit merveilleuse* (1800).

    Laurence Sterne owned a considerable number of French erotica published after 1750: see *A Facsimile Reproduction of a Unique Catalogue ...* (NY, 1970), passim.

43 Paulson, *Representations of Revolution*, 148–63.

44 *Ibid.*, 218–25; and Foxon, *Libertine Literature*, 51. See also Mario Praz, *The Romantic Agony* (second edition, 1970); and R.F. Brissenden, *Virtue in Distress: Studies in the Novel of Sentiment from Richardson to Sade* (1974).

45 See Cranfield, *The Press and Society*, 54–7.

46 See W. Graham, *The Beginning of the English Literary Periodicals*, chapter II.

47 *Ibid.*, 44–6. On the *Mercure galant* see F. Moureau, *op. cit.*

48 On *The Ladies Magazine* (1749–53) see Francis Place, MS f 90. The BL owns four imperfect volumes of this periodical. See Cranfield, *op. cit.*, 54, on *The Entertainer*.

49 The plates in volumes 1–7 of *The Town and Country Magazine* are reproduced and collected in an additional volume of this periodical.

50 See Mayo, *The English Novel in the Magazines*, especially pp. 351, 370–1; and 423.

51 For brief discussions of the erotic magazines see Ashbee, *Catena*, 322–40; D. Thomas, *A Long Time*, 117–20; Naumann, *Keyhole*, 428 n. 25; Hurwood, *The Golden Age of Erotica*, chapter 4; F. Hoffman, *Analytical Survey of Anglo-American Traditional Erotica* (Bowling Green, Ohio, 1973), 41 f. The most detailed study to date is H. Nitschke's thesis cited above, see especially pp. 59–117 and the summary, in English, on pp.

130–1. The quotation is from *The Bon Ton Magazine* of April 1793, p. 39.

52 For a classification and discussion of the various erotic sections in these magazines see Nitschke, *op. cit.*, 79–86, 135–7. Nitschke also has a list of these periodicals on pp. 132–5 and an excellent bibliography of serialised erotic novels published in *The Covent Garden Magazine, The Rambler's Magazine*; and *The Bon Ton Magazine*.

53 See *The Bon Ton Magazine*, April 1793, 40–2; and November 1793, 319–22.

54 See Nitschke, *op. cit.*, 82–6. Paul Englisch, in his *Geschichte der erotischen Literatur*, p. 655, argues that the English licentious magazines of the eighteenth century are a unique literary phenomenon without parallels in other countries. This is to be doubted. In the major areas of erotica England imitated France, and it would indeed be a surprise if France, after the *Mercure galant*, had not produced any erotic periodicals whatsoever. I have not been able to pursue this question further but I assume that French periodical erotica did exist. Rose lists *La gazette de Cythère* of 1773, but this says it is 'traduit de l'Anglais'.

55 For a discussion of *Sodom* see Thompson, *Unfit*, 125 f.; and Rabenalt, *Voluptas Ludens*, 183–213.

56 By 1700 Collier had published his *A Second Defence of the Short View of The Prophaneness and Immorality of the English Stage*. In 1706 Arthur Bedford joined him with *The Evil and Danger of Stage-Plays: Shewing their Natural Tendency to Destroy Religion and Introduce a General Corruption of Manners*. See also LeRoy J. Morrissey, *The Erotic Pursuit: Changing Fashions in Eroticism in Early Eighteenth-Century English Comic Drama*, doct. diss. (U. of Pennsylvania, 1964). The causes and effects of the Licensing Act are adequately discussed by Leonard W. Conolly, *The Censorship of English Drama 1737–1824* (San Marino, Cal., 1976). See *A Vindication of the Reformation* ..., 33–4.

57 See Conolly, *op. cit.*, 152; and Emmett L. Avery *et al.*, *The London Stage 1660–1800* (Carbondale, Ill., 1968), volume V, 170–1. Avery notes that it is of interest to study Dougal MacMillan, *Catalogue of the Larpent Plays in the Huntingdon Library* (San Marino, Cal., 1939). John Larpent was Examiner of Plays between 1778–1824, and the catalogue describes the manuscripts of 2,502 plays, some never published. See also the reprint series, *The Best of Bell's British Theatre*, 41 volumes, published by AMS Press, New York, which contains several illustrated volumes. On Colman's *The Genius*, see Bloch, *Sexual Life in England*, 597.

58 On the French erotic and obscene theatre of the eighteenth century see Englisch, *Geschichte der erotischen Literatur*, 413–23; Rabenalt, *Voluptas Ludens*, 45–212. See also *Sittengeschichte des Theaters*, published as volume V of *Sittengeschichte der Kulturwelt*, ed. Leo Schidrowitz (Vienna, second edition 1927): see especially pp. 127–92, where the fashion of employing castrato singers in England is discussed. Older surveys, but still useful, are those by Henri d'Alméras, *Les théâtres libertins au XVIIIe siècle* (1905); B. de Villeneuve, *Le théâtre d'amour au XVIIIe siècle*

(1910); and the anthology of French theatrical erotica by Raoul Vèze, *Le théâtre d'amour au XVIIIe siècle* (1910), with plays by Leyrand, Grandval, Collé, and others. A scholarly survey in German, with no special treatment of erotica, of the eighteenth-century theatre is Heinz Kindermann, *Theatergeschichte Europas* (Salzburg, 1964–1976), volumes III–IV.

For titles of plays in eighteenth-century catalogues and inventories see, for instance, the *Catalogue of the Printed Books and Manuscripts Bequeathed by Francis Douce, Esq., to the Bodleian Library* (Oxford, 1840), which has a whole page of entries under 'plays', and the catalogue of Laurence Sterne's library cited above.

59 See Rabenalt, *Voluptas*, 315, and the illustrations. On the private erotic theatres see Englisch, *Geschichte der erotischen Literatur*, 418–23; and *Bilderlexikon der Erotik*, IV, 834–7.

Two collections of erotic and ribald plays are *Théâtre gaillard*, of which a number of illustrated editions were published in Paris and London between 1776 and 1803: see Kearney, *Private Case*, for details; and *Recueil de comédies et de quelques chansons gaillardes* (Paris?, 1775); and *Recueil de comédies gailliardes* [sic] (Paris?, 1761). For collections of revolutionary plays, many of them licentious and obscene, see Jacques Truchet, ed. *Théâtre du dix-huitième siècle*, volume II (1972–4); and *Théâtre de la Révolution* (1877; reprinted 1971), with an introduction by Louis Moland. On the plays of de Sade see Rabenalt, *Theatrum Sadicum* (Emsdetten, 1963).

60 See Rabenalt, *Mimus Eroticus*, 5 volumes (Hamburg, 1965–7), volumes II and III. On Rowlandson's erotica see Gert Schiff, *The Amorous Illustrations of Thomas Rowlandson* (NY, 1969), xxxvii. George Alexander Stevens' *Lecture on Heads* was published spuriously in 1770; the first authentic edition is from 1785: see also the later version, edited by C.L. Lewis in 1808, with twenty-five humorous prints by George M. Woodward.

For comments on Hogarth's tavern scene in *A Rake's Progress* see Burke/Caldwell, *Hogarth*, and for a discussion by a contemporary, Georg Christoph Lichtenberg, *Der Weg des Liederlichen* (Frankfurt, 1968).

8 PICTORIAL EROTICA

1 On the Errington case see *A New and Complete Collection of Trials for Adultery* (1796), I, 37. The book illustrators are discussed by Hanns Hammelmann, *Book Illustrators in Eighteenth-century England* (1975), which includes an alphabetical list of illustrators and their works.

For a discussion of the caricaturists see William Feaver, *Masters of Caricature* (NY, 1981), 40–54; and Dorothy M. George, *English Political Caricature*, 2 vols. (Oxford, 1959). Major figures have, of course, found their biographers and critics. On Gillray see Draper Hill, *Mr Gillray, The Caricaturist* (1965); and his *Fashionable Contrasts: A Hundred Caricatures by James Gillray* (1966); in addition, see the earlier

study by Joseph Grego, *The Works of James Gillray, The Caricaturist;
With the History of his Life* (1873). On Rowlandson see Gert Schiff, ed.,
The Amorous Illustrations of Thomas Rowlandson; and Ronald Paulson, *Rowlandson: A New Interpretation* (NY, 1972); and his *Representations of Revolution*, chapter 5. See also G. Paston, *Social Caricature
in the Eighteenth Century*, and the various works by Eduard Fuchs cited
in the bibliography. An interesting, albeit ignored, figure of the late
eighteenth century is George M. Woodward, who worked in the tradition
of Rowlandson and Gillray. His graphic works, some published in *An
Olio of Good Breeding* (1801), and *Something Concerning Nobody*
(1814), remain to be mined. Similarly, George Morland and Richard
Newton are usually ignored in surveys of eighteenth-century English
pictorial erotica. For a brief discussion and description of some of their
erotic art works see Bloch, *Ethnological and Cultural Studies of the Sex
Life in England* (NY, 1934; repr. 1972), 349–55.

2 On the literary influence of Hogarth's pictorial series see Derek Jarrett,
The Ingenious Mr Hogarth (1976); Robert E. Moore, *Hogarth's Literary
Relationships* (NY, 1969), chapters II–V; and the editions of his works
by John Nicholas and George Stevens in 3 volumes (1808–17) now being
prepared for a reprint edition by G. Olms Verlag. See also the standard
scholarly editions by Ronald Paulson, *Hogarth: His Life, Art and Times*,
2 vols. (1971); and Burke/Caldwell, *Hogarth*. Ronald Paulson has discussed in several of his books the interdependence of eighteenth-century
art and literature.

3 Discussions of the history of *Aretine's Postures* can be found in Thomp-
son, *Unfit for Modest Ears*, chapters I and X; and Peter Webb, *The Erotic
Arts* (1975), appendix I, where on p. 348 he quotes sonnet no. 4 of
Aretino's poems.

   In addition to Nogaret's collection see also the late eighteenth-century
L'Arétin d'Augustin Carrache ou receuil de postures érotiques of which
there are editions in the BL and BN. The title alludes to two pornographers, Aretino and the sixteenth-century painter Agostino Carrachi,
an artist whose works were in demand until well into the nineteenth
century. On the prosecution of the vendor of obscene prints and the
publication of *The Amours of Peter Aretine* see Thomas, *A Long Time
Burning*, 190.

4 Books imitating classical art included Hancarville's *Monumens du culte
secret des dames Romaines* (1784). See also his books listed in the
bibliography.

5 This interest in foreign and classical cultures, which finally brought about
Neoclassicism, was alive at the very beginning of the century and was not
limited to the erotic or sexual. See, for instance, such sober reports and
descriptions as Louis de Gaya's *Marriage Ceremonies: As Now Used in
All Parts of the World ... Put into Modern English, by Mr Tho. Brown*
(1704); and 'Uxorius', *Hymen: an Accurate Description of the
Ceremonies Used in Marriage, by Every Nation in the Known World*
(1760). The literary predilection and the taste for the oriental towards the

middle of the eighteenth century were just one consequence of this interest in exotic cultures.

Other well-known English Epicureans living and working in Italy were Sir Horace Man and Lord Pembroke. R.P. Knight also tried his hand at painting and imitated Fuseli before 1800. On Knight's art and life see Peter Conrad, 'The Sensual Connoisseur', *Observer Magazine*, 31 January 1983, 18–23; and Michael Clarke/Nicholas Penny, *The Arrogant Connoisseur – Richard Payne Knight 1751–1824* (Manchester, 1982). Knight's *Account* is discussed by Ashbee, *Index*, 3–12; Hyde, *A History of Pornography*, 105; and Webb, *The Erotic Arts*, 64–5, whom I have quoted.

6 See Paulson, *Representations of Revolution*, 206–9, for a discussion of *Modern Antiques* and the relations between Nelson and the Hamiltons.

7 On Casanova cheating Winckelmann see Henri Herbedé's postscript to the German edition of Hancarville's *Monumens de la vie privée* (1979), 249–58; and on the Bertazzi case, Thomas, *A Long Time Burning*, 190.

8 For a good survey of erotic art in the Baroque and Rococo periods see Webb, *The Erotic Arts*, chapter IV. In addition, see Hurwood, *The Golden Age of Erotica*, chapter 12; and Englisch, *Geschichte der erotischen Literatur*, 497–501. Jean H. Hagstrum's discussion in his *Sex and Sensibility* of Watteau and Greuze is authoritative, especially his treatment of Watteau's *The Embarkation*: see chapter 11 and particularly pp. 297–303, and 310–16. But Hagstrum's general survey of erotic art is as sadly disappointing as his study of literary texts. He tucks away Rowlandson's pornography in a footnote on p. 282 and ignores Hogarth's erotica.

A great many pictorial examples from the Baroque and Rococo periods are contained in *Bilderlexikon der Erotik*; in the five volumes of *Allmacht Weib* (Vienna/Leipzig, 1928–30); and in the books by Fuchs and Kind cited in the bibliography. For French erotica see especially Borel, *Cent vignettes érotiques gravées par Elluin pour illustrer sept romans libertins du XVIIIe siècle* (Nyoms, 1978); *Cent quatre gravures libertines pour illustrer Andréa de Nerciat et John Cleland* (Nyoms, 1979); *Bigarrures coiro-pygo-glotto-chiro-phallurgiques* (1799; reprinted Paris, 1981); John Grand-Carteret, *Les moeurs et la caricature en France*; and his *Le décolleté et le retroussé*. See also Henri Cohen, *Guide de l'amateur de livres à gravures*.

Webb, *The Erotic Arts*, p. 139, attributes *Jupiter with Leda and the Swan* to Antoine Coypel, but with a question mark. If it is by him, it was certainly not produced in 1750, for Antoine Coypel died in 1722. However, if 1750 is the date of its creation (unless Webb refers to the *Histoire universelle*) it could well be by Charles-Antoine Coypel (1694–1752), the son of Antoine.

9 For a comparative study of erotic and pornographic book illustrations and single prints in France, England, and Germany in the age of Enlightenment see my bilingual book (published with English and German texts), *Lust und Liebe im Rokoko/Lust and Love in the Rococo Period*

(Nördlingen: Greno; 1986). On Gravelot's influence on English painters and engravers see Hammelmann, *op. cit.*, 38. For discussions of the French engravers see also B. Dighton/H.W. Lawrence, *French Line Engravings of the Late Eighteenth Century* (1910); Alain Guillerm, 'Le système de l'iconographie galante', *DHS* 12 (1980), 177–94; Cornelius Gurlitt, *Das französische Sittenbild des 18. Jahrhunderts im Kupferstich* (Berlin, 1912); and Webb, *The Erotic Arts*, 140.

10 See Webb, *op. cit.*, 145–58, for a brief discussion of English erotica of the eighteenth century. In addition, see Fuchs, *Geschichte der erotischen Kunst*; and his *Illustrierte Sittengeschichte*: vol. 'Die galante Zeit'.

For discussions of, and comments on, Hogarth's outdoor and indoor scenes of *Before* and *After* see Ronald Paulson, *The Art of Hogarth* (1975, plates 12 and 13, and pp. 43–4) and *idem, Hogarth: His Life, Art, and Times*, abridged by Anne Wilde (New Haven, Conn., 1974), 100–102; and J. Burke and C. Caldwell, *Hogarth: The Complete Engravings* (1968; reprinted 1974), notes to plates 165–6.

For comments on *Strolling Actresses Dressing in a Barn* see Ronald Paulson, *The Art of Hogarth*, plate 49; and *ibid., Hogarth*, 175–6. On Reynolds see Hagstrum, *Sex and Sensibility*, 280–81.

11 On Rowlandson see Gert Schiff, ed., *The Amorous Illustrations*, p. xxxvi; Webb, *The Erotic Arts*, 147–50; and Paulson, *Representations of Revolution*, 158–61, where the *Exhibition Stare-Case* is discussed. Paulson interprets this picture more in terms of the representation of the crowd and Revolution.

12 For a discussion of Fuseli's erotica see Gert Schiff, *Johann Heinrich Füssli*, 2 volumes (Zurich, 1972), passim; and Webb, *The Erotic Arts*, 150–58. See *ibid.*, 158 f., for an analysis of Turner's erotic works. Thomas, *A Long Time Burning*, 190–91, comments on the censoring of obscene prints around 1800.

9 EROTICA IN EARLY AMERICA

1 See the discussion of the slanted view of the Puritans from the seventeenth to the twentieth century in my *Puritan Attitudes Towards Recreation in Early Seventeenth-Century New England* (Frankfurt, 1982), chapter I; and Dunton's *Letters*, 112–13; and Edward Ward, *A Trip to New England* (1699). It is not quite clear whether Ward, who slandered the New England Puritans as well, ever visited their colonies; cf. the contradictory views of Thompson, *Unfit*, 55 n. 24, and George P. Winship's edition of *The Trip*, published in 1905 and reprinted in 1970.

2 See the colonial records cited in my *Puritan Attitudes*; and Emil Oberholzer, Jr, *Delinquent Saints* (NY, 1956); Edmund S. Morgan, 'The Puritans and Sex', *NEQ* 15 (1942), 591–607. In addition, see E.A. Evans, 'Literary References in New England Diaries 1700–1730', doct. diss. (Harvard University, 1940); W.C. Ford, *The Boston Bookmarket: 1679–1700* (Boston, 1917); G.E. Littlefield, *Early Boston Booksellers, 1642–1711* (Boston, 1900; reprinted NY, 1969); K.A. Lockridge, *Literacy in Colo-*

nial New England (NY, 1974); S.E. Morison, *Harvard College in the Seventeenth Century*, 2 vols. (Cambridge, Mass., 1936); *idem*, *The Intellectual Life of Colonial New England* (Ithaca, NY, 1956); J.L. Sibley, *Biographical Sketches of Graduates of Harvard University in Cambridge, Massachusetts*, 3 vols. (Cambridge, Mass., 1873); T.G. Wright, *Literary Culture in Early New England 1620–1730* (New Haven, 1920); Elnathan Chauncy, 'Commonplace Book', *PCSM* XXVIII, pp. 1–24; Seaborn Cotton, 'Commonplace Book', *PCSM* XXXII, pp. 307–418; Edmund Quincy, 'Notebook', *NEHGR* 38 (1884).

On Puritan reading, see R. Thompson, 'The Puritans and Prurience: Aspects of the Restoration Book Trade', in H.C. Allen/R. Thompson, *Contrast and Connection* (London, 1976), 36–65. In·his *The Intellectual Life*, 132, Morison notes that Rochester's *Poems* were sold in New England before 1700. See also R. Thompson, ' "The London Jilt" ', *HLB* (1975), 289–94; J.P. Seigel, 'Puritan Light Reading', *NEQ* 37 (1964), 185–99, especially pp. 193 and 198. For a discussion of the books owned by preachers, see J.H. Tuttle, 'The Mather Libraries', *PAAS* XX, 269–356; and the catalogues of books listed in G.L. McKay, *American Book Auction Catalogs, 1713–1934* (NY, 1967), which includes many inventories of ministers' libraries. Aspects of Puritan 'erotic' literature are discussed by D.J. Hibler, 'Sexual Rhetoric in Seventeenth-Century American Literature', doct. diss. (Notre Dame University, 1970); Karl Keller, 'Reverend Mr Edward Taylor's Bawdry', *NEQ* 44 (1970), 382–406; and D.E. Stanford, 'Edward Taylor and the "Hermaphrodite" Poems of John Cleveland', *EAL* 8 (1973), 59–61. For a more general survey of light reading, including erotic poetry and pornographic fiction, see J.D. Hart, *The Popular Book* (NY, 1950; reprinted 1976), 1–60.

3 See Davis, *A Colonial Southern Bookshelf: Reading in the Eighteenth Century* (Athens, Georgia, 1979); *Intellectual Life in the Colonial South, 1585–1763*, 3 vols. (Knoxville, Tennessee, 1978); and *Literature and Society in Early Virginia, 1608–1840* (Baton Rouge, Louisiana, 1973). See also H. Lehmann-Haupt *et al.*, *The Book in America* (second edition, NY, 1952), 50; and, for a critical view of the statements made there, Robert D. Harlan's essay in *SECC* 5 (1976), 368. Also of interest are George Smart, 'Private Libraries in Colonial Virginia', *AL* 10 (1938), 24–52; and M.C. Watkins, *The Cultural History of Marlborough, Virginia* (Washington, D.C., 1968).

4 A full critical evaluation of erotica in early America can be found in my article 'Eros Goes West: European and "Homespun" Erotica in Eighteenth-Century America', in *The Transit of Civilisation from Europe to America. Essays in Honor of Hans Galinsky*, ed. Winfried Herget and Karl Ortseifen (Tübingen: G. Narr, 1986), 145–65.

5 See Jones, 'The Importation of French Books in Philadelphia, 1750–1800', *MP* 32 (1934–5), 157–77. Jones was not interested in pornography, arguing on pp. 170–71 that 'much is not identifiable or worth identification', surely a strange statement for someone who attempts a

scholarly analysis of the book trade. But he does admit that erotica were imported. See also *Le Courier de l'Europe* (1781–88), continued as the *Courier de Londres*.

6 See W.H. Peden 'Thomas Jefferson: Book Collector', doct. diss. (University of Virginia, 1942); E.M. Sowerby, *Catalogue of the Library of Thomas Jefferson*, 5 vols. (Washington, D.C., 1952–9), vol. IV, 440–560; and Jefferson's suggestion for a library to Robert Skipwith in *A Virginia Gentleman's Library. As Proposed by Thomas Jefferson to Robert Skipwith in 1771* (Williamsburg, Va., 1961).

7 On chapbooks in early America, some of them containing trial reports and crim. con. cases, see H.B. Weiss, *American Chapbooks* (privately printed, Trenton, N.J., 1938); *idem, American Chapbooks, 1722–1842* (NY, 1945); and his *A Book About Chapbooks* (Hatboro, Pa., 1969).

On the demand for anti-papist literature in early New England see Thompson, *Unfit*, 140 and 156 n. 22. Hurwood, *The Golden Age of Erotica*, notes on p. 80 that Gavin's *Master Key to Popery* was reprinted many times in America, but Evans, s.v. 'Gavin', merely lists one reprint in Newport, Rhode Island, in 1773. See Evans' bibliography.

8 There were many versions of the *Aristotle* works, such as the *Master-Piece*, the *Compleat Midwife* and the *Problems*.

9 See R.B. Austin, *Early American Medical Imprints: A Guide to Works Printed in the United States, 1668–1820* (Washington, D.C., 1961); Francisco Guerra, *American Medical Bibliography, 1639–1783* (NY, 1962). For reprints of the Aristotle works and of the *Onania* see also Evans' bibliography. In addition, see O.T. Beall, Jr, ' "Aristotle's Master Piece" in America: a Landmark in the Folklore of Medicine', *WMQ* 20 (1963), 207–22; T.H. Johnson, 'Jonathan Edwards and the "Young Folks' Bible" ', *NEQ* 5 (1932), 37–54, especially pp. 47 and 50–4. The works of Hunter, Smellie, Hamilton, and anonymous works are listed in Austin's bibliography.

10 For American editions of Sterne's novels see *Catalogue of All the Books Printed in the United States* (Boston, 1804); and the entries, s.v. 'Sterne', in Evans, *op. cit.* See also J.D. Hart, *The Popular Book*, 56–65; Lodwick, Hartley, 'The Dying Soldier and the Love-lost Virgin: Notes on Sterne's Early Reception in America', *SHR* 4 (1970) 69–80; and S.J. Rogal, 'A Checklist of Eighteenth-Century British Literature Published in Eighteenth-Century America', *CLQ* 10 (1973), 231–56. On Isaiah Thomas' aborted attempt to print *Fanny Hill*, see Ralph Thomson, 'The Deathless Lady', C I. 2 (1935), 207–20; and on Lewis' *The Monk*, see Hart, *op. cit.*, 65.

11 On censorship in eighteenth-century America, see Leo M. Alpert, 'Judicial Censorship of Obscene Literature', *HLR* 52 (1938), 40–76, especially 53 f.; C.L. Duniway, *The Development of Freedom of the Press in Massachusetts* (NY, 1906), 43–8; A.L. Haight, *Banned Books* (1978). The first case occurred in Philadelphia, in 1815, when a certain Sharples and five associates were convicted for having sold obscene prints, and in 1821 a person was prosecuted in Boston in connection with the sale of

Memoirs of a Woman of Pleasure. While the laws on obscene libel seem to have been strict, personal behaviour was apparently allowed more freedom if P. Ackroyd is to be believed, who notes in his *Dressing Up* (1979), 84–6, that Edward Hyde, Governor of New York and New Jersey (1702–8) paraded the streets in female attire.

12 See papers such as the *American Weekly Mercury* (Philadelphia); the *Boston Gazette*; the *New England Courant*; the *Maryland Gazette*, the *New Hampshire Gazette*. Also see *The Origin of the Whale Bone-Petti-coat. A Satyr* (1714) and *Bostonian Scintillations* (1787).

13 On American erotic and bawdy satire see H.C. Carlisle, *American Satire in Prose and Verse* (NY, 1962); B.L. Granger, *Political Satire in the American Revolution 1763–1783* (Ithaca, NY, 1963); G.F. Horner, 'A History of American Humour to 1765', 2 vols., doct. diss. (University of North Carolina, 1936); and T.L. Kellogg, 'American Social Satire Before 1800', doct. diss. (Radcliffe College, 1929). Two good bibliographies of poetry are Leo Lemay, *A Calendar of American Poetry in the Colonial Newspapers & Magazines & in the Major English Magazines Through 1765* (Worcester, Mass., 1972): see particularly nos. 22, 640, 695, 882, 1883, and 1916; and O. Wegelin, *Early American Poetry* (NY, 1903).

'Upon A Fart' is quoted by K.W. Howland, *Laughter in the Wilderness: Early American Humor to 1783* (Kent State University Press, 1976), 131. For a discussion of the authorship see John H. O'Neill/Cameron C. Nickels, 'Upon the Attribution of "Upon A Fart" to William Byrd of Westover', *EAL* 14 (1979), 143–8; and Professor Dolmetsch's answer as well as the authors' reply in *EAL* 15 (1980–81), 276–9. A slightly different version of the poem appears in the article by O'Neill/Nickels, cited above, p. 145.

14 See P.M. Zall, 'The Old Age of American Jestbooks', *EAL* 15 (1980), 3–13, and appendix. The letter is from Howland, *op. cit.*, 185–9.

15 On early American prose fiction see the bibliographies by O. Wegelin, *Early American Fiction, 1774–1830* (Gloucester, Mass., 1963); Lyle H. Wright, *American Fiction 1774–1900*, 3 vols. (San Marino, Cal., 1939–66); and *idem*, 'Eighteenth-Century American Fiction', *Essays Honoring Lawrence C. Wroth* (Portland, Maine, 1951), 457–74; and E.W. Pitcher, 'Fiction in the *Boston Magazine* (1783–86): a Checklist with Notes and Sources', *WMQ* 37 (1980), 473–84.

On Byrd's library see John Spencer Bassett, ed., *The Writings of Colonel William Byrd of Westover in Virginia, Esq* (New York, 1901), appendix Λ. Byrd's 'The Female Creed' was first edited by Maude H. Woodfin/Marion Tinglin, *Another Secret Diary of William Byrd of Westover, 1739–1741. With Letters and Literary Exercises 1696–1726* (Richmond, Va., 1942), appendix IV, which I quote from 449–57. After reading the manuscript in the possession of the *Virginia Historical Society* I have suggested a different form of the satire based on the Catholic Creed: see my article on 'The Female Creed' in the special European number of *Early American Literature*, ed. J.F. Béranger (1984), 122–38.

16 On Franklin's 'bagatelles' see Richard E. Amacher, *Franklin's Wit and*

Folly. The Bagatelles (New Brunswick, NJ, 1953); Bruce Ingham Granger, *Benjamin Franklin. An American Man of Letters* (Norman, Oklahoma, 1976), 181–209; Leo Lemay, 'The Public Writings and the Bagatelles', in Brian M. Barbour, ed., *Benjamin Franklin. A Collection of Critical Essays* (Englewood Cliffs, NJ, 1979), 146–60; and Claude-Anne Lopez, *Mon Cher Papa. Benjamin Franklin and the Ladies of Paris* (New Haven, 1966), *passim*.

On Franklin's 'Letter of Advice to a Young Man . . .', see Alfred Owen Aldridge, *Benjamin Franklin. Philosopher and Man* (Philadelphia/NY, 1965), 88–89; and Howland, *Laughter in the Wilderness*, who quotes it on pp. 203–05.

On the letter 'To the Royal Academy of Brussels', reprinted in R.E. Amacher, *Franklin's Wit and Folly*, 66–69, see B.I. Granger, *op. cit.*, 203–5; A.O. Aldridge, *Benjamin Franklin*, 326. The letter was written before 1782; in January 1782 Franklin dispatched a copy to William Carmichael in Spain, discussing the difficulties involved with translating and appreciating the many puns. On Smyth's remark see his edition of Franklin's works, published in New York, 1905–1907, vol. VIII, 369. A new edition of *The Papers of Benjamin Franklin*, ed. Leonard W. Larabee *et al.* (New Haven, 1959 f.) is in progress.

17 See Aldridge, *Benjamin Franklin*, 281–96; and Lopez, *Mon Cher Papa*, *passim*.

18 On Franklin's familiar letters to Madame Brion and Madame Helvétius see Aldridge, *Benjamin Franklin*, 282–93; Granger, *op. cit.*, 196–202; and Lemay, 'The Public Writings', *loc. cit.*, 155–60.

Anecdotes by and on Benjamin Franklin, some of them bawdy or erotic, have been collected by Paul M. Zall, ed., *Ben Franklin Laughing* (London and Los Angeles, 1980): see, for instance, nos. 54 and 192.

19 On the Tuesday Club see E.G. Breslaw, 'Wit, Whimsy, and Politics: the Uses of Satire by the Tuesday Club of Annapolis, 1744–1756', *WMQ* 32 (1975), 295–306, quoted from p. 296; and Carl Bridenbaugh, *Gentleman's Progress: The Itinerarium of Dr Alexander Hamilton, 1744* (Chapel Hill, N.C., 1948), xvi–xix. The records of the Tuesday Club are in the possession of the Maryland Historical Society. The Historical Society of Pennsylvania has kindly provided me with a microfilm of the records of the Homony Club, which I quote from p. 200.

CONCLUSION

1 Noteworthy exceptions are Lawrence Stone's *The Family, Sex and Marriage in England 1500–1800* (1977), and Robert Darnton's *The Literary Underground of the Old Regime* (1982) as well as his latest work, *The Great Cat Massacre and Other Episodes in French Cultural History* (1984): see especially chapters i and iv.

2 See Peter Nagy, *Libertinage et révolution* (1975), chapter ii. 2.

3 See Keith V. Thomas, 'The Double Standard', *JHI* 20 (1959), 206–13.

4 The following discussion of Pope and Richardson has greatly profited

from two seminal studies by Boucé, 'The Secret Nexus: Sex and Literature in Eighteenth-Century Britain', in Alan Bold, ed., *The Sexual Dimension in Literature* (1982), 70–89; and 'Sex, Amours and Love in *Tom
Jones*', in *SVEEC* 228 (1984), 25–39.

5 For a detailed discussion of the links between medical and para-medical
erotica on the 'virgo intacta' and major eighteenth-century novels, see
Boucé, 'The Secret Nexus', 74–5.

6 *Ibid.*, 82–3.

7 See also my discussion of pictorial representations, and the significance of
lapdogs in eighteenth-century erotic engravings in *Lust und Liebe/Love
and Lust in the Rococo Period* (Nördlingen: Greno, 1986) and *L'Enfer
de la Bibliotèque Nathionale*, vol. III, 280–82.

8 See also Boucé, 'The Secret Nexus', 75.

9 *Ibid.*, 83.

10 See Samuel Richardson, *Pamela*. Introduction by M. Kinkead-Weekes
(1962), volume I, p. 50.

11 *Ibid.*, 174–9.

12 See also Boucé, 'The Secret Nexus', 74–5.

13 See Boucé, 'Sex, Amours and Love'. On p. 28, Boucé discusses Fielding's use of medical lore, in this case myths propagated by books on
midwifery and obstetrics as well as by sex guides. On pp. 31–3, he
analyses Fielding's fictional treatment of such hotly debated subjects
as masturbation and of pictorial pornography, sexual jokes, and *double
entendre*.

14 See Herbert Marcuse, *Eros and Civilization. A Philosophical Inquiry into
Freud* (1966), 166–70.

15 On the 'ars amoris' of the Greeks and Romans see Paul Brandt, *Sexual
Life in Ancient Greece* (1932); Jacques Antoine Dulaure, *The Gods of
Generation: A History of Phallic Cults Among the Ancients and Moderns*
(NY, 1934); T. Hopfner, *Das Sexualleben der Griechen und Römer*
(Prague, 1938); and O. Kiefer, *Sexual Life in Ancient Rome* (1934).
Good studies of the place and significance of erotica in classical literature
are Paul Englisch, *Geschichte der erotischen Literatur*, 23–87; Peter
Green, 'Sex and Classical Literature', in Alan Bold, ed., *The Sexual
Dimension in Literature*, 19–48; and, also by Green, the introduction to
Ovid. *The Erotic Poems* (1982), 15–85. See also the recent edition of
classical erotic fiction, *Im Reich des Eros. Sämtliche Liebes- und Aben-
teuerromane der Antike* (Munich, 1983).

In his *Un temps pour embrasser. Aux origines de la morale sexuelle
Occidentale* (1983) Jean-Louis Flandrin has shown that from the seventh
century on priests demanded penitence from their flock if sexual conti-
nence was not observed during certain times of the year. Especially the
men in the lower classes seem to have resisted such demands.

The reprint series, *The Augustan Translators: Restoration and
Eighteenth-century English Translations of the Classics*, published in 26
volumes by AMS Press, New York, provides an idea of the scope of
erotica translated into English from 1666 to 1819.

16 See Jean-Louis Flandrin, *Le sexe et l'occident. Évolution des attitudes et des comportements* (1981), 83–96; and Stone, *The Family*, 644–5.

17 On the rise of pornographic biography see LeRoy W. Smith, 'Daniel Defoe: incipient pornographer', *LP* 22 (1972), 173.

18 See Michel Foucault, *The History of Sexuality* (NY, 1978), *passim*; and Hans Giese/Eberhard Schorsch, *Zur Psychopathologie der Sexualität* (Stuttgart, 1973), 37 ff., and 90–3.

19 See, for instance, the front page of the *Guardian* of March 10, 1981: 'Life for M5 Rapist'.

20 See *Private Eye* no. 507 ff.: especially no. 509, p. 17; and *Lui* (French edition), July 1981, 46–50.

21 See, for instance, *Private Eye*, no. 510, p. 5; and no. 511, p. 8. See also e.e. cummings, *Complete Poems* (NY, 1972), 248.

22 See Peter Porter, *Collected Poems* (Oxford, 1984), 277. Porter's laconic view of sex is also obvious in his poetry from the 1970s; see, for instance, 'Sex and the Over Forties', *ibid.*, 160.

23 For an excellent discussion of some of these genres, including films, see the revised version of Peter Webb's *The Erotic Arts* (1983): appendices v and vi.

24 See especially Kosinski's *Steps* (NY, 1968) and *Pinball* (1982); John Hawkes, *Virginie* (1983); and Updike's trilogy, *Rabbit, Run* (1964), *Rabbit Redux* (1972), and *Rabbit is Rich* (1982).
    I have analysed love and death as central themes in recent American fiction in 'Eros und Thanatos oder der Tod im Eros. Zur Funktion zweier Grundmotive der Literatur in Jerzy Kosinskis *Pinball* und John Updikes *Rabbit is Rich*', in Konrad Tuzinski, ed., *Motive in der englischen und amerikanischen Literatur des 20. Jahrhunderts* (Kiel, 1988).

25 On the association in literature of Eros and Thanatos see also Jean H. Hagstrum, *Sex and Sensibility*, 18–19.

26 See Michel Foucault, *The History of Sexuality*, 23 and 57–8.

Bibliography

With English titles, the place of publication, when not indicated, is London, and with French titles, Paris. NY = New York. The spelling of eighteenth-century sources has been modernised, and doubtful places of publication have been put in inverted commas. Extant editions are cited by the year. English and American sources are listed in one section. To facilitate checking for the reader, the section on pictorial erotica contains bibliographies, critical literature, and sources.

I BIBLIOGRAPHIES AND DICTIONARIES

Apollinaire, Guillaume, *et al.*, *L'Enfer de la Bibliothèque Nationale: Icono-Bio-Bibliographie descriptive, critique et raisonnée, complète à ce jour de tous les ouvrages composant cette célèbre collection avec un index alphabétique des titres et noms d'auteurs* (1919, repr. Geneva, 1970).

Ashbee, Henry Spencer [Pseudonym: Pisanus Fraxi], *Catena librorum tacendorum. Being notes bio-biblio-iconographical and critical on curious, uncommon and erotic books* (1885, repr. 1960; NY, 1962).

——. *Centuria librorum absconditorum* (1879, repr. 1960; NY, 1962).

——. *Index librorum prohibitorum* (1877, repr. 1960; NY, 1962).

Austin, Robert B., *Early American medical imprints: a guide to works printed in the United States, 1668–1820* (Washington, DC, 1961).

Backscheider, Paula, *et al.*, *An annotated bibliography of twentieth-century critical studies of women and literature, 1660–1800* (NY/London, 1977).

Baldner, Ralph W., *Bibliography of seventeenth-century French prose fiction* (NY, 1967).

Barbier, Olivier and René, and Paul Billard, *Dictionnaire des ouvrages anonymes*, 4 vols. (Paris, 1872–9; repr. Hildesheim/NY, 1963).

Beasley, Jerry C., *English Fiction: 1600–1800. A guide to information sources* (Detroit, 1978).

Bécourt, Daniel, *Livres condamnés. Livres interdits. Régime juridique du livre. Outrages aux bonnes moeurs. Arrêts d'interdiction* (1961).

[Gay, Jules], *Bibliographie des ouvrages relatifs à l'amour, aux femmes, au mariage et des livres facétieux, pantagrueliques, scatologiques, satyriques, etc.*, 4 vols. (1893–1900).

Bibliography of the eighteenth-century holdings of the Institute for Sex Research. Compiled, and with an introduction, by Susan Matusak (Bloomington, Indiana, 1975).

[Schidrowitz, Leo, ed.] *Bilderlexikon der Erotik. Ein bibliographisches und biographisches Nachschlagewerk, eine Kunst- und Literaturgeschichte für die Gebiete der erotischen Belletristik ... von der Antike bis zur Gegenwart*, 4 vols. (Vienna, 1928–31; repr. with two supplement volumes, Hamburg, 1961).

[Highfill, Philip H. Jr., *et al.*], *A biographical dictionary of actors, actresses, musicians, dancers, managers & other stage personnel in London, 1660–1800*, 12 vols. published to date (Carbondale, Ill., 1973 f.).

Block, Andrew, *The English Novel 1740–1850. A catalogue including prose romances, short stories, and translations of foreign fiction* (1939; new and rev. edition 1968).

——. *Key book of British authors 1600–1932* (1933).

[Bodleian Library: *Catalogue of books in the Φ section*]

Brodhurst, Audrey C., 'The French revolutionary collections in the British Library', *British Library Journal* II (1976), 138–59.

Brunet, Gustave, *Anthologie scatologique* (1862).

Bullough, Vern L. *et al.*, *An annotated bibliography of homosexuality*, 2 vols. (NY, 1975).

Bullough, Vern L. *et al.*, *A bibliography of prostitution* (NY, 1977).

Case, Arthur E., *Bibliography of English poetical miscellanies: 1521–1750* (Oxford, 1935); enlarged by Norman Ault in *Cambridge Bibliography of English Literature*, vol. II (1940), 173–256.

Catalogue de l'histoire de la Révolution Française [1789–1799], 6 vols. (Paris, 1936–69).

Catalogue du cabinet secret du prince G ... [Galitzin]. *Collection de livres et objets curieux et rares concernant l'amour, les femmes et le mariage* (London, 1975).

Catalogue of all the discourses published against popery during the reign of King James II, 20 vols. (1683–1701).

The catalogue of printed books in the Wellcome Historical Medical Library, vol. II: books printed from 1641–1850 (1966).

Catalogue of prints and drawings in the British Museum. Division I. Political and personal satires (1689–1800), vols. II–VII (1870–1954).

Cioranescu, Alexandre, *Bibliographie de la littérature française du dix-huitème siècle*, 3 vols. (1969).

——. *Bibliographie de la littérature française du dix-septième siècle*, 3 vols. (1969).

Cordasco, Francesco, *Eighteenth-century bibliographies. Handlists of critical studies relating to Smollett, Richardson, Sterne, Fielding, eighteenth-century medicine, the eighteenth-century novel, Godwin, Gibbon, Young, and Burke. To which is added John P. Anderson's bibliography of Smollett* (Metuchen, NJ, 1970).

Damon, Gere and Lee Stuart, *The lesbian in literature: a bibliography* (San Francisco, 1976).

Deakin, Terence John, *Catalogi librorum eroticorum. A critical bibliography of erotic bibliographies and book-catalogues* (1964).

Dictionnaire de biographie française. Ed. Roman d'Amat and R. Limouzin-Lamothe (1967 f.).

Dictionnaire des oeuvres érotiques: domaine française. Ed. Gilbert Minazzoli et al. (1971).

Dictionnaire d'amour par le berger Sylvain [by Maréchal] (1788).

Dictionnaire comique, satirique, critique, burlesque, libre et proverbial par Joseph Philibert Leroux (Amsterdam, 1718; repr. 1752 and 1786).

Dictionnaire française, contenant les mots et les choses [by Richelot], 2 vols. (Geneva, 1680; repr. Amsterdam, 1685 and 1706; and Geneva, 1693 and 1710).

Dreux du Radier, Jean-François, *Dictionnaire d'amour* (The Hague, 1741).

——. *The Dictionary of Love* [translated by John Cleland] (1753).

Drujon, Fernand, *Catalogue des ouvrages écrits et dessins de toute nature poursuivis, supprimés ou condamnés depuis le 21 octobre 1814 jusqu'au 31 juillet 1877* (1879).

——. *Essai bibliographique sur la destruction volontaire des livres ou bibliolytie* (1889).

The eighteenth century: a current bibliography, vol. I (Philadelphia, 1978); vol. II (NY, 1979; published by AMS Press for the American Society for Eighteenth-Century Studies); vols. III–VIII (NY, 1980–86).

Eighteenth-century British books. An author union catalogue: extracted from the British Museum General Catalogue of printed books, the catalogues of the Bodleian Library, and of the University Library, Cambridge, 5 vols. (Folkestone, 1981), ed. G. Averly *et al.*

——, *Eighteenth-century British books. A subject catalogue: extracted from the British Museum General Catalogue of printed books,* 4 vols. (Folkestone, 1979).

The eighteenth-century Gothic novel: an annotated bibliography of criticism and selected texts. With a foreword by Devendra Varma and Maurice Lévy (Folkestone, England, and NY, 1975).

Ellis, Albert and Albert Abarbanel, eds., *The encyclopedia of sexual behaviour,* 2 vols. (1961).

English literature 1680–1800: a bibliography of modern studies compiled for Philological Quarterly. By R.S. Crane *et al.* Vol. I–IV, 1926–60 (1950–62).

English literature, 1660–1800: a current bibliography; published by Philological Quarterly (1926–date).

Fleischmann, Hector, *Les pamphlets libertins contre Marie-Antoinette. D'après des documents nouveaux et les pamphlets tirés de l'Enfer de la Bibliothèque Nationale* (1908; repr. Geneva, 1976).

——, *Marie-Antoinette, Libertine. Bibliographie critique et analytique des pamphlets politiques, galants et obscènes contre la reine* (1911).

Foxon, David F., *English Verse 1701–1750,* 2 vols. (Cambridge, 1975).

Fryer, Peter, ed., *Forbidden books of the Victorians* [a reprint of Ashbee's *Index librorum prohibitorum* of 1877] (1970).

Gartrell, Ellen G., comp., *Electricity, magnetism and animal magnetism: a checklist of printed sources 1600–1850.* Comp. for the American Philosophical Society (Wilmington, NJ, 1975).

Gesamtkatalog der Preussischen Bibliotheken, vols. 1–14 (Berlin, 1931–9).

Grose, Francis, *A classical dictionary of the vulgar tongue* (1785 and later; repr. 1963).

Guerra, Francisco, *American medical bibliography, 1639–1783* (NY, 1962).

Guiraud, Pierre, *Dictionnaire historique, stylistique, rhétorique, étymologique, de la littérature érotique* (1978).

Halkett, Samuel, and John Laing, *Dictionary of anonymous and pseudonymous English literature. New and enlarged edition* by J. Kennedy *et al.,* 7 vols. (1926–34); vol. VIII ed. D.E. Rhodes and A.E.C. Simoni (1956).

——, *A dictionary of anonymous and pseudonymous publications in the English language.* Third revised and enlarged edition, ed. John Harden, vol. I (1980).

Hart, William H., *Index expurgatorius anglicus: or a descriptive catalogue of the principal books printed or published in England, which have been suppressed, or burnt by the common hangman, or censored, or for which the authors, printers, or publishers have been prosecuted* (1872; repr. NY, 1969).

Hayn, Hugo, *Bibliotheca erotica et curiosa monacensis. Verzeichnis französischer, italienischer, spanischer, englischer, holländischer und neulateini-*

scher Erotica und Curiosa, von welchen keine deutschen Übersetzungen bekannt sind (Berlin, 1887).

—— [pseudonym: H. Nay], *Bibliotheca Germanorum erotica. Verzeichnis der gesamten deutschen erotischen Literatur mit Einschluss der Übersetzungen* (Leipzig, 1875).

——, *Bibliotheca Germanorum erotica et curiosa. Verzeichnis der gesamten deutschen erotischen Literatur mit Einschluss der Übersetzungen, nebst Beifügung der Originale.* Ed. Paul Englisch, 9 vols. (Munich, 1912–29).

Index Librorum Prohibitorum [Catholic Church] (Rome, 1938).

Jacob, P.L., ed., *Catalogue de la bibliothèque dramatique de Monsieur de Soleinne*, vol. III (1844).

Jannet, Paul, *et al.*, *Bibliotheca scatologica* (Paris, 1850).

Kearney, Patrick J., *The Private Case: an annotated bibliography of the Private Case erotica collection in the British (Museum) Library.* Introd. Gershon Legman (1981).

Knafla, L.A., 'Crime and criminal justice [1550–1800]: a critical bibliography', in J.S. Cockburn, ed., *Crime in England 1550–1800* (1977), 270–98.

Laporte, Antoine, *Bibliographie clérico-galante. Ouvrages galants ou singuliers sur l'amour, les femmes, le mariage, le théâtre, etc. Écrits par des abbés, prêtres, chanoines, religieux, religieuses, évêques, archévêques, cardinaux et papes. Par l'apôtre bibliographe* (1879).

Lemay, J. Leo, *A calendar of American poetry in the colonial newspapers & magazines & in the major English magazines through 1765* (Worcester, Mass., 1972).

Le Pennec, Marie-Françoise, *Petit glossaire du langage érotique aux XVIIe et XVIIIe siècles* (1979).

Littré, Emile, *Dictionnaire de la langue française* (1975).

Lund, Roger D., *Restoration and early eighteenth-century English literature 1660–1740. A selected bibliography of resource materials* (NY, 1980).

McBurney, William H., *A check list of English prose fiction 1700–1739* (Cambridge, Mass., 1960).

——, comp., *English prose fiction, 1700–1800, in the University of Illinois Press* (Urbana, Ill., 1965).

Maxted, Ian, *The London book trades, 1775–1800. A preliminary checklist of members* (Folkestone, 1977).

Michaud, Louis-Gabriel, ed., *Biographie universelle ancienne et moderne*, 45 vols. (1843–65; repr. 1966–70).

Miller, C. William, *Benjamin Franklin's Philadelphia printing: a descriptive bibliography* (Worcester, Mass., 1974).

Mooney, James E., and Clifford K. Shipton, *National index of American imprints through 1800: the Short Title Evans*, 2 vols. (Worcester, Mass., 1969).

Morgan, Bayard Quincy, *A critical bibliography of German literature in English translation 1481–1927* (1938; second edition 1965).

The New Cambridge Bibliography of English Literature, 5 vols. (Cambridge, 1969–77).

The Oxford History of English Literature, vol. VIII, ed. John Butt (Oxford, 1979).

Pargellis, Stanley MacCrory and Dudley Julius Medley, *Bibliography of British history: the eighteenth century 1714–1789* (Oxford, 1951).

Perceau, Louis, *Bibliographie du roman érotique au XIXe siècle*, 2 vols. (1930).

Pia, Pascal, *Les livres de l'Enfer. Bibliographie critique des ouvrages érotiques dans leurs différents éditions du XVIe siècle à nos jours*, 2 vols. (1978).

Pitcher, Edward W., 'Fiction in the *Boston Magazine* (1783–1786): a check-list with notes and sources', *WMQ* 37 no. 3 (1980), 473–84.

Plomer, Henry Robert, *A dictionary of the printers and booksellers who were at work in England, Scotland and Ireland from 1726–1775*, 2 vols. (1922 and 1932).

Quérard, J.M., *Les supercheries littéraires devoilées*, 3 vols. and 1 supplement (1869).

Reisner, Robert G., *Show me the good parts: the reader's guide to sex in literature* (NY, 1964).

Rogal, Samuel J., 'A checklist of eighteenth-century British literature published in eighteenth-century America', *CLQ* series 10 no. 4 (1973), 231–56.

Rose, Alfred [Pseudonym: Rolf S. Reade], *Registrum librorum eroticorum* (1936; repr. as *Register of Erotic Books*, 2 vols., NY, 1936).

Sabin, Joseph, *et al.*, *Bibliotheca Americana. A dictionary of books relating to America from its discovery to the present time*, 29 vols. (NY, 1868–1936).

Sallander, Hans Frederick, *Bibliotheca Walleriana. The books illustrating the history of medicine and science collected by Dr Erik Waller and bequeathed to the Royal University of Uppsala*, 2 vols. (Stockholm, 1955).

Sauvy, Anne, *Livres saisis à Paris entre 1678 et 1701* (The Hague, 1972).

Speculator Morum [i.e., William L. Clowes], *Bibliotheca arcana seu catalogus librorum penetralium, being brief notices of books that have been secretly printed, prohibited by law, seized, anathemized, burnt or Bowdlerized* (1885).

Summers, Montague, *A Gothic bibliography* (1941).

Tanselle, G. Thomas, *Guide to the study of United States imprints*, 2 vols. (Cambridge, Mass., 1971).

Tobin, James E., *Eighteenth-century English literature and its cultural background. A bibliography* (NY, 1939; repr. 1967).

Warré, M., *Table alphabétique des auteurs et personnages cités dans les 'Mémoires secrets'* (1866, repr. 1970).

Wedeck, Harry E., *Dictionary of erotic literature* (NY, 1962; repr. London, 1963).

Wegelin, Oscar, *Early American fiction, 1774–1830: a compilation of the titles of works of fiction, by writers born or residing in North America, north of the Mexican border and printed previous to 1831* (NY, 1929; third edition, Gloucester, Mass., 1963).

Wegelin, Oscar, *Early American poetry. A compilation of the titles of volumes of verse and broadsides, written by writers born or residing in North America, and issued during the seventeenth and eighteenth centuries* (NY, 1903).

Who's Who in Classical Mythology (1973).

Williams, Judith B., *A guide to the printed materials in English social and economic history, 1750–1850*, 2 vols. (NY, 1926).

Wright, Lyle H., *American fiction 1774–1900. Vol. I 1774–1850. A contribution toward a bibliography* (San Marino, Cal., 1939; second edition 1969).

——, 'Eighteenth-century American fiction', *Essays honoring Lawrence C. Wroth* (Portland, Maine, 1951), 457–74.

Young, Ian, *The male homosexual in literature: a bibliography* (Metuchen, NJ, 1975).

II ANTHOLOGIES

Ashton, John, *Chap-books of the eighteenth century; with facsimiles, notes, and introduction* (1882).

The Augustan translators: Restoration and eighteenth-century English translations of the classics [an AMS reprint series], 23 titles in 26 vols. (1666–1819).

Bell, John, *The Best of Bell's British Theatre.* With an introduction on John Bell and the theatre of the Restoration and eighteenth century, and new play prefaces by Byrne R.S. Fone, 41 vols. (1797; repr. NY, 1977).

——, *Bell's British Theatre, consisting of the most esteemed English plays. Illustrated*, 21 vols. (1776–81; repr. NY, 1977).

——, *Supplement to Bell's British Theatre*, 4 vols. (1784; repr. NY, 1977).

——, *Selected plays from Bell's British Theatre*, 16 vols. (1791–1802; repr. NY, 1977).

Bold, Alan, ed., *The bawdy beautiful: the Sphere book of improper verse* (1979).

——, *Making love: the Picador book of erotic verse* (1978).

——, *Mounts of Venus. The Picador book of erotic prose* (1980).

Bredvold, Louis I. *et al.*, eds., *Eighteenth-century poetry and prose.* The third edition, prepared by John M. Bullitt (NY, 1973).

Contes et facéties galantes du XVIIIe siècle. Ed. A. van Bever (n.d.).

Les conteurs libertins du XVIIIe siècle, 2 vols. (1904–5).

Correspondance secrète inédite sur Louis XVI, Marie-Antoinette, la cour et la ville de 1777 à 1792. Ed. M.F.A. de Lescure, 2 vols. (1866).

Cray, Ed., ed., *The anthology of Restoration erotic poetry* (California, 1965).

——, ed., *Bawdy ballads: a history of the bawdy songs* (1970).

De Vries, Leonard and Peter Fryer, *Venus unmasked, or, an inquiry into the nature and origin of the passion of love, interspersed with curious and entertaining accounts of several modern amours: an eighteenth-century anthology* (1967).

L'Enfer de la Bibliothèque Nationale. [nos. 3 and 4] *Oeuvres anonymes du 18e siècle.* Introd. Michel Camus. I (1985), II (1986).

Fryer, Peter, comp., *The man of pleasure's companion. A nineteenth-century anthology of amorous entertainment* (1968).

Hair, Paul E.H., ed., *Before the bawdy court; selections from church court and other court records relating to the correction of moral offences in England, Scotland, and New England 1300–1800* (1972).

Im Reich des Eros. Sämtliche Liebes- und Abenteuerromane der Antike. Mit einer Einleitung und Anmerkungen. Herausgegeben von Bernhard Kytzler (Munich, 1983).

Pauvert, Jean-Jacques, ed., *Anthologie historique des lectures érotiques: de Guillaume Apollinaire à Philippe Pétain*, 2 vols. (1979–80).

Petit Enfer poétique du XVIIIe siècle présenté par Henry Muller (1954).

Recueil de comédies et de quelques chansons gaillardes (1775).

Recueil de comédies gaillardes (1761).

Théâtre de la révolution. Ou choix de pièces de théâtre qui ont fait sensation pendant la periode révolutionnaire (1877; repr. Geneva, 1971).

Théâtre de campagne, ou les débauches de l'esprit (London/Paris, 1755).

Théâtre gaillard ('Glascow', i.e., Paris/London, 1776; 1787; 1788; 1803; reprinted in 2 vols., Brussels, 1867).

Truchet, Jacques, ed., *Théâtre du XVIIIe siècle*, 2 vols. (1972–4).

III BOOK CATALOGUES

Brigham, Clarence S., 'American booksellers' catalogues, 1734–1800', in *Essays Honoring Lawrence C. Wroth* (Portland, Maine, 1951), 31–67.

Catalogue of all the books printed in the United States (Boston, Mass., 1804).

Catalogue of books belonging to the late Bishop Parker's [Samuel Parker] *library, for sale at auction, at S. Bradford's office* (Boston, Mass., 1805).

Catalogue of books. To be sold by George Hunter and Co. At their store in Queen-Street (NY, 1793).

A catalogue of choice and valuable books (Philadelphia: Ben Franklin, 1744).

A catalogue of the entire and valuable library of the books of the late Henry Fielding, Esq. Which will be sold by auction by Samuel Baker on Monday, Feb. the 10th, and the three following evenings (1755).

Catalogue of the entire stock in trade of the late Ebenezer Larkin (Boston, Mass., 1814).

Catalogue of the printed books and manuscripts bequeathed by Francis Douce, Esq. to the Bodleian Library (Oxford, 1840).

A catalogue of rare and valuable books, being the greatest part of the library of the late Reverend and Learned Mr. Joshua Moodey, and part of the library of the Reverend and Learned Mr. Daniel Gookin. With a valuable collection of books, imported in October last from London ... to be sold by auction (Boston, Mass., 1718).

A facsimile reproduction of a unique catalogue of Laurence Sterne's library. Ed. Charles Whibley (London/NY, 1930; repr. NY, 1973).

McKay, George L., *American Book Auction Catalogues, 1713–1934* (NY, 1937).

[Montgomerie, John, governor of New York], *New York anno 1732. Sales of a collection of books being the library . . . of John Montgomerie.*

Sowerby, Emily Millicent, *Catalogue of the library of Thomas Jefferson*, 5 vols. (Washington, DC, 1952–9).

Valuable catalogue of books; being the extensive library belonging to John Dabney, Esq. (Salem, Mass., 1818).

A Virginia Gentleman's Library. As proposed by Thomas Jefferson to Robert Skipwith in 1771 (Williamsburg, Va., 1961).

Winship, George P., 'Old auction catalogues', *The American Collector* (September 1927).

IV SOURCES

1 *Classical*

Alciphron, *The letters of Alciphron, Aelian and Philostratus*, with an English translation by A.R. Benner and F.H. Fobes (1962).

Anacreon, *Carmina anacreonta.*

——, *Anacreon, Sapho, Bion et Moschus, traduction nouvelle en prose, suivi de la veillée des fêtes de Vénus* (1773).

——, *Fawkes's Anacreon, Sappho, Bion* (1760).

——, *The works of Anacreon and Sappho, by several hands* (1713).

——, *The works of Anacreon and Sappho, translated by F. Fawkes* (1760).

——, *The works of Anacreon and Sappho. With pieces from ancient authors, and occasional essays* (1768).

Aristaenetus, *The love epistles of Aristaenetus*, second edition (1773).

Ovid, *Ovid's Art of Love, in three books. Together with his 'Remedy of Love'. Translated into English verse by several hands. To which are added, 'The Court of Love. A tale from Chaucer'. And The 'History of Love'* (1735; repr. 1764).

——, *The Metamorphoses* (1732).

——, *The Erotic Poems.* Translated by Peter Green (Harmondsworth, 1982).

Martial, *Epigrammata.* Ed. W.M. Lindsay (Oxford, 1929).

Pervigilium Veneris.

Petronius, *The Satyricon* (translated into English in 1694, 1708, 1710, 1713 and 1714).

Priapeia (Cologne, 1655; Leyden, 1644; Amsterdam, 1669).

Sappho, see entries under Anacreon.

Juvenal, *The Satyrs of Decimus Junius Juvenalis*, sixth edition (1735; repr. NY, 1979).

2 *Italian*

Aretino, Pietro, *Ragionamenti* (Rome: part I, 1534; part II, 1536).

——, *Ragionamenti* (London, 1584; repr. 1597).

——, *The Crafty Whore: or, the mistery and iniquity of bawdy houses laid*

open [a translation of the third dialogue of part I of *Ragionamenti*] (1658).
——, [*Sonetti lussuriosi*] *Les sonnets luxurieux* [Italian and French] (Paris, 1882).
Baffo, Giorgio, *Le poësie di Giorgio Baffo, patrizio Veneto* (London, 1771).
——, ——. *Nuova edizione* (London, 1789).
——, *Raccolta universale dell opere di Giorgio Baffo Venete*, 4 vols. ('Cosmopoli', i.e. London?, 1789).
Beccadelli, Antonio, *Hermaphroditus* [*Ermafrodito*] (Bologna, 1425).
Boccaccio, Giovanni, *Contes et nouvelles de Boccace*, 2 vols. (The Hague, 1777).
——, *Contes de J. Boccace*, 10 vols. ('À Londres', i.e., Paris, 1777–9).
——, *Le Decaméron de Jean Boccace*, 5 vols. (London, 1757–61).
Bracciolini, 'Poggio' (Gian Francesco), *Liber facetiarum* (*c.* 1470).
——, *The Facetiae of Giovanni Francesco Poggio Bracciolini*. Translated by Bernhardt J. Hurwood (NY, 1968).
Franco, Niccolo, *La Puttana Errante* (*c.* 1659–60).
——, *La Putain Errante* (Lampsaque, 1760).
——, *Histoire de vie de l'Arétin ou entretiens de Magdalen et de Julie. Nouvelle édition* (1783).
——, *La Putain Errante … Nouvelle édition* (1791).
——, *The Wandring Whore* (Title and characters, but not the content, taken from *La Puttana Errante*) (1660).
Leti, Gregorio, *Il Putanismo di Roma* (Amsterdam, 1667).
——, *Il Putanismo Romano* (London, 1669; repr. 1670, 1675).
Pallavicino, Ferrante, *La retorica delle puttane* (1642).
——, *The Whores Rhetorick* (1683 and later).

3 German

Braun, Friedrich August, *Dissertatio juridica de mitigatione poena in crimine sodomiae. Von Milderung der Strafe beym Laster der Sodomiterey* (Frankfurt, 1750).
Briefe über die Galanterien von Frankfurt am Mayn ('London', i.e., Leipzig, 1791).
Cregut, Friedrich C., *Gründliche Wiederlegung eines ungegründet angebrachten Facti* (Frankfurt, 1743).
Detharding, Georg, *Disputatio inauguralis medica, de erotomania. Von der Krankheit da man verliebt ist* (Rostock, 1719).
Eunuchi conjugium. Die Kapaunen-Heyrath (Halle, 1697?; Jena, 1730 and 1737).
Grupen, Christian Ulrich, *Schediasma de amoris illecebris. Von Liebes-Caressen und Charmiren* (Frankfurt/Leipzig, 1715; repr. 1750).
Koch, Christian Gottlieb, *De obscoenis pontificorum decimis* (Flensburg, 1707).
Lichtenberg, Georg Christoph, *Der Weg der Buhlerin. The Harlot's Progress. Ausführliche Erklärung der Hogarthischen Kupferstiche* (1794–1835; repr. Frankfurt, 1969).

——, 'Der Weg des Liederlichen. The Rake's Progress', in *Aufsätze, Entwürfe, Gedichte, Hogarth-Erklärungen* (Frankfurt, 1968), vol. III, 1–2.

Die Mysterien der Liebe und des Lebensgenusses. Eine Gallerie von Cabinets Stücken für philosophische Lüstlinge (Philadelphia, 1800; repr. 1805).

Pikante Abenteuer von einem Abenteurer selbst erzählt (Leipzig, 1800).

Schurig, Martin, *Embryologia Historico-Medica* (Dresden/Leipzig, 1732).

——, *Gynaecologia Historico-Medica* (Dresden/Leipzig, 1730).

——, *Muliebra Historico-Medica* (Dresden/Leipzig, 1729).

——, *Parthenologia Historico-Medica* (Dresden/Leipzig, 1729).

——, *Spermatologia* (Frankfurt, 1720).

——, *Syllepsilogia Historico-Medica* (Dresden/Leipzig, 1731).

Stentzel, Christian Gottfried, *Dissertatio medico-iuridica de philtro rite examinandis et diiudicandis. Von Liebes-Träncken* (Wittenberg, 1726).

Wolfart, Johann Heinrich, *Tractatio juridica de sodomia vera & spuria hermaphroditi. Von ächter und unächter Sodomiterey eines Zwittern* (Frankfurt, 1742).

4 French

L'abbateur de noisettes, ou recueil de pièces nouvelles des plus gaillardes (The Hague, 1741).

L'Académie des Pays Bas, ou l'école des voluptueux, ouvrage didactique (n.p., 1769).

Almanach Anacréontique, ou les ruses de l'amour (c. 1735).

Almanach des cocus (c. 1735).

Almanach des folies de l'amour ou le tribut de l'amitié (c. 1735).

Almanach des honnêtes femmes pour l'année 1790. Avec une gravure satyrique ... sur la duchesse de Polignac (repr. c. 1870).

Les amours de Charlot et Toinette. Pièce dérobée à V[ersailles] (1779; repr. 1789 and 1790).

Les amours de Sainfroid Jésuite, et d'Eulalie fille dévote (1729).

Les amours et les aventures du Lord Fox (Geneva, 1785).

Amours, galanteries, intrigues, ruses et crimes des capuchins et des religieuses, 4 vols. (Amsterdam and Paris, 1788).

Amusement de la garde-robe (1712).

Anandrina, ou confessions de Mademoiselle Sapho. Contenant les détails de sa réception dans la secte anandrine, sous la présidence de Melle Raucourt ('En Grèce', i.e. Paris, 1789).

Ancillon, Charles, *Traité des eunuques* (1707; repr. 1978).

Andréa de Nerciat, André-Robert, *Les Aphrodites ou fragments thalipriapiques pour servir à l'histoire du plaisir* (Lampsaque, 1793).

——, *Le diable au corps. Oeuvre posthume du très-recommendable docteur Cazonne, membre extraordinaire de la joyeuse faculté phallo-coiro-pygo-glottonomique*, 3 vols. (Mézières, 1803; repr. Paris, 1980).

——, *Le doctorat impromptu* ('Londres', 1788 and later).

——, *Les écarts du temperament, ou le catéchisme de Figaro* [first part of *Le diable au corps*] ('Londres', 1785).

——, *Félicia ou mes fredaines* (1775).

——, *Monrose ou le libertin par fatalité* (1792).

Anecdotes pour servir à l'histoire secrète des ébugors (*c.* 1733).

L'année galante ou étrenne à l'amour. Contes (1773).

Apparution de Thérèse-Philosophe à Saint-Cloud. Ou le triomphe de la volupté. Dédié à la reine. Ouvrage volé dans la poche d'un aristocrate (1790).

Argens, Jean-Baptiste, Marquis de, *Mémoires historiques et secrets concernant les amours des rois de France* (1739).

——, *Thérèse philosophe, ou mémoires pour servir à l'histoire de P. Dirrag & Mademoiselle Eradice* (The Hague, *c.* 1748; and 'À Londres', 1750, 1771, 1780, 1782, and later).

Argenson, René de Voyeur, Comte de, *Notes de René d'Argenson, lieutenant général de police, intéressantes pour l'histoire des moeurs et de la police de Paris à la fin du règne de Louis XIV* (1866).

——, *Rapports inédits du lieutenant de police René d'Argenson, publiés d'après les manuscrits conservés à la Bibliothèque Nationale* (1981).

L'art de bien baiser (n.p., 1781).

Aulnoy [or Aunoy], Marie-Cathérine, Comtesse de, *Mémoires historiques de ce qui c'est passé de plus remarquable en Europe, depuis 1672 jusq'au* [sic] *1679 ...*, 2 vols. (1692).

——, *Mémoires de la cour d'Espagne*, 2 vols. (1690).

L'Autrichienne en goguette, ou l'orgie royale, opéra proverbe (1789).

Bachaumont, Louis Petit de, *Mémoires secrets pour servir à l'histoire de la république des lettres* [Bachaumont edited the first four volumes and half of the fifth. The series was continued by Pidansat de Mairobert *et al.* and published several times in 36 volumes], 36 vols. (London, 1777–89; reprinted Westmead, England, 1970).

Barret [or Baret], Paul, *Mademoiselle Javotte, ouvrage peu moral* (1757 and 1788).

Barrin, Jean, *Vénus dans le cloître* (Cologne, 1692; repr. 1702 and at Amsterdam, 1758; and The Hague, 1761; another edition was published 'À Londres', 1737).

Beauchamps, Pierre-François Godard de, *Histoire du prince Apprius &c.* ('À Constantinople', 1728).

La belle cauchoise, ou mémoires d'une jolie normande, devenue courtisane célèbre (1788).

Beverland, Adrian, *État de l'homme dans le péché original* (1714).

Bret, Antoine (?), *La belle allemande ou les galanteries de Thérèse* (1740; repr. 1745 and 1774).

Bernard, J.F., *La gazette de Cythère, ou aventures galantes et récentes arrivées dans les principales villes de l'Europe; avec le précis de la vie de la Comtesse du Barry* ('Londres', 1774).

Bernard, Pierre Joseph ['Gentil-Bernard'], *L'art d'aimer* (1775).

Bibliothèque de la cour (1781).

La bibliothèque des paillards ou choix de poésies érotiques. À Paris. Chez Madame Belle Monte ... Au temple de la volupté (*c.* 1800).

Bienville, J.D.T., *La nymphomanie, ou traité de la fureur utérine* (Amsterdam, 1771; repr. 1778 and 1784; London, 1789).

Les bijoux du petit neveu de l'Arétin, ou étrennes libertines dédiées aux femmes ci-devant de qualité, & sensibles, s'il s'en trouve; aux honnêtes représentants de la nation, dont le nombre est limité; aux chastes écclésiastiques, dont l'âge cède au plaisir; enfin, aux spectateurs voluptueux des plaisirs de l'amour ... (1791).

La blondine, ou aventures nocturnes entre les hommes et les femmes (Amsterdam, 1762).

Boileau, Jacques, *Histoire des flagellants* (Amsterdam, 1701).

Bonaventure, Charles [pseudonym], *Le synode conjugal ou Aloisia sacra*, 2 vols. (1796).

Bonnefons, Jean, *Johannis Bonefoni arverni carmina* (Lóndon, 1720).

——, *Pancharis* (Paris, 1587; reprinted Amsterdam, 1725 and 1727; and at Paris in 1757 and 1779).

Borde, Charles, *Parapilla, poème en cinq chants. Traduit de l'Italien* (1776; reprinted 1780, 1782, and 1790).

Bordel apostolique institué par Pie VI, pape, en faveur du clergé de France (1790).

Bordel national sous les auspices de la reine, à l'usage des confédérés provinciaux, dédié et présenté à Melle Théroigne, présidente du district des cordeliers, & du club des jacobins (1790; repr. as *Bordel patriotique* in 1791).

Le bordel, ou Jean-Foutre puni (1736; repr. 1747).

Bord ... R ... [Bordel royal]. Suivi d'un entretien secret entre la reine et le cardinal de Rohan, après son entrée aux États-Généraux (1789).

Boudoir de Madame de Pooo (1789).

Bougeant, Guillaume-Hyacinthe, *Le nouveau Tarquin, comédie en 3 actes* (Cologne, 1731; Amsterdam, 1732).

Le branle des capucins ou le mille et unième tour de Marie-Antoinette. Petit opéra aristocratico-comico-risible en deux actes (1791).

Brantôme, Pierre de Bourdeille, Sieur de, *Mémoires de Messire Pierre de Bourdeille, Sieur de Brantôme, contenant des vies des dames galantes de son temps* (Leyden, 1666).

Bussy-Rabutin, Roger, Comte de, *Histoire amoureuse des Gaules* (1665; often republished under different titles, such as *La France galante; Amours des dames illustres de nostre siècle; et al.*).

Le cabinet d'amour et de Vénus (Cologne, 1700 and 1750).

Le cabinet de l'amour (1793).

Le cadran des plaisirs de la cour, ou les aventures du petit page Chérubin, pour servir de suite à la vie de Marie-Antoinette, ci-devant reine de France. Suivi de la confession de Mademoiselle Sapho (c. 1795).

Cagliostro, Comte de [adopted name of Giuseppe Balsamo], *Mémoire pour le Comte de Cagliostro, accusé, contre M. le procureur-général, accusateur; en présence de M. le cardinal de Rohan, de la comtesse de la Motte &.* (1786).

Le caleçon des coquettes du jour (The Hague, 1763).

Le canapé couleur de feu (1714; repr. 1717, 1733, 1734, 1737, 1741, 1742, 1745, and 1775).

Cantiques et pots pourris ('À Londres', 1789).

Les capucins; ou le secret du cabinet noir. Histoire véritable, par l'auteur des Forges Mystérieuses (1808).

Caquire. À Chio de l'imprimerie d'Avalons, en chez Foireux (c. 1780).

Caroline et Belleval, ou les leçons de la volupté, 2 vols., third edition (Avignon, 1797).

Causes célèbres et intéressantes avec les jugements qui les ont décidées. Ed. François Gayot de Pitaval (1734).

——, *rédigées de nouveau par M. Richer, ancien avocat au Parlement*, 22 vols. (Amsterdam, 1772–88).

——, 22 vols. (Amsterdam, 1773–92).

Caylus, Anne-Claude-Philippe de Tubières de Grimoard de Pestels de Lévis, Comte de, *Oeuvres badines complètes du Comte de Caylus*, 12 vols. (Amsterdam/Paris, 1787).

——, *Nocrion. Conte allobroge* (1747).

Les cent nouvelles nouvelles (1486).

La chasteté du clergé dévoilée ou procès-verbaux des séances du clergé chez les filles de Paris. Trouvés à la Bastille (1790).

Chavigny, François de la Bretonnière [pseudonym: abbé de Prat], *Les entretiens de la grille, ou le moine au parloir* (Cologne 1682; 1721).

——, *La galante hermaphrodite, nouvelle amoureuse* (Amsterdam, 1683; 1687; Geneva, 1683).

Choderlos de Laclos, Pierre Ambroise François, *Les liaisons dangereuses* (1782).

Choisy, François-Timoléon de, *Histoire de Madame la Comtesse des Barres ... à Madame la Marquise de Lambert* (Anvers, 1735).

——, *Mémoires pour servir à l'histoire de Louis XIV*, ed. Georges Mongredien (1966).

Chorier, Nicolas, *L'académie des dames* (Amsterdam, 1680 and later).

——, *Aloisiae Sigaea Toletana satyra sotadica de arcanis amoris & veneris* (c. 1660; numerous eighteenth-century French versions).

——, *Joannis Meursii elegantiae latini sermonis* (A different title for *Aloisiae Sigaea*; many French versions published in the eighteenth century: 1720, 1750, 1757, 1770, 1774, *et al.*).

——, *Le Meursius françois ou entretiens galans* [sic] *d'Aloysia* (another version of *Aloisiae Sigaea*; numerous editions; 1782).

Chronique Arétine, ou recherches pour servir à l'histoire des moeurs du dix-huitième siècle (1789, repr. Neuchâtel, 1872).

La chronique scandaleuse; nos. 1–33 (1790–91).

Les cinq jouissances amoureuses de Clindar et Céphire. Précédées des sept béatitudes et jeux de l'amour, & suivies de la douche de Priape, & des plaisirs de la vie. Par M.D.C. (1759).

Cleland, John, *Nouvelle traduction de Woman of Pleasur* [sic] (1760, 1776).

Collé, Charles, *Accidents ou les abbés* (Amsterdam, 1786).

La confédération de la nature ou l'art de se reproduire ('À Londres', 1790).

Confessions de Sapho, où sont révélées les mystères les plus secrets d'une secte voluptueuse (1795).

La consolation des nonnes (1791).

Le courrier extraordinaire des fouteurs écclésiastiques, ou correspondance intime, secrète et libertine de quelques prélats de qualité, de plusieurs prêtres paillards, et d'un certain nombre de prestolets luxurieux (1790).

Coventry, Francis, *La vie et les aventures du petit Pompée* (Amsterdam, 1752; repr. 1784).

Crébillon, Claude Prosper Jolyot de [Crébillon *fils*], *L'écumoire ou Tanzaï et Néardarné. Histoire japonaise* (1734, 1735; also published as *Tanzai et Néardarné*).

——, ——, ed. Ernest Sturm (1976).

——, *Les égarements du coeur et de l'esprit ou mémoires de M. de Meilcour* (1736–8).

——, *Lettres de la Marquise de M ... au Comte de R ...* (1732, and later).

——, *Le sopha. Conte moral* (1742).

——, *Le sylphe* (1730).

Les dégoûts du plaisir: frivolité (Lampsaque, 1755; repr. Brussels, 1850).

Delmas, Augustin, *L'amour apostat ou les aventures de M. de ... et de Melle de ...* (Metz, 1739).

Denon, Dominique Vivant, *Point de lendemain* (1800; later published as *La nuit merveilleuse*).

Desboulmiers, Jean-Auguste Jullien [called Jullien, Jean Auguste], *Honi soit qui mal y pense ou histoire des filles célèbres du XVIIIe siècle*, 2 vols. (1760; enlarged edition, 'Londres', 1766).

Description de l'île des hermaphrodites (Cologne, 1724; 1726).

Diderot, Denis, *Les bijoux indiscrets* (1748).

——, *Ceci n'est pas un conte* (1773).

——, *Oeuvres complètes*. Ed. Jean Varloot, 23 vols. (vols. 1–13 and 23 have been published to date, 1975 ff.).

——, *Oeuvres*. Ed. André Billy (Bibliothèque de la Pléiade no. 25, 1978).

——, *La religieuse* (1796).

Le dieu des vents, ou les aventures d'école: métamorphose en p.t., ou simplement le dieu Pet; badinage en vers libre ... (The Hague, 1776).

Dorval, Jean Louis Claude Taupin, *Le jésuite misopogon séraphique, ou l'ennemi de la barbe des capucins. Par l'Alguasil Dom Diego Balayas y Caramuera* (1762).

Duclos, Charles Pinot, *Acajou et Zirphile* (1744).

——, *Confessions du Comte de ...* (1741).

——, *Mémoires pour servir à l'histoire des moeurs du XVIIIe siècle* (n.p., 1751).

Dulaurens, Henri Joseph, *L'Arétin, ou la débauche de l'esprit en fait de bon sens* (1763).

——, *L'Arétin moderne* (1772).

——, *La chandelle d'Arras* ('Berne', 1765).

——, *Le compère Mathieu* (1766).

Dunoyer, Anne-Marguerite Petit, Dame, *Lettres et histoires galantes* (Amsterdam, 1780).

——, *Lettres historiques et galantes* (Cologne, 1713).

——, ——, 5 vols. (Amsterdam 1720; 1732; published in 6 vols. 'Londres', 1739; in 5 vols. 'Londres', 1741; and in 9 vols. 'Londres', 1757).

Duvernet, Théophile Imarigon de, *Les dévotions de Madame de Betzamooth et les pieuses facéties de Monsieur de Saint-Ognon* (1789).

——, *La retraite, les tentations et les confessions de Madame la Marquise de Montcornillon* (1790).

Les enfants de Sodome à l'Assemblée Nationale, ou députation de l'ordre de la manchette (1790).

Eon de Beaumont, Charles, Chevalier de, *Les loisirs de Chevalier d'Eon de Beaumont sur divers sujets importans* [sic] *d'administration etc. pendant son séjour en Angleterre* (Amsterdam, 1774).

La facétieuse loterie de Pantalon Pasquinet, commissaire général des vents méridionaux, et intendant des bizes du nord (1706).

Favier, Jean Louis, *Mémoires secrets de Mylord Bolingbroke sur les affaires d'Angleterre depuis 1710 jusqu'en 1716 et plusieurs intrigues à la cour de France* ('Londres', 1754).

Foigny, Gabriel de, *Les aventures de Jacques Sadeur* (1692, repr. 1705; and Amsterdam, 1732 and 1788).

Fougeret de Monbron, Louis Charles, *La capitale des Gaules ou la nouvelle Babylone* (La Haye/Paris, 1759).

——, *Margot la ravaudeuse* (London, 1749/50; repr. 'à Hambourg', 1772 and 1800; and Paris, 1784).

Les fouteries chantantes, ou les récréations priapiques des aristocrates en vie (1791).

La France constipée ou Paris foiré. Poème odoriférant, suivi de la chiropédie. Foiropolis, chez le docteur Chirouec (1760?).

Fredaines lubriques de J . . . F . . . Maury, prêtre indigne de l'Église Catholique Apostolique et Romaine (1790).

Gallet [song writer], '*La pétarade ou Polichinel auteur, poème qui n'a pas encore paru en foire*' (n.p. n.d., repr. in *Voltaire âne . . . [1750]*).

Gervaise de Latouche, Jacques Charles, *Histoire de Dom B[ougre], portier des Chartreux, écrite par lui-même* ('A Rome', i.e., London, 1745).

——, *Histoire de Gouberdom, portier des Chartreux* (another edition of *Histoire de Dom B.*, 'Rome', 1786).

——, *Mémoires de Saturnin, ou le portier des Chartreux* (another edition of *Histoire de Dom B.*, 1787).

Godard d'Aucour, Claude, *Mémoires turcs* (1743).

——, *Thémidore ou mon histoire et celle de ma maîtresse* (The Hague, 1745).

Le godmiché royal suivi du Mea culpa (1789).

Gomez, Madeleine-Angélique Poisson, Dame de, *Les cent nouvelles nouvelles de Madame de Gomez*, 19 vols. (1732–9; repr. in 8 vols., 1758).

Grandval fils [real name: Charles François Racot], *Les deux biscuits* ('Astracan', 1751).

——, *La nouvelle Messaline. Tragédie en un acte par Pyron, dit Prépucius. Se vend à Chaud-Conin & à Babine, elle est dit-on de Grandval. L'on y a joint le Sérail de Delis & la Description du Temple de Vénus. À Ancome, chez Clitoris Librairie rue du sperme, vis-à-vis la fontaine de la semence à la verge d'or* (1773).

——, *Sirop-au-cul ou l'heureuse délivrance, tragédie héroi-merdifique* (n.p., n.d.).

——, *Le tempérament* (1770).

Grandval *père* [real name: Nicolas Racot], *La comtesse d'Olonne* (1738).

——, *Le pot de chambre cassé, tragédie pour rire etc. À Ridiculomanie* (1742).

Grécourt, Jean Baptiste, *Recueil de pièces choisies par les soins du cosmopolite.* À Ancome … (1735).

[Hamilton, Anthony, publications on], *Mémoires de la vie du Comte de Grammont, contenant … l'histoire amoureuse de la cour d'Angleterre sous le règne de Charles II* (Cologne, 1713; new augmented edition Utrecht, 1732; repr. 1741; repr. in 2 vols. 1760 and later).

L'hermaphrodite de ce temps (1611?).

Histoire de Mademoiselle Brion, dite Comtesse de Launay (1754).

Histoire du clergé séculier et régulier: nouvelle édition tirée de plusieurs auteurs. 4 vols. (Amsterdam, 1716).

Histoire d'un pou françois, ou l'espion d'une nouvelle espèce (1779).

Histoire et aventures de Milord Pet, conte allégorique par Mme Jeanne Fesse, dédié à MM. les vidangeurs de la ville et généralité de Paris (The Hague, 1755).

Histoire de la secte anandryne, ou la nouvelle Sapho (1794).

Histoire et vie de l'Arétin, ou entretiens de Magdalen et de Julie (a translation of Franco's *La Puttana Errante*; 1783).

Histoire secrète du Prince Croqu'étron et de la Princesse Foirette (1701).

Holbach, Paul Thiry Heinrich Dietrich, Baron de, *Le Christianisme dévoilé* (1767).

——, *De l'imposture sacerdotale* ('Londres', 1767).

——, *Les prêtres démasqués* ('Londres', 1768).

——, *Système de la nature* ('Londres', i.e., Neuchâtel, 1770, and later).

Hurtault, Pierre T.N., *L'art de péter: essay théori-physique et méthodique etc. Suivi de l'histoire de Pet-en-l'air etc. Chez Florent-Q, en Westphalie* (Paris?, 1775; repr. 1776).

Imbert, Guillaume, *La chronique scandaleuse, ou mémoires pour servir à l'histoire des moeurs de la génération présente, par Guillaume Imbert* (1783).

——, ——, 4 vols. (1785; repr. 1786; and in 5 vols. 1788–91).

——, ——, ed. Octave Uzanne (1879: a reprint of the edition of 1785).

Imbert, Guillaume, François Métra *et al.*, *Correspondance secrète, politique et littéraire, ou mémoires pour servir à l'histoire des cours, des sociétés et de la littérature en France, depuis la mort de Louis XV* (1774 ff.; reprinted in 18 vols., 'London', i.e., Maestricht, 1787–90).

Intrigues monastiques, ou l'amour encapuchonné, nouvelles espagnolles, italiennes, et françoises (The Hague, 1739).

La journée amoureuse ou les derniers plaisirs de Marie-Antoinette (1792).

La Fite de Pelleport, Anne-Gédéon, *Le diable dans un bénitier, et la métamorphose du gazetier cuirassé en mouche, ou tentative du sieur Receveur, inspecteur de la police de Paris, pour établir à Londres une police à l'instar de celle de Paris* (London, c. 1784).

——, *Les petits soupers et les nuits de l'Hotel Bouill-n. Lettre de Milord Comte de . . ., à Milord . . ., au sujet des récréations de M. de C-stri-s, ou de la danse de l'ours. Anecdote singulière d'un cocher qui s'est perdu à l'Hotel Bouill-n, le 31 décembre 1778, à l'occasion de la danse de l'ours* (n.p., 1783).

Lafontaine, Jean de, *Contes*, 4 vols. (I, 1655; II, 1666; III, 1675; IV, 1685).

——, *Contes et nouvelles en vers* (published in several parts in 1665, 1666, 1671, 1674, and later).

——, —— (Amsterdam, 1762).

——, —— ('Londres', 1780).

Lagarde, Philippe Bridard de [or Bridard de Lagarde, Philippe], *Lettres de Thérèse . . ., ou mémoires d'une jeune demoiselle de province pendant son séjour à Paris*, 2 vols. (The Hague, 1739, and later).

La Mettrie, Julien Offray de, 'L'art de jouir' [1748], in *Oeuvres philosophiques* (London, 1751; Amsterdam, 1753; Berlin, 1764 and 1796).

——, *L'école de la volupté* (Cologne, 1747).

——, *L'homme machine* (Leyden, 1748).

——, *L'homme plante* (Potsdam, 1748).

——, *La volupté* (1748).

——, *Vénus métaphysique, ou essai sur l'origine de l'âme humaine* (Berlin, 1752).

La Morlière, Charles Jacques Louis Auguste, *Angola* (1746).

——, *Les délices du cloître, ou la none* [sic] *éclairée* ('À Paris', 1757; reprinted The Hague? 1761; also published as *La religieuse en chemise, ou la nonne éclairée*, Paris?, 1763).

——, *Les lauriers ecclésiastiques ou campagne de l'abbé T . . . Seconde édition* (1748; repr. 1774, 1793, 1797).

——, ——. *Augmentée avec Les délices du cloître* (1760).

——, ——. *Avec Le triomphe des religieuses* (1764?).

Lamotte, Jeanne de St-Rémy de Valois, *Mémoires justificatifs de la Comtesse de Valois de la Motte, écrits par elle-même* (London, 1788).

La Sale, Antoine de, *Les quinze joies de mariage* (1740).

Lasolle, Henri-François de, *Mémoires de Versorand, ou le libertin devenu philosophe* (Amsterdam, 1751; repr. 1774).

Le Corvaisier, Pierre Jean, *Le Zéphirartillerie, ou la Société des Francs-Péteurs* (1743).

La légende joyeuse, ou les cent une leçons de Lampsaque, 2 vols. ('À Londres', 1749–50; repr. 1751 and 1760).

Lenoir, Jean-Pierre, *De l'administration de l'ancienne police concernant les libelles, les mauvaises satires et chansons, leurs auteurs coupables, délin-*

quants, complices ou adhérents (Bibliothèque municipale d'Orléans, MS 1421–3).

Le Sage, Alain René, *Histoire de Gil Blas de Santillane* (published in four parts between 1715–35).

Lesage, Georges-Louis, *Remarques sur l'état présent de l'Angleterre … dans les années 1713 et 1714* (Amsterdam, 1715).

Leti, Gregorio, *La vie du pape Sixte cinquième* (1717).

Lettres galantes et philosophiques de deux nonnes, publiées par un apôtre du libertinage (1777; repr. 'À Rouen', 1797).

Lettres portugaises traduites en françois (1669; also published as *Lettres d'amour d'une religieuse portugaise escrites au Chevalier de C.* Cologne, 1669).

La liberté, ou Mlle Raucour à toute la secte anandrine, assemblée au foyer de la Comédie Française ('À Lèche-con', … 1791).

Ligne, Charles-Joseph, Prince de, *Contes immoraux* (*c.* 1785; repr. 1964).

Linguet, Simon Nicolas Henri, *La cacomoade: histoire politique et morale. Traduite de l'Allemand du Docteur Pangloss, par le Docteur lui-même, depuis son retour de Constantinople* ('À Cologne', 1766; repr. 1767; 1797).

Liste de tous les prêtres trouvés en flagrant-délit chez les filles publiques de Paris, sous l'ancien régime; avec le nom et la demeure des femmes chez lesquelles ils ont été trouvés, et le détail des différens amusements qu'ils ont pris avec elles. Tirée des papiers trouvés à la Bastille (1790).

Louvet de Couvray, Jean Baptiste, *Les amours du Chevalier de Faublas* (1787–90; repr. in 4 vols. 1798).

Macé, René-A., *L'abbé en belle humeur, nouvelle galante* (1700; often reprinted).

Mairobert, Mathieu-François Pidansat de, *Confessions de Mlle Sapho* (1789).

——, *L'espion anglois, ou correspondance secrète entre Milord All'Eye et Milord All'Ear*, 11 vols. (London, 1780–89; abridged in 2 vols., 1809).

——, *L'observateur anglois*, 4 vols. (1777–8).

Mandeville, Bernard, *Vénus la populaire, ou apologie des maisons de joye* (London, 1727).

Manuel des boudoirs ou essais érotiques sur les demoiselles d'Athènes (1787).

Manuel gaillard, ou anecdotes voluptueuses recueillies par un bon-vivant à l'usage des concitoyens ('Glascow', 1776).

Manuel, Louis Pierre, *Coup d'oeil philosophique sur le règne de St. Louis* (1786).

——, *La police de Paris dévoilée*, 2 vols. (1791?).

——, *et al.*, *La Bastille dévoilée* (1789).

Marchadier [Abbé], *L'isle de France ou la nouvelle colonie de Vénus* (Amsterdam, 1752).

Marie-Antoinette dans l'embarras, ou correspondance de la Fayette avec le roi, la reine, la Tour-du-Pin & Saint-Priest (*c.* 1790).

Marivaux, Pierre Carlet de Chamblain de, *Le paysan parvenu ou les mémoires de M ...* (1734–35).

——, *La vie de Marianne* (1731–42).

La masturbomanie, ou jouissance solitaire. Stances ornées de 57 gravures (Paris?, *c.* 1830).

Mayeur de Saint-Paul, François-Marie, *L'odalisque. Ouvrage traduit du turc. Par Voltaire. À Constantinople* (1779; repr. 1787 and 1796).

Mémoires secrets sur les règnes de Louis XIV et de Louis XV, par feu M. Duclos, 2 vols. (1790).

Mercier de Compiègne, Claude François, *La bougie de Noël, ou la messe à minuit. Comédie en deux actes en prose* (1793).

——, *La calotine, ou la tentation de Saint Antoine* (1800).

——, *Élogue du pet, dissertation historique, anatomique, et philosophique* (1799).

——, *Les veillées du couvent ou le noviciat d'amour* (1793).

La Messaline française, ou les nuits de la Duch[esse] de Pol[ignac]. Et aventures mystérieuses de la Pr[inces]se d'Hé[nin] ... Ouvrage fort utile à tous les jeunes gens qui voudront faire un cours de libertinage. Par l'abbé, compagnon de la suite de la Duch[esse] de Pol[ignac]. À Tribaldis, de l'imprimerie de Priape (1789).

Meusnier de Querlon, Anne-Gabriel, *Histoire de la tourrière des Carmélites, servant de pendant au P[ortier] des C[hartreux]* (*c.* 1745; often reprinted).

——, *La tourrière des Carmélites* (another edition of *Histoire de la tourrière* 1777).

——, *Sainte Nitouche, ou histoire galante de la tourrière des Carmélites* (another edition of *Histoire de la tourrière*).

——, *Psaphion ou la courtisane de Smyrne, fragment érotique du grec de Mnasias ... où l'on a joint Les hommes de Prométhée* (London, 1748).

Les mille et une nuits, contes arabes traduits en françois; translated by Jean-Antoine Galland, 12 vols. (1704–17).

Millot, Michel, Jean l'Ange, *L'Escole des filles* (1655).

Mirabeau, Honoré Gabriel Riquetti, Comte de, *Errotika Biblion* ('Rome', 1783; repr. Paris, 1792, 1801).

——, *Hic et hec, ou l'art de varier les plaisirs de l'amour* (1798).

——, *Histoire secrète de la cour de Berlin* (n.p., 1789; repr. 1825).

——, *Le libertin de qualité ou ma conversion* (1783, repr. 1784).

——, *Le rideau levé ou l'éducation de Laure* (1796).

——, *L'oeuvre du Comte de Mirabeau. Introduction, essai bibliographique et notes par Guillaume Apollinaire* (1921).

Le moine galant ou la vie de Dom F ..., Bernardin, écrite par lui-même (1756).

Momus redivivus, ou les saturnales françaises. Ed. Mercier de Compiègne (1796).

Le mondalisme, histoire galante, écrite par une ex-religieuse ('Rome', 1777).

La morale des sens ou l'homme du siècle. Extrait des Mémoires de M. le Chevalier de Bar ... ('Londres', 1792).

Morande, Charles Thévenot de, *Anecdotes secrètes sur la Comtesse du Barry* (London, 1776).

——, *La correspondance de Mme Gourdan* (London?, 1784).

——, *La gazette noire par un homme qui n'est pas blanc; ou oeuvres posthumes du gazetier cuirassé* (London, 1784).

——, *Le gazetier cuirassé, ou anecdotes scandaleuses de la cour de France* (London, 1771).

——, *Mélanges confus sur des matières fort claires* (London, 1771).

——, *Le philosophe cynique* (London, 1771).

——, *Le portefeuille de Mme Gourdan* (London?, 1784?; attributed to Morande).

——, *Vie d'une courtisane du dix-huitième siècle* (London, 1776).

Mouhy, Charles de Fieux, Chevalier de, *L'amante anonyme ou histoire secrète de la volupté, avec des contes nouveaux de fées* (The Hague, 1755).

——, *Mémoires d'Anne-Marie de Moras, Comtesse de Corbon, écrits par elle-même et addressés à Mlle d'Au ..., pensionnaire au couvent du Cherche-Midi*, 4 vols. (The Hague, 1739; 2 vols. Amsterdam, 1739).

——, *Mémoires d'une fille de qualité qui ne s'est point retirée du monde*, 4 vols. (Amsterdam, 1747).

——, *Les mémoires de Madame la Marquise de Villenemours*, 2 vols. (The Hague, 1747).

——, *Mémoires de Monsieur le Marquis de Fieux*, 4 vols. (1735–6).

——, *La mouche, ou les aventures de M. Bigand traduites de l'italien* (1736).

Navarre, Marguerite de, *L'Heptaméron des nouvelles de très illustre et très excellente Princesse Marguerite de Valois, Royne de Navarre* (1559; first published in a shortened version, *Histoire des amans fortunez*, in 1558. Often published as *L'Heptaméron*, e.g. Bern, 1780–81).

——, *L'Heptaméron*. German edition (Munich, 1965); English edition (Harmondsworth, 1984).

Nogaret, François-Félix, *L'Arétin françois par un membre de l'Académie des Dames* ('À Londres', 1787).

——, *Contes en vers*, 2 vols. (1798).

——, *Les épices de Vénus ou pièces diverses du même académicien* (Part II of *L'Arétin françois*, 1787).

Les nones galantes ou l'amour embéguiné (sometimes attributed to the Marquis d'Argens; The Hague, 1740).

Nougaret, Pierre Jean Baptiste, *La capucinade, histoire sans vraisemblance* (1765; reprinted in 1797 as *Aventures galantes de Jérome, frère capucin*).

Le nouveau merdiana, ou manuel scatologique, par une société de gens sans gêne (1729; 1789; repr. 1870).

La nouvelle Académie des Dames, ou histoire de Mlle B ... (1774 and 1776; a reprint of *Histoire de Mlle Brion*, 1754).

Ode aux bougres (1789).

L'origine des cons sauvages, la manière de les apprivoiser, le moyen de prédire toutes choses ... Plus le bail à ferme desdits cons ... Plus la source du gros fessier des nourrices, et la raison pourquoi elles sont si fendues entre les jambes ('À Lyon', 1797).

Outhier, Reginald [or Renaud], *Dissertation théologique sur le péché du confesseur avec sa pénitente* (Gênes, 1750).

Parny, Évariste-Désiré-Desforges, *Les galanteries de la Bible* (1805; 1808).

Pauw, Cornelius de, *Recherches philosophiques sur les Américains*, 3 vols. (Paris, "an III"; repr. in 3 vols. Berlin 1768–70).

Perrin, Jacques-Antoine-René, *Les égarements de Julie* ('À Londres', 1776; repr. Brussels, 1883).

Les petits bougres au manège, ou réponse de M. ..., Grand Maître des enculeurs, et de ses adhérents, défendeurs, à la requête des fouteuses, des macquerelles et des branleuses, demanderesses ... À Enculos, chez Pierre Pousse-Fort (1791?).

Piron, Alexis, *Contes et nouvelles en vers*, 4 vols. (1778).

——, *Oeuvres badines* (1796; repr. 1797).

——, *Oeuvres érotiques* (Neufchâtel, 1775).

Les plaisirs du cloître, comédie en trois actes et en vers libres (1773).

Pöllnitz, Karl Ludwig, Freiherr von, *Amusements des eaux d'Aix-la-Chapelle*, 3 vols. (Amsterdam, 1736).

Le portefeuille d'un talon rouge. Contenant des anecdotes galantes et secrètes de la cour de France (1779).

Prévost-d'Exiles, Antoine François, *Histoire du Chevalier des Grieux et de Manon Lescaut* (1731; repr. 1733 and 1753; also published under the title, *Les aventures du Chevalier des Grieux*).

Le putanisme d'Amsterdam; livre contenant les tours et les ruses dont se servent les putains et les maquerelles; comme aussi leurs manières de vivre (Amsterdam, 1681; repr. Brussels, 1883).

Les putains cloîtrées. Parodie des visitandes en deux actes ... (1796).

Les quarante manières de foutre, dédiées au clergé de France. À Cythère, au temple de la volupté (1790).

Quillet, Claude, *Callipédie, ou l'art d'avoir de beaux enfants* (1655).

Les religieux et religieuses laborieux, ou les fruits de la liberté (1790).

Le rendez-vous de Madame Elisabeth, soeur du roi, avec l'abbé de S. Martin ... dans le jardin des Tuileries (1790).

Requête et décret en faveur des putains, des fouteuses, des macquerelles et des branleuses; contre les bougres, les bardaches et les brûleurs de paillasses. L'an second de la régénération foutative (1791?).

Restif de la Bretonne, Nicolas Edmé, *L'Antijustine, ou les délices de l'amour. Par M. Linguet* (1798).

——, *Le paysan perverti, ou les dangers de la ville* (1776).

——, *Le paysan et la paysanne pervertis* (1787).

——, *La paysanne pervertie* (1784).

——, *Le pornographe, ou idées d'un honnête homme sur un projet de règlement pour les prostituées propre à prévenir les malheurs qui occasione le publicisme des femmes* ('Londres', 1769).

Roe, Richard [pseudonym], *Concubitus sine lucina, ou le plaisir sans peine. Réponse à la lettre intitulée: Lucina sine concubitu* ('Londres', 1776).

Sade, Donatien Alphonse François de, *Aline et Valcour ou le roman philosophique* (1795).

——, *Justine, ou les malheurs de la vertu*, 2 vols. ('Hollande', 1791; third edition, 'Philadelphie', 1794).

——, *Oeuvres complètes*, 16 vols. (1973).

Sauve la peste, ou relation d'un accident terrible, véritable et remarquable, arrivé aux latrines du Palais-Royal (1790).

Senac de Meilhan, Gabriel, *La foutromanie. Poème lubrique en six chants.* (*c.* 1775; first dated edition 1780).

Les sérails de Londres, ou les amusements nocturnes (1801; a translation of *Nocturnal Revels* ..., second edition, London, 1779).

Siri, Vittorio, *Anecdotes du ministère du cardinal de Richelieu*, 2 vols. (Amsterdam, 1717).

——, *Mémoires secrets tirés des archives des souverains de l'Europe, depuis le règne de Henri IV. Traduit de l'italien ... par Jean-Baptiste Requier*, 50 vols. (Amsterdam and Paris, 1775–84; first published in 16 vols., Amsterdam, 1665–74).

Soirées amoureuses du général et de la belle Antoinette. Par le petit épagneul de l'Autrichienne. À Persépolis ... (1790).

Stretser, Thomas, *Description topographique, historique, critique et nouvelle du pays et des environs de la Forêt-Noire, situés dans la province du Merryland. Traduction très-libre de l'anglais. À Boutentativos* (Paris?, 1770?; reprinted 1790; a translation of *A New Description of Merryland*).

Swift, Jonathan [possible author], *L'art de méditer sur la chaise percée, par l'auteur de Gulliver l'aîné. Avec un projet pour bâtir et entretenir des latrines publiques dans la ville et faubourgs de Paris, sous la direction d'une compagnie, dans laquelle on pourra s'intéresser en prenant des actions. Dublin, de l'imprimerie du docteur Swift* (Paris?, 1743).

——, [possible author], *Le grand mistère, ou l'art de méditer sur la garderobe, renouvelé et dévoilé par l'ingénieux docteur Swift, avec les observations historiques, politiques et morales, qui prouvent l'antiquité de cette science et qui contiennent les usages différents des diverses nations par rapport à cet important sujet. Traduit de l'anglais (par l'abbé Desfontaines)* (The Hague, 1729).

Tallemant, Paul, *Le second voyage de l'isle de l'amour* (1664).

——, *Le voyage de l'isle de l'amour* (1663).

——, *Les deux voyages* (The Hague/Paris, 1713).

Tallemant des Réaux, Gédéon, *Les historiettes. Mémoires pour servir à l'histoire du XVIIe siècle* (Written between 1657 and 1669; first published in 1834/5).

La tentation de S. Antoine, ornée de figures et de musique (1781; repr. 1782 and 1795; attributed to Sedaine. Part II, *Le pot-pourri de Loth*, attributed to Poisinet, is bound with this title).

Thomas, Artus, Sieur d'Embry, *Les hermaphrodites. Discours de Jacophile à Limne* (1605; reprinted 1610?).

Tissot, Samuel Auguste André David, *L'onanisme, ou dissertation physique sur les maladies produites par la masturbation* (Lausanne, 1760; first published in Latin, *Tentamen de morbis ex manustupratione*, 1758; third edition of the French version, Lausanne 1764; eighth edition, 1785).

Le triomphe de la fouterie, ou les apparences sauvées. Comédie en deux actes et en vers (1791).

Venette, Nicolas, *Tableau de l'amour considéré dans l'estat de mariage* (published anonymously and pseudonymously in several editions, 1687 and 1688; later published as *De la génération, ou tableau de l'amour conjugal*).

Le vidangeur sensible, drame en trois actes et en prose, par M. . . . (1777).

Vie de Marie-Antoinette d'Autriche, reine de France, femme de Louis XVI, roi des Français, depuis la perte de son pucelage jusqu'au premier mai 1791 (1793).

Vies et actions des coquettes, maîtresses . . . les plus célèbres d'Angleterre (London, 1721).

Vie privée des écclésiastiques (1791).

Vie privée libertine et scandaleuse de Marie-Antoinette d'Autriche . . . depuis son arrivée en France, jusqu'à sa détention au temple, 3 vols. (1791–3).

Vie privée et publique du ci-derrière Marquis de Villette, citoyen rétroactif (1791?).

[*Vie voluptueuse*] *Le bordel monacal; ou vie voluptueuse des capucins et des nonnes* (Cologne, 1755; repr. Brussels, 1875).

Vie voluptueuse entre les capucins et des nonnes, par la confession d'un frère de l'ordre (Cologne, 1759; repr. 1764, 1773, 1774, 1775).

——, *augmentée d'une* [sic] *poème héroi-comique . . . et de plusieurs autres pièces* (Cologne, 1775).

Villaret, Claude, *Antipamela ou mémoires de M.D. . . .* (1742).

Villiers, Jacob de, *L'apoticaire de qualité* (1670).

Voisenon, Claude-Henri de, *Exercises de dévotion de M. Henri Roch avec Mme la Duchesse de Condor. Par feu l'abbé de Voisenon* ('À Vaucluse', 1786).

——, *Histoire de la félicité* (1751).

——, *La journée de l'amour, ou heures de Cythère* (1776).

——, *Romans et contes* (1767; London, 1785).

——, *Tant mieux pour elle, conte plaisant* (1760).

Voltaire, François-Marie Arouet de, *La pucelle d'Orléans, poème divisé en quinze livres* (c. 1761–2, 'Londres', 1762, 1764, 1775, 1780).

——, *Zaïre*.

5 English and American Sources

5.1 English newspapers and magazines

The Annual Register (1760–90).

The Bon Ton Magazine; or Microscope of Fashion and Folly (1791–5).

The Brittanic Magazine; or Entertaining Repository of Heroic Adventures and Memorable Exploits (1793–1807).

The Britannic Magazine and Chronological Repository (1807–9).

The Country Journal: or The Craftsman (1727 ff.).

Courier de l'Europe (1781–8).
Courier de Londres (1788–1826).
The Court and City Magazine, or Fund of Entertainment for the Man of Quality (1761–4).
The Court, City and Country Magazine (1764–71).
The Covent Garden Magazine or Amorous Repository: Calculated Solely for the Entertainment of the Polite World (1772–5).
The Daily Advertiser (1730 ff.).
The Daily Gazetter (1735 ff.).
The Daily Journal (1720 ff.).
The Daily Universal Register (1785–8: then *The Times*).
The English Chronicle (1786 ff.).
The Entertainer (1754).
The Evening Advertiser (1754 ff.).
The Gazetter (1748 ff.).
The General Evening Post (1758 ff.).
The Gentleman's Magazine (1731–1914).
The Grub-Street Journal (1730–37).
The Independent Chronicle (1769–70).
The Ladies Magazine: or, the Universal Entertainer (1749–53).
Lloyd's Evening Post (1757 ff.).
The London Advertiser (1769 ff.).
The London Chronicle or Universal Evening Post (1757 ff.).
The London Daily Post (1741 ff.).
The London Evening Post (1758 ff.).
The London Magazine (1732–85).
The Magic and Conjuring Magazine, and Wonderful Chronicle (1795).
The Maccaroni and Theatrical Magazine (1772–4).
The Matrimonial Magazine, or Monthly Anecdotes of Love and Marriage, for the Court, the City and the Country (1775).
The Middlesex Journal (1770 ff.).
The Monthly Catalogue (1714–17; repr. in the *English Bibliographical Sources*, series I, no. 1, 1964).
The Monthly Magazine (1796–1843).
The Monthly Review (1749–89, 1790–1825).
The New Weekly Chronicle (1758 ff.).
The Oracle (1789 ff.).
Parker's Penny Post (1725 ff.).
The Post Man, and the Historical Account (1696).
The Publick Advertiser (1657).
The Public Ledger (1769 ff.).
The Rambler's Magazine; or, The Annals of Gallantry, Glee, Pleasure, and the Bon Ton (1783–90).
The Ranger's Magazine, or the Man of Fashion's Companion (1795).
The Star (1788 ff.).
The St. James's Chronicle & Other Evening Posts (1761 ff.).
The Tatling Harlot (1709).

The Times (1788 ff.).
The Town and Country Magazine, or Universal Repository of Knowledge, Instruction and Entertainment (1769–92).
The Turkish Spy (1687 ff.).
The Universal Chronicle (1758 ff.).
The Wandering Whore (published by John Garfield in 1660).
The Weekly Journal (1715–30).
The Weekly Miscellany (1732–41).
The Westminster Journal (1742 ff.).
The Westminster Magazine (1773–85).
Woodfall's Diary (1789 ff.).
The World (1787 ff.)

5.2 *American newspapers and magazines*

Albany Gazette (New York, 1784–1820).
American Mercury (Connecticut, 1784–1820).
American Weekly Mercury (Pennsylvania, 1719–49).
Augusta Chronicle (Georgia, 1789–1820).
The Boston Chronicle (Massachusetts, 1767–70).
The Boston Evening Post (Massachusetts, 1735–75).
The Boston Gazette (Massachusetts, 1719–98).
The Boston News-Letter (Massachusetts, 1704–76).
The Boston Post-Boy (Massachusetts, 1734–75).
The Columbian Sentinel and Massachusetts Federalist (1800).
The Connecticut Courant (1764–1820).
The Connecticut Gazette (1755–68).
The Connecticut Journal (1767–1820).
The Continental Journal (Massachusetts, 1776–87).
The Daily Advertiser (New York, 1785–1806).
Dunlap's American Daily Advertiser (1793 ff.).
The Evening Post (Massachusetts, 1778–84).
Die Germantowner Zeitung (Pennsylvania, 1762–99).
The Georgia Gazette (1763–76).
Hochdeutsch-Pennsylvanische Geschicht-Schreiber, oder, Sammlung wichtiger Nachrichten aus dem Natur- und Kirchenreich (1739–46).
Kentucky Gazette (1787–1820).
The Litchfield Monitor (Connecticut, 1784–1807).
The Maryland Gazette (1727–34; 1745–1820).
The Maryland Journal (1773–97).
The Massachusetts Sentinel (1784 ff.).
The Middlesex Gazette (Connecticut, 1785–1820).
Moniteur de la Louisiane (1794–1814).
The New England Courant (Massachusetts, 1721–7).
The New England Weekly Journal (Massachusetts, 1727–41).
The New Hampshire Gazette (1756–1820).

The New London Gazette (Connecticut, 1763–73; continued as the *Connecticut Gazette*, 1774–1820).

The Newport Mercury (Rhode Island, 1758–1820).

The New York Evening Post (1744–53; 1782–83; 1794–1820).

The New York Gazette, or Weekly Post Boy (1747–73).

The New York Mercury (1752–68; 1779–83).

The New York Weekly Journal (1733–51).

The Norwich Packet (Connecticut, 1773–1802).

The Pennsylvania Chronicle (1767–74).

The Pennsylvania Evening Post (1775–84).

The Pennsylvania Gazette (1728–1815).

The Pennsylvania Journal (1742–93).

The Pennsylvania Packet, and Daily Advertiser (1771 ff.).

The Pennsylvania Packet, or The General Advertiser (1771 ff.).

Pensylvanische Berichte [sic] (1746–62: a continuation of *Hochdeutsch-Pennsylvanische Berichte*).

Porcupine's Gazette (Pennsylvania, 1797–1800).

Providence Gazette (Rhode Island, 1762–1820).

The Salem Gazette (1774 ff.).

The South-Carolina Gazette (1732–75).

The Virginia Gazette (1736–1800).

5.3 *Trial Reports and related sources*

An Act to Restrain Persons who shall be divorced for the Crime of Adultery, from Marrying, or contracting Matrimony, with the Party (1771).

Adultery Anatomized in a select collection of trials (1761).

Atherton, John, publications on.

——. *Bishop Atherton's case discussed, in a letter to the author of a late pamphlet intitled 'The Case of John Atherton'* (1711).

——. *The Case of John Atherton, Bishop of Waterford in Ireland; Who was convicted of the sin of uncleanness with a cow, and other creatures, for which he was hanged at Dublin ... To which is added The Sermon preach'd at his funeral ... The whole written by Nicolas Barnard* (1710).

——. *The Case of John Atherton, Bishop of Waterford in Ireland: fairly represented* (1710).

——. *The Penitent Death of a woeful sinner. Or, the penitent death of John Atherton ...* (Dublin, 1641; London, 1642; third edition 1651).

——. *The life and death of John Atherton, Lord Bishop of Waterford and Lysmore within the Kingdom of Ireland ... who for incest, buggery and many other enormous crimes ... was hanged* (1641).

Aubrey (or Hobry), Marie, publications on.

——. *A hellish murder committed by a French midwife on the body of her husband, Jan. 27 1687/8 for which she ... received sentence of death* (1688).

The case of impotency ... 1613 ... between Robert, Earl of Essex, and the Lady Frances Howard, 2 vols. (1715).

against Robert Thistlethwayte, late doctor of divinity and warden of Wadham College, for a sodomitical attempt upon Mr. W. French, commoner of the same college (1739).

Gill, J., *A new and complete collection of trials for adultery: or a general history of modern gallantry and divorces. Containing all the most remarkable trials ... for adultery, fornication, cruelty, incest, criminal conversation, impotency, &c. From the year 1780 to the middle of the year 1797 ... By a civilian of Doctors Commons* (1796).

——. *A new collection of trials for adultery: or, general history of modern gallantry and divorces ... From the year 1780, to the present time ... A complete history of private lives, intrigues, and amours, of many characters in the most elevated and other spheres of life ... By a civilian of Doctors Commons* (1799; vol. II, 1802; two volumes in one).

——. *A new and complete collection of the most remarkable trials for adultery: or, a general history of modern gallantry and divorces. Including all the most remarkable trials from the year 1780, to the present year 1802* (1802).

Girard, Jean-Baptiste (1680–1733), publications on.

——. *The case of Mary Katherine Cadière, against the Jesuit Father John Baptist Girard* (1731).

——. *The Case of Mrs. Mary Catherine Cadière* (1732).

——. *A compleat translation of the sequel of the proceedings of Mary Catherine Cadière, against the Jesuit Father John Baptist Girard* (1732).

——. *The Defence of Father John Baptist Girard ... against the accusation of Mary Catherine Cadière. The fourth edition* (1732).

——. *Erstaunenswürdige Historie, des Jesuiten Paters Johann Baptista Girard, Rectoris zu Toulon ... welcher unter dem Schein der Heiligkeit die Jungfer Cadière ... zur entsetzlichsten Unzucht verfüret* (Cologne, 1732).

——. *Factum der Vertheididungs-Schrifft Marien Catharinen Cadière, wider den Pater Johann Baptist Girard* (n.p., 1732).

——. *Fernerer Verlauff in Sachen der Demoiselle Catharine Cadière wider den Pater ... Johann Baptista Girard* (n.p., 1732).

——. *Memoirs of Miss Mary Catherine Cadière, and Father Girard, Jesuit ... In an epistle from a person of quality at Paris to his correspondent in London* (1731).

——. *Recueil général des pièces concernant le procez entre la demoiselle Cathérine Cadière, religieuse clariste, et le P.J.B. Girard, jésuite, accusé par la soeur Cadière de viol, rapt, avortement ... etc.,* 5 vols. (Aix-en-Provence, 1731; reprinted in 8 vols., The Hague, 1731).

——. *Thirty two pieces, never before translated, of the proceedings upon the tryal of M. Cadière, and Father Girard* (1732).

——. *Tryal of Father John-Baptist Girard, on an accusation of quietism, sorcery, incest, abortion and subornation ...* (1732).

Gurney, Joseph, *The trial of John Motherhill, for committing a rape on the body of Miss Catherine Wade ... Taken in short-hand, by Joseph Gurney* (1786).

Kenrick, William, *Free thoughts on seduction, adultery, and divorce ...*

occasioned by the late intrigue between his Royal Highness the Duke of Cumberland, and Henrietta, wife of the Right Honourable Richard Lord Grosvenor (1771).

Kotzwara, Franz, publications on.

——. *The trial of Susannah Hill for the wilful murder of Francis Kotzwara, September the 2nd, 1791 at Justice Hall in the Old Bailey* [MS in the Boston Medical Library; see also the entry under Vanbutchell].

The life and amours of Lady Ann F–l–y [Foley] (1783?).

Memoirs of Mrs. Harriet Er–g–n [Errington], *containing her amours, intrigues and tête-à-têtes with the Colonel M––n, Colonel T–l–n, Captain Sm–th etc.* (c. 1785).

A new and complete collection of the most remarkable trials for adultery, 2 vols. (1780).

The Newgate Calendar or Malefactor's bloody register, 5 vols. (c. 1773).

News from Tyburn being an account of the confession & execution of the woman condemned for committing buggery with a dog, which was also hanged on a tree by her (1677).

Old Bailey Sessions Papers

[Published under varying titles from the 1680s on, such as *The proceedings of the sessions at the Old Bailey; A narrative of the proceedings at the Old Bailey; The true narrative of the proceedings; The proceedings on the King's Commissions of the peace, and Oyer and Terminer ... at ... the Old Bailey; The proceedings at the Sessions of the peace, and Oyer and Terminer, for the city of London, and County of Middlesex; etc.*]

Plowden, Francis, *Crim. Con Biography: or celebrated trials in the ecclesiastical and civil courts for adultery and other crimes connected with incontinency, from the period of Henry the Eighth to the present time*; 2 vols. (1830).

——, *Criminal conversation biography*, 12 vols. (1789).

Select trials for murders, robberies, rapes, sodomy, coining, frauds, and other offences: at the Sessions House in the Old Bailey, 2 vols. (1734–5).

She is and she is not: a fragment of the true history of Miss Caroline de Grosberg, alias Mrs. Potter, etc. Exhibiting a series of uncommon artifices and intrigues in the course of her transactions with the Earl of Lauderdale, in the years 1764 and 1765. Together with an account of the proceedings in the process she commenced against his lordship, and the substance of the evidence on both sides (1776).

A short account of some extraordinary proceedings against the person who was shot in Lincoln's-Inn-Garden. Written by himself (1742).

Trial of David Robertson, of the Jerusalem Hotel, Charles-street, Coventgarden, late master of the Standan Tavern, Leicester-fields, for an unnatural crime with George Foulton (c. 1806).

The trial of his Royal Highness the Duke of Cumberland July 5th, 1770 for criminal conversation with Lady Harriet G–––r [Grosvenor] (1770).

The trial of Isaac Prescott, Esq. ... for the most brutal and unheard of cruelties inflicted on Jane Prescott his wife, with a frontispiece (c. 1782).

The trial of John Almon ... for selling Junius's Letter to the K... (1770).

The trial of Mr. Cooke, malt distiller, of Stratford, for the crime of adultery with Mrs. Walford . . . Before Lord Kenyon, and a Special Jury . . . (1789).

The trial of Mrs. Harriet Errington in the Bishop of London's Court at Doctors Commons for committing adultery with A.M. Smith, Esq., Captain Buckley, Captain Southby, the Reverend T. Walker and many others (1785).

The trial of the Reverend Mr. James Altham . . . for adultery, defamation, and obscenity . . . (c. 1783).

The trial with the whole of the evidence between the Right Honourable Sir Richard Worsley, Bart. . . . and George Maurice Bissett . . . for criminal conversation with the plaintiff's wife . . . (1782).

Trials for adultery: or, the history of divorces. Being select trials at Doctors Commons, for adultery, fornication, cruelty, impotence etc. From the year 1760, to the present time . . .; 7 vols. (1779–81).

The Tyburn Chronicle; or villainy display'd in all its branches. Containing an authentic account of the lives, adventures, tryals, executions, and last dying speeches of the most notorious malefactors . . . who have suffered . . . in England, Scotland, and Ireland, from the year 1700, to the present time; 4 vols. (c. 1768).

5.4 Pictorial erotica

L'Arétin d'Augustin Carrache ou recueil de postures érotiques, d'après les gravures à l'eau-forte, par cet artiste célèbre, avec le texte explicatif des sujets. À la Nouvelle Cythère (Paris, 1798; repr. Brussels, 1871).

Béraldi, Henri/Roger Portalis, *Les graveurs du dix-huitième siècle*, 6 vols. (1881).

Bigarrures coiro-pygo-glotto-chiro-phallurgiques (c. 1799; repr. Paris, 1981).

Borel, Antoine, *Cent vignettes érotiques gravées par Elluin pour illustrer sept romans libertins du dix-huitième siècle* (Nyons, 1978).

Bowles and Carver's caricatures; 2 vols. (n.p., 1820).

Cohen, Henri, *Guide de l'amateur de livres à gravures du XVIIIe siècle* (1887).

Cohen, Henri/Seymour de Ricci, *Guide de l'amateur de livres à gravures du XVIIIe siècle. Supplément par E. Crottet* (Amsterdam, 1890; sixth edition, Paris, 1912).

A compleat set of charts of the coast of Merryland (1745).

Dunand, Louis/Philippe Lemarchand, *Les compositions de Jules Romain intitulées 'LES AMOURS DES DIEUX': l'art érotique sous la Renaissance. Gravées par Marc-Antoine Raimondi* (Lausanne, 1977).

Feaver, William, *Masters of caricature from Hogarth and Gillray to Scarfe and Levine* (NY, 1981).

Fuchs, Edward, *Die Frau in der Karikatur* (Munich, 1906; repr. 1928; repr. as *Sozialgeschichte der Frau*, Frankfurt, 1973).

——, *Geschichte der erotischen Kunst*, 2 vols. (Munich, 1923 and 1926).

——, *Die großen Meister der Erotik* (Munich, 1930).

[Fuchs, Eduard, see the volumes cited pp. 461–2]

Füssli, Johann Heinrich [Henry Fuseli]

Powell, Nicolas, *Fuseli: The Nightmare* (1973).

Schiff, Gert, ed., *Johann Heinrich Füssli 1741–1825* (Zurich/Munich, 1973).

George, Dorothy M., *English political caricature*, 2 vols. (Oxford, 1959).

——, *Hogarth to Cruikshank: social change in graphic satire* (1967).

Gillray, James

British political cartoons of the eighteenth century (1807; in the possession of the ISR, Bloomington, Indiana).

Grego, Joseph, *The works of James Gillray the caricaturist; with the history of his life.* Ed. T. Wright (1873).

Hill, Draper, ed., *The satirical etchings of James Gillray* (NY, 1976).

Gravures (private collection of the ISR, Bloomington, Indiana).

Grand-Carteret, John, *Contre Rome, la bataille anticléricale en Europe: 282 images françaises, italiennes, allemandes, anglaises …* (1906).

——, *Le décolleté et le retroussé, trois siècles de gauloiseries 1600–1900* (1902; reprinted in 2 vols. 1910).

——, *Die Erotik in der französischen Karikatur* (Vienna, 1909).

——, *Les moeurs et la caricature en France* (n.d. [1888]).

Guillerm, Alain, 'Le système de l'iconographie galante', *DHS* 12 (1980), 177–94.

Gurlitt, Cornelius, *Das französische Sittenbild des 18. Jahrhunderts im Kupferstich* (Berlin, 1912).

Hammelmann, Hanns, *Book illustrators in eighteenth-century England*. Ed. T.S.R. Boase (1975).

Hancarville, Pierre-François Hugues de, *Antiquités étrusques, grecques et romaines*, 4 vols. (Naples, 1766–7).

——, *Bilder aus dem Privatleben der römischen Caesaren … Mit 51 Tafeln der Original-Ausgabe* (Göttingen, 1907; Potsdam, 1907).

——, ——. *Nachwort von Henri Herbedé* (Dortmund, 1979).

——, *Denkbilder des Geheimkultes der römischen Damen* (Vienna, 1907; repr. 1908).

——, *Denkmäler des Geheimkults der römischen Damen. Nach einem Privatdruck von 1910* (Dortmund, 1979).

——, *Monumens de la vie privée des douze Césars, d'après une suite de pierres gravées sous leur règne* ('À Caprées', 1780; repr. Nancy, 1780 and 1784).

——, *Monumens du culte secret des dames romaines, pour servir de suite aux Monumens de la vie privée des XII Césars* ('À Caprées', 1784).

——, *The private lives of the twelve Caesars … Being a condensation of d'Hancarville's Monumens de la vie privée des douze Césars*. Ed. E. Haldeman-Julius (Girard, Kansas, 1949).

——, *Veneres et Priapi uti observantur in gemmis antiquis* (Leyden, n.d.; Naples, 1771; 2 vols. London, *c.* 1790 and *c.* 1800).

——, *Veneres uti observantur in gemmis antiquis* (London?, 1785).

Hogarth, William
  A harlot's progress (1732).
  The rake's progress (1735).
  Burke, Joseph, and Colin Caldwell, *Hogarth. The complete engravings* (1968; repr. 1974).
  The genuine works. Illustrated with biographical anecdotes ... By John Nichols and George Stevens, 3 vols. (1808–17).
  Jarrett, Derek, *The ingenious Mr. Hogarth* (1976).
  Klinger, Mary F., 'William Hogarth and London theatrical life', *SECC* 4 (1976), 11–28.
  Paulson, Ronald, *The art of Hogarth* (Oxford, 1975).
  Paulson, Ronald, *Hogarth: his life, art, and times*, 2 vols. (1971).
  Paulson, Ronald, *Hogarth's graphic works*, revised edition (New Haven, Connecticut, 1970).
La Chaud, Gérard de, and Gaspard Michel [alias Le Blond], *Description des principales pierres gravées du cabinet de S.A.S. Monseigneur le Duc d'Orléans, premier prince du sang*, 2 vols. (1780 and 1784).
Lawrence, H.W., and B.L. Dighton, *French Line Engravings of the late Eighteenth Century* (1910).
Nogaret, François-Félix, *L'Arétin français, par un membre de l'Académie des Dames* (1789).
Paston, George [i.e., Emily Morse Symonds], *Social caricature in the eighteenth century ... With over two hundred illustrations* (1905).
Paulson, Ronald, *Representations of revolution (1789–1820)* (New Haven, 1983).
Rowlandson, Thomas
  Allerlei Liebe. Erotische Graphik (Dortmund, 1980).
  The amorous illustrations of Thomas Rowlandson. Ed. G[ert] Schiff (NY, 1969).
  Paulson, Ronald, *Rowlandson: a new interpretation* (1972).
  Von Meier, K., *The forbidden erotica of Thomas Rowlandson* (Los Angeles, 1970).
Webb, Peter, *The Erotic Arts* (1975; revised edition 1983).
Woodward, George Moutard, *Eccentric excursions, or literary & pictorial sketches of countenance, character & country in different parts of England and South Wales* (1807).
——, *An olio of good breeding: with sketches illustrative of the Modern Graces* (1801).
——, *Something concerning nobody ... Embellished with ... etchings* (1814).

5.5 Prose, prose fiction, plays and poetry

The academy of love. Describing the folly of young men and the fallacy of women, by John Johnson (1641).
Addison, Joseph, editor and translator, *The works of Anacreon, translated into English verse ... To which are added the odes, fragments, and epigrams of Sappho* (1735).

Adollizing: or, a lively picture of adoll-worship. A poem in five cantos (1748).

The adulteress. A satire in verse (1773).

'The adventures and amours of a bar-maid, a series of facts', *The Bon Ton Magazine* 4 (1794); published in three parts between January and April.

The adventures of a black coat (1760).

The adventures of a cork-screw (1775; repr. NY, 1974).

Adventures of a gold-headed cane, 2 vols. (1783).

The adventures of a Jesuit (1771; repr. NY, 1974).

Adventures of Jonathan Corncob, loyal American refugee. Written by himself (1787).

The adventures of Miss Beverly. Interspersed with genuine memoirs of a northern lady of quality, 2 vols. (1768).

The adventures of Miss Lucy Watson. A novel (1768).

The adventures of Mr. Loveill, interspers'd with many real amours of the modern polite world, 2 vols.; second edition (1750).

The adventures of the priests and nuns, as containing many delightful stories (1725).

Adventures of a silver penny. Including many secret anecdotes of little Misses and Masters both good and naughty (1787).

Allnight, Bumper [pseudonym], *The honest fellow: or, Reveller's memorandum-book. Wherein Mars and Venus, assisted by Bacchus, are in conjunction to exhibit the humours of the world. In a collection of such jocular songs, now in vogue ... To which is added, A collection of comic sentiments, never before printed, and other matter to make an accomplished toper* (1790).

The amazement of future ages (1684).

The American bee; a collection of entertaining histories, selected from different authors, and calculated for amusement and instruction (Leominster, Mass., 1797).

Ames, Richard, *The folly of love* (1691; fourth edition, 1700).

The amorous friars or, the intrigues of a convent (1759).

The amorous gallant's tongue tipp'd with golden expressions: or, the art of courtship refined. The thirteenth edition (c. 1741).

Amorous letters between Miss Loveman and Miss Longfart ('Paris', i.e., London, 1789).

Amorous sketches: by Master Cupid. With six capital engravings; from nature and life (1796).

'Amours of the Earl of Essex and the Countess of Rutland, supposed to be written by herself, and addressed to a lady', *The Rambler's Magazine* 4 (July–November, 1786; published in five parts).

The amours of Edward the IV. An historical novel. By the author of the Turkish spy (1700; repr. NY, 1973).

Amusements in high life; or, Conjugal infidelities in 1786. In a series of confidential letters, between ladies who have distinguished themselves by the multiplicity and singularity of their amours (1786).

The anatomist dissected: or the man-midwife finely brought to bed. Being an examination of the conduct of Mr. St. Andre. Touching the late pretended Rabbit-bearer; as it appears from his own narrative (1727).

Ancillon, Charles, *Eunuchism display'd, describing all the different sorts of eunuchs etc.* (1718).

Annet, Peter [pseudonym: Gideon Archer], *Social bliss considered: in marriage and divorce; cohabiting unmarried, and public whoring ... With The speech of Miss Polly Baker; and notes thereon* (1749).

Anstey, Christopher, *The new Bath guide, or, Memoirs of the B–r–d family. In a series of poetical epistles* (1766; repr. Hildesheim/NY, 1988).

An apology for a Latin Verse in commendation of Mr. Marten's 'GONOSO-LOGIUM NOVUM'; or, appendix to his 6th edition of the venereal disease; proving that the same liberty of describing the ... diseases of the secret parts of both sexes, and their cure (which ... is said by some to be obscene) has been ... us'd both by ancient and modern authors ... By a physician in the country (1709).

Arbuthnot, Archibald, *Memoirs of the remarkable life and surprising adventures of Miss Jenny Cameron, a lady, who by her attachment to the person and cause of the Young Pretender, has render'd herself famous by her exploits in his service* (1746).

Arbuthnot, John [pseudonym: Lemuel Gulliver], *The pleasures of marriage, in ten books* (1745).

Archenholtz, Johann Wilhem von, *A picture of England: containing a description of the laws, customs, and manners of England ... Translated from the original German ...* (1797).

Aristotle's Master-Piece

> *Aristotle's Masterpiece compleated, in two parts: the first containing the secrets of generation, in all the parts thereof, treating, of the benefit of marriage, and the prejudice of unequal matches, signs of insufficiency in men and women ..., a discourse of virginity. Of the organs of generation in women ... The use and action of the genitals ... With a word of advice to both sexes in the act of copulation* (1700).
>
> *Aristotle's Master-Piece: or, the secrets of generation display'd in all the parts thereof* (1690; 1700; 1704).
>
> *Aristotle's Master-Piece compleated in two parts* (1697; 1698).
>
> *Aristotle's Compleat Master-Piece. In three parts. Displaying the secrets of nature in the generation of man. The eleventh edition* (c. 1725; nineteenth edition, 1733; thirty-first edition, 1776).
>
> *Aristotle's Complete and experienced midwife. In two parts; the thirteenth edition* (1776).
>
> *Aristotle's book of problems; the thirteenth edition* (1776).
>
> *Aristotle's last legacy* (1776).
>
> *The complete works of Aristotle ... Containing his Master-Piece ... The Family Physician ... His experienced midwife* (1786).
>
> *The Works of Aristotle. In four parts. Containing ... I. His Complete Master-Piece. II. His Experienced Midwife. III. His Book of Problems. IV. His Last Legacy* (1777; repr. 1779, 1796, 1800; and Edinburgh, 1784).

American editions:

Aristotle's Master Piece completed. In two parts (NY, 1788; repr. 1793, 1794, 1798, and later).

Aristotle's Compleat Master Piece. In three parts (first edition *c.* 1766; twenty-sixth edition, 1755; twenty-eighth edition, 1766; Worcester, Mass., 1795; thirtieth edition, NY?, 1796).

The experienced midwife (Philadelphia, 1799).

Armstrong, John, *The art of preserving health: a poem* (1744; often reprinted until the end of the century).

——, *The oeconomy of love. A poetical essay* (1736).

——, *A synopsis of the history and cure of venereal diseases* (1737).

The art of knowing women: or, the female sex dissected in a faithful representation of their virtues and vices. Written in French, by the Chevalier Plante-Amor, and by him published at the Hague, 1729 (1730).

The art of tickling trouts; showing, the method how all faculties and professions in the world affect the false arts of wheedle, cant and flattery, to please fools and deceive wise men (1708).

Astruc, Jean, *Astruc on the venereal disease* (1754).

Atall, John, *Libertina sine conflictu; or, a true narrative of the untimely death of Doctor Atall* (1752).

Aulnoy [or Aunoy; or La Mothe], Marie-Cathérine, *The Earl of Douglas, an English story. From the French of the Countess D'Anois* [sic]. *By the translator of Dorval*, 3 vols. (Lynn, 1774).

——, *The history of the Earl of Warwick, sirnam'd [sic] the King-Maker ... To which is added, the remaining part of the unknown lady's pacquet of letters, taken from her by a French privateer* (1708).

——, *History of Hypolitus, Earl of Douglas* (1741).

——, *The history of John of Bourbon, Prince of Carency. Containing a variety of entertaining novels ... The second edition* (1723).

——, *Hypolitus, Earl of Douglas. Containing some memoirs of the court of Scotland* (1708).

——, *Ingenious and diverting letters of the Lady's* [the Countess d'Aulnoy's] *travels into Spain* (1697; repr. 1708, 1717, 1735).

——, *Memoirs of the court of England* (1707; repr. 1708).

——, *Memoirs of the court of France* (1692; repr. 1697).

——, *Memoirs of the court of Spain* (1692).

——, *Memoirs of the present state of the court and councils of Spain* (1701).

——, *The Prince of Carency: a novel* (1719).

——, *Secret memoirs of the Duke and Dutchess of O...* [Orleans] (1708).

The authentic memoirs of the countesse de Barré, the French King's mistress, carefully collated from a manuscript in the possession of the Dutchess of Villeroy. By Sir Francis N... (1771).

An authentic narrative of the celebrated Miss Fanny Davies, the celebrated modern amazon, who received sentence of death at the last Chelmsford Assizes, by Mr. Justice Ashurst, for stealing above £1250 in money and notes, from Mr. Wrigglesworth, a country grazier ... Interspersed with interesting moral reflections, and entertaining anecdotes, delineating her amorous parleys with her kind keepers in high-life. The second edition (1786).

The Bacchanalian Magazine. Composed principally of new convivial and amorous songs with easy and familiar tunes (1793).

Bancks, John, *Miscellaneous works, in verse and prose. Adorned with sculptures and illustrated with notes*, 2 vols. (1738).

——, *Poems on several occasions: consisting of tales, epistles, songs, odes, epigrams, and other miscellaneous pieces* (1733).

Barrin, Jean, *Venus in the cloister: or, the nun in her smock* (second edition, 1725).

The bauble, a tale (1721).

The bawd. A poem. Containing all the various practices these diabolical characters make use of to decoy innocent beauty into their snares, with their behaviour to them, and the means they are made to employ to entertain their numerous gallants ... By a distinguished worshipper in the temple of Venus (n.d., c. 1782).

Beauchamps, Pierre François Godard de, *History of King Apprius, &c. Extracted from the chronicle of the world, from the creation thereof* (Dublin/London, 1728).

Bedford, Arthur, *The evil and danger of stage-plays: shewing their natural tendency to destroy religion, and introduce a general corruption of manners* (Bristol/London, 1706).

The behaviour of the cl–gy as well as their traditions, destructive of religion: or, a succinct history of priestcraft, throughout all ages (1731).

The benefits and privileges of cuckolds ... The whole beautifully illustrated with several late notable intrigues that have been carried on in many parts of the beau-monde. *Humbly dedicated to Mother H–gg–r* (1728).

Betterton, Thomas, *The amorous widow, or the wanton wife* (1706; second edition 1710).

Beverland, Adrian, *Although my innocence is shelter'd ...* (1709; repr. 1712?).

——, *Hadriani Beverlandi de fornicatione cavenda admonitio* (1697 and later).

——, *A Hue and Cry after the Bulls of Bashan* (1710?).

——, *Seignior Perin del Vago's letter to Mr. Hadrian Beverland* (1702 and later).

Bienville, J.D.T., *Nymphomania, or, A Dissertation concerning the furor uterinus. Clearly and methodically explaining the beginning, progress, and different causes of that horrible distemper ... Written originally in French by M.D.T. de Bienville, M.D., and translated by Edward Sloane Wilmot, M.D.* (1775).

Boerhaave, Hermann, *Opera omnia medica* (Venice, 1742).

Boileau, Jacques, *Historia flagellantium de recto et perverso flagrorum usu apud Christanos* (Paris, 1700).

——, *Memorials of human superstition, imitated from the Historia Flagellantium of the abbé Boileau* (1785).

Bonnefons, Jean, *Pancharis, Queen of love: or, woman unveil'd. Being the Basia of Bonefonius ... Translated by several hands* (1721).
——, *Pancharis, Queen of love: or, the art of kissing ... The second edition* (1722).
Bostonian scintillations, or, A war of words. Being the productions of Visibilis, Invisibilis, etc. (Boston, Mass., 1787).
James Boswell
    James Boswell: the earlier years, 1740–69. Ed. Frederick A. Pottle (1966).
    Boswell for the defence. Ed. William K. Wimsatt and Frederick A. Pottle (1960).
    Boswell in extremes, 1776–1778. Ed. C. McC. Weis and Frederick A. Pottle (NY, 1970).
    Boswell's London journal, ed. Frederick A. Pottle (1950).
    Boswell: the ominous years, 1774–1776. Ed. C. Ryskamp and Frederick A. Pottle (1963).
    Boswell on the Grand Tour: Italy, Corsica and France, 1765–1766. Ed. F. Brady and Frederick A. Pottle (1955).
    Boswell in search of a wife, 1766–1769. Ed. F. Brady and Frederick A. Pottle (1956).
    The private papers of James Boswell. Ed. G. Scott and Frederick A. Pottle (NY, 1932–4).
Bridges, Thomas, *The adventures of a bank note*, 4 vols. (1770–71; repr. 1772).
Brown, John, *The elements of medicine* (1780; revised by T. Beddoes, Portsmouth, New Hampshire, 1803).
Brown, Thomas, *Amusements serious and comical* (1700; repr. in the series 'Les introuvables anglais', ed. Georges Lamoine, 1980).
——, *Letters from the dead to the living* (1702–3; 1707).
——, *The fourth and the last volume of the works of Mr. Tho. Brown* (fourth edition, 1719).
Buchan, William, *Observations concerning the prevention and cure of the venereal disease: intended to guard the ignorant and unwary against the baneful effects of that insiduous malady* (1803).
Bumography: or, a touch at the ladies tails; being a lampoon (privately) dispers'd at Tunbridge-Wells [Published by John Dunton] (1707; the second edition was entitled *The rump: or, a touch at the ladies tails*, 1708).
[Butler, Samuel?] *Dildoides. A burlesque poem. By Samuel Butler, gent. With a key explaining several names and characters in Hudibras* (1706).
A butler's diary, or, the history of Miss Eggerton. A novel, 2 vols. (1792).
Byrd, William, of Westover in Virginia
    Another secret diary of William Byrd of Westover, 1739–41. With letters and literary exercises 1696–1726, ed. Maude H. Woodfin and Marion Tinling (Richmond, Va., 1942).
    'The Female Creed', in *Another secret diary ...*, appendix IV.
    The secret diary of William Byrd of Westover, 1709–12. Ed. Louis B. Wright and Marion Tinling (Richmond, Va., 1941).

The prose works: narratives of a colonial Virginian. Ed. Louis B. Wright (Cambridge, Mass., 1966).

William Byrd of Virginia. The London diary (1717–21) and other writings. Ed. Louis B. Wright and Marion Tinling (Oxford/NY, 1958).

The writings of Colonel William Byrd of Westover in Virginia, Esq. Ed. John Spencer Bassett (NY, 1901).

The cabinet of amorous curiosities. In three tales. Highly calculated to please the votaries of Venus (1786).

The cabinet of love (1709).

The cabinet of love, or, Cupid's pastime (York? '1810'; probably *c.* 1718).

Cagliostro, Comte de [i.e., Giuseppe Balsamo], *Memorial, or brief, for the Comte de Cagliostro, defendant, against the king's Attorney-general, plaintiff: in the cause of the Cardinal de Rohan, Comtesse de la Motte, and others ... With an introductory preface. By Parkyns Macmahon* (1786).

Cannon, Thomas, *Ancient and modern pederasty investigated and exemplified* (1749?).

A canting academy, or, the pedlar's French dictionary (*c.* 1741).

Casanova, Giacomo di Seingalt, *History of my life. First translated into English in accordance with the original French manuscript by William R. Trask, with an introduction by the translator*, 6 vols. (1967–72).

——, *The memoirs of Giacomo Casanova di Seingalt. Translated ... by Arthur Machen*, 12 vols. (1922).

——, *The memoirs of Jacques Casanova de Seingalt, 1725–1798. Now carefully annotated for the first time in English. The memoirs and notes translated by Arthur Machen & introduced by Havelock Ellis*, 8 vols. (Edinburgh, 1940).

——, *The memoirs of Jacques Casanova de Seingalt ... The first complete and unabridged English translation by Arthur Machen. Illustrated with old engravings*, 6 vols. (London/NY, 1958–60).

Chauncy, Elnathan, 'Commonplace book', *PCSM* xxviii, pp. 1–24.

The cherub: or, Guardian of female innocence. Exposing the arts of boarding schools, hired fortune tellers, corrupt milliners, apparent ladies of fashion (1792).

A Chinese tale. Written originally by that Prior of China the facetious Sou ma Quang, a celebrated Mandarine of letters; under the title of Chamyamt-chochang, or Chamyam with her leg upon a table ... With a curious frontispiece, taken from a large CHINA *punch-bowl just come over ...* (1740).

Choderlos de Laclos, Pierre Ambroise François, *Dangerous connections ...*; 4 vols. (1784).

The choice spirits museum. A collection of songs. By H. Howard (1756).

Chorier, Nicolas, *A dialogue between a married lady and a Maid* [an abridged adaptation in English of *Aloisiae Sigeae satyra sotadica*] (1682; 1740; 1786).

——, *Aretinus redivivus, or the ladies' academy* [an adaptation of *Aloisiae Sigeae*] (1745).

——, *The school of love containing severall dialogues between Tullia and Octavia* [an adaptation of *Aloisiae Sigeae*] (1702).

——, *The schoole of women* [an adaptation of *Aloisiae Sigeae*] (1682).

Churchill, Charles, *The rosciad* (1761).

Clarke, John, 'The batchelor-keeper', in Edmund Curll, ed., *Atterburyana* (1727).

——, 'The virgin-seducer', in Edmund Curll, ed. *Atterburyana* (1727).

Cleland, John, *Memoirs of a coxcomb* (1751).

——, *Memoirs of a woman of pleasure* (1748–49; for extant eighteenth-century editions see Patrick Kearney's bibliography of the Private Case collection in the British [Museum] Library).

——, *Memoirs of a woman of pleasure*. With an introduction for modern readers by Peter Quennell (NY, 1963; repr. 1975).

——, ——. With an introduction by J.H. Plumb (NY, 1965; repr. 1978).

——, ——. Edited and with an introduction by Peter Sabor (Oxford/NY, 1985).

——, *Fanny Hill or Memoirs of a woman of pleasure*. Edited and with an introduction by Peter Wagner (Harmondsworth, 1985).

——, *The romance of a day; or an adventure in Greenwich Park, last Easter* (1760; repr. in *The surprizes of love*, 1765).

——, *The romance of a night; or, a Covent-Garden adventure* (1762; repr. in *The surprizes of love*, 1765).

——, *The surprizes of love* (1765).

The cloister; or, the Amours of Sainfroid, a Jesuit, and Eulalia, a nun (1758).

The cloisters laid open, or, adventures of the priests and nuns. With some account of confessions, and the lewd use they make of them ... Also, the Adventures of the Bath (n.d.; probably published between 1750 and 1800).

College-wit sharpen'd: or the head of the house with a sting in the tail ... The Wadhamites, a burlesque poem (1739).

Collier, Jeremy, *A second defence of the short view of the prophaneness* [sic] *and immorality of the English stage* (1700).

Colman, George (the elder), *The genius of nonsense* (1780).

Coltheart, P., *The quacks unmask'd. Which detects, and sets in a true light, their pernicious and destructive practice* (1727).

Comazzi, John Baptista, *The morals of princes: or, an abstract of the most remarkable passages contain'd in the history of all the emperors who reign'd in Rome ...* (1729).

Combe, William, *The devil upon two sticks in England: being a continuation of Le diable boiteux of Le Sage*, 4 vols. (1790; 6 vols. 1790–91).

The comforts of whoreing and the vanity and chastity of the unreasonable-ness of love (1694).

A comical new dialogue. Between Mr. G...f, a pious dissenting parson, and a female-Quaker (1706).

The complaint (1676).

The compleat academy of complements: containing first, choice sentences, with variety of similitudes, and comparisons; also the best complemental letters. Second, the art of courtship and genteel breeding, with discourses proper for this ingenious age ... Together with a collection of the newest songs that are sung at court house and play-house (1705).

The compleat midwife's practice enlarged. Corrected and much enlarged by John Pechey (fifth edition, 1698).

A compleat set of charts of the coasts of Merryland wherein are exhibited all the parts, harbours, creeks, bays, rocks, settings, bearings, gulphs, prom-ontories, limits, boundaries &c. (1745).

The complete modern London spy for the present year 1781 or, a real and universal disclosure of the secret, nocturnal and diurnal transactions in and about ... London ... written by a gentleman of fortune (1781).

Confession of Count de Harcourt, containing his amours, with several ladies of quality in the courts of France, Italy, and England. With a frontispiece (1743).

Confessions of a beauty. From the French. 2 vols. (1798).

The confessions of a coquet. A novel. In a series of letters (1785).

A congratulatory epistle from a reformed rake, to John F.....g, Esq. Upon the new scheme of reclaiming prostitutes (1758).

'Conjugal infidelity, or authentic memoirs of Lydia Lovemore. In a series of letters to Eliza', *The Rambler's Magazine* no. 7 and 8 (1789–90: published in five parts).

Consummation: or the rape of Adonis (1741).

Cotton, Charles, *Scarronides, or Virgile Travestie* (1664, 1670, 1691, 1700, 1709, etc.).

Cotton, John, *Erotopolis* [in Greek letters]. *The present state of Betty-Land* (1684; repr. in *The potent ally*, 1741).

Cotton, Seaborn, 'Commonplace book', *PCSM* xxxii, pp. 307–418.

The Covent Garden jester; or, The rambler's companion ... By Roger Ran-ger, Gent. (1785).

Coventry, Francis, *The history of Pompey the little: or, The life and adven-tures of a lap-dog* (1751; five editions in the eighteenth century; repr. NY, 1974).

The court and city vagaries, or intrigues, of both sexes (1711; repr. NY, 1970).

The court of adultery: a vision. The sixth edition. With additions (1778).

Court secrets: or, the lady's chronicle historical and gallant from the year 1671 to 1690. Extracted from the letters of Madam de Sevigne [sic] (published as part II of Edmund Curll's *Atterburyana*, 1727).

Court whispers: or, a magazine of wit. A satyr for the country (1743).

Courtney, John (?), *The rape of Pomona. An elegiac epistle, from the waiter at Hockerel to the Hon. Mr. L[y]tt[elto]n. The third edition* (1773).

The crafts and frauds of physic. Third edition (1703).

Crébillon, Claude Prosper Jolyot de [Crébillon *fils*]
    The amours of Zeokinizul king of the Kofirans (1749).
    Letters from the Marchioness de M..., to the Comte de R... (1735; repr. 1737, 1738, 1766).

The night and the moment (1770).

The skimmer; or, the history of Tanzai and Néardarné (1735; repr. 1742 and 1748).

The sopha. A moral tale (1742; eighteen editions appeared between 1742 and 1801).

The wanderings of the heart and mind: or, Memoirs of Mr de Meilcour (1751).

Croft, Herbert, *Love and madness – a story too true, in a series of letters between parties whose names would perhaps be mentioned, were they less known, or less lamented* (1780).

The cuckolds' cap garland. Containing some of the merriest songs (Newcastle, 1765?; repr. 1780?).

The cuckold's curse, against the state of matrimony. And a satire, on my Lady Tinder A–se (Dublin, 1757).

Culpeper, Nicholas, *Directory for midwives* (1651; many eighteenth-century editions).

Cummings, Edward E., *Complete Poems: 1913–1962* (NY, 1972).

Cupid and Hymen, or a voyage to the isles of love and matrimony, containing a most diverting account of the inhabitants of those two vast and populous countries ... to which is added the Batchelor's estimate of the expenses attending a married life, The married man's answer to it ... (1742).

Cupid's beehive, or the sting of love. Translated from Bonefonius, by several hands (1721).

'The curious and diverting history and adventures of a bedstead', in *The Rambler's Magazine* (1784; repr. by W. Dugdale in 1840–41).

A curious collection of novels (1731).

The curious maid. A tale (1720–21) [see Hildebrand Jacobs].

The curious maid continued (1721) [see Hildebrand Jacobs].

Curll, Edmund (editor and publisher), *Atterburyana. Being miscellanies, by the late Bishop of Rochester, &c.* (1727).

——, *De secretis mulierum; or the mysteries of human generation fully revealed* (n.p., n.d., published in the early eighteenth century).

——, *Post-office intelligence: or, universal gallantry. Being a collection of love-letters, written by persons in all stations, from most parts of the kingdom* (1736).

Cythera, or new poems upon love and intrigue (1723).

Dalton, James, *A genuine narrative of all the street robberies committed since October last, by James Dalton, and his accomplices ... To which is added, a key to the canting language ... Taken from the mouth of James Dalton* (1728).

Defoe, Daniel, *Conjugal lewdness or matrimonial whoredom* (1727).

——, *Moll Flanders* (dated 1721; published in 1722).

——, *Roxana* (1724).

——, *Some considerations upon street-walkers* (1726).

Delolme, J.L., *The history of the flagellants: otherwise, of religious flagellations among different nations, and especially among Christians. Being a*

paraphrase and commentary on the Historia Flagellantium of the Abbé
Boileau ... The second edition (1783).

The devil divorced; or the diabo-whore (1782).

A dialogue concerning the practice of physic (1735).

Dialogue of a Quaker and his maid (1786).

Diderot, Denis, *Les bijoux indiscrets* or *The Indiscreet Toys*, 2 vols.
(1749).

——, *The nun ... Translated from the French*, 2 vols. (Dublin/London,
1797).

——, *The nun* (1966; repr. 1972).

——, *Memoirs of a nun* (1928; repr. 1959 and 1960).

*Did you ever see such damned stuff? Or, so-much-the-better. A story without
head or tail, wit or humour* (1760).

Diemar, E.M., *The history and amours of Rhodope* (1780).

*Dirty dogs for dirty puddings. Or, memoirs of the luscious amours of several
persons of both sexes, of quality and distinction* (1732).

*A discovery of the island Frivola; or, the frivolous island. Translated from the
French, now privately handed about at Paris* (1750).

*A dissertation wherein the meaning, duty, and happiness of kissing are
explained* (Norwich, Swaffham, Lynn, n.d.).

Douglas, G. Archibald, *The nature and causes of impotence in men, and
barrenness in women, explained* (1758).

Douglas, John, *A dissertation on the venereal disease. Wherein a method of
curing all the stages of that distemper will be communicated* (1737).

*'Drive on Coachman.' An humorous tale. Occasioned by an affair lately
discover'd in a family of quality* (1739).

Dryden, John, *Marriage à la mode* (1671).

Duclos, Charles Pinot, *A course of gallantries; or, the inferiority of the
tumultuous joys of the passions to the serene pleasures of reason: attested
by the confession of a nobleman who had tried both*, 2 vols. (1775; a
translation of *Confessions du Comte de ...* of 1741).

Dunton, John, *Athenian sport: or, two thousand paradoxes merrily argued*
(1707).

——, *John Dunton's Letters from New England.* Ed. W.H. Whitmore (Boston, Mass., 1867).

——, *The life and errors of John Dunton* (1705; repr. in 2 vols, NY, 1969).

——, *The night walker, or, evening rambles in search after lewd women, with
the various conferences held with them, dedicated to the whores and
whoremasters of London and Westminster* (c. 1700?).

D'Urfey, Thomas, *The intrigues at Versailles; or, A jilt in all humours, a
comedy* (1697).

——, *Love for money; or, the boarding school. A comedy* (1691).

——, *The marriage-hater match'd* (1692).

——, *Wit and mirth: or pills to purge melancholy*, 6 vols. (1719–20; repr.
NY, 1959).

Eden, Adam [pseudonym], *A vindication of the reformation, on foot, among
the ladies to abolish modesty and chastity, and restore the native simplicity*

of going naked. And an attempt to reconcile all opposers to it, and make them join in a speedy completion of this glorious design (1755).

Egane, Anthony, *The book of rates now used in the sin custom-house of the Church and Court of Rome* (Edinburgh, 1779).

An elegy on the lamented death of the electrical eel (1778).

Elysium: or, the state of love and honour in the superior regions of bliss (1702; repr. NY, 1973).

Entertainments of gallantry: or remedies of love (1712; repr. NY, 1970).

An epistle from L(ad)y W(orsle)y to S(i)r R(ichar)d W(orsle)y Bart. The third edition (1782).

An epistle from Mademoiselle d'Eon to the Right Honourable L(or)d M(ansfiel)d. . . . on his determination in regard to her sex. Sixth edition (1778).

An epistle from Mr. Banks, voyager, monster-hunter, and amoroso, to Oberea, Queen of Otaheite . . . The second edition ('Batavia', i.e., London, 1773).

An epistle from Oberea, Queen of Otaheite, to Joseph Banks, Esq. (1774).

An epistle from the platonick Madam B...ier [Barbier] *to the celebrated Signor Car–ino* (1734).

An epistle from John James H...dd...g–r [Heiddegger], *Esq. on the report of Signor F–r–n–lli's being with child* (1736).

An epistle to the most learned Doctor W...d...d [i.e., John Woodward] *from a prude, that was unfortunately metamorphos'd on Saturday Dec. 29, 1722* (1723).

'An essay on matrimony', in *The sixpenny miscellany. Or, a dissertation upon pissing* (1726), 19–25.

An essay on wind. With curious anecdotes of eminent peteurs, etc. Written for the edification of windbound ladies and gentlemen (1783).

Ettmüller, Michel, *Etmullerus abridg'd . . . Translated from the last edition of the works of Michael Etmullerus* (1699).

——, *Michaelis Ettmulleri opera omnia theoretica et practica* (1685).

An examination into the origin, and meaning of the words empiricism, empirick, quack doctor and quack. And, an exact account of the present state of physick (1749).

Exhibition of female flagellants in the modest and incontinent world. Proving from indubitable facts, that a number of ladies take a secret pleasure in whipping their own, and children committed to their care, vol. I (1777), vol. II (1785), repr. 1872.

Explanatory remarks upon the life and opinions of Tristram Shandy; wherein the morals and politics of this piece are already laid open. By Jeremiah Kunastrokius (1760).

The fair adultress, or the treacherous brother. Being the secret memoirs of a certain noble family in the island of Cyprus. Interspersed with several original letters. Translated from the Greek. (1743).

The fair adultress. A novel (1774).

The fair concubine: or the secret history of the beautiful Vanella. Containing, her amours with Albimarides, P. Alexis, &c (1782).

The festival of love; or, a collection of Cytherian poems. Procured &

selected by G–e P–e and dedicated to his brother. The sixth edition (1770?).

Fielding, Henry, *The female husband: or, the surprising history of Mrs. Mary, alias Mr. George Hamilton. Who was convicted of having married a young woman of Wells and lived with her as her husband. Taken from her own mouth since her confinement* (1746; repr. and ed. C.E. Jones, Liverpool, 1960).

——, *Shamela* (1741).

——, *Tom Jones* (1749).

The fifteen comforts of cuckoldom. Written by a noted cuckold in the New-Exchange in the Strand (1706).

The fifteen comforts of matrimony. Or, a looking-glass for all those who have enter'd in that holy and comfortable state (1706).

The fifteen comforts of a wanton wife: or the fool well fitted. Dedicated to the London cuckolds (1706–7).

The fifteen comforts of whoring, or, the pleasures of town-life. Dedicated to the youth of the present age. By the author of the Fifteen comforts of matrimony (1706).

The fifteen plagues of a lawyer, a quack doctor ... To which is added, the fifteen plagues of a foot-man (1711?).

The fifteen plagues of a maidenhead [published by James Read and Angell Carter] (1706–7).

The fifteen pleasures of a virgin. Written by the suppos'd author of the Fifteen plagues of a maidenhead (1709).

The finish'd rake; or gallantry in perfection (1733; repr. NY, 1970).

The folly, sin, and danger of marrying widows, and old women in general, demonstrated; and earnestly address'd to the batchelors of Great Britain (1740?).

The f[ond] mother's garland, composed of several excellent new songs (Newcastle, *c.* 1770).

Foote, Samuel, *The minor* (1760).

A fortnights ramble through London, or a complete display of all the cheats and frauds practised in that great metropolis, with the best methods for eluding them (1792; repr. 1795).

Foster, Hanna, *The coquette; or, the history of Eliza Wharton* (Boston, Mass., 1797).

The four contented cuckolds (1790?).

Frailties of fashion, or the adventures of an Irish smock (1782).

Franklin, Benjamin, 'The Elysian fields' (1780; repr. in Richard E. Amacher, *Franklin's wit and folly. The bagatelles*; New Brunswick, NJ, 1953, 53–6).

——, 'The ephemera' (1778; repr. in Amacher, *Franklin's wit*, 48–52).

——, 'The flies' (n.d.; repr. in Amacher, *Franklin's wit*, 58–9).

——, 'Letter of advice to a young man on choosing a mistress' [also known as 'Old Mistress Apologue'], (1745; repr. in *The papers of Benjamin Franklin*. Ed. L. Larabee *et al.*, New Haven Conn., 1959 f., vol. III, 30–31).

——, 'The speech of Miss Polly Baker' (1747; repr. in Max Hall, *Benjamin Franklin and 'Polly Baker'*, Chapel Hill, NC, 1960, 157–68).

——, 'To the Royal Academy of Brussels' (*c.* 1781; repr. in Amacher, *Franklin's wit*, 66–9).

——, *The papers of Benjamin Franklin*. Ed. Leonard Larabee *et al.*; 23 vols. to date (New Haven, Connecticut, 1959 f.).

——, *The writings. Collected and edited with a life and introduction by Albert Henry Smyth*, 10 vols. (NY, 1905–7, repr. 1970).

The frauds and villainies of the common practice of physick (1705).

Free thoughts on quacks and their medicines, occasioned by the death of Dr. Goldsmith and Mr. Scawen; or, a candid and ingenious inquiry into the merits and dangers imputed to Advertised Remedies (1776).

Freeman, Charles, *et al.*, *The lover's new guide; or, a complete library of love. Giving full instructions for love, courtship, and marriage* (1780?).

The frisky songster ... The ninth edition (1802).

The fruit shop. A tale; 2 vols. (1765).

A full and true account of a dreaded fire that lately broke out in the Pope's breeches (1713).

Funny, Ferdinando [pseudonym], *The merry Andrew* (1772).

The gallant companion: or, an antidote for the hype and vapours (1746).

Garlick, Thomas, *A mechanical account of the cause and cure of a virulent gonorrhea in both sexes ... by topical applications only ... To which is added ... a short account of the cause and cure of the whites in women* (1719).

Gavin, Antonio, *The frauds of Romish monks and priests* (1691; fifth edition, 1725; for vol. II of this title see below).

——, *A master-key to popery* (Dublin, 1724; second edition, 3 vols., London, 1725–6).

——, —— (Newport, Rhode Island, 1773).

——, *Observations on a journey to Naples. Wherein the frauds of Romish monks and priests are further discuss'd* (fifth edition, 1725; this is vol. II of *The frauds of Romish monks and priests*).

Gay, Joseph, *The petticoat* (1716).

Gaya, Louis de, *Marriage ceremonies; as now used in all parts of the world ... Put into modern English, by Mr. Tho. Brown* (1704).

Genuine and authentic memoirs of a well-known woman of intrigue ... 2 vols. (1787; repr. *c.* 1880).

Genuine memoirs of the celebrated Miss Maria Brown. Exhibiting the life of a courtezan in the most fashionable scenes of dissipation; 2 vols. in 1 (1766; repr. NY, 1975).

The genuine memoirs of Miss Faulkner; otherwise Mrs. D...l...n, or Countess of H...x in expectancy. Containing the amours and intrigues of several persons of high distinction, and remarkable characters: with some curious political anecdotes, never before published (1770).

Gifford, William, *The baviad* (1791).

Girard, Jean Baptiste, publications on. [See also p. 417.]

    Spiritual fornication. A burlesque poem. Wherein the case of Miss Cadière and Father Girard are merrily display'd. In three canto's [sic] (1732).

Graham, James, '*Il convito amoroso!*' *or a serio-comico-philosophical* lecture on the causes, nature, and effects of love and beauty ... and in praise of the ... celestial bed. As delivered by Hebe Vestina ... at the Temple of Hymen in London (1782).

Grassal, Georges Joseph [alias Hugues Rebell], *The memoirs of Dolly Morton: the story of a woman's part in the struggle to free the slaves: an account of the whippings, rapes, and violences that preceded the civil war in America, with curious anthropological observations on the radical diversities in the female bottom and the way different women endure chastisement* (Paris, 1899; repr. London, 1970).

Great news from Hell, or the devil foil'd by Bess Weatherby. In a letter from the late celebrated Miss Betsy Wemyss ... To the no less celebrated Miss Lucy C...r (1760).

Grosley, Peter J., *A tour to London; or, new observations on England and its inhabitants* (1772).

Gueulette, Thomas Simon, *Mongul tales, or, the dreams of men awake*; 2 vols. (1736; repr. NY, 1973).

Hamilton, Alexander, *The family female physician: or, a treatise on the management of female complaints* (Worcester, Mass., 1793).

——, *Outlines of the theory and practice of midwifery* (Philadelphia, Pa., 1790; Worcester, Mass., 1794 et al.).

——, *A treatise on the management of female complaints* (NY, 1792; repr. 1795).

Hamilton, Anthony, publications on.
    Memoirs of the Comte de Grammont, edited with an introduction by David Hughes (1965).

Hamilton, Thomas, 6th Earl of Haddington, *Forty select poems, on several occasions* (1753).

——, *Monstrous good things!! Humorous tales in verse, for the amusement of leisure minutes. Written by the late ingenious Earl Hadding(to)n. Printed at Crazy Castle* (London?, 1785).

——, *New crazy tales, or ludicrous stories, facetiously told for the entertainment of young gentlemen and ladies ... Mulberry Hill. Printed at Crazy Castle* (1783).

——, *Select poems on several occasions in the luscious taste, by the Right Honourable Earl of H...n. To which is added several curious originals* [a new edition of *New crazy tales* of 1783] (1787).

The happy courtezan: or, the prude demolish'd (1735).

The harlot's progress: or, the humours of Drury-Lane. In six cantos [contains six prints by Hogarth] (1732).

Harris's list of Covent-Garden ladies: or New Atlantis for the year 1761. To which is annexed The ghost of Moll King or a night at Derrys (1761).

Harris's list of Covent-Garden ladies: or, Man of pleasure's kalender for the year 1788 [and 1789–93]. *Containing the histories and some curious anecdotes of the most celebrated ladies now on the town or in keeping, and also of their keepers*, 4 vols. (1788–93).

Harvey, Gideon, *The French pox, with all its kinds, causes, signs and prognosticks* ... *All comprised in this fifth edition of Little Venus unmask'd* (1685; sixth edition, 1700?).

——, *Great Venus unmasked: or, a more exact discovery of the venereal evil. Second edition* (1672).

[Haslewood, Joseph] *The secret history of the Green Rooms, containing authentic memoirs of the actors and actresses in the three Theatres Royal* (1790; second edition in 2 vols., 1792; third edition, 1793).

——, ——. *New edition, with improvements. To which is prefixed a sketch of the history of the English stage*, 2 vols. (1795).

Hawkesworth, John, *Almoran and Hamet; an Oriental tale* (1761; repr. NY, 1974).

The Hell-Fire-Club: kept by a Society of Blasphemers. A satyr ... With the king's Order in Council, for suppressing Immorality and Prophaneness (1721).

Hell upon earth: or, the town in an uproar (1729).

The He-Strumpets. A satyr on the Sodomite-club (1707; fourth edition, 1710).

Hickey, William, *Memoirs of William Hickey*. Ed. Alfred Spencer (1913).

——, *Memoirs of William Hickey*. Ed. Peter Quennell (1960; repr. 1975).

Hilaria. The festive board (1798).

Hill, John, *Exotic botany illustrated, in thirty-five figures of curious and elegant plants; explaining the sexual system, and tending to give some new lights into the vegetable philosophy* (1759).

——, *The history of a woman of quality: or, the adventures of Lady Frail* (1751).

——, *The letters and papers of Sir John Hill*, ed. G.S. Rousseau (NY, 1982).

——, *Lucina sine concubitu. A letter humbly addressed to the Royal Society; in which is proved, by the most incontestable evidence, drawn from reason and practice, that a woman may conceive and be brought to bed, without any commerce with man* (1750; repr. 1761, 1762, 1771).

——, *The vegetable system*, 26 vols. (1759–75).

Hill, Richard, *The blessings of polygamy displayed, in an affectionate address to the Reverend Martin Madan; Occasioned by his late work, entitled Thelyphthora, or, a treatise on female ruin* (1781).

The history and adventures of a lady's slippers and shoes. Written by themselves (1754).

The history of Charles Jones, the footman (1796; repr. 1797 and 1800?).

The history of a French louse; or the spy of a new species, in France and England (1779).

The history of the human heart, or the adventures of a young gentleman (1749; repr. in 1827 as *Memoirs of a man of pleasure*; and, with the original title, NY, 1974).

History of the matrimonial adventures of a banker's clerk, with the pretended Lady Ann Frances Caroline Boothby, otherwise sister to the Duke of Beaufort (1762).

The history of Miss Katty N——, by herself (1757).

The history of Pego the Great (1733).

The history of Tom Jones, the foundling, in his married state (1750).

The history of Signor del Dildo, formerly confessor to several eminent nunneries abroad, and now resident incognito in England (1732).

The history of Will Ramble, a libertine. Compiled from genuine materials, and the several incidents taken from real life, 2 vols. (1755).

[Holloway, Robert] *The Phoenix of Sodom, or the Vere Street coterie* (1813).

Homony Club of Annapolis, Maryland, *Records of* [1770–73] (Philadelphia, Pa.)

The honest London spy: exhibiting the base and subtle intrigues of the town, in a number of essays, serious and comical. By Peeping Tim. To which is added, The obliging husband and imperious wife, in a number of pleasant dialogues (1779).

Hunter, John, *A treatise on the venereal disease ... Abridged by William Currie* (1786; repr. Philadelphia, Pa., 1787 and 1791).

Hutchinson, John, *Glory or gravity* (1732).

——, *Moses's principia* (1724).

——, *Power essential and mechanical, or what power belongs to God and what to his creatures, in which the design of Sir I. Newton and Dr. Samuel Clark is laid open* (1732).

——, *The religion of Satan, or Antichrist delineated* (1736).

The impotent lover. Described in six elegies on old-age; in imitation of Cornelius Gallus, with a satyre on our modern letchers, shewing the many new inventions they have to raise their lust, viz. flogging, etc... [followed by] *Remains of the Right Honourable John, Earl of Rochester, Being satyrs, songs and poems never before published* (1718).

The inamorata. Addressed to the author of the Electrical Eel. By a lady (1777).

Intrigues à-la-mode. Biographical memoirs of Charles Augustus Fitzroy, Duke of Grafton, including some remarkable particulars in the life of the celebrated Miss Anna Bella Parsons (c. 1812).

Jacob, Giles, *The rape of the smock* (1727).

Jacobs, Hildebrand, *The curious maid* (1720–21).

——, *A merry conversation which lately pass'd between a very noted Quaker and his maid, upon a very merry occasion. To which is added, The members to their sovereign, and, The button hole. A riddle* (1739).

——, *The works. Containing poems on various subjects, and occasions* (1785).

Jackson [Reverend], *Sodom and Onan, a satire, inscribed to* [Samuel Foote] *Esq., alias the Devil upon two sticks* (c. 1776).

James, Robert, *A medicinal dictionary, including physic, surgery, anatomy, chymistry, and botany ... Together with a history of drugs,* 3 vols. (1743–5).

Johnstone, Charles, *Chrysal: or, the adventures of a guinea ... By an adept,* 2 vols. (1760; enlarged edition: 4 vols. Dublin, 1766; repr. in 2 vols., ed. Ronald Paulson, NY, 1979).

Jones, Erasmus, *A trip through London containing observations on men and things. The second edition* (1728).

Jones, Stephen, *The life and adventures of a fly* (1789).

Kick him, Jenny. A tale (in verse). The eleventh edition to which is added The female contest, a merry tale (1737).

Kidgell, John, *A genuine and succinct narrative of a scandalous ... libel, entitled, An essay on woman, etc.* (1763).

——, publications on.

An expostulary letter to the Reverend Mr. Kidgell (1763).

The priest in rhyme (1763).

Killegrew, Tom, Jr [pseudonym], *The merry quack doctor; or, The fun box broke open* (1778?).

Kilner, Dorothy, *Adventures of a hackney coach* (1781).

——, *The life and perambulations of a mouse* (1783–4).

King, Richard, *The frauds of London detected* (1795).

King, William [alias Frederick Scheffer], *The toast, an epic poem in four books. Written in Latin by Frederick Scheffer, done into English by Peregrine O'Donald, Esq.* [vol. I] (Dublin, 1732).

——, *The toast. An heroick poem in four books, written originally in Latin, by Frederick Scheffer: now done into English, and illustrated with notes and observations by Peregrine O'Donald, Esq.* (Dublin, 1736; repr. London, 1736 and 1747).

Kitty's Attalantis for the year 1766 (1766).

Kitty's stream, or the noblemen turned fisher-men. A comic satire. Addressed to the gentlemen in the interest of the celebrated Miss K(itt)y F(ishe)r by Rigdum Funidas (1759).

Knight, Richard Payne, *An account of the remains of the worship of Priapus, lately existing at Isernia, in the kingdom of Naples: in two letters; one from Sir William Hamilton, K.B., His Majesty's minister at the court of Naples, to Sir Joseph Bancks, Bart. President of the Royal Society; and the other from a person residing at Isernia: to which is added A Discourse on the worship of Priapus, and its connexion with the mystic theology of the ancients* (1786).

Lackington, James, *The confessions of James Lackington, late bookseller ... in a series of letters to a friend* (1804).

——, *Lackington's confessions, rendered into narrative* (1804).

——, *Memoirs of the forty-five first years of the life of James Lackington ... in forty-seven letters to a friend* (1791; eighth edition, corrected and much enlarged, 1794).

The ladies dispensatory, or, every woman her own physician. Treating of the nature, causes and various symptoms of all the diseases, infirmities and disorders ... that most peculiarly affect the fair sex etc. (1739; repr. 1740).

The ladies physical directory; the eighth edition (1742; first published in 1716 as *A rational account of the natural weaknesses of women*).

The lady's delight. Containing, 1. An address to all well-provided Hibernians. 2. The Arbor Vitae: or, tree of life. A poem. Shewing whence it took its root; how it has spread its leaves all over Christendom; being extremely useful to students in all branches of polite literature. 3. The natural history of the arbor vitae: or, tree of life, in prose. Printed from the original manuscript. 4. *Ridotto all'fresco. A poem. Describing the growth of a tree in the famous Spring-Gardens at Vaux-Hall, under the care of that ingenious botanist Dr. H–gg–r* (1732).

Lamotte, Charles, *An essay upon poetry and painting, with relation to the sacred and profane history with an appendix concerning obscenity in writing and painting* (1730).

Lamotte, Jeanne de St. Rémy de Valois, *Authentic adventures of the celebrated Countess de la Motte ... Translated from the French. To which is added, a narrative of her escape to London, as stated by herself. Also memoirs of her sister, under the character of Marianne* (1787).

——, *The life of Jane de St. Rémy de Valois, heretofore Countess de la Motte ...*, 2 vols. (1791).

——, *Memoirs of the Countess de Valois de la Motte; containing a compleat justification of her conduct ...* (1788).

Lancaster, Nathaniel, *The pretty gentleman* (1747).

Learned, John, *The rambling justice; or, the jealous husbands* (1678).

Lesage, Alain René, *The devil upon two sticks. Translated from the Diable boiteux of M. Le Sage. To which are prefixed, Asmodeus's crutches ... and Dialogues between two chimneys of Madrid* (Edinburgh/London, 1770).

Leti, Gregorio [alias Marforio], *The court of Rome* (1654).

——, *The history of the whores and whoredoms of the popes, cardinals and clergy of Rome* (1678).

——, *The life of Pope Sixtus the Vth* (1704; repr. 1754, 1766, 1778, 1779).

Lewis, Matthew Gregory, *The Monk* (1796; repr. NY, 1952; Oxford, 1973 and 1980).

The life and adventures of a cat (1760).

The life and adventures of William B–a–w [Bradshaw] *commonly called Devil Dick*, 2 vols. (1755).

'The life and opinions of Timotheus Randy, stay-maker', *The Covent Garden Magazine* 2 (April–June 1773; published in three parts).

Linnaeus [or Linné], Carl, *Nemesis divina*. Ed. Wolf Lepenies and Lars Gustafsson (Berlin, 1981).

——, *Systema naturae* (Leyden, 1735).

List of all the sporting ladies who is [sic] *arrived from the most principle* [sic] *towns in Great Britain and Ireland to take their pleasure at Leith races on Tuesday the 22nd of July 1777* (Edinburgh, 1777).

List of the sporting ladies (London?, c. 1770).

London: a satire. Containing prosaical strictures on prisons, inns of court, courts of justice, justices of the peace, sheriffs offices, prostitutes, play and opera houses, gaming, churches, tower, custom-house, East-India-House, Excise-office, bank, bedlam, Royal-Exchange, Mansion-House, Guildhall, Heralds-Office, Doctors Commons, court of admiralty, college of physicians, Bridewell, Westminster Abbey and St. Stephen's Chapel &c. Third edition (n.d.; 1782?).

The London-Bawd: with her character and life. Discovering the various and subtile intrigues of lewd women. The fourth edition (1711).

The London belles, or a description of the most celebrated beauties in the metropolis of Great Britain (1707).

The London jilt: or, the politick whore. Shewing, all the artifices and stratagems which the ladies of pleasure make use of for the intreguing [sic] *and decoying of men; interwoven with several pleasant stories of the misses ingenious performances* (Second edition, 1683).

Louvet de Couvray, Jean Baptiste, *The life and adventures of the Chevalier de Faublas, including a variety of anecdotes relative to the present king of Poland*, 4 vols. (1793).

Love given over, or, a satyr against the pride, lust and inconstancy, etc. of women (1709).

Love in all its shapes: or the way of a man with a woman. Illustrated in the various practices of the Jesuits of the Maison Professe at Paris, with divers ladies of quality and fashion at the court of France (1734).

The love-encounter. At Cnidus (n.p., n.d.).

Low-life: or one half of the world, knows not how the other half live ... (1764).

Luisinus, Aloysius, *Aphrodisiacus. Containing a summary of the ancient writers on the venereal disease. Under the following heads: I. Of its original. II. Of the symptoms. III. Of the various methods of cure. Extracted from the two tomes of A. Luisinus. With a large preface by Daniel Turner, of the College of Physicians in London* (1737).

——, *Aphrodisiacus, sive de lue venerea*, 3 vols. (vols. I and II printed at Leyden; vol. III at Jena; 1728–89).

Lyser, Johannes, *Polygamia triumphatrix* ('Londoni Scanorum', i.e., Amsterdam, 1682).

Mackenzie, Henry, *The man of feeling* (1771).

Maclauchlan, Daniel, *An essay upon improving and adding, to the strength of Great-Britain and Ireland, by fornication, justifying the same from scripture and reason* (Dublin, 1735; repr. in an enlarged edition in 1755).

Madame Birchini's dance. A modern tale. With considerable additions, and original anecdotes collected in the fashionable circles. Now first published by Lady Termagant Flaybum (1777; repr. 1872).

Madan, Martin, *An account of the triumphant death of F.S.: a converted prostitute who died April 1763, aged 26* (n.d., reprinted Boston, Mass., 1763).

——, *The Magdalen: or, dying penitent, exemplified in the death of F.S. Who died April, 1763, aged twenty-six years* (Dublin, 1789).

——, *Thelyphthora, or a treatise on female ruin*, 3 vols. (1780).

Mandeville, Bernard, *A conference on whoring ... By Phil Pornix* (1725; one of the several versions of *A modest defence of publick stews*, 1724).

——, *A modest defence of publick stews; or, an essay upon whoring, as it is now practis'd in these kingdoms. Written by a layman* (1724; repr. with an introduction by Richard I. Cook, Los Angeles, 1973).

—— [alias Luke Ogle] *The natural secret history of both sexes: or a modest defence of publick stews. With an account of the present state of whoring in these kingdoms. The fourth edition* [published by Edmund Curll] (1740).

Manley, Mary de la Rivière, *The adventures of Rivella or the history of the author of the Atlantis* (1714).

——, *Court intrigues, in a collection of original letters from the island of New Atalantis* (1711).

——, *Memoirs of the life of Mrs. Manley, containing not only the history of her adventures, but likewise an account of the most considerable amours in the court of King Charles the IId ... To which is added, a compleat key. Third edition* (1717; repr. NY, 1971).

——, *The secret history of Queen Zarah and the Zarazians* (1705; repr. NY, 1972).

Manningham, Richard, *An exact diary of what was observ'd during a close attendance upon Mary Toft, the pretended Rabbet-Breeder of Godalming in Surrey, from ... Nov. 28, to ... Dec. ... 7 following. Together with an account of her confession of the fraud* (1726).

Manuel, Juan, *The Spanish Decameron: or, ten novels ... translated by Sir Roger Lestrange. Third edition* (1712).

Manuel, Pierre, *Anecdotes recorded by the police of Paris, of all the affairs of gallantry which have occurred in that metropolis for several years past; with biographical sketches of the Parisian women of pleasure ... from Manuel's History of the police of Paris* (1792?).

Marini, Giovanni Battista, 'The why and the wherefore: or, the lady's two questions resolved.' ... Taken from the Priapeian collection of the Chevalier Marino (1765).

Marivaux, Pierre Carlet de Chamblain de, *The fortunate villager*, 2 vols. (Dublin, 1765).

——, *The life of Marianne*, 3 vols. (1736–42; repr. 1743).

——, *The life and adventures of Indiana, the virtuous orphan* (1746).

——, *The virtuous orphan*, 2 vols. (1747; repr. 1765, 1784).

Marten [or Martin], John [alias T.C. Surgeon], *The charitable surgeon: or, the best remedies for the worst maladies, reveal'd. Being a new and true way of curing (with mercury) the several degrees of the venereal distemper in both sexes ... To which is subjoin'd, a new discovery of the true seat of claps in men and women* [published by Edmund Curll] (1709).

——, *Gonosologium novum, or a new system of all the secret infirmities and diseases natural accidental and venereal in men and women ... written by way of appendix to the 6th edition of his book of the venereal diseases* (1708; second edition, 1711).

——, *A treatise of all the degrees and symptoms of the venereal disease. The sixth edition* (1708; seventh edition, 1711).

Mather, Cotton, *Bonifacius: an essay upon the good that is to be devised and designed* (Boston, Mass., 1710).

Mathias, Thomas James, *The pursuits of literature, or what you will: a satirical poem, in dialogue* (1794; third and revised edition, 1797).

Maubray, John, *The female physician, containing all the diseases incident to that sex in virgins, wives and widows ... To which is added, the whole art of new improv'd midwifery* (1724).

Meibomius, John Henry [Heinrich Meibom], *A treatise of the use of flogging in venereal affairs. Also of the office of the loins and reins ... Made English from the Latin original* [*De usu flagrorum* (Leyden, 1639; second edition, Frankfurt, 1670)] *by a physician* [i.e. George Sewell]. *To which is added a Treatise of hermaphrodites* [by Giles Jacob] (1718).

Memoirs and adventures of a flea (1785).

Memoirs and interesting adventures of an embroidered waistcoat (1751).

Memoirs of a man of pleasure. The third edition (1751; a translation of Henri-François de La Solle's *Mémoires de Versorand, ou le libertin devenu philosophe*, Amsterdam, 1751).

Memoirs of the amours, intrigues and adventures of Charles Augustus Fitz-Roy, Duke of Grafton, with Miss Parsons. Interspersed with a faithful account of Miss Parsons' amours with other persons of distinction (1769).

Memoirs of Antonina, Queen of Abo. Displaying her private intrigues, and uncommon passions. With family sketches, and curious anecdotes of great persons. Translated from the French (1791).

Memoirs of the Bedford coffee house. By a genius (1763).

Memoirs of an Oxford scholar, containing his amour with the beautiful Miss L., of Essex ... written by himself (1756; repr. NY, 1975).

Memoirs of love and gallantry; or the various foibles of the fair, display'd in a real history of several persons of distinction (1732).

Memoirs of the love and state-intrigues of the court of H[anover] ... (1743).

Memoirs of Marie-Antoinette, cidevant Queen of France (printed at Paris; American translation 1794: 'published according to Act of Congress'.).

——, (n.p., 1794: this is a shorter version with the same title).

Memoirs of the nobility, gentry, &c. of Thule: or, the island of love (1742; third edition, 1751).

Memoirs of Sir Financial Whimsey and his lady, interspersed with a variety of authentic anecdotes (1782).

Memoirs of the voluptuous conduct of the Capuchins in regard of the fair sex [probably an adaptation of the French *Le capucin démasqué par la confession d'un frère de l'ordre*, 1714; reprinted in 1759 and later as *Vie voluptueuse entre les capucins et les nones ...*] (1755).

The merry cuckold and kind wife (1775).

The merry-thought: or, the glass-window and bog-house miscellany (1731).

The midnight ramble: or the adventures of two noble females: being a true and impartial account of their late excursion through the streets of London and Westminster ... accompanied by their milliner ... in pursuit to discover their husbands' intrigues (1754).

The midnight spy (1766).

[Miller, Joe] *Joe Miller's jests* (1739; often reprinted).

Miller, Philip, *Catalogus plantarum ... a catalogue of trees, shrubs ... which are propagated for sale, in the gardens near London ... By a Society of Gardeners* (1730).

Miller, Vincent, *The man-plant: or, scheme for increasing and improving the British breed. The second edition* (1752).

Millot, Michel and/or Jean L'Ange, *The school of Venus* (1688; 1744; a translation of *L'Escole des filles*, Paris, 1655).

——, ——. Introduction by Donald Thomas (NY, 1971, and London, 1972).

Mirabeau, Honoré Gabriel Riquetti, Comte de, *The secret history of the court of Berlin* (1789; repr. NY, 1978).

Mocking is catching or, a pastoral lamentation for the loss of a man and no man [a satire on the castrato singer Senesino] (1726).

The modern lovers: or, the adventures of Cupid, the god of love: a novel (1756).

A modest apology for the prevailing practice of adultery (1773).

A modest defence of the ladies, in answer to a scurrilous pamphlet intituled, A rod in piss for hooped-petticoats (1719).

Moore, Edward, *Fables for the female sex. The fourth edition* (1755).

Monsieur Thing's origin: or Seignior D——o's adventures in Britain (1722).

Montague, John, Fourth Earl of Sandwich, publications on.
   The life, adventures, intrigues and amours of the celebrated Jemmy Twitcher (c. 1770).

Morris, Charles, *The festival of Ancareon* [sic]. *Being a complete collection of songs by Captain Morris. The ninth edition* (1788; repr. 1789).

——, *Hilaria* (1798).

——, *The plenipotentiary* (1787).

The mouse's tail ... Dedicated to Lord Sceggs (n.p., 1753).

Much ado about nothing: or, a plain refutation of all that has been written or said concerning the rabbit-woman of Godalming. Being a full and impartial confession from her own mouth (1727).

Nakedness consider'd: or reasons for not wearing of clothes. By a gentleman of great parts (1729).

The natural history of the frutex vulvaria or flowering shrub. By Philogynes Clitorides (1741).

Neville, Henry, *The isle of Pines or, A late discovery of a fourth island near Terra Australis incognita. By Henry Cornelius Van Sloetten* (1668; repr. with *The parliament of ladies* in 1768).

——, *The parliament of ladies* (1768).

A new Atalantis for the year one thousand seven hundred and fifty-eight. The second edition (1758).

New Attalantis for the year 1762; being a select portion of secret history containing many facts strange but true (1762).

The new boghouse miscellany, or a companion for the close-stool (1761; reissued as *The wit's miscellany* in 1762).

A new canting dictionary: comprehending all the terms, antient and modern, used in the several tribes of gypsies, beggars, shoplifters, highwaymen, foot-pads, and all other clans of cheats and villains (1725).

The new monk, a romance (1798).

A new song called The contented cuckold (1790?).

Nihell, Elizabeth, *A treatise on the art of midwifery* (1760).

Nocturnal revels or the history of King's Place and other modern nunneries,
containing their mysteries, devotions, and sacrifices ... By a monk of the
order of St. Francis. The second edition; 2 vols. (1779).
The northern Atalantis: or York spy. Displaying the secret intrigues and
adventures of the Yorkshire gentry; more particularly the amours of Mel-
isse, by ... Dr. W. King [probably published after 1732].
The northern cuckold: or, the gardenhouse intrigue (1731).
Nunnery tales (1727).
The old serpent's reply to the electrical eel (1777).
Oldmixon, John, ed., *The court of Atalantis ... Intermixt with fables and*
epistles in verse and prose. By several hands (1714).
——, *Court tales, or a history of the amours of the present nobility. To which*
is added a compleat key [a reissue of *The court of Atalantis*] (1717; second
edition, 1732).
Onania, and related publications.
The crime of Onan (together with that of his brother Er, punished with
sudden death, Gen. 38.10) or, the hainous vice of self-defilement, with
all its dismal consequences stated, 2 vols. (1724).
Eronania, on the misusing of the marriage bed by Er and Onan. ... Or the
hainous crime of self-defilement, with its nine miserable consequences in
both sexes, laid open to all those, who may ever have been guilty of this
ill action (1724: this is vol. II of *The crime of Onan*).
Eronania, on the crimes of those two unhappy brothers Er and Onan ...
Or the hainous vice of self-defilement, with all its dismal consequences
considered in all those who may ever have misfortunately injured them-
selves by this abominable practice ... containing all that can be said of
this unnatural vice (1724).
Onania; or the heinous sin of self-pollution, and all its frightful conse-
quences in both sexes considered (1708/9; repr. 1710; fifteenth edition,
1730; nineteenth edition, 1759).
A supplement to the Onania, or the heinous sin of self pollution ...
containing many remarkable, and ... surprising instances of the health
being impair'd, and genitals spoil'd, by that filthy commerce with ones
self, which is daily practised, as well by adults as youth, women as men,
married as single, as their letters inserted manifest ... with an answer to a
late scurrilous libel, call'd Onania examin'd and detected (1724; sixth
edition, 1730; tenth edition, 1759).
Onania examined and detected; or the ignorance, error, impertinence and
contradiction of a book call'd Onania, discovered and exposed (1723).
Onanism display'd: being. I. An enquiry into the true nature of Onan's sin. II.
Of the modern onanists. III. Of Self-pollution, its causes and conse-
quences. IV. Of nocturnal pollutions ... V. The great sin of self-pollution
... VI. A dissertation concerning generation, with a curious description
of the parts ... Made English from the Paris edition. The second edi-
tion [published by Edmund Curll] (1719). (See also the entries under
Tissot.)
The origin of the whale bone-petticoat. A satyr (Boston, Mass., 1714).

Osterwald, Jean-Frédéric, *The nature of uncleanness consider'd ... To which is added, a discourse concerning the nature of chastity, and the means of obtaining it* (1708).

The parasite, 2 vols. (1765).

Parker, George, *A view of society and manners in high and low life, being the adventures ... of Mr. G. Parker*, 2 vols. (1781).

Parsons, James, *A mechanical and critical enquiry into the nature of hermaphrodites* (1741).

A peep through the key-hole, or the secret history of some people and some things (1761?).

Pepys, Samuel, *The diary of Samuel Pepys* (London/NY, 1934).

——, ——. Ed. Robert Latham and William Matthews, 3 vols. to date (1970–77).

Perry, James, *The electrical eel: or, gymnotus electricus ... Inscribed to the honourable members of the R...l S...y* [Royal Society], *by Adam Strong, naturalist* (1777).

——, *Mimosa or the sensitive plant. A poem. Dedicated to Mr. Banks, and addressed to Kitt Frederick, Dutchess of Queensberry, elect* (1779).

Petis de la Croix, François, *The Persian and the Turkish tales*, 2 vols. (1714; repr. 1977).

The philosophy of pleasure: or, the history of a young lady, of luxurious temperament and prurient imagination, who experienced repeatedly the dangers of seduction, and whose escapes from the snares of love are truly wonderful, depicting many and various luscious scenes with her lovers ... Freely translated from the French (1774).

Pigott, Charles, *The female jockey club: or, a sketch of the manners of the age* (Dublin and London, 1794; seven editions in one year).

——, *The jockey club: or a sketch of the manners of the age* (1792; thirteen editions in one year).

Pilkington, Laetitia [alias Constantia Phillips], publications on.
Apology for the conduct of Mrs. Teresia Constantia Phillips (1748).
Memoirs of Mrs. Laetitia Pilkington (1748).

'The pissing conflict', *The Covent Garden Magazine* (1773).

Place, Francis, *The autobiography of Francis Place (1771–1854)*. Ed. Mary Thale (Cambridge, 1972).

——, *Place manuscript* (British Library, Add. MSS 27825 ff. 20–164).

The pleasures of coition; or the nightly sports of Venus: a poem. Being a translation of the Pervigilium Veneris of the celebrated Bonefonius, with some other love-pieces. The second edition [published by Edmund Curll] (1721).

The pleasures of matrimony, intermixed with a variety of merry and delightful stories, etc. (1743).

The pleasures of a single life, or, the miseries of matrimony. Occasionally writ upon the many divorces lately granted by Parliament. With The Choice, or, the pleasures of a country-life (1710?).

Pöllnitz, Karl Ludwig, Freiherr von, *Les amusemens de spa: or, the gallantries of the spaw in Germany*, 2 vols. (1737; repr. NY, 1978).

———, *La saxe gallante or, the amorous adventures and intrigues of Frederick-Augustus II* (1734; repr. NY, 1972).

Poetical epistle from Florizel to Perdita with Perdita's answer and a preliminary discourse upon the education of princes. Third edition (1781).

The polite road to an estate, or, fornication one great source of wealth and pleasure (1759).

Pollen, Thomas, *The fatal consequences of adultery, to monarchies as well as to private families: with the defence of the Bill, passed in the House of Lords in the year 1771, intituled, 'An act to restrain persons who shall be divorced for the crime of adultery, from marrying, or contracting matrimony, with the party,' and an historical account of marriage* (1772).

Polwhele, Richard, *The unsex'd females* (1798).

The polygamist: or, the lustful priest. Giving an account of one James Christie, a clergyman, who is now confin'd in Derby jail, for having two wives. Written by an Irish laureat (1738).

Popery display'd: or, the Church of Rome described in her true colours (1713).

Porter, Peter, *Collected Poems* (Oxford, 1984).

Post-office intelligence: or, universal gallantry [published by Edmund Curll] (1736).

The potent ally: or succours from Merryland. With three essays (in verse) in praise of the cloathing of that country: and the story of Pandora's box ... To which is added Erotopolis the present state of Merryland. Second edition (1741).

A practical essay upon old maids. Setting forth the most probable means of avoiding the deplorable state of antiquated virginity written, from woful experience, by an old maid (1768).

The praise and profit of cuckoldom. A consolatory oration delivered by an eminent teacher, to the two great congregations of London and Westminster (1743).

The present state of matrimony: or, the real causes of conjugal infidelity and unhappy marriages. In a letter to a friend (n.d.).

Pretty doings in a Protestant nation: being a view of the present state of fornication, whorecraft, and adultery, in Great Britain, and territories and dependencies thereunto belonging. Inscrib'd to the bona-roba's in the several hundreds, chaces, parks, and warrens, north, east, west, and south of Covent-Garden; and to the band of petticoat pensioners, etc. (1734).

The pretty gentleman; or, softness of manners vindicated from the false ridicule exhibited under the character of William Fribble, Esq. (1747; repr. in *Fugitive pieces on various subjects by several authors*, 1771, vol. I, 195–221).

The priest gelded: or popery at the last gasp. Shewing ... the necessity of passing a law for the castration of Popish ecclesiastics in Great Britain, as the only means to extirpate Popery etc. To which is added a list of the ... religious houses abroad maintained by the English Papists (1747).

The priest in rhyme: a doggerell versification of Kidgell's narrative, relative to the Essay on woman. By a Member of Parliament, a friend of Mr. Wilkes, and to liberty (1763?).

Prior, Matthew, *The genuine history of Mrs. Sarah Prydden, usually called Sally Salisbury, and her gallants* (1723).

——, *The literary works of Matthew Prior.* Ed. H. Bunker Wright and Monroe K. Spears, 2 vols. (Oxford, 1959).

——, *The writings of Matthew Prior*, ed. A.R. Waller, 2 vols. (Cambridge, 1904).

The progress of a rake: shewing the various intrigues and dangers he met with ... To which is prefixed ... A poem, called The rake's night (1732).

The prostitutes of quality; or adultery à-la-mode. Being authentic and genuine memoirs of several persons of the highest quality (1757).

The puzzle: being a choice collection of conundrums (1745).

Quillet, Claude, *Callipaedia. A poem. In four books. With some other pieces. Written in Latin by Claudius Quillet, made English by N. Rowe* (1710, 1712, and later).

——, *The joys of Hymen, or, the conjugal directory: a poem, in three books* (1768; an adaptation of *Callipaedia* of 1712).

Quincy, Edmund, 'Notebook', *NEHGR* 38 (April 1884).

Ranger's impartial list of the ladies of pleasure in Edinburgh (1775).

A rational account of the natural weaknesses of woman. The second edition (1716; later published as *The ladies physical directory*, 8th edition, 1742).

Ravenscroft, Edward, *The London cuckolds. A comedy* (1682).

Reason against coition. A discourse deliver'd to a private congregation. By the Reverend Stephen M... To which is added, A proposal for making Religion and the clergy useful: with the author's observations on the cause and cure of the piles, and some useful directions about wiping the posteriors. The second edition (Dublin, n.d.; repr. London, 1732).

Reasons humbly offer'd for a law to enact the castration of Popish ecclesiastics, as the best way to prevent th[e] growth of Popery in England (1700).

Records of the most ancient and puissant Order of the Beggar's Benison and Merryland, Anstruther (Edinburgh, 1892; repr. Edinburgh, 1982).

Reflections on the Marriage Act; with some hints for a new law: humbly offered to the consideration of Parliament (1764).

The reformer; exposing the vices of the age, in several characters [possibly by Edward Ward] (1700).

Richardson, Samuel, *Pamela* (1740–41).

Ridotto all'fresco. A poem. Being a curious representation of the humorous assembly of Spring Gardens, Vaux-Hall (1732).

Roach's London pocket pilot, or stranger's guide through the metropolis (1793).

A rod in piss for hooped-petticoats (1719?).

Roe, Richard (pseudonym), *A letter to Dr. Abraham Johnson* [i.e., John Hill] *on the subject of his new scheme for the propagation of the human species: in which another method of obtaining that great end, more adequate to the sentiments of the ladies, is proposed; and, the reflections that author has cast upon the Royal Society of London, are answered* (1750).

Ryder, Dudley, *The diary of Dudley Ryder, 1715–1716. Transcribed from shorthand and edited by William Matthews* (1939).

Sade, Donatien Alphonse François de, *The Marquis de Sade: three complete novels, compiled and translated by Richard Seaver and Austryn Wainhouse* (NY, 1966).

Saint André, Nathaniel, *A short narrative of an extraordinary delivery of rabbets, perform'd by Mr. John Howard ... published by Mr. St. André, surgeon and anatomist to his Majesty* (1727).

——, publications on.

A letter from the male physician, in the country, to the author of the Female physician [i.e. John Maubray] *in London, plainly shewing that for ingenuity ... he far surpasses the author of the Narrative* [St. André] (1726).

Salgado, James, *The fryer: or an historical treatise. Wherein the idle lives, vitiousness, malice, folly, and cruelty of the fryers, is described* (1680).

——, *Symbiosis, or an intimate conversation between the Pope and the devil* (1681).

A sapphic epistle from Jack Cavendish to the honourable and most beautiful Mrs. D.... (n.d., *c.* 1782).

The sappho-an. An heroic poem, of three cantos. In the Ovidian stile, describing the pleasures which the fair sex enjoy with each other. According to the modern and most polite taste. Found amongst the papers of a lady of quality, a great promoter of Jacobitism (n.d.).

Satan's harvest home: or the present state of whorecraft, adultery, fornication, procuring, pimping, sodomy, and the game of flatts (Illustrated by an authentick and entertaining story). And other Satanic works, daily propagated in this good Protestant kingdom (1749).

Saumery, P.L., *The devil turn'd hermit: or, the adventures of Astaroth, banish'd from hell. A satirical romance. Exposing, with great variety of humour, in a series of conversations between that demon and the author, the scandalous frauds, lewd amours and devout mockery of the monks and nuns; the intrigues of courts; the ambition, avarice, and cruelty of ministers ... interspersed with the portraits and secret history of most of the considerable persons that have lived in Europe within these thirty years past. Translated from the original French of Mr. de M...* (1741).

Savage, Richard, *The progress of a divine. A satire* (1735).

——, *The poetical works of Richard Savage*, 2 vols. (Edinburgh, 1780).

A scheme, humbly offered, for making R–l–g–n and the c–rg–y useful. With the author's observations on the cure of the piles, and some useful directions about wiping the posteriors (Dublin, second edition, 1732).

The school of Venus, or the lady's miscellany. Being, a collection of original poems and novels relating to love and gallantry [published by Edmund Curll] (1739).

Scott, H., *The adventures of a rupee* (1782).

The secret history of Betty Ireland. The sixth edition (1750?).

The secret history of an old shoe. Inscribed to the most wondrous-wonderful of all wonderful men and lovers (1734).

The secret history of Mama Oella (1733; repr. NY, 1970).

The secret history of Pandora's box (1742).

The sedan (1757).

The settee; or, Chevalier Commodo's metamorphosis (1742: a translation of the anonymous *Le canapé couleur de feu*, Amsterdam, 1714).

Shebbeare, John, *The marriage act. A novel ... the second edition* (Dublin, 1774).

A short dissuasive from the sin of uncleanness (1701).

Sibly, Ebenezer, *The medical mirror, or treatise on the impregnation of the human female. Showing the origin of disease ... with remarks on the effects of sea-bathing* (c. 1770).

Sinibaldus, Ioannes Benedictus, *I.B. Sinibaldi Geneanthropeiae sive de hominis generatione decateuchon* (Rome, 1612).

——, *Rare verities, or the cabinet of Venus unlocked and her secrets laid open. Being a translation of part of Sinibaldus, his Geneanthropeia and a collection of some things out of other Latin authors never before in English* (1657–8).

The sixpenny miscellany. Or, a dissertation upon pissing (1726).

Smellie, William, *An abridgment of the practice of midwifery: and a set of anatomical tables with explanations ... A new edition* (Boston, Mass., 1786).

——, *A set of anatomical tables, with explanations, and an abridgment of the practice of midwifery, with a view to illustrate a treatise on that subject, and a collection of cases* (Worcester, Mass., 1793; Philadelphia, Pa, 1797).

Smollett, Tobias, *Advice and reproof. Two satires, first published in the year 1746* (1748).

——, *Ferdinand Count Fathom* (1753).

——, *Peregrine Pickle* (1751; fifth edition, 1773).

——, *Roderick Random* (1748; second edition in 2 vols., 1748).

Snell, Hannah, *The female soldier, or the surprising life and adventures of Hannah Snell* (1750).

The sooterkin dissected, in a letter ... to John Maubray ... By Philalethes (1726).

La souricière. The mousetrap, a facetious and sentimental excursion through part of Austrian Flanders and France, etc. by Timothy Touchit, Esq. (1794).

The Spanish libertines (n.d.).

Spinke, John, *Quackery unmask'd; or, reflections on the sixth edition of Mr. Martin's treatise of the venereal disease ... and the pamphlet call'd the Charitable surgeon* (1709).

——, *Quackery unmask'd ... containing I. Reflexions on the sixth edition of Mr. Martin's Treatise of the venereal disease. II. An examination of the Charitable surgeon, the Generous surgeon, Venus's tomb, and G. Warren's new method of curing this disease. III. A brief enquiry into the ancient and present state of the practices of physick and surgery ... The second edition* (1711; repr. 1715).

——, *A short discourse preliminary to the second edition of Quackery unmask'd. Containing some useful observations . . . on the seventh edition of Mr. Martin's Treatise of the venereal disease* (1711; repr. 1715).

——, *Venus's botcher; or the seventh edition of Mr. Martin's (comical) Treatise of the venereal disease examin'd and expos'd* (1711).

'The spirit of the ring. Containing secret anecdotes of many illustrious personages of this and the neighbouring kingdoms', *The Bon Ton Magazine* 5 (September 1795–February 1796; published in five parts).

A spy on mother midnight: or, the templar metamorphos'd. Being a lying-in conversation. With a curious adventure. In a letter from a young gentleman in the country, to his friend in town (1748).

Sterne, Laurence, *A sentimental journey through France and Italy by Mr. Yorick* (1768–9; repr. 1790).

——, —— (NY, 1795: seven American editions were printed from 1768–1795).

——, *Tristram Shandy* (1759–67; repr. in 3 vols., Dublin, 1779).

Stevens, George Alexander, *The adventures of a speculist; or, a journey through London*; 2 vols. (1788).

——, *A lecture on heads, by G.A. Stevens, with additions, as delivered by Mr. Charles Lee Lewes. To which is added, An essay on satire. Embellished with twenty-five humorous characteristic prints, from drawings by G.M. Woodward, Esq.* (1785; repr. 1808, and Athens, Georgia, 1984).

Stevenson, John Hall, *Crazy tales* (1762; third edition, 1769).

——, *Fables for grown gentlemen* (1722?; repr. 1761 and 1770).

——, *The works of John Hall-Stevenson*, 3 vols. (1795).

Stretser [or Stretzer], Thomas, *Arbor vitae: or, the natural history of the tree of life* (1741).

——, *The natural history of the arbor vitae, or tree of life* (1732).

——, *Merryland display'd: or plagiarism, ignorance, and impudence, detected. Being observations, on a pamphlet intituled A new description of Merryland* ('Bath', i.e., London, 1741; Edmund Curll issued two editions of this piece).

——, *A new description of Merryland* (1740; by 1741 seven editions had appeared).

Swift, Jonathan, *A beautiful young nymph going to bed. Written for the honour of the fair sex . . . to which is added, Strephon and Chloe. And Cassinus and Peter* (Dublin/London, 1734).

—— [doubtful author], *The benefit of farting explained: or, the fundamentall cause of the distempers incident to the fair sex inquir'd into: proving à posteriori most of the disordures in-tail d on 'em are owing to flatulencies not seasonably vented. Wrote in Spanish, by Don Fart in hando Puff-in dorst, Professor of Bum bast in the University of Craccow. Translated into English, and at the request and for the use of the Lady Damp-Fart, of Her-fart-shire. By Obadiah Fizle, Groom of the stool to the Princess of Arse-mini in Sardinia. The sixth edition revis'd by the College of Fizz-icians* (1722).

——, *The complete poems*. Ed. Pat Rogers (Harmondsworth, 1983).

—— [doubtful author], *The grand mystery, or art of meditating over an house of office ... after the manner of Dr. S––ft* (1726).

——, *Gulliver's Travels* (1726).

—— [doubtful author], *Human ordure, botanically considered* (1733; repr. 1748).

——, *Swift's poems.* Ed. Harold Williams (second edition, 1966).

——, *A Tale of a Tub* (1704).

Tauronomachia or a description of a bloody and terible [sic] fight between two champions, Taurus and Onos, at Gresham-College (1719).

The tell-tale, or the invisible witness (1711; repr. NY, 1970).

The temple of prostitution. A poem dedicated to the greatest ... [whore?] in his Majesty's Dominions. [i.e., Lady Worsley] *Written by a woman of fashion* (1779).

The temple rakes, or innocence preserved (1735; repr. NY, 1970).

Teague-root display'd: being some useful and important discoveries tending to illustrate the doctrine of electricity, in a letter from Paddy Strong-cock to W...m W...n [i.e., William Watson], *author of a late pamphlet on that subject* (1746).

Thompson, Edward, *The court of Cupid*, 2 vols. (1770: contains the publications listed below).

——, *The demi-rep* (second edition, 1756; repr. 1770).

——, *The meretriciad courtesan* (1765; repr. 1770).

——, *The temple of Venus* (1763; repr. 1770).

Tissot, Samuel Auguste André David, *Onanism, or, a treatise upon the disorders produced by masturbation, or, the dangerous effects of secret and excessive venery, by M. Tissot. Translated from the last Paris edition by A. Hume* (1766; third edition, 1766; fourth edition, 1772; repr. London and Bath, 1781).

——, *A treatise on the crime of Onan; illustrated with a variety of cases, together with the method of cure. Translated from the third edition of the original* (1766).

Three new poems. Viz. I. Family duty: or, the monk and the merchant's wife. Being the shipman's tale from Chaucer. Moderniz'd. II. The curious wife ... by Mr. Fenton. Moderniz'd. III. Buckingham-house, a poem (1721; reissued in *The altar of love*, 1727).

The torpedo, a poem to the electrical eel. Addressed to Mr. John Hunter, surgeon: and dedicated to the Right Honourable Lord Cholmondely. The fourth edition (1777).

Travels of Mons. Le post-chaise. Written by himself (1753).

A treatise on the gonorrhoea. By a surgeon of Norfolk, Virginia (Norfolk, Va, 1787).

The trial of wit, or, a new riddle-book: some of which were never before published ... (Glasgow, 1782).

The tricks of the town laid open (Dublin, c. 1740; fourth edition, London, 1755).

The true friend, or essays on the evils of celibacy, and the advantages of polygamy (n.p., 1748).

The true story of the Chevalier d'Eon, or the modern hermaphrodite by one who knew it (c. 1828).

Tuesday Club of Annapolis, *Tuesday Club record book, 1744–56* (Baltimore, Md: Maryland Historical Society; MS).

The two cuckolds … two tales in the Scottish dialect (Edinburgh, 1796).

Uchtmann, Alard, *Vox clamantis in deserto ad doctissimum juvenum Hadrianum Beverlandum* (Middleburg, Netherlands?, 1700?).

The union of the breeches and petticoat … (1746).

Useful hints to single gentlemen respecting marriage, concubinage, and adultery. In prose and verse … by Little Isaac (1792).

Uxorius [pseudonym], *Hymen: an accurate description of the ceremonies used in marriage, by every nation in the known world … Dedicated to the ladies of Great-Britain and Ireland* (1760).

Valera, Cipriano de, *A full view of Popery, in a satirical account of the lives of the Popes, &c… To this is added a confutation of the Mass, and a vindication of reform'd devotion … Written by a learned Spanish convert, and address'd to his countrymen: now faithfully translated from the second and best edition of the original* (1704).

Vanbutchell, Martin [possible author], *Modern propensities; or an essay on the art of strangling, &c. Illustrated with several anecdotes. With memoirs of Susannah Hill, and a summary of her trial at the Old Bailey, on Friday, Sept. 16, 1791, on the charge of hanging Francis Kotzwarra* (n.d., probably late 1792; partly reprinted in *The Bon Ton Magazine* no. 31, September 1793).

Variety, or which is the man. A poem dedicated to Lady W(or)sl(e)y (1782).

Venette, Nicolas, *Mysteries of conjugal love reveal'd* (1703; second edition, 1707).

Venus in Boston: a romance of city life (NY, 1849).

A view of London and Westminster, or the town spy (1725).

Villiers, Jacob de [*L'apoticaire de qualité*, 1670], English versions and translations.

——, *The artful lover, or the French count turned doctor* (1751).

——, *The female apothecary deprived of her office, or a dose of French physic to the ladies* (1753).

——, *The gentleman apothecary* [translated by Roger L'Estrange] (1670; 1677, 1678, 1693).

——, *The gentleman 'pothecary* [published by Edmund Curll] (1726; repr. 1736, 1739, 1740, and later).

——, *Nobilis pharmacopola …* (1739).

——, *The surprize.…* (1739).

Voisenon, Claude Henri de, 'Tant mieux pour elle! or the marriage of Tricolore' (translated from the French by T. Dutton) *The Bon Ton Magazine* 5 (March–June, 1795; published in four parts).

Voltaire, François Marie Arouet de, *The maid of Orleans. Translated from the French of Voltaire. Canto the first* (1780).

——, *La pucelle; or the maid of Orleans* [translated into English by Catherina Maria Bury, Countess of Charleville], 2 vols. (1796).

A voyage to Lethe. By Captain Samuel Cock, sometime commander of the good ship Charming Polly. Dedicated to the Right Worshipful Adam Cock, Esq., of Black Mary's Hole, Coney Skin Merchant (1741).

The waiting woman, or the galanteries of the times (1775).

Walker, Charles [pseudonym], *Authentic memoirs of the life, intrigues and adventures of the celebrated Sally Salisbury* (1723).

Ward, Ned [Edward], *The amorous bugbears: or, the humours of a masquerade* (1725).

——, *A dialogue, between a depending courtier, who would have sacrific'd the chastity of his wife to a certain great man ... and his virtuous lady, who was avers'd to a compliance* (1735).

——, *The English nun: or, a comical description of a nunnery* (1700).

——, *History of the London Clubs* (1710 and 1711).

——, *The insinuating bawd and the repenting harlot* (1699).

——, ——. *To which is added, love. An ode to a lady. By a marry'd gentleman* (1755?).

——, ——. *To which is added, the six nights rambles* (1758).

——, *Marriage dialogues or, a poetical peep into the state of matrimony* (1709).

——, *The metamorphosed beau: or, the intrigues of Ludgate* (1700).

——, *The rambling rakes: or, London libertines* (1700).

——, *Three nights adventures or accidental intrigues* (1701).

——, *A trip to New England* (1699).

——, *The whole pleasures of matrimony: or scenes in life: interspersed with sundry delightful and comical stories* (n.d., c. 1714).

Ward, Ned, junior [pseudonym], *The comforts of matrimony: or, love's last shift: consisting of matrimonial dialogues, between persons of all ranks and degrees, from the peer to the peasant* (1780).

Wesley, John, *Primitive physick: or, an easy and natural method of curing most diseases* (n.p., 1747).

Whitehead, Paul, *The poems and miscellaneous compositions of Paul Whitehead.* Ed. Captain Edward Thompson (1770).

——, *Satires* (1748; repr. 1760).

Wilmot, John, Earl of Rochester, *The complete poems of John Wilmot, Earl of Rochester*, ed. David M. Vieth (New Haven, Connecticut, 1968).

——, *Poems on several occasions* (1710, 1712, and later).

—— [possible author], *Sodom: or, the quintessence of debauchery* (published in the seventeenth century; in 1707 John Marshall was prosecuted for publishing the playlet).

The whim!!! or the Maidstone bath: a Kentish poetic dedicated to Lady Worsley (1782).

Whipping-Tom; or, a rod for a proud lady, bundled up in four feeling discourses, both serious and merry. In order to touch the fair sex to the quick (1722).

The whore: a poem. Written by a whore of quality ... This truly sapphic production is confessedly written by a priestess of the Cyprian deity and by her recommended to those sincere whorshipers, the ladies L...r [Ligonier],

G...r [Grosvenor], W...y [Worsley], *Mrs. N... [Newton], Mrs. R...n, A...nd, who sacrifice largely to the loose rob'd goddess of delight, and tender dalliance* (n.d., *c.* 1782).

The whores rhetoric, calculated to the meridian of London; and conformed to the rules of art. In two dialogues (1683; repr. Edinburgh, 1836).

Wilkes, John, *The dying lover* (1763; appended to *An essay on woman*).

——, *The universal prayer* (1763; appended to *An essay on woman*).

——, *Veni creator; or, The maid's prayer* (1763; appended to *An essay on woman*).

—— and Thomas Potter, *An essay on woman* (1763; repr. by J.C. Hotten in 1871; and in 1972).

Wisdom revealed: or the tree of life discover'd and describ'd. A tale. By a studious enquirer into the mysteries of nature. To which is added The crab tree, or Sylvia discover'd (1750).

Wright, W., *England's witty and ingenious jester: or the merry citizen and jocular countryman's delightful companion. The seventeenth edition with new additions* (1780?).

Wycherley, William, *The complete works.* Ed. Montague Summers; 4 vols. (1924).

——, *The country-wife; a comedy* (1675).

V CRITICAL LITERATURE

Ackroyd, Peter, *Dressing up – transvestism and drag: the history of an obsession* (NY, 1979).

Adams, J. N., *The Latin sexual vocabulary* (1982).

Aden, John M., 'Those gaudy tulips: Swift's "unprintables"', in Larry S. Champion, ed., *Quick springs of sense: studies in the eighteenth century* (Athens, Georgia, 1974), 15–32.

Aldridge, Alfred Owen, *Benjamin Franklin, Philosopher and man* (NY, 1965).

——, ed., *Early American literature: a comparatist approach* (Princeton, NJ, 1982).

——, 'Polygamy and Deism', *JEGP* 47 (1949), 343–60.

——, 'Polygamy in early fiction', *PMLA* 65 (1950), 464–72.

Allen, H.C./Roger Thompson, eds., *Contrast and connection. Bicentennial essays in Anglo-American history* (1976).

Allmacht Weib: 6 vols. (Leipzig/Vienna, 1928–30).

I. Scheuer, O.F., and F.L. Wangen, *Das üppige Weib. Sexualleben und erotische Wirkung, künstlerische und karikaturistische Darstellung der dicken Frau vom Urbeginn bis heute* (Leipzig/Vienna, 1928).

II. Birlinger, Johannes R., *Das grausame Weib. Sexualpsychologische und pathologische Dokumente von der Grausamkeit and Dämonie der Frau* (Leipzig/Vienna, 1928).

III. Welzl, Joachim, *Das Weib also Sklavin. Die Frau in gewollter und erzwungener Hörigkeit* (Leipzig/Vienna, 1929).

IV. Hoyer, Erik, *Das lüsterne Weib. Sexualpsychologie der begehrenden, unbefriedigten und schamlosen Frau* (Leipzig/Vienna, 1929).

V. Brettschneider, Rudolf, *Das feile Weib. Triebleben und Umwelt der Dirne* (Leipzig/Vienna, 1929).

VI. Eszterházy, Gräfin Agnes, ed., *Das lasterhafte Weib. Bekenntnisse und Bilddokumente zu den Steigerungen und Aberrationen im weiblichen Triebleben*; supplement to *Allmacht Weib* (Leipzig-Vienna, 1930).

Alméras, M. Henri de, *Les amours de la reine Marie-Antoinette* (1907).

——, *Marie-Antoinette et les pamphlets royalistes et révolutionnaires. Avec une bibliographie de ces pamphlets* (1907; repr. 1908 and 1921).

——, *Les théâtres libertins au XVIIIe siècle: l'amour sur la scène et dans les coulisses, spectacles des petits apartements* (1905).

Alpert, Leo M., 'Judicial censorship of obscene literature', *HLR* 52 (1938), 40–76.

Alter, Robert, '*Tristram Shandy* and the game of love', *American Scholar* 37 (1968), 316–23.

Amacher, Richard E., *Franklin's wit and folly. The bagatelles* (New Brunswick, NJ, 1953).

Ariès, Philippe, *The hour of our death* (Harmondsworth, 1983).

Aron, J.P., and R. Kempf, *Le pénis et la démoralisation de l'occident* (1978).

Ashton, John, *Eighteenth century waifs* (1887).

Atkins, John, *Sex in literature*, 4 vols. (1970–82).

Avery, Emmett *et al.*, *The London stage 1660–1800. A critical introduction*, 5 vols. (Carbondale, Ill., 1968).

Bachmann, Albert, *Censorship in France from 1715 to 1750: Voltaire's opposition* [publications of the Institute of French Studies] (NY, 1934).

Baker, Sheridan, 'Henry Fielding's *The Female Husband*: fact and fiction', *PMLA* 74 (1959), 214–24.

Barber, Giles, 'Books from the old world and for the new: the British international trade in books in the eighteenth century', *SV* 150 (1976), 185–224.

Barbour, Brian M., ed., *Benjamin Franklin. A collection of critical essays* (Englewood Cliffs, NJ, 1979).

Baring-Gould, William S., *The lure of the limerick* (1968).

Bataille, Georges, *L'Érotisme* (1957).

——, *Les larmes d'Éros* (1961).

Beall, Otho T., Jr, '*Aristotle's Master Piece* in America: a landmark in the folklore of medicine', *WMQ* 20 (1963), 207–22.

Becker-Cantarino, Barbara, ed., *Die Frau von der Reformation zur Romantik. Die Situation der Frau von dem Hintergrund der Literatur- und Sozialgeschichte* (Bonn, 1980).

Belin, Jean Paul, *Le commerce des livres prohibés à Paris de 1750 à 1789* (1913; repr. NY, n.d.).

Bennett, William, *John Baskerville, the Birmingham printer. His press, relations, and friends*, 2 vols. (Birmingham, 1937–9).

Bingham, Caroline, 'Seventeenth-century attitudes toward deviant sex', *JIH* 1 (1971), 447–67.

Blackett-Ord, Mark, *Hell-Fire Duke. The life of the Duke of Wharton* (1983).

Blackman, Janet, 'Popular theories of generation: the evolution of *Aristotle's Works. The study of an anachronism*', in John Woodward, and David Richards, eds., *Health care and popular medicine in nineteenth-century England* (1977), 56–88.

Blaicher, Günther, *Freie Zeit – Langeweile – Literatur. Studien zur thera-peutischen Funktion der englischen Prosaliteratur im 18. Jahrhundert* (Berlin, 1977).

Blanchot, Maurice, 'Sade', in *The Marquis de Sade: three complete novels*, compiled and translated by Richard Seaver and Austryn Wainhouse (NY, 1966), 37–73.

Bleackley, Horace William, *Ladies fair and frail. Sketches of the demi-monde during the eighteenth century ... With sixteen illustrations* (NY/London, 1909).

——, *Life of John Wilkes* (1917).

Bloch, Iwan [alias Eugen Dühren], *Englische Sittengeschichte*, 2 vols. (second and revised edition, Berlin, 1912: previously published as *Das Geschlechtsleben in England*, Berlin, 1901–3).

——, *Ethnological and cultural studies of the sex life in England illustrated. As revealed in its erotic and obscene literature and art. Translated and edited by Richard Deniston* (NY, 1934; repr. 1972).

——, *Das Geschlechtsleben in England*, 3 vols., I (Charlottenburg, 1901), II and III (Berlin, 1903).

——, *A history of English sexual morals. Translated by William H. Forstner* (1936).

——, *Marquis de Sade's anthropologia sexualis of 600 perversions, 120 days of Sodom; or, the school for libertinage; and the sex life of the French age of debauchery; from private archives of the French government, by Dr. Iwan Bloch. Illustrated with numerous half-tones after eighteenth-century masters* (NY, 1934).

——, *Der Marquis de Sade und seine Zeit. Ein Beitrag zur Sittengeschichte des 18. Jahrhunderts* (Berlin/Leipzig, 1900; repr. Munich, 1978).

——, *Marquis de Sade, the man and his age. Studies in the history of culture and morals of the eighteenth century* (Newark, NJ, 1931).

——, *Neue Forschungen über den Marquis de Sade und seine Zeit* (Berlin, 1904).

——, *Odoratus sexualis. A scientific and literary study of sexual scents and erotic perfumes* (NY, 1934; repr. 1976).

——, *Sexual life in England past and present* (1965; a translation of *Das Geschlechtsleben in England*).

Bloch, Olivier, ed., *Le matérialisme du XVIIIe siècle et la littérature clandes-tine* (1982).

Bold, Alan, ed., *The sexual dimension in literature* (1982).

Bolen, Carl van, *Geschichte der Erotik*, fourth edition (Munich, 1967).

Bollême, Geneviève, 'Littérature populaire et littérature de colportage au dix-huitième siècle', in François Furet, ed., *Livre et société dans la France du dix-huitième siècle*, 2 vols. (1965 and 1970), 61–93.

Bond, Richard, P., ed., *Studies in the early English periodical* (Chapel Hill, NC, 1957).

Botsford, Jay Barrett, *English society in the eighteenth century as influenced from oversea* (NY, 1924).

Boucé, Paul-Gabriel, 'Aspects of sexual tolerance and intolerance in eighteenth-century England', *BJECS* 3 (1980), 173–92.

——, 'Livres de médecine populaire et mythes sexuels en Grande-Bretagne au XVIIIe siècle', *Cahiers de l'université de Pau et des pays de l'Adour* 10 (1980).

——, *The novels of Tobias Smollett* (1976).

——, 'Quelques aspects de la sexualité au dix-huitième siècle', in Michèle Plaisant, ed., *L'excentricité en Grande-Bretagne au XVIIIe siècle* (Lille, 1976).

——, 'Sex, amours and love in *Tom Jones*', *SVEC* 228 (1984), 25–39.

——, ed., *Sexuality in eighteenth-century Britain* (Manchester, 1982).

Bougard, Roger Gilbert, *Érotisme et amour physique dans la littérature française du XVIIe siècle*. PhD dissertation (Chapel Hill, NC, 1974).

Bourke, John Gregory, *Scatological rites of all nations* (Washington, 1891).

Bowles, John, *A view of the moral state of society at the close of the eighteenth century* (1800; repr. 1804).

Boyce, Benjamin, *Tom Brown of facetious memory* (Cambridge, Mass., 1939).

Brady, Frank, '*Tristram Shandy*: sexuality, morality, and sensibility', *ECS* 4 (1970), 41–56.

Brahmini, Denise, 'La sexualité dans l'anthropologie humaniste de Buffon', *DHS* 12 (1980), 113–26.

Brandt, Paul, *Sexual life in ancient Greece, by Hans Licht* [pseudonym]. Ed. Lawrence H. Dawson (1932; repr. NY, 1974).

——, *Sittengeschichte Griechenlands. Neu herausgegeben, bearbeitet und eingeleitet von Herbert Lewandowski* (Stuttgart, 1959).

Braudy, Leo, '*Fanny Hill* and materialism', *ECS* 4 (1970), 21–40.

Breslaw, Elaine G., 'Wit, whimsy, and politics: the uses of satire by the Tuesday Club of Annapolis, 1744 to 1756', *WMQ* 32 (1975), 295–306.

Brewer, John, *Party ideology and popular politics at the accession of George III* (Cambridge, 1976).

Bridenbaugh, Carl, *Gentleman's progress: the itinerarium of Dr. Alexander Hamilton, 1744* (Chapel Hill, NC, 1948).

Brigham, Clarence S., *History and bibliography of American newspapers 1690–1820*, 2 vols. (Worcester, Mass., 1947: repr. Westport, Conn., 1976).

Brissenden, R.F., 'La philosophie dans le boudoir; or, a young lady's entrance into the world', in *SECC* 2 (1972), 113–41.

Bristow, Edward J., *Vice and vigilance: purity movements in Britain since 1700* (Dublin, 1977).

Brochon, Pierre, *Le livre de colportage en France depuis le XVIe siècle. Sa littérature – ses lecteurs* (1954).

Brooks, Peter, *The novel of worldliness: Crébillon, Marivaux, Laclos, Stendhal* (Princeton, NJ, 1969).

Brown, Ford K., *Fathers of the Victorians. The age of Wilberforce* (Cambridge, 1961).

Brown, Norman Oliver, *Life against death. The psychoanalytical meaning of history* (1959).

Brown, Wallace C., *Charles Churchill, poet, rake, and rebel* (Lawrence, 1953).

Buchen, Irving, ed., *The perverse imagination: sexuality and literary culture* (NY, 1970).

Bullough, Vern L., *Homosexuality: a history* (NY and London, 1979).

——, *Prostitution: an illustrated social history* (NY, 1978).

——, *Sex, society and history* (NY, 1976).

——, *Sin, sickness and sanity: a history of sexual attitudes* (Los Angeles, 1977).

Burgess, Anthony, 'What is pornography', in Douglas H. Hughes, ed., *Perspectives on pornography* (NY, 1970), 4–9.

Burke, Peter, *Popular cultures in early modern Europe* (1978).

Bush, Clive, 'Erasmus Darwin, Robert John Thornton, and Linnaeus' Sexual System', *ECS* 7 (1974), 295–320.

Butt, John/Geoffrey Cornall, eds., *The Oxford history of English literature: the mid-eighteenth century* (Oxford, 1979).

Cadéac, Marcel, *Le chevalier d'Eon et son problème psycho-sexuel. Considérations sur les états psycho-sexuels et sur le travestisme* (1966).

Calverton, Victor F. [alias George Goetz], and Samuel D. Schmalhausen, eds., *Sex in civilization* (1929).

Capon, Gaston, *Les maisons closes au XVIIIe siècle: académies de filles et courtières d'amour, maisons clandestines, matrones, mères-abbesses, appareilleuses et proxénètes; rapports de police, documents secrets, notes personnelles et tenancières* (1903).

——, *Les petites maisons galantes de Paris au XVIIIe siècle: maisons de plaisance et vide-bouteilles; d'après des documents inédits et des rapports de police* (1902).

Carlisle, Henry C., *American satire in prose and verse* (NY, 1962).

Carter, Angela, *The Sadeian woman: an exercise in cultural history* (1979).

Castle, Terry, 'Matters not fit to be mentioned: Fielding's *The Female Husband*', *ELH* 49 (1982), 602–23.

Chalker, J., '"Virtue rewarded": the sexual theme in Richardson's *Pamela*', *Literary Half-Yearly* 2 (1961), 58–64.

Chancellor, Edwin Beresford, *The lives of the rakes*, 6 vols. (1924–5).

——, *The eighteenth century in London* (1920).

Chandler, Frank W., *The literature of roguery*, 2 vols. (NY, 1907; repr. 1977).

Chartier, Pierre, 'Asmodée ou l'effraction', *DHS* 12 (1980), 209–18.

Clarke, Michael, and Nicholas Penny, *The arrogant connoisseur – Richard Payne Knight 1751–1824* (Manchester, 1982).

Cockburn, J.S., ed., *Crime in England 1550–1800* (1977).

Cohen, Ralph, 'On the interrelations of eighteenth-century literary forms', in Phillip Harth, ed., *New approaches to eighteenth-century studies* (NY and London, 1974).

Collins, A.S., *Authorship in the days of Johnson. Being a study of the relation between author, patron, publisher and public, 1726–1780* (1927).

——, 'The growth of the reading public during the eighteenth century', *RES* 2 (1926), 284–93; 428–38.

——, 'The growth of the reading public, 1780–1800', *Nineteenth Century* 101 (1927), 749–58.

Collison, Robert, *The story of street literature. Forerunner of the popular press* (1973).

Comfort, Alex, *The anxiety makers* (1967).

Conant, Martha Pike, *The Oriental tale in the eighteenth century* (NY, 1908).

Conolly, Leonard W., *The censorship of English drama 1737–1824* (San Marino, Cal., 1976).

Conrad, Peter, 'The sensual connoisseur', *Observer Magazine* (January 31, 1982), 18–23.

Cook, Malcolm C., 'Politics in the fiction of the French Revolution 1789 – 1794', *SVEC* 201, ed. Haydn T. Mason (Oxford, 1982).

Copeland, Edward W., '"Clarissa" and "Fanny Hill": sisters in distress', *Studies in the Novel* 4 (1972), 343–52.

Coryn, Marjorie Stella, *The Chevalier d'Eon 1728–1810* (1932).

Coulet, Henri, *Le roman jusqu'à la Révolution* (1967).

Coulon, Marcel, *La poésie priapique dans l'antiquité et au Moyen Age* (1932).

Cox, C.B., and Norman St. John-Stevas, eds., 'Symposium: pornography and obscenity', *CQ* 3 (1961), 99–123.

Cranfield, G.A., *The press and society. From Caxton to Northcliffe* (NY and London, 1978).

Cressy, D., 'Literacy in preindustrial England', *Societas* 4 (1974).

Crow, Joan, 'The "Quinze joyes de mariage" in France and England', *MLN* 59 (1964), 571–7.

Curtis, T.C., and W.A. Speck, 'The societies for the reformation of manners: a case study in the theory and practice of moral reform', *LH* 3 (1976), 45–64.

Darnton, Robert, *The Great Cat Massacre and Other Episodes in French Cultural History* (NY, 1984).

——, 'The Grub Street style of revolution: J.-P. Brissot, police spy', *Journal of Modern History* 40 (1968), 301–27.

——, 'The high enlightenment and the low-life of literature in pre-revolutionary France', *Past and Present* 51 (1971), 81–115.

——, *The literary underground of the Old Régime* (Cambridge, Mass., 1982).

——, *Mesmerism and the end of the enlightenment in France* (Cambridge, Mass., 1968; repr. 1971).

——, 'Reading, writing, and publishing in eighteenth-century France: a case study in the sociology of literature', *Daedalus* (1970), 214–57.

Davis, Richard Beale, *A colonial Southern bookshelf: reading in the eighteenth century* (Athens, Ga., 1979).

——, *Intellectual life in the colonial South, 1585–1763*; 3 vols. (Knoxville, Tennessee, 1978).

——, *Literature and society in early Virginia, 1608–1840* (Baton Rouge, Louisiana, 1973).

Davis, William, *An olio of biographical and literary anecdotes* (1814).

Dawes, Charles Reginald, *A study of erotic literature in England* [typescript] (Gotherington, Cheltenham, Gloucester, 1943).

Day, Martin S., 'Anstey and anapaestic satire in the late eighteenth century', *Journal of English Literary History* 15 (1948), 122–46.

Delcourt, Marie, *Hermaphrodite. Mythes et rites de la bisexualité dans l'antiquité classique* (1958).

Delon, Michel, 'Le prétexte anatomique', *DHS* 12 (1980), 35–48.

Denizot, Paul, 'La vieille fille, personnage excentrique du XVIIIe siècle', in Michèle Plaisant, ed., *L'excentricité en Grande-Bretagne au 18e siècle* (Lille, 1976), 37–58.

Descher, Karlheinz, *Das Kreuz mit der Kirche. Eine Sexualgeschichte des Christentums* (Munich, 1977).

Dingwall, Eric J., *Very peculiar people. Portrait studies in the queer, the abnormal and the uncanny* ... (1950).

Dobrée, Bonamy, *English literature in the early eighteenth century 1700–1740: The Oxford History of English Literature*, vol. 7 (Oxford, 1959).

Dolmetsch, Carl, 'Letter to the editor and a response', *EAL* 15 (1980/81), 276–9.

Donnison, Jean, *Midwives and medical men: a history of inter-professional rivalries and women's rights* (1977).

Dubro, James R., 'The third sex: Lord Hervey and his coterie', *ECL* 2 (1976), 89–95.

Duca, Lo, *Die Geschichte der Erotik* (Munich, 1965).

Dufrénoy, M.-L., *L'Orient romanesque en France 1704–89*; 2 vols. (Montreal, 1947).

Dulaure, Jacques Antoine, *The gods of generation: a history of phallic cults among the ancient and moderns. Translated from the French by Adolph Frederich Niemöller* (NY, 1934).

Duniway, Clyde Augustus, *The development of freedom of the press in Massachusetts* (NY, 1906).

Durant, Will and Ariel, *The age of Voltaire: The Story of Civilization*, vol. 9 (NY, 1965).

——, *Rousseau and Revolution: The Story of Civilization*, vol. 10 (NY, 1967).

Dworkin, Andrea, *Pornography: men possessing women* (NY, 1981).

Englisch, Paul, *Geschichte der erotischen Literatur* (Stuttgart/Berlin, 1927; repr. 1932 and 1963).
——, *Irrgarten der Erotik* (Leipzig, 1931; repr. Magstadt, 1965).
——, *Das skatologische Element in der Literatur, Kunst, und Volksleben* (Stuttgart, 1928).
——, *Sittengeschichte Europas* (Berlin, 1931).
Epton, Nina Consuelo, *Love and the French* (1959).
Epstein, William H., *John Cleland: a biography* (NY, 1974).
Ernst, Morris L., and William Seagle, *To the pure . . . a study of obscenity and the censor* (NY, 1929).
Evans, E.A., *Literary references in New England Diaries*, PhD dissertation (Harvard University, 1940).
Faderman, Lillian, *Surpassing the love of men: love between women from the Renaissance to the present* (NY, 1981).
Flandrin, Jean-Louis, 'Amour et mariage', *DHS* 12 (1980), 163–76.
——, *Le sexe et l'occident. Évolution des attitudes et des comportements* (1981).
——, *Un temps pour embrasser. Aux origines de la morale sexuelle occidentale* (1983).
Ford, Worthington C., *The Boston bookmarket 1679–1700* (Boston, Mass., 1971).
——, *The Isle of Pines, 1668. An essay in bibliography* (Boston, Mass., 1920).
Foucault, Michel, *Histoire de la sexualité*, vol. I. *La volonté de savoir* (1976).
——, *The history of sexuality*, vol. I. (NY, 1978).
——, *Madness and civilization: a history of insanity in the age of reason* (NY, 1965).
Fowell, Frank/Frank Palmer, *Censorship in England* (1913).
Foxon, David, *Libertine literature in England 1660–1745* (New Hyde Park, NY, 1965).
Fränzel, Walter, *Geschichte des Übersetzens im 18. Jahrhundert* [*Beiträge zur Kultur- und Universalgeschichte*, vol. 25] (Leipzig, 1914).
Frankl, George, *The failure of the sexual revolution* (1974).
Frantz, David, 'Leud priapians and Renaissance pornography', *SEL* 12 (1972), 157–72.
Frost, William, 'Dryden's versions of Ovid', *CL* 26 (1974), 193–202.
Fryer, Peter, *Mrs. Grundy. Studies in English prudery* (1963).
Fuchs, Eduard, *Illustrierte Sittengeschichte vom Mittelalter bis zur Gegenwart*
    I *Die Renaissance* (Munich, 1909).
      Erzgänzungsband [supplement] (Munich, 1909).
    II *Die galante Zeit* (Munich, 1910).
      Erzgänzungsband (Munich, 1911).
    III *Das bürgerliche Zeitalter* (Munich, 1912).
      Erzgänzungsband (Munich, 1912).
    I–III repr. Berlin, 1981 (without supplements).

——, *Die Karikatur der europäischen Völker vom Altertum bis zur Neuzeit*, 2 vols. (Berlin, 1901 and 1903).

Fuchs, Eduard/Alfred Kind, *Die Weiberherrschaft in der Geschichte der Menschheit*, 2 vols. (Munich, 1913).

Fuller, Ronald, *Hell-Fire Francis* (1939).

Funke, Hans-Günther, *Crébillon fils als Moralist und Gesellschaftskritiker* (Heidelberg, 1972).

Furber, Donald, and Anne Callahan, *Erotic love in literature from medieval legend to romantic illusion* (NY, 1981).

Galvin, Thomas, *The Boston book trade, 1760–1789*, M.A. thesis (Boston: Simmons College, 1956).

Gay, Peter, *The Enlightenment. An Interpretation*, 2 vols. (1967 and 1970; repr. 1973).

George, M. Dorothy, *London life: the eighteenth century* (1966).

Giese, Hans, *Das obszöne Buch* [*Beiträge zur Sexualforschung*, vol. 35] (Stuttgart, 1965).

——, ed., *Die Sexualität des Menschen* (second edition, Stuttgart, 1971).

——, Eberhard Schorsch, *Zur Psychopathologie der Sexualität* (Stuttgart, 1973).

Gilboy, Elizabeth Waterman, 'Wages in eighteenth-century England' [*Harvard Economic Studies*, vol. 45] (Cambridge, Mass., 1934).

Gilmore, Thomas B., Jr, 'The comedy of Swift's scatological poems', *PMLA* 91 (1976), 33–43 and 464–67.

Glaser, Horst Albert, ed., *Wollüstige Phantasie; Sexualästhetik der Literatur* (Munich, 1974).

Göller, Karl Heinz, *Romance und novel. Die Anfänge des englischen Romans* (Regensburg, 1972).

Goldgar, Bertrand A., *Walpole and the wits: the relation of politics to literature 1722–42* (Wisconsin, Nebraska, 1976).

Goncourt, Edmond and Jules, *Histoire de Marie-Antoinette* (1907).

Goodwin, Albert, *The friends of liberty. The English democratic movement in the age of the French Revolution* (1979).

Goreau, Angeline, *Reconstructing Aphra. A social biography of Aphra Behn* (Oxford, 1980).

Gorsen, Peter, *Das Prinzip obszön. Kunst, Pornographie und Gesellschaft* (Reinbek bei Hamburg, 1969).

Goulemot, Jean-Marie, '"Prétons la main à la nature ..." Fureurs utérines', *DHS* 12 (1980), 97–112.

Graham, Walter, *The beginning of English literary periodicals. A study of periodical literature 1665–1715* (NY, 1926).

Granger, Bruce Ingham, *Benjamin Franklin. An American man of letters* (Norman, Oklahoma, 1976).

——, *Political satire in the American Revolution 1763–1783* (Ithaca, NY, 1963).

Green, Peter, 'Introduction', in P. Green, ed., *Ovid. The erotic poems* (Harmondsworth, 1982), 15–85.

——, 'Sex and classical literature', in Alan Bold, ed., *The sexual dimension in literature* (1982), 19–48.

Greene, Donald, 'On Swift's "scatological" poems', *Sewanee Review* 75 (1967), 672–89.

Greiner, Martin, *Die Entstehung der modernen Unterhaltungsliteratur. Studien zum Trivialroman des 18. Jahrhunderts* (Hamburg, 1964).

Griffin, Susan, *Pornography and silence. Culture's revenge against nature* (1981).

Guha, Anton A., *Sexualität und Pornographie. Die organisierte Entmündigung* (Frankfurt, 1976).

Guicciardi, Jean-Pierre, 'Hermaphrodite et le prolétaire', *DHS* 12 (1980), 49–78.

Haac, Oscar, 'L'amour dans les collèges de Jésuites: une satire anonyme du XVIIIe siècle', *SVEC* 18 (1961), 95–111.

Hagstrum, Jean H., *Sex and sensibility: ideal and erotic love from Milton to Mozart* (Chicago/London, 1980).

Haight, Anne Lyon, *Banned books: informal notes on some books banned for various reasons at various times in various places* (NY, 1934). *Updated and enlarged by Chandler B. Grannis* (NY, fourth edition, 1978).

Hall, Max, *Benjamin Franklin and Polly Baker: the history of a literary deception* (Chapel Hill, NC, 1960).

Halpert, Herbert, *et al.*, 'Symposium on obscenity in folklore', *JAF* 75 (1962), 189–265.

Halsband, Robert, *Lord Hervey: eighteenth-century courtier* (1973).

Hambridge, Roger A., '"Empiricomany, or an infatuation in favour of *empiricism* or *quackery*": the socio-economics of eighteenth-century quackery', in *Literature and science and medicine. Papers read at the Clark Library summer seminar 1981* (Los Angeles, 1982), 45–102.

Hamilton, Adrian, *The infamous Essay on Woman: or, John Wilkes seated between vice and virtue* (1972).

Hamilton, Bernice, 'The medical professions in the eighteenth century', *EHR* 4 (1951), 141–69.

Hanson, Laurence William, *Government and the press, 1695–1763* (Oxford, 1936).

Hare, E.H., 'Masturbatory insanity: the history of an idea', *JMS* 108 (1962), 1–25.

Harlan, Robert D., 'A colonial printer as bookseller in eighteenth-century Philadelphia: the case of David Hall', *SEEC* vol. 4, ed. Ronald C. Rosbottom (1976), 355–71.

Hart, James D., *The popular book. A history of America's literary taste* (NY, 1950; repr. 1976).

Hartley, Lodwick, 'The dying soldier and the love-lorn virgin: notes on Sterne's early reception in America', *SHR* 4 (1970), 69–80.

Harvey, A.D., 'Prosecution for sodomy in England at the beginning of the nineteenth century', *HJ* 21 (1978), 939–48.

Hatin, Eugène, *Les gazettes de Hollande et la presse clandestine aux XVIIe et XVIIIe siècles* (1865).

Henriot, Émile, *Les livres du second rayon, irréguliers et libertins* (1926; repr. 1948).

Heriot, Angus, *The castrati in opera* (1956).

Herold, J. Christopher, *Love in five temperments* (1961).

Hervé-Piraux, F.R. [pseudonym of François Bournand and Raphaël Viau], *Histoire des petites maisons galantes*.
    Vol. I *Les temples d'amour au XVIIIe siècle* (1910).
    Vol. II *Les folies d'amour au XVIIIe siècle* (1911).

Hervez, Jean [pseudonym of Raoul Vèze] see Vèze, Raoul.

Hibbert, Christopher, *The road to Tyburn: the story of Jack Sheppard and the eighteenth-century underworld* (NY/London, 1957).

——, *The roots of evil. A social history of crime and punishment* (Boston, Mass./London, 1963; repr. Westport, Conn., 1978).

Hibler, D.J., *Sexual rhetoric in seventeenth-century American literature*. PhD thesis (Notre Dame University, 1970).

Hildeburn, Charles S.R., *A century of printing. The issues of the press in Pennsylvania, 1685–1784* (Philadelphia, 1885–6).

Hill, Christopher, *Society and Puritanism in pre-revolutionary England* (1964; repr. 1969).

Hoffmann, Frank, *Analytical survey of Anglo-American traditional erotica* (Bowling Green, Ohio, 1973).

Hoffmann, Paul, *La femme dans la pensée des lumières* (1977).

Holbrook, Stewart H., *The golden age of quackery* (NY, 1959).

Homberg, Octave, *Un aventurier au XVIIIe siècle. Le Chevalier d'Eon* (1904).

Hopfner, T., *Das Sexualleben der Griechen und Römer* (Prague, 1938).

Horne, Colin J., 'Swift's comic poetry', in J.C. Hilson *et al.*, eds., *Augustan worlds: new essays in eighteenth-century literature* (NY, 1978), 51–67.

Horner, George F., *A history of American humor to 1765*; 2 vols., PhD dissertation (University of North Carolina, 1936).

Houlahan, Michael O., *Sexual comedy in* Tristram Shandy. PhD dissertation (Northwestern University, 1970).

Howland, Kenney W., ed., *Laughter in the wilderness: early American humour to 1783* (Kent, Ohio, 1976).

Howson, Gerald, *Thief-taker general. The rise and fall of Jonathan Wild* (NY, 1970).

Hughes, Douglas A., ed., *Perspectives on pornography* (NY, 1970).

Hughes, Peter, 'Wars within doors: erotic heroism and the implosion of texts', *ES* 60 (1979), 402–21.

Hunt, Morgan Magill, *The natural history of love* (1960).

Hurwood, Bernhardt J., *The golden age of erotica* (Los Angeles, 1965; repr. London, 1968).

Hyde, H. Montgomery, *A history of pornography* (1964).

——, *The other love. An historical and contemporary survey of homosexuality in Britain* (1970; published as *The love that dared not speak its name*, Boston, 1970).

Ivker, Barry, 'John Cleland and the Marquis d'Argens: eroticism and natural morality in mid-eighteenth-century English and French fiction', *Mosaic* 8 (1975), 141–8.

Jaeger, Muriel, *Before Victoria* (1956).

Jahoda, Marie, *The impact of literature: a psychological discussion of some assumptions in the censorship debate* (NY, 1954).

Jameson, Eric, *The natural history of quackery* (1961).

Jarrett, Derek, *The begetters of revolution: England's involvement with France 1759–1789* (1973).

——, *England in the age of Hogarth* (1974; repr. 1976).

Johnson, Thomas H., 'Jonathan Edwards and the "Young Folks' Bible"', *NEQ* 5 (1932), 37–54.

Jones, Howard Mumford, 'The importation of French books in Philadelphia 1750–1800', *MP* 32 (1934–5), 157–77.

Jones, Louis Clark, *The clubs of the Georgian rakes* (NY, 1942).

Jordanova, L.J., 'Natural facts: a historical perspective on science and sexuality', in Carl MacCormack and Marilyn Strathern, eds., *Nature, culture, and gender* (Cambridge, 1980).

Jousselin, Frenand, *D'Eon de Beaumont. His life and his times* (1911).

Jullien, Adolphe, *La cour et l'opéra sous Louis XVI: Marie-Antoinette et Sachini; Salieri; Favart et Gluck. D'après des documents inédits conservés aux Archives de l'État et à l'Opéra* (1878; repr. NY, 1976).

Karl, Frederick R., *A reader's guide to the development of the English novel in the eighteenth century* (1974).

Kearney, Patrick J., *A history of erotic literature* (1982).

Keller, Karl, 'Reverend Mr. Edward Taylor's bawdry', *NEQ* 44 (1970), 382–406.

Kellogg, Thelma Louise, *American social satire before 1800: based on a study of representative newspapers, magazines, and miscellaneous works, with special reference to social satire in the American Almanac.* PhD dissertation (Radcliffe College, Harvard University, 1929).

Kiefer, Otto, *Sexual life in Ancient Rome* (1934).

Kindermann, Heinz, *Theatergeschichte Europas*; 10 vols. (Salzburg, 1964–76).

King, Lester S., *The medical world of the eighteenth century* (Chicago, 1958).

——, *The philosophy of medicine: the early eighteenth century* (Cambridge, Mass., 1978).

——, 'Rationalism in early eighteenth-century medicine', *JHM* 18 (1963), 257–71.

Knaurs Sittengeschichte der Welt. Von Paul Firschauer.
  Vol. I *Vom Paradies bis Pompeji* (Munich, 1973).
  Vol. II *Von Rom bis Rokoko* (Munich, 1974).
  Vol III *Von Paris bis Pille* (Munich, 1974).

Knox, Ronald A., *Enthusiasm. A chapter in the history of religion* (Oxford, 1950).

Korshin, Paul J., ed., *Studies in change and revolution. Aspects of English intellectual history 1640–1800* (Menston, England, 1972).

Kronhausen, Eberhard and Phyllis, *Bücher aus dem Giftschrank. Eine Analyse der verbotenen und verfemten erotischen Literatur* (Bern/Munich, 1969).

——, *Erotic fantasies. A study of the sexual imagination* (NY, 1970).

——, 'The psychology of pornography', in *The encyclopedia of sexual behaviour*, ed. Albert Ellis and Albert Abarbanel (NY, 1961), 848–59.

——, *Walter, the English Casanova. A presentation of his unique memoirs 'My Secret Life'*, 2 vols. (1967).

Kropf, C.R., 'Libel and satire in the eighteenth century', *ECS* 8 (1974–5), 153–68.

Labatut, Jean-Pierre, *Les noblesses européennes de la fin du 15e siècle à la fin du 18e siècle* (1978).

Lachèvre, Frédéric, *Le libertinage au XVIIe siècle* (1920).

Lamoine, Georges, *La vie littéraire de Bath et de Bristol 1750–1800*, 2 vols. (Lille, 1978).

Landon, Richard G., 'Small profits do great things: James Lackington and eighteenth-century bookselling', *SECC* 5, ed. R.C. Rosbottom (1976), 387–400.

Langbein, John H., 'The criminal trial before the lawyers', *The University of Chicago Law Review* 45 (1978), 263–316.

——, *Prosecuting crime in the Renaissance: England, Germany, France* (Cambridge, Mass., 1974).

Lange, Bernd-Peter, *Die Theorie literarischer Gattungen in der englischen Aufklärung. Poetische Regeln und bürgerliche Gesellschaft* (Munich, 1979).

Lange, Victor, *Die Lyrik und ihr Publikum im England des 18. Jahrhunderts. Eine geschmacksgeschichtliche Untersuchung über die englischen Anthologien von 1670–1780* (Weimar, 1935).

Laprade, William Thomas, *England and the French Revolution, 1789–1797* (Baltimore, Md, 1909; repr. NY, 1977).

——, *Public opinion and politics in eighteenth-century England to the fall of Walpole* (NY, 1936; repr. 1977).

Laroch, Philippe, *Petits-maîtres et roués. Évolution de la notion de libertinage dans le roman français du XVIIIe siècle* (Laval, Canada, 1979).

Laslett, Peter, *Family life and illicit love in earlier generations. Essays in historical sociology* (Cambridge, 1977).

Lasserre, François, *La figure d'Éros dans la poésie grecque*. PhD dissertation (Lausanne, 1946).

Lawrence, David Herbert, *Pornography and obscenity* (1929).

Leavis, Queenie D., *Fiction and the reading public* (1932; repr. 1965 and 1968).

Leduc, Jean, 'Le clergé dans le roman érotique français du XVIIIe siècle', in *Roman et lumières au XVIIIe siècle* (1970).

Lee, Jae Num, *Swift and scatological satire* (Albuquerque, New Mexico, 1971).

Lee, Vera, *The reign of women in eighteenth-century France* (Cambridge, Mass., 1975).

Legman, Gershon, *The horn book. Studies in erotic folklore and bibliography* (New Hyde Park, NY, 1964; repr. London, 1970).

——, *The limerick. 1700 examples, with notes, variants and index* (1974).

——, *Rationale of the dirty joke: an analysis of sexual humor*; 2 vols. (NY, 1968 and 1975).

——, 'Toward a motif-index of erotic humor', in *JAF* 75 (1962), 227–48; repr. in *The horn book*, pp. 454–94.

Lehmann-Haupt, Helmut, *et al.*, eds., *The book in America: a history of the making, the selling, and the collecting of books in the United States* (NY, 1939; second edition, 1952).

Leibbrand, Annemarie and Werner, *Formen des Eros. Kultur- und Geistesgeschichte der Liebe*, 2 vols. (Freiburg/Munich, 1972).

Lemay, Joseph A. Leo, ed., *The oldest revolutionary: essays on Benjamin Franklin* (Philadelphia, 1976).

——, 'The public writings and the bagatelles', in Brian Barbour, ed., *Benjamin Franklin. A collection of critical essays* (Englewood Cliffs, NJ, 1979), 146–60.

——, 'The text, rhetorical strategy and themes of the *Speech of Miss Polly Baker*', in Leo Lemay, ed., *The oldest revolutionary*, 91–120.

Leppmann, Wolfgang, *Winckelmann. Ein Leben für Apoll* (Munich, 1983).

Le Roy Ladurie, Emmanuel, *Montaillou. Cathars and Catholics in a French village 1294–1324* (Harmondsworth, 1980).

Leventhal, Herbert, *In the shadow of the enlightenment: occultism and Renaissance science in eighteenth-century America* (NY, 1976).

Linebaugh, Peter, *et al.*, eds., *Albion's fatal tree: crime and society in eighteenth-century England* (1975; repr. 1977).

Linebaugh, Peter, 'The ordinary of Newgate and his account', in James S. Cockburn, ed., *Crime in England: 1550–1800* (1977), 246–69.

Link, Viktor, 'Literatur vor Gericht: zur Wechselbeziehung von Literatur und Landeskunde', in Kuno Schumann, ed., *Anglistentag 1979: Vorträge und Protokolle* (Berlin, 1979), 121–39.

——, 'The reception of Crébillon's *Le sopha* in England: an unnoticed edition and some imitations', *SVEC* 132, ed. Theodore Besterman (1975), 199–204.

Littlefield, George E., *Early Boston booksellers, 1642–1711* (Boston, Mass., 1900; repr. in 2 vols., 1907, and in 1 vol., NY, 1969).

Lloyd, Alan, *The wickedest age: the life and times of George III* (Newton Abbott, 1971; the American edition appeared under the title, *The king who lost America*).

Lockitt, C.H., *The relations between French and English society, 1763–93* (London/NY, 1920).

Lockridge, Kenneth A., *Literacy in colonial New England* (NY, 1974).

Lockwood, Thomas, *Post-Augustan satire. Charles Churchill and satirical poetry, 1750–1800* (1979).

Longworth, Clifton T., *The devil a monk would be: a survey of sex and celibacy in religion* (1936).

Lopez, Claude-Anne, *Mon cher papa. Benjamin Franklin and the ladies of Paris* (New Haven, Conn., 1966).

Loth, David G., *The erotic in literature. A historical survey of pornography as delightful as it is indiscreet* (1962).

Lough, John, *An introduction to eighteenth-century France* (1964).

——, 'Locke's list of books banned in France in 1679', *French Studies* 5 (1951), 217–22.

Lounsberry, Barbara, 'Sermons and satire: anti-Catholicism in Sterne', *PQ* 55 (1976), 403–17.

Lovett, Robert M., 'Sex and the novel', in Victor F. Calverton/Samuel D. Schmalhausen, *Sex in civilization* (1929), 677–92.

Low, Donald A., *Thieves' kitchen. The Regency underworld* (1982).

Lüsebrink, Hans-Jürgen, 'Les crimes sexuels dans les *Causes Célèbres*', *DHS* 12 (1980), 153–62.

——, *Kriminalität und Literatur im Frankreich des 18. Jahrhunderts* (Munich/Vienna, 1983).

MacCormack, Carl, and Marilyn Strathern, eds., *Nature, culture, and gender* (Cambridge, 1980).

Macdonald, Robert H., 'The frightful consequences of onanism: notes on the history of a delusion', *JHI* 28 (1967), 423–31.

Mainusch, Herbert, and Edgar Mertner, *Pornotopia. Das Obszöne und die Pornographie in der literarischen Landschaft* (Frankfurt, second edition, 1971).

Mannix, Daniel Pratt, *The Hell-Fire Club* (1970).

Marchand, Henry L., *The French pornographers, including a history of French erotic literature* (NY, 1933; repr. 1965).

Marcus, Steven, *The other Victorians: a study of sexuality and pornography in mid-nineteenth-century England* (NY, 1967).

Marcuse, Herbert, *Eros and civilization. A philosophical inquiry into Freud* (Boston, 1955; repr. London, 1966).

——, *Obscene: the history of an indignation* (1965; a translation of the German version, *Obszön: Geschichte einer Entrüstung*, Munich, 1962).

Margetson, Stella, *Leisure and pleasure in the eighteenth century* (1970).

Marshall, Dorothy, *The English poor in the eighteenth century. A study in social and administrative history* (1926).

Martin, Henri-Jean, *Livre, pouvoirs et sociétés à Paris au XVIIe siècle (1598–1701)* (Geneva, 1969).

Mass, Edgar, *Literatur und Zensur in der frühen Aufklärung. Produktion, Distribution und Rezeption der* Lettres persanes (Frankfurt, 1981).

Mauzi, Robert, *L'idée du bonheur dans la littérature et la pensée françaises au XVIIIe siècle* (1960).

May, George, *Diderot et* La religieuse (1954).

Mayo, Robert D., *The English novel in the magazines 1740–1815. With a catalogue of 1375 magazine novels and novelettes* (Oxford/London, 1962).

Mertner, Edgar, see entry under Mainusch, Herbert.

Meyer-Spacks, Patricia, '"Ev'ry woman is at heart a rake"', *ECS* 8 (1974), 27–46.

Michelson, Peter, *The aesthetics of pornography* (NY, 1971).

Molnar, John Edgar, *Publication and retail book advertisements in the Virginia Gazette. 1736–1780*. PhD dissertation, 2 vols. (University of Michigan, 1978).

Monselet, Charles-Pierre, *Les galanteries du XVIIIe siècle* (1862; repr. in 1875 as *Les amours du temps passé*).

——, *Les oubliés et les dédaignés, figures littéraires de la fin du XVIIIe siècle* (Alençon, 1857; repr. Paris 1876 and 1885).

Moore, Robert Etheridge, *Hogarth's literary relationships* (NY, 1969).

Morgan, Edmund S., 'The Puritans and sex', *NEQ* 15 (1942), 591–607.

Morison, Samuel E., *Harvard College in the seventeenth century*, 2 vols. (Cambridge, Mass., 1936).

——, *The intellectual life of colonial New England* (Ithaca, NY, 1956; repr. 1960).

Morison, Stanley, *The English newspaper. Some account of the physical development of journals printed in London between 1622 and the present day* (Cambridge, 1932).

Morrissey, LeRoy J., *The erotic pursuit: changing fashions in eroticism in early eighteenth-century English comic drama*, PhD dissertation (University of Pennsylvania, 1964).

Mortier, Roland, 'Libertinage littéraire et tensions sociales dans la littérature de l'ancien régime: de la "Picara" à la "Fille de joie"', *Revue de Littérature comparée* 46 (1972), 35–45.

Mossiker, Frances, *The Queen's necklace* (NY, 1961).

Moureau, François, 'Le *Mercure Galant* de Dufresny (1710–1714) ou le journalisme à la mode', *SVEC* vol. 206, ed. Haydn Mason (Oxford, 1982).

Muchembled, Robert, *Culture populaire et culture des élites dans la France moderne (XVe–XVIIIe siècles)* (1978).

Murtuza, Athon, 'Twentieth-century critical responses to Swift's scatological verse: a checklist', *Bulletin of Bibliography* 30 (1973), 18 ff.

Mylne, Vivienne, *The eighteenth-century French novel. Techniques of illusion* (Manchester/NY, 1965; repr. with minor amendments, 1970).

Nabakowski, Gislind, *et al.*, *Frauen in der Kunst*; 2 vols. (Frankfurt, 1980).

Nagy, Peter, *Libertinage et révolution* (1975).

Naumann, Peter, *Keyhole und Candle: John Clelands* Memoirs of a woman of pleasure *und die Entstehung des pornographischen Romans in England* Anglistische Forschungen, no. 115 (Heidelberg, 1976).

Nelli, René, *Érotique et civilisations* (1972).

Neumann, R.P., 'Masturbation, madness, and the modern concepts of childhood and adolescence', *JSH* 8 (1975), 1–28.

Nicoll, Allardyce, *A history of early eighteenth-century drama* (Cambridge, 1925; second edition, 1929).

——, *A history of late eighteenth-century drama, 1750–1800* (Cambridge, 1927).

Nitschke, Hansgeorg, 'Die Darstellung der Sexualität bei John Cleland und in englischen Magazinen der zweiten Hälfte des 18. Jahrhunderts', unpublished dissertation [1. Staatsexamen] (Technische Universität Braunschweig, 1982).

Nixon, Edna, *Royal spy. The strange case of the Chevalier d'Eon* (1965).

Nobile, Philip, ed., *The new eroticism: theories, vogues, and canons* (NY, 1970).

Norell, L., 'The cuckold in Restoration comedy', unpublished PhD dissertation (University of Florida, 1962).

Nussbaum, Felicity, 'Juvenal, Swift, and *The Folly of Love*', ECS 9 (1975/6), 540–52.

——, *The brink of all we hate. English satires on women 1660–1750* (Lexington, Kentucky, 1984).

Nutz, Walter, *Der Trivialroman. Seine Formen und seine Hersteller* (Cologne, second edition, 1966).

Ogg, David, *Europe of the Ancien Régime 1715–1783* (Glasgow, 1965).

O'Neill, John H., and Cameron C. Nickels, 'Upon the attribution of "Upon a Fart" to William Byrd of Westover', EAL 14 (1979), 143–8.

O'Neill, John H., 'Sexuality, deviance, and moral character in the personal satire of the Restoration', ECL 2 (1972), 16–19.

Parks, Stephen, *John Dunton and the English book trade: a study of his career with a checklist of his publications* (London/NY, 1976).

Partridge, Eric, *Shakespeare's bawdry: a literary and psychological essay and a comprehensive glossary*, revised edition (1960).

Paulhan, Jean, 'The Marquis de Sade and his accomplice', in Richard Seaver and Austryn Wainhouse, comp., *The Marquis de Sade: three complete novels* (NY, 1966), 3–37.

Paulson, Ronald, *Popular and polite art in the age of Hogarth and Fielding* (Notre Dame, Ind., 1979).

——, *Satire and the novel in eighteenth-century England* (New Haven, Conn./London, 1967).

Pearsall, Ronald, *The worm in the bud: the world of Victorian sexuality* (London/NY, 1969).

Peckam, Morse, *Art and pornography: an experiment in explanation* (NY, 1969; repr. 1971).

Peden, William H., *Thomas Jefferson: book collector*. PhD dissertation (University of Virginia, 1942).

Perrin, Noel, *Dr Bowdler's legacy: a history of expurgated books in England and America* (NY, 1969).

Perry, Ruth, 'Anality and ethics in Pope's late satires', BJECS 4 (1981), 139–55.

Petermann, Renate, ed., *Theater und Aufklärung. Dokumentation zur Ästhetik des französischen Theaters im 18. Jahrhundert* (Munich, 1979).

Pikoul, Valentin, *Le Chevalier d'Eon et la guerre de sept ans* (1983).

Pinkus, Philip, *Grub St. stripped bare. The scandalous lives & pornographic works of the original Grub St. writers* (1968).

Pintard, René, *Les libertins érudits.*

Pitcher, Edward W., 'Changes in short fiction in Britain 1785–1810: philosophic tales, gothic tales, and fragments and visions', *SSF* 13 (1976), 331–54.

——, 'On the conventions of eighteenth-century British short fiction: part I 1700–1760; part II 1760–1785', *SSF* 12 (1975), 199–212; 327–41.

Plongeron, Bernard, *La vie quotidienne du clergé français au XVIIe siècle* (1974).

Plumb, John Harold, *The commercialisation of leisure in eighteenth-century England* (Reading, 1973).

Porter, Roy, *English society in the eighteenth century* (Harmondsworth, 1982).

——, 'Medicine and the Enlightenment in eighteenth-century England', *BSSHM* 25 (1979), 27–40.

——, 'Mixed feelings: the Enlightenment and sexuality in eighteenth-century Britain', in P.G. Boucé, ed., *Sexuality in eighteenth-century Britain* (Manchester, 1982), 1–28.

——, '"The Secrets of Generation Display'd": *Aristotle's Master-Piece* in Eighteenth-century England', *ECL* 9 (1985), 1–21.

——, 'Sex and the singular man: the seminal ideas of James Graham', in 'Sex and Eighteenth-century English culture'; *SVEC* 228 (1984), 3–25.

——, and G.S. Rousseau, eds., *Sexual Underworlds of the Enlightenment* (Manchester, 1988).

Postgate, Raymond W., *That devil Wilkes* (1930).

Pottinger, David, *The French book trade in the Ancien Régime, 1500–1791* (Cambridge, Mass., 1958).

Power, Sir d'Arcy, 'Aristotle's Masterpiece', in *idem, The foundations of medical history* (Baltimore, Md, 1931), 147–78.

Praz, Mario, *The romantic agony* (second edition, 1970).

Preston, John, *The created self. The reader's role in eighteenth-century fiction* (1970).

Quinlan, Maurice J., *Victorian prelude. A history of English manners 1700–1830* (NY, 1941).

Rabenalt, Arthur M., *Mimus eroticus*, 5 vols. (Hamburg, 1965–7).

——, *Theatrum Sadicum. Der Marquis de Sade und das Theater* (Emsdetten, 1963).

——, *Voluptas ludens. Erotisches Geheimtheater. 17. 18. und 19. Jahrhundert* (Munich, 1962).

Real, Hermann J., and Heinz J. Viencken, 'The syphilitic lady,' *The Scriblerian and the Kit-kats* 15 (1982), 52–54.

——, '"Those odious common whores of which this Town is full": Swift's "A Beautiful Young Nymph Going to Bed"', *AAA* 6 (1981), 241–59.

Redwood, John, *Reason, ridicule and religion. The age of Enlightenment in England 1660–1750* (Cambridge, Mass., 1976).

Rees, Christine, 'Gay, Swift, and the nymphs of Drury-Lane', *Essays in Criticism* 23 (1973), 1–21.

Rémo, Félix, *La vie galante en Angleterre* (1888).

Reuilly, Jean de, *La Raucourt et ses amies, étude historique des moeurs saphiques au XVIIe siècle* (1909).

Reynolds, Myra, *The learned lady in England, 1650–1760* (Gloucester, Mass., 1920; repr. 1964).

Richetti, John J., *Popular fiction before Richardson: narrative patterns 1700–1739* (Oxford, 1969).

Richmond, H.M., *The school of love. The evolution of the Stuart love lyric* (Princeton, NJ, 1964).

Rist, Ray C., *The pornography controversy. Changing moral standards in American life* (New Brunswick, NJ, 1975).

Rives-Child, John, *Casanova* (Paris, 1983).

Robiquet, Paul, *Thévenau de Morande: étude sur le XVIIIe siècle* (1882).

Roe, Shirley A., *Matter, life, and generation: eighteenth-century embryology and the Haller–Wolff debate* (Cambridge, 1982).

Rogal, Samuel J., 'Enlightened enthusiasm: anti-Methodism in the literature of the mid and late eighteenth century', *EE* 5 (1974), 3–13.

——, 'The selling of sex: Mandeville's *Modest Defence of Publick Stews*', *SECC* 5 (1976), ed. R.C. Rosbottom, 141–50.

Rogers, Katherine M., '"My female friends": the misogyny of Jonathan Swift', *TSLL* 1 (1959), 366–79.

——, *The troublesome helpmate: a history of misogyny in literature* (Seattle, 1966).

Rogers, Pat, *The eighteenth century* (1978).

——, *Hacks and dunces: Pope, Swift and Grub Street* (London/NY, 1980).

Rollins, Hyder E., 'A contribution to the history of the English Commonwealth drama', *Studies in Philology* 18 (1921), 267–333.

Rolph, Cecil H., ed., *Does pornography matter?* (1961).

Rousseau, George S., 'Doctors and medicine in the novels of Tobias Smollett', PhD dissertation (Princeton University, 1966).

——, 'John Wesley's Primitive Physick, 1747', *HLB* 16 (1968), 242–56.

——, '"Sowing the wind and reaping the whirlwind": aspects of change in eighteenth-century medicine', in Paul J. Korshin, ed., *Studies in change and revolution. Aspects of English intellectual history 1640–1800* (Menston, England, 1972), 129–59.

Rowse, A.L., *Homosexuals in history. A study of ambivalence in society, literature and the arts* (1977).

Rudé, George, *Paris and London in the eighteenth century; studies in popular protest* (NY, 1973).

Runte, Roseann, 'La Fontaine: precursor of the eighteenth-century libertine', *ECL* 3 (1976), 47–51.

Rustin, Jacques, *Le vice à la mode. Étude sur le roman français du XVIIIe siècle de* Manon Lescaut *à l'apparition de* La nouvelle Héloïse *(1731–1761)* (1979).

Sadleir, Michael, *Forlorn sunset* (1947).

St. John-Stevas, Norman, *Obscenity and the law* (1956).

Saisselin, Rémy G., 'Room at the top of the eighteenth century: from sin to aesthetic pleasure', *Journal of Aesthetics and Art Criticism* 26 (1967/8), 345–50.

Sanger, William W., *The history of prostitution* (NY, 1859; repr. 1972).

Sasse, Klaus, *Die Entdeckung der 'courtisane vertueuse' in der französischen Literatur des 18. Jahrhunderts. Rétif de la Bretonne und seine Vorgänger.* PhD dissertation (Hamburg, 1967).

Schakel, Peter J., *The poetry of Jonathan Swift. Allusion and the development of a poetic style* (Madison, Wisc., 1978).

Schelsky, Helmut, *Soziologie der Sexualität: über die Beziehungen zwischen Geschlecht, Moral und Gesellschaft* (Reinbek bei Hamburg, 1955).

Schivelbusch, Wolfgang, *Das Paradies, der Geschmack und die Vernunft* (Munich/Vienna, 1980).

Schlaffer, Heinz, *Musa iocosa. Gattungspoetik und Gattungsgeschichte der erotischen Dichtung in Deutschland* [Germanistische Abhandlungen, vol. 37] (Stuttgart, 1971).

Schlamm, William S., *Vom Elend der Literatur. Pornographie und Gesinnung* (Stuttgart, 1966).

Schöwerling, Rainer, *Chapbooks. Zur Literaturgeschichte des einfachen Lesers. Englische Konsumliteratur 1680–1840* [Regensburger Arbeiten zur Anglistik und Amerikanistik, vol. 18] (Frankfurt, 1980).

Schumann, Kuno/Joachim Möller, *Jonathan Swift* [Erträge der Forschung, vol. 159] (Darmstadt, 1981).

Schulz, Dieter, 'The coquette's progress from satire to sentimental novel', *Literatur in Wissenschaft und Unterricht* 6 (1973), 77–89.

Scott, George Ryley, *Into whose hands: an examination of obscene libel in its legal, sociological and literary aspects* (1945).

Seigel, Jules Paul, 'Puritan light reading', *NEQ* 37 (1964), 185–99.

Selden, Roman, *English verse satire 1590–1765* (1978).

Seligman, S.A., 'Mary Toft – the rabbit breeder', *Medical History* 5 (1961), 349–60.

Sgard, Jean, 'La littérature des *Causes Célèbres*', in *Approches des lumières, Mélanges offerts à Jean Fabre* (1974).

Shahar, Shulamith, *Die Frau im Mittelalter* (Königstein/Taunus, 1981).

Shapiro, N.R., *The comedy of Eros: medieval French guides to the art of love* (Urbana, Ill., 1971).

Shepard, Leslie, *The broadside ballad: a study in origins and meaning* (1962).

——, *The history of street literature: the story of broadside ballads, chapbooks, proclamations, news-sheets, election bills, tracts, pamphlets, cocks, catchpennies and other ephemera* (Newton Abbot, 1973).

Shinagel, Michael, '"Memoirs of a Woman of Pleasure": pornography and the mid-eighteenth-century English novel', in Paul J. Korshin, ed., *Studies in change and revolution* (Menston, England, 1972), 211–36.

Sibley, John L., *Biographical sketches of graduates of Harvard University in Cambridge, Massachusetts*, 3 vols. (Cambridge, Mass., 1873).

Siebert, Frederick S., *Freedom of the press in England 1476–1776: the rise and decline of government control* (Urbana, Ill., 1952; repr. 1965).

Silver, Rollo G., 'The Boston book trade, 1790–1799', in *Essays honoring Lawrence C. Wroth* (Portland, Maine, 1951), 279–303.

Sinclair, Reid Baytop, *What the world calls obscene: Swift's ugly verse and the satiric tradition*. PhD dissertation (Vanderbilt University, 1965).

Singer, Herbert, *Der galante Roman* (Stuttgart, second edition, 1966).

Sittengeschichte der Kulturwelt und ihrer Entwicklung in Einzeldarstellungen, ed. Leo Schidrowitz, 11 vols. (Vienna, 1926–30).

   I *Sittengeschichte des Intimen: Bett, Korsett, Hemd, Hose, Bad, Abtritt. Die Geschichte und Entwicklung der intimen Gebrauchsgegenstände* (Vienna, 1926).

   II *Sittengeschichte des Lasters: die Kulturepochen und ihre Leidenschaften* (Vienna, 1927). Supplement volume (Vienna, 1927).

   III *Sittengeschichte von Paris: die Grosstadt, ihre Sitten und ihre Unsittlichkeit* (Vienna, 1926).

   IV *Sittengeschichte des Proletariats: der Weg vom Leibes- zum Maschinensklaven, die sittliche Stellung und Haltung des Proletariats* (Vienna, 1926).

   V *Sittengeschichte des Theaters. Eine Darstellung des Theaters, seiner Entwicklung und Stellung in zwei Jahrhunderten* (Vienna, second edition, 1927).

   VI *Sittengeschichte der Liebkosung und Strafe. Die Zärtlichkeitsworte, Gesten und Handlungen der Kulturmenschheit und ihr Gegenpol der Strenge.* (Vienna, 1928).

   VII *Sittengeschichte des Geheimen und Verbotenen. Eine Darstellung der geheimen und verborgen gehaltenen Leidenschaften der Menschheit, die Einstellung der Staatsgewalt zum Geschlechtsleben der Gesellschaft* (Vienna, 1930).

   VIII *Sittengeschichte des Hafens und der Reise. Eine Beleuchtung des erotischen Lebens in der Hafenstadt, im Hotel, im Reisevehikel. Die Sexualität des Kulturmenschen während des Reisens in fremdem Milieu* (Vienna, 1927).

   IX *Sittengeschichte der Revolution. Sittenlockerung und Sittenverfall, Moralgesetze und sexualethische Neuorientierung in Zeiten staatlicher Zersetzung und revolutionären Umsturzes* (Vienna, 1930).

   X *Sittengeschichte des Intimsten. Intime Toilette, Mode und Kosmetik im Dienst der Erotik* (Vienna, 1929).

Slepian, B., and L.J. Morrissey, 'What is *Fanny Hill*?', *Essays in Criticism* 14 (1964), 65–75.

Sloterdijk, Peter, *Kritik der zynischen Vernunft*, 2 vols. (Frankfurt, 1983).

Smart, George, 'Private libraries in colonial Virginia', *AL* 10 (1938), 24–52.

Smith, Le Roy W., 'Daniel Defoe: incipient pornographer', *LP* 22 (1972), 165–78.

Smith, Margarette, 'Smollett and matrimonial bawdry', *SVEC* 228 (1984), 39–47.

Smith, Norah, 'Sexual mores in the eighteenth century: Robert Wallace's *Of Venery*', *JHI* 39 (1978), 419–33.

Solomon, Harry M., 'Difficult beauty: Tom D'Urfey and the context of Swift's "The Lady's Dressing Room"', *SEL* 19 (1979), 431–44.

Solomon, Miller, '"To steal a hint was never known": the Sodom apple motif and Swift's "A Beautiful Young Nymph Going to Bed"', *Tennessee Studies in Literature* 22 (1977), 105–16.

Sontag, Susan, 'The pornographic imagination', in Douglas H. Hughes, ed., *Perspectives on pornography* (NY, 1970), 131–70.

Sossaman, Stephen, 'Sex, love and reason in the novels of John Cleland', *MSE* 6 (1978), 93–106.

Soupel, Serge, 'Science and medicine and the mid-eighteenth-century novel: literature and the language of science', in *Literature and Science and Medicine. Papers read at the Clark Library Summer Seminar 1981* (Los Angeles, 1982), 1–43.

Speck, W.A., 'The harlot's progress in eighteenth-century England', *BJECS* 3 (1980), 127–39.

Spufford, Margaret, *Small books and pleasant histories. Popular fiction and its readership in seventeenth-century England* (1981).

Stanford, Donald E., 'Edward Taylor and the "Hermaphrodite" poems of John Cleveland', *EAL* 8 (1973), 59–61.

Steiner, George, 'Night words', in *idem, Language and silence. Essays 1958–66* (1979), 91–101.

Stephen, Leslie, *English literature and society in the eighteenth century* (1904).

——, *A history of English thought in the eighteenth century*, 2 vols. (1902; repr. 1927).

Stern, Bernhard, *Geschichte der erotischen Literatur aller Völker und Zeiten*; 2 vols. (Vienna/Leipzig, 1908).

Stiverson, Gregory A., 'Books both useful and entertaining: reading habits in mid-eighteenth-century Virginia', *Southeastern Librarian* 24 (1975), 52–8.

Stone, Lawrence, *The Family, Sex and Marriage in England 1500–1800* (1977).

Straus, Ralph, *The unspeakable Curll* (1927).

Streeter, Harold Wade, *The eighteenth-century English novel in French translation: a bibliographical study* (NY, 1936).

Sturm, Ernest, *Crébillon fils et le libertinage au XVIIIe siècle* (1970).

Summers, Montague, *The gothic quest. A history of the gothic novel* (1938; repr. 1950).

Sutherland, James R., 'The circulation of newspapers and literary periodicals 1700–1730', *The Library* 15 (1935), 110–24.

Sutherland, James, *A preface to eighteenth-century poetry* (Oxford, 1963).

Tannahill, Reay, *Sex in history* (1980).

Tarczylo, Théodore, '"Prêtons la main à la nature ..." L'Onanisme de Tissot', *DHS* 12 (1980), 79–36.

——, *Sexe et liberté au siècle des lumières* (1983).

Taylor, Gordon Rattray, *The angel makers. A study in the psychological origins of historical change 1750–1850* (1958; rev. ed., 1973).

——, *Sex in history* (1959).

Telfer, John Buchan, *The strange career of the Chevalier d'Eon de Beaumont* (1885).

Thalmann, Marianne, *Der Trivialroman des 18. Jahrhunderts und der romantische Roman. Ein Beitrag zur Entwicklung der Geheimbundmystik* (Berlin, 1923).

Thomas, Donald, *A long time burning: the history of literary censorship in England* (1969).

——, *The Marquis de Sade* (1976).

Thomas, Keith V., 'The double standard', *JHI* 20 (1959), 206–13.

Thomas, K. Bryn, *James Douglas of the pouch and his pupil, William Hunter* (1964).

Thompson, Charles John Samuel, *The mysteries of sex: women who posed as men and men who impersonated women* (1938; repr. NY, 1974).

——, *The quacks of old London* (London/NY, 1928).

Thompson, Roger, 'The London Jilt', *HLB* (1975), 289–94.

——, 'The Puritans and prurience: aspects of the Restoration book trade', in H.C. Allen and Roger Thompson, eds., *Contrast and connection. Bicentennial essays in Anglo-American history* (1976), 36–65.

——, *Unfit for modest ears. A study of pornographic, obscene and bawdy works written or published in England in the second half of the seventeenth century* (1979).

——, *Women in Stuart England and America: a comparative study* (1974).

Thomson, Ann, 'La Mettrie et la littérature clandestine', in O. Bloch, ed., *Le matérialisme du XVIIIe siècle* (1982).

Thomson, Ann, 'La Mettrie et la littérature clandestine', in O. Bloch, ed., *Le matérialisme du XVIIIe siècle* (1982).

Thomson, Ralph, 'The deathless lady', *C* 2 (1935), 207–20.

Thornton, John Leonard, 'Medical books from 1701–1800', in *idem, Medical books, libraries and collectors: a study of bibliography and the book trade in relation to the medical sciences*, revised edition (1966).

Towers, A.R., 'Sterne's cock and bull story', *ELH* 24 (1957), 12–29.

Trevelyan, George Macaulay, *Illustrated English social history*. Vol. III: *The eighteenth century* (1951; repr. 1964).

Troyer, Howard W., *Ned Ward of Grubstreet. A study of sub-literary London in the eighteenth century* (Cambridge, Mass., 1946).

Trumbach, Randolph, 'London's sodomites: homosexual behavior and Western culture in the eighteenth century', *JSH* 2 (1977), 1–33.

——, *The rise of the egalitarian family: aristocratic kinship and domestic relations in eighteenth-century England* (NY/London, 1978).

Tucker, Joseph E. 'English translations from the French 1650–1700: corrections and additions to the CBEL', *PQ* 21 (1942), 391–404.

Tuttle, Julius H., 'The Mather libraries', *Proceedings of the American Antiquarian Society* 20, 269–356.

Tyson, Gerald P., *Joseph Johnson: a liberal publisher* (Iowa City, Iowa, 1979).

Underwood, Dale, *Etherege and the seventeenth-century comedy of manners* (New Haven, Conn., 1957).

Van Eeghen, Isabella Henrietta, *De Amsterdamse Boekhandel*, 6 vols. (Amsterdam, 1961–78).

Varma, Devendra P., *The gothic flame: being the history of the gothic novel in England: its origins, efflorescence, disintegration and residuary influence* (1957).

Vartanian, Aram, 'Érotisme et philosophie chez Diderot', *Cahiers de l'association international des études françaises* 13 (1961), 367–90.

——, 'La Mettrie, Diderot and sexology in the Enlightenment', in Jean Macary, ed., *Essays on the age of the Enlightenment in honor of Ira O. Wade* (Geneva, 1977), 347–67.

Versini, Laurent, *Laclos et la tradition* (1968).

Vèze, Raoul [alias Jean Hervez], *Correspondance d'Eulalie ou tableau du libertinage de Paris* (1911).

——, *La galanterie parisienne au XVIIIe siècle. La régence galante; le libertinage sur le trône; un harem royal ...* (1905).

——, *La galanterie parisienne sous Louis XV et Louis XVI. D'après les mémoires, les rapports de police, les libelles, les pamphlets, les satires, chansons du temps* (1910).

——, *Les maîtresses de Louis XV d'après les mémoires ...* (1910).

——, *Les sociétés d'amour au XVIIIe siècle* (1906).

Wade, Ira O., *The clandestine organization and diffusion of philosophic ideas in France from 1700 to 1750* (Princeton, N.J., 1938; repr. NY, 1967).

Wagner, Horst, *Crébillon fils. Die erzählerische Struktur seines Werkes* [Münchener Romanistische Arbeiten, vol. 37] (Munich, 1972).

Wagner, Peter, 'Eros Goes West: European and "Homespun" Erotica in Eighteenth-Century America', in Winfried Herget and Kan Ortseifen, eds., *The Transit of Civilization from Europe to America* (Tübingen, 1986), 145–65.

——, '"The Female Creed": a new reading of William Byrd's ribald parody', *EAL* 19 (1984), 122–37.

——, 'Puritan attitudes towards recreation in early-seventeenth-century New England', *Mainzer Studien zur Amerikanistik* 17, ed. Hans Galinsky (Frankfurt, 1982).

——, 'Researching the taboo: sexuality and eighteenth-century English erotica', *ECL* 8 (1983), 108–15.

——, ed., 'Sex and eighteenth-century English culture', in H.T. Mason, ed., *SVEC* 228 (1984), 1–67.

——, 'The discourse on sex – or sex as discourse: eighteenth-century medical and paramedical erotica', *Sexual underworlds of the Enlightenment*, ed. Roy Porter and George Rousseau (Manchester, 1988).

——, 'The veil of science and morality: some pornographic aspects of the *Onania*', *BJECS* 6 (1983), 179–84.

Warner, James H., 'Eighteenth-century English reactions to the *Nouvelle Héloïse*', *PMLA* 52 (1937), 803–19.

Watkins, C. Malcolm, *The cultural history of Marlborough, Virginia* (Washington, DC, 1968).

Watson, Eric, 'An Essay on Woman', *NQ* 9 (1914), 121–3, 143–5, 162–4, 183–5, 203–5, 222–3, 241–2.

Watt, Ian, *The Rise of the Novel* (Harmondsworth, 1972).

Weinstein, Leo, *The metamorphoses of Don Juan* [Stanford Studies in Language and Literature] (Stanford, 1959).

Weiss, H.B., *American chapbooks* (Trenton, NJ, 1938).

——, *American chapbooks, 1722–1842* (NY, 1945).

——, *A book about chapbooks. The people's literature of bygone times* (Hatboro, Pa, 1969).

Whitley, Raymond K., 'The libertine hero and heroine in the novels of John Cleland', *SECC* 9, ed. Roseanne Runte (1980), 387–404.

Whitney, Lois, *Primitivism and the idea of progress in English popular literature of the eighteenth century* (Baltimore, 1934).

Wilcoxon, Reba, 'Rochester's sexual politics', *SECC* 8, ed. Roseanne Runte (1979), 137–49.

Wiles, Roy M., *Freshest advices. Early provincial newspapers in England* (Columbus, Ohio, 1965).

——, *Serial publication in England before 1750* (Cambridge, 1957).

William, Harold H., *The Toast: an heroick poem. A paper* (privately printed, 1932).

Williams, Guy, *The age of agony: the art of healing c. 1700–1800* (1975).

Williams, Harold, *Dean Swift's library* (Cambridge, 1932; repr. 1974).

Williams, J.B., *A history of English journalism to the foundation of the gazette* (1908).

Wolfe, Richard J., 'The hang-up of Franz Kotzwara and its relationship to sexual quackery in late eighteenth-century London', *SVEC* 228 (1984), 47–67.

Wright, Lawrence, *Clean and decent: the fascinating history of the bathroom and the water closet* (1960).

Wright, Thomas, G., *Literary culture in early New England 1620–1730* (New Haven, Conn., 1920).

Wunderer, Richard, *Jocus pornographicus*, 2 vols. (Schmiden bei Stuttgart, 1969).

Young, Wayland Hilton, *Eros denied. Studies in exclusion* (1965; second edition, 1968).

Zall, Paul M., *Ben Franklin laughing. Anecdotes from original sources by and about Benjamin Franklin* (London/Los Angeles, 1980).

——, 'The old age of American jestbooks', *EAL* 15 (1980), 3–15.

Index

Note: *Figures in italics refer to illustrations*